Psychology for Professional Groups

Psychology and Medicine

Psychology for Professional Groups

Series Editors: Antony J. Chapman and Anthony Gale

Psychology for Professional Groups is a new series of major textbooks published with the British Psychological Society. Each is edited by a teacher with expertise in the application of psychology to professional practice and covers the key topics in the training syllabus. The editors have drawn upon a series of specially commissioned topic chapters prepared by leading psychologists and have set them within the context of their various professions. A tutor manual is available for each text and includes examination questions, practical exercises and projects, further reading and general guidance for the tutor. Each textbook shows in a fresh, original and authoritative way how psychology may be applied in a variety of professional settings, and how practitioners may improve their skills and gain a deeper understanding of themselves. There is also a general tutorial text incorporating the complete set of specialist chapters and their associated teaching materials.

Published with this book
Psychology for Physiotherapists. E. N. Dunkin

Subsequent titles
Psychology and Management. Cary L. Cooper
Psychology for Social Workers. Martin Herbert
Psychology for Teachers. David Fontana
Psychology for Occupational Therapists. Fay Fransella
Psychology for Nurses and Health Visitors. John Hall
Psychology for Careers Counselling. Ruth Holdsworth
Psychology for Speech Therapists. Harry Purser
Psychology and People: A tutorial text. Antony J. Chapman
    and Anthony Gale

Psychology and Medicine

David Griffiths

First published 1981 by THE BRITISH PSYCHOLOGICAL SOCIETY
and THE MACMILLAN PRESS LTD.

Distributed by The Macmillan Press Ltd, London and
Basingstoke. Associated companies and representatives
throughout the world.

ISBN 0 333 318 625 (hard cover)
ISBN 0 333 318 773 (paper cover)

Printed in Great Britain by Wheatons of Exeter

Note: throughout these texts, the masculine pronouns have
been used for succinctness and are intended to refer to both
females and males.

The conclusions drawn and opinions expressed are those of
the authors. They should not be taken to represent the
views of the publishers.

To Susan, Timothy and Matthew

Contents

Preface

K. Rawnsley

British medical schools nowadays include psychology in the undergraduate curriculum, though the subject attracts mixed feelings both from students and from some members of staff. Its 'relevance', as indeed that of other basic sciences, may not dawn until the student has first-hand experience of clinical life. He may then begin to realize that he is perforce dealing with complex sentient beings (including himself) and that diagnosis and treatment depend upon much more than a knowledge of anatomy, physiology and pathology.

By that time it is not necessarily too late and the present book, if he has not already encountered it, will offer him a most readable, up-to-date and expert review of many areas of psychology bearing upon clinical medicine. The young student, in his early peregrination of the wards, may well turn initially to the chapter by Griffiths on communication between doctors and patients. He is, after all, placing his foot upon the first rung of a ladder which he will continue to climb throughout the whole of his medical career - learning clinical skills of which the linch-pin is interviewing. If he is puzzled by the strange ways in which patients and staff behave in hospital settings he will find illumination in Orford's chapter on institutional climates.

During his paediatric clerkship there are several chapters of immediate relevance on abilities and behaviour (Foss); social development (Schaffer); and clinical child psychology (Griffiths).

When working on the medical and surgical wards and in the out-patient departments he will be impressed by the high proportion of elderly patients and the chapter by Coleman offers a sensitive and valuable perspective. He may realize early on that the giving and receiving of drugs and the response to these substances involves more than can be understood in purely chemical terms. Griffiths' chapter on this topic will interest him.

Many students have their first experience of death during the clinical years. They will have to cope with their own feelings on encountering patients with fatal illnesses and they may or may not be helped by their seniors. Carr's chapter on death and bereavement will provide some insight.

Traditionally students are brought up in the orderly antiseptic world of the teaching hospital with the emphasis on high technology medicine and on the study of patients divorced from their natural habitat. General practice, however, is what most students will eventually do after qualification and so, belatedly, this is being incorporated in a small way into the undergraduate menu. It is in this setting par excellence that the medical student will appreciate the ubiquity of 'psychological problems'. Several chapters have an immediate bearing: counselling and helping (Hopson); psychopathology (Shapiro); insomnia, obesity, sexual behaviour (all by Griffiths); the family (Frude); understanding and managing personal change (Hopson); stress (Griffiths); pain (Ray).

Psychological medicine, a peculiarly British term, though permeating throughout clinical medicine, retains as its main focus the study and management of mental disorders. Psychology, of course, has a very special link with this discipline and the student will find valuable material in the chapter on personality and individual assessment (Kline); how human behaviour is changed (Beech); biological bases of behaviour (Martin) and mental handicap (Griffiths).

Some doctors, like some children, are late developers but may make up for lost time and even surpass their peers. This book, capably edited by David Griffiths and written with understanding and skill by a team of carefully selected contributors, will facilitate their growth admirably.

Kenneth Rawnsley
Department of Psychological Medicine
Welsh National School of Medicine
Cardiff

Foreword

This book is one of a series, the principal aims of which are to illustrate how psychology can be applied in particular professional contexts, how it can improve the skills of practitioners, and how it can increase the practitioners' and students' understanding of themselves.

Psychology is taught to many groups of students and is now integrated within prescribed syllabuses for an increasing number of professions. The existing texts which teachers have been obliged to recommend are typically designed for broad and disparate purposes, and consequently they fail to reflect the special needs of students in professional training. The starting point for the series was the systematic distillation of views expressed in professional journals by those psychologists whose teaching specialisms relate to the applications of psychology. It soon became apparent that many fundamental topics were common to a number of syllabuses and courses; yet in general introductory textbooks these topics tend to be embedded amongst much superfluous material. Therefore, from within the British Psychological Society, we invited experienced teachers and authorities in their field to write review chapters on key topics. Forty-seven chapters covering 23 topics were then available for selection by the series' Volume Editors. The Volume Editors are also psychologists and they have had many years of involvement with their respective professions. In preparing their books, they have consulted formally with colleagues in those professions. Each of their books has its own combination of the specially-prepared chapters, set in the context of the specific professional practice.

Because psychology is only one component of the various training curricula, and because students generally have limited access to learned journals and specialist texts, our contributors to the series have restricted their use of references, while at the same time providing short lists of annotated readings. In addition, they have provided review questions to help students organize their learning and prepare for examinations. Further teaching materials, in the form of additional references, projects, exercises and class notes, are available in Tutor Manuals prepared for each book. A comprehensive tutorial text ('Psychology and People'), prepared by the Series Editors, combines in a single volume all the key topics, together with their associated teaching materials.

It is intended that new titles will be added to the series and that existing titles will be revised in the light of changing requirements. Evaluative and constructive comments, bearing on any aspect of the series, are most welcome and should be addressed to us at the BPS in Leicester.

In devising and developing the series we have had the good fortune to benefit from the advice and support of Dr Halla Beloff, Professor Philip Levy, Mr Allan Sakne and Mr John Winckler. A great burden has been borne by Mrs Gail Sheffield, who with skill, tact and courtesy, has managed the production of the series: to her and her colleagues at the BPS headquarters and at the Macmillan Press, we express our thanks.

Antony J. Chapman
UWIST, Cardiff

Anthony Gale
University of Southampton

May 1981

I

What is Psychology? Introduction
David Griffiths

What is psychology?

Aims, scope and methods

What is psychology? Psychology can be defined as the science that studies the behaviour of man and animals or, more simply, the scientific study of behaviour. An alternative to this definition refers to psychology as the scientific study of 'behaviour and experience'. This is preferred by some on the grounds that the term 'behaviour' is traditionally used to refer to actions and events which are directly observable (running, laughing, crying and so on), whereas many important aspects of human 'experience' are not observable in this way. For example, feelings and emotions, attitudes, beliefs and moods are important and common aspects of our lives and yet cannot be observed directly.

In theory, we can experience emotions or moods without any necessary external manifestations. In practice, however, these aspects of our experience are inferred from behaviour. Smiling suggests the presence of a pleasant emotional state; depression or sadness will often be evident from other facial expressions. Much of our experience is also evident from what we say; in a clinical situation, our understanding of a patient will often depend extensively on his self-report in interview. Facial expression and verbal report are, of course, observable behaviours, so that the two definitions have in common that behaviour is a major source of interest to the psychologist. But this is not to suggest in any way that experience is not. On the contrary, it is an important and essential concern of psychology.

Any broad definition of psychology requires to be supplemented by a further consideration of three questions. First, exactly what is its subject matter? Second, what are its aims? Finally, what methods does it use to secure those aims?

The subject matter of psychology

The interests of psychologists in behaviour and experience involve, in practice, three sets of events. It must be emphasized that in reality these events are closely integrated; however, it is useful to differentiate between them. What are these sets of events? As we shall see, they coincide to some extent with the distinction between 'behaviour' and 'experience' which has already been mentioned. Psychology concerns itself with:

1. 'OVERT' BEHAVIOURS: these are activities which can be directly observed. Most involve motor activities and we are concerned with such actions as talking, crying, facial expressions, walking, running and so on. The attractiveness of these events to psychologists resides partly in the fact that they can be observed and recorded with relative ease. They are, therefore, more amenable to objective evaluation. Indeed, technological advances such as audio- and videotapes are now available to provide a permanent and objective record of a wide range of 'overt' events.

2. 'COVERT' EVENTS OR EXPERIENCE: when we are concerned with feelings and moods, attitudes and beliefs, direct observation is not possible. Inference is necessary if we are to derive some impression of their presence, intensity and qualitative characteristics. Such inference is based primarily on observations of 'overt' behaviours and, if we remind ourselves that verbal descriptions of feelings and beliefs are also examples of 'overt' behaviour, then it becomes obvious that all inferences about 'covert' events are based on 'overt' behaviour. Though experience is not as amenable to objective assessment as behaviour, its existence cannot be denied on this basis and few psychologists would, these days, deny the relevance of subjective feelings and other facets of experience. At one time introspection - based on observation and reporting of one's own experience - was the main method used by psychology. Its limitations soon became evident, however: for example, unreliability in self-report; and more recently psychologists have become concerned with other sources of information, notably behavioural and physiological changes.

3. PHYSIOLOGICAL CHANGES: it is well known that behaviour and experience are often associated with characteristic physiological changes. Anger and anxiety, depression and elation are accompanied by changes in heart rate, the electrical conductivity of the skin and so on. Psychologists have become interested in these changes both in their own right and because of their relationships to overt behaviour and experience. For example, what physiological changes occur when an individual experiences a panic attack or intense anxiety? Is it possible to differentiate emotional states in terms of patterns of physiological change? Is it possible to train the individual to control his own muscular tension or blood pressure? In addition to the theoretical significance of physiological change, psychologists have also been interested in these variables since they again offer an additional opportunity for objective and precise measurement (Hilgard, Atkinson and Atkinson, 1971).

The aims of psychology
Psychology has three major sets of aims in relation to its subject matter. These are set out below.

1. OBSERVATION AND ASSESSMENT: all scientific disciplines attempt to accumulate a body of information and facts, so that observation and assessment is naturally an important step. The chapters which follow in this book are a compendium of information which has been gathered from extensive and systematic observation. Calibration and quantification are important aspects of scientific enquiry and we often have cause to note that many aspects of behaviour can be quantified and measured. For example, measures of intelligence are based on problems to be solved by the individual (e.g. arithmetic, logical reasoning, spatial arrangement of shapes); the intelligence quotient is usually based on a count of the correct items, or a measure of the time taken to solve selected problems. Alternatively, the extent of the individual's fear in relation to a phobic object such as a snake can be assessed by observing how near he can get or how long he can tolerate close contact.

2. EXPLANATION AND UNDERSTANDING: psychologists share with other scientific disciplines a strong interest in the identification of those factors and mechanisms which cause or maintain behaviour and experience. In relation to a patient, for example, it might be important to establish why he cannot tolerate the company of others, why he attempts to end his own life or why he fails to succeed at school or work. In relation to broad dimensions of behaviour, such as intelligence or anxiety, it might be important to determine those general factors which determine these characteristics. Eysenck (1976) suggests that one of the distinctive features of psychology as a scientific discipline is that it is concerned with the contribution of both biological and environmental factors. It is therefore a 'bio-social' science. For example, the study of the determinants of intelligence and emotionality has involved evaluations of the importance of heredity on the one hand and of past experience on the other.

The identification of aetiology is of theoretical interest, but it also involves a number of important practical implications. For example, special teaching or experience cannot be expected to produce dramatic improvements in intellectual level if the research has established that heredity is a major determinant of intelligence. This is not to suggest that teaching and experience should not be attempted; it does suggest, however, that there might be limits on the extent of the effects.

3. PREDICTION, AND MODIFICATION OR CONTROL, OF BEHAVIOUR: these are important practical aims for applied psychology. Prediction and control are also, however, important tests of the validity of our observations and explanations. For example, our confidence in the accuracy and validity of an intelligence test is likely to be increased if it is established that the test results are good

predictors of an individual's success at work and school
(see chapter 11). In relation to the individual, a hypothesis which suggests that a person's depression is caused
by the discomfort of a high level of anxiety is given some
support by the demonstration that his depression improves
following a course of treatment to reduce his anxiety. Such
an observation is not, however, an infallible test of the
hypotheses since it is also known that depressive states
improve spontaneously even in the absence of treatment
(Rachman, 1973). The chapters in this book provide many
examples of the involvement of psychology in both prediction
and modification. In relation to the modification or control
of behaviour, recent years have seen important developments
in the application of psychological techniques to the reduction of human misery and the amelioration of functioning in
a wide range of spheres. We often take the opportunity to
refer to these developments in view of their obvious interest to the medical reader. Psychological treatments are
reviewed, for example, in chapters 6, 12 and 13, but are
also considered in many other chapters.

Psychology as a science

Psychology is basically a scientific discipline. But what
does this mean? In essence, it means that psychology shares
the same aims and methods which are commonly and traditionally used by other sciences such as physics, chemistry
or physiology.

   The overall aims of scientific enquiry are to observe,
explain, and predict or control natural phenomena. It is
important to emphasize, however, that the status of psychology as a science is not seriously affected by the many
ethical and practical problems which have tended to retard
progress in the observation, explanation, prediction and
control of behaviour. For example, social and ethical considerations have prevented direct observations of sexual
behaviour in humans until relatively recently. Precise
measurement of the physiological changes accompanying
behaviour have similarly been delayed until the technology
which is required has become available. Progress in these
respects, however, has been made and it is important to
remember - in answer to any criticism that psychology has
not made the same degree of progress as other sciences -
that psychology has 'a long past but a short history'
(Eysenck, 1976). What this means is that, though psychological curiosity is as old as mankind, scientific techniques have only been applied in psychology very recently.

   As we see in the chapters which follow, psychology also
shares the basic methods of scientific enquiry. Science has
a basic strategy which is carefully designed to ensure that
reliable facts are established and observations can be
repeated or replicated by independent investigators.

   Whilst there is some variation, the main steps in
scientific enquiry are: (i) observation and assessment; (ii)
the categorization and classification of observations and

the selection of specific categories which are of special interest; (iii) the formulation of hypotheses, models or theories to link observations and explain them; (iv) the derivation of objectively testable predictions in order to validate or test hypotheses, models and theories; (v) the collection of further observations (often within the setting of an experiment) to test predictions and establish their truth and accuracy; and finally (vi) the acceptance, rejection or modification of hypotheses, models or theories on the basis of new observations and established 'facts'.

Two important principles in this strategy involve, first, the importance of evidence which is factual and empirical; second, the application of the hypothetico-deductive approach which involves the derivation of testable deductions from explicitly stated hypotheses. This model is the best framework used by psychologists to investigate a wide range of phenomena and the following chapters provide many examples.

It is also important to emphasize that many of the activities of psychologists are not 'scientific' to the extent that they follow this pattern of five basic steps. Once again, however, this is also true of other disciplines. For example, astronomy is limited to verification of its theories by testing predictions since control of planetary and other movements is obviously not possible.

Within an applied context, the clinical psychologist will often be required to treat a patient on the basis of a set of unproven assumptions. He might have been able to accumulate evidence, formulate a model which identifies the factors responsible for the patient's problems, and establish that his model is consistent with the known evidence; the time available, however, and also the patient's interest and welfare, might often dictate that treatment be undertaken immediately rather than after any extensive testing of the theoretical assumptions which are made.

In some instances it is possible to combine intervention with a testing of hypotheses. For example, an individual whose stammer had been suggested to be caused by high anxiety was observed under three controlled conditions. One involved observations of his speech after a tranquillizer had been administered; another involved similar observations after the adminstration of a placebo or inactive substance; a third set of observations was made without any intake of tablets. The results demonstrated that speech interruptions were much less common after the tranquillizer and were relatively unaffected by the placebo. This conclusion provided support for the aetiological role of anxiety, and also had important implications for treatment. The example is, nevertheless, the exception which proves the rule in clinical practice that, for both practical and ethical reasons, an extensive testing of assumptions is often not feasible.

At this point, it would be useful to consider the methods commonly used by psychologist to collect information and test assumptions. The following section provides a brief summary of the major methods of psychology.

Methods of psychology

Direct observation

This involves the observation of the organism, often but not always in a number of natural surroundings, and with a minimum of interference from the observer. Ethology is a branch of enquiry which studies animals in their normal habitat, but the observational methods involved have been applied to a wider range of human behaviour (Hutt and Hutt, 1970). For example, developmental and child psychology has involved extensive and systematic observations of the behaviour of children. Norms or 'milestones' of development - whether in motor activities, speech, social or emotional responses - have been accumulated primarily from careful observation of children at different ages. Similarly, clinical observations have established the behaviours which cluster together to constitute the wide range of disorders listed in textbooks of psychiatry and abnormal psychology (see, for example, Davison and Neale, 1974).

Observational studies involve a number of decisions by the observer. In the first instance, the observer must decide on the aspects of behaviour which interest him. For example, he might be interested in intelligence or problem solving, in social and interpersonal responses, or in motor activities. When such decisions are made, observations inevitably become selective since the observer records certain events but disregards others.

Observers must also select a site where observations are to be made. Patients might, for example, be observed in a ward setting or in their homes; children might be observed either at home or school. The setting for observations is important since behaviour can be quite specific to a setting (Mischel, 1968). Behaviours observed in one setting might not therefore be representative of the individual's behaviour in general, or in other settings. Observers might also have to decide whether or not to alter the environment in order to establish whether changes in the environment are associated with changes in the individual's behaviour. For example, clinical studies have established that seating arrangements on a ward can exert significant effects on the interaction between patients. Seating can therefore be altered as an independent variable and further observations conducted to establish the effects in terms of behavioural change. In this instance, direct observation is complicated by the interventions associated with a controlled experiment.

Observation is an important method and, without doubt, it is the most important step in strategies of scientific enquiry. Observations suggest hypotheses and are also used to test hypotheses. As with most methods, however, observation in both natural and 'contrived' settings can involve a number of problems.

One difficulty is that, for both practical and ethical reasons, direct observation is sometimes not possible. For example, direct observation of sexual behaviour has become permissible and available only very recently in the history of objective enquiry (Belliveau and Richter, 1977). Another problem is that the presence of an observer can have significant effects on behaviour. The behaviour of a child can be influenced by the presence of an adult. The behaviour of an anxious individual can be dramatically altered by the presence of a trusted professional. Social behaviour, in interview or group discussions, is known to be sensitive to the presence of observers, and selection interviews would hardly be an ideal setting for the observation of the interviewee's 'natural' behaviour. Once again, the investigator's dilemma will be to decide whether the presence of the observer has produced a sample of behaviour which is atypical.

A third problem involves disagreement between observers, for it has been established that observer agreement or 'reliability' can be very poor unless precautions, such as a careful definition of rating categories, are taken. It is, in fact, sometimes difficult to differentiate between error due to observers and variation in the behaviour which is observed since it is well known that behaviour varies considerably with situations. In other words, behavioural characteristics such as punctuality, honesty or anxiety can be specific to certain settings (Mischel, 1968). If observers record their impressions in different settings (as has been demonstrated where the assessments of parents and teachers are compared), then the differences due to observer error and behavioural variation in the observed can be difficult to disentangle.

One final problem associated with direct observation is that there are many questions which cannot be resolved in this way and require further refinements in technique. For example, to some extent it is possible to observe and assess the individual's intelligence or problem-solving skills through the use of standard tests, but it is not possible to ascertain on this basis whether the individual's intellectual level is influenced more by heredity than his environment and experience. Other observations, such as comparisons of identical and non-identical twins, have been necessary to establish the contribution of heredity to the determination of intellectual competence. Nevertheless, direct observation plays a very important role in the process of psychological enquiry and is essential to the investigation of all psychological functions.

Observation and theory are closely interrelated. On the one hand, observations contribute to the derivation of theories. For example, observations of the behaviour of a patient might suggest that he is suffering from excessive anxiety or depression. Observations of the social incompetence of the mentally handicapped in institutional settings might suggest that their behaviour is influenced by a lack of stimulation or training. On the other hand, theories usually direct the attention of the observer to certain observations and often suggest to the observer that certain of these observations might be related. Freudian theory, for example, suggests that personality is influenced by early experience. Investigators have therefore been keen to relate aspects of the behaviour of mature individuals to early experiences such as weaning and toilet training. Another example relates to the determinants of intelligence. Suggestions about the importance of heredity have led investigators to compare the intelligence test results of identical twins, who have the same genetic endowment, with non-identical twins, who do not, in order to discover whether identical twins are more similar than non-identical twins in their test scores (Shields, 1962).

Introspection, self-observation and self-report
Introspection was at one time the main data source for psychology. In practice, the individual was required to observe his own feelings or functioning, and to report on these to the psychologist. Though the 'armchair' phase was probably very comfortable for participants, it was increasingly seen to be a rather sterile technique which had serious shortcomings. Self-reports of experience are difficult, and sometimes impossible, to validate; consistency in the self-reports of groups of observers might have reflected little more than the effects of suggestibility or group pressures; and discrepancies in self-reports are difficult to evaluate unless the investigator has recourse to other sets of data. Introspection, therefore, lost ground to other techniques, the main trend being to study behaviour directly and to bias psychology to the investigation of the observable.

The present status of self-report is that most psychologists accept that it should not be disregarded. At the same time, its limitations are known and the data gathered from individuals' or patients' self-report are normally corroborated by, or at least compared with, other observations. For example, the neurotic patient's complaints about severe anxiety are compared with the existence of other signs of anxiety. Anxiety might be expected to be evident in some aspects of overt behaviour. Anxiety associated with heights, open or enclosed spaces would involve avoidance or escape from cliffs, open spaces or small rooms. In addition, anxiety might also be associated with physiological changes such as muscular tension or a rapid pulse. If these other changes were present, then the inference of an anxiety state might be justified. If not, the self-report of discomfort might be inferred to be indicative of a mild degree of discomfort or, alternatively, simply an inaccurate communication.

Many aspects of self-report are indeed not difficult to validate. For example, a client's complaint that he is impotent or failing at his job could be corroborated by interviews with his sexual partners or an employer. Other aspects of self-report - such as indications of vague or indefinable internal sensations or discomforts - are difficult or impossible to corroborate in this manner. More recent research has also indicated that self-report can actually produce changes in behaviour. For example, the maintenance of diary records has been shown to be associated with interesting changes in eating and smoking (Thoreson and Mahoney, 1974).

Surveys

Surveys usually involve the collection of relatively large amounts of information. For example, opinion surveys involve interviews or questionnaires, which are administered to large samples of the general population. The most widely known survey is probably that conducted by Kinsey and his colleagues on aspects of sexual behaviour in post-war America (Kinsey, Pomeroy and Martin, 1948). Many thousands of individuals were interviewed about their attitudes to sex, their sexual preferences and sexual behaviour. This information was then analysed to demonstrate trends, and these trends were related to factors such as age, marital status, geographical area, education and social class.

Surveys can provide information which is valuable, theoretically important and practically useful. For example, Kinsey's findings demonstrated the wide variation in sexual behaviour and the difficulty of defining normality in a narrow manner. Surveys on the attainments and behaviour of children have contributed to developmental norms which allow clinicians and educationists to identify the limits of normality at different ages, and to identify the retarded or precocious child who might need special provisions to ensure that his needs are adequately met. The correlational data yielded by survey research have also made some contribution to the identification of those factors which affect or determine behaviour. For example, surveys of the changes in the intelligence test scores of the mentally handicapped in hospitals have demonstrated the importance of the individual's home background before admission (Clarke and Clarke, 1965). Patients from worse or deprived homes tend to make relatively larger improvements in test performance after admission, suggesting that the environment can both depress and stimulate their competence and attainments.

Surveys also have limitations which must be recognized. For example, many surveys involve self-report which is difficult to corroborate or verify. The information on sexual behaviour collected by Kinsey and his colleagues has often been challenged on this basis. One safeguard in this respect is to repeat surveys in different geographical areas in order to establish the reliability of any findings, and Kinsey's investigations did indeed include some checks of this kind.

Another problem for surveys involves the adequacy of samples. It is usually impractical or impossible to survey a whole population, so that samples of individuals need to be selected. These samples need to be representative of the population from which they are drawn. In practice, samples need to be as large as possible and also to be selected in a random manner so that every member of a population which is of interest (such as eight-year-old children or middle-class students in a specific town) has an equal chance of selection for assessment (Phillips, 1973). If samples are not representative of their parent population, then the results of a survey investigation are of doubtful value.

The controlled experiment
Psychology has a long and respectable history of laboratory experimentation which extends back to the nineteenth century (Boring, 1950). More recently, both laboratory and practical research have played important roles in the development of psychology as an objective and scientific discipline. Whereas in the past experimentation was often concerned with the behaviour of animals, or with limited aspects of human behaviour such as reaction time or shape perception, more recent research has been concerned with behaviours whose relevance to human welfare is more direct. There has, for example, been an increasing amount of objective evaluation of psychological treatments (Rachman, 1973). In addition, two important areas of psychological research - the experimental tradition and the psychology of individual differences - have been integrated in a manner which increases both the theoretical and practical value of the results.

The controlled experiment in psychology is usefully illustrated by considering an example. A clinical example is described in order to demonstrate the value of experimentation in the case of individuals who are suffering from a psychological problem. Our example involves individuals who are suffering from phobic anxiety conditions; the investigation is designed to establish whether treatment is effective, and also to identify the essential ingredients of the treatment programme. The steps involved in an objective investigation are provided in figure 1, though it must be stressed that this is one of a number of designs which might be employed.

This design allows the investigator to identify the effects of relaxation and exposure to the feared situation (e.g. the presence of others or exposure to open spaces) on a group of patients who suffer from a phobic-anxiety condition. Initial assessment, the first step in our experiment, provides 'baseline' or 'pre-treatment' data on such factors as the type and intensity of the individual's difficulties; characteristics such as age, sex, social background and personality might also be assessed in order to establish whether such factors are related to subsequent improvement and could be used as predictors of outcome. Random allocation to the four groups, the second step, should ensure homogeneity, but a check at this point will serve to confirm this. The four groups are therefore initially similar in terms of the severity of their disorder. Separate 'treatments' are then provided over the same time period for three groups whilst the fourth group is used as a 'no treatment' control. Reassessment then establishes whether the groups

Figure 1

(1)	(2)	(3)	(4)	(5)
Identify and assess patients	Random allocation to treatment groups	A. Relaxation training and exposure to fear situations OR B. Discussion of feared situations OR C. Relaxation alone OR D. No treatment control group	Reassessment	Follow-up

are homogeneous after intervention. If relaxation and graded exposure are essential to the modification of anxiety and phobic behaviour, Group A should be significantly better than the others at reassessment. Groups B and C are available to allow for the possibility that relaxation alone, or discussion alone, can produce similar effects. Follow-up assessments, which can be conducted at variable periods of time, establish whether any improvements which occur are stable over time and thus of greater practical value to the client.

Assessment procedures in clinical psychological research often involve several measures - such as self-report, ratings and direct measures of overt behaviour, and physiological assessment - since it has been demonstrated that treatments can have specific rather than general effects on behaviour. For example, an agoraphobic might improve to the point where he can walk in open space, but still feels subjectively very uncomfortable. Furthermore, some aspects of behaviour appear to change more rapidly than others in response to treatment.

The above example utilized a group design which has been used frequently in psychological research. Such designs have commonly analysed changes in terms of the average effect which follows the introduction of a treatment or other procedure. Individual difference in response is common, however, and important differences of this kind are missed if analyses are exclusively concerned with group effects. At least one study (Griffiths and Gillingham, 1978) has demonstrated that, in response to an experimental treatment, some individuals improve whilst others deteriorate. If an average effect is calculated, gains and losses cancel each other out, and the treatment can appear to have no effect at all. This means, of course, that the careless use of group designs can conceal important effects rather than lead to improvements in our knowledge of the changes associated with psychological treatment procedures. As an important supplement to group procedures, techniques have more recently been developed to allow objective investigations to be applied to the behaviour of the individual.

Experimental investigations of the single case (Hersen and Barlow, 1976) combine objective measurement with the use of the individual as his own control. The overall aim is to demonstrate links between modification procedures and behavioural change, and to establish cause-effect relationships. An example again suffices to illustrate important elements of single case methodology. A number of studies have recently reported on the evaluation of social skills training in the modification of disordered social and interpersonal behaviour. Social skills training procedures (cf. Trower, Bryant and Argyle, 1978) involve a combination of demonstration, guidance and feedback procedures which have been developed to remedy social inadequacy. These procedures might be applied to a client whose social behaviour had been observed, and found to be deficient to the extent that he tended to talk too little, to converse in an excessively quiet manner, to talk excessively about his weakness and to avoid eye contact during social interactions. Such deficiencies would be established by repeated observation and would be considered as 'targets' for modification.

The initial steps of a single case evaluation would involve repeated 'baseline' measures of the four target behaviours. In practice, the client's interaction with others would be observed and recorded on a number of occasions. Repeated assessment would also demonstrate whether or not the behaviours in question were stable when the individual was involved in social contact with different individuals (ideally of both sexes). If instabilities in any of the targets were identified, it might be possible to relate these to stimulus factors (e.g. whether the other person involved in an interaction was talkative or older than the client) or alternatively to variables (such as anxiety level) 'within' the client.

When baseline measures had been established, training procedures would then be applied to the first 'target' (e.g. a tendency to talk too little) but not to the others. The effectiveness of the treatment would be inferred from the existence and extent of change in the target, whilst the other responses would constitute controls and would not be expected to vary in the same manner. The other 'targets' would be subjected to training at different times, and the effectiveness of the training would be reflected in the association between the onset of treatment procedures and changes in the behavioural target. Repeated follow-up assessments would, in addition, establish the stability of any improvements whilst similar assessments in other situations would enable investigators to establish whether there was any generalization of treatment effects from the clinical setting (Griffiths, 1980). The following (figure 2) is a diagrammatic representation of findings on a hypothetical case.

Figure 2

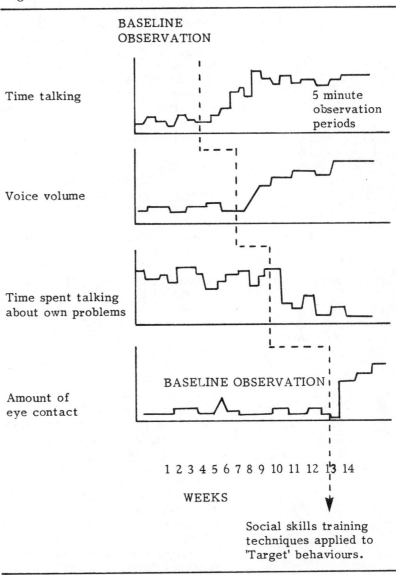

In some instances, it is possible to 'reverse' treatment procedures to ascertain the mechanisms which are essential for behavioural change. For example, psychological research on the importance of rewards suggests that it is important to provide rewards immediately or soon after a behavioural

response if that response is to be modified. One investigation of the importance of the timing of rewards compared
the effects of two procedures (Ayllon and Azrin, 1965). One
of these involved the provision of rewards which were contingent on the appearance of selected activities (such as
washing and dressing) in chronic ward psychiatric patients.
The other involved the provision of rewards which were
given independently of the patient's behaviour. The associated changes in activity indicated that, as had been
predicted, contingent or immediate rewards were indeed
responsible for improvements in patients' behaviour.
Activity levels decreased to pre-treatment levels when
rewards were provided but were not linked with selected
behaviours.

Ethical aspects of controlled research are not considered in any detail here, but it is important to remember
that ethical issues are raised in psychological experimentation which involves, for example, the withholding or delay
of treatments. The situation is not, however, simple and
uncomplicated to the extent that many of the treatments in
common use have not been objectively evaluated. The possibility that they have limited or no effects, or even disadvantages, cannot therefore be excluded. Careful psychological research is an important approach to ascertaining
whether treatments are effective and also to identifying the
variables and mechanisms which determine treatment effects.

References

Ayllon, T. and Azrin, N.H. (1965)
The measurement of and reinforcement of behaviour in
psychotics. Journal of Experimental Analysis of
Behaviour, 8, 357-383.
Belliveau, F. and Ritcher, L. (1977)
Understanding Human Sexual Inadequacy. London: Hodder
& Stoughton.
Boring, E.G. (1950)
A History of Experimental Psychology. New York: Appleton-
Century-Crofts.
Clarke, A.D.B. and Clarke, A.M. (1965)
Mental Deficiency, the Changing Outlook (2nd edn).
London: Methuen.
Davison, G.C. and Neale, J.M. (1974)
Abnormal Psychology: An experimental clinical approach.
New York: Wiley.
Eysenck, H.J. (1976)
Psychology as a bio-social science. In H.J. Eysenck and
G.D. Wilson (eds), A Textbook of Human Psychology.
Lancaster: MTP Press.
Griffiths, R.D.P. (1980)
Social skills and psychological disorder. In W.T.
Singleton, P. Spurgeon and P.R. Stammers (eds), The
Analysis of Social Skill. New York: Plenum Press.
Griffiths, R.D.P. and Gillingham, P. (1978)
The influence of videotape feedback on the self

assessments of psychiatric patients. British Journal of
Psychiatry, 183, 156-161.

Hersen, M. and Barlow, D.H. (1976)
Single case experimental designs. New York: Pergamon.

Hilgard, E.R., Atkinson, R.G. and Atkinson, R.L. (1971)
Introduction to Psychology (5th edn). New York: Harcourt
Brace Jovanovich. ('Physiology of Emotion', 336-340.)

Hutt, S.J. and Hutt, C. (1970)
Direct Observation and Measurement of Behaviour.
Springfield, Ill.: Thomas.

Kinsey, A.C., Pomeroy, W.B. and Martin, C.E. (1948)
Sexual Behavior in the Human Male. Philadelphia:
Saunders.

Mischel, W. (1968)
Personality and Assessment. New York: Wiley.

Phillips, J.L. (1973)
Statistical Thinking: A structural approach. San
Francisco: Freeman.

Rachman, S. (1973)
Psychological treatment. In H.J. Eysenck (ed.), Handbook
of Abnormal Psychology (2nd edn). London: Pitman Press.

Shields, J. (1962)
Monozygotic Twins Brought Up Apart and Brought Up
Together. London: Oxford University Press.

Thoresen, C.E. and Mahoney, M.J. (1974)
Behavioral Self Control. New York: Holt, Rinehart &
Winston.

Trower, P., Bryant, B. and Argyle, M. (1978)
Social Skills and Mental Health. London: Methuen.

Questions

1. What is the subject matter of psychology? What would psychologists find the main areas of interest?
2. What are the main aims of psychology? Illustrate these aims by reference to clinical examples.
3. Is psychology a science? What does the term 'science' mean? Compare the scientific status of psychology with that of anatomy, physiology and sociology.
4. What are the problems and limitations of a scientific discipline such as psychology in a clinical setting?
5. Discuss the subject matter, aims and methods of psychology. Provide examples of the applications of psychology in a clinical context.
6. What are the major methods of psychology? Discuss each method critically.
7. Compare and contrast the contributions made to psychological knowledge by direct observations, surveys and controlled experiments.
8. What contribution can psychology make to medicine?
9. What contribution can psychology make to medical training? Discuss the place of psychology in the training of medical students.
10. What are the similarities and differences between psychology, psychiatry and psychoanalysis?

2

Psychology and Medicine: This Book
David Griffiths

There are two broad aspects of psychology which are important for doctors. One of these consists of those skills in interacting with others which the doctor needs if he is to make an effective contribution to the welfare of his patients and of the Health Service in general. The second consists of the broad range of psychological knowledge and information which has been accumulated by psychologists and others (e.g. Rachman, 1977) and is again relevant to the provision of effective and efficient services to both individual patients and groups.

Examples of skills required by the doctor and which involve a significant psychological and behavioural component are not difficult to find. They are epitomized for many by the stereotype of the BBC's Dr Finlay figure whose bedside manner combines a humanitarian sympathy for the patient with a basic competence in the essentials of diagnosis and treatment. A more specific example involves the doctor's need to acquire interview skills which both allay patients' anxieties, recognize their expectations and, at the same time, allow him to gather the information which he needs. Doctors will often need to administer treatments which involve some discomfort to the patient in a manner which reduces stress and controls the possibility of patient refusal or non-compliance. Considerable skill is also needed to explain the nature and consequences of many disorders to patients; to inform patients or relatives about the presence of an incurable disease or the imminence of death; to inform parents that their child is mentally handicapped; or to control patients' eating or smoking habits in a manner which is uncomfortable in the short term but to their advantage in the long term. These and other achievements involve cognitive components (e.g. an awareness of the various ways of approaching issues and patients), and also perceptual sensitivity and a number of complex behavioural and communicative skills (Trower, Bryant and Argyle, 1978).

Psychological information and an understanding of the relevance of psychological and social factors to both normal and abnormal behaviours are also essential to the doctor. For example, he will benefit from an understanding of the factors which influence and determine the individual's anxiety and tension levels in relation to surgical or other procedures (cf. chapter 14). Doctors also clearly need to be aware of the research on the effects of short-term hospitalization on children, or of long-term institutional care on the social competence of the mentally handicapped. In addition, of course, they will need to know about the measures which can be adopted to prevent or ameliorate adverse responses to both short- and long-term hospitalization. In rather a different speciality, doctors clearly need to acquaint themselves with the current status of knowledge on the aetiology of sexual problems (cf. chapter 21). What are the limits of normality in sexual activity? To what extent are impotence or frigidity 'physical' in origin, and to what extent are they caused and maintained by psychological factors such as anxiety? As a final example, what methods are available to help patients to control their eating or smoking and, more generally, to follow treatment instructions given to them by their doctors? There are, of course, many examples of knowledge which must be regarded as essential to modern medicine. A literature on psychology and medicine has become increasingly available (e.g. Eysenck, 1973; Rachman, 1977; Rachman and Philips, 1978) and this book contains a selection of up-to-date reviews of relevant psychological knowledge.

These two aspects of psychology - skills and knowledge - are closely integrated in practice. For example, a doctor who interviews a patient presenting with a sexual difficulty will need a basic knowledge of sexual behaviour and problems but will also need the skills to elicit relevant information without embarrassing or antagonizing the patient. Alternatively, a doctor who needs to evaluate a child will often need some acquaintance with developmental norms and also the skills to elicit information on the child's behaviour from direct observation or interviews with the parents. Clinical child psychology is discussed in chapter 6.

Whilst recognizing that knowledge and skill are often integrated in practice, there are important reasons for distinguishing between them in theory. One is that it is possible for the doctor to be competent in one sphere but not the other. He might, for example, have an understanding of the psychology of sexual behaviour but not the skills which are required to elicit relevant information from patients. Alternatively, his interview skills might be adequate but redundant to the extent that he does not know enough about the psychological factors associated with sexual problems to ask the right questions. There is also another reason for distinguishing between psychological skills and information: they are acquired in quite different ways.

Skills cannot be acquired from books or lectures alone. The acquisition of skills requires demonstration and explanation, preferably by the competent and 'expert', but the trainee also requires the opportunity to practise extensively, to receive feedback on his performance and to modify his behaviour appropriately (Holding, 1965). Doctors and

medical students learn these skills from their clinical
supervision by consultants and other senior doctors and
there is no alternative to the observation of models,
practice and feedback. It cannot be assumed that trainees
are necessarily exposed to good 'models' and adequate
feedback since there is some evidence to indicate, for
example, that doctors are not always effective in communicating with their patients (cf. chapter 18). Nevertheless,
it is certainly not necessarily true that psychologists
would be more appropriate or effective models or trainers in
these respects. In any case, psychologists would have
limited experience of most of the clinical problems which
need to be handled by the doctor (e.g. preparing a patient
for surgery or giving advice about family planning), so that
there is no real alternative to training by senior doctors
who normally have very extensive experience and expertise
in their speciality fields.

In relation to psychological 'knowledge', however,
psychologists do have a stronger claim to be regarded as
'experts' since the accumulation of information about the
aetiology, assessment and modification of behaviour is an
important part of their contribution. The remaining sections
of this book provides summaries of psychological knowledge
and theory in relation to a number of topics. Some of these
topics (e.g. aspects of child development) involve normal
functioning whilst others (e.g. insomnia and mental
handicap) involve disorders and problems.

How is this information relevant to the needs of the
practising doctor, whether he is in training or is already
trained? Listed below are six aspects of the usefulness of
this information to medicine.

*   Psychological research often provides a rational basis
    for clinical activities in relation to both individual
    patients and categories of disorder, and also in rela-
    tion to the planning and provision of services. For
    example, research on the biological determinants of
    anxiety provides a rational basis for the application of
    medication to control predispositions to develop high
    anxiety. Complementary research on the importance of
    environmental determinants (e.g. life stresses) and
    psychological mechanisms (e.g. conditioning of emotional
    responses) provides a rational basis for the explanation
    of disorders and also the application of psychological
    treatment techniques. As another example, survey re-
    search which has demonstrated wide individual differ-
    ences in sexual behaviour and preferences has alerted
    clinicians to the wide limits of normality in sex.
    Finally, investigations of the importance of the envi-
    ronment in determining the social competence of the
    mentally handicapped have provided a rational basis for
    activity programmes and training procedures.
*   Psychological research often identifies problems of
    practical and clinical relevance. It has been

demonstrated, for example, that many of the symptoms
and handicaps associated with psychiatric disorders or
mental handicap are functions of the environment (e.g.
lack of stimulation) rather than of a biologically
determined disease process. This work indicates the need
to provide an interesting and stimulating environment,
and also the problems to be expected if institutional
environments are not adequate in these respects. Investigations of the modification of obesity and smoking
have demonstrated another problem. Whilst it is sometimes not difficult to reduce weight or stop smoking,
follow-up indicates that relapses are common, so that it
is considerably more difficult to maintain long-term
changes in behaviour.

* An understanding of the psychology of many disorders
  will often influence the selection of treatment goals.
  It can be seen from the following chapters that research
  associated with surgical stress (chapter 14) has demonstrated the importance of information given to the
  patient. The work of Philip Ley and his colleagues
  (chapter 18) has further demonstrated the need to communicate effectively with patients. The evidence on the
  problems and needs of the terminally ill and their
  families (chapter 8) also indicates many of the goals
  relevant to adequate care.
* Psychological knowledge does not necessarily produce
  skilled social behaviour, but it can nevertheless
  contribute to the development of skills and expertise,
  for knowledge is invariably an important element in
  expertise. In relation to most disorders, and irrespective of the presence or importance of a psychological
  component, the doctor will need to know where his attention and enquiry should be directed. In relation to
  sexual problems, for example, he might need to consider
  the importance of emotional state, beliefs and attitudes, personality, previous experience and family background. Alternatively, the doctor's awareness of the
  importance of information in controlling stress associated with surgery might motivate him to communicate
  carefully with his patients. Finally, his awareness of
  the wide limits in sexual preferences might guide his
  assessment of the sexual behaviour of his patients (cf.
  chapter 21).
* Psychological enquiry has provided a considerable body
  of information which could not be derived from clinical
  experience. There are many questions, for example, which
  contact with patients could not answer and which require
  the refinements of controlled research. In relation to
  psychological treatments, clinical observation might
  establish that there are improvements in a client's
  behaviour. Controlled studies might be needed, however,
  to identify the factors which are responsible for such
  changes. Professionals, including both doctors and
  psychologists, are often involved with client groups who

are by definition 'abnormal'; for this reason, their impressions of 'normality' are likely to be biassed and possibly inaccurate. Surveys are, therefore, potentially useful to the extent that they sample the behaviour of more representative groups of the population, and provide a more reliable and valid basis for the evaluation of the individual.

* Summaries and discussions of the products of psychological enquiry are also useful to the extent that they acquaint doctors with the aims, methods and contributions of psychologists. The profession of psychology is relatively small and has been given official recognition very recently in the history of the Health Services in Great Britain (Trethowan Report, 1977). Clinical psychologists have, however, become increasingly involved in areas of the Health Service outside psychiatry, and recognize that their contribution to patient welfare is likely to be maximized if they can both demonstrate and communicate to others the ways in which psychology is relevant to patient care. This text should make some contribution to that goal.

Psychology and medicine: this book

This book is a selective discussion of the relevance of psychology to a number of areas which should be of some interest to doctors. It is important to emphasize that it is not a comprehensive handbook. In spite of the time which has elapsed since the Royal Commission report on medical education (1968), we have not yet reached the point where there is agreement or uniformity in selecting those aspects of psychology which are relevant to doctors. Indeed, it is unlikely that a standard syllabus will ever be agreed, since the limits of our knowledge continue to be extended by psychological enquiry and investigation.

The sections which follow have in common a basic set of aims. First, each chapter attempts to provide a summary of psychological knowledge and opinion in a particular area. Each contributor has some claim to be regarded as an expert and the summaries provided are up-to-date synopses of contemporary information. Second, each chapter has been selected since it presents psychology in a manner which is interesting and relevant. For the most part, reviews are concerned with issues of practical importance and relevance to Health Service professionals and others. Comprehensive reviews of psychological research on such functions as learning, personality and human development are not provided, but are available elsewhere if the reader should wish to pursue an interest in such fields (Hilgard, Atkinson and Atkinson, 1971; Eysenck, 1973; Chapman and Gale, in press). The emphasis on relevance and practical interest in this text is intended to increase the value of this particular volume to doctors and others involved in Health Care.

A third aim, already mentioned, is that the chapters available in this book should contribute to the development of clinical expertise. As we have seen, knowledge of the kind provided here does not necessarily produce skills but it does, nevertheless, make a potentially important contribution to that closely integrated package of skill and information which is more appropriately labelled as clinical expertise or competence. In relation to psychological matters, the reader should benefit to the extent that his opinions will, whether they are subsequently correct or otherwise, have had the opportunity to be informed.

How should this book be used?

Since it is a collection of chapters which have been written independently, it follows that it can be read either in its entirety or piecemeal. Though a reading of the whole book will provide the reader with a more comprehensive view of the relevance of psychology, a selection of specific sections will provide the same goal in relation to limited areas of application such as counselling (chapter 13), the use of standardized tests (chapter 11), mental handicap (chapter 20), or obesity (chapter 23). Each contribution is, of course, dependent on the skill and knowledge of its author and there can be no guarantee that conclusions and recommendations are valid in every instance. Chapters should therefore be read critically and the reader will continually need to relate the content to his own experience. On the other hand, it is also to be hoped that the reader will be able to relate his own experience and views to the conclusions and information provided by each chapter. In order to increase the teaching potential of each chapter further, discussion with both teachers and other students is to be encouraged. In this respect, the relatively short length of most chapters increases their suitability as bases for group discussions and seminars.

References

Chapman, A.J. and Gale, A. (in press)
Psychology and People: A tutorial text. London: Macmillan/British Psychological Society.

Eysenck, H.J. (1973)
Handbook of Abnormal Psychology (2nd edn). London: Pitman.

Hilgard, E.R., Atkinson, R.C. and Atkinson, R.L. (1971)
Introduction to Psychology (5th edn). New York: Harcourt Brace Jovanovich.

Holding, D.H. (1965)
Principles of Training. Oxford: Pergamon Press.

Rachman, S. (1977)
Contributions to Medical Psychology, Volume 1. Oxford: Pergamon Press.

Rachman, S. and Philips, H.C. (1978)
Psychology and Medicine. Harmondsworth: Penguin.

Royal Commission on Medical Education (1968)
Report 1965-1968. Cmnd. 3569. London: HMSO.

Trethowan Report (1977)
The Role of Psychologists in the Health Services. Report of the Sub-committee. London: HMSO.
Trower, P., Bryant, B. and Argyle, M. (1978)
Social Skills and Mental Health. London: Methuen.

Questions

1. Discuss the ways in which psychology can be relevant to medicine.
2. What are the limitations imposed by teaching psychology to medical trainees through lectures?
3. What provisions are needed to ensure that trainee doctors acquire psychological skills in addition to psychological knowledge?
4. In relation to the teaching of psychology in medical schools, what aims and methods should guide the teaching?
5. How do medical trainees normally view the relevance and importance of psychology to (a) their training and (b) the care of patients? Examine the evidence for and against a variety of views of the relevance and importance of psychology.

Annotated reading

Davison, G.C. and Neale, J.M. (1974) Abnormal Psychology: An experimental clinical approach. New York: Wiley.
This is a well-written, illustrated and clear account of clinical psychological aspects of psychiatry. It also contains an introductory section on theory and empirical research in psychology, and then reviews the contribution of psychology to the various categories of psychiatric disorder such as depression, schizophrenia, etc.

Eysenck, H.J. (1976) Psychology as a bio-social science. In H.J. Eysenck and G. Wilson (eds), A Textbook of Human Psychology. Lancaster: MTP Press.
This is a useful contemporary introduction to psychology as a discipline which attempts to integrate biological and social approaches in the explanation of behaviour and psychological functioning.

Rachman, S. and Philips, H.C. (1978) Psychology and Medicine. Harmondsworth: Penguin.
This should be read as a companion volume to the Davison and Neale textbook since it reviews the contribution of psychology to a selection of clinical problems outside psychiatry. Among the topics covered are aspects of child care, headaches and sleep problems.

3

Biological Bases of Behaviour
Irene Martin

Opening remarks
DAVID GRIFFITHS

A discussion of the biological determinants of behaviour is an appropriate part of our introduction to psychology in medicine for at least two reasons. The first is that biological factors are important components of the aetiology of human behaviour. We have already seen (chapter 1) that psychology is a bio-social discipline. The broad assumption made by most psychologists is that human behaviour is determined by a complex aetiology which involves both biological and environmental 'causes'.

In the past, the proponents of 'biological' and 'environmental' models tended to belong to schools of thought which were mutually exclusive. The assumption was that behaviour was a function of either biology or environment but not both. More recently, however, it has been increasingly realized that both biology and environment (or 'nature' and 'nurture') are involved. The focus of controversy now involves the relative contribution of the two sets of determinants and their interaction to produce the broad range of psychological functioning, and also individual differences. Irene Martin's brief has been to examine the relevance and importance of biological factors, whilst some of the chapters which follow (e.g. Jim Orford's discussion of institutions and Neil Frude's review of the family) are more concerned with the importance of the environment as a context for human behaviour.

A second reason for the inclusion of this chapter is that a medical readership will be more acquainted with an organic model than with environmental and social determinants of behaviour. Doctors will also tend to be more interested in biological determination, though they will be more accustomed to examining the organic determinants of physical pathology rather than human behaviour. An examination of biological determinants is, therefore, a convenient starting point since it is an area of common interest to medicine and psychology. Irene Martin's discussion refers to both examples of biological aetiology (such as the role of heredity and brain damage) and also, very importantly, to some of the mechanisms which have been postulated to explain how biological factors influence behaviour (e.g. the role of conditioning and arousal).

Irene Martin's review also discusses some of the problems involved in relating behaviour to its biological

aetiology. An investigation of brain-behaviour relationships, for example, has obviously been hampered by a broad
range of practical problems and humanitarian considerations.
Experimental techniques, such as the observation of the
effects of induced lesions, would have provided answers to
many questions but are simply not possible for reasons which
need hardly be emphasized. Progress has therefore tended to
be slow and patchy but has nevertheless occurred, and this
chapter is to be welcomed as a useful and broad introduction
to the current status of our knowledge of the biological
bases of behaviour.

Introduction
IRENE MARTIN

Effective human survival on this earth is achieved by
adaptive behaviour, made possible by the evolution of a
brain and nervous system which bear the imprint of solutions
to survival over millions of evolutionary years. For man,
some large part of his knowledge has been acquired during
his lifetime, but for him as for all living creatures there
are innate programmes which regulate many functions. Whatever we do, my writing, your reading, our sitting, breathing
and wakefulness involve countless electrical and chemical
events within us, most quite beyond conscious awareness.

The focus in this chapter is on adaptive behaviour, and
includes attention, emotionality, ways of evaluating events
in the environment, conditioning, and mechanisms of coping
with stress. First we need to consider what is meant by the
term 'behaviour', and how it can be classified, described
and explained; next, we consider the relationship which
psychological concepts have to the brain and nervous system.
Individual differences form an important part of this examination: individuals differ markedly in almost all aspects of
behaviour, in memory, learning, intelligence, and in their
general ability to cope with life events. Some theories of
personality are discussed which relate differences between
people to differences in the reactivity of physiological
systems. The question of maladaptive behaviour is considered
in such contexts as excessive anxiety, stress, and psychosomatic reactions, and modes of investigations described in
which psychological and physiological principles interact.

We begin by asking such questions as: what kinds and
classes of behaviour interest us, what is their importance,
and what theories can account for them? These questions are
asked with specific reference to the contribution which
psychology can make to a general biological view of man.

What is behaviour?

To begin with human behaviour at its most acccessible level,
we can watch the individual in action, speaking, socializing, playing games, and going to work: that is, performing
the usual range of human activities and interactions with
the world around. Suppose we begin like modern ethologists
- those who study the behaviour of animals in natural settings - and extend the study to man so that we become man-

watchers. Suppose, further, that just as in the study of animals we cannot ask the people we are watching why they do certain things or what they are feeling: we simply observe. We would see how people greet one another, dress, flirt, fight and demonstrate. It might be useful to use some classification such as parental behaviour, work behaviour, social behaviour, or illness behaviour.

However, parental behaviour is very broad. It includes reproduction, home-making, maternal/paternal roles, feeding, education and development of the young. For purposes of analysis it needs to be broken down, and when this is done we quickly arrive at hundreds of small units of behaviour: feeding the baby, cuddling and contact, organizing a daily schedule, and so on. If we ask one simple question, such as how does a baby's perception of the mother's face develop, we need to take careful measurements in a laboratory-type setting, comparing and measuring reactions to 'mother's face' with reactions to other faces and objects in the environment. In this way psychologists are led from the straightforward observation of the stream of life to much more detailed aspects of activities and behaviour; and in doing so they encounter charges of living within ivory towers removed from real-life situations. But the breaking down of what we observe into manageable segments is essential for understanding and measurement, as all sciences have recognized.

Rapid advances in a science often follow the identification of a meaningful and measurable unit: for example, the cell in physiology, the neuron in neurophysiology, the gene in genetics. It may be that psychology has not yet found the most appropriate units for describing behaviour, and at present it deals with both narrow (e.g. reflexes) and broad (e.g. play) types of responses. Once meaningful and measurable units of behaviour have been identified there are several features which have to be considered. An important one relates to measurement such as assigning a ranking or rating to the unit of interest. Suppose our unit is a set of responses used to define aggressive behaviour. We might then record how often a child engages in this aggressive behaviour: very frequently, often, sometimes, rarely or never? Having made a measurement for one child a next step is to interpret this. Is it unusual? An individual measurement needs to be compared with the norm of an appropriate sample; boys, for example, may show aggressive behaviour more commonly than girls; fourteen-year-old boys more commonly than six year olds.

The ultimate usefulness of any isolated unit or concept of behaviour lies in its relation to explanation; at a more fundamental level there are theories about aggression as about many kinds of behaviour. What motivates what we do? Just as important, how long do we persist or when do we stop what we are doing? It is understandable that we eat when hungry, but why do some people never know when to stop?! Behaviour like eating is clearly directed towards certain ends: food alleviates certain tissue deficiencies and its intake restores equilibrium: it may have analogies with people feeling 'better' when they have had a good cry or a good row.

This, then, is an outline of some of the factors which govern behavioural analysis and its interpretation. They range from the need to define appropriate units of behaviour, to measurement which involves norms and variation, to the abstraction of certain concepts and to theories which postulate underlying principles of behaviour such as seeking and enjoying an equilibrium of functioning.

Evolution

The opening of this chapter emphasized the role of the brain. It is possible for evolutionary development to follow many routes, each of which offers a specific adaptive advantage. Some animals survive better in their environments because of their strength, speed or camouflage. The story of man's evolutionary development centres on the brain, and the elaboration of the brain and nervous system in conjunction with developing manual dexterity. Lowly organisms do not possess a recognizable brain, but gradually it develops to become the complex structure which we know.

One consequence of an evolutionary approach is to view behaviour as being adaptively fitted to a given environment. This can be achieved by the inheritance of instinctive responses which are built into the nervous system as part of its inherited structure, and which appear virtually ready-made at their first performance. Even these, however, typically improve in efficiency with experience. The ability to modify behaviour through learning and experience characterizes all animals, but man above all.

It also follows from an evolutionary perspective that man's behaviour can be viewed as continuous with that of other animals and explanations of motivation, emotion and learning should be applicable across species. In the case of learning principles this has been a good workable assumption: all animals habituate to a repeated event which is harmless and many show critical periods at which learning is optimally effective; they shape their behaviour according to principles of reward or punishment.

In other instances, for example speech and concept formation, such an assumption has been questioned. It may be that spoken language is species-specific to man, and that infra-human animals do not have the brain structure or development which makes such language possible. Attempts to teach spoken language to chimpanzees have not progressed far. Complex forms of non-verbal communication exist among most social animals: in gesture, in the proximity or distance which we put between ourselves and other people, in eye-gaze and direction, and in a very extensive set of facial expressions and vocalizations. It is possible to gain at least as much information about social interactions from these sources as from the spoken word.

The development of language and abstract concepts lead to the co-existence in man of an elaborate cognitive structure based on strong emotional-motivational foundations. Although he learns to fulfil and express these primitive requirements in socially acceptable ways, sexual needs, needs for dominance, interdependencies, rivalries and infant care, all form a basic and powerful set of motivations which interact in complex ways with the more sophisticated set of cognitive skills.

Attempts to assess the relative contribution of these factors in human behaviour have generated a number of controversies in which protagonists often take an overly simplistic point of view. Some have maintained that behaviour is dominated by instincts; others by learning; some that intelligence (and personality and illness) is inherited, others that it is a result of the environment; some that man's emotionality is powered by physiological drives, and others that it results from a cognitive interpretation of life events. As is often the way with extremist arguments, the work of analysing the real issues is laborious, lengthy and technical.

The nature/nurture debate has recently been carried on within the context of sociobiology; this is defined by Wilson (1975) as the study of the biological basis of social behaviour, particularly of animal societies but also early human and contemporary human societies. It seeks to extend genetic analysis to human social organizations and argues that such socio-cultural systems represent a new stage of evolution. This viewpoint has been vigorously attacked by those who object to the 'biologizing' of human society because of complex ethical and political implications.

A biologically-based psychology has to make assumptions about the working organization of the brain. Textbook descriptions point out that it has an input sensory system which provides information about the world through eyes, ears, touch, taste, etc., a central processing unit which stores, codes and elaborates the input, and an output muscular system, through which we move and act in the environment. This provides a convenient descriptive structure within which sensations, perceptions, memory and motor skills can be studied.

While an input/central-processor/output description of the brain may be a useful shorthand device it tends to over-emphasize the importance of structural divisions. In practice, most behaviour is a patterning of perceptions, learning and executive skills which are linked in complex ways. The act of attention, for example, involves the bodily alignment of the sense organs to receive information, a high degree of selectivity of sensory input, an interpretive element, and the preparation for movement should the attended-to signal require prompt action. A view which emphasizes function rather than structure is preferable in that it stresses the active, organizing role of the brain; it reflects the way in which the individual is actively scanning his world, interpreting and evaluating what goes on in terms of what is important for survival and effective behaviour.

A fundamental assumption is that an organism cannot survive unless it has an innate mechanism which tells it when it is favourably or unfavourably correlated with its environment. This carries the implication that the only way it can 'get the message' is by some form of subjective awareness of its own welfare and comfort, including the machinery for not liking to be uncomfortable.

A welfare system

Bodily activity ensures that we approach or move away from different classes of events; towards those which are good, benefit us and promote welfare, and away from those which are bad, dangerous and destructive of life.

Detection of the positive and negative in the world is an innate feature of all forms of life. A plant turns towards the sun and light through mechanisms of phototropism; it absorbs water and minerals as required. For animals, positive or negative evaluations are accompanied by a pattern of physiological changes organized towards approach or withdrawal. In the natural environment many stimuli will be neutral while others, such as extremes of temperature and pressure, will produce an unlearned evaluative response on every exposure.

These positive and negative evaluations and perceptions of beneficial and harmful factors can be generalized to other environmental events through processes of conditioning, and in this way many likes and dislikes can be acquired. Experiments with humans have shown that if neutral stimuli are paired closely in time either with pleasant conditions (a good lunch) or unpleasant (putrid odours), the neutral stimuli will subsequently be rated as more pleasant or more unpleasant. It is a common experience that tastes which were once pleasant become disagreeable or even revolting when they have been associated with discomfort or nausea. An enormous advantage is gained when new evaluations can be acquired through this process of conditioning in that they permit the anticipation of favourable or unfavourable events and enable the organism to ensure a better adjustment to its environment.

Concepts of behaviour

Arousal

One of the most striking and easily observable features of human activity is its shift along a dimension of arousal. Humans, in line with many animals, show phases of sleep, wakefulness and high energy output. At high levels of arousal, many cognitive functions such as speed of reacting, memorizing, learning, etc., improve. But there is a limit for every individual, and once past this limit performance tends to decline. The spur of high arousal when writing examination papers must be a common experience; extreme agitation, on the other hand, can exert an unpleasant handicapping effect. It seems that up to a certain optimal point arousal acts as a spur to do well, but when it becomes too intense and spills over into anxiety, behaviour is disorganized and people are unable to perform efficiently on a whole range of tasks.

The psychological concept of general arousal and its relationship to performance has been made more plausible by the discovery of a structure within the brain, the reticular formation, which seems to serve as a general arousal system for the cortex. Traditional sensory physiology recognized that sensory pathways travel from the peripheral sense organs up through the brainstem to the appropriate sensory region of the cortex. It is now known that neural messages going along the classical sensory pathways also send messages into the ascending reticular activating formation and the diffuse thalamocortical system which in turn send arousal messages to the cortex, serving to maintain its level of wakefulness and alertness. Thus the function of these arousal systems includes the maintenance of cortical and behavioural arousal.

As individuals become more aroused and excited, a higher level of energy mobilization (i.e. release of stored energy from the liver, muscles, etc.) is required to support the energetic activity which may be required. At the sleep end of the continuum, sleep itself has been broken down into a variety of stages which are differentiated according to the pattern of brain (electro-encephalographic) activity. One of them is called REM (rapid eye movement) sleep, or dream sleep, in which muscle relaxation co-exists with electro-cortical arousal, muscle twitches and often dramatic increases in autonomic activity.

Evidence indicates that the sleep-waking cycle is regulated by a stable internal clock, with characteristics peculiar to the individual. It is a dimension of relevance to the understanding of individual differences, since people vary in their level of arousal throughout the 24-hour cycle and the experience of stress tends to be associated with disturbed sleep and arousal patterns.

Emotion

Another important concept which links the study of behaviour and brain is that of emotion, a term which can be viewed from a hundred different viewpoints but which in the present context is examined with respect to its physiological implications.

Many observations indicate that emotionality is related to the activity of the autonomic nervous system, and internal bodily upheaval is one of the surest signs we have that we are emotionally disturbed. It was an imaginative leap, however, to suggest that this disturbance has a biological utility which lies in preparation for action. Cannon (1963) assigned an 'emergency' function to the sympathetic division, pointing out that pain and major emotions such as fear and rage are manifested in the activity of the sympathetic nervous system. He demonstrated that the wide distribution of sympathetic fibres permits diffuse action throughout the body, whereas the cranial and sacral divisions of the parasympathetic system with their restricted distributions allow for more specific action.

Sympathetic impulses to the heart make it beat faster. They cause constriction of the blood vessels of the gut and control blood flow in such a way as to direct more blood to brain and skeletal muscles. Sympathetic effects are closely connected with the release of hormones which circulate in the blood to augment and prolong sympathetic neural effects.

The importance of Cannon's work was his experimental approach in linking emotional behaviour with its physiological substrate, in pointing to the utility of these bodily changes in terms of mobilizing the organism for prompt and efficient fight or flight, and in trying to elucidate the physiological structures within the brain which govern this type of behaviour. Those implicated are located in the visceral brain (limbic system): that is, the hippocampal structures, amygdala, cingulum and septum. This part of the brain plays an important role in elaborating the emotional feelings that guide behaviour.

Investigations with human subjects have attempted to elucidate the role of cognitions in the experience of emotion. It is not known how many emotions there are which can be differentiated in terms of physiologically based activity (fear and anger are emotions which are likely to show different patterns of autonomic and muscular activity, but the range could be much wider) or whether emotion refers to a general state of arousal which we learn to label as love, depression, envy, etc., depending upon the situation and the interpretation of the events which have produced the arousal.

The significance of concepts of arousal and emotionality lies in their linkage with the brain and nervous system, and in their role in stress, health and well-being. Man no longer lives in a jungle but the 'emergency' services he has inherited still act as though he did; the signs of danger are not from predators but become conditioned to stimuli, events and people in the course of everyday interaction with the environment. Excessive physiological arousal occurs in states like anxiety, generalizes to all kinds of stimuli and is highly unpleasant to experience.

Motivation

One popular conception of motivation is that of 'drives' which energize behaviour in specific directions, that is, towards food, water and sexual partners and away from pain and punishment. Animals deprived of fundamental biological needs become restless and active, cross obstructions and learn different responses in order to achieve their goals. It is therefore implied in many theories of motivation that organisms act mainly to reduce basic drives, and that many forms of responding are learned because the reduction of drives (by eating, drinking, etc.) is rewarding.

In a general biological sense both motivation and emotion can be viewed as a complex integration of behaviour involving selective attention to certain events, a heightened physiological state of excitement, and certain probable patterns of action. These patterns of action are common to most higher species of animals and have a clear biological utility in coping with the environment and with survival. However, it has always seemed evident that biological theories of motivation are thinly stretched when it comes to human experience. Various social needs relating to achievement, power, affiliation, etc., have been postulated which do not readily fit into existing drive theories, and to date no single satisfactory theory of motivation has been formulated in human psychology.

Conditioning

We learn to do certain things and learn not to do others. Of the skills we learn, some of the most dramatic involve muscular co-ordination, as in tennis, skating or swimming. Another set involves mental skills, such as extensive memorizing and the development of concepts about the world. There is another category of responses – evaluations, perceptions, feelings and emotions, many of which occur outside normal conscious awareness – which are believed to be learned through the process of conditioning. This mechanism is also useful as an explanation of the development and maintenance of maladaptive habits such as persistent and neurotic anxiety which involve the wide-ranging physiological concomitants which have been discussed. Since conditioning can occur in physiological systems of such diversity as the viscera, the endocrine and the immunosuppressive system, it has been implicated in the physiological stress responses associated with psychosomatic disorders.

The process of conditioning relates to the pairing in time of a 'neutral' with a 'significant' stimulus. Most people are familiar with the outline of Pavlov's conditioning methods with dogs, in which a quiet tone (neutral conditioned stimulus, CS) is followed by food (a significant unconditioned stimulus, UCS). Pavlov recorded the salivation which occurred as a natural response (unconditioned response, UCR) to the food, and demonstrated that the salivary response gradually comes to be given to the CS (a conditioned response, CR). Though the outline may be familiar, however, the connection between salivating dogs and human behaviour, personality and illness is not self-evident.

Suppose we replace the terms CS and UCS with life events and the CR and UCR with widespread physiological responses related to emotionality and pain. The implications become clearer. If one has ever been in a car crash, the general constellation of events – sounds, place, people, shouting – act as a significant and traumatic UCS, arousing great fear and widespread bodily reactions (UCRs). Return, even many years later, to the place where the accident occurred and the once neutral cues of the road and surrounding terrain will probably re-evoke the previous sensations and emotions (as CRs) quite powerfully. The significant aspects of conditioning are that two events have become associated in such a way that feelings and bodily reactions can be activated by certain stimuli, once of themselves 'neutral' but having preceded important events, come to exert strong and lasting effects on our feelings and reactions. In laboratory situations the CS and UCS are usually paired on many occasions, but in real life (as well as some laboratory conditions) a single pairing is sufficient if the events are sufficiently great in their impact.

Once the CR is acquired it will be reliably given provided that the CS-UCS pairing is continued. If, however, the UCS is omitted and the CS is given alone, the CR will extinguish: that is, it will gradually die away. Conditioning experiments usually include an acquisition phase, during which the CR develops, and an extinction phase during which it disappears.

The development of conditioned fears has obvious biological utility in preparing for and avoiding dangerous situations which might lead to pain and death. However, many human fears become attached to a variety of relatively harmless objects such as birds and insects, high places and aeroplanes, having injections, walking in the streets, or up stairs: that is to say, situations in which it is inappropriate to have anything more than a mild anxiety response. How some people acquire conditioned fears, who they might be, and what can be done about it are themes which are considered later.

Problems with concepts in psychology

Terms like arousal, emotion and conditioning have been derived from the analysis and observation of behaviour, and are related to underlying physiological mechanisms. Psychologists are divided, however, as to whether (i) they want to relate psychological concepts to physiology and the brain, and (ii) even if they want to, whether this is always a feasible thing to do. There is, therefore, a recurring debate as to the meaning which a psychological concept can have if it is independent of physiology. In practice, of course, a great deal of psychological research has continued quite successfully with the analysis and development of concepts such as attention, memory and learning without any reference to the nervous system.

In trying to develop purely behavioural concepts, one influential group of psychologists (the behaviourists) turned their attention to the nature of the interaction of the individual with his environment. They attempted to identify those situational/environmental factors (the general term 'stimulus' is used in this context) which precede certain kinds of responses, and to establish regularities ('laws') between stimuli and responses. In such a stimulus-response analysis the on-going state of the person may be important, but it need not refer to a physiological condition. A purely psychological description is possible of an individual's cognitions and perceptions of the stimulus events and of his decisions to act.

This leads to one of the greatest difficulties in psychology. If we want to know how a person perceives or feels in a situation, what kind of information do we gain when we ask him? This requires him to 'introspect' and requires us to accept his verbalization of his judgements and reasons about how he feels. Clinicians frequently have to rely on the patient's answers to such questions as 'How do you feel?' or 'Where is the pain?' Many psychological studies have tried to investigate this problem, recognizing that in its basic form none of us has more than a very limited access to our own mental and physiological processes, and that what people say and what they feel and do are often not very highly related. Therefore asking a person how he feels may not provide an adequate answer: (i) he may be so 'mixed up' he genuinely does not know how he is feeling; (ii) he may not want to be truthful, for a whole variety of reasons; or (iii) he may have learned to use words like 'anger', 'anxiety', 'pain' and 'depression' in an unusual way. Without very precise definitions there is no way we can be sure that your use of words to describe subjective experience is the same as mine.

When Van Gogh paints a chair and a physicist describes the atomic properties of wood they are looking at the same object from completely different perspectives. When psychologists use terms such as 'emotions' and 'stress' they are using everyday, common-sense language, used freely by everyone, but they may mean something quite different. Common-sense explanations insist that people have expectations, awareness, emotions, beliefs, etc. Psychological concepts have to be developed in accordance with scientific criteria: that is to say, they must be properly defined, have minimal ambiguity, and ultimately have implications for causal analyses. In such a goal it will almost certainly be necessary to clear up some of the misunderstandings between the use of terms as 'ordinary language' explanations and as scientific concepts.

Individual differences

There are many ways of considering variations in human behaviour. Not all of them relate to the brain and nervous system, but in this section we concentrate on those which relate personality to arousal and emotion systems of the brain. Medical and veterinary clinicians, animal breeders and observant farmers have long been aware of marked individual differences in the susceptibility of different animals to disease, responsiveness to injury, and drugs; yet recognition of individual differences in people has often been neglected.

One set of investigations, originating with Pavlov's observations on dogs, has postulated that a dimension of general cortical excitability ranging from high (excited) to low (inhibited) states underlies individual differences in behaviour. As neuro-physiological knowledge has grown, this simple system has become elaborated to refer to the functions of the frontal cortex and of sub-cortical regions, particularly the reticular activating system (involved in arousal) and the hypothalamic/pituitary circuit (involved in emotionality). In addition, the concept has been extended to include the regulation of function between the two hemispheres.

Subsequent workers have added their refinements to Pavlov's original observations, but have kept the general notion clear that individuals differ in levels of cortical arousal and emotional arousability, and that these differences are directly due to brain and nervous system functioning.

Eysenck, for example, has retained the Pavlovian concept of a balance of inhibition/excitation and postulates that individuals range along this continuum, with a few at either end and the majority centrally placed in the distribution, but has changed the description of the basic mechanisms. In his formulation, extraverts have a chronically lower level of cortical arousal than introverts, who have a relatively high level. Because of this, the introvert has a reduced need for external stimulation to attain his optimal level of arousal. Thus a high level of internal excitation (arousal) accounts for the introvert's relative aversion to stimulating activities, exciting events and social contact. By contrast, the extravert's low level of internal arousal leads to a search for external stimuli in order to achieve the optimum level of arousal; he is impelled to seek noise, excitement, new experiences and many social contacts. If he is prevented from seeking these kinds of varied stimuli he becomes bored and readily distracted.

Eysenck's personality scheme also includes dimensions of neuroticism and psychoticism. The former has been related to excessive activity of the autonomic nervous system; people who are high on the neuroticism dimension are described as having strong and labile emotions, while those at the other end experience less strong and more stable emotions. Taken together, the two dimensions of extraversion-introversion and neuroticism form four quadrants. Those people who are both introverted and unstable tend to be moody, anxious, reserved, unsociable; those both introverted and stable tend to be calm, even-tempered, careful and thoughtful. People who are both extraverted and unstable tend to be touchy, restless, aggressive, excitable and impulsive; those who are both extraverted and stable are lively, easy-going, outgoing, carefree people. Further descriptions refer to the introvert as reacting to low levels of sensory stimuli, as amplifying stimuli and as being especially sensitive and reactive to frustration.

Other personality scales measure such traits as impulsiveness (e.g. the tendency to act on the spur of the moment without planning) and sensation–seeking, which refers to unusual activities such as sky-diving, speed-racing, taking drugs, etc. Attempts have been made by many investigators to relate personality measures derived from such questionnaires to general autonomic reactivity, cortical excitability, adrenalin/noradrenaline output, and, more recently, to a number of biochemical variables.

Contemporary studies are recognizing the importance of biogenic amines such as serotonin, dopamine and noradrenaline in psychiatric illness, since the discovery that both anti-psychotic and anti-depressant drugs interfere with the turnover of one or several of the amine neurotransmitters. Investigators are working on the assumption that biochemical variables may not be directly related to psychiatric illness as such but rather to a constitutional vulnerability which is evidenced in personality types and which may lead to illness and breakdown, provided other factors (psychosocial or somatic) are present.

Intelligence is another source of variation between individuals which is believed to have a biological/genetic basis. Conventional tests of intelligence (IQ) usually measure cognitive tasks similar to those involved in scholastic examinations, and might give disadvantageous results for members of minority groups from different cultural and educational backgrounds. This has stimulated a search for alternatives to the usual IQ test, and in recent years measurements of small electrical changes obtained from surface scalp electrodes have been made as indices of 'neural efficiency', the hypothesis being that when a stimulus occurs, neurons which are fast and efficient generate characteristic waves of evoked potential.

Several studies have reported correlations between these measures and intelligence, but it is too early to say whether this approach will have any practical value in the intelligence issue.

The application of conditioning principles

Many writers have implicated a mechanism of conditioning to account both for the acquisition of emotional responses and for their failure to extinguish. Following from this, neurotic behaviour can be regarded as learned behaviour, and distinguished from other types of behaviour in that it is maladaptive; that is, it produces actions with predominantly unfavourable and unsatisfactory consequences. In spite of this they may persist over a period of months, years or a lifetime.

It is impossible to trace back through an individual's history in order to establish how he acquired neurotic behaviour patterns. One can, however, investigate the ease with which different individuals condition to different stimuli both in the acquisition and extinction phase, and once a conditioned emotional response has been acquired its extinction can be followed in time. Though we cannot be sure how conditioned fears and phobias have developed (such as those to small insects like spiders, the dark, heights, etc.), we know that they are common in small children and usually extinguish over the years. However, some people extinguish slowly, if at all, and for them persistent emotional responding to certain stimuli can last a very long time indeed. And, of course, in human subjects conditioning stimuli become generalized, verbalized, and symbolized; that is, they become extended both in range and in power.

This extreme resistance to extinction is difficult to treat. However, these reactions can sometimes be extinguished in accordance with well-known principles of conditioning, which try to remove, step by step, the series of responses to a range of related stimuli of which such fears and phobias are invariably made up. This could involve training in techniques of relaxation and skills in the evocation of pleasant imagery and thoughts which counteract fear and desensitize the individual to aspects of the feared object. Subsequently he is encouraged to apply learned coping skills to those real-life situations which evoke the fear.

The fundamental conditioning research on which basis clinical application is possible is carried out in laboratory studies, frequently with laboratory rats, in which noxious (i.e. disliked, unpleasant) stimulation such as electric shock is used as a UCS to produce an 'emotional' UCR and, after pairing of CS and UCS, an emotional CR. These have shown that the CR can become associated not only to the specific CS but also to any object in the environment, the room, and even the experimenter. Thus a process of generalization takes place such that the conditioned fear spreads rapidly to a whole series of stimuli. This makes very plausible the notion that in real-life situations the acquisition and spreading of fear to many different stimuli can readily occur.

Environmental stressors

Conditions on which life and health depend are found both inside and outside the living organism. Within there is the whole complex machinery which regulates the internal environment, that is, the circulating organic liquid which surrounds and bathes all the tissue elements. An important principle in physiology, first stated by Claude Bernard, the French physiologist, emphasizes that the aim of physiological mechanisms is the preservation of the constancy of this internal environment.

Outside the living organism are all the changing features of the environment which require powers of adaptation and learning to cope with change. Most animals are innately equipped to deal with the specific changes of importance they are likely to encounter; but a more flexible response repertoire is evident in higher animals who in the case, for example, of reaction to danger tend to inherit an 'alarm reaction' which is triggered by a wide range of rather general danger signals, such as moving objects, novel stimuli, or stimuli of sudden or unusually high intensity. This mechanism, with its associated wide range of behavioural tactics, ensures that they are on guard against most of the usual risks of life, and an equally important mechanism of habituation damps down responding when responding is no longer necessary. Thus animals once alarmed by the irregular rattle of passing trains will soon learn that they can safely graze in adjacent fields without generating continuous fear responses to them.

Such adaptive mechanisms seem to ensure survival and also a kind of equilibrium of physiological functioning in relation to the constant flux of external events. Presumably they help conserve bodily resources since any animal failing to take appropriate action would die, yet if responding interminably to events around would rapidly become exhausted.

There are several theories of stress which involve the concept of the individual being driven beyond his powers of coping or adaptation such that equilibrium is not easily restored, and beyond some optimum at which he can function most effectively.

It has already been suggested in the case of sensory stimulation that individuals have a preferred optimum, and seek to maintain that optimum. Some individuals will prefer to reduce sensory stimulation when it is excessive, while others will seek to increase it when it falls below a certain level. Experiments in which volunteers have been deprived of practically all sensory input, by eliminating visual, auditory and tactile stimuli, have revealed marked individual differences in the degree of tolerance to these conditions, with some individuals finding them unbearable. Periods ranging from a few hours to several days under such conditions produce deficits in a wide variety of intellectual and perceptual tests, and often hallucinations and dream-like states occur in which coherent thinking is difficult. Such studies demonstrate that normal behaviour disintegrates when the general sensory input falls in amount below a certain level. There are also studies which show the deleterious effect of too much noise, as suffered, for example, by workers in factories and people living in flight paths near airports.

The psycho-biological use of the term 'stress' had its origins in the work of Selye in Canada, who sees stress as a succession of physiological stages within the organism following failure of the normal mechanisms of adaptation. If stressor agents (Selye's work was mainly with rats and involved such stressors as intense heat, cold, virus infections, intoxicants, haemorrhage, muscular exercise, drugs, injury and surgical trauma) are applied intensely or long enough, they produce certain general systemic changes which represent the animal's attempt to cope with the situation. These changes seem to be common to quite different stressors, and according to Selye they constitute the response pattern of systemic stress. They include autonomic excitability, adrenalin discharge, and such symptoms as an increased heart rate, decreased body temperature and muscle tone, anaemia, blood sugar changes and gastro-intestinal ulcerations. These changes occur as an initial response to the stressor agent and Selye labelled them the alarm reaction. If noxious stimulation continues but is not too severe a second phase occurs, labelled the stage of resistance, in which the adaptive powers of the body act to counteract the stressor. If noxious stimulation persists, this stage gives way to the final stage of exhaustion which may ultimately lead to death.

It is important to know whether psychological stimuli can also induce a systemic stress syndrome, with similar physiological response patterns occurring in similar stages. Men in stressful situations such as paratroopers, submariners, pilots and combat infantrymen, have demonstrated that life-threat and social-status-threat situations can induce symptoms of systemic stress, the degree of stress depending on the type, intensity and duration of the threat and on certain pre-stress sensitizing factors such as personality and previous conditioning experiences. However, the attempt to extend Selye's idea of general systemic stress to include psychological aspects has met with many problems. Psychological stress factors are less easy to define, measurements of the physiological changes are less easy to make and there are obvious ethical limitations on laboratory research with human volunteers.

Certain issues in psychological stress are more readily amenable to laboratory-type investigations with both human and animal subjects, and one theme explored in recent years relates to general 'coping behaviour', particularly with reference to the control which an individual has over frustrating situations. These studies indicate that stress reactions to aversive stimuli which are unavoidable and uncontrollable are much more severe than those resulting from exposure to situations over which the individual can develop control. It seems to be not only the exposure to, say, painful and unpleasant stimuli which leads to distress, but the knowledge of not being 'in control' of them which leads to feelings of helplessness in susceptible individuals. Contemporary life provides many frustrating situations over which we have little or no control: for example, bureaucratic decisions, cancellation of scheduled trains, being treated rudely when no retaliation is possible, and so on: situations in which there may be few successful methods of coping. One speculation is that repeated exposure to such conditions can generate feelings of hopelessness and helplessness which may contribute towards lack of motivation and possibly even to depression.

Relations between physiology and behaviour

A fundamental assumption is that the unique character of human beings, their ability to think, feel, learn and remember, lies in the brain and in the pattern and chemistry of inter-connections between neurons. Exactly how information is received about the world, how it is processed, interpreted, learned, memorized and stored are questions being pursued in pharmacology, neurochemistry, electrophysiology and psychology using an enormous range of sophisticated techniques. These include recordings of electrical events within single cells and multiple units, and the analysis of the biochemical events occurring in synaptic transmission. Many brain regions are being explored, for it is still unsettled whether memory and learning can be localized within specific areas or whether they are multiply represented throughout the brain. Most of our knowledge about neuronal changes comes f om animal experiments, whereas information about cognitive processes comes from recordings of cortical potentials from human subjects.

Given the broad scope of this work, the boundaries between different disciplines is loosening, and terms such as neurobiology, neuroscience, brain research and physiological psychology are being used interchangeably and often overlap in their interests. Illustrations from the latter two categories are given in the following sections. Two other disciplines, those of psychosomatic illness and psychophysiology, focus entirely on human behaviour and the interacting effects of psyche and behaviour, but differ inasmuch as the former relates to clinical and the latter to research problems.

Brain research

Studies involving brain implantation techniques, that is, the placing of electrical or chemical stimulation devices in strategic brain tissues, have provided many illustrations of how brain stimulation affects motivational and emotional behaviour. Another line of investigation has shown the dramatic effects of destroying localized regions of the brain. Ablation of portions of the limbic system in the temporal lobe has produced monkeys that are extremely tame and hypersexual; and wild, unmanageable animals have been transformed into gentle creatures that could be fed by hand. Other procedures have produced a state of violent rage even in very tame laboratory rats, a state labelled 'septal rage' since it is produced by destruction of the septal area of the limbic circuit.

As a result of the development of surgical techniques and the powerful effects of brain intervention observed on behaviour, a large number of neurosurgeons throughout the world performed operations on selected psychiatric patients in the 1950s and 1960s (of which leucotomy is perhaps the best known) with the hope that appropriate surgery might afford some relief from severe suffering. The advantages and disadvantages of the approach have been debated, and few operations of this kind are performed today. The original hope that a physical, anatomical abnormality of the brain could be detected and corrected in psychiatric patients has not been realized.

More recently it has been discussed whether brain intervention might alleviate severe and intractable behaviour problems such as hyperexcitability and violent, destructive and uncontrollably aggressive behaviour, and some exploratory attempts have been made in this direction. It is not easy to evaluate the results of these operations: on the whole there is always a cost-benefit factor in neurosurgery. No miraculous recovery is ever accomplished with the kinds of very severe behavioural problems which have been referred, and although relief from disabling symptoms may be obtained there is always the possibility that it will create other difficulties. A very readable account of this work and thoughtful discussion of its results are available in Valenstein's 'Brain Control'.

Innumerable ethical problems are associated with brain surgery. Some people have argued that violent prisoners should be treated by surgical means rather than spend a lifetime in prison. Others feel that because the brain is the reservoir of creativity and individuality it should never be disturbed unless it is clearly diseased or injured.

Many brain-behaviour studies arise from accidental brain lesions, following which a variety of disorders have been noted in speech, motor behaviour, memory and perception. These vary in extent and quality as a function of the nature and place of injury, and detailed mapping of the disability can lead to a better understanding of how speech, memory, etc., are organized psychologically and within the brain. Sometimes the nature of the deficits is minutely recorded by the patients themselves, and these provide insight into the disruptions in ability to think, talk, and understand the speech of others. One particularly careful account as experienced by a soldier and observed by a Russian neuropsychologist is described in Luria's 'Man with a shattered world' (1973). The patient describes the fragmentation of his visual and perceptual world following a gunshot wound and of his struggle to re-combine the fragments, and Luria relates the disorders to the sites of the injury which in this case had destroyed that part of the brain which combines the multiple impressions received by the brain into a coherent whole.

Accurate assessment of cognitive deficits associated with perception, speech and memory may be assisted by the development of appropriate tests. In the case of emotional deficits no tests are available, and assessment is more difficult. As a result, much less is known about the effects of brain and central nervous system damage on normal human feelings. Again, some of the information which is available has been obtained from accidental lesions, and there are some reports on the emotional life of paraplegics and quadriplegics obtained through structured interview and concerning sexual excitement, anger, fear, grief and sentimentality. These suggest a reduction in the intensity of feeling, and an awareness of a more 'mental' kind of emotional response than of a powerful physiological drive.

Recent work has highlighted the psychological importance of brain chemistry. There are good reasons to believe that it is involved in the control of sleep, eating, sexual and aggressive behaviour, neuropsychological processes such as attention and sensitivity to pain, and in mood and emotionality. One theory, for example, is that levels of catecholamines in the brain determine a person's mood, high levels being correlated with euphoria and low levels with depression. If amines act in this way, it might seem to follow that a correction for imbalance could be achieved by the administration of drugs such as monamine-oxidase inhibitors; and contemporary pharmacological research, some carried out on laboratory animals and some on patients in clinical trials, is investigating this hypothesis. There are, however, many complications when human beings are involved in assessments of this kind, for as well as direct pharmacological effects, psychological factors such as expectancies of both the therapist and patient and aspects of the therapeutic setting also play a part. An incidental and related observation made in the context of hallucinogenic drugs similarly suggests that the effects which are experienced are partly due to setting and expectation. Another interesting finding which is well-documented is that some patients claim satisfactory pain relief from placebos (i.e. completely inactive, 'dummy' tablets) for many kinds of symptoms, and attempts have been made, so far without clear resolution, to identify who these people are and what the mechanism is by which the effect is produced.

Physiological psychology

Among the important psychological functions investigated are those of memory and learning, a major question being whether there is a single anatomical site or physiological process responsible for learning. Forms of learning which are most often studied are habituation to a repeated stimulus, and simple classical conditioning: that is, situations where both stimuli and responses can be precisely controlled and measured. A traditional method of studying this question is by lesions in specific regions of the brain to examine the effect on a previously learned response. On the whole, extensive cortical lesions appear to have no adverse effect on classical conditioning, and confirm the belief that this type of learning can occur sub-cortically. This does not deny the importance of the cortex in analysing complex stimuli or the possibility that the cortex is involved in more complex forms of conditioning.

Another approach is to correlate electrical events within the brain in the course of learning as observed in external responding. The evidence is clear that widespread electrical changes in neuronal activity occur throughout the brain, especially during the initial phases, and that this generalized activity decreases leaving activity at only the primary sensory and motor response areas. Which aspects of neural activity are causes or consequences of learning and which are associated with the motivational and attentional variables essential to learning can only be determined with the use of careful control procedures, and in many studies these have not been incorporated.

In recent years there has been a particular interest in the role of the hippocampus in learning and the storage of short-term memories: the hippocampus has inputs from many sensory modalities, access to motor systems, and connections with parts of the limbic system allegedly concerned with reinforcement and reward. In humans, bilateral lesions associated with this area have been shown to cause a severe and lasting memory deficit characterized by the inability to learn new information. Patients with such lesions appear to have undiminished powers of perception, but they are largely incapable of incorporating new information into their long-term store.

Synaptic connections between the neurons of the brain have long been thought to relate to learning and memory, and progress has been made in identifying the various chemical transmitters at the synaptic junction, in mapping their distribution in the brain and in analysing their mode of action. Instead of searching for a unique memory molecule, many investigators are trying to analyse the metabolism of neurons responding to various kinds of stimulation. They feel that the physical basis of memory is likely to comprise a complex chain of metabolic reactions, with initial chemical changes occurring in short-term memory and different changes subsequently mediating the transfer to long-term memory. The final chemical changes associated with long-term memory must be stable and long-lasting in order to preserve the memory trace from degrading.

A topic of profound importance is how we register and record the events of the world about us. Research in the past decade has revealed the existence of cells within the brain which appear to react quite specifically to different aspects of a sensory stimulus. They have been termed 'feature detectors' in that some cells will fire at the onset of a stimulus, others to its colour, and others again to its duration, intensity and localization in space. Some neurons are specially tuned to respond to complex stimuli, to time characteristics and to novelty. Thus incoming stimuli leave traces of their characteristics within the nervous system. These traces or 'neuronal models' preserve information about the intensity, quality, duration and so on of past stimuli, and it is against these stored models that new events are compared. Several theorists have proposed that there is an analysing mechanism within the brain which assesses the novelty and significance of incoming events in such terms as: is this event new or has it happened before? Is it significant or irrelevant? It then activates the appropriate response or damps down responding (as in habituation) if the event has occurred many times before and is unimportant. In this way we build up an internal picture of the external world, and act on that information.

Again, theorists have pondered whether the basis of perception and cognitive processes is to be sought in single cells or localized anatomical structures; the facts are that while some degree of brain localization occurs it is also true that information and function in any one sensory modality is redundantly distributed throughout anatomically extensive regions.

The brain appears to have two halves (hemispheres) which were once assumed to be similar in function, as are the two kidneys and two lungs. Actually, there are some specialized functions which are found only in one or other of the two sides. The best example is that of language: damage to a particular region of the cortex on the left side of the brain leads to aphasia; damage to the corresponding area on the right side leaves the faculty of speech intact. This asymmetry is also reflected in memory defects arising from lesions in a single temporal lobe. A left temporal lobectomy can impair the ability to retain verbal material but leave intact the ability to remember spatial locations, faces, melodies and abstract visual patterns.

One of the most interesting recent findings is that different emotional reactions follow damage to the right and left sides of the brain. Comprehension of the affective components of speech is impaired with right but not with left temporal-parietal lesions, and the comprehension of humorous material is different in patients with left and right hemisphere lesions. Under special laboratory conditions it is possible to ensure that information from the world reaches only one hemisphere at a time, and if pictures are shown either to the right or the left hemisphere, those on the right are rated more emotionally and as being more unpleasant. While this specialization of hemispheres should not be over-exaggerated, it does suggest a unique kind of specialization within the human brain.

Psychosomatic medicine

One of the most striking features of psychosomatic illness is the marked individual difference in susceptibility to illness, in modes of precipitation and in the patterning of symptoms. Why one patient should develop gastric ulcers while another develops hypertension is a question that has often been asked and not yet satisfactorily answered.

There is reasonably general agreement that deleterious physiological effects can arise from prolonged stress; that the functional disturbance of a vegetative organ or system can be caused by emotional disturbances which include conflict, stress and life events, and that chronic functional disturbance may lead to tissue change and organic disease. Some of the possible mechanisms have been outlined in Cannon's concept of an organism preparing for fight or flight, and in Selye's work on systemic reaction to prolonged, severe stressors.

There have been many theories concerning the psycho-physiological specificity, or patterning of response, which is a feature of psychosomatic disorders. One possibility is a genetic component which determines the organ system involved; another is that this combines with a learning process such as classical conditioning. Conditioned visceral responses and associated feelings of anxiety can occur to all sorts of stimuli and can be remarkably persistent over time. They are of particular interest in that, while these organs have cortical representation, the activity of the organs is not easily discriminated and is generally below normal conscious awareness. This suggests that an individual might become conditioned to respond to inappropriate internal or external stimuli over long periods of time during which he would have no knowledge of the progressive disturbance of function.

Another factor which seems to be significant in the precipitation of symptoms is the recent occurrence of conflict, emotional upheaval or environmental stress. Attention has been focussed on recent changes in individuals' lives prior to illness onset and an association between them has been repeatedly documented. However, even the highest of these correlations is relatively modest, suggesting that recent life changes alone do not exert a strong primary effect on illness onset. What effect they do exert is influenced by the way in which an individual perceives them, as well as by the individual's coping capabilities and illness behaviour characteristics.

It is clear that of the people who experience recent life changes there are far more who do not go on to report illness symptoms than there are those that do. Therefore a major research question is how do the majority of individuals tolerate their recent life change experience and remain healthy? Certainly a good deal needs to be done in the systematic quantification of subjects' stress tolerance characteristics.

Investigations into coronary heart disease (CHD) both in the USA and Europe have reported a constellation of personality traits, attitudes and life styles alleged to characterize this illness. A 'Type A' behaviour pattern comprising ambitious, driving, competitive work behaviour with a sense of urgency towards deadlines and associated with more intense cardio-vascular reactions has been compared with the more placid, less reactive 'Type B' individual who is less inclined to develop CHD. However, no clear-cut method of dividing patients into 'Type A' or 'Type B' categories is available, and correlations between behaviour patterns and illness are still at a p eliminary stage.

A fully satisfactory explanation of psychosomatic illness has to account for the continuity, chronicity and specificity of symptoms which recur throughout time, and explanations of these phenomena, which are still being sought, are likely to be multifactorial in nature. The specificity of diagnosis is also important. Psychosomatic disorders traditionally include asthma, gastric ulcers, some cardio-vascular disorders, hypertension, and tension headaches. These are very globally defined illness categories, and what is needed is the identification of subforms of the illnesses. Different subforms of a disease may arise from

different aetiologic or pathogenic mechanisms. Conversely,
the same mechanism may produce different lesions or disturbances. To illustrate specifically, allergic mechanisms
play a role in only 30-50 per cent of all patients with
bronchial asthma. In the rest, viral infections combined
with psychological factors play a part in exciting asthmatic
attacks. Progress in psychosomatic investigations could be
enhanced in the future by characterizing patient groups
according to the subforms of the disease from which they
suffer. The subforms could then be compared socially and
psychologically with one another.

Psychophysiology

Attention, interest, thinking and feelings are accompanied
by generalized changes throughout the brain and nervous
system. Against this background are the specific excitations
required for specific tasks: looking at a picture entails a
complex mosaic of eye movements, playing tennis involves the
patterning of muscle action potentials, and attending to a
speaker requires the inhibition of other sensory input.

How the psychological constructs of attention, thinking
and feeling interact with physiological changes, and what
the nature of their interaction is, remains a complex and
fascinating research problem. The direction of causality is
obscure: is it the perception of a threatening situation
which arouses the physiological concomitants of anxiety, or
does the physiological arousal come first and determine the
nature of the perception?

Psychophysiology is an area of study which concentrates
on human behaviour, and tries to analyse the cognitive,
verbal and psychological aspects of behaviour in relation to
the physiological. The term physiological in this context
refers to those variables which can be recorded by means of
small disk electrodes attached to the surface of the skin.
The range of variables which can be recorded in this way is
very wide and includes heart rate, palmar skin resistance
(attributable to palmar sweating), skin temperature, blood
flow, respiration and cortical potentials recorded from the
surface of the brain.

Most of these variables show constant on-going activity:
the heart, lungs and cortical potentials show rhythmic
changes and also show quite striking changes in response to
simple stimuli such as lights and tones. More complex situations, such as verbal instructions, conversation, calling
the individual by name, mental arithmetic tasks, and so on,
can produce significant changes of long duration. In addition, many of these systems show a considerable amount of
spontaneous activity, that is, changes which occur in the
absence of any clearly defined event.

When the individual is left quietly to relax this
activity shows a steady decline. If now an unexpected
stimulus is given, a startle or orientating ('what is it?')
response occurs. When the same stimulus is repeated, the
response becomes smaller on each subsequent occasion until

it no longer occurs: that is, it has habituated. If a mild stimulus (CS) is paired with an unpleasant stimulus (UCS) such as an electric shock, conditioned responding occurs. Among psychophysiologists there is substantial interest in the physiological changes which occur in habituation, in the acquisition of conditioned autonomic responses, and in the nature of reactivity of different individuals to mild stressors such as unpleasant noises, pictures, etc. There is a great deal of variation between individuals and characteristic response profiles have been described in which high reactivity is evident in one aspect of responding - certain skeletal muscle groups or cardiac changes or blood pressure - while other aspects show minimal activity. Whether such a pattern of 'response specificity' relates to symptom patterns in certain individuals awaits longitudinal studies.

A major source of information concerning the neurophysiology of cognitive processes in humans is the scalp-recorded event-related potential (ERP). The combined electrical activity of millions of neurons in the brain as a whole is recorded in these and allied electro-encephalographic (EEG) recordings. There is clear evidence that certain components of the ERP are related to the physical attributes of the stimulus such as sensory modality and intensity, while other components reflect the individual's evaluation of the significance or meaning of the stimulus.

Selective attention to one stimulus and not to another can be demonstrated by instructions to subjects to monitor one stimulus and to ignore another: components of the cortical potential response to the monitored stimulus are enhanced as compared with those to the irrelevant stimulus. Various studies in schizophrenia have attempted to relate observed behavioural abnormalities to aspects of psychophysiological responding within the context of deficits in arousal and/or attention. It has been hypothesized that in the acute stage of his illness the schizophrenic is constantly aware of a wide range of stimuli other than those which should strictly be in the forefront of his attention; that he orientates to these irrelevant stimuli and does not habituate to them. This can be tested not only by recording and comparing cortical evoked responses to different tones, some of which carry information while others are irrelevant as indicated above, but also by recording autonomic activity to assess the rate at which habituation occurs to significant and non-significant stimulus events.

Psychophysiological responsivity has often been considered in relation to clinical anxiety. Anxious patients frequently report trembling, sweating, shortness of breath, palpitations and muscular tension, and these have been recorded in situations where the patient is at rest trying to relax and also in response to different stimuli. There are several reports of anxious groups typically responding more readily, habituating more slowly, and taking longer to recover from stimulation. The effect of training and biofeedback on levels of physiological activity is the subject of much contemporary research.

Another area has concentrated on whether psychophysiological reactivity is an indicator of 'good' performance; that is, whether it correlates with speedy reactions, better perception, memory, etc. Recordings of cortical potentials have been related to the way in which people process information, and to such concepts as expectancy, attention and vigilance. Recordings of brain activity during sleep have been used to delineate the function of sleep, to define quantitatively what is good sleep, effects of drugs on sleep, and what role sleep plays in illness and well-being.

Psychophysiological measures can provide useful indicators of autonomic and cortical reactivity in response to stimuli of many kinds. They are helpful in their demonstration of individuals' idiosyncratic response profiles, in the study of habituation, relationship to task performance, processing of information, and in their indication of the variety of changes which occur along the sleep-wakefulness continuum. Perhaps the future may also see further links between psychophysiological research and the problems of psychosomatic medicine and psychiatry.

Concluding comments

If the aim of psychology is to clarify man's behaviour in this world it must accord a central position to biology, since this of all disciplines is the most directly linked to the understanding of living beings. The biological basis of behaviour refers to evolutionary, genetic, physiological and brain-behaviour mechanisms, and more recently has been extended to human social behaviour. Triumphs of molecular biology, of technology and field observation have been accomplished. The discovery of deoxyribonucleic acid (DNA) and the theory of the genetic code tell us how the information is coded which determines that a new life will inherit the characteristics of its parents; technological developments make it possible to record electrical events from single neurons within the brain, and to measure minute traces of brain chemicals. Studies by ethologists have made us familiar with the behavioural repertoire of animals in their natural habitat.

The evolution of the brain and central nervous system has led to the increasing role of learning as a strategy whereby the organism attains information about the environment and itself during its own lifetime. This implies an increasing flexibility of gene/behaviour interaction, though a genetic basis of learning probably resides in the emotional/motivational states that help define reward and punishment. These aspects of behaviour are augmented by the evolution of socio-cultural organizations in which knowledge and ideas are perpetuated through socialization and teaching.

There are many challenges to the understanding of human nature. The work which psychologists have to do centres on the analysis of behaviour into useful segments, and the derivation of meaningful concepts such as attention and arousal, emotion, memory and stress. It must contend with individual variation, possibly along dimensions such as extraversion, neuroticism and impulsiveness, and elucidate the psychophysiology of neurosis and stress reactions.

These in turn can be examined in relation to practical issues. Some would account for the genesis of neurosis in terms of maladaptive patterns of learning, and aim to treat anxieties and phobias according to conditioning principles. Psychophysiological illnesses such as the psychosomatic disorders can be viewed as a combination of genetic predisposition, faulty learning and environmental stress, and each of these factors needs to be studied. The contribution of physiological arousal, perceptions and attitudes in the experience of emotion remains to be unravelled.

The goal which lies ahead in the biological context is the fitting together of psychological facts and factors with the patterns of bodily activity which form the basis of human individuality and welfare.

References

Cannon, W.B. (1915)
Bodily Changes in Pain, Hunger, Fear and Rage. New York: Harper & Row.
Luria, A.R. (1973)
The Man with a Shattered World. London: Jonathan Cape.
Valenstein, E.S. (1973)
Brain Control: A critical examination of brain stimulation and psychosurgery. New York: Wiley.
Wilson, E.O.
Sociobiology: The new synthesis. Cambridge, Mass.: Belknap.

Questions

1. Describe and discuss the ways in which the biological determinants of behaviour are being investigated by psychologists and others.
2. 'Human behaviour has an enormously complex aetiology, and the importance of specific factors must always be evaluated against this background.' Discuss.
3. What is the nature-nurture controversy? Discuss and elaborate with reference to examples of human behaviour.
4. Discuss the claim that human behaviour can be adequately assessed, explained and modified without any reference to physiological, biochemical or other organic factors.
5. Describe, and discuss critically, the experimental and clinical techniques which have been used to investigate the biological determinants of human behaviour.
6. Consider the following: (a) the relevance of animal experimentation to understanding human behaviour; (b) the aims, methods and limitations of physiological psychology; (c) the contributions of brain research to the explanation and modification of behaviour.

7. Discuss the clinical implications of the research on the biological determinants of behaviour. Consider in particular whether the research has or can make any contribution to the practical aspects of patient care. Does the research have practical as well as theoretical implications?
8. Provide examples of the clinical relevance and importance of the following: (a) the concept of arousal; (b) conditioning; (c) individual differences; (d) biological determinants of the stress response.

Annotated reading

Eysenck, H.J. (1976) Psychology as a bio-social science. In H.J. Eysenck and G.D. Wilson (eds), A Textbook of Human Psychology. Lancaster: MTP.

> An introduction to psychology as the study of behaviour with special reference to the interaction of social and biological factors.

Martin, I. (1976) Emotions. In H.J. Eysenck and G.D. Wilson (eds). A Textbook of Human Psychology. Lancaster: MTP.

Strongman, K.T. (1978) The Psychology of Emotion (2nd edn). Chichester: Wiley.

> The above two references discuss a number of facets concerning the study of emotion.

Boddy, J. (1978) Brain Systems and Psychological Concepts. Chichester: Wiley.

Van Toller, C. (1979) The Nervous Body: An introduction to the autonomic nervous system and behaviour. Chichester: Wiley.

> Two useful books, both in very readable style, which cover in much greater depth the topics outlined in the biological bases chapter. They are detailed and informative, and worth sampling on topics which interest the student.

Gray, J. (1971) The Psychology of Fear and Stress. London: Weidenfeld & Nicolson.

> Deals not only with innate and acquired features of fear and stress but also with mechanisms of conditioning and reinforcement.

Valenstein, E.S. (1973) Brain Control: A critical examination of brain stimulation and psychosurgery. New York: Wiley.

> An interesting account of a number of topics involving brain and behaviour studies, including a good discussion of the effects of psychosurgery in psychopathological disorders.

4

Abilities and Behaviour in Childhood and Adolescence
B. M. Foss

Opening remarks
DAVID GRIFFITHS

This is the first of three chapters concerned with the early stages of human development up to adolescence. Brian Foss is concerned with abilities and behaviour; Rudolph Schaffer considers social development and David Griffiths discusses the role of the psychologist in understanding and modifying problem behaviours in children.

Doctors who work with children and adolescents clearly need to have an extensive knowledge of human development. The chapter by Brian Foss is a discussion of two important aspects of growth and development. The first is the pattern of development: more generally, what can children do at various ages and how do differing aspects of behaviour relate to each other? What can the infant perceive and understand? When do specific skills develop and how broad are individual differences? His second theme involves those factors and mechanisms which influence the speed and pattern of development. He discusses, for example, the role played by reinforcement and the child's tendency to imitate. Both aspects of development - the pattern of change and its determinants - are clearly relevant to the work of paediatricians and other doctors and deserve attention by trainees since they are important parts of the expertise of the doctor who works with children.

Trainees in medicine might also need to be reminded of the specific ways in which an understanding of the psychology of development is likely to be useful in a clinical setting. Examples of the relevance of psychology are not difficult to find. A knowledge of developmental norms, for instance, is basic to assessments of whether a child's behaviour is abnormal: it can also enable the clinician to evaluate change in the child's activities and to monitor the effects of treatments and other procedures. In addition, an acquaintance with normal milestones and patterns of development will also need to be supplemented by an understanding of those factors and processes which influence the rate, pattern and extent of development. Such an understanding will often be necessary for treatment since it will imply the courses of action which need to be considered. For example, the importance of reinforcements (rewards and punishments) as determinants of behaviour might imply, in practice, that adaptive behaviour or skills are likely to increase or develop only if the appropriate level and type of reward is available in the child's natural environment. A broad understanding of development might also suggest, however, that specific behaviours and skills are not likely to appear or flourish until specified age levels have been reached, so that the effects of rewards are dependent on maturational processes. Biological and environmental factors therefore interact to influence both development and the effects which any intervention might be expected to exert.

Childhood
B. M. FOSS

Psychological information about children comes from a variety of sources of which the main ones are:

* catalogues of development stages;
* child psychology: the study of children 'for their own sake';
* clinical studies, especially of abnormal children;
* educational studies, especially of backwardness;
* studies of process: perception, learning, thinking, etc., for the sake of understanding how the processes develop;
* experiments on infants, often involving newly discovered techniques which allow the study of their abilities;
* 'social' psychological studies, especially of inter-action between infant and mother;
* studies arising from theories of child psychology, especially those of Freud, Piaget and the learning theorists.

Different sources have often used very different methods, and sometimes the findings are in conflict. For instance, some experimental techniques used with infants give results that suggest that a young infant's perceptual discrimina-tions and learning ability are more advanced than earlier, different studies suggested. In what follows a consensus view is given, the discrepancies being mentioned only when they are of particular interest.

Early development
Before birth, the foetus behaves spontaneously and will respond to stimulation and there is evidence that some learning occurs in the form of conditioning to sounds, but it is doubtful if this has importance for later behaviour. Immediately after birth there is a whole range of reflexes which can be observed, some of them quite complex. One of these is the 'rooting reflex' in which a touch on the cheek of the infant results in his turning his head so that the mouth comes towards the stimulus, and this eventually leads to sucking. New-born infants also show grasping, swimming movements, walking movements and also some reflexes which disappear during development. Even at birth the differences between infants are very great, and the range of abilities and behaviour which can be called normal is large at all

ages. This is a point which is made repeatedly in what
follows. The newborn spends most of its time sleeping (say
80 per cent) but the depth of sleep varies, as does the
level of arousal when the child is awake. In assessing the
performance of infants and also older children it is
important to pay attention to the state (as Heinz Prechtl
has called it) of the individual. The level of performance
which a child shows varies very much with state. When
neonates are assessed, for instance, with the Brazelton
Neonatal Assessment Scale, the responses of the infant are
observed while the state varies from deep sleep to being
highly aroused and back again to a quieter final state.
There are quite a few observations which suggest that the
infant is most receptive of new experiences when it is in
a quiet contented state: for instance, immediately after
eating but before falling asleep. The quality of sleep in
infants is different from that in older children in that
there is a much higher percentage of rapid-eye-movement
(REM) sleep. At birth, something like 60 or 70 per cent of
the time spent asleep is in a REM state, but that percentage
falls fairly rapidly following birth when deep sleep begins
to take up a greater proportion of the time.

Apart from sleeping, the newborn seems to spend most
of his time eating, excreting or crying. There are several
kinds of cry which most mothers can distinguish from each
other and which can be analysed using spectographs (which
break up the sound into its frequency components). The birth
cry appears to be unique. Then there is a basic cry, sometimes called a hunger cry, which is the common pattern, and
the pain cry, which may be elicited on the first day, for
instance when a blood sample is taken. It is characterized
by an initial yell followed by several seconds of silence
during which the baby maintains expiration and which finally
gives way to a gasp and loud sobbing, which in its turn
reverts to a basic cry. There is also a frustration cry
which is rather like a diminished version of the pain cry.
Many mothers have also recognized a different kind of cry
which starts at, say, the fourth week. It seems to be a sham
cry in the sense that it is caused by no specific need but
seems simply to be a way of calling for attention. Presumably this kind of cry develops into the distress which older
children show when separated from their mothers.

What things does the infant attend to? Can it recognize
its mother's face and voice, or are these learnt gradually
over a period of time? Until recently it was believed that
recognition of faces and voices did not occur until the
infant was several months old, but it now looks as though
infants become competent in this way very much earlier, as
many mothers suspected. At least, what they can do is distinguish between different voices and faces probably as
early as the third week of life, and it is likely that they
can tell difference in smell between different people as
early as the second week of life. There are several newly-
developed ways in which these earlier responses of children

can be studied. One method is simply to look at the direction of gaze of the infant. If he is given two objects to look at and gazes significantly more at one of them, then it is inferred that he can tell the difference between them and probably finds one more interesting than the other. Another technique is to use the fact that if an infant is shown any one thing or listens to any one thing for a period of time he will habituate to the stimulus and stop responding to it. If that stimulus is replaced by a different one and the infant now starts attending all over again it is assumed that he can tell the difference between the new stimulus and the old one. Yet a third technique is to get the infant to control his own environment by providing him with an artificial teat. When the infant sucks, a pressure transducer results in changes in the flow of electric current and these in turn can be made to change the infant's environment. For instance, an infant may learn to suck for the reward of being played one particular voice on a tape-recorder. Using these kinds of techniques it looks as though infants are visually attracted by brightness, movement and contours of objects. There is some evidence that at even two weeks of age infants are particularly attracted to representations of the human face. This is a topic on which there is a conflict of evidence. Until the mid-1970s most experiments suggested that infants studied the contours of figures including faces, but did not pay any attention to the configuration generally. These were followed by experiments using new techniques (for instance, imitation of facial gesture), claiming that in the first week or two of life children in fact were reacting to the features of the face generally; but there are yet further experiments which show that there may have been methodological flaws. What is clear, though, is that most babies have a great deal of opportunity to get to know faces in that mothers play face-to-face games with their babies from the very first days of life; indeed, where they are allowed to be with the baby from birth they will tend to play these games immediately. By the time the baby is three weeks old it gets 'turned off' if, when face to face with an adult, the adult fails to react to the baby's changes in facial expression.

By the time he is four or five months old the baby has already learnt to categorize faces in a way which is not understood but which is obviously fundamental to the whole of his future development. By this time he can definitely recognize an individual face in a variety of orientations but can also tell the difference between those orientations; so he has already acquired categories of sameness and difference for faces as a whole, but also sameness and difference for orientation. Shortly after this it is clear that he can recognize objects when they are presented in different modalities: for instance, he can recognize by touch something which he knows visually, and it is clear then that he has some idea of definite objects. However, he still has some problems with 'object permanence', because when an object disappears behind a screen and reappears at the other side the event appears to be unexpected.

Perception

The development of perception obviously relates to both sensation and attention. Sensory deficiencies will delay or prevent perceptual development in that particular modality (e.g. vision, hearing, touch, etc.), but will also have consequences for development generally; and the way in which perception develops through experience will depend on what things the child notices. To take an extreme case, a child in a visually exciting environment will develop visual perceptual categories earlier, especially if his sound environment is dull. The situation is not simple though. There are reports of a child of deaf mute parents who sat for hours in front of a television set but still did not pick up language. What seems vital for perceptual learning is some kind of interaction with the environment. In describing what happens it is useful to think in terms of perceptual categories. For instance, an infant is able to categorize movement and discriminate it from lack of movement, and also to categorize various colours, probably from birth. It would be reasonable then to suppose that very soon after birth the infant's nervous system will deal differently with red moving stimuli and all other kinds of stimuli, and the infant may well be able to tell the difference. If, later in life, the infant reaches out to touch such objects, he may come across a red moving object which is a flame and as a result of touching it his behaviour will have an outcome which is different from that when he touched other kinds of objects. In such a way he will learn to discriminate the sub-category of red moving objects. Movements of all kinds - eye movements, head movements, and body movements, and all kinds of interaction with the environment - seem to be important for the development of new perceptions, and this leads to the possibility that the child's perceptual development will be affected by his interests (in the wider sense, i.e. matters of concern), because he is more likely to attend to, and interact with, those aspects of the environment which are relevant to those interests. One can see evidence for this kind of effect in the many cross-cultural studies that show, for instance, that Eskimos have many categories for snow. Similarly, small boys may have many categories for motor cars. It will be seen that the psychological idea of a percept is not very different from a concept. One's perception of a dog is not only affected by the sight of the dog, but also knowing what it sounds like, feels like to be patted, or to be bitten by, and smells like; and if one happens to be a dog fancier one's perception of the dog will involve very much finer discriminations than those made by other people. Perception, then, is affected not only by the present state of affairs - the stimuli from the environment, the perceiver's attention, his motivation and emotional state - but also by his whole previous history, and this leads to the possibility that different kinds of people have rather different perceptions. The members of a gang will perceive that gang's symbols (hair-cut and clothing, favourite music, favourite drink, etc.) quite differently from the way they would be perceived by a member of an opposing gang.

Skills

It is only about halfway through the first year of life that a child begins to show good evidence for integrating its movements with its perception by being able to get hold of objects in an obviously intentional way. The gradual development from these early stages through walking and various kinds of play activity to complex skills involved, for instance, in sports, are well documented (some are listed briefly at the end of this chapter). It may be useful to have a model of the way in which such skills are acquired, and one such model is to regard the skill as based on a hierarchy of lower-order habits. For instance, a child learning to write must have first learnt to hold a pencil (there is an innate grasping reflex but the child will have to relinquish this method of grasping for one using finger and thumb opposition), will have had to learn to move the pencil across the paper hard enough to leave a mark but not break the paper, will have had to learn to match shapes, to move from left to right across the page, to distinguish between mirror image letters, and so on. Many of these habits can be learnt only in a fairly definite sequence because one will depend on the acquisition of previous habits. Eventually the child will have a whole hierarchy of writing and drawing habits, and at some stage these will have to be integrated with other hierarchies of talking and hearing habits, if he is to become an ordinary literate person. The establishment of these hierarchies depends obviously on having the necessary sensory and motor abilities. They also depend on practice (one cannot learn to drive a car just by reading a book), by knowledge of results (otherwise movements will not become perfected) and on having the motivation to continue learning. One of the characteristics of these skill hierarchies is that the lower-order habits become automatic, and the skilled person does not have to think about them at all but can concentrate on the 'higher' aspects of what he is doing. Such a model helps to throw light on some of the reasons why children may fail to develop skills necessary for everyday life; for instance, some sensory or motor abilities may be deficient, an essential lower-order habit may be missing, there may have been difficulty in integrating one or more hierarchies, or there may have been inadequate motivation.

Solving problems

Investigation of problem solving has been one of the main ways in which psychologists have studied thinking. A main impetus in the study of the development of this kind of ability was the work of the Swiss psychologist Piaget. He based an elaborate theory on the way in which children develop concepts of number, space, relationships, etc., and claimed that the thinking of a child develops through a series of definite stages, rather as in the development of a skill hierarchy. His results and his theory have been open to question, and although many psychologists do not agree with his theoretical formulation, many of his empirical results have been replicated in a variety of cultures. There has, though, been a tendency to show that some of the problems which Piaget posed can be solved by children at a slightly earlier age given a different method of presenting the problem, and it turns out that sometimes the child fails to solve a problem for reasons other than those given by Piaget. For instance, the child's short-term memory may be inadequate for him to store the information necessary if he is to solve the problem. One of the most interesting classes of problems he has used concerns what he calls conservation. For instance, in testing a child's ability to show conservation of volume, the child is faced with two identical beakers filled with equal amounts of, say, lemonade. If the child agrees that there is an equal amount in each beaker, the lemonade from one is then poured into a tall thin glass. The child who has not acquired the concept of conservation will choose the lemonade in the tall thin glass in preference; it will appear greater in quantity to him. According to Piaget, it is only in middle childhood that children acquire conservation concepts, and it is only when they are about 11 or 12 that full logical thinking is possible.

One major concern of psychologists has been to determine how important language is in the development of a child's thinking abilities. Perhaps it is because educationists themselves are rather verbal people that many believe language to be the most important single thing. However, there is some contrary evidence. For instance, deaf mutes who have very little vocabulary or syntax may nevertheless be rather competent in dealing with a whole range of problems varying from those found in ordinary intelligence tests to complicated problems in logic. Of all the tests which have been tried, it happens to be that conservation problems are those which seem most affected by lack of adequate language. In dealing with questions of this kind it is important to realize that there are several kinds of thinking and of intelligence. For instance, when a very broad range of intelligence tests are analysed by a technique such as factor analysis (which is essentially a way of classifying tests), it usually turns out that there are two broad groups of tests: those involving language and those which do not, but may depend more on being able to manipulate space and pattern, for instance. There are also large individual differences between people in this matter. Some seem to use language very much more in ordinary thinking, and there is some evidence across cultures that on the whole girls are better at language skills and boys better at spatial skills.

There is one kind of problem whose solution seems to depend on developmental stages and which may hold the key to some of the changes which occur with age. If a young child is given a series of objects varying in colour, size and shape, and asked to sort them, he may do so by their colour or their shape or their size, but having sorted by one method he will be unable to see that there is a second or third method of sorting them, and it is only when children are considerably older that they can see from the start that there is an ambiguity about how sorting should be done.

Play

Play in animals and humans is usually easy to recognize but not so easy to define. Most play does have the property of appearing to be 'not for real', but there are difficult borderline cases. For instance, when children are playing together with toys there may be frequent episodes where there is competition for toys or for territory and this may involve aggression which certainly appears real. Play at first tends to be solitary even when other children are there. There may be 'parallel play' in which children pursue the same tasks though with no obvious co-operation. Fully co-operative play is not seen much before children are three or four years old. In most cultures it seems that there are sex differences in typical play. Boys tend to play more with boys and girls with girls, and boys show much more of what has come to be called 'rough and tumble play'. This is the sort of play where there is a lot of wrestling and tumbling about and rolling over, sometimes with open-handed arm beating (often without contact) and rapid jumping up and down, sometimes with arm flapping, and the whole thing is often accompanied by laughter. Where there is a largish group of children, one variant is that there is a great deal of group running, usually in a circle and often occurring with a lot of laughter. Chasing is another very common variant. Another sex difference is observed when children play with their mothers, in that girls tend to have closer proximity to the mother than boys do, at least on average. When play is solitary, dolls and other playthings and pets are sometimes made to stand for parents and for children. Such play is often taken to reveal a child's preoccupations, and play therapy is based on the notion that emotional pre-occupations can be acted out. In older children a lot of play becomes competitive. The dominance fighting to establish a 'pecking order', which can be seen in all social animals, is very evident in children. Some of it may be symbolic and indirect, especially in girls, where dominance fighting is more likely to be verbal than physical.

Arguments about the functions of play are centuries old, and the theories are on the whole untestable (as are most functional theories). However, there is now a certain amount of evidence from animals and from children regarding the effects of deprivation of play. Harlow's experiments at Wisconsin on the effects of various kinds of upbringing on later behaviour in rhesus monkeys have shown that, if small monkeys are deprived of play, especially rough and tumble play, they may become maladroit later at both sexual and social behaviour. It is possible that play has this kind of functional importance in humans also. A more popular theory is that play in humans is essential for cognitive development. Many educationists believe this and they get theoretical support from Piaget's notion that the growth of understanding depends heavily on the child's actions with respect to the environment. An intervention programme has been reported in which children who appeared to be intellectually backward as a result of malnutrition were given regular structured play sessions with toys, and as a result showed considerable development compared with children not given such a programme.

Individual differences

From birth children show individual differences in every measurable aspect of behaviour. These are determined genetically but also by events during pregnancy and at birth. The measures will also be affected by the way the measurements are made and by the state of the infant at the time. For decades people have been attempting to discover if any of these differences at birth correlate with differences in early childhood and later, and in general it appears that only in extreme cases, for instance where there are physical or psychological disabilities, is there any kind of continuity. This lack of correlation seems to hold also when differences in infancy are compared with differences in early childhood or later childhood. From time to time claims are made that there are some traits which are relatively invariant, but these are nearly always followed by counter claims. It looks as though the generally held belief that later personality depends on events in early childhood has been very much exaggerated. It is true that if measures of Developmental Quotient taken at, say, six months, are compared with measures of Intelligence Quotient taken at, say, eight years, there will be a small correlation, but it is so small as to make predictions in individual cases impossible. One of the most commonly used measures of personality is extraversion-introversion, but this again has not been shown to be invariant through childhood and into adulthood. There are, of course, gross differences when groups of children are compared rather than individual children, and it is quite likely that some sex differences will continue to be found in the majority of cultures. For instance, on the whole girls are better at tasks involving the use of words, whereas boys are better at tasks involving manipulation of space. Naturally, individual children do develop interests and attitudes which will remain with them for many years. The term 'sex typing' is used for all those kinds of learning which serve to emphasize the male and female roles within the child's sub-culture. Even before the age of three children tend to choose toys associated with the appropriate sex role, and this kind of learning may even become exaggerated between the years of six and, say, twelve. Other differences between large groups are: institutionalized children tend to be delayed in the first appearance of many kinds of behaviour, including smiling, for instance; social class differences are often found: for example, before one year of age middle-class children tend to fixate an object longer than working-class children, and in middle and late childhood middle-class children tend to develop a more complex language, this sometimes being accentuated by different types of schooling experienced by different social classes.

Leaving aside the problem of whether or not there is continuity in individual differences from birth to maturity, there are of course a very large number of individual differences which may be measured at any one age and which will show invariance probably for several years. Some important ones are general intelligence, specific abilities, kinds of imagery, cognitive style, extraversion-introversion, neuroticism, etc.

Explanatory principles

A large number of theories have been propounded regarding the way in which a child develops, two of the most influential being those of Freud and Piaget. Apart from these theories there are also various explanatory principles which are used by many theorists and which are mentioned briefly here because they have some generality.

Maturation of nervous system
At birth the weight of the brain is only one-quarter of its adult weight and much of its structure is very immature. It is especially lacking in fibres interconnecting different parts of the brain, so that it is likely that co-ordination of different kinds of sensory information with each other and with movements is going to be of a very limited kind. At three months of age that part of the brain concerned with the control of movement is one of the best developed areas, especially the part concerned with movements of the hand. The primary sensory areas are less well developed and the visual areas less so than the auditory areas. At this age there is an increasing number of interconnecting fibres. One measure of maturity of nerve fibres is the extent to which the fibres have acquired a sheath known as a myelin sheath, which is important for the more rapid transmission of impulses. At three months myelination is most advanced for the trunk, arm and forearm regions of the parts of the brain concerned with both movement and sensation. The auditory and visual areas come next and are about equal, but in other parts of the cortex there is still a general lack of myelination. At the age of 15 months, areas concerned with movement are still ahead, the region for the hand being best developed and the region concerned with the legs being least well developed. At this age a child's abilities seem to be

fairly consistent with the degree of maturation of the nervous system. This is an age at which many children are still unable to walk and at which not many can do so skilfully. (Here again the individual differences are of course very big and there are also some group differences: for instance, the development of locomotion occurs significantly earlier in Black children of Jamaican origin compared to indigenous Whites in the UK.) Between the second and fifth years there is some evidence that the mechanisms concerned with control of emotional behaviour become more mature, and this may be reflected in emotional development generally; but structural changes continue in the lower parts of the brain up to the age of puberty, and development continues in the higher parts of the brain until the third decade of life or perhaps later in some parts of the cortex. On average, at year ten the brain is 95 per cent of adult weight and electrical activity has reached the adult form at about the time of puberty. All of this development is controlled by heredity but also by many other factors, especially hormones secreted by the endocrine glands, drugs, disease, physical injury (especially at birth), malnutrition and lack of stimulation in a very broad sense. To what extent does the stage of development of the nervous system put limitations on the child's capabilities? It may be more than coincidence that the age at which Piaget believes fully logical and abstract thought is possible is also the age at which electrical activity in the brain is fully matured. However it must be stressed that no one has yet shown any close one-to-one relationships between state of maturation of the nervous system and maturation of intellectual and behavioural development. It would seem reasonable to suppose, though, that a person with a fully matured brain must be different in some ways psychologically.

Reinforcement
This is the notion that behaviour is controlled by its consequences. In the sense in which 'reinforcement' is used by B. F. Skinner, a reinforcing state of affairs is one which, when it follows a response of an animal or human, will reinforce that response so that the probability of that response occurring in similar circumstances in the future will increase. Much of the fundamental work on reinforcement has been done on rats and pigeons but also on a very wide variety of other animals and also on humans, and it is the basis for many of the techniques used in behaviour modification. In a typical experiment a rat learns to press a lever which results in the delivery of a food pellet which is reinforcing to the hungry rat. Using such a simple set-up it is possible to investigate the effects of a wide variety of variables on the rate of learning. If, after the animal has learnt, food is no longer delivered when the lever is pressed (extinction trials), the animal will go on pressing for a while and then cease, but there may be spontaneous recovery. If the animal has been put on a 'schedule' of reinforcement, in which reinforcement is not given for every

response but only now and again, either regularly or irregularly and unpredictably, then the animal tends to be much more persistent in pressing the lever and will go on doing so for very much longer when food is no longer delivered at all. In other words, after a schedule of reinforcement, especially if the reinforcement has been irregular, the behaviour is much more 'resistant to extinction'. A rat can also be put very much under the control of the environment in that, if a light is always on during reinforced trials but never on during unreinforced trials, the animal will learn quite rapidly to press the lever only when the light is on. The light is then described as a 'discriminative stimulus'. A wide variety of things may act as reinforcers. For instance, isolated monkeys will press a lever for a view of the monkey colony or for a tape-recording of the noises of other monkeys and these stimuli act as reinforcers. These kinds of experimental results have to be applied to humans with a good deal of caution. It is not clear how a human's behaviour is modified if he knows that he is being subjected to a pattern of reinforcement, nor is it clear what the effects are of having language and being able to conceptualize the set-up. Apart from behaviour modification techniques as used by therapists, the following are some applications which may be made.

There is one kind of crying, which was mentioned earlier, whose function seems to be to get attention even though there is nothing physically wrong with the child. Such attention-getting crying may be very persistent and attempts have been made to extinguish it by not attending to the child when he produces this kind of cry. There are several published papers indicating that this kind of procedure is effective. Getting attention, presumably benign attention, is an important reinforcer for many children. There are reports, for instance, of a child who spent most of his time in a horizontal position and crawling, and as a result obtained a lot of attention which presumably reinforced his crawling behaviour. The teachers were trained to attend to the child only when he approximated to standing up and not to attend to him when he was crawling, and as a result the child learnt to produce more normal behaviour. One famous experiment controlled the smiling of babies by reinforcing them with smiles and pleasant noises whenever they smiled. A comparison was made of babies who had been reinforced at every smile with those who had been put on a schedule, that is, they had been reinforced only at every fourth smile. As predicted, the babies on the schedule smiled more and the smiling was more resistant to extinction. It is not known, though, how long this kind of learning persisted. One prediction of the theory would be that if a child produced a certain kind of behaviour to obtain affection, then that behaviour would be more persistent if the affection were given capriciously and, for the child, unpredictably. As Skinner himself has pointed out, in everyday life most reinforcers are irregular rather than regular. This is particularly true in gambling and it is quite likely that one of the mechanisms at work in the persistent gambler is the direct result of unpredictable reinforcement. Bearing in mind the way in which an animal's behaviour can be controlled by a discriminative stimulus in the environment, one could argue that it would be much easier for a child to learn appropriate behaviour if it were made quite clear in the environment when that behaviour was appropriate and when not. To caricature the situation, if a father wore a tie whenever the child was expected to behave in a fairly orderly fashion, but did not wear a tie during playtime, then it should be much easier for the child to discriminate between those two situations. It must be very difficult indeed for a young child to know what is appropriate behaviour in a typical supermarket when everyone else is taking goods off the shelves but he himself is not allowed to do so. The use of reinforcers can be incorporated in methods of training in the way described by Skinner. Using 'methods of approximation', behaviour can be gradually 'shaped' in a desired direction. For instance, if a pigeon is to be taught to turn twice in a clockwise direction, the procedure is as follows. If the pigeon turns very slightly to the right it is reinforced; next time it turns a bit further to the right it is reinforced again and the reinforcement is given more the closer the bird approximates to what is wanted and given less when it is still only making tentative movements towards the right. Eventually it is reinforced only for turning two full whole circles and not reinforced at all for any other behaviour. This is a technique which has been used more or less by animal trainers for centuries, but there has been very little application of it to the training of children, though Skinner did believe that to some extent he was using this kind of thing in the 'programmed learning' techniques which he developed.

Imitation
There is some evidence that infants will imitate facial expressions when they are only a few weeks old. For instance, they will put out their tongue apparently imitatively at two or three weeks. However, it may not be true imitation since the infant will also put out his tongue at a pencil pointed at him at the same age. In the second half of the first year, though, a great deal of facial imitation goes on. Detailed analysis on videotape shows that in most cases it is the mother imitating the infant and not the other way round. A lot of this imitative play seems to be a precursor of language and conversation but it is not yet known how important it is. In the second and third year and later, there is a great deal of imitation, much of it apparently important for 'sex typing'. For instance, a three-year-old girl will spend a great deal of time imitating her mother's activities about the house. There have now been many studies of the extent to which imitation or copying occurs in middle childhood from grown-ups or from television. Boys in particular tend to copy aggressive movements especially if the

person they are imitating is a man, and more especially if
the man appears to be rewarded for what he is doing. It is
still very unclear to what extent this sort of behaviour
persists as a result of such imitation. It is still also not
known in general what people children imitate most. For
Freud, the central concept in child development is identification, and he believed that imitation was one of the best
behavioural signs that identification existed. Very early in
life he believed that identification with the mother figure
occurred and that later, at about the time the super-ego
develops, identification with the aggressor (the aggressive
aspects of either mother or father figure) took place. It is
clear that there are many kinds of imitation, all of which
require psychological explanation, so that imitation is not
itself a really good explanatory concept, but at a descriptive level it allows one to account for many changes occurring in child development and in adolescence. It is clear
already in pre-adolescent gangs that there is imitation of
clothing, hair style, tastes in food and drink and music,
etc.

The role of language
Many psychologists believe that the possession of language
is one of the more important things distinguishing man from
the higher apes, but the dividing lines are not clear. For
instance, apes are able to solve complicated problems, and
some have also been taught a certain amount of vocabulary
and a little syntax. However, in man it is assumed that
language is essential for intellectual development, but in
practice it has been difficult to demonstrate just how
important it is. For instance, adults who have brain damage
which affects their language functions (the aphasias) may
still be able to do complex reasoning; and deaf mutes who
have a minute vocabulary and practically no syntax can do
remarkably well in a wide variety of intellectual tasks.
Perhaps one of the problems is that educators tend to be
rather verbal people and they themselves use language a good
deal in their thinking, assuming that other people are the
same. It is clear, though, that there are many different
kinds of intelligence and different kinds of thinking and
some may be possible without the use of language, at least
in the conventional sense. It is obvious, however, that
language plays a large part in the social development of
children. Mothers talk a great deal to their infants and
young children and they do so more to girls than to boys.
Language probably also plays a large part in moral development. The way in which a child becomes socialized and
gradually adopts the morals of his sub-culture can be explained to some extent in terms of the way in which he is
reinforced for doing appropriate things and punished for
doing inappropriate things, and in terms of the way he
imitates what he sees other people doing. However, language
plays an important part because he is also given a great
deal of instruction regarding his behaviour. There have been

several retrospective studies which have shown that, when delinquents are compared with non-delinquents, the parents of the non-delinquents have used more explanation to their children regarding proper conduct. It is also typical that middle-class parents use a good deal more explanation about things in general.

Freud

Many present-day theories of child development are more or less based on classical psychoanalytic theory, and many people would consider that Freud's main contribution was to focus attention on the first five years of life as being of paramount importance in determining later personality. He suggested that during this period the child passes through stages related to the way in which the libido (instinctual energy) operates. The first stage is the oral stage, in which the child's erotic life (in Freud's rather special meaning) centres on the mouth; this is followed by the anal stage, when life centres on excretion; then the phallic stage in which sexual (but of course pre-pubertal) interests centre on the genitals and the body surface as a whole. There then follows a latent period during which there is little development until the genital period is reached at adolescence. Mental illness in later life was seen as originating from traumatic experiences occurring during these periods. The situation is complicated for boys by the Oedipus situation in which the five-year-old sees himself as competing with his father for the love of his mother. Some of these ideas were elaborated by other psychoanalysts by devising personality typologies which were based on infantile experience. For instance, an orally-accepting type of person would be a lover of food and drink, a smoker, fond of words; the phallic type might be a lover of the body beautiful, perhaps an exhibitionist or an admirer of sculpture. Needless to say, it is extremely difficult to test the validity of such speculations.

Piaget

Piaget founded what is sometimes called the Geneva School of Child Study. He set out to discover how logical thinking develops, and in doing that had little to say about emotion, motivation and social pressure. His most important technique was to carry out small experiments or demonstrations on individual children, and to question them when they were old enough. One of these typical experiments on conservation of volume has already been described. Another rather different example is concerned with relationships. For instance, Piaget might ask a boy, 'How many brothers have you got?' 'Two: Peter and James.' 'And how many brothers has Peter got?' 'One: James.' Using such methods Piaget found that the child's cognitive development could be best described in terms of a sequence of stages which always occurs in the same order. (Other workers also find the sequence to be rather stable.) The main stages are: the sensori-motor stage (roughly 18 months) during which the child's behaviour does not indicate internal representation of things or any reflective thought; the stage of symbolic thought (until about four years) in which play and language and thinking are integrated but may still be idiosyncratic and often dominated by perception (e.g. the child is unable to conserve volume in the experiment in which liquid is poured from one beaker into another); the stage of concrete operations where the child begins to show mature thinking except that he does not show general propositional thinking; and the stage of formal operations in which fully logical thought is possible.

These are descriptions of the various stages as Piaget saw them. He also constructed a rather complex theory with its own terminology. Piaget saw the child as having a complex of cognitive structures which adapt more or less to changes in the environment. That adaptation occurs by means of two mechanisms: assimilation, in which new events in the environment are assimilated to what the child already has; and accommodation, in which the child's existing structures do change so as to accommodate the new environmental events. Intelligent behaviour involves a suitable balance between these two things. For development to occur, according to Piaget, the child needs feedback from his own actions, so that interaction between the child and its environment is a necessity.

Adolescence

In the first half of this century adolescence was treated as a period of 'storm and stress', of rebellion, of altruism, and searching for an identity. Some of these characteristics of adolescence now seem to be specific to the cultures in which the originators of the ideas lived, and this is particularly true for the notion that adolescence is a period of storm and stress. From anthropological and other studies, it is clear in some cultures that such a period does not exist. The last few decades have seen major changes occurring in the adolescent world so that many of the old generalizations apply no longer. A few decades ago the situation could be stated in fairly black and white terms: the young adolescent was economically dependent; he was sexually capable but not expected to have, or even legally forbidden from having, intercourse; and his social roles were essentially non-adult. In the course of a decade he was expected to go through a fairly clear series of transitional stages until he inevitably reached the desired position in an adult society in which his economic, sexual and social roles would all have changed utterly. At the present day sexual intercourse is often practised soon after the onset of puberty; many children, including working-class children, have considerably more spending money than their parents had at the same age; and there are now so many sub-cultures all the way from pre-adolescence to adulthood that at any age a child can find himself fully accepted within a culture as a full member of the society.

Biological factors

It is now generally accepted that the onset of puberty
occurs earlier as time passes. The results of the onset of
puberty on the child seem to depend very much on what the
child and his peers expect those effects to be. For instance, there are large differences in the extent of menstrual pain, and those differences vary somewhat between
cultures and seem to reflect the expectations within those
cultures. Some studies suggests that menarche affects performance at school, whereas there are other studies giving
contrary evidence. Here again much may depend on expectations. It is likely that if a child reaches puberty long
before or long after other children in his age group, this
may have a considerable effect on his own behaviour and
attitudes. It may be that ignorance of biological factors is
detrimental in individual cases, but no one has yet shown
what is the best way to carry out sex education, or indeed
yet shown that sex education is a good thing (and it would
be extremely difficult to show, since the investigator would
have the problem of deciding what sex education is good
for).

Social factors

Not many generations ago a person was unlikely to survive
if he did not belong physically to a group of people. The
need to belong to a group is still as great, though little
is known about the psychological mechanisms involved.
Avoidance of loneliness is one powerful drive. In modern man
this need may be satisfied by simply identifying with the
group and not necessarily belonging to it physically. A
century ago a person's choice of group was limited usually
to the family, the immediate neighbourhood, work, church,
and perhaps hobbies and sport. Now, especially in cities or
where people are mobile, groups are based more on common
interests. It is very easy for a person to find other people
who want to behave in the same way or have common goals.
There is a tendency for members of a group to come to look
alike, talk alike, make the same choices in food, music,
beliefs, etc., and these tendencies are often seen in an
exaggerated form in adolescent groups, especially where the
identification with the group is so complete that the person
sees himself as belonging to that group only and no other.
One very noticeable thing about human groups of all kinds
(and this applies to groups at all levels of sophistication)
is that they are not only bound together by common likes but
also by common dislikes. All groups are against something.
Anything which lessens old group allegiances will also make
new groupings easier, so that one would expect gangs to be
especially prevalent in new high-rise housing estates, or
with people who have just left school. One idea about adolescence, which seems not to have changed over the centuries, is that there is something called 'adolescent revolt'.
It has been observed in many cultures (though not in all),
that soon after puberty there tends to be a reaction against

the parental ways of life. The idea that there is something primitive and possibly biological about this has been re-inforced by many observations of primate societies which show that young males tend to form breakaway groups and also start fighting for dominance within the old group.

Dominance fighting is well accepted as an explanatory concept applied to social animals of all kinds, and some biologists and psychologists see it as a main source of competitiveness in human behaviour. Besides the pressures to belong to a group and to conform to it, there are still these largely competitive tendencies which may take the form of wanting to be unique, and to have a role of one's own within the group. Very often such a role involves being best at something. Being best may involve owning things, being the most daring, or beautiful, or cleverest. With small boys, competitiveness may show itself in actual dominance fighting. Psychologists of various kinds have talked a lot about the adolescent need for having an identity. It is pos-sible that that need may be partly and perhaps completely satisfied once the person finds a role within a group, especially if the role and the group are of high esteem.

Attitudes and beliefs

Sociologists and social psychologists use the concept 'reference groups'. A market researcher may want to know how to advertise a certain kind of cosmetic product. If it is intended to be attractive to adolescent girls, he may well use the technique of finding out which reference group is relevant. For instance he may, using questionnaire tech-niques, ask questions of the kind designed to find out who adolescent girls identify with when buying cosmetics. In general, one's reference group is the group of people with whom one identifies with respect to one's attitudes, beliefs and values. Developmental studies show that for young child-ren the home provides the main reference group, but in mid-dle childhood already there is a tendency to adopt values of heroes from stories or from television, and this becomes very marked in pre-adolescence. In adolescence there may be a complete change of reference groups as has already been suggested, and if this change is very radical then it may be a source of conflict. The way in which the conflict ex-presses itself will, of course, vary between individuals, and any of the usual clinical manifestations are possible: anxiety, depression, hysterical reactions, aggression, and in some cases an attempt at a rational solution of the conflict. Attitudes towards choice of work will be affected by group pressures in just the same way as all other atti-tudes. The situation is affected by the fact that in many adolescent sub-cultures all the heroes and heroines are roughly of the same age as members of the sub-culture, and there is no need to look ahead to what is going to happen when one belongs to an older age group. In such cases atti-tudes towards work are likely to be unrealistic in terms of planning ahead.

Some early developmental stages

Here are given only rough indications. The normal variation is very large indeed. (The following are adapted from tables prepared by B. M. Foss in 'Introductory Psychology', edited by John Coleman and published by Routledge & Kegan Paul.)

First month (neonatal period)

Notable reflexes: Moro, Babinski, sucking, grasping, 'stepping', 'swimming', yawning, blinking, vomiting, hiccoughing, sneezing: penis erections in the male. All these are there at birth, or within a few hours. At one month, when awake, the neonate lies on back with head to preferred side, and brings it to mid-position only momentarily. The chin may be lifted (to illustrate the very large range: some infants can raise their heads at birth; others do not do so until more than two months old, even though they are perfectly healthy). Feet are pressed against the observer's hand.

There are perceptual 'preferences' for moving objects, brightness, colour, pattern complexity, possibly for symmetry and possibly also for patterns resembling the human face. The head is moved to track a moving object, sometimes after only a few days.

'Emotional' reactions are limited to startle (Moro) and varying levels of general distress, shown in tearless crying, thrashing about and turning red. Crying simply to get attention occurs towards the end of this period. 'Pleasure' and 'burp' smiles appear, but not 'social' smiling. Classical and operant conditioning have been demonstrated in the first month.

Months 2 and 3

Head is held up when infant is supported in a sitting position. It comes more often to the mid-line. Child takes some weight on legs if supported in standing position. Transition occurs from hands mainly closed to mainly open. Starts to reach out to dangling objects, but this response may be very much delayed in unstimulating surroundings.

Accommodation of lens of eye is more or less complete by end of period (some exists at birth), and eyes converge on approaching object. Blinking at fast-approaching object occurs at about two months, and eye can trace object through wide arc. Head is turned to familiar sound.

Crying is now accompanied by tears. Child feeds a great deal; for instance, still twice at night. Colicky babies are often free of colic by three months.

'Social' smiling, at a face, mask, etc., starts in this period. At about two months, if the infant is in an attentive state, he will react strongly when talked to, as though trying to answer.

Months 4–6

Transition from sitting supported to beginning to sit alone. Grasps, but inefficiently. When prone and awake, head tends to be kept in mid-line, but is turned in direction of unfamiliar sound (i.e. later than to a familiar one). Towards end of this period will continue to smile at familiar face, but react coolly to strange ones. Grasped objects tend to be brought to mouth. Finger-thumb opposition is not yet possible. Arm movements still tend to be ambidextrous or symmetrical. Some bi-manual co-ordination.

Starts to sleep through the night, but this is often accompanied by screaming at bedtime. This particular kind of crying seems particularly susceptible to operant conditioning; it is easily increased by reinforcement, and extinguished by ignoring it. Gurgles and babbles to people.

Yet more anticipatory behaviour, for instance before being picked up. Will wait expectantly for a meal.

Months 7-12
Transition from crawling to going rapidly on all fours, and standing by pulling himself up, and walking if led. Now grasps efficiently and can throw with a thrusting movement. May hold out arms to be picked up at the beginning of this period, but some children are much later. In first half of period objects are banged repetitively, and often thrown away repetitively for someone to retrieve. Infant highly amused by 'peek-a-boo'. Many understand 'no' halfway through period, and many speak two or three words by one year.

Emotional expression becomes much more differentiated. Frustration at being deprived of toy comes halfway through period. Fear of strangers is often shown. Shows definite affection and signs of attachment. Enjoys reciprocal 'games', but will play on his own for long periods. Gives up object when asked. Can put one object in another. Appears to realize that there is more to an object than he can see.

During the first year, much of the child's behaviour seems to be concerned with integrating information from the various senses and with body movements. Also he seems to be learning the limits of his own body, that is, learning his 'body schema'. For instance, it is only in the second half of the first year that the infant seems to learn that his feet are part of himself, so that when he bites them they will hurt.

According to Freud, the child is dominated by orality during this period. According to Piaget, there is a transition from reflexive behaviour to primary and secondary 'circular reactions' in which repetition plays the important part; for example, repetition of movements with pleasurable ends. These learned reactions are gradually integrated, and lead to trial and error behaviour which in turn leads to desired goals.

Months 12-18
Progresses from walking alone to creeping up and down stairs without help. Begins to jump with both feet. Moves from constantly throwing things to rolling them and piling things on each other. Scribbles. Uses cup and spoon.

Can locate sounds well, knows own name, enjoys nursery rhymes and tries to sing. Enjoys picture books and can identify pictures of well-known things. Changes from few words and much babbling and jargon to use of about a dozen intelligible words. Can obey single orders. Imitates mother at household jobs.

According to Piaget, during this period the child starts problem-solving to some extent symbolically; that is, without actually carrying out the actions in a trial and error fashion.

Months 19–24

Becomes able to stoop, and later to kick, without falling over. Runs and jumps well. Imitates walking backwards. Builds up six or seven cubes at beginning of this period; and pours from cup to cup. Later washes and dries hands; dresses himself. Makes circular scribbles rather than just strokes.

Produces two-word sentences and, towards the end of the period, talks volubly, using pronouns. Plays along with other children, but individually.

During this period, sex differences appear in 'aggressiveness', 'fearfulness' and interest evoked by toys.

During the second year, separation from the mother or mother-substitute is very traumatic.

According to Freud, this is the anal period, during which erotic satisfaction is related to excretion, both expulsion and retention. There is no doubt that in our culture toilet training often leads to conflicts with parents during the second year.

Years 2–5

The child progresses in body control until he can skip on both feet (but not hop); gross body movements are replaced by more differentiated fine movements: for example, tying a shoe-lace becomes possible. Can copy squares, triangles, etc., and the drawing of a man changes from a basic circle with long descending, radiating lines to a conventional child's drawing-of-a-man, with discernible head and limbs.

In about the fourth year the child may distinguish left from right in some conditions. Things are often seen animistically and, later, as being under the control of outside, mysterious agencies.

Play develops from individual forms, with egocentric monologues, to co-operative play, and then organization into groups with leaders and rapid changes of roles. Play with dolls, etc., is highly imaginative, and imaginary companions are common.

Speech at the beginning of this period usually involves lisping and stuttering.

Years 6–12

This is the period during which, especially according to Piaget, there is a great change in a child's thinking ability. At the beginning of this period children are unable to conserve volume, which means that they do not realize that a given amount of liquid does not change when it is poured from a vessel of one shape to one of a different shape. They are also unable to see things from a different point of view. At the beginning of this period they are in general unable to see from the start that it is possible to categorize objects and people in several ways, but at the end of the period children have already achieved or will soon achieve logical thinking. During this period most children in our society stop thinking out loud and often practise deliberate deception. They seem to take pleasure in having a world of their own to which grown-ups cannot have access. During this period too they start playing more in gangs and, if there are sufficient children around to make it possible, these gangs will very often be of a single sex. In many sub-cultures the differences of role between boys and girls tend to become exaggerated. Hero and heroine worship becomes marked and there is a great deal of emulation of favourite pop singers and sportsmen, and children often build up large collections of pictures, discs and so on associated with them.

Questions

1. Discuss the ways in which an understanding of the pattern and determinants of development in childhood is important to doctors.
2. What are the psychological and behavioural changes associated with adolescence?
3. Is adolescence inevitably a period of turmoil and stress?
4. How important is play to the growing child?
5. Discuss the assessment and explanation of individual differences in childhood. Are individual differences determined more by biological than psychological factors?
6. What contributions did theorists such as Freud and Piaget make to our knowledge of development?
7. Discuss critically the methods which are used to assess and explain the behaviour of the child.
8. 'The child is father of the man.' Discuss.
9. Discuss the development of three aspects of psychological functioning and behaviour up to adolescence. Mention any social or psychological factors which might affect the development of these functions.
10. Discuss the ways in which a knowledge of developmental norms is important for the paediatrician. Mention some of the practical problems encountered in the assessment of young children.

Annotated reading

Hadfield, J.A. (1962) Childhood and Adolescence. Harmondsworth: Penguin.

Sandstrom, C.I. (1968) Psychology of Childhood and Adolescence. Harmondsworth: Penguin.

These cover both childhood and adolescence. The book by Hadfield is particularly useful for parents. The one by Sandstrom is a little dated though there is a revised edition from 1979.

Bower, T. (1977) Perceptual World of the Child. London: Fontana.

Garvey, C. (1977) Play. London: Fontana.

Donaldson, M. (1978) Children's Minds. London: Fontana.
These belong to a series of short books on children called The Developing Child and edited by Jerome Bruner, Michael Cole and Barbara Lloyd. The last of these three references is particularly good on cognitive growth and its relevance to education.

Turner, J. (1975) Cognitive Development. London: Methuen.

Green, J. (1974) Thinking and Language. London: Methuen.
These are part of a series called Essential Psychology, and are particularly relevant.

Watson, R.I. and Lindgren, H.C. (1979) Psychology of the Child and the Adolescent (4th edn). New York: Collier Macmillan.
This is an American book, but covers the non-American work well, and is slightly more advanced than the other suggested readings.

5

Social Development in Early Childhood

H. R. Schaffer

Opening remarks
DAVID GRIFFITHS

The relevance of Rudolph Schaffer's chapter to doctors is implied in his introductory discussion of the reasons for psychologists' interest in children; for psychologists and doctors are interested in development for similar reasons. The first of these is an uncomplicated interest and curiosity in understanding the process and determinants of development. To quote Schaffer, 'they want to find out how a helpless, naive and totally dependent baby manages in due course to become a competent, knowledgeable adult'.

The second reason is more practical and immediate. An understanding of development is, as we have already noted in discussing Brian Foss's chapter, relevant to many practical decisions. Many of the questions considered in this chapter are directly relevant to decisions and actions which will confront the clinician. Does it matter whether a child is reared by his biological mother or a foster mother? Is the 'natural' mother necessarily better for the child? Do the children of working mothers suffer as a consequence? Why do some parents become baby batterers? Are the early years special to the extent that they determine adult personality? What are the effects of maternal deprivation on the child? What effects, in the short and long term, do one-parent families have on children?

Doctors will also be relieved to see that Schaffer provides answers to quite a number of these questions. Psychologists will be delighted to realize that these answers are based on objective results. Uncertainties, where they remain, are recognized but it is important to have an evaluation of existing evidence, albeit incomplete evidence, since many of the questions facing clinicians are too urgent to await conclusive answers based on further investigation.

Introduction
H. R. SCHAFFER

Child development is one of the fastest growing fields of psychology. In the last few decades a considerable body of knowledge has accumulated regarding the nature of development from conception onward. As a result we know quite a lot about how children behave at various ages; we are also beginning to disentangle the much more difficult question as to the causes of behaviour: that is, why children behave as they do.

There are two basic reasons why psychologists study children. In the first place they want to investigate the nature of development: to discover what it is that accounts for the helpless, naïve, and totally dependent new-born baby becoming in due course a competent, knowledgeable adult capable of such skills as language, creative thought, and forming relationships with other people. The second reason stems from the many social problems associated with childhood: in today's rapidly changing society especially questions continually arise as to the 'right way' of bringing up children. Should we protect children from viewing violence on television? Are children of mothers who go out to work more likely to become delinquents? Does hospitalization in the early years produce later difficulties? How can one mitigate the effects of divorce on children? Why do some parents become baby batterers? Increasingly the psychologist is asked to examine these and many other such problems and produce answers useful to society. It is primarily to this aspect of child psychology that we pay attention here.

Let us first of all distinguish two ways of tackling the problems of child rearing. One is represented by the advice-givers, the professional experts, from Dr Spock onwards. Their large number - as found on radio and television, on bookshelves and in the women's magazines - is a striking feature of today's society and is surely a response to the considerable uncertainty which parents feel about their task. But however well-intentioned and experienced these advice-givers may be, we have to recognize that their statements generally reflect only their personal opinions and prejudices, and rarely the results of systematically carried out research investigations. Take the question of the mother going out to work. In the last 30 or 40 years there has been a dramatic increase in the number of women taking up employment, and this has included a large number of those with young children. Are such children harmed thereby? A heated debate has raged around this question, often carried out at a 'some cases I have known' level. Experience of individual cases may well provide a useful insight, but the numbers involved are generally few, they may well be atypical, and the conclusions are usually based on subjective impressions. No wonder different people then arrive at different answers. Contrast this with the second way in which such problems may be tackled: that is, with the approach of the social scientist. Care will be taken to select a reasonably large and representative sample of working mothers and their children; this will be compared with a group as similar as possible except that the mothers are not at work; and both groups will be assessed by means that, as far as possible, will eliminate the influence of any subjective biasses that the investigator may have. If, moreover, several studies of different groups all arrive at the same conclusion, one is justified in having faith in their findings. This is indeed what has happened in this case: comparisons of the children of working and non-working mothers have generally shown no differences between them: in some cases, for example, when the child is in some form of suitable day care, the children of working mothers may even have gained from their increased opportunities of contact with other children and adults.

By the use of methods such as these child psychology is gradually accumulating knowledge about the factors that play a part in furthering or, alternatively, holding back children's development. In this chapter we examine this knowledge, with particular reference to the child's social development in the early years.

The child's socialization

How a child develops depends to a quite large extent on the people around him. From them he learns the skills and values needed for social living: from the use of knives and forks to knowing the difference between right and wrong. Other people are always near the child, influencing him by example and command, and none more so at first than the members of his own family. On them depend the initial stages of his socialization.

Disadvantaged children and their families

It is, of course, only too apparent that not every family carries out its socializing task with equal effectiveness. By way of illustration, let us look at the way in which the child's intellectual development is shaped by his social environment.

We have long ago given up the idea that intelligence is entirely determined by an individual's innate endowment and not at all influenced by the circumstances of his own life. Studies of infants brought up in grossly depriving institutions have drawn attention to the powerful effect a child's environment may exert on his development. Such a child, reared in conditions that provide him with little stimulation through play and social interaction, may progressively deteriorate and, irrespective of his original endowment, end up grossly retarded. With improvements in such features as the staff-child ratio of the institution and the introduction of a more stimulating regime, the child's deterioration can be halted and even be reversed.

Less dramatically but on a more extensive scale, a similar phenomenon has been described in relation to school failure. In the United States in particular, increasing concern came to be expressed a number of years ago regarding the large number of children, generally from the economically and socially most deprived sectors of the community, who are at a severe disadvantage when first starting school. Such children (as someone once put it) 'have learned not to learn'. Their failure in the education system, in other words, is ascribed not so much to some genetic inferiority as to factors operating in the home which result in an inability to make use of whatever intellectual capacities they have.

A great many schemes have been launched to counter this situation. Some of the early 'Operation Head Start' experiments, designed to give children some extra training in basic cognitive skills before school entry, were clearly inadequate. Whatever effects such one-shot inoculations produced were of short duration and soon disappeared. This is partly because the schemes were too brief, partly because they were started too late in the child's life, but partly also because they were directed at the child alone and left untouched the home situation. Given a conflict of values about education between home and school it is highly likely that the home will win. It is therefore significant that more recent efforts have been directed at much younger children (some schemes starting even in infancy) and that they have attempted to involve the parents as well as the child, or even to work solely through the parents.

There is now little doubt that parents can enhance or suppress the child's educational potential. The question is how they do so. Work by Basil Bernstein has indicated language use to be one of the main factors that differentiate the mothers of various social groups and that may well be implicated in shaping children's intellectual development. Not only are there social class differences in the style of language adopted (at least for the English mothers studied by Bernstein), but some American work has also shown that mothers from disadvantaged homes engage in face-to-face talking with their infants less frequently and for shorter periods than middle-class mothers. The child from a poor family may live in extremely noisy surroundings, where the overcrowded conditions and the constant blare of radio or television might appear to provide him with far more linguistic stimulation than is the case for the middle-class child in his quiet suburban home. Yet to profit from stimulation the young child must be exposed to it under the intimate, personalized, challenging conditions that only the to-and-fro reciprocity of a face-to-face situation can provide, and it is in this respect that many children from deprived backgrounds are at a disadvantage.

Child effects on adults

We must not now jump to the conclusion that the development of children is totally a matter of what parents do to them, and that the child is merely a passive organism wholly at the mercy of those around him. Socialization would then become a kind of clay-moulding process: the child, that is, arrives in the world as a formless lump of clay and society, as represented by mothers and fathers and other authority figures, proceeds to mould him into whatever shape it desires. The end product could then be wholly explained in terms of the actions of these people, and if by chance this product turned out to be undesirable it would be entirely the responsibility of the socializing agents.

Such a view is misleading. How parents bring up their child is not just a matter of their own ideas, preferences and predispositions; it depends also on the nature of the child, which from the very beginning can exert a definite influence on how the parents treat him. Even the very youngest baby is already a psychologically active being, with demands which he has no hesitation in making known and peculiarities to which other people must adjust. He brings these demands and peculiarities to even the very earliest encounters with others, whose behaviour towards him he will thereby affect.

Take an obvious example: babies cry and thereby draw attention to themselves. They may not yet be able to speak and so call the mother by name; they may not yet be capable of walking and so fetching the mother to help. However, nature has equipped them with a very powerful device that will influence from the very beginning both the amount and the timing of attention which others provide. It is a sound that can have a most compelling effect on the adult: we have all heard of the mother who can sleep through a thunderstorm, but is immediately awoken by her child's whimper in the next room. What is more, there are several quite distinctive types of cry, signalling hunger, anger and pain respectively. Mothers can distinguish these, and the last in particular tends to arouse them to immediate action. The baby, that is, initiates the interaction; he can also maintain it by use of another powerful device, namely the smile, which mothers generally find so delightful that they will want to remain with the child.

Another illustration of children's influence on parents comes from the marked differences that exist in the behaviour of even quite young babies. Some are highly active and restless, others quiet and content; some are sensitive and liable to be upset by the slightest change in routine, others are emotionally robust and easy-going. The kind of care provided for one is therefore inappropriate for another, and any sensitive mother will therefore find herself compelled to adopt practices suitable for her individual child. A good example is provided by babies' differences in 'cuddliness'. Not all babies love being held and cuddled: some positively hate it and resist such contact by struggling and, unless released, by crying. It has been found that these 'non-cuddlers' tend to be much more active and restless generally, and to be intolerant of all types of physical restraint (as seen when they are being dressed or tucked into bed). Their behaviour with the mother is thus an expression of a general disposition and has little to do with the way in which the mother has been handling the child. The mother, however, is forced to treat her child in a manner that takes into account his 'peculiarity': when frightened or unwell these children cannot be comforted by being held close, but have to be offered other forms of stimulation such as bottles, biscuits or soothing voices. Each mother must therefore show considerable flexibility in adjusting to the specific requirements of her child.

There is one further, and perhaps unexpected, example one can quote of the way in which parents are influenced by their children. It concerns the phenomenon of baby battering, which has attracted so much attention in recent years. It is by no means a new phenomenon: historically speaking, it is probably as old as the family itself, and there are indeed indications that in previous centuries the killing of young children (and especially of new-born infants) was far more prevalent than it is today. What is new is public concern that such a thing can happen, and this in turn has given rise to the need for research into such cases. As a result of various investigations it is now widely agreed that violence results from a combination of several factors: the presence of financial, occupational and housing problems facing the family; the parents' emotional immaturity which makes it difficult for them to deal with such problems; their social isolation from potential sources of help such as relatives and neighbours; and, finally, some characteristic of the battered child that singles him out as a likely victim.

It is the last factor that is particularly relevant to us, for it illustrates once again that the way in which parents treat their children is influenced by the children themselves. There is evidence that children most likely to be battered are 'difficult': they are more likely to be sickly, or to have been born prematurely, or to have feeding and sleeping problems. Being more difficult to rear they make extra demands that the parents are just not able to meet. The child's condition acts on the parent's inadequacy, and so the child, unwittingly, contributes to his own fate.

Mother-child mutuality

It is apparent that children do not start life as psychological nonentities. From the beginning they already have an individuality that influences the adults around them. Thus a mother's initial task is not to create something out of nothing; it is rather to dovetail her behaviour to that of the child.

Such dovetailing takes many forms. Take our previous example of the non-cuddlers. Such a child demands a particular kind of contact that might well not tally with the mother's own preferences. After all, she too has certain requirements of her own which she brings to the relationship and wishes to fulfil therein; if, however, she has a preference for close physical contact with the baby which the latter then rejects, some mutual readjustment will need to take place. This cannot happen if the mother rigidly insists on providing her child with a type of stimulation that he is unable to accept. Fortunately most mothers quickly adjust and find other ways of relating to the child. It is only when they are too inflexible, or interpret the baby's behaviour as rejection, that trouble can arise from a mismatch.

Mutual adjustment is the hallmark of all interpersonal behaviour; it can be found in even the earliest social interactions. The feeding situation provides a good example. Should babies be fed by demand or by a rigid, pre-determined schedule? Advice by doctors and nurses has swung fashion-wise, sometimes stressing the importance of exerting discipline from the very beginning and of not 'giving in', at other times pointing to the free and easy methods of primitive tribes as the 'natural' way. In actual fact each mother and baby, however they may start off, sooner or later work out a pattern that satisfies both partners. On the one hand, there are few mothers who can bear to listen for long to a bawling infant unable as yet to tell the time; on the other hand, one should not under-estimate the ability of even very young babies to adjust to the demands of their environment. An example is provided by an experiment, carried out many years ago, in which two groups of babies were fed during the first ten days of life according to a three-hour and a four-hour schedule respectively. Within just a few days after birth each baby had already developed a peak of restlessness just before the accustomed feeding time, and this became particularly obvious when the three-hour group was shifted to a four-hour schedule and so had to wait an extra hour for their feed. In time, however, these babies too became accustomed to the new timetable and showed the restlessness peak at four-hourly intervals. We can see here a form of adaptation to social demands that must represent one of the earliest forms of learning.

When one examines in detail the manner in which feeding proceeds, yet other kinds of mutual adjustment become clear. Feeding is, of course, not a one-sided task like shovelling coal into a boiler, for the baby has an active say in determining just how things proceed. Babies suck in bursts, with pauses in between: a rhythmic form of behaviour controlled by inborn mechanisms in the brain. Mothers need to adjust their own behaviour to this rhythm. As detailed film analyses of bottle- or breast-feeding sessions have shown, they do so by being generally quiet and inactive during bursts; during pauses, on the other hand, they jiggle, stroke and talk to the baby, thereby setting up a kind of dialogue in which the partners take it in turns to be actor and spectator. Thus the mother allows herself to be paced by the baby, fitting in with his natural sucking pattern, responding to his signals such as ceasing to suck, and accepting the opportunity to intervene offered by his pauses. At the same time the baby too shows that he has learned about the mother's patterning by, for instance, responding to the end of her jiggling with resumed sucking. A to-and-fro thus occurs from which both parties may gain satisfaction.

Not surprisingly, the major responsibility for mutual adjustment lies initially with the adult. The degree of flexibility one can expect from very young children is limited. Yet the fact that they are involved in social interactions from the very beginning of life means that they have the opportunity of gradually acquiring the skills necessary to become full partners in such exchanges. Observations of give-and-take games with babies at the end of the first year have made this point. Initially the baby knows only how to take: he has not yet learned that his behaviour is just one part of a sequence, that he needs to take turns with the other person, and that the roles of the two participants are interchangeable (one being a giver, the other a taker). Such and other rules of behaviour he will learn in time; they form the basis for much of social intercourse, and it is through social intercourse that the child acquires them in the first place.

Socialization is sometimes portrayed as a long drawn-out battle, as a confrontation between wilful young children and irritated parents that must at all cost be resolved in favour of the latter. Goodness knows such battles occur, yet they are far from telling us everything about the process of socialization. There is a basic mutuality between parent and child without which interaction would not be possible. The sight of the mother's face automatically elicits a smile from the baby; that produces a feeling of delight in the mother and causes her in turn to smile back and to talk or tickle or pick up, in this way calling forth further responses from the baby. A whole chain of interaction is thus started, not infrequently initiated by the baby. Mother and child learn about each other in the course of these interactions, and more often than not mutual adjustment is brought about by a kind of negotiation process in which both partners show some degree of flexibility. On the mother's part, this calls for sensitivity to the particular needs and requirements of her child which is an ingredient of parenthood that we return to subsequently; on the child's part, it refers to one of the most essential aspects of social living that he must learn early on.

Some conditions that foster development

If the environment in which a child is reared can have marked effects on him, it is necessary to learn how this is brought about. We need to identify those factors in the child's experience that promote mental health and social integration in order then to try and eliminate whatever obstacles there may be to the child's optimal development. And if this smacks of social engineering, it is in fact none other than the strategy so successfully used in the field of physical health. Any action taken to identify and eliminate the causes of infant mortality, tuberculosis or polio needs no defence; any action required to get rid of deprivation, maladjustment and antisocial behaviour is similarly justified.

Let us admit immediately that we are still woefully ignorant as to what the factors are that bring about inadequate or undesirable development in children. It is easy to make guesses and put all the blame on not enough parental discipline, too much violence on television, the declining influence of religion, the social isolation of today's family, too much pocket money ... the list of favourite explanations could go on for a long time yet. It is, however, much more difficult to substantiate the influence of any one factor, for to produce research findings sufficiently credible to form the basis for social action is a long and painful process. There are, nevertheless, some conclusions to which we can point.

The blood-bond: myth or reality?

Is it essential, or at least desirable, that children should be brought up by their natural parents? Is a woman who conceived and bore a child by that very fact more fitted to care for this child than an unrelated individual?

This is no academic question. Children have been removed by courts of law from the foster parents with whom they had lived nearly all their lives and to whom they had formed deep attachments, in order to restore them to their biological mother from whom they may have been apart since the early days of life, and all because of the 'blood-bond'. Yet such a thing is a complete myth. There is nothing at all to suggest that firm attachments cannot grow between children and unrelated adults who have taken over the parental role. The notion that the biological mother, by virtue of being the biological mother, is uniquely capable of caring for her child is without foundation.

Were it otherwise, the whole institution of adoption would be in jeopardy. Yet there is nothing to suggest that adoptive parents are in any way inferior to natural parents. In a study by Barbara Tizard (to which we refer again), children who had been in care throughout their early years were followed up on leaving care. One group of children was adopted, another returned to their own families. It was found that the latter did less well than the adopted children, both in the initial stages of settling in and in their subsequent progress. The reason lay primarily in the attitudes of the two sets of parents: the adoptive group worked harder at being parents, possibly just because the child was not their own. There have been a good many studies which have examined the effects of adoption, and virtually all stress the high proportion of successful cases to be found. And this can happen despite the difficulties such children may have had to face, such as problems in the pre-adoption phase and the knowledge gained later on of the fact of their adoption. Successful parenting is a matter of particular personality characteristics that need to be identified, not of 'blood'.

Fathers as parents: more myths?

Men go out to work and earn a livelihood; women stay at home and look after the children. Such division of labour is clear-cut and traditional. It suggests that women are specifically fitted for child care and that they, not men, should be encouraged to devote themselves to this task.

The facts of modern family life tell a different story. Over the last few decades men have increasingly come to participate in the care of their children. They push prams, change nappies and give bottles to their babies. They are no longer the stern and distant figures that Victorian writers such as Freud depicted. And with increasing unemployment it is no longer uncommon to find families in which a complete role reversal has taken place: mother, having found a job, goes out to work, leaving her unemployed husband in charge of home and children. Fortunately there is no evidence to indicate that the biological make-up of men makes them unfit for this task or even, necessarily, inferior to women in this respect. Parenting is unisex; the reasons for the traditional division of labour (such as the need to breast-feed the child and the importance of using men's greater physical strength for hunting and tilling the fields) are no longer applicable.

A father's prolonged absence from a family (because of military service, for instance) can produce some harmful effects on a child. A number of studies have described these, with particular reference to the absence of a model for a boy to imitate. Whether sex-appropriate behaviour is indeed acquired through such imitation remains controversial; on the other hand, the need for the often onerous task of parenting to be shared is widely agreed upon. We have here one of the reasons why the children of single-parent families can be so vulnerable, for the remaining parent must cope with a great multiplicity of stresses: financial, occupational and emotional. This applies particularly when the single-parent status is due to illegitimacy, desertion, divorce or death. In nearly all these cases it is still mostly the woman who is left holding the baby. If one then finds ill-effects in the children it is usually very difficult to single out the particular factors that brought these about: the absence of the father, or any of the other concomitant stresses.

Nevertheless, there is one respect in which the fatherless child is usually deprived, and that is the opportunity early on to diversify his social relations. We have long ago given up the idea that social development can be explained in terms of the mother-child relationship alone. On the contrary, the child needs to be provided with other relationships that will increasingly acquaint him with the complexities of the social world. The very fact that he has two parents helps him to learn from the start that not all people are alike and that he must adapt his own behaviour according to their different characteristics and different demands upon him. A child isolated with his mother and caught up in one all-encompassing relationship does not have the same chance of learning this vital lesson, and his social development may well be impoverished thereby. It is in this sense, more than any other, that fathers matter in the early years.

Parenthood: full-time or part-time?
In the early 1950s, as a result of a report drawn up by John Bowlby, people became aware of the harmful effects that maternal deprivation might bring about. The children in whom

these effects had been found were mainly those who had spent a large part of their childhood in institutions or had suffered long-term hospitalization: an experience that we look at in a later section. However, in the years following Bowlby's report, the idea that children require continuous mothering was taken to an extreme which Bowlby himself never implied. There were many parents, as well as professional workers and public authorities, who thought it was the mother's duty to stay with her child night and day, 24 hours on end, throughout the pre-school years. As a result, mothers felt guilty if they left the child for just an afternoon; a halt was called to the expansion of nursery school facilities; and a propaganda drive to declare mothering a full-time total commitment was launched in order to save the mental health of young children. But is such a commitment really necessary or even desirable?

We can look at this situation from both the mother's and the child's point of view. As far as mothers are concerned, a crucial consideration is the recent finding of an extremely high incidence of depression among house-bound women. This applies particularly to working-class women, and is associated with such factors as the lack of a close relationship with the husband, having three or more children under the age of 14 at home, and not being employed. In short, these women suffer from being isolated. On the other hand, as the Court Committee on the future of the Child Health Services made clear in its 1976 report, mothers who go out to work are less likely to suffer from depression, anxiety and feelings of low self-esteem. And yet 'the sad truth is that our society has in no way come to terms with this social fact nor tried to use the opportunity it could afford through day care and education to improve the quality of services for children'.

As far as the children are concerned, there is some evidence that those remaining at home during the pre-school years with their depressed mothers are more likely to be developmentally delayed in functions such as language, as well as being emotionally more vulnerable. In general (as we mentioned earlier on) children of mothers going out to work do not suffer adverse effects. However, an important proviso concerns the quality of their care. For one thing, there is a need for consistency: a young child always being left with different people is likely to become bewildered and upset. And for another, we have the enormous problem of illegal childminders looking after an estimated 100,000 children in Britain. According to recent findings, the quality of care provided by such childminders is only too frequently of an unsatisfactory nature, being marked by ignorance and neglect that in some cases can be quite appalling.

However, officially provided facilities such as nursery schools often do have beneficial effects, both intellectually and socially. The intellectual effects have been of most interest in relation to children from deprived backgrounds. Despite some earlier doubts, it is now becoming

clear that compensatory schemes such as Operation Head Start
in the United States can be successful in improving children's educational progress. They are even financially worth
while, in that they save the need for subsequent expensive
remedial action. As to effects on social development, there
has been some concern that day care might in some way
'dilute' the child's attachment to the mother and danger-
ously weaken this basis for security. The most recent
evidence does not support this view: a daily period away
from the mother need not impair the relationship; fostering
the tie between mother and child is not a 24-hours-a-day
activity.

One undoubted advantage for the child's social development which day care does usually bring with it is the
opportunity to play with other children. This important
topic deserves a separate section.

Relationships with other children

Until quite recently child psychologists paid little attention to this aspect. This was partly, once again, due to the
idea that no relationship matters other than that with the
mother. It was partly also because of the idea (originally
put forward by Piaget, the influential Swiss psychologist)
that children are totally self-centred in the early years,
to the extent that they are incapable of playing with others
in any significant way.

A closer look at children's groups has shown this to be
manifestly untrue. Children as young as one year can meaning-
fully interact with one another: usually briefly, sometimes
violently, but already in a manner very different from the
'parallel play' that was supposed to be the only joint activity of which young children are capable. The form which
these interactions take rapidly becomes more and more complex: given the opportunity, children will soon acquire the
great variety of social skills that playing with others
demands. Thus, by the age of four, children are already
capable of taking turns in reciprocal games like hide-and-
seek, of holding a question-and-answer conversation, of
helping or providing comfort, and many other such ingredients of the ability to relate to another person.

The opportunity of regular experience with other children has two sorts of effect. The first takes us back to a
previously mentioned point: the importance of diversifying
social behaviour. The more a child is encouraged to adapt to
a variety of other individuals, the more his repertoire of
social skills will grow. Learning that an aggressive, self-
assertive playmate needs to be handled differently from a
quiet, shy one is the kind of lesson that may be most useful
for survival.

The second effect concerns the socializing influence of
other children. The values and ideals children acquire do
not all come from their parents; from middle childhood on
especially, but also earlier, the peer group can exert a
considerable influence. This may happen in some cultures

more than in others: the Soviet Union, for instance, lays
great stress on techniques of collective upbringing; as a
result, it has been claimed, Russian children develop a
concern for others and a sense of community at quite an
early age. In the Israeli kibbutz system the peer groups
play an even greater role in the child's socialization:
though not surprisingly, for the child is part of the group
from birth, having all along spent the major portion of his
daily life in the communal nursery rather than in the family
home. Yet even in our culture peer influence is marked: on
choice of clothes, musical taste, and television viewing;
but also on racial prejudice, religious beliefs, and
delinquency.

Sensitive and insensitive parents

A child's development does not take place in a vacuum; it
occurs because the people responsible for his care carefully
and sensitively provide him with the kind of environment
that will foster his growth. They do so not only by such
conscious decisions as to what toys to buy for Christmas or
which nursery school to send him to, but also quite unconsciously by the manner in which they relate to him.

Take the language which adults use in talking to a
child. This is in many ways strikingly different from
language addressed to other adults: in fact it constitutes a
quite distinctive style of address which has recently been
given the horrible label 'motherese'. The characteristics of
motherese are not just a restricted vocabulary, but also a
considerably simplified grammar, a great deal of repetition,
a slowing down of speech, a high pitch of voice, and the use
of special intonation patterns. Not only mothers but most
adults, confronted by a young child, will quite unconsciously adopt this style. What is more, the younger the
child the more marked are the features of motherese. If one
films mothers talking to their babies and then plays back
the film in slow motion, one can see clearly what highly
exaggerated gestures and facial expressions mothers use in
this situation, as though they are trying to ensure that the
child attends and continues to attend to them. Their vocal
phrases are greatly slowed down, with long pauses in between, as though they are making allowance for the fact that
the child can absorb only a limited amount of information at
a time. The mothers, that is, appear to be highly sensitive
to the abilities and requirements of the particular child
and are continously adjusting their input to him to ensure
that he can assimilate it. It is believed that the child's
task of learning language is made easier thereby.

Such examples of quite unconscious sensitivity in relating to children are numerous. They occur all the time: in
the feeding situation, when (as we have seen) the mother
makes sure that her stimulation does not clash with the
baby's bursts of sucking; during mutual play, when the
mother carefully adjusts the speed and the manner with
which she offers the baby a toy in the light of his still

uncertain skills in reaching and grasping; or even when the child is merely sitting on the mother's knee and looking around him, and she quite automatically follows the direction of his gaze in order then to share his interest. In relating to their children mothers do not arbitrarily descend on them bolt-out-of-the-blue fashion; they mostly take the child's own interests, abilities and on-going activities as their starting point, in order then to provide him with the 'right' kind of stimulation.

Sensitivity is the capacity to see things from the child's point of view, to be aware of his requirements and to be able to respond to them appropriately. There are indications that it is an essential part of helping a child to develop. Children brought up in institutional environments, in which they are all treated the same and where care is never personalized, become developmentally retarded. Most adults quite naturally display sensitivity in their contacts with children. Unfortunately (as social workers so often find out to their cost), some parents seem to be devoid of this vital part of parenting. Why this is so we still do not know for certain. It does seem, however, that parents who themselves had a depriving childhood and did not experience sensitive care are more likely to show the same attitude to their own children. Case work, counselling, and educational programmes may be measures that need to be employed for the sake of short-term solutions in such families. In the long-term, however, it is essential for us to find out far more about the conditions that foster or hinder parental competence.

Are the early years 'special'?

That children need to be studied for their own sakes requires no justification. If we are to provide better methods of child care and education it is imperative that we find out precisely how children at particular ages and stages function and how their behaviour is affected by the various kinds of social environments that adults create for them. Childhood is therefore of interest because of concern for the child per se.

There is, however, another reason for this interest, namely the fact that children become adults. A widespread belief exists that experience in childhood, and particularly so in the earliest years, has a crucial formative influence on later personality, that the child is father to the man, and that what happens to him early on will in some way mark him for the rest of his life. It follows from such a belief that the earliest years are more important than subsequent years and that special care needs to be taken during this period to protect the child against experiences that might well leave their irreversible imprint on him. The idea that the very young child is particularly vulnerable may seem plausible, but what is the evidence?

The influence of child-rearing practices
It is easy to assert that early experience is important, but

the problem is in fact a complex one. What sort of experience? How early? Important in what way?

More than any other individual, Freud had attempted to provide answers to these questions. Children, he suggested, pass through a series of phases (oral, anal, genital) during which they are specially sensitive to certain kinds of experience. During the oral phase, for example, the baby is mainly concerned with activities such as sucking, chewing, swallowing and biting, and the experiences that matter to him most are those that impinge on these activities. These include the extent to which his need to suck is gratified, whether feeding is timed according to his own requirements or some pre-arranged schedule, whether weaning is gradual and late or sudden and early, and so on. When these experiences are congenial to the child he passes on to the next developmental phase without difficulty; when they are frustrating and stressful, however, he remains 'fixated' at this stage in that, even as an adult, he continues to show characteristics such as dependence and passivity in his personality make-up that distinguish babies at the oral stage.

Freud's theory therefore suggests that there are definite links between particular kinds of infantile experiences on the one hand and adult personality characteristics on the other. If borne out, such a theory would help to explain why people's personalities can differ so dramatically; what is more, it would enable parents to choose among particular infant-care practices should they wish to foster a particular kind of personality in their child.

The theory, however, has not been borne out. A large number of investigations have compared breast-feeding with bottle-feeding, self-demand with rigidly scheduled regimes, early with later weaning, and other aspects of the child's early experience that could be expected to produce lasting after-effects. No such effects have been found. The sum total of these investigations adds up to the conclusion that specific infant-care practices do not produce unvarying traces that may unfailingly be picked up in later life. Whatever their impact at the time, there is no reason to believe that these early experiences mark the child for good or ill for the rest of his life.

And just as well! Were it otherwise we would all be at the mercy of some single event, some specific parental aberration, that we happened to have encountered at some long-distant point in our past. Freud's theory made little allowance for the ameliorating influence of later experience, yet the more we study human development the more apparent it becomes that children, given the opportunity, are able to recuperate from many an early misfortune. Let us consider some other examples that make this point.

Maternal deprivation
The biologist Konrad Lorenz once suggested that the young of certain species, such as chicks and ducklings, are able to form a lasting attachment to the parent animal only

during a quite specific critical period in the earliest
stage of development. They do so by merely being with the
parent for a few crucial hours; if they miss this opportunity and have no contact with the parent during the critical period they are unable ever again to form attachments.

There are many who have generalized Lorenz's findings
to human beings, believing that the child too goes through
a period (albeit a more extended one) during which he must
be with his mother if he is to develop the ability to form
affectionate relationships with other people. Deprived of a
relationship with a mother-figure at that time, such an
ability will never develop. This view was most clearly
formulated by Bowlby, whose 1951 report reviewed the evidence on the after-effects of maternal deprivation. This
evidence, he believed, showed that children in institutions,
long-stay hospitals, and other such impersonal settings,
where they had no opportunity to form a continuous and
emotionally meaningful relationship with one specific mother
figure, showed various pathological characteristics in
subsequent years. The main syndrome of these after-effects
was labelled by Bowlby as 'affectionless character', referring to the inability of the individual to make anything but
highly superficial relationships with other people, be it
with wife or husband, children, friends or colleagues. In
short, the child became like Lorenz's isolated duckling: he
had missed out on a vital experience, namely being mothered,
and as a result was mentally crippled for life.

Bowlby's theory suggests a definite link between early
experience and later pathology. A continous loving relationship with the mother in the early years is necessary if the
child is to become capable of forming meaningful bonds with
other people. We need to learn to love, and can only do so
in the context of a secure relationship with a mothering
person. Bowlby was, moreover, quite specific as regards the
age range within which this had to occur, proposing that the
first two and a half years constitute the critical period in
which the bond with the mother has to be formed. If for any
reason (such as prolonged hospitalization or being in care)
this does not take place at that time, no amount of good
mothering subsequently can remedy the situation. The child
is condemned to become an 'affectionless character'.

There is no doubt about the tremendous influence on the
practice of caring for children that Bowlby's ideas have
had. And no wonder, for so many children are thereby implicated. Take the annually issued statistics on children in
care: in England and Wales more than 100,000 children were
in care in 1978, representing some 7 per 1,000 of the estimated population under the age of 18. In Scotland the proportion was even greater, being approximately 11.5 per 1,000
children. Not all these children are, strictly speaking,
'maternally deprived' (some even continue to live at home,
though under the supervision of the local authority). Nevertheless, many have suffered the kind of disruption in family
life that Bowlby regarded as pathogenic. The same applies to

hospitalized children: here, too, a considerable proportion of the childhood population is affected by the traumatic separation from the mother to which Bowlby drew attention. Anything that can be done to improve the lot of so many children is therefore worth considering, and there is no doubt that in the last two decades a great deal has been done. Children's institutions have become less impersonal with the introduction of family group systems; there is greater emphasis on fostering children with ordinary families; and, most important, far more stress is placed on prevention and keeping children with their own parents. Similarly, the psychological care of children in hospitals has improved greatly during this period: visiting by parents is nowhere near as restricted as it was at one time; mother-baby units make it possible for parents to stay with their children; and again the emphasis on prevention means that rather more thought is now given to the need to admit the child in the first place.

Anyone who has ever seen a young child separated from his mother and admitted, say, to a strange hospital ward, where he is looked after by strangers and may be subjected to unpleasant procedures like injections, knows the extreme distress that one then finds. It is perhaps difficult for an adult to appreciate the depth of a child's panic when he has just lost his mother: a panic that may continue for days and only be succeeded by a depressive-like picture when the child withdraws into himself from a too painful world. Parents also know only too well about the insecurity which the child shows subsequently on return home, even after quite a brief absence, when he dare not let the mother out of sight. There is no doubt about these dramatic short-term effects, and for their sake alone the steps taken to humanize procedure have been well worth while.

Far more problematic, however, is the question of long-term effects: that is, the suggestion that periods of prolonged maternal deprivation in the early years impair the child's capacity to form interpersonal relationships. What evidence we have here suggests that things are not as cut and dried as Bowlby indicated, and to make this point we can do no better than to turn to the report by Barbara Tizard to which we have already referred.

Tizard investigated the development of children who had spent all their early life in institutions. All had originally been admitted to care in the early weeks of life, and all were reared in children's homes which provided them with good physical care but with no opportunity to form any stable attachments to any adult. Indeed, by the age of two these children had been looked after by an average of 24 different people: by four and a half years they had had as many as 50 different mother-figures. In their social behaviour these children were, not surprisingly, totally indiscriminate.

At varying ages, but mainly beyond the end point of Bowlby's critical period of two and a half years, some of these children were adopted. One might have expected them by now to be so marked by their earlier experience that they were incapable of forming ties to their adoptive parents: to show all the irreversible signs, in other words, of the affectionless character. Yet this proved not to be the case. Nearly all these children developed deep attachments to their adoptive parents, and this included even a child placed as late as seven years of age. Compared with a control group of normally reared children the adopted group did show a number of aberrant symptoms, such as poor concentration at school and being over-friendly with strangers. There was no indication, however, that the inevitable outcome of their earlier upbringing was the 'affectionless character'.

Once again we can conclude that a child's experience in the early years does not necessarily and irreversibly mark him for life. There are now a number of reports available that make the same point. In each case the crucial factor concerns the nature of the new environment in which the child is placed. Had the children studied by Tizard continued to live under the same impersonal regime they might well have become affectionless; as it was, the adoptive parents involved were prepared to invest a great deal of time, effort and emotion into the care of the child: perhaps rather more than one might normally find in parents' relationships with their own children. Given such favourable circumstances, the outlook for children would appear to be good: they need not be condemned by previous misfortune; their recuperative powers should not be under-estimated.

Mother-baby contact in the new-born period
The idea that the bond between mother and child must not be broken, particularly during certain critical periods of development, has recently surfaced again, though in a somewhat different form. Again the idea originated with observations on animals. Female goats and sheep, it has been found, must remain close together with their new-born young for a specified period of some hours after birth. If they are separated, the mother will subsequently butt the young away and refuse to have anything to do with it. Mothering in these animals can therefore only emerge if nothing interferes with this early contact.

Two American paediatricians, Marshall Klaus and John Kennell, have generalized this idea to human mothers. According to their observations, the practice adopted by most western maternity hospitals of separating mother and baby except for feeding periods impairs the mother's subsequent ability to look after the child. Mothers, on the other hand, who are allowed to keep their baby during this time show more interest in and a higher commitment to the child who in turn is more likely to thrive. Moreover, Klaus and Kennell believe that this effect is not confined to the period in the maternity hospital: when they followed up two groups of mothers and children, identical except in the amount of contact during the first few days of the child's life, they claim to have found differences months, even years, later. The mothers belonging to the extended contact group were more devoted, more sensitive; the children's development was more advanced both socially and intellectually: supposedly all because of a few hours of being together just after the child's birth.

Again, it is useful to distinguish between short-term and long-term effects. The work of Klaus and Kennell has been most influential in humanizing practices in maternity hospitals in many different countries. In particular, it has drawn attention to the need for extra stimulation of babies in Special Care Units, kept isolated in incubators. More generally, it has made medical and nursing staff consider carefully the way in which the psychological relationship between mother and her new-born baby should be managed. From that point of view, it may well be that greater contact in those early days produces beneficial results for both parties concerned. As to long-term effects, however, the situation is quite different. A number of other investigators have in fact completely failed to replicate Klaus and Kennell's findings: according to them, whatever short-term effects there may be disappear quite soon. The relationship between mother and child is thus not determined forever by that one specific experience occurring at one specific point of time. And just as well, for the sake of all those mothers who are too drugged or too ill in the immediate post-natal period to care at once for their babies, and, for that matter, for the sake of adoptive mothers who may have no contact at all with the child till he is several months or even years old. As we saw from Tizard's study, such mothers may well be 'super-mums', just because they missed out on the child's earlier development.

Birth abnormalities and social class
Some children arrive in the world so severely damaged that no amount of good care will rectify the handicap. They can certainly be helped to make full use of whatever capacities they do have, yet the limits imposed by nature are such that functioning as normal members of society will always be beyond their reach.

In less severely affected cases the course of development is not so easy to predict. Two children coming into the world with the identical kind of pathology may develop along quite different lines. In one case, the child's condition at birth may give rise to a whole sequence of problems that continue and even mount up throughout his life; in the other, the difficulty is surmounted and the child functions normally.

Take such a birth complication as anoxia, the severe shortage of oxygen in the brain. This is a considerable trauma to the child's system at so early a point of its life, and several studies have followed up such children in the full expectation that they will turn out to be impaired in their intellectual and other functions. Yet this has not been the case: some children may indeed show the apparent after-effects of this condition, yet in others they may disappear completely. Or take another birth hazard that has traditionally been associated with later difficulties, namely prematurity. A very low birth weight means that the child arrives in the world in a very precarious condition, and his future development may be affected accordingly. Or so at any rate it was thought, for recently it has become clear that, as with anoxia, the expected unfortunate consequences are by no means inevitable. In many cases, though deficits may be evident in the early stages of development, complete recovery has taken place by the time the child reaches school age. In other, apparently identical cases, the deficit remains.

The answer to this paradox lies in the different kinds of social environment in which the children develop. Where these are favourable the effects of the initial handicap may be minimized and in due course be overcome altogether. Where they are unfavourable the deficits remain and may even be amplified. The outcome, that is, depends not so much on the adverse circumstances of the child's birth as on the way in which his family then copes with the problem. And this, it has been found, is very much related to the social class to which the family belongs.

Social class is in many respects a nebulous concept, particularly in these days of rapidly changing educational and occupational opportunities. Nevertheless, it does help one to pinpoint the extent to which families may be advantaged or disadvantaged, and especially so in relation to the care of their children. Moreover, it represents a continuing influence: poor housing, poor health, poor job prospects, inadequate educational facilities; such a constellation of factors is not easily reversed and thus defines the environment in which a child may spend all his formative years. It is therefore not surprising that social and economic status turn out to have a much stronger influence on the course of development than some specific event at birth.

Thus even organic damage, just as the other aspects of a child's early experience, cannot in and of itself account for the particular course which that child's development takes. The irreversible effects of early experience have no doubt been greatly overrated. To believe in such effects is indeed dangerous for two reasons: first, because of the suggestion that during the first few years children are so vulnerable that they are beyond help if they do encounter some unfortunate experience; second, because it leads one to conclude that the later years of childhood are not as important as the earlier years. All the evidence indicates that neither proposition is true: the effects of early experiences are reversible if need be, and older children may be just as affected by unfortunate circumstances (though possibly different ones) as are younger children.

Conclusions

A child's development always occurs in a social context. Right from the beginning he is a member of a particular society, and the hopes and beliefs and expectations of those around him will have a crucial bearing on his psychological growth. There is nothing inevitable about a child's development: he may come into the world with the capacity for language, but when he begins to speak, in what way and for what purposes depends on the kind of environment in which he is reared. And that environment is a complex affair: psychologists are still, as it were, taking it to pieces in order to see what parts of it are crucial to the child. We may not have got very far yet with this task, but at least we can make one negative statement with some very positive implications: development can never be explained in terms of single causes. Thus we have seen that isolated events, however traumatic at the time, do not on their own bring about lasting change; that early experiences do not preclude later influences; that the one relationship with the mother does not account for everything. For that matter, development is not simply a matter of the environment acting on the child, for the child too can act on his environment. Not surprisingly, when confronted with a specific problem such as child abuse, we find invariably that a combination of circumstances needs to be considered if one is to explain it. Simple-minded explanations of the kind 'juvenile delinquency is due to poverty (or heredity or lack of discipline)' will not do justice to such a complex process as a child's development. And similarly, action taken to prevent or treat which focusses only on single factors is unlikely to succeed.

At a time of rapid material progress the conditions under which children are brought up can change drastically. The invention of the feeding bottle, the great reduction in infant mortality, the introduction of television, the availability of central heating and of washing machines: these are just some of the material changes which in turn have changed the task of those responsible for children's upbringing. Unfortunately, we do not usually become aware of the psychological implications until well after the new technological developments have been instituted: high rise blocks of flats are built, and we discover only subsequently what living on the twentieth floor may mean to families with young children; television can be beamed into every home in the country, and only now are questions being asked about the possible harmful effects of children viewing certain types of programme. Ideally, psychological implications ought to be considered from the beginning; let us for the present at least recognize that they exist and need to be monitored. The same applies to social changes: the increasing number of single-parent families, the rising incidence of divorce and remarriage, the various experiments in communal living that have been instituted, the changing roles of the sexes: there are many features of today's society that can have profound effects on children's development. All may bring problems of adjustment which various professional workers are then asked to solve. This cannot simply be done by guesswork; fortunately child psychology is increasingly able to offer some help and guidance on the basis of objective investigations into the nature and course of development.

Questions

1. 'Child rearing practices have often been determined more by myths than scientific fact.' Discuss.

2. Is it true that children should, wherever possible, be brought up by their biological mothers?

3. It has been suggested that the personality of the 'mature' adult is determined in the first five years or so of his life. Subsequent experiences are seen as less important. Is this true?

4. Discuss the suggestion that children have as much effect on their parents' behaviour as the latter have on them. What are the clinical implications of this area of research?

5. Imagine that you have to lecture about social development in early childhood to a group of nurses and health visitors. What points would you wish to emphasize, bearing in mind that your audience will often be required to give practical advice about child rearing to parents?

6. Discuss the suggestion that children who lose their mothers are doomed to become abnormal adults, and consider in particular the clinical implications of this issue.

7. Discuss the effects of the following in young children, and mention the clinical implications in each case: (a) long-term hospitalization; (b) short-term admission to hospital; (c) adoption; (d) one-parent families.

8. Make a list of factors which could accelerate or retard the development of young children. Are the effects of damaging environments or experiences inevitable and irremediable?

9. What advice, in general terms, would you consider giving in the following: (a) a divorced mother worried about the effects of the absence of a father on her five-year-old child; (b) a 25-year-old father bringing up a three-year-old child after the death of his wife; (c) staff on a paediatric unit who are keen to reduce the ill-effects of admission on young children; (d) a deaf mother anxious about the effects of her impairment on the development of her baby?

Annotated reading

Booth, T. (1975) Growing up in Society. London: Methuen (Essential Psychology Series).

A general account of the influences that determine the way in which people grow up together. It takes into account not only the contribution of psychology but of such other social sciences as sociology, anthropology and social history. Its main value lies in the way child development is seen as occurring within the social context of each particular culture.

Bowlby, J. (1965) Child Care and the Growth of Love. Harmondsworth: Penguin.
A more widely available version of Bowlby's classic report, first published in 1951, concerning the link between maternal deprivation and mental pathology. It should be read in conjunction with Rutter's book (see below).

Clarke, A.M. and Clarke, A.D.B. (1976) Early Experience: Myth and evidence. London: Open Books.
A collection of contributions by different authors, all concerned with the question whether early experience exerts a disproportionate influence on later development. A wide range of research studies is reviewed, and the consensus is against seeing the early years as in some sense more important than later stages of development.

Dunn, J. (1977) Distress and Comfort. London: Fontana/Open Books.
Discusses some of the issues that concern parents during the early stages of the child's life, with particular reference to the causes and alleviation of distress, but places these issues in the wider context of the parent-child relationship and its cultural significance.

Kempe, R.S. and Kempe, H. (1978) Child Abuse. London: Fontana/Open Books.
An account by the foremost experts on child abuse of the state of knowledge regarding all aspects of this vexed area: causation, treatment and prevention.

Lewin, R. (1975) Child Alive. London: Temple-Smith.
Various researchers summarize in brief and popularized form what we have learned about child development in recent years. Most contributions deal with young children, and the book as a whole emphasizes how psychologically sophisticated even babies already are.

Rutter, M. (1972) Maternal Deprivation Reassessed. Harmondsworth: Penguin.
A systematic review of the evidence on this controversial topic that has accumulated since Bowlby highlighted its importance. Discusses the various studies that have been carried out on the effects, both short- and long-term, of early deprivation of maternal care.

Schaffer, H.R. (1971) The Growth of Sociability.
Harmondsworth: Penguin.
  A description of work on the earliest stages of social
  development. It shows how sociability in the early years
  has been studied, and reviews what we have learned about
  the way in which a child's first social relationships
  are formed.

Schaffer, H.R. (1977) Mothering. London: Fontana/Open
Books.
  An account of what is involved in being a parent. Brings
  together the evidence from recent studies of the mother-
  child relationship, and examines different conceptions
  of the parent's task. Gives special emphasis to the
  theme of mutuality in the relationship.

Tizard, B. (1977) Adoption: A second chance. London: Open
Books.
  An account of an important research study on children
  in residential care who were subsequently adopted.
  Raises some crucial issues regarding the effects of
  early experience and the public care of young children.

6

Clinical Child Psychology

David Griffiths

Childhood is free of serious and persistent psychological
problems for the majority of developing children. Nevertheless, a substantial minority does require specialized
psychological help: in some cases, the help is needed on a
long-term basis (as in mental handicap), whilst in others
(e.g. the problem of bedwetting) short-term intervention is
sufficient. This discussion is concerned with some of the
problems which affect children and, more specifically, with
aspects of the detection, assessment and management of
psychological and behavioural problems.

How are psychological and behavioural problems in
children referred for specialist help? Referral comes from
a potentially large number of sources. In many instances,
parents become concerned with some aspect of their child's
behaviour and seek medical advice from their general practitioner or paediatrician. Referral to specialist resources
might also be made from schools, or courts dealing with
legal offences involving children, when it is thought that
the problems presented by children or young offenders
indicate a degree of disturbance which requires help.

Specialist help is available at a number of potential
places and normally involves the activity of a multi-
disciplinary team of individuals rather than treatment by
one professional. Teams of paediatricians, child psychiatrists, social workers and clinical psychologists might be
based at Health Services or local authority child guidance
clinics, or possibly at departments of child health linked
with local hospitals. Though the initial assessment often
involves co-ordinated team effort (e.g. the assessment of
physical causes, psychological development and the family
situation), the programme of management or treatment will
often require the skills of individual professionals. In
addition to doctors, social workers and psychologists, this
help might be provided by specialist teachers, speech
therapists or physiotherapists.

Psychological problems affecting children

What kind of psychological and behavioural problems affect
children? There is a wide range of potential difficulties
and it is beyond the scope of this discussion to review all
of the problems which can affect infants, school-age

children and adolescents. The following, however, are some specific examples of problems which can appear during the developing years.

Developmental retardation

Development is normally orderly and progressive. This means that it is possible to define the behaviour of the normal two, eight or ten year old in terms of what we know to be 'normal' behaviour at these ages. For example, norms are available for motor development, aspects of social competence such as eating and dressing skills, and also communication and language abilities. Some examples of developmental norms are provided in chapter 4. In some cases, however, assessment indicates that the child is 'behind'. In other words, he is not developing as expected. The degree of retardation might be minimal or severe; it might affect most aspects of behaviour as in severe mental handicap. Alternatively, some aspects of behaviour might be affected whilst others would be quite normal (as in enuresis).

Educational problems

These might involve the difficulties of the child whose attainments at school are below the 'average' for his age group. For example, the child whose reading or arithmetic competence is well below that of his peers. As we shall see, the detailed assessment of such a child might indicate that though his behaviour is abnormal when compared with other children of the same age, it might not be inappropriate when his specific abilities and situation are considered. For example, the child's reading attainment might be retarded by two years at the age of seven years; but if assessment indicates that he is mentally handicapped, then his reading attainment might be considered to be satisfactory for his intellectual growth.

Emotional problems

Anxieties and fears are quite normal in childhood (cf. chapter 14) and tend to be transient and to disappear as the child grows and develops the capacity to cope adequately with his environment. One instance of this is that fear of animals and strangers is common in infants, but considerably less so in groups of schoolchildren. Some children, however, develop fears which are so intense or handicapping as to require special attention. For example, the infant whose fear of dogs is so intense that he is reluctant to leave his mother's side and panics even at the sight of dogs on television. Other children become anxious about some aspect of their schooling (e.g. failure at specific school subjects or bullying from other children) and develop a 'school phobia' so that they refuse to go to school. If the refusal to attend school continues over a prolonged period of time, this might cause other difficulties which add to the seriousness of the problem. School refusals might miss important lessons in a particular subject so that integration into further schooling becomes progressively more difficult.

Behaviour or 'conduct' problems

Once again, varying degrees of aggressiveness, destructiveness and generally antisocial behaviour are not uncommon in children. Temper tantrums, often associated with frustration, are common in infancy and their frequency reaches a peak in two year olds. Older children also frequently lose their tempers, as indeed do adults! One American survey (Lapouse and Monk, 1959) showed that a sample of six to twelve year olds manifested temper loss quite often; in fact, 48 per cent of them had a temper loss at least twice per week. Whilst these problems might require little more than careful handling by parents, other instances of aggressive behaviour are clearly more serious. Delinquency involves a wide range of problems which extend from theft and truancy to physical assault and sexual misdemeanours. Such behaviours require careful assessment and management and there are clear indications that their aetiology often resides in the environment rather than any psychological pathology which can be identified 'within' the offender. For example, adolescent groups often engage in various activities which offend against society's mores. Within such groups, however, the individual might be subjected to pressures such as social ostracism and punishment which have the effect of making him comply with the group norm. Whilst society might not wish to tolerate various aspects of delinquency, such behaviours might nevertheless be normal and acceptable within the group.

Habit training

Urination and defecation are examples of involuntary and necessary responses which have to be brought under voluntary control. The process of learning involved is, for various reasons, not successfully accomplished by some individuals. One consequence of failure is enuresis and another is encopresis (soiling). Once again, the abnormality of bed-wetting and soiling has to be evaluated against the general background of the child's development. Enuresis is quite common before the age of three but subject to increasing concern after this age. Its frequency is another important variable, since infrequent wetting of the child's bed at night might not be a problem which requires special attention. One survey, for example, indicated that 17 per cent of a six- to twelve-year-old group had wet their beds in the previous year; 8 per cent had wet their beds at least once a month.

When is a child's behaviour abnormal?

Deciding whether a child's behaviour is abnormal and requires specialized attention is not necessarily as easy as might be assumed. Indeed, the abnormal often merges into the normal. Herbert (1974), for example, comments that

'Emotional problems, signs of psychological abnormality are, by and large, exaggerations, deficits, or handicapping combinations of behaviour patterns common to all children'. What then are the criteria which are used to identify abnormal behaviour and to decide when specialized treatment procedures are required?

The following are the main factors which must be considered when deciding whether or not the behaviour of a child requires specialized professional attention.

Age and the stage of the child's development

Whether or not many behaviours are considered abnormal will depend on the child's age. Behaviours which are common and normal at some ages are abnormal at others. For example, temper tantrums are common in pre-school children and peak during the second year; many mothers will have learnt about the 'Terrible two's' from experience! Enuresis, as we have seen, is common during the second and third year but abnormal in an eight or ten year old. Fears of animals and the unknown are normal in pre-school children but less normal in secondary-school children whose fears are now more concerned with social behaviour and physical appearance. Herbert's (1974) review stresses the transitoriness of many developmental problems, and longitudinal surveys of problems in children demonstrate clearly that about two-thirds of children seen in child guidance clinics improve spontaneously. Furthermore, change is more closely related to environmental factors (such as family stress) than to treatment.

Frequency

Many behaviours are normal if they occur infrequently but abnormal if they are common features of the child's behaviour. Most children have one or two fears and these tend to disappear spontaneously and without specialized help. The presence of a large number of fears might, however, indicate an abnormal degree of fearfulness or timidity. Similarly, temper tantrums or outbursts were reported to occur once a month or more in the six- to twelve-year-old sample studied by Lapouse and Monk (1959). More frequent temper outbursts might indicate the presence of an abnormality, though the clinician might exercise his discretion in making a judgement since 11 per cent of the survey group continued to have tantrums at least once a day.

Intensity

We have already seen that fears are quite normal but, in some children, the intensity of their discomfort is such that treatment is necessary. For example, approximately one in three children show some reluctance in going to school. School phobics, however, are anxious to the point where they panic if attempts are made to take them to school. Excessive fear will be obvious from the child's physiological state (heart rate, muscular tension, etc.), his subjective feelings of discomfort and the attempts to avoid or escape from

school. In relation to conduct disorders, some destructiveness is normal in children but it might involve harm to
objects and other individuals to an extent that requires
special help.

Duration

Many behaviours are considered abnormal if they endure and
the need for investigation and treatment is sometimes
indicated by the persistence of behaviours such as aggression and tantrums, fears and phobias, depressive reactions
and bedwetting or soiling. The persistence of many problem
behaviours is also potentially serious since it can lead to
secondary complications. For example, the child who refuses
to attend school will fall further behind in scholastic
attainment and will miss opportunities to acquire both
educational and social skills.

The child's environment

This can be important in a number of ways. For example, many
children would appear to receive specialized help not because their behaviour is abnormal but because of the degree
of anxiety and concern expressed by the parents. For this
reason, a number of studies have failed to distinguish between the behaviour of clinic attenders and the behaviour of
non-attenders. The differences, in other words, reside in
the behaviour of the parents rather than the children. In
fact, in some cases the child's behaviour might appear to be
abnormal but, on closer scrutiny, be seen to be a normal
response to an abnormal situation. The abnormality resides
in the environment rather than in the child. Abnormal
degrees of aggression in children might, for example, be the
consequences of the child's modelling or imitating parental
behaviour. Alternatively, the child's aggression might be a
consequence of the frustration of his needs within a restrictive and rigid family code of behaviour. There are, in
fact, relationships between parents' behaviour and patterns
of delinquency (Hewitt and Jenkins, 1946). For example,
misdemeanours such as theft and truancy which are committed
by groups of adolescents have been found to be related to
parental attitudes of indifference. In such circumstances,
the youngster relates to his peer group rather than his
parents and follows the norms of the group. Within the
group, activities such as theft and truancy might be normal;
this is, of course, another example of the causal contribution of the environment rather than pathology 'within' the
individual.

   This brief discussion indicates that many factors need
to be considered when the abnormality of the child's behaviour is being assessed. It is clearly not sufficient to
limit observations to the child's behaviour in isolation.
Herbert (1974) suggests that two questions will always need
to be asked. First, 'Is the child's behaviour appropriate to
his age, intelligence and social situation?' Second, 'What
are the consequences - favourable or unfavourable - of the
child's pattern of traits and ways of behaving?'

If the answer to these questions confirms that action needs to be taken, what form should this take? The next section considers the three main steps: assessment, formulation, and treatment or management.

Assessment

When a child has been referred for specialized help, assessment is naturally the first step which needs to be taken. Assessment will attempt to specify those aspects of behaviour which are problematic; an equally important secondary aim will be to identify those factors which cause and maintain these behaviours. An identification of the child's problem and its causes will naturally be a basis for management and treatment. The assessment of children normally involves three sets of observations.

Direct observations of the child's behaviour

The child's behaviour is observed in the clinic setting and also increasingly at home and school if opportunities for this are available. Direct observation will indicate whether there are any abnormalities in, for example, the child's motor, social or emotional behaviour. Motor behaviour might be abnormal in terms of specific or general deficiencies (e.g. inability to walk or grasp objects) or 'excess' responses (such as tics or general hyperactivity). Observation of social behaviour might suggest an abnormal degree of shyness or withdrawal, or alternatively dominance or aggression towards either children or adults. Examples of emotional abnormalities might be excessive fears or a general absence of any emotional response (associated perhaps with withdrawal or retardation).

Play activities can be an important source of information, especially in view of the child's natural tendency to play and also the absence or inadequacy of communication skills so that the child cannot explain or describe his problem. In a clinic setting, play with dolls might be encouraged in order to assess the perceptions of the child; for example, his responses to mother and father figures might be very apparent in his responses to the appropriate doll figures. The problems of direct observation have already been discussed in chapter 1; observations of the child's behaviour in the clinic setting also have a number of shortcomings. Children's behaviour can be very sensitive to environmental factors. Since the clinic setting will be strange, the child's behaviour might be atypical. For example, a normally aggressive or destructive child might behave in a docile manner when faced with the novelty of a clinic. Variation and specificity (rather than consistency) in behaviour is, in fact, quite normal in children and adults, and traits such as honesty vary considerably between settings. This means that the individual child could be honest in some situations but quite dishonest in others. The practical implication of these findings is that the child's behaviour needs to be observed in a variety of representative settings.

Observations in different settings will often indicate that, though behaviour varies, it does so consistently. For example, the American psychologist Sears observed children's aggression in two situations. One involved aggression in doll play; the other involved observations of aggression in the child's school playground. Aggression in these two settings was generally unrelated, so that observation in one setting could not be used to predict behaviour in the other. There was, however, more consistency when the mother's response to aggression was considered. If aggressive acts were punished severely, the child's aggression in doll play and school was less likely to be consistent; if aggression was tolerated without punishment, the level of aggression was more consistent. In order to make a more accurate prediction in these circumstances, however, the clinician would clearly have needed additional information about both the behaviour of the child and his parents.

Standardized or test assessment
Here the child is presented with a structured situation, often an assortment of problems to solve, and his response is recorded and assessed. For example, he is asked to define a word, to build a tower of bricks or to draw a picture of a man. His responses are then compared with normative data. In many intellectual tests, comparison of the child's score with the distribution of scores for his own (or other) age groups will then allow inferences about his level of intelligence. Developmental testing involves observations of the child's competence at a wide range of tasks and uses this information to determine the level of the child's development both generally and in relation to specific areas such as motor performance and communicative skills.

The developmental testing of babies and young infants is commonly required in paediatric settings and is based on several principles. One principle is that behaviour and psychological skills change with age and the pattern of attainments is related to age in such a way that the individual child's performance allows his level of development to be identified. For example, a six year old might be retarded to the extent that his attainments are at the three-year level. He might then be said to have a developmental age of three, which is three years below his chronological age.

The characteristic behaviours at specific age levels have been identified by observation and investigation which has produced sets of norms. Developmental tests compare the behaviour of the child with the norms for varying age groups. As we have seen, the results allow the clinician to relate the child's developmental age to his actual age and to decide on the degree of retardation or precocity. Development, however, is not necessarily consistent in different areas of functioning. The child can be advanced or retarded in some respects but not others: for example, motor, speech, social or emotional behaviours. It is therefore very helpful to use a battery which assesses the various areas of development and establishes whether the individual child's development is consistent or better in some respects than others. Specific disabilities (e.g. motor or speech impairment) clearly need to be detected, since they can have serious effects on many other aspects of the child's growth.

Once again, standardized assessments can involve a number of difficulties. One problem is that testing requires the co-operation of the child, sometimes over prolonged periods. Test results can therefore be affected by the child's co-operation and motivation and the assessment of young children can be unreliable because of the difficulty of sustaining their co-operation. Another problem is that children's rates of development vary quite considerably; some children have spurts of development, others develop at a constant rate. Individual differences are determined by such factors as the amount and quality of stimulation in the child's environment, but endogenous factors (e.g. sensory deficiencies) can also have important effects. The practical implication of these observations of inconsistencies in development is that results can become unreliable if change occurs. Periodic re-assessment is therefore necessary to ensure that assessments are up to date and accurate.

The topic of assessment is discussed more generally in chapter 11.

Reports and interview information from parents, teachers and others who know the child

This is probably the most common source of information about the child and it can also be the most unreliable. For example, a small number of studies have investigated the accuracy of self-report and other information provided by parents and have found this information to be a poor guide to overt behaviour. Parents have, for example, been shown to be inaccurate in their reports of their responses to children's misdemeanours. Self-report is not, therefore, an accurate guide to behaviour. As we have seen, however, behaviour does tend to be inconsistent so that it might be quite unreasonable to require individuals to report on their response to children's naughtiness. In real life, there is likely to be variation in their response, depending on such factors as the nature and severity of the misdemeanour and the presence of other people. For example, a mother is less likely to slap her child if the misdemeanour is slight and other people are present.

Observers can also disagree in their assessments. This was demonstrated dramatically in a survey of maladjustment conducted on 10- and 11-year-old children in the Isle of Wight (Rutter, Tizard and Whitmore, 1970). Both parents and teachers completed questionnaires on a group of children and the results were compared with specialized individual assessment. On the questionnaire, 284 children were above a cut-off point which had previously been shown to indicate disturbance requiring specialized help. Approximately 6 per cent of the group was identified by this score as in need of such help. However, further inspection revealed that there was little overlap between the children identified as being maladjusted by the parents and the teachers. Only 19, out of a total of 284, were identified by parents and teachers. Why were there such discrepancies? One important factor would appear to be specificity of behaviour. In other words, problem behaviours were apparent in school or at home but not in both settings. A high proportion of children were, in fact, diagnosed as manifesting specific rather than general problems. The practical implication is, once again, that (in both clinical and survey assessments) assessment must involve information from the most important settings for each individual child.

Observations limited to clinic or home or school will often not be sufficient, and important factors might be missed.

Formulation and aetiology

When assessment has been completed, the next stage involves a formulation of the child's difficulties. This includes a statement of the areas of behaviour which are abnormal. For example, the difficulties might affect intellect (e.g. mental handicap or specific verbal deficits), emotional responses (e.g. a phobia), social behaviour (such as withdrawal or aggression) or educational attainment (e.g. specific or general backwardness in school work). In addition to the identification of problem areas, management and treatment will often be affected by suggestions about those factors which have caused or are maintaining the problem behaviours; in other words, some indication of aetiological factors.

A comprehensive review of the aetiology of disordered behaviour in children is not attempted but it would be useful to consider some examples. The following are three broad categories of potentially causal agents which could be involved in producing and maintaining abnormal behaviours.

Constitutional and temperamental variables
Many aspects of behaviour, both normal and abnormal, appear to be innately or biologically determined (cf. chapter 3). Observation of the behaviour of neonates suggests, for example, that individual differences in the level of activity, rhythmicity, response to stressors and sleep patterns are apparent soon after birth, when the environment has not really had enough opportunity to exert significant effects (Thomas, Birch et al, 1963). Eysenck and his colleagues have demonstrated that abnormal behaviours such as anxiety and antisocial behaviours are related to the personality dimensions of extraversion-introversion and neuroticism. For example, neurotic introverts are more likely to develop dysthymic disorders (anxiety problems, fears, moodiness, etc.) whereas neurotic extraverts are more likely to present with conduct problems such as truancy and stealing (Eysenck

and Rachman, 1965). Evidence from carefully conducted twin studies (Shields, 1962) suggests that both neuroticism and extraversion are determined to a significant extent by genetic mechanisms. Eysenck has also attempted to identify the mechanisms whereby genetic factors determine behaviour. He suggests, for example, that neuroticism is determined in part by the responsiveness of the individual's autonomic nervous system. The neurotic is assumed to have a 'weak' or labile sympathetic system so that he over-responds to a wide range of stressors.

Pre- and peri-natal factors

Disorders and problems linked with pregnancy and birth are associated with a higher incidence of behavioural and psychological problems, though the exact nature of the links (and, more specifically, the manner in which psychological abnormality is produced by organic damage) is not well understood. Correlations between organic damage and psychological abnormality do not necessarily imply a cause-effect relationship. Nevertheless, it seems very likely that organic damage is an important determinant of a wide range of behavioural abnormalities. For example, anoxia at birth is associated with a higher incidence of perceptual motor deficits, over-excitability and retarded development during the first two years. Babies who are born precipitately, after a short labour, or after difficult pregnancies, are more likely to be irritable, hyperactive and difficult. Premature babies have a substantially higher risk of developing a range of behavioural abnormalities which include excessive distractability, hyperactivity, hyper-irritability, impaired intelligence and educational attainment (Herbert, 1974). It must be stressed, however, that pre- and peri-natal problems do not necessarily lead to psychological problems and deficits. Many individuals who are born prematurely, or after difficult births, are completely normal. Once again, individual differences are apparent and co-exist with the higher probability of abnormalities. Even when organically determined deficits are present, as in the case of the effects of anoxia, there are wide differences between individuals in the subsequent development of these problems, and their effects on other behaviours. Many deficits can be remedied and reduced by the effects of training and a stimulating environment.

Experience and the environment

The organism develops within its environment and, whatever its innate potential, development is clearly influenced by this environment. For example, retarded infants who are reared in a stimulating environment are subsequently more capable and successful than equally handicapped individuals who are reared in poorer surroundings (Skeels, 1966). Mentally handicapped individuals admitted to hospitals from poorer and neglected homes subsequently manifest more significant intellectual improvements than those who come from better homes. This finding probably reflects the adverse and retarding effects exerted by poor home environments (Gunzburg, 1968). It is now more generally agreed, however, that deprivations early in life do not necessarily have permanent adverse effects. For example, the loss of a mother does not have serious consequences as long as a satisfactory substitute environment is available to the child (Rutter, 1975). In general, research evidence suggests that the consequences of early experience (such as weaning and toilet training) are not as irrevocable and total as Freud suggested (cf. chapters 4 and 5). Human behaviour continues to be flexible and to change in response to experience and environmental factors which are present both in childhood and the more mature years (Clarke and Clarke, 1972).

Two further distinctions need to be made in relation to the aetiology of childhood problems. The first relates to the difference between an original 'cause' and a subsequent 'maintaining' agent. The two can be quite different. A problem can be produced by one factor but maintained by another. For example, mental handicap can be caused by brain or nervous system damage but its effects (such as the number and severity of functional handicaps) are clearly influenced by the quality of the environment and opportunities for training. The skills of the handicapped might be influenced by organic deficits, but their number and adequacy are invariably a reflection of environment. A further example involves the aetiology of phobic problems. A child's fear of dogs might be caused both by an innate response to large, unpredictable, moving objects and a traumatic event such as a bite by a dog; the fear of dogs might be maintained, however, by a repeated avoidance of dogs and escape from situations where dogs are present. The distinction between cause and maintenance has many practical implications. It is often impossible to rectify an original cause (e.g. organic damage or traumatic experience) but it is often quite possible to modify a condition by the management of those factors which are maintaining it (by training, or the careful control of avoidance and escape).

The second distinction which needs to be made is between primary and secondary causes. Causation often involves a sequence of events which are related; abnormalities in specific aspects of behaviour can produce problems in other areas. For example, sensory deficiencies (such as deafness or poor vision) can retard the development of intellectual or communication skills (such as vocabulary level or language); intellectual or communication deficits can, in turn, impair the child's ability to relate to others or benefit from school experiences. When the child is being assessed, it will often be important to distinguish the relative importance of various causal factors so that treatment and management procedures are developed to ensure that the most important causal entities are reduced or, failing this, fully recognized.

Treatment and management   Treatment and management are the final stages of what should ideally be a closely integrated sequence of activities whose aim is to help the child and his family. Although the selection of treatment is influenced by the assessment and formulation of the problem, it is also affected by a number of other factors. The local availability of resources (e.g. residential treatment facilities or the presence of specialists such as speech therapists) is obviously one factor. Under ideal circumstances, the evidence about the efficacy of treatment programmes should be another. In practice, however, such evidence is often not available. Alternatively, the selection of treatment is determined more by therapists' bias rather than objective evidence. Indeed, the beliefs and theoretical biasses of clinicians are important determinants of the treatment which is provided. For example, divergent views exist as to the nature and cause of enuresis or bedwetting. The psychodynamic school views enuresis as the superficial symptom of a more widespread disturbance; unconscious mechanisms and conflicts are seen to be the most important problems. The consequence is that treatment is concerned with underlying conflicts rather than the enuresis. Psychodynamic therapists have argued that superficial treatment of the enuresis will neglect the most important problem; they have therefore predicted that such treatments will not be effective or, alternatively, will produce substitute problems. Behavioural psychologists, on the other hand, view enuresis as a failure to acquire the habits of continence; in other words, as a learning problem. Their treatment has been directly concerned with the enuresis and with attempts to facilitate the child's acquisition of behaviours compatible with night-time continence. In due course, we consider the relative value of these approaches when we discuss enuresis in more detail.

A detailed review of psychological treatments used with children is not undertaken at this point. The following are some examples of treatment provisions available to help children.

Educational and training techniques

These involve such facilities as speech therapy to reduce communication problems and remedial teaching to improve educational attainment. Though such facilities might be related to specific behavioural or skills deficiencies, their effects can be widespread since many specific deficiencies have serious and general effects. For example, a speech problem can have serious effects on the child's social skills and educational progress. In relation to the child with more widespread problems - such as the mentally handicapped child - programmes are needed both to identify the range of problems and as a basis for comprehensive and goal-directed training.

Psychotherapy

It is very difficult to discuss psychotherapy briefly since

the term refers to a large number of approaches which differ in their theoretical assumptions and practical aspects of the treatment techniques. The Freudian approach is the best known but there are many others (cf. chapter 13). Most of these approaches tend to share the general assumption, however, that the presenting problem should be viewed as a superficial symptom of a more basic pathology. The general pathology is often assumed to involve conflicts at the unconscious level and these conflicts often involve aspects of the child's relationship with significant individuals, such as the parents.

Psychotherapy tends to use a range of techniques with children. Since the communicative skills of many children are undeveloped, language cannot be used to the same extent as it might be with adults. Play activities are used to take advantage of the child's natural propensity to engage in play. Doll play, for example, is assumed to provide useful information about the child's fantasies, perceptions and anxieties in relation to his environment. Play activities are also used to modify the child's problems. For example, the child might be encouraged to express his aggression through lively activity involving dolls or materials such as sand or paint. Through play, the child might also be encouraged to develop alternative perceptions of his world, or to overcome anxieties and fears. Though psychotherapy is still a common component of treatment programmes, the issue of its effectiveness continues to be a matter of debate (Rachman, 1973).

Behaviour therapy
As with the psychotherapies, behaviour therapy refers to a number of different techniques and approaches. For example, conditioning techniques such as the 'bell and pad' apparatus are used to treat enuresis. This is placed in the child's bed and the alarm is activited by the urine expelled by the child. Operant behaviour modification methods are quite different and involve the control of the child's behaviour by the careful and contingent application and withdrawal of reward. Habits and skills such as dressing, speaking and eating might be taught to the mentally handicapped by the careful application of rewards. Undesirable behaviours (such as destructiveness and self-mutilation) might be reduced by the withdrawal of such reinforcements as adult attention or, in extreme cases, the use of punishments. Other behaviour therapy techniques involve the provision of models which the child can imitate; for example, fears and phobias in children can be reduced by allowing the child to observe other children who act in a fearless manner in the presence of the fear stimulus. Relaxation techniques can be used to treat fears in older children but, in younger children, a gradual approach to the object of the fear (e.g. dogs) can be combined with eating or play activities; in other words, activities which are likely to inhibit the development of anxiety.

Behaviour therapy techniques have two general aims. One is to facilitate the development of adaptive behaviours (e.g. self-help, communication and social skills); the other is to reduce and eliminate undesirable and maladaptive behaviours (such as aggressive and destructive responses). Though the techniques are diverse, their common element is that they are derived from basic research in psychology on the factors which produce and maintain behaviour. Their original source, in fact, has been the experimental laboratory rather than the clinic. Though the behavioural techniques have been developed more recently than psychotherapy, the experimental tradition which has distinguished their development has also produced a substantial body of objective evaluation. Many questions about the effectiveness of these techniques are unanswered, but the availability of empirical evidence on many treatments has allowed other questions to be resolved. For example, there is little or no evidence to support the predictions made by psychotherapists about the adverse consequences of direct symptomatic treatments (Rachman, 1973). Behaviour therapy is discussed in more detail by Beech in chapter 12.

In relation to all treatment approaches, it is important to remember that treatment and management normally involves the child and his environment. Parents have been increasingly involved, for example, and their involvement has frequently included a therapeutic role. One instance of this is the training of the mentally handicapped, where professional attention is now directed as much to the family as to the child. In practice, the family is encouraged to act as both therapist and trainer. This gives parents and others an important role and purpose, reduces feelings of helplessness in the face of disability and is an efficient application of specialist effort since parents and other individuals are important parts of the child's natural environment. Another example of the 'environmentalist' approach is seen in family therapy. Much of family therapy is based on a 'systems' approach; it views the problem as residing in the 'system' of family interaction rather than in any pathology 'within' the child. Therapy is consequently directed not at the child in isolation but at the whole family. Such a focus, which emphasizes those aspects of the environment which cause or maintain problem behaviour, might be expected both to resolve current problems and to prevent the development of future difficulties. A considerable amount of careful evaluative research is required, however, to establish whether theoretical expectations are confirmed by practical results (Rutter, 1975).

Specific conditions

We have now completed our general discussion of the steps involved in the provision of help for problem behaviours in childhood: assessment, formulation and treatment. In order to complete our discussion, the remaining part is concerned with a more detailed consideration of specific types of disorder and their treatment. The problems which we consider now are (i) enuresis or bedwetting, (ii) hyper-activity, and (iii) anxieties, fears and phobias.

Enuresis

Enuresis, more commonly known simply as bedwetting, involves the persistent tendency to empty the bladder during sleep. Urination at night is sometimes associated with waking, but this is often not so and the enuretic wakes at the normal time to find that the bed is wet, sometimes drenched, with urine.

The identification of enuresis as a problem requiring specialist help is dependent on age since the child's mus-culature must develop to the point where it is sufficiently strong and under a degree of voluntary control. When matur-ation allows this, the child is potentially able to learn to inhibit the initially involuntary processes involving the elimination of urine. For these reasons, assessment and treatment are not seriously considered until three or four years of age. At the age of $2\frac{1}{2}$, approximately 60 per cent of children are dry at night; this subsequently rises to 97 per cent by the age of 12, so that approximately 3 per cent of the population is enuretic.

It is hardly surprising that enuresis is associated with a number of other problems. Clinical experience and surveys indicate a raised incidence of difficulties such as a lack of confidence, anxiety and tension and also guilt. In addition, there are often restrictions on the child's social functioning since he cannot sleep away from home without the risk of wetting the bed. The families of enuretics are also under some stress, partly because of the extra work (e.g. washing bedclothes) and also the concern as to the nature and effects of the problem in the growing child. Whilst some clinicians believe that enuresis is a symptom of a more pervasive disturbance of personality, it seems equally plausible to suggest that low confidence and anxiety are consequences of the difficulties associated with enuresis. This possibility is further supported by the observation that confidence and self-evaluation often improve after successful treatment. Enuresis is more common in boys than girls. Though it is associated with encopresis (soiling) in approximately 10 per cent of cases, the large majority of enuretics have no apparent problem in acquiring bowel control.

Enuresis is not, in fact, a unitary and consistent entity. There are at least two categories which differ from each other in important respects. In 'primary' enuresis, the individual never achieves continence. The failure to acquire bladder control appears to have an organic basis in approxi-mately 10 per cent of cases, so that a routine medical assessment is necessary. The role of organic factors in predisposing the other 90 per cent of enuretics to the problem requires further investigation, but there is evi-dence to suggest that physical factors could be involved.

Enuretics have been shown to have a smaller maximum bladder capacity than control subjects and there is also an indication that they have more spontaneous bladder contractions (Taylor and Turner, 1975). The significance of these findings obviously needs further investigation. An alternative explanation is that failure to achieve continence can be viewed as a failure of learning. Toilet training obviously involves learning; it is suggested that, for various reasons, some children fail to achieve this learning. Parents might, for example, train inappropriately or with a degree of enthusiasm which antagonizes or frightens the child. The child might, in consequence, be too highly aroused for efficient learning; failure to respond might produce punishments which further increase the child's arousal.

'Secondary' enuresis refers to the child who has achieved continence but lost it at a later age. In other words, the child relapses after a period of being dry at night. In some cases of secondary enuresis, the problem appears to be a response to stress. The most common precipitants of this development are the birth of a sibling or a change of school. Further investigation of secondary enuresis is obviously desirable but it seems possible that in at least some of these cases the loss of continence is part of a stress syndrome. It is well known, of course, that learnt behaviours can be disrupted by a range of life stresses.

How is enuresis modified? A number of techniques have been used with varying degrees of success.

* REDUCING FLUID INTAKE: most parents have tried to treat their child's enuresis by reducing fluid intake in the evening and some doctors continue to recommend this. Clinical experience suggests very clearly, however, that the technique is not effective. Many enuretics continue to wet the bed even when the volume of urine in the bladder is very small.

* WAKING DURING THE NIGHT: parents sometimes try to modify enuresis by waking their child to go to the toilet at regular intervals. The approach is generally unsuccessful. Enuretics either do not respond or relapse when they are not woken.

* MEDICATION: various drugs have been tried, but controlled studies have failed to provide convincing evidence for the efficacy of medication in the management of enuresis. Stimulant drugs have been used in association with conditioning techniques; their use facilitates the response to conditioning procedures but the relapse rate when the drug is withdrawn has been very high.

* PSYCHOTHERAPY: this has been attempted on the assumption that enuresis is a symptom of a more pervasive disorder and, more specifically, of unconscious conflicts. The value of psychotherapy has not, however, been demonstrated to be impressive and the validity of

the claims about the importance of unconscious factors is not supported by demonstrations that enuresis can be treated successfully, and with no adverse consequences, by superficial techniques which do not attempt to modify the individual's psychodynamic conflicts.

* CONDITIONING TECHNIQUES: on the basis that enuresis can be viewed as a failure of learning, various techniques have been used to facilitate the learning process. The 'bell and pad' technique involves the use of an alarm which is installed in the enuretic's bed; when the enuretic wets the bed, the urine completes an electrical circuit which rings the alarm. The child wakes and then goes to the toilet whilst the parents re-set the apparatus. Records of the frequency and extent of bedwetting are maintained by the parents and the technique does appear to be the most successful to date (Taylor and Turner, 1975). Taylor and Turner suggest, however, that a number of problems remain to be resolved. Parental co-operation cannot be guaranteed and many attempts at treatment are unsuccessful because the parents refuse to or are unable to co-operate for the period of months required by the treatment.

Relapse rates have also been consistently high and vary from 10 to 30 per cent. In many cases, relapses are easily treated by a repetition of the treatment. Relapse rates have also been reduced by modifications to the treatment procedures. For example, relapse is less likely if (towards the end of the treatment programme) the child's fluid intake is increased to one or two pints per evening. It is argued that this might increase the bladder's capacity and provide the individual with the opportunity for 'overlearning'. Another modification involves techniques designed to encourage the child or family to cope with various life stresses since it is known that relapse is often preceded and presumably caused by a stress such as the birth of a sibling.

In spite of the problems which have been encountered, conditioning techniques continue to be the single most effective treatment. More recently, American psychologists have developed and evaluated rapid toilet training techniques which use combinations of modelling (using dolls and humans), high fluid intake and rewards (Azrin and Foxx, 1975). It is claimed that these techniques can be effective within 24 hours and can be used both with normal children and the retarded. As we have seen, the evidence suggests that techniques based on learning procedures are the most successful. In view of this it is also interesting to note Taylor and Turner's conclusion that the mechanisms underlying the development and modification of enuresis continue to be a matter for hypotheses and conjecture.

Hyperactivity
This condition refers to a syndrome of disruptive and

difficult behaviours. As the term suggests, the most obvious abnormality is the child's overactivity; as we shall see, however, the hyperactive child also has a number of other problems. The problems and modification of hyperactivity are considered by Bidder, Gray and Pates (1981). In the group of pre-school children studied by Bidder and her colleagues, restlessness and almost continuous activity were the most obvious features. Hyperactive children changed their activities, on average, every minute or so whilst a control group changed every five minutes. The hyperactive children were, not surprisingly, viewed as difficult and disruptive by their parents, who also noted a number of other difficulties. Parents complained, for example, of difficulties in controlling their children, poor concentration and short attention span, poor sleep patterns, a domineering and often aggressive attitude towards other children and also difficulties in toilet training, dressing and other necessary activities.

The children studied by Bidder and her colleagues had, on average, five or six of these problems. The condition is not necessarily easy to diagnose and this is partly because precise norms on such factors as activity level and concentration for young children are simply not available. Diagnosis is usually dependent on complaints from parents, and the stress involved in coping with such a child can be quite considerable. Indeed, the presence of problems such as hyperactivity increases the probability of child abuse and non-accidental injury, though it must be stressed that the large majority of hyperactive children are not involved in this danger. If the hyperactive behaviour continues over a prolonged period, however, then parents' tempers are bound to be frayed by problems such as disrupted sleep, lack of co-operation, and even destruction of property.

How serious is the problem? In addition to the adverse effects of the condition on parents and family and the increased risk of aggression directed towards the child, there are also other difficulties. The child's learning can be seriously disrupted by the problems associated with hyperactivity, so that the acquisition of essential social skills and educational progress could be either retarded or even prevented. If this occurs, a vicious self-maintaining cycle of difficult behaviour and retarded development could be set up, which is clearly to the disadvantage of both the child and the family. Modification of the hyperactive syndrome is therefore clearly necessary.

What techniques are available to control the hyperactive child's behaviour and how effective are management procedures? As usual, the standard medical treatment has involved medication. The busy doctor may, of course, have little time to do more than prescribe drugs. Bidder, Gray and Newcombe's (1978) review suggests clearly, however, that medication has not proved to be a satisfactory treatment. Drugs appear to have little or no effect or, at best, to have transient effects which disappear when they are withdrawn. The value of medication is further reduced by the possibility of side effects. It is therefore clear that alternatives to drugs need to be explored. Bidder and her colleagues have, in fact, conducted carefully controlled evaluations of behavioural training procedures.

The behavioural treatment of hyperactivity involves a number of steps. First, the child's behaviour is carefully observed in order to identify the most troublesome behaviours and their frequency. Ideally, this is done in the home situation and involves recording by the parents and also clinical observers. Such observations can establish, for example, that the main problems are frequent changes of activity, destructive acts and refusal to comply with requests from the parents. Observation can also establish baseline, pretreatment, frequencies of all troublesome behaviours. Second, training programmes are introduced with the help of the parents. For example, the child is encouraged to persist at selected tasks by the provision of rewards or 'reinforcements'. Alternatively, parents might be required to withhold attention when the child is performing maladaptive actions such as pestering or destructiveness. Aggressive or destructive acts might be controlled with 'time out' procedures; in practice, the child is removed to a bare or uninteresting room whenever he misbehaves. One final example involves the techniques of 'over-correction'; the child is required to 'correct' the consequences of his behaviour. For example, the untidy child has to clean up the mess; the destructive child is compelled to repair whatever damage has been caused, and so on. Though the exact programme is geared to suit the needs of each child, these are the major techniques which are used. In essence, the treatment involves precise problem identification, goal setting and parental training. The parents carry out the programme and the child's progress is monitored by repeated observations of the relevant behaviours.

How effective is this technique? The work of Bidder and her colleagues involves comparisons of treated and untreated groups and suggests three overall conclusions. First, hyperactivity can be brought under control in as little as six to twelve weeks and with a modest degree of professional involvement. Hyperactivity is therefore a condition which appears to be sensitive to environmental manipulation. Second, the changes are maintained over follow-up periods of three to six months. Third, training programmes can be maintained by parents. In addition, the skills in child management acquired by parents can subsequently be used to prevent the development of further problems. Parents function, in effect, as therapists to their own children. Further work remains, as usual, to be done. For example, follow-up studies over periods in excess of six months are needed in order to monitor the long-term maintenance of gains and also the effects on the child's development. Furthermore, hyperactivity can be associated with a number of causal factors (including physical conditions and family management practices). Further research will need to establish whether behavioural management techniques are effective with all variants of the condition.

Anxiety, fears and phobias

Anxiety, especially in relation to specific fear objects, is sufficiently common in childhood to be considered as a normal phenomenon. For example, Lapouse and Monk's (1959) survey involved interviews with the mothers of 482 children aged 6-12 years. In 43 per cent of the group, the mothers reported the presence of seven or more worries and fears. The majority of childhood fears are, however, transient and disappear without any specialized treatment. Furthermore, surveys of children who attend child guidance clinics indicate that they do not have a greater number or range of worries and fears than control children who are not receiving professional help.

One of the most extensive surveys of fears in children was conducted by the American psychologist, Jersild. The study is reviewed by Herbert (1974) and involved a large sample of children between 5 and 12 years of age. Fears were shown to be universal; only 5 per cent of the sample did not admit to any fears. The objects of fear varied considerably and involved imaginary figures (monsters, witches), animals and strangers. The most common fears also change with age. For example, young infants tend to fear strangers and, more generally, unknown entities; fear of animals develops later in the pre-school phase; anxieties about physical appearance, self-presentation and social contacts appear later still during the school years and adolescence. The content of fears tend to reflect aspects of the child's environment and the stage of development. For example, during early adolescence worries concerned with school experiences are more common than worries about home.

What factors determine the development and persistence of fears and worries? Eysenck and Rachman (1965) have listed a number of factors involved in the aetiology of anxiety and can be assumed to be relevant to the behaviour of both adults and children. These are discussed more fully in chapter 14, but since it would be useful to list them here, the following are the major determinants of anxiety.

1. PERSONALITY: some individuals are more likely to develop anxiety than others and this predisposition has been related to personality characteristics such as neuroticism. The neurotic individual, it is suggested, is predisposed to respond physiologically to any stress. Physiological responses, controlled by the autonomic nervous system, occur more quickly, intensely and persistently. Such a theory is supported by a number of clinical and research studies. For example, neuroticism measured by questionnaires is correlated with the number of irrational fears reported by individuals. School phobic children have been shown to be generally timid and sensitive away from home: in one study,

only 8 per cent of a group of school phobics were rated as domineering and aggressive.

2. CONFINEMENT: anxiety is more likely to be generated if the individual's movement is restricted and escape is difficult. Humans can, of course, be confined by both social and physical barriers. The practical implication is that the child who is confined in some way (e.g. in a classroom during a thunderstorm) is more likely to develop a strong phobic response.

3. INTENSITY OF THE FEAR STIMULUS: some fear stimuli will be inherently more frightening than others. For example, a loud noise is more likely to produce anxiety than a quiet whisper.

4. AGE: as we have already seen, age is related to the manifestation and development of fears. Younger children are generally more fearful, and fears are also related to the child's physical size and coping abilities.

5. PAST EXPERIENCE: past experience can have contradictory effects. On the one hand, repeated exposure to even weak fear stimuli (e.g. dogs) can accumulate to produce intense anxiety. On the other hand, repeated exposure can also immunize the individual and prevent the development of intense phobias. Eysenck and Rachman refer to the observation that school refusals are less likely in children who have previously attended nursery schools.

6. CONFLICT: fear and anxiety are more likely to occur if certain types of conflict situation are present. Ambivalent situations, where the individual is torn between approach and avoidance, are particularly likely to produce stress and anxiety. School refusals, for example, experience this type of conflict very often; their need to go to school (partly to avoid parental censure) is in conflict with such problems as difficulty in coping with school work and backwardness. Many fears are maintained because the individual is able to avoid contact with the feared stimulus, or escape from it; for example, a fear of dogs or heights can be maintained by the opportunities to avoid and escape.

7. STRENGTH OF COMPETING RESPONSES: anxiety is less likely to develop if exposure to a potentially fearful stimulus is associated with the presence of factors which are antagonistic to anxiety. For example, the child is less likely to be afraid if the parent is present, or indeed if other children are present who are not showing any indications of fear. Children often imitate the fears of others, and parents are particularly important models whose behaviour either inhibits or facilitates the development of fears in their children. As we see shortly, the young child's susceptibility to anxiety can also be reduced by

such activities as eating: in fact, by any activity which
is incompatible with anxiety and fear.

What techniques are available for the management of anxiety
and fears? It should be stressed that decisions about the
need for treatment must be made with a full understanding
that many fears are quite normal and often disappear in time
without specialized help. Treatment might often be justified, however, if the fear is having adverse and potentially
serious effects on the child and his family. For example,
the school phobic is missing the opportunity to acquire both
social and educational skills and, in Great Britain,
persistent inattendance at school can render the parents
liable to prosecution. Within the context of development,
some long-lasting phobic conditions can handicap the child
seriously if important experiences and opportunities to
learn are lost. In other words, the consequence of persistent anxiety problems can involve the development of
secondary handicaps. These contribute in turn to a dimi-
nishing degree of competence in the child and a self-
perpetuating vicious circle of difficulties.

Progress in the management of anxiety and phobias has
fortunately been very impressive (cf. chapter 12) and the
technology needed to control fears and phobias is now
available to us. Tranquillizers are, of course, the most
easily available methods to reduce anxiety but their use in
childhood has tended to be restricted to older school-age
children and adolescents. Psychological techniques are now
freely available and the most commonly used technique
involves gradual exposure to feared objects under conditions
where the anxiety response is maintained at a low level. For
example, several techniques are available to modify the
anxiety of the child who fears dogs. One essential ingredient is that the exposure to dogs is gradual and controlled.
For instance, he is initially exposed to pictures of dogs
rather than live specimens; alternatively, he is initially
exposed to dogs in the distance. When the child's discomfort
subsides, the dogs are gradually brought nearer. Alternatively, he is initially exposed to small dogs or puppies. In
addition to graded exposure, other techniques are used to
control the child's anxiety. Anxiety might be inhibited by
an activity such as eating, or by the presence of attractive
toys or other children who behave in a non-fearful manner.

Other techniques can also be used both to prevent and
control fears and anxiety. The provision of non-anxious
models has already been mentioned. The development of skills
(including language) which allow the child to cope with his
environment (e.g. physical and social skills) can also reduce the probability of anxiety. Finally, verbal explanation
and opportunities to become acquainted with potentially
frightening stimuli can also be helpful. Play activities can
be useful in this respect since the child will naturally use
play to adapt himself to situations which he finds threatening. Doll play, as we have already seen, can be used both to

diagnose and identify the child's fear and also to facilitate the processes of control and de-sensitization which are needed if the child is to overcome his problems.

In addition to those procedures which are likely to reduce anxiety, it is also important to be aware of those methods which are not effective, or even exacerbate the child's anxiety. Forcefully exposing a child to a fear stimulus can often increase the extent of the fear since it involves the element of constraint; ridiculing the child for his weakness is another technique which, though often used by frustrated parents, is not effective. Ignoring the child's fears, or removing the fear object, can be useful ploys to reduce the child's stress but, in many instances, the fear persists to the extent that behavioural treatment is required. Once again, however, it is important to remember that many fears are transient and disappear without special help. Since attention can act as a reinforcement for a range of behaviours, including fear behaviours such as avoidance, a generally non-emotional and neutral attitude together with a minimum of fuss has much to recommend it.

References

Azrin, N. and Foxx, R. (1975)
Toilet Training in Less than a Day. London: Macmillan.

Bidder, R.T., Gray, O.P. and Newcombe, R. (1978)
Behavioural treatment of hyperactive children. Archives of Disease in Childhood, 53, 574-579.

Bidder, R.T., Gray, O.P. and Pates, R.M. (1981)
Brief intervention therapy for hyperactive, behaviourally disturbed pre-school children. Child: Care, Health and Development, 7, 21-30.

Clarke, A.D.B. and Clarke, A.M. (1972)
Consistency and variability in the growth of human characteristics. In W.D. Wall and V.P. Varma (eds), Advances in Educational Psychology. London: University of London Press.

Eysenck, H.J. and Rachman, S. (1965)
Causes and Cures of Neurosis. London: Routledge & Kegan Paul.

Gunzburg, H.C. (1968)
Social Competence and Mental Handicap: An introduction to social education. London: Ballière, Tindall and Cassell.

Herbert, M. (1974)
Emotional Problems of Development in Children. London: Academic Press.

Hewitt, L.E. and Jenkins, R.L. (1946)
Fundamental Patterns of Maladjustment: The dynamics of their origin. Springfield, Ill.: Thomas.

Lapouse, E. and Monk, M.A. (1959)
Fears and worries in a representative sample of children. American Journal of Orthopsychiatry, 29, 803-818.

Rachman, S. (1973)
Psychological treatment. In H.J. Eysenck (ed.),

Handbook of Abnormal Psychology (2nd edn). London: Pitman.

Rutter, M. (1975)
Helping Troubled Children. Harmondsworth: Penguin.

Rutter, M., Tizard, J. and Whitmore, K. (eds) (1970)
Education, Health and Behaviour. London: Longmans.

Shields, J. (1962)
Monozygotic Twins Brought Up Apart and Brought Up Together. London: Oxford University Press.

Skeels, H.M. (1966)
Adult status of children with contrasting early life experience: a follow-up study. Monographs of the Society for Research in Child Development, 31, No. 105.

Taylor, R.D. and Turner, R.K. (1975)
A clinical trial of continuous, intermittent and overlearning 'bell and pad' treatments for nocturnal enuresis. Behaviour Research and Therapy, 13, 281-293.

Thomas, A., Birch, H.G., Chess, S., Hertzig, M.E. and Karn, S. (1963)
Behavioural Individuality in Early Childhood. New York: International University Press.

Questions

1. Provide as many examples as possible of childhood problems which require psychological intervention. In relation to each example, explain clearly how the problem is defined as abnormal. In other words, specify the criteria which would indicate that the behaviours in question are to be regarded as abnormal.

2. What are the main steps which need to be taken in relation to the psychological evaluation and investigation of psychological difficulties in childhood? Illustrate each step by referring to: (a) mental retardation; (b) fearfulness and timidity; (c) truancy and stealing; (d) backwardness in school.

3. Discuss some of the theoretical and practical problems associated with: (a) the assessment of young children; (b) identifying the causes of psychological problems in childhood.

4. Describe and discuss critically the major psychological approaches to the treatment of disordered behaviour in childhood.

5. Discuss the claim that abnormal behaviour in the child (e.g. school difficulties, antisocial behaviour, or anxiety) is inevitably a reflection of difficulties in the child's family. What are the broad categories of determinants which cause or maintain behavioural and psychological problems in children?

6. Discuss the contributions which a clinical psychologist might make to the work of a paediatric department.

7. Describe and discuss the contribution of the psychologist to the assessment, explanation and modification of: (a) bedwetting; (b) hyperactivity; (c) fears and phobias.

8. Discuss some of the practical and ethical problems asso-
    ciated with the application of behaviour modification
    techniques to children. Does the application of beha-
    viour modification techniques involve any ethical
    problems which are not experienced in psychotherapy or
    medical treatments?

Annotated reading

Herbert, M. (1974) Emotional Problems of Development in
Children. London: Academic Press.
    This is a comprehensive and clear review of the causes,
    assessment and management of problems in childhood and
    adolescence. One of its impressive characteristics is
    that it combines a competent review with a clear style,
    and a practically useful consideration of assessment and
    treatment. It can be used as a reference source, and
    read either in its entirety or in relation to specific
    topics.

Rutter, M. (1975) Helping Troubled Children. Harmondsworth:
Penguin.
    This is a comprehensive review of the aetiology and
    management of problems in childhood. It is probably not
    as easy to read as Herbert's book, but is nevertheless
    an extremely useful text both in its entirety and as a
    reference source. The author, Michael Rutter, has a
    strong claim to be regarded as the most eminent child
    psychiatrist in the UK.

7

Ageing and Social Problems
Peter G. Coleman

Opening remarks
DAVID GRIFFITHS

Peter Coleman reminds us in his introduction to ageing that
the number of old people in our society has increased dramatically. The over-65s in the UK now account for one in seven
of the total population. It has become increasingly obvious,
however, that the problems and needs of the elderly must be
studied and understood if they are to receive the support
and practical help which they deserve. The chapter combines
a review of the psychological and social changes experienced
by the elderly with an enthusiastic and committed argument
for the need to provide them with sympathetic and effective
care. He also reminds the reader that the majority of professionals who care for the elderly are likely to be young,
so that an acquaintance with both the normal and abnormal
aspects of ageing cannot necessarily be assumed. This review
must, however, be considered as a useful foundation for the
development of a relevant body of knowledge. It avoids the
tedium of extensive lists of problems, signs and symptoms,
and yet addresses major issues such as intellectual functioning, social activity and self-esteem in old people.
Whilst Peter Coleman recognizes that old age is often associated with difficulties - physical, psychological and
social - he also emphasizes that two-thirds of the elderly
continue to enjoy good health and do not require medical or
other specialized services to any significant extent. This
is not to suggest, however, that this majority of old people
are free of problems; the suffering associated with loneliness, social isolation and loss of self-esteem can be
particularly acute.

The chapter is likely to be of interest to various
groups of doctors. Certainly to trainees, whose knowledge
of the elderly might often be limited to their own relatives and relationships within their social groups; possibly also to clinicians whose contact with the elderly will
tend to be limited to those presenting with medical and
other difficulties. Finally, the discussion is also relevant
to administrative doctors who contribute to the planning and
organization of services. Indeed, the following discussion
is no less relevant to many other professional groups, and
any individuals who are concerned with old people.

What is it to be old?
PETER G. COLEMAN

The study of ageing and problems associated with it are now recognized as important. This is not surprising, for older people have become the major clients of the health and social services. They also have a lot of free time at their disposal. If there is to be an expansion in adult education and opportunities for creative leisure activities, the benefits should go especially to retired people.

What is surprising is that it has taken so long for the social sciences to pay attention to ageing and old age. So many young professionals are called on to devote their attention to the needs of people at the other end of the life span, yet they are likely to have received little in the way of stimulating material about the distinctive psychological features of old age.

Professional people do nevertheless have to be introduced to the subject of ageing, and it is interesting to note how that introduction has come to take on certain standard forms over the last ten years. There are two very popular, almost obligatory it seems, ways to begin talking or writing about ageing. The first way is to present the demographic data about the increasing numbers of elderly people in the population; the second way is to discuss the negative attitudes people have about working with the elderly.

The common introduction to ageing

In important respects old age as we know it today is a relatively modern phenomenon. Though there may have been individual societies in the past where a comparably large part of the population was old, it is clear that there has been a dramatic change in developed countries since the turn of the century. At that time in Britain those over the age of 65 constituted one in 20 of the population; today they constitute one in seven.

In recent years much more use is being made of the statistic 'over the age of 75', since it has become clear that this is the group in the population which makes the largest demands on the health and social services. This has highlighted the worrying news for service planners in a time of economic constraints that, while the total number of those over 65 will not increase very much in the coming years, the population of those over 75 has already passed 5 per cent of the total population and will reach 6 per cent by the end of the 1980s.

However, expressing concern simply at the number of elderly people in the population is misleading. Why after all should it be a problem that 15 per cent rather than, say, 10 per cent or 5 per cent of the population is over the age of 65, or that 6 per cent rather than 4 per cent or 2 per cent is over the age of 75? A lot of the issues have to do with economics. The state must find the means to continue paying adequate and perhaps even improved pensions, and to provide welfare services to larger numbers of people.

Yet perhaps the more fundamental issues are the availability and willingness of people, whether relatives, neighbours, professionals or volunteers, to give assistance to large numbers of disabled people in the population. For ageing, as any introduction to the subject makes abundantly clear, is associated with an increasing likelihood of developing chronic disability.

Global estimates of disability in daily living (in getting around the house and providing for oneself) indicate that the need for assistance is present in 15-20 per cent of the age group 65-74, rising to 35-40 per cent in the 75-84 age group and over 60 per cent in those above 85. If one adds on the number of people living in institutions (hospitals and old people's homes), which is about 4-5 per cent of the total elderly population, one can conclude that about 30 per cent, or nearly one in three, of all people over the age of 65 are disabled and in need of help.

A typical introduction to ageing then goes on to present further numerical data on the social position of the elderly. Almost one-third of people over 65 have been found to live alone and large numbers are lonely. Many live in poor housing, lack basic amenities and so on.

The need for a life-span perspective

Large numbers of elderly people, large numbers of disabled elderly people, and large numbers of elderly people live in deprived circumstances; such is a typical introduction to old age. But there are vitally important perspectives missing. No wonder indeed that we should be concerned with attitudes, with finding enough people prepared to work with the elderly, enough geriatricians, enough nurses, enough social workers and so on, when the only image we present of old age is a negative one. If the only perspective we emphasize is one of endless problems, often insoluble because of irremediable physical and mental deterioration, we cannot expect many people to have the courage to become involved.

Old people are people like the rest of us. What is special about them is not that they may be mentally deteriorated, disabled or isolated. The majority, after all, is none of these things and many people reach the end of their lives without suffering any disadvantages. What is special about old people is that they have lived a long time. They have had all the kinds of experience we have had and many, many more. They are moving towards the end of life it is true, but it is every bit as important how one ends one's life as how one begins it.

The perspective on ageing that is needed is one which takes into account the whole life span. The discovery any student of old age has to make is not only that old people have a long life history behind them but that their present lives, their needs and wishes, cannot be understood without an appreciation of that life history.

If we really talk to old people all this will become evident. But how often do we do this? A most eloquent

testimony of our neglect is a poem (88 lines long) that was
found in the hospital locker of a geriatric patient. (It can
be found in full, quoted in the preface of the recent Open
University Text, Carver, V. and Liddiard, P. (1978), 'An
Ageing Population', Hodder & Stoughton.)

What do you see nurses
   What do you see?
Are you thinking
   When you are looking at me
A crabbit old woman
   Not very wise,
Uncertain of habit
   With far-away eyes

....

Then open your eyes nurse,
   You're not looking at me.

The writer emphasizes the continuity between her identity as
an old person and her identities at previous stages in the
life cycle. She is still the small child of ten with a large
family around her, still the 16 year old full of hopes and
expectations, still the bride she was at 20 and the young
woman of 30 with her children growing up fast. At 40 her
children are leaving home, and she and her husband are on
their own again. But then there are grandchildren for her to
take an interest in. Years pass and she has lost her husband
and must learn to live alone. She is all of these people.
But the nurse does not see them.

Psychological changes with age

It is only proper to admit at the outset that the main activity of psychologists interested in ageing, with some exceptions, has not been of a life span perspective. Their
work has mainly been concerned with trying to establish what
psychological changes, usually changes of deterioration,
occur with advancing age, with understanding the bases of
such changes and finding ways of compensating for them.
These are obviously important questions.

Cognitive deterioration

It would be wishful thinking to deny that there is any
deterioration with age. Physical ageing is a fact which is
easy to observe, though it may occur at different rates in
different people. Performance in everyday tasks in which we
have to use our cognitive ability to register things we see
or hear, remember them and think about them also deteriorates. Absent-mindedness is one of the most common complaints
of older people in everyday life.

In more recent cross-sectional studies of the performance of different age groups on experimental tasks, psychologists have tried their best to control for obvious factors
which might produce differences in their own right, like
education, illness, sensory impairment and willingness to
carry out the tasks in question. Of course, certain question

marks remain over differences in attitude and perceived role: for instance, whether older people see the purpose of such tasks in the same way as younger people. Nevertheless, certain conclusions can be drawn about the abilities which seem to change the most as one grows older. In the first place, older people take much longer to carry out tasks and this is not only because their limb movements are slower. In tasks in which they have to divide their attention ('try to do two things at once'), decline with age is very marked and is already evident in those over 30. Ability to remember things we have seen or heard declines, as does the ability to hold associations in mind.

However, in some older people decline is not evident at all. Particular experiences, for example particular occupational backgrounds, may develop certain abilities in an individual to such an extent that they remain well developed throughout old age. Retired telephone operators who have no difficulty in dividing attention between a number of messages are a case in point. The prominence of so many older people in public life where they reap the fruit of years of experience in political dealings is also an obvious illustration. Moreover, it seems to be true that in some old people deterioration does not, in fact, occur. There are studies which indicate that the cognitive ability of a sizeable minority of elderly people, perhaps as many as one in ten, cannot be distinguished from that of younger people.

This, then, is evidence that age itself is not the important thing. Indeed it seems better to view age simply as a vector along which to measure the things that happen to people. Some things that happen with age are universal. They occur at different times, but they are unavoidable. These things we can, if we like, describe as 'age' changes. But a lot of the things we associate with old age are not due to ageing processes and are not universal. There is a great variation in the extent to which people are hit by physical and social losses as they grow old. Some people are fortunate, some people are unfortunate.

From the point of view of cognitive ability, the most unlucky are those people who suffer from the various forms of dementia or brain diseases which lead to a progressive deterioration in mental functioning. But health is by no means the only extrinsic factor influencing mental state in old age. A lot of research has been done recently on the psychological effects of such brain-washing treatments as isolation and sensory deprivation. Disorientation and confusion are common results. Yet we are often slow to recognize that old people may be living in circumstances where by any ordinary standards they are extremely isolated and deprived of stimulation. No one calls to see them, to engage them, to remind them of their names, roles and relationships. Disorientation in time and space, and confusion about identity and relationship with others, can be a natural result. From our own experience we know how time can lose meaning after one has been ill in bed for a day or two, away from the normal daily routine.

Other social and psychological factors play a role too. Motivation to recover or maintain abilities is obviously a crucial factor, and a number of studies have shown that amount of education remains one of the major factors in cognitive ability and performance throughout life.

Personality and life style

Scientific work on personality and style of life in old age does not match the amount that has been done on cognitive functioning. The evidence we do have, however, relates both to change and stability.

One clear finding from research is that introversion or interiority increases with age. This means that as people grow old they become more preoccupied with their own selves, their own thoughts and feelings and less with the outside world. This change is only relative, of course, but it is evident both from responses to questionnaires and also from projective tests, where people are asked to describe or react to stimuli they are presented with, such as pictures of family and social situations.

The term disengagement has been used to describe such a change in orientation; a decreased concern with interacting with others and being involved in the outside world and an increased satisfaction with one's own world of memories and immediate surroundings. However, critics have been quick to point out the dangers of exaggerating the extent to which disengagement is a 'natural' development in old age. Most of the decreased interaction and involvement of older people is forced upon them by undesired physical and social changes: disability, bereavement, loss of occupational roles and so on. Moreover, there is also clear evidence that old people are happier when there is a good deal of continuity between their past and present activities.

Indeed, in contrast to any change in personality that may occur, the stability that people show in their characteristics and style of life over a period of time is far more striking. Longitudinal studies show that people continue to enjoy the same interests and activities. When striking negative changes occur in a person's interests or familiar mode of activities, or ways of coping with life in old age, for no obvious reason, this is often a sign of psychiatric illness, especially depression.

Some of the most valuable studies on personality in old age are, in fact, those which have shown how important it is to take into reckoning a person's life style, for instance in explaining why people react differently to changes and losses such as retirement, bereavement and living alone, or a move to a residential home. Any research finding about old people usually has to be qualified by a reference to life style. This is mentioned again when talking about adjustment to relocation.

Growth and development

Though deterioration has been the main perspective of
psychological research on ageing up to now, it is not the
only one. Certainly in literature old age has been treated
much more generously. The works of Nobel prize winners, such
as Patrick White ('The Eye of the Storm', 1973), Saul Bellow
('Mr Sammler's Planet', 1969) and Ernest Hemingway ('The
Old Man and the Sea', 1952), present vivid and compelling
pictures of old age that, like King Lear, have to do with
deterioration and change but also with growth in understanding and the values of existence.

Indeed, a characteristic theme in literature is of old
age as a time of questioning; of one's own achievements, of
the meaning of one's life, of the values one lived by and of
what is of lasting value. It is as if an old person, freed
from the strait-jacket of society, suffering losses in his
ability to function and in his social position - perhaps
indeed precisely because of them - is, somehow, let free to
question life. Psychologists have only begun tentatively to
approach these issues, but there is a lot in writers like
Jung to consider.

Adaptation to loss in old age

From what has already been said it should be clear that old
age is a time of great inequality. It is a time when losses
occur, loss of physical and mental abilities, loss of people
who were close to one, loss of roles and loss of activities.
These losses are not inevitable; they do not occur in the
same degree to everyone; but adapting to loss is a characteristic feature of old age.

Attitudes to health and well-being

Severe disability is one of the major losses of old age and
its central importance in shaping the rest of an individual's life is one of the most common findings to emerge
from investigations on social aspects of ageing. People who
are disabled have more problems in maintaining their desired
styles of life and are more dissatisfied than people who are
not disabled. This is not surprising.

What is more surprising, or at least not logically to be
expected, is the fact that, in general, levels of well-being
do not decline with age. This is despite the fact that the
incidence and severity of disability tend to increase with
age and have a great influence on well-being. The key to
understanding this comes from studies on subjective health.

The clear evidence from both longitudinal and cross-
sectional studies is that whereas objective health and
physical functioning of elderly people tend to deteriorate
with age, the same is not true in regard to how they feel
about their health. The most likely explanation has to do
with expectations. People expect to become somewhat more
disabled with old age. If they do, they accept it. But if
their physical functioning remains stable they may in fact
experience this as a bonus and feel better as a result.

Only if their health deteriorates beyond the expected norm are they likely to feel badly about it.

This argument applies strictly only to feeling well, but it has a wider implication for well-being generally and for reactions to other losses in old age. Expectation is a very important aspect of reaction to loss. It is what people expect and what people find normal that determines how they react to things and how satisfied they feel with their situation. This kind of consideration also leads one to reflect how different things could be if old people's expectations changed. This is in fact not so unlikely. Future generations of elderly people may be far less accepting of lower standards of health and also, for instance, of income. They may expect things to be a good deal better for them. And if things are not going to be better they are going to be less happy as a result.

Adjustment to relocation
Another misfortune often following from disability is that people can find themselves being obliged to move, sometimes quite unexpectedly and against their will, to different environments, particularly institutional settings, where they often have to remain for the rest of their lives. Though this is usually done to them 'for their own good' (they are judged incapable of looking after themselves in their own homes), the end result may be much worse than leaving them alone: for instance, further deterioration and loss of interest in life.

There has been growing realization of the extent to which environmental changes can contribute to physical illness and psychiatric disorders. Even where it is voluntarily undertaken and has otherwise favourable effects, there are indications that rehousing can undermine a person's health. There is also a great deal of variation between individuals in their reactions, so it is important to discover which factors might predict the ability to adjust easily to new surroundings.

Among psychological factors cognitive ability is clearly crucial. There appear to be two major reasons why cognitively impaired old people react worse to relocation. In the first place, their lack of ability to anticipate and prepare means that they experience more stress on making the move. Second, because of their poor short-term memory and orientation abilities it may take them a long while to understand their new surroundings.

Personality is important too. We are not sufficiently sensitive to the fact that the institutional environments we provide may be fine for one kind of elderly person but not for another. American studies have shown the importance, for instance, of rebellious and aggressive traits, as opposed to passive and compliant ones, in predicting survival and lack of deterioration after relocation to institutional settings. Vital as well, of course, are attitudinal factors concerned with what the move means to the person, whether he wants to go, and how he sees his own future in the new setting.

Self-esteem and its sources: the lynchpin of adjustment?
Disability and environmental change have been picked out for
consideration as two of the negative changes associated with
old age. There are others, of course. Bereavement requires
a major adjustment which seems to follow certain definite
stages. Grieving is a normal, healthy part of the process,
and the support and understanding of those around in allowing the bereaved person to express himself may be very
important to it. Loss of occupational role with retirement
is another big change. Indeed, adjustment to it is often
thought of in the same terms as adjustment to the old age
role itself. Most people make good adaptations, but not all,
and retirement can be a major precipitating factor in the
onset of late life depression.

Then again, a very significant loss for many people as
they grow older is that of income: they must adapt to making
do with less. There has been almost no psychological investigation of this kind of adaptation. From what one can see
it would seem that a lot of old people positively take pride
in stretching their money. This, of course, may also have a
lot to do with their experience of deprivation in the past.

Naturally, in all these adaptations much depends on the
characteristics of the individual person involved, and one
is led to ask whether there are any general ways in which
one can conceptualize how a person adapts to the various
losses and changes that occur with old age. Some authors
talk in terms of the individual possessing particular qualities: for instance, 'coping ability'. But the most valuable
index of adjustment in old age is that of self-esteem.

Maintenance of positive attitudes to oneself seems to be
one of the key issues in old age. An especially important
component of self-image is a sense of being in control of
one's own life. Development in childhood and adulthood is
associated with an increasing sense of effectiveness and of
impact on the external world. In old age this sense may well
be taken away.

Intrinsic to this conception of self-identity is the
notion that it must have roots outside itself. Therefore, if
an individual is to maintain his self-esteem he has a
continuing need of sources from which he can define an acceptable image of himself to himself. For some people these
sources can exist in past relationships and achievements or
in an inner conviction about the kind of person one is, but
in the main they depend on the present external circumstances of their lives; their roles in the family, in
relation to other people, in work and in other activities.

When these circumstances change, as they often do in
old age, a person may have to find alternative sources to
maintain a positive view of himself. Here again it is vital
to understand a person's life history. A person whose sense
of self has been based on one particular kind of source, for
instance relationships with members of his close family, is
going to suffer especially if he loses such family contacts
through death.

One way to investigate sources of self-esteem is to ask people directly what makes them say that they feel useful or feel useless, for instance. Not surprisingly, lack of infirmity and contact with other people including the family emerge as the major sources of self-esteem. Especially in disabled people, being able to do things for oneself, and in particular to get around, appear to be key factors; also being a source of help and encouragement to others is very important.

In this context it is worth putting in a good word for residential care and other types of grouped housing schemes. In a previous part of this section it was noted that a move to an institutional setting can be damaging for certain types of individual, but a good institutional setting can also be of great benefit to certain people. This is possible when sources of self-esteem are likely to be strengthened rather than weakened by the move.

For instance, some people could be said to be 'living independently in the community'. But in reality they may be extremely isolated and totally dependent on the services being brought to them. Once they have moved to a genuine communal setting the burden of infirmity and consciousness of being alone can be diminished. Precisely because they are better able to cope for themselves in the new environment and to be of importance to others, they may gain a new lease of life.

Helping old people

Not all the loss and trauma of old age can be countered from an individual's own resources. The modern welfare state provides a range of services for the elderly; housing, health and social services. These are, of course, limited, subject to decisions about what level of services the country can 'afford'. We do not know what a perfect service for the elderly would be like, but we certainly do know that what we provide at present falls a long way short of it.

However, the achievement of the present level of services needs to be respected if we are to develop further, and it is important that people in the various caring professions who carry out these services remember their responsiblities. One of the real dangers is taking the operation of a service for granted and applying it automatically or mindlessly. The people on the receiving end then cease to be considered as individuals.

A key element, it seems to me, in any work with elderly people is the individual assessment, and it is here that the psychological perspective has a vital role. We need a good assessment not only of people's physical condition and capabilities and of their social situations, but also of their individual needs, their abilities and interests, which should include a good picture of how they used to be.

Besides helping in assessment, psychology can also play a role in the actual provision of therapeutic interventions both to old people themselves and to those around them.

Applied psychology should be able to show the best way: for example, to help recover abilities that seem to be lost or to mend social relationships that have become tense.

Maintenance of interests, activities and functioning

One of the most tragic images we have of old age is that of an old person with shoulders sunk, sitting collapsed in a chair, totally uninvolved in the world around. In a previous section the question of 'disengagement' in old age was raised, and let us repeat the point made there that, although some decline in activity may be an intrinsic part of growing old, most of such decline is the result of physical disability and environmental trauma.

When there is a dramatic decline in a person's activities for no obvious reason, we need to alert ourselves to the possibility that the person may be depressed. Loss of well-established habits and activities and lack of interest or anxiety about trying to regain them may be symptoms of the kind of depression which will respond to treatment, even though the person may not admit to having depressed feelings. But, of course, there also has to be some activity and interests for the person to go back to. Particularly if someone is disabled there may be few possibilities open to him and the person is then likely to decline again. It is also quite clear that prolonged inactivity has deleterious effects both on physical and psychological functioning. Skills that are not exercised tend to atrophy.

In recent years a lot of new initiatives have been taken in geriatric hospitals in providing opportunities for patients to engage in different types of activity, arts and crafts, music discussion and so on. Generally, staff report improvements in elderly people who do take part in such activities, which can be seen in their personal appearance, in their physical and mental functioning and in their contact with others.

An even greater challenge is offered by people who are mentally deteriorated. In the first place it is very important to distinguish elderly people who really have irretrievable brain disease from those who only appear to have because they are depressed. Indeed, it may be symptomatic of someone's depression that he thinks his brain is rotting. It may be no easy matter to distinguish this, because it is difficult to motivate someone who is depressed actually to demonstrate his abilities. With the right treatment and support depressed people can be encouraged to regain their old abilities.

However, elderly people who clearly are deteriorating mentally should not be abandoned to their fate. Tests have shown that such people, given encouragement and help, can still acquire and retain new information and maintain skills. But the effort needed from outside is great. A good example is the use of so-called 'reality orientation', where people around the elderly person, either informally throughout the day or in concentrated formal classes, systematically try to help remind the person of time, place and season, of names of people, of objects, and of activities and so on.

Psychologists have a lot to do applying findings from the study of learning and memory to help old people. The trouble at present is that such people are often left alone, and this only exacerbates their condition. Dementia is a progressive illness, but what happens between its onset and death is important. If in the future we find medical means of slowing down its progress, it will become an even more urgent matter to find means as well to allow people to maintain their optimum potentialities in the time that remains left to them.

Family relationships

Another vital issue is the relationship between disabled elderly people and their families. Many more of such people are supported by their families than live in institutions for the elderly. For instance, in the case of severe dementia, there are four to five times as many suffering from such a condition living in the community as live in residential homes or hospitals. Yet often families who are doing the caring get pitifully little in the way of support services.

If they become overburdened by the stress of their involvement, both they and their elderly relatives suffer. The old person's mental condition may well be aggravated by tired and irritable relatives, and if there is a breakdown in care and there is no alternative but to take the old person into an institution, the family members are likely to suffer greatly from feelings of guilt. They often want to care for a relative until that person dies, but need help in carrying it out.

It is an important principle to accept that work with families is an integral part of work with elderly people. Family ties after all usually form a substantial part of an individual's identity. If those ties are damaged, so is the person's identity. The physical and mental deterioration that affects many people as they grow older and their ensuing state of dependency can put a strain on many relationships. Men, for instance, usually do not expect to outlive their wives. They can encounter great problems if they find instead that they have to spend their old age looking after a physically or mentally deteriorated wife, especially if in the past it was their wives who ran the household. Children too often find difficulty in taking over responsibility for ailing parents.

The actual symptoms, particularly of mental disturbance in old age, can be very disturbing. In some forms of dementia (probably dependent on the part of the brain that has been affected) the behavioural changes that can occur, caricaturing the person's old personality, increasing aggression or leading to a loss in standards of cleanliness, can be very painful for relatives to bear. It may be difficult for them to accept that the patient is not simply being difficult or unreasonable.

Families need counselling about the nature of the illness and, in the case of dementia, of its progressive nature, and preferably, too, promise of continued practical support. Group meetings held for relatives of different patients by doctors, social workers or other professionals can also be useful in allowing relatives to share common experiences and problems. Groups for the bereaved, particularly husbands or wives, can also play their part. The last years of their lives may have revolved around the care of a sick spouse and they must now find new meaning in life.

The future

In discussing ageing and social problems it may seem strange to end with a note about the future. But from what has been said it should be obvious that great improvements need to take place, both in society's provision for the elderly and in the attitudes of each and every one of us to the elderly people we live among.

For most people old age is not a particularly unhappy time, though for some it is. In part that may be, as we have suggested, because old people have low expectations. They quietly accept a society that treats them meanly and as somehow less important. In the future that may all change. We may see new generations of elderly people, foreshadowed in today's Grey Panthers in America, who will mobilize their potential power as a numerically important part of the electorate and pressurize society to give them a better deal.

On the other hand, old people may continue to remain on the sidelines. They may refuse to see their own material and other interests as being of central importance to society, in which case the rest of the population must see they are not forgotten.

The most important changes indeed are the attitudinal ones. We must recognize that old people are ourselves. They are our future selves. There is a continuity in life both between their past and present and between our present and future.

Old people remain the same people they were. Indeed, if we really want to know about a person's needs and wants and how they could be satisfied, the best introduction would be to let them tell us about their life history. Whatever new steps are taken in the future must follow on from this and make sense in relation to it.

Better provision would follow from such a recognition. If we really respected people's individuality we would provide them with choice about the circumstances and activities with which they end their days, not just enforce certain standard solutions. In short, we must allow people to grow old in ways that suit them, perhaps to explore new avenues of development in order to make the most of the years that remain. Also, when we consider those who need our help, who suffer in old age and perhaps are dependent upon us, we should not forget these wider perspectives.

Bibliography

Birren, J.E. and Schaie, K.W. (eds) (1977)
Handbook of the Psychology of Ageing. London: Van Nostrand Reinhold.

Brearley, C.P. (1975)
Social Work, Ageing and Society. London: Routledge & Kegan Paul.

Bromley, D.B. (1974)
The Psychology of Human Ageing (2nd edn). Harmondsworth: Penguin.

Carver, V. and Liddiard, P. (eds) (1978)
An Ageing Population (Open University text). Sevenoaks: Hodder & Stoughton.

Chown, S.M. (ed.) (1972)
Human Ageing. Harmondsworth: Penguin.

Dibner, A.S. (1975)
The psychology of normal aging. In M.G. Spencer and C.J. Dorr (eds), Understanding Aging: A multidisciplinary approach. New York: Appleton-Century-Crofts.

Gray, B. and Isaacs, B. (1979)
Care of the Elderly Mentally Infirm. London: Tavistock.

Kastenbaum, R. (1979)
Growing Old - Years of Fulfilment. London: Harper & Row.

Kimmel, D.C. (1974)
Adulthood and Ageing. An interdisciplinary developmental view. Chichester: Wiley.

Miller, E. (1977)
Abnormal Ageing. The psychology of senile and presenile dementia. Chichester: Wiley.

Neugarten, B. and associates (1964)
Personality in Middle and Later Life. New York: Atherton Press.

Questions

1. What are the main differences between young and old people? Are these differences related to the biological aspects ageing and are they inevitable?
2. Consider four old people (over 60) whom you know reasonably well. Compare them with four people of your own age. What are the main differences in behaviour and psychological functioning? What factors could account for these differences?
3. Describe and discuss the main changes in intellectual functioning, personality and social behaviour which occur with ageing. When you mention changes for the worse, consider whether and how these could be prevented or reduced.
4. What factors should be considered in the design and organization of residential homes for the elderly?
5. Are residential homes the ideal setting for old people? Consider the advantages and disadvantages of residential care institutions for the elderly.

6. Imagine that you are asked to contribute to the counselling of individuals in preparation for retirement. What are the most important bits of information and advice which you would like to give?
7. Discuss the advantages and disadvantages of old people living with their younger relatives. In relation to potential areas of dfficulty, consider how these could be avoided or reduced.
8. Consider ways in which the elderly could be more usefully integrated into contemporary society.
9. What are the most important psychological and social aspects of ageing which the doctor should consider in assessing and helping an old person?
10. Consider ways in which current services for the elderly could be improved.

Annotated reading

Kastenbaum, R. (1979) Growing Old - Years of Fulfilment. London: Harper & Row.
>A short introduction to the subject written by an American psychologist. He presents a balanced approach to old age, giving due weight to positive perspectives. The book is also attractively illustrated.

Bromley, D.B. (1974) The Psychology of Human Ageing (2nd edn). Harmondsworth: Penguin.
>A much longer book written by a British psychologist. It gives a very thorough coverage of subjects such as changes in performance and cognitive skills with age, and is good on the methodological issues involved in doing research on ageing.

Carver, V. and Liddiard, P. (eds) (1978) An Ageing Population (Open University Text). Sevenoaks: Hodder & Stoughton.
>A collection of readings prepared for the Open University course. The papers have been drawn from a variety of sources to provide a multidisciplinary perspective on the needs and circumstances of the elderly.

Brearley, C.P. (1975) Social Work, Ageing and Society. London: Routledge & Kegan Paul.
>A book written for social workers, bringing together a wide range of material from medicine, psychology and sociology.

Gray, B. and Isaacs, B. (1979) Care of the Elderly Mentally Infirm. London: Tavistock.
>A more specialized book on the elderly mentally infirm also intended for social workers, written jointly by a geriatrician and a social worker.

8

Dying and Bereavement
A. T. Carr

Opening remarks
DAVID GRIFFITHS

The emphasis placed by modern medicine on the treatment of
pathological conditions, and its concern on occasions with
the more dramatic applications of complex technology, can
encourage us to forget that death is, at best, delayed
rather than prevented. Doctors, whether they work in hospitals or the community, are inevitably involved in the
management of death and its consequences. The content of
this chapter is therefore very appropriately included in
this book and Tony Carr's review treats a sensitive subject
in a very competent and sympathetic manner.

Expertise in the management of the dying, and also the
bereaved, can only really be acquired through practical
experience. What then is the value of a review of our
understanding of death and bereavement? Its justification
must surely be that it makes a useful contribution to the
development of expertise. It discusses many questions which
a trainee is likely to ask but which can be difficult to
answer on the basis of limited clinical experience. What are
the main causes of distress for the dying and their relatives? How can the dying, and those close to them, be helped
to cope with inevitable stresses? What should patients and
their relations be told? What are the consequences of telling them the truth? What are the most important features
of bereavement, and what can professionals and others do to
help? Whilst it is always easier to pose these questions
than to answer them with certainty, the following review
provides an impressive and interesting synopsis of current
understanding of the psychology of death and bereavement.
It is certainly likely to encourage the development of skill
and sensitivity which patients can reasonably expect of
their doctors when they are themselves coping with the most
stressful experience in their lives.

Demographic trends
A. T. CARR

If you had been born at the beginning of this century, your
life expectancy at birth would have been 44 years if you
were male or 48 years if you were female. If you were born
today, your initial life expectancy would be 70 years or 76
years respectively. These figures reflect an ageing of the
population that has occurred in all western industrial
societies over the past 80 years. Although we all will die,

most of us will do so at a relatively advanced age. Although we all will be bereaved, most of us will not suffer this until we are young adults or until we are in our middle years.

The fatal conditions of the present day, once hidden by the mass diseases, are those associated with longevity. In 1978, almost 590,000 people died in England and Wales and 85 per cent of these deaths were attributable to only three categories of illness: diseases of the circulatory system (heart and blood circulation), neoplasms (cancer) and diseases of the respiratory system (OPCS, 1979). Also, more than two people in every three now die in institutions of one form or another.

In the absence of any radical changes of events, the vast majority of us will die aged 65 years or over, in an institution of some sort and as a result of a disease of our circulatory system, or respiratory system, or of cancer. This underlines an important feature of dying and death at the present time: they have become unfamiliar events that take place in unfamiliar surroundings, watched over by unfamiliar people. We all know that we will die and that we may be bereaved, yet we have very little relevant experience upon which to develop our construing or anticipation of these events and states.

Telling

The majority of fatally ill people realize, at some point, that they will not recover, even if they have not been informed of the nature of their illness. However, it would appear that only about half of all fatally ill people appreciate their condition before significant changes in health force the conclusion 'I am dying'. This is almost certainly an under-estimate: there will be some people who know that they will not recover but who do not communicate this.

Although about one-half of terminally ill people appear to appreciate the seriousness of their illness, this awareness is usually achieved independently, informally and indirectly. No more than 15 per cent of terminally ill cancer patients are told of their prognosis either by their general practitioner or by a hospital doctor (Cartwright et al, 1973). This contrasts markedly with the experiences of their close relatives. Almost 90 per cent of the close relatives of terminally ill patients are aware that the patient's illness is terminal and most of them are informed of this by a general practitioner or by a hospital doctor. There are several implications of these data, the two most obvious being that fatally ill people and their principal carers often do not share the same information about the illness, and that doctors usually are unwilling to tell patients when they have a disease that will kill them. Perhaps the most serious consequence is that one or more of the familial participants has to cope with the demands of this most stressful period without adequate support.

It is remarkable how little emphasis is placed upon the wishes of the patient. Most people, including doctors, whether they are young or old, ill or well, say they would want to know if they had a fatal illness or that they are glad they do know. Several studies have examined this issue and the results are consistent in showing that more than 70 per cent of all the samples used say they would want to be informed if they had a terminal disease. It is clear that most people say they would want to be informed of the seriousness of their illness, most doctors say that they would want to be told and yet the majority of fatally ill patients are not told. Also, the existence of a real threat to life does not reduce the very high proportion of people who want to know if they have a fatal illness.

In general, learning that one has a fatal illness is followed by a period of disquiet, even grief, although the emotional response may be concealed from others. It is worth noting that some patients do not 'hear' or at least appear not to remember, what they have been told regarding their prognosis. Although it has been proposed that the defence mechanism of denial is a ubiquitous response to learning of a fatal prognosis (Kubler-Ross, 1969), there are other more mundane possibilities. The first is the use of terminology that may have very precise meanings for a professional but which may mean nothing, or something very different, to the patient. To inform a patient of 'malignant lymphoma' or 'secondary metastases' may not constitute communication. Even when the words that are used are understood reasonably well, they may not convey what was intended. For some individuals, the knowledge of their impending death will be extremely distressing; in such cases the person may be quite unable to accept what is plain to everybody else. They may become distraught as their bodies show increasing signs of impending death while they continue to deny that they are dying. Such extreme responses, as a terminal illness progresses, correspond to denial as elucidated by Kubler-Ross (1969). However, it would be inappropriate to regard as denial a person's failure to comprehend or to recall initial statements of his prognosis. Quite apart from the communication problems mentioned above, if a person has no prior suspicions that his condition may be terminal it is probable that he will be unable to accept a fatal diagnosis. It is not that he refuses to accept such information, but he is unable to accept it. It demands a radical revision of a person's view of the world and such a major psychological adjustment takes time. Initially, such news is not disbelieved, but on the other hand, it cannot be fitted into a person's perception of the world: it cannot be accommodated. The revised view of the world will need to be tested, amended and confirmed in the light of further information. The person will seek such information in what people say, how they behave and how his body feels. It is only when the revised view of the world 'fits', in the sense that it is not violated by new observations or new information, that the person is able fully to accommodate the 'truths' that have been offered. An individual who has prior suspicions about the seriousness of his illness has already constructed, at least in part, a view of his world that includes himself as a dying person.

Our aim must be to maintain dignity, to alleviate suffering and to help the person live as fully as possible for as long as he is able: he should be told what he is prepared to hear at a time when he is prepared to listen. The same principle might be kept in mind when dealing with relatives. There are indications that those who are told with care show improved family relationships, less tension and less desperation during their terminal illnesses than those who are not (Gerle et al, 1960). Helping a person towards fuller awareness of, and adjustment to, a fatal prognosis is the beginning of a communication process which is itself an integral part of caring for the terminally ill.

Terminality and dying

The two words terminality and dying are being used to draw a distinction that can have important implications for the way in which fatally ill people are managed and treated. The main implication is that of regarding someone as terminally ill, but nevertheless living and with some valuable life remaining, rather than regarding him as dying with all the negative attitudes this provokes. Once an illness has been diagnosed as terminal we need to regard the patient as living and possibly living more intensely than the rest of us, until he clearly is dying. Terminality, then, begins when a terminal diagnosis is made but dying starts later, usually when death is much closer and when the person is prepared to relinquish his biological life in the absence of valuable, functional life.

Sources of distress

Effective and appropriate care of the fatally ill requires an awareness of potential sources of distress so that distress can be anticipated and thus be avoided or alleviated. Of course, distress is not confined to the patient: effective care and support for those who are close to the patient is merited not only on humanitarian grounds, but also because of the exacerbation of the patient's suffering that can result from the distress of relatives and friends. Table 1 summarizes some of the most common sources of distress for the patient and those who are close to him.

The listing contained in table 1 is by no means exhaustive, but it illustrates a number of points. First, given some capacity for empathy on the part of the survivor(s) there is little that the terminally ill person must endure that the survivor can avoid. This commonality of the sources of distress argues strongly for the need to attend to the welfare of survivors before they become bereaved. Second, it is clear that almost all the potential sources of distress are psychological in nature. Even some of the physical symptoms such as incontinence or smells are distressing because of our values and expectations. Also, pain itself is an experience that is subject to psychological factors rather than a sensation that is elicited by an appropriate stimulus.

Although we cannot examine in detail the physical distress of terminal illness, our discussion would be incomplete without a summary of this. Cartwright et al (1973) and Ward (1974) identified retrospectively the physical symptoms experienced by their samples of terminal cancer patients, 215 and 264 individuals respectively. These data are summarized in table 2.

It is striking that the rank order of symptoms is the same for both samples and a significant proportion of patients in each sample experienced each of the symptoms listed. Other common physical symptoms were breathing difficulties, 52 per cent; coughing, 48 per cent (Ward); and sleeplessness, 17 per cent (Cartwright et al).

Distress and coping

An examination of tables 1 and 2 points to a number of psychological processes that predispose people to react with depression and anxiety during a terminal illness. Current approaches to depression emphasize the role of loss and helplessness as aetiological factors. Loss refers to the real or imagined loss of a valued object, role, activity, relationship, etc. The individual relevance of the concept of loss lies in the individual differences of our value systems. For example, a pe son who highly values physical abilities, physical appearance, etc., is likely to be more at risk for depression as a result of physical debility, tiredness and deterioration in appearance, than someone for whom such attributes are low in his hierarchy of values.

Helplessness describes a state that is characterized by an awareness that one's behaviour is unrelated to the events which impinge upon oneself. When a person is subjected to aversive events whose occurrence, intensity, duration, etc., is quite independent of behaviour, a characteristic state may ensue. This state, which occurs in the majority of subjects tested, is known as learned helplessness. There are individual differences in susceptibility to learned helplessness, but the more aversive the events and the more frequently they are experienced as independent of behaviour the more likely it is to develop. It is a generalized state characterized by apathy, dysphoric mood, psychomotor retardation (i.e. slowness in thought and action), and feelings of hopelessness. Many clinical depressions are explained most fully in terms of the development of helplessness and there is evidence that sudden death is not an uncommon consequence of learned helplessness in laboratory animals. There can be little doubt about the relevance and importance of helplessness to our consideration of the welfare of the terminally ill.

Let us now return to the sources of distress summarized in tables 1 and 2. It is clear that some of these are intrinsically uncontrollable, and others duplicate the procedures that are used in experimental work to induce

Table 1

Common sources of distress

Fatally ill person (P)	Those who love P
Awareness of impending death	Awareness of impending bereavement
Anticipation of loss	Anticipation of loss
Physical sequelae of disease process, e.g. tumours, lesions, nausea, incontinence, breathlessness, unpleasant smells	Empathic concern, aversion, etc.
Frustration and help-lessness as disease progresses	Frustration and help-lessness as disease progresses
Uncertainty about the future welfare of the family	Uncertainty about the future welfare of the family
Anticipation of pain	
Empathic concern	Caring for P, night-sitting, tiredness, etc.
Changes in roles with family, friends, etc.	Changes in roles with family, friends, etc
Changes in abilities as illness progresses	Empathic concern
Changes in appearance as illness progresses	Empathic concern, aversion, etc.
Uncertainties about dying	Empathic concern
Dying	Empathic concern
	Discovery of death, directly or indirectly
	Practicalities, funeral, etc.
	Grief
	Role changes
	Reconstruction of life

Table 2

Symptoms suffered by terminal cancer patients

Symptom	Per cent in sample of Cartwright et al	Per cent in sample of Ward
Pain	87	62
Anorexia	76	61
Vomiting	54	38
Urinary incontinence	38	28
Faecal incontinence	37	20
Bedsores	24	13

helplessness in that they are aversive, uncontrollable and repeated: for instance, urinary incontinence and vomiting. Furthermore, many patients undergo physical investigations and treatments that they do not understand, that they find unpleasant or painful and about which they feel they have little choice other than to accept them passively. It is not surprising to find that depression is commonly encountered in the terminally ill. A significant minority of fatally ill people and their next-of-kin become moderately or severely depressed (about one in five people in each group). Those most at risk are adolescents, young parents with dependents, those who have many physical symptoms and those who experience lengthy hospitalization.

The reciprocal interaction of physical and psychological processes must not be overlooked. We have already considered the depressive role of repeated, unpleasant physical symptoms. However, the interaction also proceeds in the other direction: adverse emotional states such as depression and anxiety augment pain and other physical discomforts. The essential point is that pain is not a simple response to an appropriate physical stimulus such as tissue damage: it is an experience that is compounded of the stimulation and the person's response to that stimulation. The motivational and emotional state of the person acts, as it were, to colour the sensation and to produce the experience we call pain. Without such 'colouring' and evaluation the sensation may be perceived but not experienced as painful.

It is the experience of most who work in terminal care that the relief of anxiety or depression through appropriate support, communication and practical help reduces the pain of patients and, not insignificantly, reduces the need for medication. The point is not that attention to the psychological state of the patient removes the need for relevant medication but that it reduces the dosages that may be required to bring relief. There are many obvious advantages that derive from this, not the least of which is the ability to alleviate pain without resorting to medications that render the patient confused, drowsy or comatose.

Anxiety arises when a future event is appraised as threatening. This appraisal is the evaluation of an event in terms of its harmful implications for the individual, harm being the extent to which continued physical and psychological functioning is endangered. Threat appraisal is a highly subjective process that depends upon the subjective likelihood of an event - that is, how probable the person feels the event to be - and the degree of harm that will result, this again being subjectively assessed. So a terminally ill person is anxious to the extent that the events that he anticipates are both likely and harmful in his own terms: if they are not perceived as likely or harmful then they will not provoke anxiety.

Anxiety is an essentially adaptive emotion, in that it motivates us to initiate behaviours that prevent the anticipated harm being realized. To the extent that a person accepts that he is dying and is unable to reduce or eliminate the harmful consequences of this process, he is liable to remain anxious. An inspection of tables 1 and 2 reminds us that there are many potential types of harm that the fatally ill person is motivated, by anxiety, to alleviate. It is reassuring to note that the intense panic that is such a common feature of clinical anxiety states occurs rarely in terminal illness except, perhaps, in those who continue to deny the imminence of death as the end approaches and those for whom breathing is difficult. However, moderate anxiety is by no means uncommon in the terminally ill. This is not only an extra burden of suffering for the person but it also exacerbates other discomforts including pain.

There are few systematic reports of anxiety in terminal illness but from the data that do exist it is clear that moderate anxiety is experienced by between one-quarter and one-half of patients. The anxiety may be readily discerned in those people who are able to verbalize their fears, and who are given the opportunity to do so, but it may be less obvious in those who communicate less well verbally. However, the physiological and behavioural concomitants of anxiety are good indicators of the presence of unspoken fear. Often it is difficult to distinguish between physiological signs of anxiety such as gastric upset, nausea, diarrhoea, muscular pains, etc., and symptoms of the disease process or side effects of treatment. Nevertheless, the possibility that a patient might be persistently anxious should not be overlooked.

Given the subjective nature of threat appraisal, the causes of an individual's anxiety can be surprisingly idiosyncratic, but there are a few consistencies that may provide some clues. Younger adults expect to be distressed by pain and parting from the people they love, whereas the elderly fear becoming dependent and losing control of bowel and bladder functioning. Hinton (1972) reports that almost two-thirds of his patients who died aged 50 years or less were clearly anxious but this was true of only one-third of those aged 60 years and over. There is a clear and understandable trend for young parents of dependent children to be more anxious than other groups. Perhaps it is not insignificant that younger patients also tend to experience more physical discomfort during their terminal illnesses.

According to Hinton (1963), anxiety is more common in people with a lengthy terminal illness. He found more than 50 per cent of those who had been ill for more than one year to be clearly anxious, but only 20 per cent of those who had been ill for less than three months showed similar levels of anxiety. Although anxiety levels fluctuate during a patient's terminal illness, there is no general trend for anxiety to increase as the person draws closer to death. Some people become more apprehensive as their illnesses progress, but others become more calm during the last stages of their lives.

Some specific experiences of illness may be potent sources of anxiety. Prior episodes of intolerable pain can provoke great anxiety when they are recalled or when their return is anticipated. Difficulties in breathing are commonly associated with anxiety and a tendency to panic. Also, in the context of a mortal illness there are a number of sources of distress that are intrinsically uncontrollable and uncertain, such as the final process of dying, death and the nature of the world in which one's dependent survivors will be living. When anticipated harm remains and the person perceives it as beyond his ability to influence, he becomes liable to the state of helplessness. If this is severe he may become depressed, as we have discussed: if less severe, then he may exhibit the resignation that has been termed 'acceptance' (Kubler-Ross, 1969). If he persists in his attempts to control and influence events that are beyond his reach he is likely to remain anxious and even to become more anxious as he approaches death.

For the fatally ill child under five or six years of age, anxiety takes the form of separation anxiety, loneliness and fears of being abandoned. The young child does not appear to fear death and its implications, but his fears are aroused by those aspects of illness and hospitalization which elicit fear in most ill children who require hospital treatment.

Between the ages of six and ten or eleven years, separation fears persist, but the child is increasingly prone to anxiety over painful treatments and bodily intrusions. Such fears of mutilation and physical harm are intensified in the absence of familiar, trusted adults. Some children in this age group, because of differing prior experiences or more advanced cognitive development, are also aware of the cessation of awareness and bodily functioning consequent upon death.

Although there is some dispute as to whether the child under ten years of age is aware of his impending death at a conceptual level, there is little doubt that many young children perceive that their illness is no ordinary illness. This is a frequent clinical observation and there is a good deal of evidence that it is so whether or not the diagnosis is discussed with the child (Spinetta, 1974). Of course there are many cues that may indicate to the child that something very serious and threatening is happening, quite apart from his numerous tests, treatments and visits to hospital. Most children are finely tuned to detect meaningful and subtle signs in the verbal and non-verbal behaviour of adults: the things that are not talked about, tone of voice, eye contact, posture, etc. Also, there are many cues that the child would find it hard to overlook: whispered conversations, unusually frequent and intense bodily contact, unusual generosity and freedom of choice with regard to presents and treats, and so on.

Parents and others usually begin to grieve for the fatally ill child soon after they accept the prognosis. Their ability to cope with this grief is an important determinant of their effectiveness in supporting the child. Since familiar adults and siblings are likely to be the child's greatest potential source of comfort and reassurance, it is important that time and attention is devoted to these significant others for the sake of the child's welfare. There are indications of a high incidence of psychological difficulties in family members, particularly siblings, during the terminal illness of a child. Clearly parents, who are themselves struggling with their own emotions, may have difficulty sustaining the other children in the family, let alone in providing comfort and reassurance to the one who is ill.

Adolescents and some younger children will be aware of the finality of death. Although dependent upon adults in a functional sense, they may perceive themselves as having important roles to play in the welfare of others and thus be subject to fears for the well-being of their survivors in much the same way as adults with dependents. The very young child may endure a terminal illness with striking calmness and acceptance of his lot, provided that his separation fears are allayed, but once he is past the age of six or seven years he becomes prone to a wide range of fears that exceed those of his 'normally ill' counterpart with severe, chronic, but non-fatal illness. Although children may be reluctant to express their fears, or may express them unclearly and indirectly, they should be anticipated in all aspects of care.

We have examined the range of potential sources of distress in terminal illness and the most common types of distress that result from these. Pain, anxiety and depression are sufficiently frequent and severe to merit attention when services are being planned and delivered. However, a majority of fatally ill people do not become severely anxious, deeply depressed or suffer from unrelieved pain. This does not minimize the awful suffering of the large minority or the pressing need for improvements in care to which this suffering testifies. It indicates only that, with whatever help they receive, most people who endure a terminal illness cope reasonably well, keeping their levels of distress within limits that are acceptable to themselves and to those who care for them.

The responses of people who are faced with impending death show sufficient uniformity to enable observers to write of stages, phases and patterns of coping (e.g. Kubler-Ross, 1969; Falek and Britton, 1974). Quite apart from doubts about the uniformity and progressive nature of stages of coping in terminal illness (e.g. Schulz and Aderman, 1974), it cannot be assumed that any particular individual NEEDS to negotiate these stages in order to cope most effectively with his impending death. The emotional responses and their dependent behaviours are indicators of the difficulties, and triumphs, experienced by people in their attempts to cope. The absence of a specific emotion does not mean that the person has omitted a necessary stage of the 'normal' coping pattern and that this omission detracts from his adjustment. Provided we do not equate typical with ideal or necessary, an awareness of the emotional stages or phases that are commonly encountered in terminal patients can help us to understand the problems they face, to provide the types of help and support that might be beneficial and to improve our ability to cope with the emotions that their behaviours arouse in relatives and in ourselves.

However, there are a number of general points that can be made about a stage model of terminal illness. The responses delineated, including denial, anger, bargaining, depression and acceptance (Kubler-Ross, 1969), are not specific to people who are facing death; they have been observed in many other stressful situations that involve loss and uncontrollable harm, such as bereavement, amputation and imprisonment. The generality evidenced by these observations does not confirm the progression of the stage model: it highlights the normality of disbelief, anger, sadness, etc., in the face of irretrievable and severe loss.

Often it is difficult to decide which stage or phase a person is in. Without reasonable certainty in the identification of stages, the predictive value of a stage model is severely impaired. This predictive aspect of the model is also reduced if the stages are not ubiquitous and if they are not successive. Clinical observation suggests that the emotion displayed by a person is responsive to many internal and external events. Perhaps all that can be said with any certainty is that some responses, when they occur, are likely to predominate earlier in a terminal illness, for example denial, and some are more likely to appear later, for example depression and acceptance.

We must take care not to lose sight of the individual in anticipating responses to a terminal illness. The fatally ill person brings with him his own particular view of himself, his family, his future, doctors, death, etc. The importance of individual differences during the terminal phase of life is well illustrated by the work of Kastenbaum and Weisman (1972). They found that their patients could be divided into two broad groups, both of which were aware of the imminence of death but which differed markedly in their behavioural styles. One group gradually withdrew from their usual activities and social contacts, remaining inactive until their final illness. The other group was characterized by involvement: patients in this group remained busily engaged in everyday activities until death occurred as an interruption in their living.

Dying

The relationship between a patient's reactions to a terminal illness and his dying is not only that these are the psychological context within which the final process occurs, but also there are increasing indications that they influence the timing of death (see Achterberg and Lawlis, 1977). Whereas blood chemistries reflect on-going or current disease status, psychological factors are predictive of subsequent disease status and longevity. Poorer prognosis and shorter survival occurs in patients who, typically, show great dependence upon others, who deny the severity of their conditions, who have a history of poor social relationships and who do not have access to, or do not utilize, supportive social relationships during their illnesses. These patients tend to become more withdrawn, pessimistic and depressed as their illness progresses. Longer survival is associated with patients who maintain good personal and social relationships in the context of an existing network of such relationships. They can be assertive without hostility, asking for and receiving much medical and emotional support. They may be concerned about dying alone and seek to deter others from withdrawing from them without their needs being met. These patients also experience less pain, or at least complain less about pain and discomfort.

Dying is a process rather than an event that occurs at one point in time. This final process that constitutes the transition from life to death is usually of short duration, a matter of hours or days. For the vast majority of people it is not dramatic. Most people, both ill and well, express a desire to die peacefully or to die in their sleep. There is little doubt that this wish is fulfilled in most cases. Although there are a few people for whom pain or breathlessness may increase near the end, most slip knowingly or unawares into the unconsciousness that continues until their dying is finished.

After a terminal illness lasting some months, most patients are tired and wearied by their experiences. During his last days, apart from having his needs tended, a patient may wish to be alone or to avoid news and problems of the 'outside world'. He may well become less talkative and pre-fer shorter visits. Communication tends to shift increas-ingly towards the non-verbal. In terms of interaction he may want little more than somebody to sit with him in silence, perhaps holding his hand. It is clear from those who wish to talk briefly in their last hours of life that there is an experience of 'distance' from life. As Saunders (1978) so aptly puts it, 'They were not frightened nor unwilling to go, for by then they were too far away to want to come back. They were conscious of leaving weakness and exhaustion rather than life and its activities. They rarely had any pain but felt intensely weary. They wanted to say good-bye to those they loved but were not torn with longing to stay with them'.

Euthanasia

Euthanasia, meaning a gentle and easy death and the act of bringing this about, has been a source of discussion and controversy for many years. The level of current interest is evidenced by the large number of recent publications on the topic in the professional literature and the increasing support of the public for such organizations as the Volun-tary Euthanasia Society in the UK and the Euthanasia Educa-tion Council in the USA.

The public support for euthanasia is probably based upon an expectation that death will come as a result of a lengthy illness, an illness that may well be prolonged unduly by the application of current medical knowledge and techniques. It is based upon fears of the physical and psychological in-competence, dependence, indignity and pain that may result from a chronic or terminal illness. Even those professionals who oppose euthanasia on ethical, religious or practical grounds readily concede that such fears are not unjustified for many people. We have already examined the potential distress of terminal illness but, for many people, support for euthanasia is prompted by thoughts of an unwanted, useless existence where biological life is maintained artificially and against their wishes in a hospital, nursing home or geriatric ward. Sadly, such thoughts are all too often reinforced by cases that Saunders (1977) rightly describes as 'truly horrendous'. As a society we cannot escape the reality that far too many elderly people end their days in loneliness, isolation and degradation. Even when the physical care provided is good, the psychological distress can be great. The prima facie case for euthanasia appears to be strong.

The many logical, philosophical and ethical arguments relating to the legalization of voluntary euthanasia, both active and passive, have been well stated several times (e.g. Rachels, 1975; Foot, 1978), and space precludes their consideration here. However, these arguments frequently take little account of relevant practical and psychological issues. In drawing up the necessary guidelines for the legalization of voluntary euthanasia there are major problems in guarding against error and potential abuse, both by relatives and professionals. Nevertheless, many of these problems could be surmounted by the use and recognition of the Living Will. This document, as distributed by the Euthanasia Educational Council, is signed and witnessed when the person is in good health. Its aim is to avoid an existence in dependence, deterioration, indignity and hopeless pain.

Doctors spend their lives preserving the lives of others and alleviating their suffering. It can be argued that, in recent years, the pendulum has swung too far in the direction of the maintenance of life at the expense of the relief of distress, but the activities of doctors make demands upon their energies and their personal time that few other professions would tolerate. This degree of commitment is consistent with, and continually reinforces, a value system that places a very high priority upon the preservation of life and actions that serve this end. For an individual in whom such values relate closely to his self-concept, the active termination of a patient's life may be damaging to his self-regard and to his concept of his own worth as a person. Although there is little difference between active and passive euthanasia on moral and logical grounds, for an individual doctor the difference may be vast and unbridgeable in terms of his own psychology. It would be quite unjustifiable to place such men in a position where society expected them to implement active euthanasia.

From the patient's point of view, the availability of euthanasia has a wider potential than the avoidance of further suffering. People who are given control over aversive and painful stimulation, by having the facility to terminate, reduce or avoid it in some way, are better able to cope with the experience. Even though the available control is rarely exercised, the aversive stimulation is better tolerated and provokes less distress. Provided that the patient is quite sure that his life can be terminated when he wishes, and only when he wishes, he is likely to cope better with the effects of his illness or condition and to be less distressed by them.

To allow a patient to die in order to release him from hopelessness and irreducible suffering, while continuing to treat his current distress, is thoroughly compatible with the humanitarian principle of care. Whether or not one wishes to describe this as passive, voluntary euthanasia is a matter of personal choice. There are grounds for a more widespread recognition of this compatibility and for more weight to be given to the wishes of patients and their families. Of course, the same grounds demand that more effort, time and resources should be devoted to improving the quality of care that is offered. All such improvements weaken the case for regarding death as a desirable release from suffering, as a release that is needed so frequently that its use should be regularized. In the long term, and certainly in the shorter term, there are likely to be some people for whom death is the preferred option. It is a problem that will become more acute as our society continues to age and as the life-preserving techniques of medicine continue to develop.

Bereavement is a state characterized by loss. The main focus of interest is upon the loss occasioned by the death of a significant person but people are bereaved by other losses such as loss of role, loss of status, separation and amputation. The state of loss serves as the stimulus for the bereavement response, a response that is manifested culturally and individually. The cultural response constitutes mourning and is a pattern of behaviour that is learned from and supported by one's immediate culture as appropriate following bereavement. Grief is the individual response and is the main area of concern for researchers and clinicians alike. In that grief typically follows a reasonably consistent course over time, ending ultimately in its resolution, it can be regarded as an individual process that occurs in response to individual loss.

The nature of grief

Although the major features of grief are known to most of us either intuitively or through personal experience, the chief findings of the many descriptive studies can be summarized broadly as follows:

* grief is a complex but stereotyped response pattern that includes such physical and psychological 'symptoms' as withdrawal, fatigue, sleep disturbance, anxiety and loss of appetite;
* it is elicited by a rather well-defined stimulus situation, namely the real or imagined loss of a valued object or role, and it is resolved when new object relations are established;
* it is a ubiquitous phenomenon among human beings and appears in other social species, especially higher primates;
* it is an extremely stressful response both physically and psychologically, but grief-related behaviour is often antithetical to the establishment of new object relations and hence to the alleviation of the stress. For example, fatigue and withdrawal make it much more difficult for the bereaved person to develop new roles and new personal relationships in place of those lost through bereavement.

The complexity and stress of grief is readily appreciated when the number and nature of its components are considered. Hinton's (1972) description of grief adumbrates the most commonly observed characteristics: shock, denial, anxiety, depression, guilt, anger and a wide variety of somatic signs of anxiety. Other components include searching behaviour, suicidal thoughts, idealization of the lost person, panic, a heightened vulnerability to physical illness and to psychological disorders.

The nature of grief as a process is emphasized by the designation of stages by many observers and authors. Although there is a sequential character to the process it would be incorrect to anticipate an orderly progression through the stages in all people. As with the notion of stages in dying that was discussed earlier, the component responses of the various stages overlap and merge into one another. Also, there are frequent 'regressions' to earlier stages. Again, it is better to think in terms of components, some of which will predominate earlier in the process and others that will predominate later. In general, three stages or phases have been delineated and labelled according to inclination: perhaps the best descriptive labels are shock, despair and recovery.

Initially there may be a period of numbness and detachment depending, to some extent, on the unexpectedness of the news of the death. During this immediate response the person may appear stoical and calm. Normal routines may be maintained especially where domestic or other factors structure the situation. Alternatively, the person may appear dazed and quite unable to comprehend the reality of the news; he may be unresponsive to his environment and in need of care and support during this period. Whatever the specific initial reaction in a particular instance, it can last from a few minutes to two weeks or so, with the stoical reaction being the more likely to persist longer. The bereaved person is less able than the terminally ill to deny successfully the reality of the situation: sooner or later, and in many different ways, powerful and pointed signs of the reality of loss occur, such as the empty place at table, the empty bed or chair, the funeral or the silent house when friends and relatives depart. As with the news of terminal diagnosis, people need time to assimilate and to accommodate to a new state of the world. Whether the period of shock and disbelief is long or short, a sense of unreality or even disbelief is likely to return periodically for several months.

As awareness of the loss develops the person may express anger at himself, at staff or at God for not preventing the death. Whether or not anger is present, the phase of acute grieving or despair is the most painful. Lindemann (1944), in his pioneering study of bereavement, observed the following 'symptoms' as common to all individuals suffering acute grief: somatic distress lasting between 20 minutes and one hour at a time, feelings of tightness in the throat, choking with shortness of breath, muscular weakness and intense subjective distress described as tension or psychological pain. This specific response, which appears to be unique to bereavement, occurs against a background of stress, anxiety and sadness or depression, together with the somatic concomitants of these emotions.

Behaviourally, the grieving person may be unable to
maintain goal-directed activity, appearing disorganized and
unable to make plans. He may be restless, moving about in
an aimless fashion and constantly searching for something to
do. He may find himself going, unwittingly, to the places
where the dead person might be found if he were alive. A
preoccupation with the lost person creates a perceptual set
that leads to misinterpretations of ambiguous sights and
sounds as indicative of his being alive. Some grieving
people report seeing the dead person with a clarity that
goes beyond illusion and misperception. Such experiences can
occur long after the phase of acute grieving is past.
Obviously, the physical and psychological demands of this
period are heavy and it is not surprising that irritability
is common, especially when the person is eating and sleeping
poorly. Anger, frustration and resentment may be directed
at friends and neighbours irrespective of merit. Such feelings may also be directed against the dead person for abandoning the survivor.

The intense anguish of the despair phase can be unremit-
ting, rising to peaks of distress with thoughts of the loved
one who has died. Most bereaved people seem unable to prevent themselves from thinking and talking about the one who
has died even though this usually exacerbates their distress. Whether this is conceptualized as 'grief-work' or as
repeated exposure leading to habituation, it appears to be
necessary to recovery from grief. A reduction in the frequency and intensity of periods of peak distress may be the
first sign that the process of recovery is beginning. Although estimates vary, the acute despair phase of grief
typically lasts for three to ten weeks.

The process of recovery from grief is a process of
reconstruction. Although some aspects of the person's
private and public 'self' may survive bereavement relatively
unchanged, it is necessary to develop new roles, new behaviours and new relationships with others. Whatever else may
or may not be changed by bereavement, the survivor must live
without one important and potentially crucial personal relationship that had existed previously: the loss of this
relationship is the loss of the psychological and practical
advantages, and disadvantages, that it conferred. Socially,
the survivor is now a widow or a widower rather than one
of a married couple: he is now a boy without a father, or
she is now a mother without a child, etc. Apart from the
direct, personal impact of such changes, they also influence
the way survivors are viewed and treated socially. The bereaved person has to develop a new private and public self
that enables him to live in a changed world.

Although a reduction in the frequency and intensity of
periods of extreme distress may herald the process of
recovery, it cannot begin in earnest until the person has
periods in which he is not overwhelmed with despair nor
preoccupied with thoughts of the one who has died. Many
bereaved people recall with clarity the moment when they

realized that they had not been preoccupied with their loss: when, for a brief period at least, their thoughts had been directed elsewhere and their emotions had been less negative, even positive. These moments of 'spontaneous forgetting', together with improvements in sleeping and appetite, provide the person with some opportunity to reconstrue and to reconstruct himself and his future. With less exhaustion and a lightening of mood, decisions and actions become more feasible and the person can begin the active process of reviving previous relationships and activities, perhaps in a modified form, and of developing new ones. This period of active readjustment may never be complete, especially in the elderly, but it usually lasts for between six and 18 months after the phase of acute grief and despair.

Determinants of grief
Strictly speaking, it is inaccurate to talk of determinants of grief for the available data do not allow us to identify the causative factors that lead to variations in the response to bereavement. However, it makes intuitive sense to talk of determinants and is in keeping with other literature on the topic. Parkes (1972) groups the factors of potential importance according to their temporal relationship to the event of death, that is, antecedent, concurrent and subsequent determinants. Among antecedent factors, the most influential appear to be life stresses prior to bereavement, relationship with the deceased and mode of death. On the whole, an atypical grief response with associated psychological problems is more likely when bereavement occurs as one of a series of life crises, when the death is sudden, unanticipated and untimely, and when the relationship with the deceased had been one of strong attachment, reliance or ambivalence.

A number of demographic variables (concurrent) relate to the nature of grief. In particular, being young, female and married to the deceased increases the likelihood of problems arising after bereavement. Of course, these factors are not unrelated to such antecedent factors as strong attachment, reliance and untimely death. Other concurrent factors with adverse implications are susceptibility to grief, as evidenced by previous episodes of depression, an inability to express emotions, lower socio-economic status and the absence of a genuine religious faith.

The presence of religious faith might be placed more appropriately with subsequent determinants, for its role is likely to be one of supporting the bereaved person during the stressful period of grief. Also, someone with an active belief system probably will be associated with a supportive social group, and there is little doubt that a network of supportive social relationships is the most advantageous of the subsequent determinants. Other subsequent factors that have positive implications are the absence of secondary stresses during the period of grief and the development of new life opportunities at work and in interpersonal relationships, for instance. Again, these are more probable when a good network of supportive social relationships exists. It is worth recalling our earlier conclusion about the value of such relationships in a person's adjustment to impending death.

Among the wide range of factors that have implications for a person's reaction to bereavement, there is most controversy about the importance of anticipatory grief. As the term implies, this refers to grief that occurs in anticipation of an expected death, particularly the death of a child or a spouse. Overall, it can be concluded that younger widows experience more intense grief, with associated problems, than those aged 46 years or over. Sudden death exacerbates the severity of the grief response for young widows but not for the middle-aged or the elderly. For the latter two groups there appears to be a small effect in the opposite direction: that is, some symptoms of grief, especially irritability, are greater after a prolonged illness prior to death. It should be noted that the potentially beneficial effects of anticipatory grief are not confined to conjugal bereavement but also mitigate the response to other losses, such as that of a child. Also, it seems possible that there is an optimum period for the anticipation of death, perhaps up to six months, after which the lengthy duration of illness may increase stress and exhaustion and increase the likelihood of adverse reactions in subsequent grief.

Illness and death after bereavement

There are clear data that reveal an elevated mortality risk after bereavement. At all ages, bereaved persons experience a higher risk of dying than married people of corresponding sex and age. The increase in risk is greater for bereaved males than females, and for both sexes, the increase is greater at younger ages.

The elevated risk of death is concentrated particularly in the first six months after bereavement especially for widowers, with a further rise in the second year for widows. The predominant causes of death are coronary thrombosis and other arterio-sclerotic or degenerative heart diseases. Most of these causes can be seen as a result of continued stress and a lack of self-care. In general, when the data from replicated studies in the UK and the USA are taken together, the risk of dying is at least doubled for widows and widowers at all ages for a great variety of diseases.

Having briefly examined the possible psychological and physical consequences of bereavement, and having considered relevant predictive factors, it is important to remember that we are talking only of probabilities. A person may be at great risk of problems following bereavement, in the statistical sense, and yet survive the experience well. Another person with only favourable indicators may suffer badly and experience severe physical or psychological problems.

The vast majority of bereaved people, with a little help from their friends, cope well with the experience and reconstruct lives that are worth while in their own terms. There are no persuasive grounds for considering the provision of professional services for the bereaved. The most useful strategy is to maintain some form of non-intrusive follow-up after bereavement with ready access to an informal support group if this should be necessary. The bereaved need somebody who will listen when they want to talk, somebody who will not try to push them into things before they are ready: somebody who will support them emotionally and practically when appropriate and just by showing that they care. This demands an informal response rather than a professional one. However, professional care and concern should not end with the death of a patient: the newly bereaved person still has a long way to go and every effort should be made to ensure that they will have access to whatever social support may be needed.

References

Achterberg, J. and Lawlis, G.F. (1977)
Psychological factors and blood chemistries as disease outcome predictors for cancer patients. Multivariate Experimental Clinical Research, 3, 107-122.

Cartwright, A., Hockey, L. and Anderson, J.L. (1973)
Life Before Death. London: Routledge & Kegan Paul.

Falek, A. and Britton, S. (1974)
Phases in coping: the hypothesis and its implications. Social Biology, 21, 1-7.

Foot, P. (1978)
Euthanasia. In E. McMullin (ed.), Death and Decision. Boulder, Colo.: Westview Press.

Gerle, B., Lunden, G. and Sandblow, P. (1960)
The patient with inoperable cancer from the psychiatric and social standpoints. Cancer, 13, 1206-1211.

Hinton, J.M. (1963)
The physical and mental distress of the dying. Quarterly Journal of Medicine, 32, 1-21.

Hinton, J.M. (1972)
Dying. Harmondsworth: Penguin.

Kastenbaum, R. and Weisman, A.D. (1972)
The psychological autopsy as a research procedure in gerontology. In D.P. Kent, R. Kastenbaum and S. Sherwood (eds), Research Planning and Action for the Elderly. New York: Behavioral Publications.

Kubler-Ross, E. (1969)
On Death and Dying. London: Tavistock.

Lindemann, E. (1944)
Symptomatology and management of acute grief. American Journal of Psychiatry, 101, 141-148.

Office of Population Censuses and Surveys (1979)
Mortality Statistics. London: HMSO.

Parkes, C.M. (1972)
Bereavement. London: Tavistock.

Rachels, J. (1975)
Active and passive euthanasia. New England Journal of Medicine, 292, 78-80.

Saunders, C. (1977)
Dying they live. In H. Feifel (ed.), New Meanings of Death. New York: McGraw-Hill.

Saunders, C. (1978)
Care of the dying. In V. Carver and P. Liddiard (eds), An Ageing Population. Sevenoaks: The Open University.

Schulz, R. and Aderman, D. (1974)
Clinical research and the stages of dying. Omega, 5, 137-143.

Spinetta, J.J. (1974)
The dying child's awareness of death. Psychological Bulletin, 81, 256-260.

Ward, A.W.M. (1974)
Telling the patient. Journal of the Royal College of General Practitioners, 24, 465-468.

Questions

1. How has the pattern of dying changed in the UK since the turn of the century? What has caused these changes and what are their consequences?
2. Who should be informed of a patient's fatal prognosis? Give reasons for your answer.
3. Summarize the most common sources of distress of the terminally ill and their families: what are the implications of these?
4. Why do terminally ill people become depressed and how large a problem is this?
5. How common is anxiety in terminal illness and why does it arise?
6. What psychological problems might arise for a fatally ill six-year-old child and his family? What steps could be taken to mitigate these problems?
7. Why should there be growing public support for the legalization of voluntary euthanasia and why is this not reflected in professional attitudes?
8. What is the bereavement response and what causes it?
9. What factors are important in influencing the nature of grief?
10. Construct a stereotypic, but detailed, character sketch of the person most likely to cope badly with a terminal illness: do the same for the person most likely to cope well. Justify your answer.
11. How would you respond to a 40-year-old dentist, with two children, who is suffering with terminal cancer, when he asks you 'What will it be like?' What points would you hope to cover in this and subsequent conversations, and why do you consider these important?

Annotated reading

General
Kastenbaum, R.J. (1977) Death, Society and Human Experience. St Louis, Mo.: Mosby.

Written by a psychologist, but for a general readership, this book provides broad coverage of the psychological and social aspects of death at a level that is readily understood, without being unduly simplistic. Relevant data are cited together with many illustrative examples. A good deal of space is given to concepts of death, from childhood to old age, and there are sections on bereavement and suicide. A few exercises for students are also included.

Terminal illness and dying

Hinton, J. (1972) Dying. Harmondsworth: Penguin.

This is an eminently readable book by a psychiatrist with much practical experience of caring for the terminally ill and the dying. This experience enables Hinton to write with some authority on practical considerations and to place research findings in perspective. Relevant data are cited appropriately throughout the text and the book contains a good deal of useful information. The best sections are upon dying and the care of the dying and there is a concluding section on bereavement.

Doyle, D. (ed.) (1979) Terminal Care. Edinburgh: Churchill-Livingstone.

This is a collection of papers arising from a multi-disciplinary conference. Accordingly, it provides useful reading for a wide range of health-care professionals including nurses, social workers and ministers of religion. In addition to examining the roles of different professions there are chapters on grief, domiciliary care and primary care.

Euthanasia

Glover, J. (1977) Causing Death and Saving Lives. Harmondsworth: Penguin.

This is a clear and concise consideration of the ethical and practical problems associated with most aspects of taking life, from abortion to euthanasia. For those who want a brief but careful consideration of euthanasia and those who are seeking to place euthanasia in a wider context, this is a most valuable book.

Russell, R.O. (1977) Freedom to Die. New York: Human Sciences Press.

Although the author examines arguments for and against the legalization of voluntary euthanasia, the tone of the volume is clearly in favour of this. The value of the book lies in its uncomplicated style, broad coverage and extensive appendices. In addition to examining the relevant arguments, the author traces the development of public awareness of euthanasia and attempts that have been made to promote the practice. The appendices include an example of the Living Will and various legislative proposals and bills that have been proposed in the UK and USA.

Bereavement

Parkes, C.M. (1972) Bereavement. London: Tavistock. This volume appeared in Pelican Books in 1975 and, although it is now beginning to age, it is probably the best single source of information on bereavement. The reader is taken progressively through the response to bereavement in its many manifestations and is provided with a clear account of grief, the factors that influence this and the nature of recovery. Illustrative examples and research findings are used throughout the text and the book concludes with a substantial section on helping the bereaved.

Smith, K. (1978) Helping the Bereaved. London: Duckworth. This is a short and unpretentious book aimed at a general readership. It is valuable for its reliance on the statements of bereaved people to convey powerfully the experience of grief and the range of emotions and events that commonly occur. The examples help one more accurately to empathize with the bereaved.

9

The Family
Neil Frude

Opening remarks
DAVID GRIFFITHS

Clinicians, especially general practitioners and other doctors working in the community, will scarcely need to be reminded of the experience of the family as a critical part of the individual's social environment. Neil Frude's review of the psychological aspects of family life is both scholarly and impressively readable. He reminds us that the interest of the psychologist has changed from a concern with the individual to a focus on human relationships. The family provides the individual with the most lasting, intense and influential relationships which he is likely to experience. Family relationships can, however, be both a help and a hindrance. On the one hand, clinicians will be particularly interested in the observation that 'some problems which were initially identified as belonging to the individual adult or child are now seen, more appropriately, as problems of the family system'. On the other hand, sick and disabled individuals are often able to survive outside institutions only because of the support and care provided by their families. The family has considerable potential as a vehicle for therapy. For instance, clinical psychologists working with the mentally handicapped often involve parents as assessors and trainers of both sub-normal children and adults. Their aim, in general terms, is to liberate the therapeutic potential which is present in the family but which often requires guidance if it is to be practically useful.

This chapter, in common with many others in the book, also attempts to summarize the evidence on critical issues of obvious clinical relevance. For example, Frude's review suggests that schizophrenia is not caused by experiences within the family; at the same time, the behaviour of significant family members can have a substantial effect on prognosis and outcome after discharge from hospital. Depression is another condition whose aetiology and outcome are influenced by family relationships. The loss which increases the individual's vulnerability to depression often involves incidents such as death, conflict or departures which arise within the family; at the same time, support from a spouse or other family member can have important effects on both vulnerability and outcome. In addition to the discussion of specific clinical conditions, the review which follows contains a great deal on issues which will help to sensitize trainees and inform the more experienced. The chapter includes a consideration of psychological aspects of marital breakdown, single-parent families, sexuality, the elderly and many other issues whose relevance to doctors hardly needs to be emphasized.

Psychology and the family
NEIL FRUDE

The psychologist may regard the family as a background against which to view the individual, asking perhaps how the parents influence the development of a child or how families of alcoholics may help the individual to overcome his or her difficulties, or alternatively the family itself may be the unit of study. The family is a small group and we can observe the patterns of communication within it, the process of mutual decision making, and so forth. It is a system, with individuals as sub-units or elements within. Typically, psychologists have focussed their interests on the biological and social nature of the individual, but they are now becoming increasingly concerned not only with individuals or even 'individuals in relationships' but with the relationships themselves.

Clinical and educational psychologists, for example, are increasingly working within the family context and some problems which were initially identified as 'belonging' to the individual adult or child are now seen, more appropriately, as problems of the 'family system'. Also, psychologists working, for example, with handicapped children have come to recognize that the powerful influence and involvement of the parents means that they can be harnessed as highly potent sources of training, and such clinicians are increasingly using these strategies to establish a far more effective educational programme than they themselves could possibly provide. But the needs of parents, and the stresses which such a high level of involvement may place upon them, are also recognized and so the psychologists may well regard themselves as involved with the problems of the family as a whole.

So there are vital problems in the area and there are some impressive results. Let us look at some of these, choosing some of those areas which relate to major social problems and some innovations which suggest methods for their alleviation.

Family planning

Current surveys of the plans of young married couples for families have shown a high level of conscious control and active planning, a reflection of the wide availability of highly effective contraceptive techniques. The number and spacing of children are controlled with varying degrees of skill and success. The number of couples who opt for voluntary childlessness seems to be increasing. In about half of such cases the couple have planned from the start not to have children, while the other half postpone pregnancy and eventually decide to remain childless.

Contraceptive use varies greatly. Despite the numerous methods available, none is perfect, for various reasons. Some men find that the sheath reduces pleasurable sensation, the pill may have side effects on health or mood, and a number of women find methods such as the cap bothersome and distasteful. The coil may involve a painful initial fitting and an extensive gynaecological involvement which some find embarrassing and disturbing. Sterilization or vasectomy may be advisable for the older and highly stable couple, but a number of people who have undergone such surgery later change their partners. They may then request reversal surgery and in many cases successful reversal will not be possible. The solution to the contraception problem is thus by no means always simple and family planning counselling, and the tailoring of recommendations to the particular needs and life stage of the couple, is a task requiring considerable skill and insight as well as knowledge of the technical features of the particular methods.

Different couples have different 'ideal family structures', often specifying not only the number of children but also their spacing and sex. There is still some preference, overall, for boys and current research makes it likely that in the near future couples will be able, with some accuracy, to determine the sex of their baby. Many will prefer to 'leave it to nature' but others will choose one option or the other. This is likely to result in a relative excess of boys, with longer-term social results which can only be guessed.

Reactions to pregnancy range from unqualified delight to profound despair. The option of abortion is now increasingly available. Reactions to this also vary from relief to regret and while, overall, the evidence is that there are rarely long-term negative consequences for the women, several studies have suggested the need for pre- and for post-termination counselling. A number of women miscarry, some repeatedly, and again this can be a very stressful experience requiring skilled intervention.

Birth and early interaction

The process of birth is biological, but the importance of social variables is also apparent. The pregnant woman may anticipate the sex and looks of her baby, but initial acceptance is by no means inevitable. Premature babies, for example, may look very unlike the baby-food advertisements which may have conditioned the mothers' expectations.

Fathers are now often present at the delivery and there is evidence that this helps the woman in the birth process itself and also helps the couple to feel that the baby is part of both of them. The demands which the baby makes may not have been fully anticipated and the initial period with the infant may call for a difficult process of adaptation and adjustment, just as the first period of the couple living together calls for give and take and the setting-up of new norms of interaction.

Not all babies are the same: they differ in their activity level, their crying and their patterns of sleep and wakefulness. Some are not easy to care for, and may be unresponsive and difficult to soothe. Baby-care makes great demands and the mother may be totally unprepared for the energy and level of skill required. Surveys show that many of them find the period of early childhood highly stressful. They may be tired and feel inadequate and, at times, very angry. If they fail to understand and control the baby their treatment of him may be poor and, sometimes, harsh.

The level of medical care in pregnancy and around the time of the birth may be high, but many mothers then feel isolated with the baby, unsure about such matters as feeding, toileting and weaning.

In assuming that a 'mother's instinct' will aid her in these tasks we may have seriously under-estimated the extent to which, in earlier times, the informal training opportunities offered to the young girl by larger family units and the close neighbourhood community helped her in her own parenting.

The developing child

In the early years interactions with parents form the major social background for the child. There is a good deal of informal teaching and the child learns by example. Guidance and discipline help the infant to establish a set of internal rules and encouragement and praise help to develop skills and intellectual abilities. Overhearing conversations between adults enables the child to learn about the structure of language and conversation and the rules of social interaction. Watching the parents' interactions and reactions enables children to develop their own emotional repertoire and social skills, and they will experiment and consciously imitate the behaviour of their parents. The child may identify strongly with a particular parent. Games of pretence enable youngsters to practise complex tasks and build a repertoire of interactive styles, and in collaboration with other young children they may rehearse a number of roles. In both competitive and co-operative play social interaction patterns are devised and perfected, children learn about rule-following and discover their strengths and weaknesses relative to their peers.

Different parents treat their children differently, and there are many styles of parenting. Some parents are warm and affectionate, others are more distant, and some are openly hostile. Some give the child a lot of freedom and exercise little control while others are very restrictive. Not surprisingly, the children reared in such atmospheres develop somewhat differently. The children of highly restrictive parents tend to be well-mannered but lack independence, the children of warm parents come to have a confident high regard for themselves, and the children of hostile parents tend to be aggressive. There are various ways in which such findings can be explained. Do the aggressive children of hostile parents, for example, behave in that way because they are reacting against the pressures which their parents put on them, are they simply imitating the behaviour of the adults around them and picking up their interactive styles, or is there perhaps some hereditary biological component which makes both parents and children hostile?

Probably, as in so many cases of such overall correlations, there is a combination of such factors. It is also possible, of course, that hostility originating in the children themselves causes a parental reaction. We must be wary of the conclusion that children simply respond to the atmosphere of their home. They also help to create that atmosphere and the relationship between parents' behaviour and the child's behaviour is a fully interactive one. Children are not shapeless psychological forms capable of being moulded totally in response to their social environment, but have dispositions and levels of potential of their own which they bring into the family.

Children have certain psychological needs which the family should be able to provide. They need a certain stability, they need guidance and a set of rules to follow and the feeling needs to be conveyed to them that they are 'prized' by their parents. In the traditional system with two parents there may be a certain safeguard for the constant provision of these needs by one or other of the parents, and for the prevention of total lack of interest or of rejection. But if the natural family with two parents is ideal in many ways as an arrangement in which to provide for the child's development, this is not to say that the child's best interests cannot also be met in alternative contexts. Most children in single-parent households fare well and develop happily. For the child living apart from the natural parents adoption seems a better option than does fostering (though long-term fostering seems to share many of the positive features of adoption) and fostering seems to be better for the child than a continued stay in an institution. Even this context, however, can provide reasonably well for the child's needs if there is stability, a high level of staffing, high intimacy between staff and children and the provision of high levels of verbal and other types of stimulation.

The family and stress

Just as the family is a principal source of a person's happiness and well-being, it can also be the most powerful source of stress. Research has now been done to try to establish inventories of the life stresses which people experience and in even a cursory glance through such a list it is difficult not to be struck by the extent to which the relationships within the family are bound up with personal change. Some of these events, like the birth of a handicapped child or the death of a child, happen to only a few people, but others, such as the older child leaving home, marital conflict, sexual problems, and the death of a parent happen to many or most. Stress precipitated by such life events has been shown to have a marked effect on both physical and mental health, and if illness is the result then this in turn will provide added hardship.

It is not only particular events which cause stress. The constant presence of ill-health, handicap or marital conflict can similarly take its toll over the years. On the other hand, the stability and comfort of the family setting and the constant presence of others seems to provide much that is beneficial. Marriage reduces the risk of alcoholism, suicide and many forms of psychological ill-health, and interviews with separated and widowed people reveal the elements which they feel they are now missing in their lives, and which in turn may help to explain why living in relative isolation tends to be associated with a greater risk of experiencing psychological problems. As well as providing the opportunity to discuss problems and providing stability, the presence of a spouse reduces loneliness. It also facilitates discussion of a variety of issues and so enables the partners to forge a consensus view of the world: it provides extra interest and social contact, the opportunity to give love and express concern, and provides constant feedback to the individuals about themselves, their value and their role. Practical tasks may be shared and the person may be aware of being prized by the other. This then fosters the sense of self-worth which has been found to be very important for overall well-being.

Of course, not all marital relationships are good and some may lead to far greater problems than those of living in isolation. Certainly recent family changes and conflict seem, in many cases, to be a trigger factor leading to subsequent admission to a psychiatric hospital. Overall, however, it seems that the emotional impact of an intimate relationship, in adult life as in childhood, is likely to involve many more gains for the individual than losses, that people value the protection which such relationships provide and that they often suffer when such support ends.

Schizophrenia, depression and the family

There is a popular notion that schizophrenic illness originates in family relationships, and that certain forms of family communication, in particular, may cause an adolescent or young adult to become schizophrenic. A considerable number of studies have now been carried out to establish whether or not there is a firm evidential basis for such an assumption and, at this point, it looks as if the decided lack of positive evidence should lead us to abandon the hypothesis that such relationship problems constitute the major cause of the illness. While no strong data to support the family interaction claim have been forthcoming, however, a great deal of evidence implicating the role of genetics in schizophrenia has been found and it now looks as if a predominantly biological explanation may eventually be given. But while there is no good evidence that family relationships are formative in schizophrenia, there is strong support for the notion that family interaction markedly influences the course of a schizophrenic illness and the pattern of relapses and remission from symptoms over the years. It seems that the emotional climate in the home and particular family crisis events often trigger renewed episodes of schizophrenic breakdown.

On the other hand, it seems that depression often has its origin in severe life events and difficulties and that the family context provides many of these. In a recent study conducted in London, Brown and Harris (1978) found that depression was more common in those women in the community who had recently experienced a severe event or difficulty. Many of the events involved loss. Women with several young children were more vulnerable than others, as were the widowed, divorced and separated. Social contact seemed to provide a protective function against the effects of severe life events and the rate of depression was lower in those women who had a close intimate relationship with their husbands. Women without employment outside the home were found to be more vulnerable and the loss of a mother in childhood also seemed to have a similar effect. Brown and Harris suggest that such early loss through the death of a parent may change the way in which the person comes to view the world and attempts to cope with the problems that arise. The study provides clear evidence that family relationship factors may make a person more or less susceptible to clinical depression, and again illustrates how the contribution of family life to personal problems is two-sided. The family may be the source of much stress, but a close supportive marital relationship will enable the individual to cope with many problems without succumbing to the threat of clinical depression.

Sexual behaviour and sexual problems

Married couples vary greatly in the frequency of their sexual contact and in the style and variety of their sexual interaction. The rate of intercourse does not seem to be related to overall satisfaction with the marriage, except that where a marriage is failing for other reasons sexual contact may be low or absent. If there is a marked discrepancy, however, between the expectations or needs of the partners then this may lead to conflict and dissatisfaction. Sex is also one of the factors which can cause problems in the early stages of adjustment to marriage.

Although several medical men and women wrote 'marriage manuals' during the nineteenth century and in the early part of this century, our knowledge of human sexuality was very limited before the studies of people such as Kinsey and Masters and Johnson. Using interviews, and later observational and physiological techniques, researchers have now provided us with extensive information about sexual practices. Masters and Johnson (1966, 1970), in particular, have supplied a thorough and detailed account of human sexual behaviour, and they have also provided insights into such questions as sexuality in the older person and sexual behaviour during pregnancy.

It has become clear that problems of sexual dysfunction affect a great many people at some stage in their marriage. Masters and Johnson have produced a range of therapies which has been shown to be highly effective, and many of these have now been adopted by other psychologists, psychiatrists and marriage counsellors. The couple, rather than the individual man or woman, is considered to be the most appropriate treatment unit, and discussion and detailed advice are followed up with 'homework assignments' which the partners carry out in the home. Anxiety about sexual performance can have a serious effect on behaviour and a vicious circle can easily form, for example, between anxiety and failure to achieve erection. Awareness of the female orgasm has increased considerably in recent years and it appears that the pattern of problems for which advice is sought has changed. Whereas the majority of sexual problems encountered by counsellors some decades ago involved a mismatch of sexual appetites, with the woman complaining about her husband's excessive demands, a dominant problem now seems to be that of the woman's dissatisfaction with her husband's ability to bring her to orgasm.

Opinions differ about how much the 'couple unit' is always the appropriate focus for treatment and how far deep-seated relationship difficulties, rather than specific sexual skills and attitudes, underlie the problems presented. It does appear that in about half of the cases seen there are other serious marital difficulties in addition to the sexual dysfunction being treated by sex therapy which is aimed at improving other aspects of the relationship.

Family conflict and violence

There is open conflict at times in most families. Sometimes the focus of disagreements is easily apparent; it may centre, for example, on matters concerning money, sex or the handling of children, but at other times the row seems to reflect underlying resentments and difficulties in the relationship. Studies have been made of how arguments start, how they escalate and how they are resolved, and some research in this area has been successful in identifying patterns of conflict which seem to predict later marital breakdown. It appears that there are right ways and wrong ways to fight with other family members. In some marriages there may be constant conflict which, however, is successfully worked through and which does not endanger the basic relationship.

Inter-generational conflict is also common. In the early years the parents have the power and may use discipline to settle matters of disagreement. Again, the way in which this is done is important and it seems that parents should not use their power in such a way that the child feels rejected.

Children should be made to feel that their behaviour, rather than their whole personality, is the target of the parents' disapproval. In the adolescent years, the child's struggle for power and independence is often the focus of conflict. Adolescence is frequently a period of stress and young people may have doubts about their status and future. It is also a time when peer-influence may conflict with that of the parents.

Marital conflict sometimes leads to physical assault and a number of wives have to receive medical attention for injuries inflicted by their husbands. Many such wives choose to return to the home after such an incident although some seek the haven of a women's refuge. Even where there is repeated violence, the wife often feels that her husband is not likely to treat her badly in the future; she may feel that drinking or stress triggered the assault, and such wives often report that the man is generally caring and responsible and that his violent outbursts are out of character. Jealousy and sexual failure or refusal are also associated with attacks on the wife, though it is also true that for some couples physical assault or restraint represents a modal response in conflict situations, and that in some marriages (and indeed in some sub-cultures) there are few inhibitions against the couple hitting one another.

Violence against children also occurs with alarming frequency in families, and it is estimated that about two children die each week in England and Wales as a result of injuries inflicted by their parents. The children involved are often very young, and it does not take much physical strength to seriously injure a small child or baby. Only a small proportion of the parents involved in these attacks have a known psychiatric history and, contrary to one popular image, they often provide well for the general needs of their children. Sadistic premeditated cases do occur but they are relatively rare. Generally the attack occurs when a child is crying or screaming or has committed some 'crime' in the eyes of the parent. The mother or father involved is often under considerable stress, and there are frequently severe marital difficulties. The parents involved are often young and may have little idea of how to cope with the crying child, and there is evidence that many abused children are themselves difficult to handle. They may be disturbed, over-active or unresponsive although, of course, many such problems may themselves be the result of longer-term difficulties in the family.

Family therapy

There has recently been a considerable growth of interest in 'family therapy'. This is practised in a variety of ways and with a number of alternative theoretical underpinnings but it claims, in all its forms, that when there is a psychological disturbance it is useful to work with the 'family system' rather than with the individual identified client. The view is often expressed that the symptom should properly be seen as an attribute not of the individual but of the family as a whole. By focussing on the structure of the group, on the emotional climate and on the pattern of relationships and communication, an attempt is made to bring about a fundamental change which will result in a well-functioning family and an alteration in the circumstances which have maintained the symptom.

Thus a child who is truanting from school may be presented as the only problem by a family who, in fact, have a number of difficulties. By focussing on or scapegoating the child in this way, the family system may preserve itself from serious conflict between other members or between the family group and another part of the wider social system. The child's problem with school is therefore in some way 'useful' to the family and any direct attempt to deal with the truanting may be directed at reducing the underlying conflict or at changing a disordered style of communication which has led to the family 'needing' the child's symptom.

In the therapeutic sessions family members are seen together. The focus is largely on the group processes operating and involves the observations of such inter-actional elements as coalitions, stratagems and avoidances. As these are further analysed, they may be revealed to the family or they may be simply 'corrected' by the direct authoritative action of the therapist. The periods inter-vening between treatment sessions are seen as being of primary importance for the family, who may then revert to original dysfunctional patterns or may continue in the direction of therapeutic change.

The role of the therapist is varied. Some therapists regard themselves primarily as analysts and concentrate on making the family aware of its interactional style, whereas some regard themselves as mediators or referees or may take sides with one or more family members to provide a necessary balance of power. If two or more therapists work as a team then they may present their own relationship as a model of open communication and in this way try, for example, to illustrate the constructive potential of conflict.

The professional background of family therapists is highly varied and their original training may be in psycho-logy, social work or psychiatry. The theoretical concepts used similarly cover a wide range including psychoanalysis, communications theory and behavioural analysis. Concepts have also been borrowed freely from general systems theory, which is predominantly a mathematical theory with applica-tions in cybernetics and biology. In behavioural family therapy the focus is on the manipulation of the family consequences of individual behaviour and the attempt is made to analyse and modify social reinforcement patterns and observational learning.

Because family therapy involves a varied and often subtle set of procedures, it is very difficult to carry out satisfactory studies to measure its effectiveness. Many of the variables said to be involved are rather intangible and the processes underlying changes in social systems are highly complex. Preliminary evidence suggests that it is often useful but this can also be said of many other forms of therapy, and the 'cost-effectiveness' considerations which play a part in treatment choice sometimes make it difficult to support a strong case for the use of family therapy. Many critics would return a general verdict of 'not proven', but the level of interest by professionals is undoubtedly high and growing. One special difficulty has been the failure of those working in this area to provide an adequate means of identifying the cases which may be most appropriately treated in this way. Any attempt to treat all conditions with a uniform approach is unlikely to return a high overall rate of effectiveness. With a more limited set of identified problems this mode of treatment may in future prove to be the optimal means of effective intervention for a range of cases. At present, family therapy reflects just one aspect of the increasing awareness of the importance of understanding the social context when dealing with a presented psychological symptom.

The effects of marital breakdown

Divorce statistics represent a very conservative estimate of marital failure and a still more conservative estimate of marital unhappiness and disharmony, but the rates are high and increasing. There are various estimates of the likely divorce rate of currently made marriages but one in four is a frequently encountered figure. There are certain known predictors of marital breakdown. It is more frequent, for example, when the couple married at an early age, when they have few friends, when they have had relatively little education and when their life style is unconventional. The marital success or failure of their own parents also bears a direct statistical relationship to the couple's chances of breakdown.

Psychological studies have shown that certain measures of personality and social style are also predictors of failure. If the wife rates her husband as being emotionally immature, if the husband's self-image is lacking in coherence and stability, or if either of the partners is emotionally unstable then marital breakdown is more likely than if the reverse holds. Good communication, a high level of emotional support and the constructive handling of conflict situations are, not surprisingly, features of relationships which are associated with high levels of marital happiness and low rates of breakdown. In many of these studies it is, of course, difficult to disentangle cause and effect.

The process of adjustment to a marriage may be a long and difficult one, and some marriages never successfully 'take'. The highest rates of breakdown therefore occur in the first years, but many relationships are stable and satisfactory for a while and are then beset with difficulties at a later stage. Divorce is usually preceded by months or years of intense conflict and may eventually come as a relief, but the evidence suggests that generally the whole process is a very painful one for many members of the family involved, both adults and children.

Research with divorcees has revealed a high degree of stress and unhappiness which may last for a very long time. On the whole, it appears that the experiences of women in this situation result in rather more disturbance than those of men, but for both sexes the status of divorce is associated with higher risk of clinical depression, alcoholism and attempted suicide. The psychological effects of a marriage breakdown may stem largely from lack of social support, the absence of an intimate relationship and a loss of self-esteem, but there are often additional pressures relating to the loss of contact with the children or of having to bring them up alone. There is a high rate of remarriage among the divorced; and divorce itself, for all the apparent risks which it brings, is still often preferable to continuing in a marriage which has failed.

The 'broken home' is associated with increased aggressiveness and delinquency in children, but there seems to be only a weak association with neurotic and other psychiatric problems of childhood. While the rate of conduct problems in the children of divorce is considerably higher than that for children of stable marriages, there is apparently little increase in such antisocial behaviour for children whose homes have been broken by the death of a parent. This suggests that it is the discord in the home which produces the effect rather than the mere absence of one parent. This is supported by the finding that conduct problems also occur with increased frequency in homes with continual discord, even when there is no separation or divorce.

Single-parent families

Children are raised in single-parent families when the mother has not married, when there has been a divorce or separation, or when one parent has died. 'Illegitimacy' is a somewhat outmoded term and an increasing number of single women now feel that they want to rear their child on their own. Social attitudes against illegitimacy and single parenthood have softened over the years and this has encouraged more mothers to keep the baby rather than have it adopted.

Single parenthood appears to be more stressful for the remaining parent than sharing the responsibilities with a partner. Lack of emotional support and of adult company are some of the reasons for this but there are also likely to be increased financial hardships, and the homes of single parents have been shown to be overcrowded and often lack both luxuries and basic amenities. During times of parental illness there may be few additional social resources to call upon, and the single parent is less likely to be able to organize a social life for herself (about 90 per cent of single parents are women). A number of self-help organizations have now been formed to fulfil some of the special needs of the single parent.

One-parent families are viable alternatives to the more traditional nuclear families, and most of the children raised in such circumstances do not appear to show any signs of disturbance or impaired development. There have been suggestions that the boy without a father might tend to be more effeminate but it has been found that most boys brought up by their mothers are as masculine as the rest. If any-thing, they tend to make fewer sex-identity based assump-tions about tasks and roles. We could say that they seem to be less 'sexist' than other boys. Similarly, the girl brought up with the father alone does not seem to lack feminine identity. These findings reflect a more general conclusion that children seem to base their own stereotypes on the wider world around them rather than on the conditions prevailing in their own immediate family.

The family life of old people

Old age is marked by declining health and mobility and by a process of disengagement from several life enterprises, notably employment. There may be low income and financial difficulties, contemporaries are likely to die, and the old person may find it difficult to replace such contacts with the result that they live in a shrinking social world. The high emphasis which some old people place on privacy may reduce the uptake of potential neighbourhood and community resources.

The major exception made to such concern with privacy is with the immediate family. Typically, contacts with children and grandchildren are highly prized and may be a major focus of interest in their lives. While there is likely to be an increase in dependency, however, this is often recognized by the old and they often respect the independence of the younger family and feel a crushing sense of obligation if they are forced through circumstance to accept aid from them. In some families there is an informal 'exchange of services' between generations with the older person, for example, looking after the grandchildren while parents are working or having a short holiday.

Recent social change has resulted in fewer three-generation households, but with increasing age and decrea-sing health, and perhaps the death of one of the parents, the younger couple may want to offer the surviving partner a place in their home. There may be doubts about how well this will work out and conflict may be initiated between the marital partners over how far feelings of duty should lead to changes which might disrupt the family. As the children become older the pressure on space may build up, and with increasing health difficulties the burden of the older person may become too great. Deafness may become an irritation, there may be restricted mobility and the elderly parent may become incontinent.

The increased strain on the family may lead to harsh feelings or even violence towards the old person as well as to a detrimental effect on the health of other members of the family. Eventually the pressure may become unmanageable and the old person may be forced to enter an institution. For many elderly people, living with a child is a halfway stage between having a home of their own and living in an old people's home. Both moves may involve their giving up possessions and pets. The quality of institutions varies greatly, but a frequent reaction is one of withdrawal, depression and depersonalization. Despite having many people around the old person may suffer from a deep sense of loneliness and isolation.

While it seems inevitable that old age will always bring unhappiness to some people, for many it is a time of contentment and fulfilment and in a number of cases the positive aspects centre on activities and memories of relationships within the family. Older women, for example, may play a major role in organizing family get-togethers and may act as a social secretary for members of the extended family, and grandmothers and grandfathers may gain great satisfaction from their relationships with their grand-children. Many of the recent social changes in housing organization and mobility, it is true, militate against a high level of interaction between the generations, and there seems as yet little awareness by policy-makers of the social costs which such changes entail.

The future of intimate life styles

Contact with intimates in the family group seems to provide the individual, overall, with considerable benefits. Significant relationships are highly potent and there may be dangers, but generally the benefits far outweigh the costs. A variety of psychological needs are very well fulfilled in the traditional family setting. The child growing in the caring and stable family setting can generally develop skills and abilities and achieve a potential for happiness better than in any other setting, and the adult can fulfil with the marital partner the needs of emotional support, freedom from loneliness, sex, stability, and the building of a mutually comfortable 'social reality'. When the basic family pattern is disturbed there can be grave consequences for each of the people involved.

There is no uniform change in western society to a single alternative life style arrangement but there is rather an increasing diversity. There are now fewer children in families, more single-parent families, more divorces and separations, and there is a high incidence of transitory relationships and less contact between generations. Several lines of evidence suggest that children are valued less than in the recent past; that women, in particular, are looking more outside the family for their role-orientation and their life satisfactions; that there is now less 'family feeling'; and that family duties and responsibilities impinge upon individual decision making less than was the case some decades ago.

We may expect this variety to increase further as ideas regarding the roles of men and women evolve, as changes in biological and 'hard' technology take place and as patterns of employment and leisure alter. It would be premature to forecast, at this stage, what effects such changes will bring to interpersonal relationships and personal life styles. What does seem certain, however, is that there will be important effects. To some extent these can be affected by direct social intervention and some undesirable effects may be prevented.

Family life, then, is a key variable in society and adverse changes may inflict an enormous social bill. For this reason the effects on individuals must be carefully monitored. Psychologists are just one of the groups which will be involved in this vitally important enterprise.

References

Brown, G.W. and Harris, T. (1978)
Social Origins of Depression. London: Tavistock Publications.
Masters, W. and Johnson, V. (1966)
Human Sexual Response. Boston: Little, Brown.
Masters, W. and Johnson, V. (1970)
Human Sexual Inadequacy. London: Churchill.

Questions

1. Write an essay on 'The family and psychology'.
2. Assess the importance of personal relationships in the lives of individuals, referring to psychological and other studies to support the analysis you present.
3. Consider some of the factors which might lead a couple to decide to remain childless.
4. Now that there are a number of highly effective contraceptive methods why do so many unwanted pregnancies occur, and how might this be changed?
5. How is a relationship between the mother and her baby likely to differ from that between the father and his baby? Why is this so?
6. Many mothers find looking after a young baby a difficult and stressful experience. Why is this?
7. Hospital births may be medically the safest, but are there likely to be psychological dangers in treating birth more as a biological than as a social and family process?
8. What are 'the needs of children' and how may they be met?
9. Critically assess the evidence relating to the effects of a mother's work outside the home on the children.
10. Write an essay on 'The family as a source of stress'.
11. Some people have maintained that schizophrenia arises as a result of problems within the family. Critically assess the evidence relating to this issue.
12. Describe current approaches to the treatment of sexual dysfunction.
13. The family seems to be the context for a good deal of violence, particularly towards children and wives. Why should this be so?

14. Write an essay on 'The after-effects of divorce'.
15. Consider the special problems of the single-parent family.
16. 'The natural social setting for old people is with their younger family.' How true is this statement? Consider the problems which may arise in a three-generation household.
17. Is the family an institution worth preserving?
18. Are there 'experts' in child-rearing? Is this process too important to be left to parents?
19. Some authors have claimed that the family is oppressive and that people should be liberated from the limits that it places on them. How far do you share this view? Give reasons.

Annotated reading

Belliveau, F. and Richter, L. (1971) Understanding Human Sexual Inadequacy. London: Hodder & Stoughton.
    Non-technical report of the work of Masters and Johnson on sexual behaviour and sexual problems, including details of treatment methods.

Herbert, M. (1975) Problems of Childhood. London: Pan.
    A comprehensive account of the problems of the early years, their treatment and prevention.

Kellmer Pringle, M. (1980) The Needs of Children (2nd edn). London: Hutchinson.
    Important review of children's needs and how they may be met both inside and outside the family. Readable and authoritative book with important implications for social policy.

Kempe, R. and Kempe, E. (1978) Child Abuse. London: Fontana/Open Books.
    The nature of treatment of violence and sexual assault on children in the family, with an account of methods of treatment and prevention.

Rutter, M. (1976) Helping Troubled Children. Harmondsworth: Penguin.
    Leading British child psychiatrist examines the nature of the more severe problems of childhood. Provides good coverage of the importance of family factors and related methods of treatment.

10

Institutional Climates
Jim Orford

Opening remarks
DAVID GRIFFITHS

Whilst the family home is the most important part of the social environment for the majority of the population, institutions constitute home for an unfortunate but large minority. This minority includes many of the psychiatrically ill, the mentally handicapped, the chronically sick and children (for instance, orphans). Although it is apparent that many of the disordered and abnormal behaviours found in these individuals are caused by internal pathology, it has also been demonstrated that significant aspects of their behaviour are maintained by the social environment within the institution. The previous chapter suggested that the outcome in schizophrenia is influenced by the patient's family. Research on chronic schizophrenia, involving long-stay patients in hospital, has similarly demonstrated that behaviours such as social withdrawal and inactivity are determined as much by unstimulating ward environments as by any biological process. When ward environments are improved, many problematic behaviours subside in both number and severity. The key to change can therefore involve environmental alteration as much as individual treatment, and institutions become a natural focus for the clinician who is keen to improve the welfare of his patients.

Jim Orford's discussion of institutions is concerned with a number of important issues. For example, what effects do size and location have on institutional 'climates'? Which aspects of institutions influence the behaviour and attitudes of staff, and how do staff influence the character of institutions? What effects, in addition, do the characteristics of patient or client groups have on institutional climates? And, last but certainly not least, what can be done to change institutions?

The answers to these questions will be of obvious concern to both clinicians and researchers. They are especially important to the clinician who is keen to explore the possibility of helping patients both through individual therapy and improving their social environment. Institutions might be undesirable and 'de-humanizing' but they nevertheless continue to be important parts of the structure of the Health Services, and in this way to affect the lives of many individuals. It therefore continues to be important to understand institutions and to consider whether and how they

should be changed to suit the needs of the individual.
Trainees who read this chapter should become be sensitized
to an aspect of their work environment which will have significant effects on both their own attitudes and behaviour,
and those of their future patients.

Introduction
JIM ORFORD

A person's behaviour is influenced by the surrounding
environment, as well as by attributes which the person
brings to that environment, such as personality, abilities
and attitudes; behaviour is a function of person and
environment. Many people either live or work in institutions
of one kind or another. For such people, the institution
constitutes an important part of their environment. For some
people it constitutes almost their total environment. Those
who work in an institutional setting cannot fail to notice
how the institution influences its members, either for good
or ill. Many will have felt frustrated by the values which
the institution seems to embody, or by the practices which
are prevalent within it, feeling that members could be
helped more if things were otherwise, or even that members
are being harmed by the institution. The great importance of
these matters has begun to be recognized in psychology and
there is a growing psychological literature on the organization of institutions and how to change them. The study of
institutions holds wider lessons for social psychology too.
An institution is a social psychological laboratory. The
experiments which take place there are naturally occurring
experiments in the psychology of social interaction, social
roles, inter-group attitudes, conflict and cohesiveness. The
study of institutions is of vital significance for both
theoretical and applied psychology.

Much of the literature on the subject concerns health
care or social service institutions such as mental hospitals
and hostels or homes for children, the elderly, or the
disabled. Although many of the examples upon which this
chapter draws are taken from such institutions, the chapter
attempts to build up a general picture of institutional life
which is equally as relevant, for example, to educational
institutions such as schools and colleges, and to penal institutions such as prisons and detention centres. These different institutions have a great deal in common. Each is a
collection of people, gathered together in a special building or group of buildings. These people are not normally
linked by family ties, but are there because of the special
'needs' (for education, care, treatment, rehabilitation, or
punishment) of inmates, users, or 'clients' (pupils, members, patients, residents). It is the responsibility of
another group of people, the staff, to provide for the
clients' needs. This they are in a position to do on account
of their special training, skills, or occupation (as teacher, prison officer, warden, doctor or nurse). Usually the
institution has been set up by, and is part of, a larger
organization which is responsible for managing the institution. Penal institutions in Britain are governed by the

complex machinery of the Home Office; hospitals by the
Department of Health and its network of Regional, Area and
District Authorities, each with a complex system of members,
officers and management teams; local authority schools and
homes by committees and sub-committees of elected and co-
opted representatives, the Authority's officers and the
institution's committee of governors or managers; and institutions run by voluntary bodies by their trustees and
management committees. Institutions are almost always influenced by people, often a large number of them, who have
control over the institution but who are not involved in
day-to-day work with the institution's clients. It is more
than purely academic to consider some of these defining
features of human service institutions. They immediately
suggest ways in which an institution differs from a person's
own home, and hence they indicate where some problems with
institutions are to be expected. The small family home
provides the clearest contrast to the large residential
institution. People are not gathered together in the former
on account of their special needs or their special qualifications, there is no demarcation between staff and clients,
and the influence of outside organizations is minimal. It is
no wonder that a great deal of thought and effort has been
devoted to the goal of making institutions as normal and
home-like as possible. Many other comparisons and contrasts
between organizations and groups could be made, and there
is no absolute definition of an institution.

**Ideal types: the total
institution and the
therapeutic community**

It is important to be clear what is meant by a 'total
institution' and by the term 'therapeutic community'. They
are important ideas which have had much influence but as
terms they are liable to be used loosely, and hence may
obscure rather than reveal the true facts about institutional climates. In his much-read and often-quoted collection of essays entitled 'Asylums: Essays on the Social
Situation of Mental Patients and Other Inmates', Goffman
(1961) noted that it is normal in modern society for people
to conduct different aspects of their life, for example
sleeping, playing and working, in different places, with
different people, and under different authorities. Total
institutions, in contrast, are places where these barriers
between different spheres of life are broken down. All
aspects of life are conducted in the same place and, most
importantly, under the same single authority. It is quite
likely that activities are tightly scheduled by those in
authority in accordance with an overall plan. He noted that
many penal and caring institutions were total institutions
in this sense. So were a number of places, with which this
chapter is less concerned, such as army barracks, ships and
monasteries. On the other hand, certain places with which
we are concerned, such as day schools and day hospitals or
centres, would not qualify as total institutions.

It is also important to recognize the variety of climates which exist even within total institutions. In their

book, 'Varieties of Residential Experience', Tizard,
Sinclair and Clarke (1975) point out the danger of general-
izing from studies of single institutions, such as Goffman's
study of an American mental hospital. Used loosely, the
expression 'total institution' can give rise to a misleading
stereotype. There is now ample evidence, some of which is
considered later in this chapter, that institutions vary
greatly, and furthermore that individual institutions can be
changed.

Nevertheless, the harm that institutions may do has
increasingly been recognized. Barton (1959) has gone so far
as to say that the symptoms of institutionalization are so
well marked that they constitute a disease entity which he
called 'institutional neurosis'. He has written:

> Institutional Neurosis is a disease characterized by
> apathy, lack of initiative, loss of interest ...,
> submissiveness, and sometimes no expression of feelings
> of resentment at harsh and unfair orders. There is also
> lack of interest in the future ..., a deterioration in
> personal habits ..., a loss of individuality, and a
> resigned acceptance that things will go on as they are.

The concept of the 'therapeutic community' is an important
one because it represents one type of ideal contrasting
markedly with the most inhumane or least therapeutic institutional climates. The model therapeutic community was the
Henderson Unit at the Belmont Hospital in Surrey. The unit,
described by Maxwell Jones (1952) and studied by Rapoport
(1960), was principally aimed at helping young adult psychiatric patients, many of whom had problems of repeated
antisocial conduct and who were difficult to accommodate
elsewhere. Amongst the ideals of the therapeutic community
are an emphasis on ACTIVE REHABILITATION as opposed to
custodialism; DEMOCRATIZATION, namely that decision making
about the unit's affairs should be shared amongst staff and
patients alike; PERMISSIVENESS: that is, that distressing or
deviant behaviour should be tolerated rather than repressed
in the interests of institutional conformity; COMMUNALISM:
that is, that the climate should be informal without the
development of highly specialized roles, and that relationships should be close but never exclusive; and REALITY
CONFRONTATION: that is, that patients should be continually given interpretations of their behaviour as other
members of the unit see it. It is important to appreciate
that the Henderson model is a very specific one.
Structurally it was a total institution and although its
climate was undoubtedly in contrast to that of many large
impersonal institutions, in some ways it was rather formal,
with a detailed programme of therapeutic and administrative
groups, work assignments and other activities. Units are
often self-styled 'therapeutic communities', but they are
rarely aiming to recreate the type of therapeutic community
unit described by Jones and Rapoport.

Structural features of institutions

There are many separate features of institutions which contribute to climate and a number of these are considered in turn.

Size

There is considerable evidence that people prefer, and are more active socially in, small units of organization. One explanation for these findings is based on the idea of 'manning'. Where there are relatively few patients, pupils or residents, there are relatively many tasks and activities for them to undertake. There is much scope for involvement in activity; the setting may be said to be relatively under-manned. In contrast, settings with relatively many individuals may be over-manned, with relatively less opportunity for involvement for all.

This is perhaps why efforts are often made to break up an institution into smaller, more manageable, groups such as classes, houses or year groups in schools, and wards and small units within hospitals. Unfortunately, the overall institution may continue to exercise a strong influence on the smaller units that comprise it. One recent study (reported in Canter and Canter, 1979) found that staff working in institutions for handicapped children adopted more institution-orientated as opposed to child-orientated practices in looking after the children when their unit was part of a larger overall institution. The size of the unit itself was unimportant. Individual units within institutions are rarely fully autonomous but continue to be dependent on the larger institution in many ways. This notion of autonomy is an important one to which this chapter returns.

Location

Location is of both symbolic and concrete significance. The isolated mental hospital symbolizes community attitudes to the mentally ill, for example. Other features of institutions may symbolize a similar relationship between institution and community. Prisons are often located in cities but their isolation is ensured by their high walls and impenetrable, fortress-like entrances; they are in the community, but not of it. It is important to consider what factors are operating to promote closeness of contact between an institution and its local community, and what factors are operating to inhibit it. It is interesting to speculate, for example, on whether a prominent sign announcing that a house is a home for the elderly eases visiting by members of the community or makes it more difficult? Certainly many small residential caring units such as hostels and halfway houses pride themselves on carrying no such institutional signboard.

Ease of access to community facilities may be crucial for those who must remain in an institution for a long time. A lack of interest in, or desire to return to, life outside are considered by Barton and others to be amongst the main features of institutionalization, and he lists loss of

contact with the outside world, loss of personal friends,
and loss of prospects outside as three of its main causes.

The issue of location illustrates an important point
about the psychology of social organizations. The point is
that no single variable is independent of others, and
consequently it is almost impossible to impute causal
significance to single features of institutions. In this
case, it is very unlikely that the location of an institution is independent of the philosophy or ideology under
which it operates, or the attitudes of staff who work in it.
A rehabilitation philosophy is likely to be associated with
close community contacts, either because the institution was
located close to the community in the first place, or
because means had been found to overcome an unsatisfactory
location.

Internal design

Large rooms with high ceilings, glossy interior wall paint
in drab colours, no change of decor from one area to
another, lack of personalization by the use of pictures,
photographs and ornaments, lack of privacy, even sometimes
extending to a bathroom and toilet, absence of individualized sleeping accommodation, few personal possessions or
places to keep them, and generally an absence of opportunity
to express individuality; these are amongst the internal
design features of an institution which contribute to an
institutional as opposed to homely atmosphere.

Once again, however, it is important to avoid over-
simple ideas of cause and effect. Two examples from Canter
and Canter's book (1979) on the influence of design in
institutions illustrate this point. One example concerns the
first several years' operation of a purpose-built unit for
disturbed children. A number of features, such as outside
play facilities, were designed by the architect with the
express purpose of reducing institutional climate. Others,
such as doors for bedrooms, were strongly advocated by the
director and were eventually installed. Observation of the
day-to-day life of the unit, however, led to the view that
the overwhelming ideology of the unit, which placed emphasis
on the children's disturbance and on the need for staff
control and surveillance, undermined the use of these design
features. Play facilities were rarely spontaneously used,
bedroom doors were hardly ever closed, and rooms which were
designed for personal use were used as seclusion rooms for
punishment. The second example concerns a purpose-built
forensic unit where it was possible to show, by a process of
behaviour mapping (a procedure whereby a map of WHO does
WHAT and WHERE is produced by observing samples of behaviour in different places at different times), the use to
which different spaces were put and the meanings that became
attached to them. Certain areas were clearly designated as
staff offices, and others as patient lounges. As a result,
segregation of staff and patients was the rule rather than
the exception.

One small-scale feature of physical layout which is relatively easily manipulated is that of SEATING ARRANGEMENT. The terms 'sociopetal' (meaning encouraging interpersonal relationships) and 'sociofugal' (discouraging relationships) have been used to describe possible seating arrangements in institutions. Seats in the lounge areas of old people's homes and other institutions are often arranged around the edge of the room or in some other sociofugal pattern, such as in rows facing a television set. Sociopetal patterns, on the other hand, have been found to lead to more interaction, more multi-person interaction, and more personal conversations. Once again, it is important to appreciate other, more human, aspects of the environment. It is often found, when attempts have been made to re-arrange furniture in a more sociopetal fashion, that there is a tendency for the seating to revert to its former arrangement. It is as if the institution has a will of its own and is in some way resistant to change. Exploring how this reversion to type comes about, and making a diagnosis of what is to blame, may provide vital insights into the nature of the institution.

It is worth speculating on the function which may be served by furniture arrangement in different types of institution. For example, why is the seating arrangement of pupils in a primary school often very different from, and usually more sociopetal in design than, that to be found in a secondary school? Is this difference accidental, or does it say something about the expected relationship between teacher and pupils, and perhaps thereby about the whole underlying philosophy of education?

Rules, regulations and routines

Studies of institutional practices

Considerable progress has been made in describing the variety which exists within health and social care residential institutions. Similar variety exists within educational establishments, and within penal settings.

Studies have compared hostels and hospitals for mentally handicapped children, and have found the latter to be much more institutional in their handling of the children: routine is more rigid, children are more likely to be treated en bloc, treatment is less personalized, and social distance between staff and children is greater. Wide variation is found in the degree of 'ward restrictiveness' in adult mental hospitals. Similar variation exists in halfway houses for ex-psychiatric patients. On average, hostels are less institutional than mental hospitals, the former having between one-half and two-thirds the number of 'restrictive practices' found in the average hospital ward in one study. However, considerable variation is found in both types of facility and there is an overlap between them. Some of the hostels, whilst being small in size, and designed to provide a link between the large institution and the community, nevertheless retain a number of institutional practices. In one instance a hostel had more institutional practices than the hospital rehabilitation ward from which most of its residents came.

A key idea linking these studies is that of clients' DECISION MAKING freedom. Table 1 provides an indication of some of the major areas of decision making considered in such studies. The list could be expanded greatly to include a large range of day-to-day activities over which most people are able to exercise personal choice. Whether an institution allows this exercise of choice to continue for its clients or whether these decision-making freedoms are curtailed is crucial in determining whether an institution creates a therapeutic climate or institutionalization.

Table 1

A range of decisions which may be allowed or restricted in institutions and which are illustrative of those considered in studies of institutional practices

What time to get up and go to bed
What to wear
What to eat for breakfast and other meals
Planning future meals
Whether to make a drink or snack
Whether to visit the local shops
Whether to go to work
Whether to go to the pictures
How to spend own money
When to have a bath
When to have a haircut
Whether to have medicine
Deciding arrangement of own room
Deciding decoration of own room
Whether to smoke
Whether to play the radio or TV
When to invite friends in
Whether to have a sexual relationship with a friend
Planning decoration or repair of the place
Deciding how to care for or control other members
Deciding policy

Staff autonomy

Reference has already been made, when considering the size of an institution, to the importance of a unit's autonomy within the larger institution. Decision-making freedom may be limited not only for clients but also for those staff who have the closest dealings with them. The advantages of the informality which can occur in a truly independent small unit are illustrated by an incident which occurred at Woodley House, an American halfway house for the mentally

ill. It concerned a dispute between pro- and anti-television
factions in the house. The former decided to convert part of
the basement of the house for their use, leaving the living
room to the others. A staff member took them in her car to
buy paint and other materials and later the same day the
newly-decorated television room was in use. Such an incident
could not easily occur in that way in a larger and more
formal institution. There are a number of reasons for this,
one being that the staff member at Woodley House was not
limited to a prescribed professional role, and there were no
other members of staff upon whose role territory she was
trespassing.

It is this variable of staff autonomy which Tizard et al
(1975) considered to be one of the strongest influences upon
the quality of staff-client interaction in an institutional
setting. The firmest evidence for this hypothesis is
contained in a chapter of their book written by Barbara
Tizard. It concerns residential nurseries run by voluntary
societies. She observed 13 such units, all of which had been
modernized in recent years to provide 'family group' care.
Mixed age groups of six children each had their own suite of
rooms and their own nurse and assistant nurse to care for
them. Despite this effort at 'de-institutionalizing', marked
differences existed in the degree to which nurses were truly
independent agents. Nurseries were divided by the research
team into three classes on the basis of the amount of unit
autonomy. The first group, it was felt, was in effect run
centrally by the matron:

> Decisions were made on an entirely routine basis or else
> referred to the matron. Each day was strictly time-
> tabled, the matron would make frequent inspections of
> each group, and freedom of the nurse and child was very
> limited. The children were moved through the day 'en
> bloc' ... The nurse had little more autonomy than the
> children, e.g. she would have to ask permission to take
> the children for a walk or to turn on the television
> set. As in hospital each grade of staff wore a special
> uniform, and had separate living quarters, and the
> nurse's behaviour when off duty was governed by quite
> strict rules.

At the other extreme was a group of nurseries which more
closely approximated a normal family setting:

> The staff were responsible for shopping, cooking, making
> excursions with the children and arranging their own
> day. The children could move freely about the house and
> garden and the staff rarely referred a decision to the
> matron. The nurse-in-charge did not wear uniform, and
> her off-duty time was not subject to rules. Her role, in
> fact, approximated more closely to that of a foster-
> mother. Since she could plan her own day and was not
> under constant surveillance she could treat the children
> more flexibly.

A third group of nurseries was intermediate in terms of independence. As predicted, the more autonomous staff were observed to spend more time talking to children, and more time playing, reading and giving information to them. Furthermore, children in units with more autonomous staff had higher scores on a test of verbal comprehension. The difficulty of teasing out what is important in complex social situations, such as those that exist in institutions, is illustrated by Barbara Tizard's findings. Autonomy was correlated with having a relatively favourable staff-to-child ratio and hence we cannot be certain that autonomy is the crucial variable.

Nevertheless, an effect of staff hierarchy was noticed which could explain the apparent importance of autonomy. When two staff were present at once, one was always 'in charge'. This had an inhibiting effect on a nurse's behaviour towards children: she would function in a 'notably restricted way, talking much less and using less "informative talk" than the nurse in charge'. This might explain differences between autonomous and less independent units, as staff in the latter type of unit would be much more likely to feel that someone else was in charge whether that person was present or not.

Flexible use of space, time and objects
Inflexible routine is one of the major charges brought against the institution by such writers as Barton and Goffman. Institutional life can be 'normalized' as much as possible by allowing flexible use of different areas of buildings and grounds, by varying time schedules, and by allowing flexible use of objects such as kitchen and laundry equipment, televisions, radios and record players. Residential institutions usually deprive adult inmates of the opportunity to take part in 'complete activity cycles'. Instead of taking part in a complete cycle of shopping for food, preparing it, eating, clearing away and washing up after it, residents may simply be required to eat what others have purchased and prepared, rather like guests in a hotel.

Staff attitudes and behaviour

Ideology
The influence of an institution's ideology or philosophy is pervasive, although its significance can be missed altogether by those taken up in the day-to-day activities of the place. Many examples could be given. The philosophy of a progressive school such as Summerhill, with its emphasis on personal development, is distinct from that of a regular secondary school with its emphasis on academic learning. The rehabilitation philosophy of Grendon Underwood prison is distinct from that of most closed penal establishments with their emphasis on custody. Many institutions have mixed and competing ideologies. These frequently give rise to conflict within the institution, the different ideologies often being represented by different cadres of staff. For example,

educational and child care philosophies compete within institutions for handicapped children, as do educational and disciplinary philosophies within institutions for young delinquents. Important shifts may take place gradually over time. For example, a general shift from a custodial philosophy to a more therapeutic ideology has occurred in mental hospitals over the last several decades. Quite recently some of those working in British prisons have detected a move in the opposite direction in response to the call for tighter security.

Words such as 'open' to describe penal institutions, 'progressive' to describe educational facilities, and expressions such as 'therapeutic community' to describe an institution for residential care, all serve as public announcements of ideology and intended behaviour. However, it has already been noted that terms such as 'therapeutic community' are frequently used loosely, and sufficient is known about the absence of a strong correlation between attitudes and behaviour to make us doubtful that ideal philosophies will always be perfectly borne out in practice.

Staff attitudes

Nevertheless, no one who has worked in an institution for very long can have failed to notice what appear to be marked individual differences in staff attitudes. In the mental hospital setting questionnaires have been devised to detect staff attitudes of 'custodialism' or 'traditionalism'. The matter is by no means simple, however, and attitudes vary along a number of dimensions. For example, one study distinguished between 'restrictive control' and 'protective benevolence'. Staff high on restrictive control tended to be described as 'impatient with others' mistakes' and 'hardboiled and critical', and not 'sensitive and understanding' and 'open and honest with me'. Those high on protective benevolence, on the other hand, were described as 'stays by himself' and 'reserved and cool', and not 'lets patients get to know him' and 'talks about a variety of things'. Staff members high on this attitude scale expressed attitudes that appeared to suggest kindliness towards patients and yet they appear to have been seen by the latter as basically aloof, distant and non-interacting.

A study of hostels for boys on probation also illustrates the complexity of the matter. This study examined the relationship between failure rate, based on the percentage of residents leaving as a result of absconding or being reconvicted, and the attitudes of 16 different wardens. Two components of attitude were identified, each positively associated with success: strictness as opposed to permissiveness; and emotional closeness, which included warmth and willingness to discuss residents' problems with them, versus emotional distance. However, the two components, each separately associated with success, were negatively associated with one another. Hence wardens who displayed more warmth and willingness to discuss problems were also likely to be over-permissive, whilst those who were relatively strict tended to be lacking in emotional closeness. The ideal combination of warmth and firmness was a combination relatively rarely encountered.

Individual staff attitudes can partly be explained in terms of individual differences in general attitudes or personality: members of staff who are more generally authoritarian in personality tend to hold more custodial attitudes. This alone, however, cannot explain differences that are found between different institutions. Although the correspondence is far from complete, it has been found to be the case that where the prevailing policy is custodial, staff subscribe to a custodial view and tend to be generally authoritarian in personality. This raises the fascinating question of how such relative uniformity comes about. It can be presumed that the same three main processes are at work as those that operate to produce consensus and similarity of attitude in any social group or organization. The three processes are (i) selection-in, (ii) selection-out, and (iii) attitude change. Selection of new staff will most likely operate in a way that increases uniformity of attitude, both because certain people are more attracted than others by the prospect of working in a particular institution, and also because certain potential staff members are thought more suitable by those responsible for the selection (selection-in). Staff remain in one place for a variable length of time, and the institution may retain for longer periods those members whose attitudes are in conformity with the prevailing ideology (selection-out).

As social psychological experiments on conformity show so clearly, it is difficult to maintain a non-conformist position in the face of combined opinion, and the third process - attitude change - is likely to be a strong factor.

Staff behaviour and staff-client social distance

Although research leads us to expect none too close a correspondence between attitudes and behaviour, a number of studies in institutions suggest that philosophy and attitudes can be conveyed to residents via staff behaviour. Studies of units for handicapped children, for autistic children, and for the adult mentally ill, suggest that staff behaviour towards clients is more personal, warmer and less rejecting or critical when management practices are more client-orientated and less institution-orientated. Large differences have also been detected in the amount of time which staff members in charge of hostel units spend in face-to-face contact with their residents. Sharing space and activities together, and spending relatively more time in contact with one another, may be the most important factors in reducing social distance.

Social distance between staff and clients was an important concept in Goffman's and Barton's analyses of institutions. Avoidance, or reduced time in contact, is a fairly universal indication of lack of affection and often of prejudiced and stereotyped attitudes. There are numerous means of preserving social distance including designation of separate spaces, such as staff offices. A clearly designated staff office makes staff and client separation easier, but such a space may be used in a variety of different ways. The door may be kept open, or closed, or even locked with a key only available to staff.

Controversy often surrounds the wearing of staff uniform in institutions. There are arguments for and against, but inevitably the uniform creates or reinforces a distinction and may therefore increase social distance. A movement away from the traditional institutional organization is very frequently accompanied by the abandonment of uniforms where these previously existed. The use of names and titles in addressing different members of a community is another indication of the presence or absence of social distance. Forms of address are known to be good signs of both solidarity and status within social groups. The reciprocal use of first names is a sign of relative intimacy, and the reciprocal use of titles (Mr, Mrs, etc.) a sign of distance. Non-reciprocal forms of address, on the other hand, are indications of a status difference, with the person of higher status almost always using the more familiar form of address (say a first name or nickname) in addressing the person of lower status, and the latter using title and surname towards the former, or even a form of address which clearly indicates the former's superior status (sir, boss, etc.). If forms of address change as people get to know one another better, it is usually the person of higher status who initiates the use of familiar forms of address first.

Hence an examination of a particular institution in terms of designated spaces for staff and others, uniforms and other visual indications of role or rank, and of forms of address, can give useful clues to status divisions and social distance within the institution. However, it is of the utmost importance to keep in mind that social distance, like all of the social psychological features of institutions considered here, is a highly complex matter. It has been suggested, for example, that there are at least two distinct forms of social distance, namely status distance and personal distance. If these aspects of social distance are relatively independent, as has been suggested, it follows that status distance need not necessarily preclude the formation of a personally close relationship.

Institutions as complex systems

The client contribution

Staff may be crucial determinants of climate, particularly senior staff, but so too are the institution's users or clients. The climate in an institution is the product of a bewildering complexity of factors which interact in ways that are far from straightforward. No simple theory which attempts to explain what goes on inside an institution in terms of physical design alone, of the attitudes of senior staff alone, or of management practices alone, can do justice to them. It would be as faulty to ignore the personalities, abilities and disabilities of the users as it would be to ignore the philosophy of the institution or the design of its buildings. This point is forcefully brought home in Miller and Gwynne's (1972) account of homes catering for people with irreversible and severe physical handicaps where the most likely termination of residence is death. They contrasted two ideologies which they believed existed in such institutions: the 'warehousing' philosophy, with its emphasis upon physical care and the dependence of residents; and the 'horticultural' philosophy, with its emphasis on the cultivation of residents' interests and abilities. They stress that each has dangers - the one of dependence and institutionalization, the other of unrealistic expectations being set - and that each is a response to the serious nature of the residents' handicaps.

There are a number of studies of social behaviour on the wards of mental hospitals which prove the point that social climate depends upon the mix of patients who are residing there. A clear instance was provided by Fairweather's (1964) study which is described more fully below. Introducing changes of a progressive nature on a hospital ward increased the level of social interaction generally but significant differences between different patient groups still persisted, with non-psychotic patients interacting most, acute psychotic patients an intermediate amount, and chronic psychotic patients the least. The mix of clients is especially crucial where group influence is considered to be one of the principal media of change (whether the change desired be educational, therapeutic or rehabilitative). Even in the relatively permissive climate of the Henderson therapeutic community, those with particularly socially disruptive personalities cannot be tolerated and, if accidentally admitted, may have to be discharged.

Under circumstances where group influence operates, it is particularly important that the client group exerts its main influence in a manner consistent with the overriding philosophy espoused by staff. This is always in danger of going wrong in secondary schools where the 'adolescent sub-culture' may exert a countervailing force, and in prisons where the 'inmate code' has to be contended with. In Canadian schools and centres for juvenile delinquents a procedure known as the 'Measurement of Treatment Potential' (MTP) has been in use to assess this aspect of climate. Where clients choose as liked fellow clients the same members as those whose behaviour is approved of by staff, then treatment potential is considered to be high. When there is a mismatch between residents' and staff choices, treatment potential is said to be low.

Climate
Many factors contributing to climate have been considered in

this chapter and there are many others which it has not been possible to consider. Repeatedly emphasized has been the complex way in which these factors interact to influence the climate of an institutional unit. 'Climate', a word used here to cover any perceptions of, or feelings about, the institution held by those who use it, work in it or observe it, is not the same thing as success, effectiveness, or productivity. However, the latter are notoriously difficult to define, let alone measure, whereas people's perceptions of atmosphere can be collected and their relationships with features of the institution analysed. A massive programme of research along these lines has been conducted by Moos (1974). He has devised a series of questionnaires to tap the perceptions of members of various types of institutions and organizations. The most thoroughly tested of these scales is the Ward Atmosphere Scale (WAS), which assesses perceptions along the ten dimensions shown in table 2. This list was based upon earlier research by others as well as a great deal of preliminary work of Moos' own. He claims that dimensions 1-3 (the relationship dimensions) and 8-10 (the system maintenance and system change dimensions) are equally relevant across a wide range of institutions including schools, universities, hospitals and penal institutions. Dimensions 4-7 (the personal development dimensions), on the other hand, need modification depending upon the setting.

Amongst the many findings from research based upon the WAS and similar scales are the following. First, when staff and patient perceptions are compared in hospital treatment settings, average staff scores are regularly found to be higher on all dimensions except Order and Organization (no difference between staff and patients), and Staff Control (patients scoring higher than staff). Second, when scores are correlated with size of unit and with staff-to-patient ratio, it has been found that Support and Spontaneity are both lower and Staff Control is higher where patient numbers are greater and staff-to-patient ratios are poorer (MTP has also been found to correlate with smallness of size and favourability of staff to pupil ratios). Third, where patients have greater 'adult status' (access to bedrooms, television, unrestricted smoking, less institutional admission procedure, etc.), Spontaneity, Autonomy, Personal Problem Orientation, and Anger and Aggression are all higher and Staff Control is lower. Fourth, all scales correlate positively with ratings of general satisfaction with the ward and with ratings of liking for staff, with the exception of Staff Control which correlates negatively with both.

Changing institutions

A knowledge of the factors discussed in this chapter should enable those involved in policy, planning and management to generate ideas for constructive change, and those in relatively junior positions to try and bring about change in their practice within the prevailing limits of autonomy.

However, major changes may require innovations or interventions from outside and it is these that are now discussed
in the remainder of this chapter.

Table 2

The 10 dimensions measured by Moos' Ward Atmosphere Scale

RELATIONSHIP DIMENSIONS

1. INVOLVEMENT measures how active and energetic patients are in the day-to-day social
   functioning of the ward. Attitudes such as pride in the ward, feelings of group
   spirit, and general enthusiasm are also assessed.

2. SUPPORT measures how helpful and supportive patients are towards other patients, how
   well the staff understand patient needs and are willing to help and encourage
   patients, and how encouraging and considerate doctors are towards patients.

3. SPONTANEITY measures the extent to which the environment encourages patients to act
   openly and to express freely their feelings towards other patients and staff.

PERSONAL DEVELOPMENT DIMENSIONS

4. AUTONOMY assesses how self-sufficient and independent patients are encouraged to be
   in their personal affairs and in their relationships with staff, and how much
   responsibility and self-direction patients are encouraged to exercise.

5. PRACTICAL ORIENTATION asses es the extent to which the patient's environment
   orients him towards preparing himself for release from the hospital and for the
   future.

6. PERSONAL PROBLEM ORIENTATION measures the extent to which patients are encouraged
   to be concerned with their feelings and problems and to seek to understand them
   through openly talking to other patients and staff about themselves and their past.

7. ANGER AND AGGRESSION measures the extent to which a patient is allowed and
   encouraged to argue with patients and staff, and to become openly angry.

SYSTEM MAINTENANCE AND SYSTEM CHANGE DIMENSIONS

8. ORDER AND ORGANIZATION measures the importance of order on the ward; also measures
   organization in terms of patients (do they follow a regular schedule? Do they have
   carefully planned activities?) and staff (do they keep appointments? Do they help
   patients follow schedules?)

9. PROGRAMME CLARITY measures the extent to which the patient knows what to expect
   in the day-to-day routine of his ward and how explicit the ward rules and procedures
   are.

10. STAFF CONTROL measures the necessity for the staff to restrict patients: that is,
    the strictness of rules, schedules and regulations, and measures taken to keep
    patients under effective control.

Innovative programmes

One of the best documented programmes of institutional
change in the mental health care system is the work reported
in a series of publications by Fairweather and his colleagues. The first report (Fairweather, 1964) described
dramatic differences in patient social behaviour between an
experimental 'small group' ward and a physically identical
'traditional' ward in a mental hospital. In the traditional
ward, staff members made final decisions on all important
matters. By contrast, on the small group ward it was the
responsibility of a group of patients to orient new fellow
patients to the ward, to carry out work assignments, to
assess patient progress, and to recommend privileges and
even final discharge. The total experiment lasted for six
months, and staff switched wards halfway through. Social
activity was at a much higher level on the small group ward,
and the climate in the daily ward meeting was quite different with more silence and staff control on the traditional
ward, and more lively discussion, less staff talk, and many
more patient remarks directed towards fellow patients on the
small group ward. Nursing and other staff evaluated their
experience on the small group ward more highly, and patients
spent significantly fewer days in hospital.

In a further report, Fairweather et al (1969) compared
the community adjustment of ex-patients who moved together
as a group from a small group ward in the hospital to a
small hostel unit in the community (the 'lodge'), and others
who moved out of the hospital in the normal way. The results
were quite dramatic, with the lodge group surviving much
better in the community in terms of the prevention of re-
admission to hospital, the amount of time in work (much of
which was organized by the ex-patient group as a consor-
tium), and residents' morale and self-esteem. This is a
particularly good example of the setting-up from scratch of
a new small institution designed to avoid many of the most
disagreeable features of large institutions.

Changes in the philosophies and modes of practice in
institutions mostly take place over a period of years as a
result of the slow diffusion of new ideas. A third report by
Fairweather et al (1974) was concerned with this process.

Having established the value of the lodge programme,
they set out to sell the idea to mental hospitals throughout
the USA. They were concerned to know the influence of a
number of variables upon the diffusion process, and consequently adopted a rigorous experimental approach. First,
they varied the degree of effort required on the part of the
hospital contacted in order to accept the initial approach
offered. Of 255 hospitals contacted, one-third were merely
offered a brochure describing the lodge programme (70 per
cent accepted but only 5 per cent finally adopted the lodge
programme), one-third were offered a two-hour workshop about
the programme (80 per cent accepted and 12 per cent finally
adopted), and one-third were offered help with setting up a
demonstration small group ward in the hospital for a minimum

of 90 days (only 25 per cent accepted but 11 per cent finally adopted the lodge). A second variable was the position in the hospital hierarchy of the person contacted with the initial approach offer. One-fifth of initial contacts were made to hospital superintendents and one-fifth to each of the four professions, psychiatry, psychology, social work and nursing. This variable turned out to be relatively unimportant: contacts were just as likely to result in the adoption of the lodge programme when they were made to people in nursing as to superintendents or those in psychiatry.

Much more important than the status of the person who initiates an idea is, according to Fairweather et al, a high level of involvement across disciplines, professions, and social status levels within the institution. When change did occur there was most likely to exist a multi-disciplinary group which spearheaded the change, led by a person who continuously pushed for change and attempted to keep the group organized and its morale high. The disciplinary gr up to which this person belonged was of little importance. Nor was change related to financial resources. The need for perseverance is stressed. The need to keep pushing for change despite 'meetings that came to naught, letters that stimulated nothing, telephone calls unreturned, and promises unkept' is a necessary ingredient of institutional change.

Action research

Fairweather's studies concerned the setting-up of new facilities or units. If, on the other hand, constructive change is to be brought about in existing institutions and their units, the total climate of the institution, and particularly the autonomy of the individual staff members, are limiting factors. A number of schemes have been described for providing helpful intervention from outside in the form of a person or team who act as catalysts or change agents. Several of these involve the process known as Action Research. For example, Towell and Harries (1979) have described a number of changes brought about at Fulbourne psychiatric hospital in Cambridgeshire with the help of a specially appointed 'social research adviser'.

The process begins when the interventionist(s) is invited to a particular unit to advise or help. It is stressed that the initiative should come from the unit and not from the interventionist, although it is clearly necessary for the latter to advertise the service being offered, and Moos (1974), for example, has argued that feeding back research data on social climate can itself initiate a change process. After the initial approach there follows a period during which the action researcher gets to know the unit, usually by interviewing as many members as possible individually, by attending unit meetings, and by spending time in the unit observing. Then follow the stages which give 'action research' its name. With the help of the action researcher, members of the unit (usually the staff group collectively) decide upon a piece of research which can be quickly mounted and carried through and which is relevant to the matter in hand. The results of this research are then used to help decide what changes are necessary. The action researcher remains involved during these phases and subsequently as attempts are made to implement changes and to make them permanent.

For example, one of the Fulbourne projects concerned a long-stay ward which had adopted an 'open door', no-staff-uniforms policy and which was designated as suitable for trainee nurses to gain 'rehabilitation experience'. The staff, however, felt 'forgotten' at the back of the hospital, felt that scope for patient improvement was not often realized, and that they were unable to provide the rehabilitation experience intended. The social research adviser helped the staff devise a simple interview schedule which focussed on such matters as how patients passed their time, friendships amongst patients, and feelings patients had about staff and their work. Each member of staff was responsible for carrying out certain interviews and for writing them up and presenting them to the group. All reports were read by all members of staff and discussed at a special meeting. The group reached a consensus that patients were insular, took little initiative, expected to be led by staff, had no idea of 'self-help', saw little treatment function for the nurses, saw little purposeful nurse-patient interaction, and had only negative feelings, if any, towards fellow patients.

Although there were no immediate or dramatic changes, a slow development over a period of 18 months was reported in the direction of a much increased 'counselling approach to care'. The research interview was incorporated into routine care. This itself involved the setting-up of a special contact between individual nurse and individual patient, a factor which is mentioned in other projects described by Towell and Harries and by many other writers who have described constructive changes in institutions. At first the social research adviser took a leading role in groups in helping to understand the material gathered in interviews. This role was later taken over by the ward doctor and later still by a senior member of the nursing staf At this point the social research adviser withdrew. Later on patients read back interview reports and there were many other signs of reduced staff and patient distance. Over the three-year period during which these changes came about, the number of patients resettled outside the hospital increased from two in the first year to eight in the second and eleven in the third.

It is stressed by those who have described 'action research' and schemes like it, such as 'administrative consultation' and the type of social systems change facilitated by a consultant described by Maxwell Jones (1976), that staff of a unit must be fully involved and identified with any change that is attempted. It is relatively easy to bring about acceptance of change on an attitudinal level, largely through talking, but to produce a behavioural commitment to change is something else. Those who have written of the 'action research' process talk of the importance of 'ownership' of the research activity. The aim is to get the unit's members fully involved and to make them feel the research is theirs.

Resistance to change

We should expect such complex social systems, whose mode of operation must have been arrived at because it serves certain needs or produces certain pay-offs for those involved, to be resistant to change. Particularly should we expect it to be resistant to change when this threatens to involve change in status and role relationships. Unfortunately, it is just such changes for which we so frequently search. The themes of decision-making autonomy and social power have been constant ones throughout this chapter; they lie at the heart of what is wrong with many of the worst institutions. Maxwell Jones (1976) believes it is almost always the required task of the social systems facilitator to 'flatten' the authority hierarchy, and to support lower status members in taking the risks involved in expressing their feelings and opinions, whilst at the same time supporting higher status members in the belief that they can change in the direction of relinquishing some of their authority.

As in most earlier sections of this chapter, examples of attempts to change institutions or parts of institutions have been taken from the mental health field. Nevertheless, the processes and problems involved can be recognized by those whose main concern is with other types of institution such as the educational and penal. In particular, those who have in any way, large or small, attempted to change such institutions can recognize the problem of resistance to change. Nothing illustrates better the need to add to our understanding of how institutions work. In the process of finding out more on this topic we learn more of man in a social context, which is part of the central core of the study of psychology.

References

Barton, R. (1959; 3rd edn, 1976)
Institutional Neurosis. Bristol: Wright.
Canter, D. and Canter, S. (eds) (1979)
Designing for Therapeutic Environments: A review of research. Chichester: Wiley.
Fairweather, G.W. (ed.) (1964)
Social Psychology in Treating Mental Illness. New York: Wiley.
Fairweather, G.W., Sanders, D.H., Cressler, D.L. and Maynard, H. (1969)
Community Life for the Mentally Ill: An alternative to institutional care. Chicago: Aldine.

Fairweather, G.W., Sanders, D.H. and Tornatsky, L.G. (1974)
Creating Change in Mental Health Organizations. New York: Pergamon.

Goffman, E. (1961)
Asylums: Essays on the social situation of mental patients and other inmates. New York: Anchor Books, Doubleday.

Jones, Maxwell (1952)
Social Psychiatry: A study of therapeutic communities. London: Tavistock (published as The Therapeutic Community, New York: Basic Books: 1953).

Jones, Maxwell (1976)
Maturation of the Therapeutic Community: An organic approach to health and mental health. New York: Human Sciences Press.

Miller, E.J. and Gwynne, G.V. (1972)
In Life Apart: A pilot study of residential institutions for the physically handicapped and the young chronic sick. London: Tavistock.

Moos, R.H. (1974)
Evaluating Treatment Environments: A social ecological approach. New York: Wiley.

Rapoport, R.M. (1960)
Community as Doctor: New perspectives on a therapeutic community. London: Tavistock.

Tizard, J., Sinclair, I. and Clarke, R.V.G. (eds) (1975)
Varieties of Residential Experience. London: Routledge & Kegan Paul.

Towell, D. and Harries, C. (1979)
Innovations in Patient Care. London: Croom Helm.

Questions

1. Discuss the characteristics of the 'total institution', and relate these to any institutional setting which you have experienced. Do you consider the concept of the 'total institution' to be clinically useful? If you do, justify your view.

2. Consider the hospital as an example of an institution. What are the factors which make a hospital into an institution? What factors tend to influence the climate of the hospital as an institution?

3. Discuss the effects of the following factors on the 'climate' of the institution: (a) size; (b) location; (c) staff behaviour; (d) clients, patients or inmates; (e) administration.

4. What does 'institutionalization' mean? Is 'institutional neurosis' a necessary consequence of long-term care in institutions?

5. Consider the example of a long-term ward for psychiatric patients which, in terms of both its physical and social characteristics, is clearly a poor environment. Would you expect this to affect patients? How? What might be done to remedy or prevent adverse effects?

6. List and discuss the ways in which institutions can be made more therapeutic for patients or inmates.
7. What contribution can the doctor make to improving the institutional care of the chronically physically handicapped in hospitals?
8. Discuss the contribution which research could make to both the understanding and improvement of institutions. Consider in particular the problems involved in applying research techniques to the institution.
9. Discuss the suggestion that institutional change is often necessary but invariably difficult. Why is it difficult to change institutions? What can the doctor do to facilitate change?

Annotated reading

Barton, R. (1959; 3rd edn, 1976) Institutional Neurosis. Bristol: Wright.
> This is now a classic, describing institutionalization as a state analogous to a disease. It is written from a medical perspective but is brief, easy to read, describes the effects of institutionalization within a hospital setting, but forcefully makes the point that the state can arise in any institutional setting.

Fairweather, G.W., Sanders, D.H., Cressler, D.L. and Maynard, H. (1969) Community Life for the Mentally Ill: An alternative to institutional care. Chicago: Aldine.
> The main part of this book describes the story of a group of mental hospital patients who left the hospital together and set up home in a 'lodge', living and working productively together. Elsewhere in the book research findings are reported. Those who enjoy reading about research findings may also wish to read Fairweather, G. W. (ed.) (1964), 'Social Psychology in Treating Mental Illness', New York: Wiley.

Goffman, E. (1961) Asylums: Essays on the social situation of mental patients and other inmates. New York: Anchor Books, Doubleday.
> Another classic, in which a sociologist describes the events and processes he saw in a large American mental hospital. The book is full of telling sociological insights, but it is important when reading 'Asylums' to have in one's mind the knowledge that not all institutions, not even all mental hospitals, are alike and that there are important differences amongst them.

Jones, Maxwell (1952) Social Psychiatry: A study of therapeutic communities. London: Tavistock. (Published as 'The Therapeutic Community', New York: Basic Books, 1953).
> Again a classic. The original description of the concept of the Therapeutic Community. Revolutionary in its time and still very well worth reading to understand the basic ideas behind the concept.

King, R.D., Raynes, N.V. and Tizard, J. (1971) Patterns of Residential Care: Sociological studies in institutions for handicapped children. London: Routledge & Kegan Paul.
This book is detailed and has quite a high research content. It is especially useful for the definitions and criteria for assessing institutional practices. Because of this it has been an influential book upon which later research has been based.

King's Fund (undated). Living in Hospital: The social needs of people in long-term care. London: Research Publications Limited.
This is an easy to digest pamphlet designed to be read by people who work in institutions. It poses a number of very detailed questions which the reader should ask himself about the environment created in his own institution for those who reside there.

Miller, E.J. and Gwynne, G.V. (1972) A Life Apart: A pilot study of residential institutions for the physically handicapped and the young chronic sick. London: Tavistock.
This is an account of a study of several homes and hospital units for a very disadvantaged group, most of whom would never leave the institutions in which they were resident. It describes several places in considerable detail and in the course of so doing raises many of the issues with which the present chapter on institutional climates is concerned.

Otto, S. and Orford, J. (1978) Not Quite Like Home: Small hostels for alcoholics and others. Chichester: Wiley.
This book is in two parts. The first reviews work on institutions and on small hostels for the mentally ill, offenders, and people with drinking problems in particular. The second part describes in detail a research study of two particular hostels for problem drinkers. It covers a great deal of important ground but is probably not so easy to read as some of the other books suggested.

Tizard, J., Sinclair, I. and Clarke, R.V.G. (eds) (1975) Varieties of Residential Experience. London: Routledge & Kegan Paul.
This book is an important collection of chapters written by different authors describing a variety of studies of residential institutions of one kind or another, mostly for children or adolescents. Particularly important are the first chapter in which the editors criticize the simplicity of Goffman's approach in 'Asylums', and the chapter by Barbara Tizard in which she shows how residential nurseries can be run in very different ways.

Towell, D. and Harries, C. (1979) Innovations in Patient Care. London: Croom Helm.

These authors describe how changes were brought about in the running of a mental hospital. Particularly inspiring in my view is chapter 2 which describes how significant change was brought about in an acute psychiatric ward and on a long-stay ward.

Rutter, M., Maughan, B., Mortimore, P. and Ouston, J. (1979) Fifteen Thousand Hours: Secondary schools and their effects on children. London: Open Books.

Here is a recent account of a detailed research project concerning the organization of a number of London secondary schools and their effect on the pupils' achievement and behaviour. The research is detailed and painstaking and the book is probably not easy to read, but for those who find statistics heavy going it contains some valuable passages about differences in school organization.

Walter, J.A. (1978) Sent Away: A study of young offenders in care. Farnborough, Hants.: Teakfield.

Walter's book describes his detailed observations and results of interviews at one Scottish List D school (the equivalent of the English Community Home or, as it used to be called, Approved School). It is a racy, easy to read account, concentrating particularly on the overall ideology or philosophy of the school and its effect upon staff and boys.

11

Personality and Individual Assessment
P. Kline

Opening remarks
DAVID GRIFFITHS

Psychological assessment is naturally an important part of
the contribution of the psychologist to the Health Services.
Assessment, both of physical and psychological variables, is
basic to many aspects of patient care. Assessments of behaviour and psychological functioning, more particularly, have
important roles in paediatrics, neurology, psychiatry and
mental handicap. In all of these specialities, assessments
contribute to diagnostic decisions, and are used to identify
patients' assets and handicaps, to facilitate the selection
of treatment goals and to monitor progress and change and
responses to therapy. The relevance of assessments will be
related to the influence which they have on decisions and
action, and psychologists will usually be keen to identify
clinically relevant questions before they undertake any
assessments of intellectual functioning, memory, social
competence, vocational interests or other aspects of personality. For example, what is the patient's current intellectual level, and is there any indication that this has
changed? Has there been any deterioration? What are the
effects of specific techniques (such as neurosurgery) on
intelligence and memory? What are the main deficits present
in the behaviour of a mentally handicapped child? Is a
patient suitable for psychotherapy? What occupations are
most likely to be suitable for an individual on the basis of
his intellectual level, personality and interests?

Psychological assessment can be a complex and specialized matter and Paul Kline's chapter provides a useful
introduction for doctors. His review is concerned with a
selection of assessment techniques: tests, the interview,
rating scales and many other devices. The rationale and
theoretical models which serve as a basis for the derivation
and use of assessments are also described and the contributions of Freud, Eysenck and others are critically evaluated.
Doctors will find this chapter particularly useful since it
combines an enthusiasm for the potential value of tests with
a caution about their limitations. Numbers and quantitative
scores are useful but they can also be misleading and seductive, and it is important for both the psychologist and
clinician to be aware of the limitations of psychological
tests. Kline's introduction places some emphasis on the need
to establish the reliability and validity of the many

techniques which are included in his review and he continues to provide many specific examples of the advantages and limitations of the more commonly used devices.

It is particularly important for doctors to note Kline's comments on the interview and clinical assessment. He suggests that, as a technique for decision making, the interview can be very unreliable. It therefore lacks validity. The dilemma posed by the evidence is that, though the interview is clearly fallible and unreliable, there is no real alternative to it since decisions have to be made. Though the solution to this problem is not provided, this part of the discussion should encourage a realistic degree of caution about clinical and interview decisions which cannot be assumed to be invariably present amongst clinicians.

The use and value of psychological tests
P. KLINE

There are more than 2,000 psychological tests currently published in the United States and Great Britain. Psychological tests are widely used daily in all branches of applied psychology. It is therefore a pertinent question to ask why they are so used, and what value they have.

Basically, whenever it is helpful to know the personal characteristics of the person with whom we are dealing, then psychological testing is valuable. Some examples will clarify this point.

* CHILD IN SCHOOL: suppose we have a child who is making poor progress in his work. It is then sensible to test his basic intelligence, and his verbal and numerical ability. If it turns out that he is dim, then we can adjust our expectations and his syllabus accordingly. If he is not, then we look elsewhere for the cause of his difficulties: for example, problems at home and so on.
* YOUNG ADULT NEEDING VOCATIONAL GUIDANCE: here it is helpful to know the range of his interests and abilities: also, perhaps, his personality. The requisite tests can tell us what we need to know far more accurately than intuitive guesses from an interview.
* HOSPITAL PATIENT, HIGHLY DEPRESSED AND AWK-WARD: in this case, a measure of anxiety and depression could well help us to establish whether this is a personality difficulty or whether it is a less fundamental reaction to the situation, in which case ameliorative tactics can be employed.

These three examples can easily be multiplied in all fields of human psychology. The point is that psychological tests allow the most accurate assessment of personal characteristics that has been devised and thus give us a factual basis on which to make our professional decisions concerning treatment and practice. There can be no doubt that psychological tests are one of the most useful things to have emerged from the study of human psychology.

However, not all psychological tests are efficient and of good quality. Hence in this chapter we examine the nature of good tests and their construction so that we can understand their value and not simply use them blindly, believing in them because psychologists claim them to be good or, conversely, not use them at all on some mystical and mythical argument that tests are bad and measure nothing but ability on tests. That is why, in this chapter, we lay the emphasis on the characteristics of good tests and the proper interpretation of the meaning of the scores. We examine individual differences among human beings, how such differences are measured, and the psychological implications of such differences for understanding personality and behaviour.

First of all we discuss psychological tests and testing techniques, for it is by the application of these measures that individual differences have been discovered.

Characteristics of good psychological tests and how these may be achieved

Efficient testing devices must be (i) reliable, (ii) valid and (iii) discriminating.

Reliability
Reliability has two meanings: first, self-consistency, which means that tests must be self-consistent, and each item should measure the same variable. Imagine an instrument, for example, which measured in part pressure as well as temperature. Second, consistency over time, which is called test-retest reliability. If a test is administered a second time to a subject, the score on the two occasions should be the same unless a change has taken place. Reliability is measured by the correlation coefficient, an index of agreement running from +1 (perfect agreement) to -1 (perfect disagreement). A correlation of 0 shows random agreement. Good tests should have a reliability coefficient of at least 0.7, which represents 49 per cent agreement (square the coefficient and convert to percentage).

1. FACTORS INFLUENCING RELIABILITY

* Test length: it can be shown that reliability increases with the length of a test. Thus the typical university essay exam, having only four items - four essays - is not highly reliable. Consider what the sources of unreliability might be for such an essay-type examination. This is one reason why most psychological tests have a large number of items. Twenty items are about the minimum necessary for reliability.
* Objective scoring: scores should be objective, there should be no personal judgement required of the scorer. Where judgement is required, as in essays, differences arise, often large, between the same marker's attempts if he re-scores the test. Thus a good test has items that are objectively scored.

If a test is reliable, then it can be valid. Notice the 'can'. It is possible to devise a highly reliable test that measures virtually nothing. A test for measuring the length of people's noses would be easy to devise and it could be very reliable, but it is unlikely to be a valid test of intelligence or personality. On the other hand, an unreliable, inconsistent test which gives different scores on different occasions cannot possibly be valid.

Validity

A test is said to be valid if it measures what it claims to measure. This may sound obvious, but many tests are quite invalid. For example, essay-type tests of scientific subjects are highly unlikely to be valid since essay writing demands verbal ability, and ability in physics is somewhat different from this. The term validity is used in psychological testing (psychometrics) in different ways.

1. FACE VALIDITY: this refers to the appearance of a test which is said to be face-valid if it looks as if it measures what it claims to measure. This is important in testing adults who may balk at doing tests which look absurd. They may simply refuse to co-operate or treat the test as a bit of a joke. Children, however, are used to overlooking such niceties. Face validity is not usually related to true validity.

2. CONCURRENT VALIDITY: this refers to studies of the validity of a test made on one occasion. For example, the concurrent validity of a new test of intelligence would be assessed by its correlation with a well-established intelligence test; that is, does the new test give a similar score to the score on the existing test? Concurrent validity studies are beset by problems of criteria: what tests or other measurement should be used in establishing the concurrent validity of a test? If other similar tests are used, and the correlation is very high, the question arises as to what value the new test has since it is measuring the same variable as the old one.

3. PREDICTIVE VALIDITY: this refers to the capacity of a test to correlate with some future criterion measure. This can be the most powerful evidence for the validity of a test. Some examples will clarify this point. Thus a good test of anxiety should be able to predict future attendance at the psychiatric clinic, and a good test of intelligence given at 11 years of age should correlate with future academic performance in O and A level examinations and at university. Thus the test predicts events external to the test itself.

4. CONSTRUCT VALIDITY: the construct validity of a test is defined by taking a large set of results obtained with the test and seeing how well they fit in with our notion of

the psychological nature of the variable which the test claims to measure. Thus it embraces concurrent and predictive validity. In effect we set up a series of hypotheses concerning the test results and put these to the test. For example, if our test was a valid measure of intelligence we might expect:

* high-level professional groups would score more highly than lower-level professionals;
* children rated as highly intelligent by teachers would score more highly than others;
* scores would correlate positively with level of education;
* scores would correlate highly with scores in public examinations;
* scores would correlate highly with scores on other intelligence tests;
* scores would not correlate with scores on tests not claiming to measure intelligence.

If all these hypotheses were supported then the construct validity of our test would be demonstrated. It is deserving of note that it is always useful to show (as in the final point mentioned above) what tests do not measure, a technique used by Socrates in his examination of the meaning of words.

Unlike reliability for which there can be clear, unequivocal evidence, the validity of a test is, to some extent, subjective. Nevertheless, most well-known tests, especially of ability, have accumulated so much evidence relating to validity that there is no dispute about them. It is more difficult to demonstrate the validity of personality tests but, as will be seen, it can be done. Many psychological tests have little support for their validity and a large number are clearly invalid. Given the list of criteria and procedure requirements set out above, you should now be in a position to ask the right questions about any new test or test results which are presented to you.

Discriminatory power
Good psychological tests should be discriminating: that is, they should produce a wide distribution of scores. For example, if we test 10 children and all score 15 we have made no discriminations at all.

If four score 13, three score 12 and another three score 14 then we have made only three discriminations. If, on the other hand, each child scores a different score, then the distribution of scores is wide. The scatter of scores in a distribution is known as the variance and the standard deviation is the usual measurement. A good test has a large standard deviation. A test can be so simple that all children pass all items, or so hard that no child passes any item; clearly, neither would provide useful information. With tests which are reliable, valid and discriminating, it is possible to investigate the nature of individual differences in human beings. In fact, this has been going on since the turn of the century when Binet began the assessment of educability of Parisian children.

Methods of assessment of individual differences

With these demands for adequate testing in mind, we can now scrutinize the various methods for the assessment of individual differences. The reader should make sure that he understands fully all that has been said so far before going on to the next section.

The interview

This is the commonest form of assessment and almost certainly the worst. The standard interview requires the subject to answer questions face to face with the interviewer or panel. This basic procedure can be varied. For example, groups of subjects can be interviewed together: the interview may have a schedule of questions which is rigid or flexible. In some cases interviewers have no predetermined set of questions. Again the interviewer may simply reflect back the answers of the subjects, in others he may respond fiercely.

However, there are so many serious problems with interviews that in most cases they are best abandoned. These problems are:

* poor interview reliability: there is poor reliability between different interviewers and between occasions if the same interviewer sees subjects twice. As we have discussed, this is fatal to the validity of the technique.
* poor validity: Vernon, working with the army in an intensive examination of the interview, found little evidence for its validity. The Halo effect (judgement on one variable being influenced by judgements of others), bias and inferences from external signs - for example, that subjects with pocket-watches are ostentatious - are all sources of error. He concluded that the interview can even lower the efficiency of selection techniques.

While careful training of interviewers can eliminate some of these faults, there is still no clear evidence that interviews are an effective method of assessment. At best they should be used only to supplement data from other sources, by eliciting information that could not be obtained by any other method. In brief, the interview often has to be used because there is no alternative, but it should be used with extreme caution when important decisions are being made.

The rating scale

Rating scales require the rater to place subjects on some point of a continuum which implies the possession of some characteristic or trait. Subjects can be rated, for example, for aggression or for neatness on a five- or seven-point scale, extending from very aggressive to very meek.

PROBLEMS WITH RATING SCALES

* In many cases, unless subjects are known to the raters for a long time and have been seen in a wide variety of contexts, ratings on some variables are literally impossible. Thus, to make an adequate judgement, the behaviours in question need to be sampled adequately. Think of the last time you were shy, or angry, or noisy: would someone observing you on just that occasion have obtained an accurate and representative sample of your behaviour?

* The inter-rater reliability is often poor. This is because ratings reflect the rater as well as the subject's behaviour. For example, some raters always use extremes, others never. Some raters always choose the middle. Their use of language, in other words, affects the scales. To overcome this problem, each point on the scale can be tied to specific behaviour. Thus 'very weak' might include 'always does what others want, never makes suggestions of his own', etc. Clearly, a great deal of work has to be done before a scale is ready to use. Not only must the items be standardized but the raters must be trained to use them reliably.

* The halo effect (see above) also affects ratings, tending to make ratings correlated. This reduces the discriminatory power of items.

* The rater's presence can affect the behaviour under observation.

* Rating scales have poor discriminating power. Generally five or seven points are about the most a rater can reliably use. Thus discriminations with such scales do not compare well with those made by a 100-item test.

From what we have said about principles of test construction, it can be seen that many of these faults are technical rather than logical and can, therefore, in principle be overcome. However, although some of these faults can be remedied by using a large number of raters, each with comparable means and standard deviations, and each rating traits separately after living with the subjects for some time, generally rating scales are clumsy and unreliable methods of assessment. This is usually because people who have devised many of the rating scales in use have not had sufficient training in psychometric procedures.

Mention should be made here of behavioural assessment. This involves the observation and counting of specific behaviours. For example, in clinical psychology it is often useful over the course of psychotherapy, especially with in-patients, to make behavioural assessments. In this the relevant behaviours can be listed and their frequency can be computed over a sample time period. Thus, if psychotherapy aimed to improve ward co-operation, appropriate examples can be listed and frequency counts made: results can be compared before and after treatments. An example of such a scale in current use is the Stott British Social Adjustment Guide for evaluating the behaviour of children, at home, at school, and at residential schools. Such measurement can be reliable if the behaviours listed are described with sufficient accuracy.

Repertory grids

A repertory grid is constructed basically of elements and constructs. Elements usually consist of the objects which we desire to know how subjects construe (i.e. think about). Thus in clinical assessment typical elements might be: mother, father, wife and child. A study of such elements would discover how the subject sees his world. In educational assessment, elements would relate to school, with mathematics, English, teacher 1, teacher 2, etc., all actually named. These elements are usually elicited from the subject himself.

The constructs are the discriminations made by a person among his elements. These are usually elicited from the subject himself. Thus, for example, if a subject says that his mother is warm but his father is aloof, then the bipolar dimension warm/aloof becomes one construct in this subject's grid.

By eliciting elements and constructs in this way we can make up a matrix, the grid, with elements along the top and constructs running vertically down. Subjects then rank or rate the elements along the dimension of each construct. This enables the grid user to see what constructs go together for this subject and what elements cluster together. For instance, it may emerge that a subject has 'attractive' and 'slim' as two correlated constructs. This means that he is unlikely to have a fat girlfriend. Similarly, if we find that 'husband' and 'father' are correlated (i.e. share the same constructs in the subject's mind) then we know the kind of marital relationship the subject is likely to have.

The repertory grid is not a test: rather it is a method particularly suited to idiographic measurement; that is, the measurement of what is private and particular to an individual. However, it must be noted that scores from different individuals are not comparable since each grid is particular to an individual. This, therefore, indicates that the basic repertory grid is useful for individual casework rather than for studies where comparability between subjects is important.

This leads us on to two further points. The first is that the grid can be used with given elements and constructs. This enables subjects to be compared and norms can be built up, so that the grid then becomes little different from a set of rating scales with norms. It clearly loses all the advantages of the grid, for the basic grid is concerned with the actual cognitive world of the subject in contradistinction to ordinary tests, which use words and concepts whose meanings may well differ for each and every subject.

The second point concerns the question of whether the grid is anything more than a carefully designed interview. Certainly much of the information from a grid could be obtained from an interview. One obvious difference, however, between the grid and the interview is that the grid yields reliable scores. However, despite the grandiose nature of much of the statistical analyses which are fashionable in the treatment of grids (including factorial analyses), it remains doubtful whether the grid data are, in fact, suited to them, since replicable factor analyses (e.g. Nunnally, 1978) require at least 200 subjects and in most grids the n is nowhere near this figure. In many instances, too, no rotations are used but principal components are interpreted, a procedure bound to confound psychological import with artifact. (For a brief description of factor analysis see section below.)

In brief, therefore, we argue that the repertory grid is probably useful in the individual case but that further than this its use is not justified. The complex statistical analyses seem dubious in the light of the data and, used normatively, the grid becomes a set of self-rating scales.

In conclusion, therefore, it can be stated that as methods of assessment:

* interviews are not sufficiently reliable or valid to merit use in isolation when important decisions have to be made;
* rating scales are too cumbersome to complete, requiring extensive knowledge of subjects by raters, and have little discriminatory power, thus contra-indicating their use;
* repertory grids are useful for the study of the individual case but results among subjects are not comparable and complex multivariate statistical analyses of the results are inevitably flawed by statistical artifact.

For all these reasons it would seem sensible, if you wish to measure individual differences, to use tests which are constructed to be reliable, valid and discriminating.

Types of tests and categories of individual differences

Individual differences among human beings fall into relatively independent categories for which different types of tests have been developed.

Intelligence and ability tests

One category of tests is concerned with human abilities. There is a great problem in psychometrics of how many abilities there are. Guilford, for example, in his work on abilities claims 120, while Thurstone in his original analysis argued that nine primary mental abilities were the most important.

Spearman, in his brilliant and original work on the factor analysis of abilities put the case for the primacy of one, 'g', general reasoning ability. So here we have three experts with apparently three very different views of the nature of human abilities.

Resolution of the dilemma: the resolution of this problem concerning the number and nature of abilities has essentially been carried out. There is now agreement among factor analysts as to what constitutes an efficient method of factor analysis that will reach replicable results, factor analysis being the statistical technique used for the analysis of individual differences.

Factor analysis: here we give a brief non-mathematical description of factor analysis to enable the reader to grasp the essentials of the method and understand the results.

1. FACTORS: the basic data for a factor analysis are test scores derived from very many test items administered to many subjects. These scores are then correlated with each other. The aim of the factor analysis is to make sense of the correlations obtained between the variables and to reveal whether there is an underlying structure which accounts for the correlations (which can, of course, be positive, negative or not significantly different from zero). So a factor is simply a linear combination of variables. In factor analysis we attempt to see if we can account for the observed correlations between a set of variables in terms of a few factors (i.e. combinations of those variables). It is thus a simplifying technique.

2. FACTOR LOADINGS: when the factor analysis is computed, each variable loads on the factors. This loading is (essentially) the correlation of the variable with the factor. Thus a factor is defined by its factor loadings. For example, a factor loading on vocabulary, verbal fluency, essay writing, passing GCE English and French, but with no loadings on mathematics, science, or mechanical ability, is clearly a factor of verbal ability.

3. INFINITY OF SOLUTIONS: a major difficulty with factor analysis resides in the fact that there is an infinite number of mathematically equivalent solutions. This is essentially because, if the aim is to reproduce a set of correlations from another set of numbers once a solution has been reached, it is possible to manipulate one figure and the other relevant figures accordingly to produce the same result.

4. SIMPLE STRUCTURE: each solution, mathematically equivalent, can be seen as a hypothesis to account for the observed correlations. Thus by the law of parsimony, Occam's razor, it makes sense to choose the simplest solution. In factor analysis it is agreed that the aim is simple structure: that is, the set of the most simple factors obtainable. In simple structure each factor has a few high

loadings and all other variables load nonsignificantly on them. The procedure by which simple structure is reached is known as rotation because if each factor is regarded as a vector or axis then it can be literally rotated relative to the others until the simplest position (as defined above) is reached. This is rotation to simple structure.

In the field of tests of ability, then, rotation to simple structure should yield the main primary ability factors. Two further points need to be mentioned about factor analysis before proceeding to examine the results.

* Primary and higher-order factors: the factors emerging from a factor analysis are primary or first-order factors. If these are correlated (oblique), then it is possible to factor-analyse these correlations (between the factors). The resulting factors are second order. First-order factors load on variables, second-order on first-orders and so on. Higher-order factors are therefore more broad than first-orders.

* Sampling subjects and variables: if factor analysis is used to explore and define an area as it is in the study of abilities, then it is essential to sample both subjects and variables as widely as possible. For example, if we include no tests of musical ability in our battery, then clearly no factor of musical ability can emerge. Similarly, if we restrict our sample of subjects to ESN children, it is unlikely that a factor of abstract reasoning would emerge. When we come to examine the primary ability factors, we must bear in mind that all variables have not, in fact, been fully tested.

5. THE PRIMARY ABILITY FACTORS: the factor analysis of abilities rotated to simple structure has yielded the following primary factors. Each factor may be regarded as a basic dimension of ability. Thus performance in any task will depend upon a subject's status on these factors. Our list of factors are those found in a study by Hakstian and Cattell and is a modification of the list presented in Kline (1979).

V   Verbal ability: understanding words and ideas. Loading on synonyms, meaning of proverbs and analogies, it is probably the best indicator of gc (crystallized intelligence).

N   Numerical factor: this is facility in manipulating numbers which is factorially distinct from arithmetic reasoning.

S   Spatial factor: the ability to visualize two or three-dimensional figures when their orientation is altered.

P   Perceptual speed and accuracy factor: which involves

assessing whether pairs of stimuli are similar or different.

Cs Speed of closure of factor: this taps the ability to complete a gestalt when parts of the stimulus are missing. Speed of verbal closure correlates 0.61 with word fluency, suggesting that familiarity with words plays a part in the results.

I Inductive reasoning: this involves induction, reasoning from the specific to the general.

Ma Associative or rote memory: memory for pairs for which no mediating link exists.

Mk Mechanical ability or knowledge.

Cf Flexibility of closure: this involves disregarding irrelevant stimuli in a field to find stimulus figures. According to Hakstian and Cattell this factor is a manifestation of Witkin's field independence.

Ms Span memory: this is the short term of digits or letters, as has long been used in the WISC and WAIS tests (see below).

Sp Spelling: recognition of mis-spelt words. Hakstian and Cattell point out that spelling has not appeared as a factor in previous research because usually there was only one test, thus making the emergence of a factor impossible. Since there are good correlations with V and W, whether spelling is a narrow primary or dependent on these two factors is not yet clear.

E Aesthetic judgement: the ability to detect the basic principles of good art. Like Mk, this would appear to depend much on previous experience.

Mm Meaningful memory: this involves the learning of links between pairs in which there is a meaningful link. The mean correlation of Mm with Ma tests is only 0.35, suggesting that Ma and Mm are behaviourally distinct.

O1 Originality of ideational flexibility: this is loaded on the multiple grouping tests of Guilford and is related to divergent thinking. There are substantial correlations between this O1 factor and O2 and F1.

F1 Ideational fluency: the ability to reproduce ideas rapidly on a given topic. This is distinct from W word fluency and associational and expressional fluency.

W Word fluency: the rapid production of words, conforming to a letter requirement, but without meaning. This factor was found as early as 1933 by Cattell and has occurred regularly in factorial studies ever since.

O2 Originality 2: as with O1 this is a relatively new factor loading on the Guilford tests where subjects have to combine two objects into a functional object.

A Aiming: involving hand-eye co-ordination at speed.

Rd Representational drawing ability: drawings of stimulus objects scored for precision of lines and curves.

D Deductive reasoning.

Mc General motor co-ordination: this is tested by the pursuit rotor, among other tests.

Amu Musical pitch and total sensitivity: found in the Seashore (musical aptitude) test.

Fe Expressional fluency: found in Guilford: verbal expression for assigned ideas.

ams Motor speed: found in Guilford.

asd Speed of symbol discrimination: found in Guilford.

- Musical rhythm and timing.

J Judgement: ability to solve problems where judgement and estimation play a part; again, found in Guilford.

These are the main dimensions of ability as revealed by factor analysis. The first three factors, verbal ability, numerical and spatial ability, are those most implicated in academic performance.

An obvious difficulty with this list of primary factors lies in their number. There are so many that nobody could hold them in their mind at once when thinking about abilities. Thus it is not a successful simplification. However, these factors are correlated and a factor analysis of their inter-correlations reveals the following five factors. It is these which give us the clear, simplified picture of abilities.

6. SECONDARY FACTORS

gf Fluid intelligence: loading on the Culture-Fair test, inference, induction, memory span and flexibility of closure. Also, it loads intellectual speed and level of tests.

gc Crystallized intelligence: this is the factor of traditional intelligence tests. Loading on verbal, mechanical, numerical and social skills factors.

gv Visualization: loads all skills where visualization is helpful, spatial orientation, formboards. This factor loads some of the tests of the Culture-Fair test, thus demonstrating that even here visualization can be useful.

gr Retrieval capacity or general fluency: loading on ideational fluency and irrelevant association tests, it is the general retrieval power which accounts for a variety of skills.

gs Cognitive speed factor: this affects speed in a wide range of tasks although it is a minor factor in solving gf problems. This factor is speed in mechanical performance, for example writing or numerical computation.

In other words, performance in any task depends upon our status on the five factors. In most academic tasks gf and gc are the two critical factors. It is these which together are equivalent to the old-fashioned factor of general intelligence. Fluid ability is close to an inherited reasoning ability while crystallized ability is fluid ability as evinced in a culture. If we were forced to assess subjects for a job with one test, then a good gc test would be our best bet.

Thus, in conclusion, the assessment and factor analysis of abilities have led to the finding that abilities can be conceptualized in terms of five broad factors of which two are critically important (fluid and crystallized ability) in almost all problem-solving tasks.

Aptitude tests

Aptitude tests comprise a group of tests related to tests of ability. Aptitude tests tend to be of two different kinds. One type may be identical with the group tests discussed above. Thus it would be difficult to distinguish between verbal ability and verbal aptitude. However, computer aptitude tests are clearly different: they should test the collection of traits (perhaps more than just abilities) necessary for this particular job. In some instances, such as clerical aptitude, the necessary skills are quite disparate and unrelated to each other because clerical jobs involve a variety of disparate skills. Generally, aptitude tests measure the separate abilities demonstrated to be important for a particular job or class of jobs.

Personality tests

Personality tests can be divided into tests of temperament, mood and dynamics. Temperament tests measure how we do what we do. Temperamental traits are usually thought of as enduring and stable, such as dominance or anxiety. Dynamic traits are concerned with motives: for instance, why we do what we do. These attempt to measure drives such as sexuality or pugnacity. Moods refer to those fluctuating states that we all experience in our lives: anger, fatigue or fear.

Temperament tests

The most used type of temperament test is the personality questionnaire. These consist of lists of items concerned with the subject's behaviour. Typical items are: 'Do you enjoy watching boxing?', 'Do you hesitate before spending a large sum of money?' Items come in various formats. Those above would usually require subjects to respond 'Yes' or 'No', or 'Yes', 'Uncertain' or 'No'. Sometimes items are of the forced choice variety. For example, 'Do you prefer: (i) watching boxing; (ii) going to a musical; or (iii) sitting quietly at home reading?'

CONSTRUCTION OF PERSONALITY QUESTIONNAIRES: given that these items are used, readers may wonder how personality questionnaires are constructed and how are the items chosen? In fact, the selection of items by item analysis is briefly described because this gives an insight into the effectiveness of personality questionnaires.

* Item writing: in the first place, items will be written which are face valid, that is, they appear to be relevant to the variable which we are trying to measure. For example, if we were attempting to measure anxiety we should include items that seemed to touch on the symptoms and feelings of anxiety both as we experience it and as we have found it delineated in the literature, such as finding it difficult to get to sleep, worrying over things one has done, feeling miserable for no good reason, having palpitations, poor appetite, and so on.
* Item analysis: in the construction of tests, the item analysis by which items are selected for a test is the critical issue. The rationale of item analysis is simple: if we are trying to measure a variable (say anxiety) then each selected item should be shown to measure anxiety. Furthermore, if the test is to be discriminating, then each item should be answered in one way (yes or no) by not more than about 80 per cent of the sample. Obviously, our sample for item trials should be drawn from the population for whom the test is intended. Item analysis therefore requires a statistical procedure which will establish that each item measures a common variable, and that each item is discriminating. Three possible procedures are used: (i) factor analysis: the items are correlated and the correlations are then subjected to factor analysis. Items loading on a general factor (unless we are constructing several scales at once) are selected. This method automatically eliminates items of low discrimination, since they will not load up properly. The items are then tried out again on a new sample to eliminate those loading by chance in the first item trial; (ii) correlations of item and total score: a

more simple method and one with less technical problems than factor analysis is to correlate each item with the total score for each scale separately. Items are chosen which correlate beyond 0.3. The endorsement rate for each item is also checked and any items of poor discriminatory power are removed. Finally, all results are checked on a new sample. Results from this method are similar to method one; (iii) criterion-keying: here the items are administered to criterion groups and those items that can discriminate between the groups are selected. The problem here is to establish sufficiently clear criterion groups to make the technique robust. Thus an anxiety scale might be given to a group of anxious patients and a control non-anxious group. In addition, if the groups differ on more than one variable – if, for example, anxiety is confounded with intelligence - the resulting scale could be heterogeneous. Thus this method is not, in our view, as powerful as methods one and two.

* Validation of the scale: finally, the scale produced by the item analysis must be validated as discussed in our section on test validity.

These methods are used in the construction of all psychometric tests which contain items (therefore excluding projective tests: see below), not only personality questionnaires. Method one was used to construct Cattell's 16PF personality questionnaire, method two for our own Ai3Q, a far less well-known test than the former, and method three was used to construct the MMPI (the Minnesota Multiphasic Personality Inventory).

The disadvantages of questionnaires are considerable, in spite of the fact that many valid and highly useful personality questionnaires have been constructed. These disadvantages are: (i) they are easy to fake: that is, subjects may not tell the truth, for one reason or another, and this makes them difficult to use in selection, although for vocational guidance or psychiatric help where subjects have no reason to fake, this is not too serious; (ii) they require a degree of self-knowledge, and some subjects (while attempting to be honest) may respond quite unrealistically; (iii) they are subject to response sets, such as the social desirability set, that is, the tendency to endorse the socially desirable response and present oneself in what one considers to be the most favourable light. For example, to the item, 'Do you have a good sense of humour?', the response 'Yes' would be given by about 95 per cent of subjects. The other serious response set is that of acquiescence, the tendency to put 'Yes' or 'Agree' as an answer regardless of content. Balanced scales, with some responses keyed 'No', obviate this to some extent.

OBJECTIVE TESTS: objective tests, defined by Cattell (cf. Cattell and Kline, 1977) as tests of which the purpose is hidden from the subject and which can be objectively scored (see section on reliability), have been developed to overcome the disadvantages of questionnaires. The aim is to reduce the possibility of faking response sets or acquiescence though the reader might wish to challenge their face validity. Ironically, because their purpose is hidden from subjects, considerable research is necessary to establish their validity, and as yet most are still in an experimental form. These tests will probably take over from questionnaires when the necessary research has been done. The following examples indicate their nature.

* Balloon-blowing: subjects are required to inflate a balloon as much as they can. Measures taken are the size of the balloon, time taken blowing it up, whether they burst it, and if they delay in beginning the task. This test may be related to timidity and inhibition.
* The slow line-drawing test: subjects are required to draw a line as slowly as possible. The measure is the length of line over a fixed time.

In fact more than 800 such tests have been listed and more can easily be developed depending upon the ingenuity of the researcher. The technique is to administer a large battery of such tests and to determine experimentally by so-called 'validity studies' what each of them measures.

PROJECTIVE TESTS: projective tests essentially consist of ambiguous stimuli to which the subjects have to respond. These are some of the oldest personality tests and one, the Rorschach Test (the inkblot test), has achieved a fame beyond psychology. The rationale of projective tests is intuitively brilliant: if a stimulus is so vague that it warrants no particular description, then any description of it must depend on what is projected on to it by the subject. Projective testers believe that projective tests measure the inner needs and fantasies of their subjects. Their ambiguity disarms the subject, thus enabling the tester to sidestep the latter's defences, or his desire to please or to fake.

A serious problem with projective tests lies in their unreliability, however. Very complex responses have to be interpreted by scorers, and often considerable training, experience and expertise is necessary. Inter-marker reliability is low. Generally, too, it is difficult to demonstrate test validity. However, the present writer has experimented with entirely objective forms of scoring these tests and some evidence has now accrued that this is a useful procedure.

PROJECTIVE TEST STIMULI: although any ambiguous stimulus could be used as a test, generally the choice of stimulus is determined by the particular theory of personality the test constructor follows. For example, a psychoanalytically orientated psychologist would select stimuli relevant to that theory, such as vague figures who could be mother and son (the Oedipus complex) or figures with knives or scissors (the castration complex). The TAT (Thematic Apperception Test) developed by Murray uses pictures which, it is hoped, tap the inner needs held by Murray to be paramount in human behaviour.

Mood and motivation tests

Mood and motivation tests are essentially similar to temperament tests, but relatively little work has been done on them and their validity is not so widely attested as that of temperament tests.

Mood tests generally use items that concentrate as might be expected, on present feelings rather than on usual ones. With such tests, high test-retest reliability is not therefore to be expected. However, fluctuations in scores should not be random but should be related to external conditions. Thus experiments can be conducted in which scores, if the tests are valid, can be manipulated. For example, subjects can take the mood test and then some can be angered, others sexually aroused, and the tests can be retaken. If the experimental manipulations are good and the tests valid, the relevant scores should change in response to these changes in mood.

The results of motivation tests should be similarly fluctuating, according to whether drives are sated or frustrated. In a well-known study by the present author the scores of a single subject over a 28-day period were related to a diary recording all that happened to her and everything she felt or thought, and it was found that the relations of scores to diary events were close. For example, the fear drive rose each weekend, when the subject went touring in a dangerous car. The career drive was flat except on the day when the subject was interviewed for a course in teacher training, and so on.

Motivation tests can be of the questionnaire variety, although objective and projective tests are more frequently used. For moods, questionnaire tests are more usually employed, though they suffer, of course, from the same response sets as bedevil questionnaire measures of temperamental traits.

Interest tests

The tests of motivation described above are very general: that is, they measure variables thought to account for a wide variety of human behaviour. Vocational and industrial psychologists, however, have long felt the need for more specific measures of motivation which assess the variables deemed to be of immediate relevance to them, such as interests. For example, we all know of motoring enthusiasts whose interest in cars appears to account for much of their behaviour and conversation.

Thus a number of interest tests have been developed which attempt to assess the individual's major interests:

outdoor, mechanical, or an interest in people for example. In some tests, the scoring of items is in terms of occupational groups. The performance of specific occupational groups on the tests is known and if, for example, foresters score high on a particular item then this item contributes to the 'interest in forestry' score. In other tests, the scoring involves little more than subjects having to rank jobs. In other words, interest tests of this type are like formalized interviews.

Generally, as has been pointed out in Buros (1972), the correlations of interest test scores with success in a job relevant to the interests are modest and little better than the correlation obtained between job success and the subject's response to the question of whether he thinks he would enjoy the job or not.

Attitude tests

Social psychologists have attempted to measure attitudes for many years now. Generally, the attitudes tested are important aspects of a person's life, such as attitudes to war, or to coloured people (in white populations) or to religion. Obviously, if efficient measures of such attitudes are possible then progress can be made in understanding how such attitudes arise and are maintained; important knowledge, it is thought, in a complex multi-racial society. There are three kinds of attitude test, differing in their mode of construction.

* THE THURSTONE SCALES: in these tests proposed items are given to judges to rank on a scale of 1-11 (favourable-unfavourable) in respect of an attitude. Items are then retained on which there is good agreement among the judges. The subject then taking the test is given the highest judged rank score of the items with which he agrees. The reason for this is clear if we consider a few examples. (1) 'War is totally evil' would probably be ranked high as unfavourable to war. (2) 'Wars sometimes have to be fought if there is no alternative': this is clearly against war but not strongly. (3) 'Wars are not always wrong': this is yet further down the scale, while the item (4) 'Wars are good: they select the finest nations' is favourable. Thus a subject who agreed with (1) would not agree with (2), (3) or (4). Similarly, a subject agreeing with (3) would not agree with (4).

    These tests are difficult to construct because much depends on obtaining a good cross-section of judges. A more simple alternative is the Likert Scale.
* LIKERT SCALES: in the Likert scales statements relevant to the attitude being measured are presented to the subject who has to state on a five-point scale the extent of his agreement. Thus a 'Hitler' would score 100 on a 20-item attitude to war scale; a 'Ghandi' would

score zero, one presumes. To make the scale less obvious, items are so written that to agree with items represents both poles of the attitude.

* THE GUTTMAN SCALE: this is a scale so constructed that if the items are ranked for positive attitudes, then any subject who endorses item 10 will also endorse items 1-9 below it. While this tends to happen by virtue of its construction with the Thurstone scale, such perfect ordering rarely occurs in practice. Guttman scales are not much used because they are extremely difficult to construct, and as Nunnally (1978) has pointed out, this perfect ordering of items can usually only be achieved by leaving huge gaps between the items (in terms of attitude) which means few items and rather coarse measurement.

Such, then, are the main types of psychological tests with which individual differences are measured in psychology. Needless to say, these are not the only kinds of test. In the remainder of this chapter we briefly describe some intelligence tests, discuss some of the substantive findings that have emerged from these tests, and examine their application in practical psychology.

Intelligence tests

Intelligence has been the most widely studied of all test variables and, since it is a topic of considerable importance in applied psychology and education, we shall examine in detail some intelligence tests, to help us to understand the nature of intelligence as conceptualized by psychologists.

Individual intelligence tests

Some intelligence tests are given to subjects individually. This enables the tester to measure not only the intelligence of the subject but also to see how he tackles problems and this is very important in educational psychology. For example, it is possible to see whether a child panics at difficulties or goes on and on obsessionally even when it is obvious that no solution will result. Similarly, it can be seen whether the child concentrates on the questions or whether he is easily distracted, which is valuable in attempting to understand any educational difficulties which he may have.

The Wechsler intelligence scale (WISC)

This consists of the following sub-tests which fall into two groups: verbal tests and non-verbal performance tests (Wechsler, 1938). A total IQ score is obtainable as are a verbal IQ and a performance IQ. Large differences between these two sub-scores are of some psychological interest and would call for further study. Some of our examples are taken from Kline (1976).

1. THE VERBAL TESTS

*   Vocabulary: a straightforward vocabulary test. Vocabulary is highly related to intelligence although social class differences in reading habits do, obviously, affect this particular sub-test. Nevertheless, if forced to have to make a selection of intelligent children or adults as quickly as possible, the vocabulary sub-test would be about the best measure obtainable.
*   Information: a test of general knowledge.
*   Arithmetic: an ordinary arithmetic test.

These three tests are heavily affected by school learning and social class. In Cattell's terms they measure gc because, in western countries, fluid ability is most heavily invested in these subjects.

*   Comprehension: this is an interesting test because it presents problems which are dependent upon how much the child is capable of making sensible decisions on its own initiative. One example (which is not in the test) might be a question like 'What would you do if you saw a burglar in the house next door?' Two points would be scored by a response such as 'Phone the police - dial 999'; one point by the response 'Run and tell mummy', and no points by 'Shoot him with my bow and arrow' or 'Push his car over'. At the higher level this sub-test requires abstract analytical reasoning on such questions as 'Why is there a Hippocratic oath?'
*   Similarities: a common form of intelligence test item, simple to write and easy to vary the level of difficulty; for example, 'What is similar about peaches and prunes?' The correct response requires that the essential similarity (fruit) is recognized.
*   Digit span (forward and reverse): digits are read out and the subjects repeat them immediately. Seven or eight digits is the usual span for bright adults.

In the majority of cases most psychologists give five of the six tests, the last two of which in part measure fluid ability.

2. THE NON-VERBAL TESTS: these are generally quite novel to most subjects. Hence they measure gf to a far greater extent. Large disparities between the verbal and performance score are often found in middle-class children whose upbringing is highly verbal. The performance sub-tests are as follows.

*   Block design: patterns are presented to the child in a booklet, and he must then make them up by arranging building blocks such that their top surfaces represent the pattern. This test can be made of varying difficulty. It is also one which indicates well how a child tackles a strange problem.

* Picture arrangement: here, series of strip cartoons tell stories. Each series is presented in jumbled order and the child must put them in their correct sequence: a neat way of testing a child's ability to work out the relationships involved.
* Object assembly: this is a timed jigsaw-like task of arranging broken patterns.
* Mazes: the child is required to trace his way through pencil and paper mazes.
* Coding: here the key to a simple cipher system is given. The child then completes as many examples as possible (presented in random order) in a fixed time.
* Picture completion: pictures with a missing element, often only a small detail, are shown to the subject who is required to spot this.

This, then, is the Wechsler Intelligence Scale, one of the standard intelligence tests. The verbal and performance IQ scores are highly reliable as is the total score: all around 0.9 or beyond.

The WISC is an individual test. It is obviously not suitable for group testing. We shall now look at some item types used in intelligence tests (rather than examine any one test in detail) for these are widely used in applied psychology.

Items used in group intelligence tests
Items can be verbal or non-verbal, testing largely fluid or crystallized ability.

1. ANALOGIES

Easy: a is to c as g is to ...
        Sparrow is to bird as mouse is to ...

Difficult: Samson Agonistes is to Comus as the Bacchae are to ...

With analogy items all kinds of relationships may be tested, as in the examples where we find sequence, classification, double classification (by author and type of play, for example), and opposites. Analogy is thus a useful form for encapsulating a wide variety of relationships. We can use shapes for this type of item, as distinct from verbal forms.

Thus is to as is to ...

Alice Heim has a special predilection for clock items where slow clocks are shown in mirrors! Her tests (e.g. AH6) are most popular for group administration. One example is set out below.

or 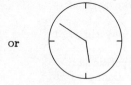 is to ⟨clock⟩ as ⟨clock⟩ is to ...

2. ODD MEN OUT items also allow us to test wide varieties of relationships in many materials. Some examples are given below.

    carrot, turnip, swede, beetroot, cabbage
    valley, coomb, hillock, gorge, chasm
    early, greasy, messy, swiftly, furry

For these three examples some knowledge is required of vegetables, geography and grammar, but this alone is not enough.

3. SIMILARITIES are essentially the same item form (where the common relationship must be worked out), but are more difficult to write for a group test because the multiple choice answer will give the game away.

Non-verbal odd-men-out items are essentially the same item form (where the common relationship must be worked out), but are more difficult to write for a group test because the multiple choice answer will again give the game away.

Non-verbal odd-men-out items are simple to produce, as shown below.

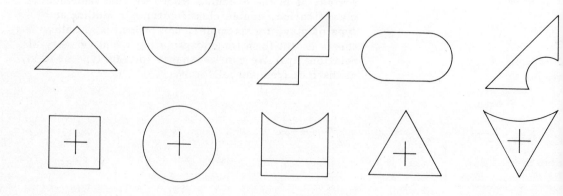

These are the kinds of items used in abstract reasoning tests.

Numbers, of course, offer easy ways of creating complex relationships without needing any special knowledge of mathematics and hence sequences are a useful item form. 20, 40, 60, 80 ... is, for example, entirely unequivocal. Sequences allow also for the development of highly complex of multiple relationships. For example,

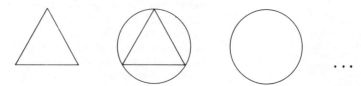

followed by a multiple choice to complete.

Raven's Matrices is an example of a test composed entirely of such sets of non-verbal items. Many forms have been produced and it is capable of extending the intelligence of subjects from about five years upwards to the limits. It is one of the best single measures of fluid ability. Despite its non-verbal appearance, however, it is related to some extent to verbal ability, presumably because verbalization improves performance. These are typical items then in tests of intelligence.

From our description of these and of WISC scale, it should be possible to get an insight into what it is that intelligence tests measure.

We have concentrated on intelligence tests in our more detailed study of tests because they have been at the centre of so much controversy, both in respect of their use as selection devices for secondary school education, and more recently in respect of their heritability. It is to this latter topic that we shall now turn, since it is of great social importance and intellectual interest, which is a further reason for ensuring that the nature of such tests is fully appreciated.

The heritability of intelligence test scores

This is so large and complex a subject that inevitably our summary must be somewhat assertive and dogmatic. To make it even more difficult, well-known writers reviewing the same evidence come to opposite conclusions. For example, Cattell (1971) and Eysenck (1971) conclude that about 80 per cent of the variance in intelligence test scores is heritable, in the West at least. Kamin (1974), reviewing the same evidence, comes to the conclusion that there are no sound data to reject the hypothesis that differences in test scores are determined by different life experiences.

To make our discussion of this matter comprehensible rather than comprehensive, we shall establish first a number of important points.

* All results of heritability studies refer only to the population from which the sample was drawn. Thus results in Great Britain are not applicable in other cultures. If culture has any effect, then in a country with a diverse cultural background (such as India), the heritability index would be smaller than in a more homogeneous culture.
* All workers in the field argue that there is an INTERACTION between genetic and environmental determinants of intelligence test scores. The disagreement lies in the matter of how large the influence of each factor is.
* In principle, an ideal method of studying the topic is to investigate the differences in intelligence test scores of monozygotic twins (i.e. twins with the same genetic endowment) reared apart. All differences in test scores within such pairs must be environmentally determined (ignoring differential effects of placental deprivations, etc., in such pairs which would exaggerate any differences).

    Critics of this approach argue that it is vitiated by the fact that twins are by definition a different population from singleton children. Furthermore, there is a tendency for identical twins to be placed in foster homes similar to each other, thus making their scores similar.
* Burt carried out the most extensive twin studies. His data, however, must be ignored. It appears, alas, that he doctored the figures.
* However, all other twin studies show the same results, namely that in America and Great Britain there is a substantial hereditary component in the determination of test scores. The critical finding is that identical twins reared apart show less differences in intelligence test scores than do non-identical twins reared together.
* Kamin's (1974) arguments attempting to refute these results are statistically weak as has been fully exposed by Fulker (1975) among others. Kamin's work may be safely ignored.
* More sophisticated methods of statistical analysis, known as biometric genetic methods, which have been demonstrated to be powerful in animal work have also been employed in the study of human intelligence test scores. These can assess the kind of gene action and the mating system in the population by analysing within and between family differences and their interactions. The results of these methods are difficult to impugn and it appears from such studies that: (i) around 70 per cent of the variance in IQ score is heritable in Great Britain and the USA; (ii) there is a polygenic dominance for IQ and that assortative mating is an important influence.
* Such biometric methods can be applied to any variable

to reveal its heritability. The major personality variables such as extraversion, neuroticism and psychoticism (see below) are also similarly highly genetically determined.

The factorial description of personality

Personality questionnaires have been subjected, over the years, to factor analyses in the hope of discovering what are the basic temperamental dimensions. The main researchers in this area have been Cattell (working in Illinois), Eysenck (in London) and Guilford (in California). Although superficially each has produced what looks like a separate set of factors, recent research in this field has enabled some sort of consensus to be arrived at (see Cattell and Kline, 1977; Kline, 1979, for a full discussion of this work). In effect, the study of individual differences has led to the establishment of the main dimensions of personality. These dimensions are therefore those that demand study, and are as outlined below.

Extraversion
The high-scoring extravert is sociable, cheerful, talkative, and does not like to be alone. He enjoys excitement, takes risks and is generally impulsive: an outgoing optimist, active and lively. The introvert is the opposite of this: cold, retiring and aloof. This dimension has been related by Eysenck to the arousability of the central nervous system. Scores on tests of this factor have a large genetic component.

Neuroticism (or anxiety)
The highly anxious subject is one who worries a lot, is moody and often depressed. He is highly emotional and takes a long time to calm down. He tends to sleep poorly and to suffer from psychosomatic disorders. This variable is claimed to be related to the lability of the autonomic nervous system.

These variables are both measured by the Cattell 16PF test and Eysenck's EPQ (the most recent version of the Eysenck personality tests). If we know an individual's status on these two factors, then already we know a good deal about his temperament.

Psychoticism
This variable has not been as extensively studied as extraversion and anxiety and only recently (1975) has it appeared in a published questionnaire, the EPQ. Nevertheless, the nature of psychoticism is clear. The high scorer on this dimension is solitary, uncaring of people, troublesome, lacking in human feeling and empathy, thick skinned and insensitive. He is cruel, inhumane, hostile and aggressive, reckless to danger, aggressive even to his own family. Naturally enough, most normal individuals score low on P,

but many criminals score high. This factor has been related by Eysenck to 'maleness', and to be related to levels of male sex hormones.

It is to be noted that these three factors have not only been clearly identified from the factor analysis of questionnaires: there is also a considerable mass of experimental data supporting their identification and nature.

These are the three second-order factors claimed by Eysenck to be the most important in accounting for temperamental differences. Second-order factors are factors arising from the correlations among first-order factors: that is, the factors accounting for the original correlations (see our discussion of factor analysis above). These first-order, or primary, factors are more problematic than the second orders but, as the work of Cattell has shown, can be of considerable power in applied psychometrics.

In brief, the factorial analysis of personality has revealed three basic dimensions, each tied to the basic physiology of man and hence largely heritable.

Of course, this factorial analysis of personality is essentially a theory of personality postulating that these three factors, physiologically and largely genetically determined, account for most of the differences in behaviour between individuals. It is interesting, therefore, to contrast this theory which is closely based upon measurement with some earlier theories of personality based on clinical observation and inference.

Psychoanalytic theories and theories of personality

Perhaps the most famous theory of personality is the classical psychoanalytic theory of Freud. Freud was a psychiatrist working in Vienna from the turn of the century to just before the outbreak of the Second World War. Eysenck has attacked psychoanalysis because it lacks quantification, is hard to verify and is not, in his view, highly successful as a therapy. Against this one must bear in mind the fact that it has attracted intelligent men all over the world because of its ability to throw light on a diverse array of human behaviours, such as totemism, painting, scientific endeavour, literary production, dreams and neuroses. Our brief description can do little justice to Freud's 24 volumes of collected papers.

Data base
The data on which psychoanalytic theory is based are the free associations of patients and their free associations to dreams: what Freud called 'the royal road to the unconscious'. Free association is the process by which a patient is required simply to say whatever comes into his head regardless of its nature.

The unconscious
A critical feature of Freudian theory is the emphasis placed upon unconscious mental activity: this is highly important in determining behaviour. Unconscious mental activity

(primary processes) is chaotic, illogical and bizarre, demanding immediate satisfaction of the drives and needs within the unconscious. Only by understanding the unconscious can we understand personality. Preconscious ideas are unconscious but capable of recall: for example, telephone numbers.

The mind

In psychoanalytic theory the mind is divided into three parts. The id, unconscious, is the repository of basic drives, sex and aggression, and what has been repressed into it. The id is the source of mental energy, demanding immediate expression. This, however, in modern society cannot be permitted. To kill and copulate at whim leads only to prison. The id is controlled, therefore, by two other mental provinces; first, the ego, the decision-making agent, developed by identification with the same sex parent and, second, the super-ego, the repository of our moral values (which are those of our parents as seen at about the age of five when the super-ego develops: see below). Thus mental health depends upon the correct balance of these three systems: too much control and the individual leads a narrow inexpressive life. If the super-ego is too strong we feel guilt-ridden and anxious, yet if there is too little control we become psychopathic criminals. The aim of psychoanalytic therapy is to make man as rational as possible: where id was, there shall ego be.

The ego maintains control by the use of mechanisms of defence, which satisfy the conflicting demands of id and super-ego and which are unconscious. The system of defences we use profoundly affects our behaviour.

Successful defences (sublimation) allow expression of the instinctual, forbidden id drive: unsuccessful defences simply prevent its expression. This is important because in Freudian theory an instinctually barred expression still demands outlet. Hence unsuccessful defences have to be used over and over again, as the id drive persists in seeking expression: the basis of the tension and weariness of neurotic illness.

Defence mechanisms

1. SUCCESSFUL DEFENCES

* Sublimation: this involves the deflection of instinctual drives so that they are expressed in a manner acceptable to the ego. For example, in Freudian theory anal drives, the desire to smear and handle faeces, are sublimated in the exercises of painting and pottery-making. Children's love of playing in mud and puddles is another example of such sublimation.

  If drives are blocked, the energy remains in the system and demands different outlets. Sublimation is important because it allows the expression of otherwise forbidden drives. Indeed, Freud (1933) regarded sublimation as the cornerstone of civilized life: the arts, the sciences, all are sublimations of sexuality. Free expression of the id, sexuality and aggression is the road to barbarism.

2.   UNSUCCESSFUL DEFENCES

*   Repression: one of the most important mechanisms of defence. There are two phases in repression: primal repression, where the ego denies the instinct entry into consciousness, and repression proper, where the instinct and all connected with it are kept out of conscious- ness. The energy still remains in the system and is expressed as anxiety. Thus repression is critical in the development of neurosis. It is, of course, unconscious.
*   Denial: this is similar to repression, except that here the ego wards off the external world by altering perception. Denial of age is a common example: the middle-aged paunch crammed into tight jeans, combined with an Afro hair-cut and cowboy boots.
*   Projection: here unacceptable impulses are attributed to others. A woman's neurotic fear of sexual attack may result from her projection of her own sexual drive and even lead to agoraphobia.
*   Reaction-formation: the feelings in the conscious are the opposite of those in the unconscious. Thus love becomes hate, while shame, disgust and moralizing are reaction-formations against sexuality. The delusions of persecution found in paranoia are in Freudian theory attributed to reaction-formation against homosexuality. Thus, 'I love him' becomes 'I hate him', which becomes, by projection, 'he hates me'.
*   Regression: to avoid conflict, people resort to earlier modes of behaviour. Thus the person regresses to earlier modes of responding which were appropriate then, but not in the present. The ego cannot solve the conflicts cre- ated by the need to develop new responses appropriate to present circumstances.
*   Isolation: here feelings and emotions are separated from the experiences which normally produce them: for example, the man who can have sexual relations only with women he despises; the isolation of love and sex.
*   Undoing: here an action 'undoes' an imaginary or real action. For example, the obsessional who washes every- thing he touches because he feels, being himself dirty, that he has made them dirty.

From this, the importance of defence mechanisms in under- standing personality must be obvious. The quality of the dynamic balance depends upon the strategy of our defences. However, another aspect of psychoanalytic theory relevant to personality is Freudian psychosexual developmental theory and this is described below. As we shall see, it is in this that the importance of the first five years is emphasized.

Psychosexual development

'Sexual life does not begin at puberty, but starts with plain manifestations soon after birth' (Freud, 1940). Indeed Freud described the infant, to the outrage of his contemporaries, as a 'polymorphous pervert'. This is because, as Freud (1940) continued, 'sexual life includes the function of obtaining pleasure from zones of the body - a function which is subsequently brought into the service of reproduction'. The infant derives pleasure initially from the stimulation of any part of the body, and this pleasure is sexual: hence the term 'polymorphous pervert', for Freud defined any sexual activity which does not have reproduction as its aim as a perversion.

* The oral stage: very soon in the infant's life the sexual drive begins to manifest itself through the mouth, which becomes the principal erotogenic zone. There is an oral-erotic phase, sucking, and an oral-sadistic phase, biting. The erotogenic pleasure is known as oral eroticism.
* The anal stage: at about two years of age, the anus becomes the most important erotogenic zone. Anal erotism also has two phases: there is pleasure in expelling faeces (anal-expulsive) and later in retention (anal-retentive).
* The phallic stage: around the age of four the penis and clitoris become the chief erotogenic zones; this is phallic erotism. Then, after the Oedipus and castration complexes, the child enters the latency period, during which he usually experiences less sexual conflict, until the final stage of sexual organization is established at puberty.
* The mature genital stage: here previous stages are reorganized and subordinated to the adult sexual aim of reproduction.

The Oedipus complex

Freud regarded the Oedipus complex not only as his greatest discovery but as one of man's greatest discoveries. It explains how, in spite of our instincts, we become law-abiding citizens, strive for perfection, and develop a conscience. Every male child is fated to pass through the Oedipus complex. At the phallic stage the boy becomes his mother's lover; he desires to possess her physically, to assume his father's place: his father becomes a rival.

However, the Oedipus complex is 'doomed to a terrible end'. It is repressed through fear of castration - a punishment for infantile masturbation - which the boy imagines will be inflicted on him by his powerful rival, his father. The result of this is that the boy identifies with his father (through fear of castration), and thus the super-ego is born. Since the child cannot have his mother sexually (as the id wishes) he adopts the compromise of vicarious pleasure, through identifying with his father. This identification involves not only sexual pleasure but subsequently the father's ideas and beliefs. Thus the cultural values of our generation are passed on to the next. Clearly, these complexes are critical for the development of the male personality.

Penis envy

For the girl, however, there is a different process. At the phallic phase she suffers from penis envy: inferiority feelings about the clitoris vis-à-vis the penis. She then turns against her mother who, she feels, has castrated her; in her mother's place she puts her father as an object of love. Thus the Electra complex begins. Oedipal attitudes are more likely to remain in women, as there is no castration complex to end them. It is through fear of losing love that the girl identifies with the same sex parent and develops the super-ego which, according to Freud, is likely to be less strongly developed in women. It follows that women are less idealistic and less troubled by conscience.

Psychosexual theory and personality

Two facts contribute to the importance of psychosexual theory in understanding personality.

* Pregenital erotism cannot all be directly expressed. Thus defence mechanisms have to be used, producing other apparently unrelated behaviours. For example, direct expression of anal erotism (sodomy) is actually illegal in Britain. Direct expression of oral erotism is allowed: connoisseurs of food, specialists in oral sex. Indeed, permanent character traits, according to Freud, are either unchanged expressions of these original instincts or defences against them. Defences against oral erotism are the oral traits of dependency, talkativeness and optimism. Defences against anality embrace the famous anal character of parsimony, perseverance, obstinacy and orderliness. Parsimony is a sublimation of the desire to retain the faeces; orderliness a reaction formation against the desire to smear them.
* Fixation at the pregenital level: we may become fixated at a particular level, as a result of being over-indulged or not sufficiently indulged during the relevant stage of infancy. Thus fixation at the oral level can be caused by sudden weaning or indulgent demand feeding. Similarly, different kinds of toilet training can cause fixation at the anal level. Fixation implies that undue importance is attached to a particular developmental phase. Fixation is also partly determined by constitutional factors, such as the sensitivity to stimulation of the particular erotogenic zone. This, of course, interacts with the environmental variables discussed above.
* The Oedipus complex: this is regarded as the kernel of neurosis. For Freud, truly maturing involves breaking away from the parents. In the neurotic this is never done. This unconscious conflict affects our lives in

ways of which we are unaware. Attitudes to women (do
we like women like our mother?), attitudes to employers
and superiors and attitudes to authority itself (rivalry
of father) are all examples of this. The castration
complex, too, is also powerful. This may be reflected
in attitudes to vivisection, to surgery, to blood
itself. Homosexuals in psychoanalytic theory are held to
have the castration complex. Their homosexuality stems
from their inability to face penisless beings or beings
that bleed from their private parts.

This brief account of psychoanalytic personality theory
makes clear its complexity in that it can account for a huge
variety of behaviours. However, it does so with a surprisingly small number of concepts.

Objections to Freudian theory
We have already mentioned the objections to psychoanalysis
on scientific grounds, objections most widely broadcast by
Eysenck. These concern:

*   the lack of clear raw data;
*   the poor sampling: the patients under Freud's care are
    clearly not samples of all mankind;
*   the lack of statistical analysis;
*   the ambiguity and vagueness of the concepts;
*   the difficulty of falsifying the theory;
*   the failure of the therapy to show itself efficacious.

Even if all these objections are admitted, does this inevitably mean that Freudian theory should be abandoned as
worthless?

The scientific study of psychoanalytic theory
A previous work (Kline, 1972) has dealt extensively with
this problem. The essence of the case that psychoanalytic
theory has some scientific validity and is deserving of
further investigation is set out below.

*   Psychoanalytic theory can be broken down into sets of
    testable hypotheses. In this sense, Freudian theory is a
    collection of theories as Farrell (1964) has claimed.
*   When this is done and the theories are put to a scien-
    tific test, using proper samples, validated tests and
    adequate statistics, certain of the psychoanalytic
    propositions can be shown to hold. For example (see
    Kline, 1972), there is reasonable evidence for re-
    pression and the Oedipus complex. To summarize the
    findings in this huge area: much of Freudian theory has
    received some objective support and it would be flying
    in the face of the evidence to reject it out of hand.

Other psychoanalytic theories
Of course, over the years a large number of variants of
Freudian theory have developed: the work of Jung, Adler,

Fromm, Horney, Sullivan and Melanie Klein, being amongst the most well known. In general, these theories have differed from those of Freud in their lesser emphasis on sexuality. For Adler the great drive was the aim of achieving superiority (hence his use of the inferiority complex). For Jung the profoundest aspects of the mind were the contents of the collective unconscious, the accumulated wisdom of the ages. While Freud believed that mental health lay in controlling the instincts of the id, Jung believed that only by allowing oneself proper contact with the collective unconscious could one develop one's full potential.

Other theories of personality

Psychoanalytic theories, especially those of Jung and Freud, have had enormous effects on the Zeitgeist; their ripples have spread far beyond the confines of psychology. For this reason alone psychoanalytic theory deserves critical scrutiny.

However, there are many other personality theorists whose work, even if influenced by dynamic theories, can in no way be called psychoanalytic. To summarize these briefly and with justice is hardly possible. However, many of these theories are old, so that a brief acquaintance is perhaps all that is necessary. More recently theories of personality have been eschewed because the field is so large. The age of grand theorizing is gone. Indeed, the nearest thing to a coherent modern personality theory is in fact the factor-analytic work of Eysenck and Cattell, which we have already discussed. To conclude this brief account of theories of personality let us simply select a few items from various different theories to illustrate the range and scope.

The work of McDougall

McDougall, a psychologist not now held in high repute, claimed that the mainsprings of human activity lay in a number of native propensities, and sentiments within which these propensities are organized. McDougall (1932) listed 18 propensities among which were: food seeking, rejecting noxious substances, sexual propensities, fear, exploratory drive, protective and gregarious propensities to name but seven. However, McDougall regarded one sentiment as all important; the self-image, the master sentiment around which much of what we do revolves. Other sentiments are (for example, money-seeking, job-seeking and so on) cultural avenues for expressing the basic propensities.

This kind of psychologizing is mainly of historical interest (i) because it is speculative rather than empirical and (ii) because the very concept of propensity is circular: that is, we observe a behaviour, such as food seeking, explain it by hypothesizing a food-seeking propensity and then use the behaviour which it seeks to explain as confirmation of the hypothesis. However, we mention it because recent factor-analytic work by Cattell in Illinois (see Cattell and Kline, 1977) gives some support for there being a number of basic propensities and sentiments, although by no means as many as McDougall claimed. It could be the case that McDougall will become more highly esteemed as more empirical work is carried out. McDougall's theory suffered neglect because of a distaste among psychologists, which lasted from the Second World War until quite recently, for any theory which was based on the notion of inborn propensities or instincts.

Murray

Murray was another important personality theorist who, in 'Explorations in Personality' (1938), attempted to develop a new subject 'Personology'. His work was based on the analysis of interviews, biographies, projective and experimental tests and involved brilliant clinical intuition from a huge amount of data from each subject. He postulated a large number of needs to account for human behaviour together with corresponding environmental presses. Although the factor analysis of motivation has not supported his list of needs, for example, to abase, to affiliate, to achieve, to be aggressive, to be different, it seems likely that Murray was looking at surface clusters of behaviours rather than the larger more basic factors of factor analysis. One of his drives, nAch, the need to achieve, has been extensively studied by McClelland and colleagues and does seem an important determinant of entrepreneurial performance at least. Murray's work is valuable because it lays stress on the importance of studying the whole person in all his aspects, yet not to the extent that generalizable laws of behaviour cannot be formulated. This is a good counterbalance against large-scale statistical studies where the unique individual can be lost.

Physique and personality

Two researchers, Kretschmer (1925) and Sheldon (Sheldon and Stevens, 1942) have claimed that physique is related to temperament. Kretschmer observed from his clinical work that schizophrenics tend to be thin, and manic depressives fat, extreme examples, in his view, of tendencies in the normal population that moody individuals are likely to be rotund, and aloof, withdrawn people of slender build.

Sheldon in his work on physique and character attempted to classify body build into three dimensions, each on a seven-point scale. Most individuals are high on one of these dimensions which are measured precisely from different parts of the body. A cluster analysis (a simple form of factor analysis) of ratings of temperament showed a close relationship between body build and character, findings which have been challenged on grounds of computing error (not that uncommon in large-scale correlational studies calculated by hand). The results were in accord with common sense and literary stereotypes. The fat individual was of Falstaffian temperament, the muscular rugby-playing type was pushy and insensitive, and the thin ectomorph cold and withdrawn.

Modern studies conducted by Eysenck and colleagues at the Maudsley and Cattell and co-workers at Illinois give

only modest confirmation of this link. Nevertheless, it is
research that has been neglected, perhaps surprisingly, and
large-scale investigations of Sheldon's typology relating it
to the main personality dimensions might prove useful.

In all these theories which we have so far mentioned it
must be noted that there are common problems. These relate
to the proper quantification of temperament and dynamics.
None of these researchers had personality tests of proven
validity and reliability.

Finally, the approach of two other psychologists must
be mentioned so that psychological testing in relation to
personality can be put into a different perspective. Our
view, as is obvious, is that precise measurement is the
'sine qua non' of any adequate personality theory. Concomitant with this is our claim that factor analysis is the
instrument by which good tests can be constructed and
validated. This indeed is the psychometric view, the implicit underpinning of the work of Eysenck and Cattell.

Allport

Allport (1938), however, has explicitly argued against
this. He admits that statistical analyses of tests can
reveal common dimensions. However, he stresses the importance of the unique components of personality that each
individual alone possesses, dependent upon the experience
that he alone has undergone. For Allport it is these personal data that are critical to understanding personality.

Two important points are raised here. First, if Allport
were correct, a science of personality would be impossible,
for each individual is essentially unique. We can, given
sufficient time, understand him but this would not help us
to understand anyone else. Thus no statements about regularities of behaviour can be made. The second point follows
from this. If Allport were correct, it would not be possible
to predict real-life behaviours from tests of personality.
In fact, however, this can be done, as the extensive hand-
books to the better personality inventories, the 16PF test,
the EPQ and the MMPI, illustrate. Allport, therefore, must
have exaggerated his case. Even so, the existence of personality scales is not incompatible with the notion of
uniqueness. In any one sample, individuals will have very
different profiles across a range of scales. This does not
mean they will not share certain characteristics or groups
of characteristics in common with other members of the
sample.

Situationalism

Mischel (e.g. 1977) has been highly influential in recent
personality theory to such an extent that many writers have
abandoned the notion of traits entirely, and hence the
measurement of personality is regarded as impossible and
worthless.

He attacks traits on the old behaviourist ground of
redundancy. We see a man violently attacking another and
say he is high on aggression, and that this aggression is

causing the behaviour. While this logical argument is sound, it can be refuted empirically if in fact wide clusters of behaviour do cohere together such that a concept of aggression can parsimoniously account for them.

His second argument is empirical. He argues that in fact there are few cross-situational similarities in behaviour. Behaviour to Mischel is situation-specific. To understand a behaviour we must examine the stimuli which elicit it.

Intuitively this is not sensible since in everyday life we do find people to be consistent. We think of A as cheerful, B as testy and so on. This is regarded by Mischel as but a halo effect, reflecting the stereotype of the observer. Thus we form a view of an individual and remember the behaviour that confirms it, forgetting what fails to fit our picture: fighting Irishmen, sad Russians, loudly-checked English gentlemen, just for example. Thus our everyday observations are set at nought.

Further, Mischel argues that the traits which raters use reflect only the categories of behaviour which raters hold, rather than any real categorization of observed behaviour, citing as evidence studies where ratings of virtually unknown subjects revealed the same factor structure as ratings of known subjects.

Finally, situationalists cite investigations where traits and ratings fail to correlate with observed criterion behaviours, thus casting doubts on the cross-situational generality of such measures.

The answer to situationalism is again an empirical one. If there is no cross-situational generality, if the responses to personality questionnaires are specific to the tests, how can it be that there are meaningful educational, clinical and occupational discriminations and correlations? These, if Mischel were correct, should not occur, yet they do and this fact alone seems to us to refute the situationalist case.

Enough has been said about theories of personality. Generally, most flounder through a lack of sound quantification and a consequent reliance on clinical impressions. Those theories that argue that common traits can never reveal the uniqueness of the individual are destroyed by the evidence, as is situationalism. The fact is that personality traits can be reliably and validly measured and these do have substantial correlations with a wide variety of external criteria. As such they should become the data base of any theory of personality.

The application of the study of individual differences to educational, clinical and occupational psychology

The study of individual differences which has been described in this chapter has implicit within it a model of man which might be called the psychometric model. Explanation of this model, which is remarkably simple, will make the application of results obvious.

The implicit psychometric model
This model states that any given piece of behaviour is

related to that individual's status on the main factors in the sphere of ability, temperament, motivation and mood. This model does not ignore past experience because this itself affects status on these variables. The psychometric model is therefore a variant of a trait model of behaviour. Thus, for example, performance at GCE depends upon intelligence, verbal and numerical ability, extraversion, anxiety, psychoticism, mood at the time of taking the exam and the various motivation variables discussed above. These main variables will account for a high proportion of the variance among the examination results. Obviously for different behaviours (e.g. exam passing and serving well behind a bar) different weights for each of the factors is required.

How important each factor is, that is, what its weight is, has to be determined empirically. In fact, the statistical technique of multiple correlation or regression does this precisely. Thus, the argument runs, we put all the test variables into a multiple correlation with the criterion and these are then weighted to achieve the highest possible correlation. These weights (beta weights) indicate the relative importance of the variable for the behaviour in question. Cattell and colleagues have done exactly this with academic success in both America and Great Britain and found multiple correlations around 0.7.

Thus in educational guidance and selection we find the beta weights of the variables and select and guide children accordingly. If X, Y and Z have the highest weights for academic success, then we select and encourage children high on these variables. In industrial psychology, too, we can find the tests most related to psychiatric breakdown or diagnose into clinical groups. Then we know who in the population is at risk and can avoid putting them into stressful conditions.

Conclusions

This brief summary of individual assessment and personality shows how precise measurement of individual differences by well-designed tests can yield a corpus of knowledge which is not only of theoretical interest but is also of considerable practical importance, for it gives a rational basis for selection and guidance both in education and industry as well as being helpful in the psychiatric clinic.

References

Allport, G.W. (1938)
Personality: Psychological interpretation. New York: Chilton.
Buros, O.K. (1972)
VII Mental Measurements Year Book. New Jersey: Gryphon Press.
Cattell, R.B. (1971)
Abilities: Their structure, growth and action. New York: Houghton-Mifflin.

Cattell, R.B. and Kline, P. (1977)
The Scientific Analysis of Personality and Motivation.
London: Academic Press.
Eysenck, H.J. (1971)
Race, Intelligence and Education. London: Temple-Smith.
Farrell, B.A. (1964)
The status of psychoanalytic theory. Enquiry, 7,
104-122.
Freud, S. (1933)
New Introductory Lectures. London: Hogarth Press &
Institute of Psychoanalysis.
Freud, S. (1940)
An Outline of Psychoanalysis. London: Hogarth Press.
Kamin, L.J. (1974)
The Science and Politics of IQ. Harmondsworth: Penguin.
Kline, P. (1972)
Fact and Fantasy in Freudian Theory. London: Methuen.
Kline, P. (1976)
Psychological Testing. London: Malaby Press.
Kline, P. (1979)
Psychometrics and Psychology. London: Academic Press.
Kline, P. and Storey, R. (in press)
The aetiology of the oral character. Journal of Genetic
Psychology.
Kretschmer, E. (1925)
Physique and Character. London: Methuen.
McDougall, W. (1932)
The Energies of Man. London: Methuen.
Mischel, M. (1977)
On the future of personality measurement. American
Psychology, 32, 246-254.
Murray, H.A. (1938)
Explorations in Personality. New York: Oxford University
Press.
Nunnally, J. (1978)
Psychometric Theory. New York: McGraw-Hill.
Sheldon, W.H. and Stevens, S.S. (1942)
The Varieties of Temperament. New York: Harper & Row.
Wechsler, D. (1938)
The Weschler Intelligence Scale for Children. New York:
Psychological Corporation.

Questions

1. How is the usefulness of psychological tests evaluated?
   Provide as many examples as you can.
2. What are the advantages and disadvantages of the interview as an assessment technique? How could some of the
   problems associated with the interview be avoided or
   reduced?
3. Describe three types of psychological test, and mention
   the method of construction and also examples of
   practical situations where each might be used.
4. In clinical situations, discuss the advantages and
   disadvantages of (a) the interview and (b) psychological

tests. Take every opportunity to compare the usefulness of these approaches in the assessment of the individual.

5. Discuss the usefulness of psychological tests in the following situations: (a) the investigation of a 30-year-old man who is suspected to be showing signs of intellectual deterioration following a road accident; (b) the assessment of a 16-year-old girl who has requested vocational guidance; (c) giving advice to a 45-year-old man who is unhappy with his job, and in danger of dismissal because of poor work performance.

6. How is intelligence determined? Discuss how an understanding of the determinants of intelligence is relevant to clinical and other practical situations.

7. Describe any personality theory, and provide a critical evaluation of its usefulness.

8. Discuss the advantages and limitations of psychological tests.

9. Consider situations where patients have (or might have) consulted you about difficulties which have psychological components. What psychological and social information did you gather? In retrospect, should you have gathered more information: if so, what information? What uses might psychological tests have had in these circumstances?

Annotated reading

Cronbach, L. (1976) Essentials of Psychological Testing. Chicago: Harper & Row.
    A clear comprehensive discussion of psychological testing and tests.

Cattell, R.B. and Kline, P. (1977) The Scientific Analysis of Personality and Motivation. London: Academic Press.
    An account of the factor analysis of personality where the results are related to clinical theories.

Freud, S. (1978) New Introductory Lectures. Harmondsworth: Penguin.
    A brilliantly told account of Freudian theory by the Master himself.

Hall, G.S. and Lindzey, G. (1973) Theories of Personality. New York: Wiley.
    A good summary of a variety of personality theories.

Vernon, P.E. (1979) Intelligence, Heredity and Environment. San Francisco: Freeman.
    Vernon is well known for his balanced account of issues relating to intelligence, its measurement, and social significance. This is one of the most recent reviews of topics in the field and is written in a lucid style.

12

Creating Change
H. R. Beech

Opening remarks
DAVID GRIFFITHS

The topic of behavioural control or 'behaviour modification'
is one which is always likely to inflame passions both
amongst the lay public and professional groups. When this
occurs, it is often obvious that complainants and critics
are not well informed about the aims, rationale and techniques which are used. In this chapter, Reg Beech provides
an introduction to all of these aspects of behaviour therapy. It is based on extensive clinical experience and is
also tempered by a sincere concern for clients and a clear
awareness that behavioural techniques have a number of
limitations.

Beech emphasizes in his introduction that whilst psychologists have developed a range of techniques to change behaviour, the eventual decision about the implementation of
these techniques must reside with society as a whole. His
review also reminds us that the application of these methods
has resulted in the reduction and avoidance of a wide range
of human suffering and impairment. For example, behaviour
therapy has improved the outlook for anxiety and phobic conditions very considerably and the application of behaviour
modification to the training of the mentally handicapped
(discussed in chapter 20) has begun to improve the prognosis
for sufferers and their families very dramatically.

The chapter also includes other examples of the applications of behaviour therapy: alcoholism, obsessional
states, sexual and marital problems, eating disorders and
bedwetting. In relation to each problem area, the reader is
allowed to become acquainted with the rationale for the
development of particular treatments and also with the
details of the treatment programme and the practical limitations involved in their clinical application. The following review goes some considerable way towards informing a
readership who are likely to be in a position to exert
significant influence on the application of these techniques
to patients, and this chapter can be recommended as a fair
and competent evaluation of behaviour therapy.

Introduction
H. R. BEECH

A desire to change behaviour must be as old as man himself
and has presented problems which have fascinated successive
generations of would-be modifiers in all walks of life.

Apart from the problems inherent in the development and use of appropriate modification procedures, there has always been the enormously difficult question of the standards of behaviour that should be applied. It is by no means easy to define what constitutes ideal or even just acceptable behaviour and thereby to provide the goals towards which behaviour modification is to be directed. This problem is primarily the concern of philosophers, politicians and, it is hoped, the public at large, who together explicitly or implicitly lay down standards of acceptable conduct.

The psychologist's main contribution does not lie in this area, since his expertise in producing changes in behaviour does not imply any particular acumen in determining suitable goals for man. These days, some psychologists are apt to confuse the two issues of goals and the modification procedures which are required to achieve them, and to become self-appointed arbiters of standards in many matters. Such confusion may be understandable when an individual possesses the power both to effect change and desire to define the appropriators of outcome, but it is also very dangerous. In addition, all too often there appears to be only a naive conception of the responsibilities involved in behaviour modification. In particular, it is easy to conclude that some aberrant conduct (e.g. indecent exposure) must be stopped and often only a little more difficult to determine what form of treatment procedure should be used to bring about the change. The main problem, which at times may be neglected, is that of what effects the intervention and resultant behaviour change will have eventually on the quality of life of the client and of those with whom he is directly concerned. For example, ignoring naughty behaviour may successfully reduce the frequency of temper tantrums displayed by a young child, but suppose that the parents learn the technique too well and apply it to other behaviour problems, without realizing the need for appropriate attention and praise at other times? It would be difficult to condone the punitive environment to which the child was exposed.

Clearly it is essential that all possible ramifications of any treatment procedure are defined and their implications understood. Naturally, most psychologists try to give careful thought to the implications of change and would be suitably cautious about embarking upon major alterations to behaviour, but there is a need for vigilance to preserve a proper balance between enthusiasm to help and an appreciation of possible consequences of such changes.

The treatment procedures that psychologists working within a behavioural framework use today have emerged as a distinct group of techniques from a plethora of strategies, some of which have been advocated for centuries, although one of their most appealing qualities is that they are not static, but evolve constantly in the light of psychological research and through the influence of work and theorizing in related disciplines. The discussion which follows attempts to place behavioural treatments in their historical setting and to describe some of the influences which have moulded their theoretical structure.

Historically, methods of treatment have been very closely linked to both theory and practical work on the cause and development of abnormal behaviour. In fact, the greatest inspiration for the clinicians has been the meticulous work of those who have studied the way in which behaviour is acquired. It is not surprising, therefore, that the means of producing alterations in behaviour have undergone a profound change since the turn of the century, primarily as a result of the work and theories of Pavlov (1927). Before then the models of Man's psychological functioning tended to be either unduly simplistic or overly complex. Implicit in most simple models was the assumption that behaviour was determined by inheritance and hence could not be modified by any means other than by physical prevention. These views tended to produce strong action with irreversible consequences since they assumed that 'bad' (unwanted) behaviour could only be dealt with by stringent means such as cutting out tongues, permanent incarceration or putting to death. By these means society could rid itself of 'dissident' and disagreeable elements and, indeed, it is difficult to see what else could have been done in the absence of more effective knowledge of appropriate means of producing changes in behaviour.

In this context the more complex models of Freud and the neo-Freudians (Munroe, 1955) were immensely important, not because they provided the technology for change but because they presented an entirely new conception of 'bad', 'wrong' or 'inappropriate' behaviour. Rather than regarding such behaviour as a reflection of defects in the very substance of Man, the emphasis was upon the part which learning and the environment play.

According to this view, undesirable and unwanted behaviours often arise out of life's early experiences and Man is more or less the hapless victim of circumstances over which he has little personal control. It is argued that such experiences help to mould three essential components of the mind, the super-ego, ego and id, and thus indirectly influence the individual's daily interactions with his environment. But in some cases experiences may become so deeply buried that a person may remain unaware of these 'sources' of his maladaptive behaviour, and prolonged therapy (psychoanalysis) may be needed to bring them to the surface again.

Although this model is strongly environmentalistic, according paramount importance to the way in which life's circumstances produce what we are, Freud himself was quite aware that another influence (heredity) was at work. His emphasis upon the environment, one assumed, was occasioned in part by interest, and in part by the recognition that one could do little about hereditary influences but perhaps rather more about remedying the consequences of learning,

so he and his followers focussed their therapeutic endeavours on the factors affecting the supposed complex
interactions between the ego, super-ego and id. Although
merely global means of describing psychological functioning,
these hypothetical constructs were often endowed with 'motivation' and influence which made them appear substantive.
This has tended to detract from Freud's more important
contribution to the realization of the significance of
environmental influences as well as heredity in determining
behaviour.

The experimental and theoretical work of Pavlov (1927)
came as a refreshing change to the empirically minded. His
work retained all the advantages of acknowledging the importance of environmental influences whilst avoiding the
trap into which Freud had fallen: that is, requiring the
postulation of almost mystical entities as determinants of
behaviour. The constructs which Pavlov adopted were testable and their effects measurable. Working extensively with
dogs, he was able to demonstrate that the salivation response could be 'conditioned' to a previously innocuous
stimulus. Having observed that dogs salivate when presented
with food, on repeated occasions he sounded a bell just
before the dog received its meal and eventually found that
the sound of the bell alone was sufficient to evoke salivation. Pavlov went on to investigate how the conditioned
response, once acquired, could be eliminated and found that,
if the bell was sounded repeatedly without the subsequent
provision of food, the salivation response gradually diminished and finally no longer occurred. These demonstrations,
including those showing how a 'neutral' cue may come to
evoke an autonomic response (or cease to do so), provided
the impetus for much experimental work and theorizing and
served as an inspiration for clinical practice.

Watson (1920) viewed stimulus response associations,
including those of the sort produced by Pavlov, as the
building blocks of even the most complex behaviour. In one
experiment, investigating how emotional responses are
acquired, he worked with Albert, an 11-month-old child of
apparently phlegmatic disposition. Briefly, the question
posed by Watson was that of whether or not emotional behaviour can be learned through a simple associative process.
Another way of putting this, at least to help the argument
along, is to ask whether or not we learn to be 'neurotic'.
Could it be that fears, anxieties and, indeed, the whole
gamut of 'abnormal' behaviours, are the product of the
Pavlovian associative process called 'conditioning'?

Perhaps a glance at the Little Albert experiment will
help to clarify the point. Watson selected for special
attention Albert's fondness of a white rat and felt that to
replace this particular feeling with one of fearfulness
would be an important demonstration of the power of learning. To achieve this he arranged for a loud noise to occur
(made by crashing two metal plates together) whenever Albert
reached out for the animal. The immediate result was to

produce a startled response in the child since apprehension in reaction to sudden, unexpected loud noises is 'natural'. With repeated association of the noise and the rat the reaction transferred to the latter and, whenever it was presented, Albert would begin to whimper, crawl away and show signs of fear. Two further points of importance were noted by Watson: first, the new fear reaction was enduring, that is, it did not diminish over a lengthy period of observation and, second, the fear was also found to transfer to objects bearing some similarity to the original, such as a ball of cotton wool.

In Watson's view, this experiment confirmed the susceptibility of emotional reactions to conditioning and provided the basis for explaining all irrational fears. Not only were they learnt by association, but the fears so acquired were lasting and showed a tendency to spread. Watson's parting shot in his famous paper was to mockingly contrast the actual circumstances in which Albert's 'neurosis' occurred with the interpretation for such anxieties which might be offered, later in life, to a middle-aged Albert lying on the psychoanalyst's couch.

This essentially Pavlovian approach to the genesis of phobias and other maladaptive emotional responses is still influential amongst behaviourally-orientated theorists, who are concerned increasingly with the way in which the acquisition of the response is affected by such variables as the temperament and emotional state of the subject and the nature of the stimulus and response which are to be associated.

Of course, neither Pavlov nor the over-enthusiastic Watson believed that man was merely a blank sheet upon which life's experiences are to be written, so that he is simply the sum total of these experiences. Pavlov, particularly, was interested in the effects of environmental experiences upon certain types of organism and conducted experiments showing that different reactions occur to noxious stimulation in dogs having 'strong' or 'weak' nervous systems (roughly corresponding to our notion of phlegmatic and excitable temperaments), and interest in the relationships between learning and temperament is also found in the work of psychologists such as Eysenck (1953) who are concerned with explaining the differences which exist between individuals. Generally speaking, these investigations indicate that behaviour is the outcome of an interaction between the existing nature of the organism and the environmental experiences to which that organism is subjected. For example, Eysenck and his co-workers have offered evidence in support of the contention that the more introverted individual tends to acquire new reactions quickly and to lose them slowly, whilst those of more extraverted temperament show the opposite tendencies.

It is most probable that habits are acquired as a result of environmental events but that the character or type of individual involved determines the speed and firmness with

which these reactions are built up. Another illustration
will serve to make these two points more clear.

Rachman (1966) conducted an investigation to examine
the acquisition of 'fetishistic' behaviour, using three male
volunteers. The idea behind the experiment was to see
whether or not sexual arousal could be transferred from
'appropriate' stimuli (pictures of attractive naked girls)
to 'inappropriate' ones (black knee-length women's boots and
black shoes). The technique of association employed was
similar to that used by Pavlov and involved showing the
experimental subject first a picture of boots and then, one
second later, a sexually arousing picture.

Although this arrangement to most people seems to be the
wrong way around, it is that which appears to produce the
'best' results. So, presenting boots followed by a sexually
exciting stimulus could be expected to result in the former
acquiring sexually arousing properties following a number of
associations. This expectation was borne out by the results
since all three subjects, following 30, 65 and 24 'trials'
respectively, began to show signs of sexual arousal to the
picture of boots alone (sexual arousal being measured by an
electro-mechanical device attached to the subject's penis).
This, of itself, is of considerable interest since it clearly demonstrates that the rule or law of association applies
to sexual arousal just as it does in other aspects of human
functioning. But, of course, it can also be observed that
the three individuals concerned learnt at different rates;
furthermore, they were found to 'lose' this newly established reaction after different amounts of retraining.

In short, while the laws of conditioning applied to all
three subjects, it would seem the individual is an important
factor in the outcome. Both Rachman and Eysenck (Rachman,
1966) share the view that these latter findings indicate the
significance which attaches to the properties of the central
nervous system of the individual.

It may be that the influence of the state of the system
is not restricted to inter-individual differences. It has
been argued (Beech, 1974) that many psychological reactions
could only be accounted for if we assume that the organism
is in a special state when such reactions are being acquired
and, in particular, a specific state of the central nervous
system may be required for an individual to learn to be
phobic. The experiments carried out to date (e.g. Vila and
Beech, 1978) tend to support this contention as applied in
the context of certain emotional states. It is observed, for
example, that women premenstrually often experience an
unpleasant emotional state and, in this condition, tend to
respond adversely to relatively mild stimuli. It was hypothesized that this particular condition could, in the
appropriate circumstances, lead to rapid learning of a
phobic (anxiety) reaction to some previously quite innocuous
stimulus, and this was found to be the case. So, although
there are some well-documented rules by which habits - both
useful and otherwise - are learnt, whether or not they are

acquired may depend upon both permanent as well as perhaps temporary states of the central nervous system.

Another factor of importance must be added before we can achieve a better perspective of the environmentalist viewpoint. This concerns the biological limitations imposed upon learning processes and has been extensively covered by Seligman and Hager (1972). Learning theorists have tended to assume that associations can be formed between any two stimuli, no matter what their character. Anything can be associated with anything else or, to put it in another way, an organism can learn to produce any given reaction to any given stimulus: sexual arousal can become attached to the sight of boots, cotton wool may come to effect a fear reaction, and so on.

Seligman and Hager have collected evidence which leads us to reject the assumption that all stimuli and responses are potentially amenable to association. Briefly, the argument is that organisms appear to have the potential to make certain connections but not others; in fact there seems to be a biologically determined predisposition to learn some things easily but others with great difficulty or not at all. It is as if nature endows a species with a certain propensity to learn because, perhaps, this will ensure its survival.

It is pointed out, for example, that dogs find it very easy to learn how to escape from an enclosed space by using their paws to operate a catch, but it is virtually impossible for a dog to learn to wag his tail to secure escape from such confinement. It appears that there is a kind of repertoire of connection-forming potential which each species possesses (Seligman calls this preparedness) and that this has biological and evolutionary value for the organism.

It might be, of course, that such mechanisms constitute a handicap to us and an example of this could be the appearance of spider phobia (and snake phobia) among populations which are not at all at risk. Obviously the question arises of whether or not these are examples of a special potential to become afraid of such creatures: that is, particular examples of a prepared biological reaction. It is not very difficult to imagine that such readiness to respond with fear has been useful in evolutionary terms.

Finally, it is worth while making some brief reference to a viewpoint which, if valid, could impose the most severe limitations upon changes in behaviour (human or otherwise). It is most starkly represented by Dawkins (1978) who argues that all creatures are merely machines, created by genes, and dedicated to survival. The different machines, corresponding to different species, are all designed to serve as an effective vehicle to ensure gene survival. In short, such a model might restrict the learning which could take place; for example, altruistic behaviour could only be acquired if genetic endowment 'allowed' such behaviour in the interest of the individual making any sacrifice. It is not difficult to think of numerous ways in which the gene machine might fail to show the flexibility ordinarily conceived to be possible by the extreme environmentalist.

Work such as that described has led to a fuller understanding of why it is that only some people, when in the presence of particular stimuli, may exhibit strong but unwanted autonomic responses. It may also be applicable to some forms of motor behaviour, but it has seldom been utilized in this context. Instead, those who have wished to explain overt behaviour responses have often turned to the work of Skinner (1953).

Skinner is an avowed environmentalist whose work shows little regard for heredity, the emotional or drive state of the organism and the importance of autonomic responses. His model of behaviour has been criticized as being too simplistic and mechanistic, but despite this it has undoubtedly made two real contributions to behaviour modification techniques. Of greatest importance is his demonstration that the consequences of any act will affect the chances that the same piece of behaviour will occur on a subsequent occasion. If positive reinforcement is applied contingently, the frequency of a response will increase, whereas punishment decreases the likelihood that the same behaviour will occur. In addition, Skinner highlighted the role of environmental stimuli in controlling behaviour. Stimuli which are present when a response has been rewarded consistently will become the cue for the execution of that response. Similarly, stimuli occurring in the context of punishment will promote non-occurrence of the response.

The pervasive influences of Pavlov's conditioning and Skinner's operant control are apparent in very many of the behaviour modification procedures which are in use today, providing both theoretical structure and empirically-based strategies for change from these underpinnings. It is no surprise to find that behaviour modification focusses upon the obvious (often overt) things that are wrong, unlike, say, psychoanalysis, which has less regard for 'symptoms' and directs attention to some presumed underlying causes. If, for example, a child is a persistent bed-wetter, the psychoanalyst would tend to deal with this problem by trying to identify and remove the mental mechanisms which are alleged to cause this behaviour to occur, such as resentment against the parents. The behavioural approaches, by contrast, would focus upon the bed-wetting itself and attempt to eliminate this by direct means.

It is not possible to provide more than a brief glimpse of the wide range of techniques and procedures which have been developed in the general context of behaviour modification. On the whole, case studies have been chosen as the best means of giving an illustrative account of the range and extent of behaviour change that can be achieved. Therefore, at first glance it may appear that most work has involved only one or a small group of patients. Of course, this involves some distortion since there has been a substantial amount of theoretical and controlled investigative research. This is how methods of intervention should and, indeed, must be developed and signs of a recent trend towards neglecting theory in favour of empiricism must be regretted. Fortunately, only a small minority of the procedures to be described lack any theoretical foundations; it is likely that this minority will founder while better proven methods survive.

Aversive treatment

One of the first techniques to become widely known and practised was that of using strong noxious stimulation to eliminate unwanted behaviour. This technique probably became best known in the treatment of alcoholism and excellent results were claimed for the method (Voegtlin and Lemere, 1942). Basically, the application of aversive treatment involved the production of the undesirable response immediately followed by the application of some unpleasant stimulus, such as a strong electric shock or an emetic drug. Repeated association of, say, taking a sip of whisky, and the administration of the shock is expected to produce a learned aversion to alcohol. Such treatment has been applied to a wide range of problems, most of which might best be described as belonging to the category of 'gratification' behaviour, such as alcoholism, homosexuality, fetishistic behaviour and gambling.

More sophisticated applications of the basic paradigm have been elaborated, one of these offering the possibility of escape from shock if the individual chooses an adaptive form of alternative behaviour. For example, shocks may be given with the presentation of pictures depicting homosexual activity, but these can be terminated when the individual presses a button that switches off such pictures and replaces them with heterosexual 'scenes'. In this way, it has been argued, one may ensure that the unwanted reaction is deterred while the 'preferred' reaction is encouraged (relief from shock is gained by exercising the heterosexual choice).

Not surprisingly, this type of treatment has met with strong and sometimes uninformed criticism from certain groups who argue that such methods are inhuman, are infringements of personal liberty and so on. In fact it is probable that this sense of outrage has tended to discourage the widespread use of aversive techniques.

What critics overlook completely, of course, is that other methods of control may have been tried and have failed and also that the individual is a volunteer for the treatment rather than the unwilling victim of sadistic acts. Furthermore, although the use of 'punishment' over the past few years has had a bad press - popular and professional - there is no doubt that it is efficient in discouraging patterns of behaviour with which it is associated and is still widely used by lay individuals and groups as a means of control (e.g. in militant action of pickets).

Indeed, it may well be argued that without the many and varied ways in which 'offences' are punished a major means of socialization would be lost to society. One might include here the whole range of 'punishments' from a slight frown or sign of irritation to swingeing fines or imprisonment.

Having said this, it is important also to say that controlling by example or by rewarding individuals for doing the right thing (as opposed to punishment for doing the wrong thing) may seem preferable as a course of action and can often be more effective. But much depends upon the behaviour to be changed, the context in which it occurs, the speed with which action is to be taken, and so on.

As an example of the application of this method to an individual case, the treatment of a compulsive gambler by Barker and Miller (1968) might be considered fairly typical. A 34-year-old executive had gambled away his earnings throughout his marriage and his wife had finally insisted that he should stop gambling or she would leave him. Thus motivated, he was treated by applying electric shocks at all stages of gambling on a fruit machine, from inserting tokens to being paid out, this regime being applied in four three-hour-long sessions. A revulsion to gambling developed and, after completion of treatment, he made no further attempt to 'play' fruit machines. This was followed by a relapse, but further treatment again restored an aversion to gambling.

Less stringent forms of aversion have been applied to minor behaviour problems and, probably because of their relative innocuousness, have not involved public protest.

For example, the problem of nail-biting was dealt with by Bucher (1968). Twenty habitual nail-biters were equipped with portable shock-boxes and were instructed to shock themselves each time they put a finger to mouth or lip. Thirteen of the group reported no nail-biting after four days of this procedure, although all relapsed later.

As a final example, consider the application of aversion therapy to smoking (Powell and Azrin, 1968). Three volunteers agreed to carry a special cigarette packet which delivered an electric shock on being opened. All reduced their smoking rate considerably when using the device, but they returned to their old level of smoking when the device was discarded.

It is obvious from the foregoing that aversion therapy produces both successes and failures, but perhaps just as important is the need to secure appropriate levels of co-operation and motivation. After all, it clearly requires a certain dedication to change if one is being subjected to strong electric shocks on a voluntary basis. It may well be argued, of course, that the problems of aversion therapy stem largely from the target areas chosen: for instance, the impulse to carry out the 'deviant' behaviour is often very strong and, in a very real sense, the individual does not 'want' to give it up. Indeed, on occasions, the individual's life style has developed around the 'unwanted' behaviour (e.g. gambling, homosexuality) and any change would be intensely disruptive.

In 1924 Jones reported upon the means by which the fears of children might be overcome and described the method which she had found to be most successful. Essentially her training procedure involved two ingredients; a gradual approach to the object or situation producing anxiety, and an attempt to eliminate such feelings at each stage. In short, if a child feared spiders, he might be shown one at a distance and then, gradually, the spider would be brought closer, while the child was being fed chocolate. In effect this means that the child was being exposed, by stages, to increasingly close contact with the feared object during the course of which he was being 'distracted' by the chocolate.

The credit goes to Wolpe (1958), however, for translating this approach into viable theoretical terms and cogent therapeutic practice. Wolpe's experimental work with cats enabled him to formulate ideas about both the acquisition as well as the removal of neurotic behaviour. He noted that if an animal were placed in a cage and exposed to electric shock there, it would soon come to fear that cage or even being brought into the experimental laboratory for testing. The response of fear had become a conditioned association to certain 'stimuli', the latter being capable of reliably triggering an automatic reaction. However, it could also be noted that the fear of the animal varied (being greater in the cage than out of it, for example) and, in particular, was much reduced by gentle sympathetic handling from the experimenter. From such observations Wolpe conceived the idea of fear being inhibited by certain events and referred to this as a process of reciprocal inhibition. Basically, his argument was that any organism can respond to only one of two antagonistic impulses at any one time: for example, sexual arousal is not found at the same time as intense anxiety, nor can great enjoyment of some situation be present at the same time as marked fear. It might follow, therefore, that if one can repeatedly produce a state incompatible with fear, it may be possible to make the inhibition of anxiety permanent.

Wolpe's extension of his experimental work to human subjects (together with that of numerous other investigators) has been extremely successful (see, for example, Eysenck and Beech, 1971) and appears amply to bear out the contention that the 'little-by-little' approach works well. In practice, of course, rules of thumb have been worked out for the efficient application of the principles involved and it is worth while describing these now.

It will occur to you that there may well be problems in arranging the steps in training so that they range from those which would cause very little discomfort to those which would occasion major anxiety attacks. In fact this is not too difficult and the construction of this 'hierarchy' is usually quite a simple matter, involving as it does the description of simple 'scenes' describing the critical elements. For example, a person afraid of heights may be able to begin by getting used to the first two steps of a short step-ladder, then progress to looking down on to the street from the window of a fifth-floor office, and, later still, standing on the high observation platform overlooking some spectacular piece of scenery. These steps would be arranged at evenly-spaced intervals so that, say, step 1 would conjure up anxiety equivalent to five units, step 2, ten units, and so on up to a situation which would produce most anxiety at 100 units.

However, another difficulty then arises. Supposing 100 units of anxiety involves looking over Niagara Falls, or sitting in Concorde and being told that one engine has failed, or giving a speech to a packed House of Commons. How can one arrange that the average height phobic, fearful air-traveller or anxious public speaker engages in these situations, or even those rather closer at hand? More to the point, if the individual sufferer is afraid of travelling on the underground train, how can we meet the requirement that the steps in the hierarchy should involve the train coming to a halt between stations for intervals of one, two or three minutes? In the real world, although such events can be expected to occur, they cannot be stage-managed to happen at the right time and in the proper sequence demanded by the hierarchy.

The solution to these problems lay in the development of a system for creating 'reality' in the imagined world of the client. The therapist, for example, would describe a scene in which the client IS floating over Niagara Falls in a barrel, or IS trapped in a lift between the tenth and eleventh floors or IS handling the paraquat which he dreads to use on his garden weeds. The instinctive objection to this, of course, is that such imagined scenes have no relevance to the fear which would be experienced in a real-life situation but, in practice, this objection appears to be relatively unimportant.

Indeed, it seems that dealing with the feared situation in imagination is almost as good as doing so in real life. Naturally, most therapists (as well as their clients) wish to confirm that what they have learned by way of controlling anxiety in the imagined situation applies to the real world too, so parallel real-life experiences are arranged to afford such reassurance.

It is obviously a very considerable advantage to make use of the 'imaginary' scenes, not only because of the greater control over what 'actually' happens, but also because it is so economical of time: in the same therapeutic hour, one can take a trip in Concorde, deliver a speech at a school prize-giving and become stuck in a lift halfway up the Empire State Building! Indeed, in imagination, everything is possible.

It will be recalled, however, that it is Wolpe's contention, endorsed by experimental findings, that the mere repetition of some experience will not of itself lead to an adjusted reaction. Simply going time and time again to the dental surgery waiting-room may do little to allay the anxiety which some people experience. In some way therapy must be arranged so that the anxiety which attaches to a particular scene must be eliminated and this, as was pointed out early in this section, involves invoking some reaction incompatible with anxiety. At one and the same time the individual must be exposed to a stimulus to anxiety and a response antagonistic to anxiety must be produced. In this way it will be possible to learn a new association; the old cue to anxiety is present, but no anxiety is experienced.

Although not always the case, in general a good level of relaxation is incompatible with the presence of anxiety, so that one could present scenes of a disturbing nature to an individual but might reasonably anticipate a lack of anxiety response providing the relaxed state was preserved.

The presentation of imagined scenes from the hierarchy, together with the relaxed condition of the client, became known as systematic desensitization in imagination.

The results of applying this method appear to be most encouraging in a wide variety of phobic conditions, including fear of travelling, heights, social situations, insects and many others. Yet there are clearly still many cases of phobic reactions which do not respond very well to this method and, in essence, there are really only two explanations we can offer. First, perhaps the method itself has limitations or, alternatively, the theoretical system upon which it is based has validity in only a proportion of cases. Perhaps an example of the latter will help to clarify the point.

The basic contention in Wolpe's model is that neurotic reactions (such as phobias) are learnt and it therefore should follow that some process of un-learning is needed to put matters to rights. It is apparent, however, that in many cases, search as one might, it is impossible to find any learning experience which plausibly accounts for the symptoms observed. If learning is implicated (and it is not enough simply to say that because Mr X was not born with his phobia he must therefore have learnt it) then it may well have a special character and require quite different theoretical models (and different techniques) to account for and produce changes.

Cognitive learning

The early behaviourists, such as Watson, were very much opposed to considering any activity which could not be directly observed; behaviour, for them, meant only the overt and readily quantifiable aspects of functioning. Hence, internal 'behaviours' - thoughts, ideas, images, fantasies - were not considered to be suitable matters for investigation. Gradually, however, this rather austere behavioural position began to give place to an acceptance of the importance of thoughts or cognitions, and a recognition that a place must be found for such functions in theoretical formulations.

Unfortunately, to date, such formulations are inadequate and fail to provide a really cogent basis for the development of treatment methods. Therefore cognitive therapies have tended to evolve through empirical trial and cognitive theories tend to emphasize the self-evident.

It is hardly surprising to find that the points of contact with earlier treatment methods deriving from the behavioural tradition are not particularly numerous or solid. To an extent some appear to be merely sub-categories of psychotherapy, with the differences being perhaps those of emphasis rather than substance. It is true, however, that in such examples of treatment the notions involved are often amenable to direct test and this openness to refutation is not commonly found in the psychotherapies. There is, in addition, no great emphasis upon any early personal experiences and their relation to the distress experienced by the client but, instead, attention is focussed upon the problems as they exist here and now. Additionally, such formulations tend to be readily understood, easily taught, and generally briefer than the psychotherapies. One of the best-known and widely practised is Rational Emotive Therapy (RET).

This type of treatment, devised by Ellis (1962), is really a good example of the middle ground between psychotherapy and behavioural treatments. The main thrust of the approach derives from the assumption that psychological disorders result from faulty thinking and that this is revealed in what people say to themselves. Such 'self-talk', it is assumed, has a major bearing upon how people act and feel, and modifying these internalized verbalizations can be beneficial.

Ellis summarizes the cycle of events involved in his ABCDE paradigm.

* A is the activating event: the troublesome real external event to which the individual has been exposed (e.g. girl tells boy their affair is over).
* B represents the self-verbalizations in response to A ('I'm a mess ... no one loves me').
* C concerns the emotions and behaviours resulting from B (depression, weeping, refusing to go out, etc.).
* D: client and therapist dispute the irrational beliefs; the patient's arguments are dissected and challenged.
* E: the client confronts his irrational beliefs and feels better as a result of putting them into perspective.

In particular the therapist is concentrating attention upon the discriminations to be made by the client between those things which are objectively true ('she doesn't love me ...') and those which are patently not ('no one loves me ... I'm a complete mess ...'). In short, therapy is focussed upon the illogicality of deducing 'I'm useless' from 'She doesn't love me'. Out of this examination it is expected that more positive emotions and behaviours will be born.

In addition to the above analysis the client is given homework in the form of tasks which disprove faulty conceptions of the kind referred to above, that is, identifying, confronting and disputing irrational ideas. Examples of such ideas have, no doubt, a certain familiarity for most of us but, perhaps for the stable individual, are more ephemeral and easy to abandon. Typical of these faulty ideas according to Ellis, are: that one MUST always appear competent; that small (or large) mistakes are a sign of fatal weakness; that one MUST have sincere love and approval from everyone all the time; that things which go wrong prove beyond doubt that life is awful, bitter and often catastrophic; that the slights and unkind remarks of some people clearly establish that no one can be trusted.

Ellis claims that this approach, over a period as short as six months, compares favourably with other forms of psychotherapy. However, the success of the method clearly depends upon the extent to which faulty ideas are generated by life events and, in turn, produce unwanted emotion reactions. Where such a causal chain can be found, and where the persistent lack of logic leads to the preservation of adverse emotions, Rational Emotive Therapy may have a good deal to commend it. One may doubt, however, that many problems which arise in this way can be disposed of simply through logical analysis, and the system has an apparent plausibility which is often denied by experience. Furthermore, in many cases of psychological disturbance it would seem that two factors are at work which are not readily dealt with in Rational Emotive Therapy; namely, the relative stability (native temperament) of the individual and the fact that, in so many examples of psychological disturbances, it is not life's events which have conspired to produce breakdown but some internal alteration of state. Let us clarify these points.

From Pavlov onwards, as has been pointed out earlier in this chapter, the evidence suggests that some organisms appear to be constitutionally vulnerable while others are more robust; some individuals appear to capitulate readily to stresses while others remain pretty unflappable. This speaks for itself and we can easily identify examples among our acquaintances who can be said to be of a 'nervous disposition'. This is what is meant by a constitutional vulnerability: to be born with an unusual sensitivity to stresses and strains. The second factor missing in the RET formulation is the way in which temporary states of an individual's central nervous system appear to influence mood, behaviour and, probably, his susceptibility to adverse learning. Again, the example of this comes from experiments which investigate the effect upon learning of the menstrual cycle (Asso and Beech, 1975; Vila and Beech, 1977; Vila and Beech, 1978). The argument advanced is that the menstrual cycle is an example of the variability in state which affects the acquisition of learning, such that at one stage in the cycle the individual may be relatively uninfluenced by noxious events but, at other stages, the opposite is true. The evidence suggests that during the four days prior to menstruation an individual female is far more likely to learn to behave 'defensively' than if the same opportunity is provided at other times in the cycle. In short, it seems that the organism becomes especially susceptible to learning a neurotic (unadaptive) reaction when such learning opportunities occur in conjunction with a special state of the nervous system. Indeed, it is argued that at such times learning can occur with great rapidity and tends to show a degree of permanence.

To the extent to which these factors are operative, therefore, the RET view of unadaptive thought and behaviour would require modification. We would need to recognize, for example, that the faulty logic with which RET purports to deal is likely to be prompted by the vulnerability of the system affected and that this altered state of the organism may well prevent more logical argument from being appreciated or acted upon.

A cognitive strategy bearing a less tenuous relationship to behaviour orthodoxy is 'thought stopping'.

There can be very few who have not, at some time, experienced a persistent and unwanted thought which simply will not go away. For most, this will have taken the form of a problem which goes unresolved and, no matter how much one thinks of it, no useful solution occurs. Other examples of this kind cover a serious mistake made, an acute embarrassment, and so on, which we live again and again in our minds, each time experiencing the same agonized feelings. Sometimes a tune may go on and on for some time in one's head, against one's will it seems. In many psychiatric states it is quite common to find that a worrying idea repeatedly presents itself to the considerable distress of the sufferer. Indeed, in one type of disorder, obsessional states, this is a major problem and what patients most desire is relief from the intolerable insistence of the thoughts which trouble them. These ruminations are often singularly unpleasant involving dirt, disease and death and, in many cases, these thoughts have become so frequent and pronounced that a normal existence is completely impossible (Beech, 1974).

At face value it seems that if only such thoughts could be removed and replaced by 'ordinary' preoccupations, then the person affected would be completely normal. At the very least it seems to be a desirable objective to help the individual to deal with such thoughts and the mental agony they occasion. Thought stopping is a technique often used for this purpose (Wolpe, 1969).

The most common variation of thought stopping involves the client deliberately producing the unwanted thought, following which the therapist may shout 'stop' and emphasize this by some signal, such as banging the table. Certainly this usually has an important and immediate interruptive effect on the adverse thoughts and it is contended that this process, after numerous repetitions, can lead to the permanent suppression or inhibition of the unwanted thought. During the course of acquiring this form of inhibition the 'control' is passed to the client who may, at first, shout 'stop' and bang the table but later find that a mere internalized signal (saying 'stop' to himself) is sufficient.

Unfortunately, not much is known in theoretical terms about how thoughts become inhibited by this strategy; nor for that matter are there any well-conducted large-scale investigations which increase our confidence in thought stopping as a means of thought control. The exercise, for example, is not usually one which simply involves stopping a thought (or trying to do so), but is one in which unwanted thoughts are, perhaps for the first time, systematically brought into mind. Furthermore, the extent to which shouting, table banging and so on are necessary is not known and, for good measure, it is pertinent to enquire about what is happening when the unwanted thought is dismissed. The latter, of course, may be a crucial question to ask since the answer may well be pertinent to securing better control over thought processes.

Is it better, for example, to emphasize the stopping process, or should one give equal or even greater weight to building up 'constructive' alternatives to the unwanted thought?

At the same time the very simplicity of the strategy and its essential directness is very much more in keeping with the conditioning models from which behaviour modification practices are derived. While it is not yet a technique which one can claim is well substantiated, useful evidence has accumulated (see Beech and Vaughan, 1978) and experience suggests that helpful results can be gained. Perhaps it will be useful to cite one indication of an area in which beneficial changes have occurred.

Although Mr C claimed he had forgiven his wife for her sexual indiscretion of some years ago, he found it impossible to rid himself of the image of her in the arms of her lover and, to his dismay, found himself repeatedly 'going over the details' with his wife. Such rehearsals did nothing to finally clear the matter from his mind or help put the past into perspective. Here, it seemed, was a case where simply 'forgetting' would help the couple to avoid unpleasant and even harrowing domestic scenes and afford an opportunity for them to get along together rather better.

A variation of thought stopping was used but basically it involved the deliberate production of the unpleasant scene and its termination. Rigorous training sessions over several weeks resulted in a decreased capacity for the unwanted thought to be brought into mind as well as increased facility in dismissing such thoughts when they did obtrude. What seems to be important, however, is that the individual concerned actually wants to be rid of the thoughts, and experience sometimes indicates that morbid preoccupations, although often painful, are not always entirely unwelcome. Indeed, in Mr C's case, the review of

his wife's indiscretion was not without a curious kind of
relish on his part.

Another cognitive technique, devised by Cautela (1966),
also translates very well from the traditional areas of
behavioural concern to the area of mental events. Covert
sensitization represents an attempt to apply the aversive
conditioning paradigm to thoughts in much the same way as
electrical shock has been used in the context of observable
behaviours, such as transvestism. Basically, the individual
is required to conjure up images or fantasies of the unwanted behaviour and, at this point, ideas of a less attractive
character are introduced. In the case of a very obese lady
given to bouts of gluttony, for example, she might be set
the task of imagining a table groaning with delicious foods
and not a soul around to inhibit stuffing herself to burst-
ing point. When her thoughts are occupied in this way the
therapist requires her to imagine that she has indeed gorged
herself beyond satiation but that she begins to vomit, over
the food, the table, the floor; he describes the feeling of
nausea, the rush of vomit, etc., and then, to bring the
scene to its climax, he depicts the room filling with dis-
gusted onlookers revolted at the sight and smell of this
pathetic creature.

Such exercises are, of course, repeated again and again
in an attempt to build up an appropriate feeling of nausea if
the client even reaches out in the direction of a cream
cake.

The difficulty is that, although the process bears a
superficial resemblance to the orthodoxies of aversive
training, in practice there is an almost total absence of
the precision which should usually be employed. One can, for
example, specify the number of shocks to be given and their
strength, but we have little idea of how harrowing the
'vomit' fantasy is, or even whether the client is paying any
real attention to it; such matters remain unobservable except through the subjective report of the individual
concerned.

As a further example of this technique, Foa's (1976)
case of transvestism may be mentioned. The patient, a 25-
year-old man, had developed a habit of dressing in women's
clothing, finding sexual gratification from this p actice.
This had brought him to the attention of the courts who
referred him for treatment, part of which involved covert
sensitization.

The patient was asked to imagine driving along in his
car when, suddenly, he sees a bra and pants on a clothes
line. He stops his car, gets out, and approaches the clothes
line with the intention of taking these items to use in his
cross-dressing. As he does so he begins to feel nauseous
and, as he touches the bra, the vomit spills out over his
own clothing and the article he is stealing, the scene being
depicted in as much unpleasant detail as possible. Then he
imagines throwing the bra away and feeling very much better.
It is worth noting that, as in this case, the tendency to

relapse following aversive treatment is a common finding and the therapist generally plans to provide 'booster' courses of treatment as the need arises. It is indeed, a general management problem of producing changes in behaviour that old 'habits' are often revived and further training is required to re-establish the new patterns of behaviour.

Operant training

It will be apparent from much of what has been said earlier that hedonism is of fundamental importance in most models of learning. Briefly, humans learn when they are rewarded for doing so and fail to learn (or begin to un-learn) when punishment is applied. The sophisticated use of rewards and punishments is central to the success of operant control of behaviour and, as any brief study will indicate, the degree of refinement in making use of the basic ideas of reward and punishment is extremely important.

To begin with, the notion of total and dramatic change is perhaps the wrong attitude with which to approach operant training; rather, one might think of both strengthening and shaping some existing behaviours as being the aim of such training. The following is a simple illustration of what we have in mind.

If you have a friend with some slight eccentricity of behaviour, such as twisting a lock of hair, or tugging at an ear lobe from time to time, then you might take the trouble to count the frequency of this behaviour over a period of an hour or so. Having noted this frequency you could set about strengthening this piece of behaviour (i.e. simply making it occur much more often) by rewarding its occurrence. In theory at least rewards (positive reinforcement) should have this effect.

Accordingly, you might be able to provide some simple reward, such as a smile or other expression of pleasant appreciation whenever your friend engages in the habit. Over the next hour, unless you have been rather clumsy and inept in your application of positive reinforcement (and your friend is disposed to enquire about your state of mental well-being) you should see a marked increase in ear-lobe tugging, hair-lock twisting, or whatever. In much the same way you might set out to discourage the behaviour - that is, reduce its frequency - by offering a negative reinforcement or punishment (e.g. a frown or audible 'humph') immediately after the habit has made its appearance.

Really, three things are required to make the training effective:

* the positive or negative reinforcement (reward or punishment) must be appreciated as such by the indivi- dual undergoing change. It is unsatisfactory if he neither sees the reward or, if he does see it, fails to appreciate it as a positive reinforcement;
* that the reinforcers are given immediately after the behaviour to be changed has been produced. It is of

little use to offer reinforcers in connection with
behaviour which has occurred some time before rewards
are applied;
* the application of reinforcement must be systematic,
at least in the beginning, and applied each time the
behaviour to be changed occurs. Later on, certain
changes in the reinforcement pattern can be made which
may even increase the effectiveness of learning.

One of the virtues of the operant approach is the extremely
wide variety of behaviour to which it has been and can be
applied, and the following examples help to illustrate this
point.

Epstein and Goss (1978) have reported upon the use of
positive reinforcement to eliminate disruptive behaviour in
the classroom. Here, Ike (aged 10) wandered about the class,
bothering other children and doing little work himself. The
therapy programme involved providing points for acceptable
behaviour which could be 'spent' playing games or on a
praise-filled note to Ike's mother. Over a period of some
seven weeks it was observed that there had been dramatic
shifts in this boy's behaviour including sitting in his own
seat for about 90 per cent of the time (as opposed to 70 per
cent formerly) and keeping his mind on school tasks for 58
per cent of the time (instead of 25 per cent before
treatment).

Although this example does seem to involve relatively
simple strategies, the exercise requires more careful
planning and implementation than is obvious.

Another example is that of Terry, aged 4, who whined and
shouted a good deal and only stopped when comforted by his
parents (Hall et al, 1972). This rather disturbing behaviour
was, it seems, being rewarded by the attention given and
the answer to the problem involved removing the positive
reinforcement (attention). The parents were instructed to
ignore the behaviour when it occurred and, if possible, to
leave the room. The result was that the whining and shouting
was drastically reduced over a period of just a few days.

These examples of behaviour, which might be regarded as
merely having nuisance value, could be replicated many times
over and illustrate how quickly and effectively control can
be exerted by the simple expedient of manipulating
reinforcements.

On the whole, less success attaches to such methods in
dealing with more complex disturbance, as one might expect,
but it would be only fair to say that where operant training
is directed to appropriate targets the results are encouraging. This point may need a little clarification. No one
would claim that operant training cures schizophrenia or
turns the child of subnormal intelligence into one of average IQ yet, in numerous cases of severe disturbance, there
can be a useful place for such training. In this connection,
developing communication with others, co-operation in

executing tasks, effective participation in social activities and the development of such 'self-help' behaviours as making appropriate visits to the toilet, maintaining reasonable standards of cleanliness and so on, have been reported. Understandably, such improvement has been not only important to the well-being of patients but has often allowed more time to be spent in creating a fuller and more meaningful existence for those in institutional care. Limited objectives, it is true, but valuable and humanitarian.

Perhaps one last example is worth citing in this section since it concerns a problem which has frequently and dramatically come to public notice. The report by Bachrach et al (1965) concerned a 37-year-old woman suffering from anorexia nervosa whose refusal to eat adequately had reduced her to a mere 47lb in weight, leaving her 'so cachetic and shrunken about her skeleton as to give the appearance of a poorly preserved mummy suddenly struck with the breath of life'. Eight previous hospital admisssions failed to produce improvement and her condition was such that grave concern was expressed for her survival. Operant control over eating was the target. The therapists transferred this lady to a 'barren experimental box' and she was informed that each of three people in charge of her treatment would eat one meal a day with her in the 'box'. Their task was to reinforce verbally any behaviour related to eating (from spearing a piece of food with her fork to swallowing it), the reinforcement taking the form of talking to her about something in which she was interested. However, steadily the amount of relevant 'food' behaviour she exhibited before being rewarded was stepped up. Later on it was possible to employ other sources of reinforcement, such as access to television, radio and a record-player. Any failure by her to meet eating requirements would lead to discontinuation of reinforcement and she would be left alone until the next meal occasion.

Subsequently, as the patient gained in weight, a greater variety of rewards was employed (walks, visitors, etc.) until, some two months after treatment began, she was discharged from hospital weighing 14lb heavier than at admission. The problem now was that of sustaining her progress outside the strict control of the hospital environment.

Fortunately, the family was willing to employ the same principles at home with the result that she continued to gain weight, levelling out at 88lb. Although remaining very thin she became active socially, took an interest in her appearance and even found a job which she thoroughly enjoyed.

In the main, as will be evident, the treatment in this case depended upon the application of positive reinforcement (rewards) for appropriate behaviour. However, it is also clear that it was necessary to begin by depriving this patient of many things in order to allow the reward system to work.

In conclusion

Behavioural treatments tend to have, certainly at first sight, a rather austere quality which does not readily secure respect and interest. The somewhat stark and mechanical procedures often appear to fit animal training rather than to be suitable for application to human behaviour. Surely, it is thought, more subtle and complex processes are characteristic of humans and, therefore, quite different approaches will be required. Psychoanalytic views, represented by the 'media', appear to endorse fully the notion that the human psyche is infinitely complicated and that only a theory which affords the richness of death wishes, oedipus complexes, fixations, and so on, will do.

On the other hand, the very simplicity of behavioural theories and techniques is perceived by adherents as the most essential and pleasing aspect. They would argue that such clarity is vital to the construction of scientific models of human functioning and that the tortuous elaborations of psychoanalytic theory are both overly complex and contradictory. A frequently quoted case in point is that of the theory and treatment of nocturnal enuresis.

Ordinarily we expect toilet training to proceed 'naturally' and that, by two or three years of age, many children will be clean and dry during the day. Becoming dry through the night usually follows before too long and, apart from the occasional accident, these habits will be preserved once established. Of course, a proportion of children (and even some adults) continue to wet their beds, often causing themselves and others great irritation, trouble and concern.

Psychoanalysts are inclined to take the view that this kind of behaviour (bedwetting) must not be taken at face value since it may well be a substitute for sexual gratification or a means by which a child can express aggression and resentment toward its parents. In sharp contrast to this somewhat convoluted reasoning is the exquisitely simple behavioural formulation: an individual learns to be 'dry' at night and some people have failed to acquire this 'skill'. It will be readily apparent that at least two deductions from the basic propositions separate the rival theories:

* if the habit of being dry has to be learned, then it should be possible to provide for such opportunity;
* if, as the psychoanalytic view suggests, the symptom (bedwetting) is merely a cover for the real problem (resentment, sexual gratification, etc.), then removing the symptom, as above, would not eliminate the underlying complex; presumably some new means of revealing the basic discontent would be sought.

In addition, since it is commonly observed that nocturnal enuresis is often found in the context of more general disturbances of behaviour, a third prediction can be made:

* if, as psychoanalysts claim, the general behaviour disturbance is only another aspect of maladjustment,

removing the symptom of bedwetting will not produce healthy adjusted behaviour. On the other hand, if the general behaviour problems are generated by the symptom of bedwetting, then removing the latter should eliminate the former.

A simple device to treat bedwetting was devised by Mowrer (1938) and, in modified form, continues to be used today. Briefly, the apparatus is designed to activate an alarm (bell or buzzer) whenever the bed is wet and this has the effect of waking the sleeper. It is argued that, gradually, the use of this method allows a new association to be formed – between bladder tension and the suppression of bladder release – so that the individual can, during sleep, continually inhibit the release of bladder contents. The point is that this method seems to work remarkably well with most enuretics, with claims of success in about 70-100 per cent of cases: in addition, the removal of this abnormality seems to be associated with a general improvement in behaviour and attitudes.

Clearly the evidence in this case is convincingly favourable to the behavioural approach: the simple explanation and the application of learning to the construction of new behaviours has effected important changes. There is no evidence that this comparatively simple strategy is a superficial attack upon the problem and no reason to believe that the difficulties were underpinned by complex psychological mechanisms of the type postulated by psychoanalysts.

Of course, the evidence of one test case of this kind does not establish that the same outcome would be found in other examples. Indeed, the great virtue of the behavioural approach, simplicity, may not always be reflected in abnormalities of conduct; nature does not owe us simplicity and some cogent explanations of abnormalities may turn out to be extremely complex. Yet at least the behavioural approach has been marked by two other characteristics of outstanding importance. In the first place the models put forward have generally been amenable to testing and scrutiny, a characteristic not always apparent in other theories of psychological function. Second, there has been an obvious willingness to conduct experiments to examine the value of the model, to test deductions made from it and, in general, to adopt an exemplary critical attitude.

The approach most certainly has shortcomings, in our view primarily because of the almost exclusive emphasis given to acquired as opposed to genetic influences, and because of the difficulties inherent in dealing with 'internal' behaviours, such as ideas and fantasies. Nevertheless, the empirical demonstrations of the power of the behavioural approaches have ensured an important place for these techniques for a long time to come.

References

Asso, D. and Beech, H.R. (1975)
Susceptibility to the acquisition of a conditioned

response in relation to the menstrual cycle. Journal of Psychosomatic Research, 19, 337-344.

Bachrach, A.J., Erwin, W.J. and Mohr, J.P. (1965)
Case Studies in Behaviour Modification. London: Holt, Rinehart & Winston.

Barker, J.G. and Miller, M.E. (1968)
Some clinical applications of aversion therapy. In H. Freeman (ed.), Progress in Behaviour Therapy. Bristol: Wright.

Beech, H.R. (ed.) (1974)
Obsessional States. London: Methuen.

Beech, H.R. and Vaughan, M. (1978)
The Behavioural Treatment of Obsessional States. New York: Wiley.

Bucher, B.D. (1968)
A portable shock box with application to nail-biting. Behaviour Research and Therapy, 6, 389-392.

Cautela, J.B. (1966)
Treatment of compulsive behavior by covert desensitization. The Psychological Record, 16, 33-41.

Dawkins, R. (1978)
The Selfish Gene. Oxford: Oxford University Press.

Ellis, A. (1962)
Reason and Emotion in Psychotherapy. New York: Kyle Stuart.

Epstein, R. and Goss, C.M. (1978)
A self-control procedure for the maintainance of nondisruptive behaviour in an elementary school child. Behaviour Therapy, 9, 109-118.

Eysenck, H.J. (1953)
Uses and Abuses of Psychology. Harmondsworth: Pelican.

Eysenck, H.J. and Beech, H.R. (1971)
Counterconditioning and related methods. In A.E. Bergin and S. Garfield (eds), Handbook of Psychotherapy and Behavior Change. New York: Wiley.

Foa, E.B. (1976)
Multiple behaviour techniques in the treatment of transvestism. In H.J. Eysenck, Case Studies in Behaviour Therapy. London: Routledge & Kegan Paul.

Hall, R.V., Axelrod, S., Tyler, L., Grief, G., Jones, F.C. and Robertson, R. (1972)
Modification of behavior problems in the home with a parent as observer and experimenter. Journal of Applied Behavior Analysis, 5, 53-64.

Jones, M.C. (1924)
The elimination of children's fears. Journal of Experimental Psychology, 7, 383-390.

Mowrer, D.H. and Mowrer, W. (1938)
Enuresis: A method for its study and treatment. American Journal of Orthopsychiatry, 8, 436-459.

Munroe, R.L. (1955)
Schools of Psychoanalytic Thought. New York: Dryden Press.

Pavlov, I.P. (1927)
Conditioned Reflexes (Transl. Anrep). London: Oxford University Press.

Powell, J. and Azrin, N.H. (1968)
The effects of shock as a punisher for cigarette smoking. Journal of Applied Behavior Analysis, 6, 63-71.

Rachman, S. (1966)
Sexual fetishism; an experimental analogue. The Psychological Record, 16, 293-296.

Seligman, M.E.P. and Hager, J.L. (1972)
Biological Boundaries of Learning. New York: Appleton-Century-Crofts.

Skinner, B.F. (1953)
Science and Human Behavior. New York: Macmillan.

Vila, J. and Beech, H.R. (1977)
Vulnerability and conditioning in relation to the human menstrual cycle. British Journal of Social and Clinical Psychology, 16, 69-75.

Vila, J. and Beech, H.R. (1978)
Vulnerability and defensive reactions in relation to the human menstrual cycle. British Journal of Social and Clinical Psychology, 17, 93-100.

Voegtlin, W.L. and Lemere, E. (1942)
The Treatment of Alcohol Addiction. Quarterly Journal of the Study of Alcohol, 2, 717-803.

Watson, J.B. and Rayner, R. (1920)
Conditioned Emotional Reaction. Journal of Experimental Psychology, 3, 1-4.

Wolpe, J. (1958)
Psychotherapy by Reciprocal Inhibition. Stanford, Ca: Stanford University Press.

Wolpe J. (1969)
The Practice of Behavior Therapy. New York: Pergamon.

Questions

1. A patient presents with a cat phobia which is so severe that he is reluctant to leave his home. What could you do to help him?

2. Outline at least three approaches to the modification of problem behaviours in humans and comment on their usefulness.

3. Individuals who suffer from, for example, mild depressions or anxiety states are often told to 'pull themselves together'. How useful is this advice? What alternative approaches are available?

4. Compare and contrast the methods of traditional psychotherapy and behaviour therapy to the modification of abnormal behaviours such as excessive fear or a lack of confidence.

5. What are the major assumptions about abnormal behaviour which are made by behaviour therapists? How are these assumptions integrated into the techniques used to treat pathological behaviours?

6. Describe and discuss the most important practical and ethical problems associated with the behaviour therapies.
7. Discuss the suggestion that behaviour therapy is degrading and inhumane, and should be used to modify behaviour only as a last resort.
8. Suggest how you would try to modify the following problems: (a) persistent over-eating; (b) transvestism; (c) head banging and self-injury in a three year old; (d) shyness; (e) bedwetting in an eight year old.
9. Discuss the factors which influence the development of common phobias (e.g. for spiders and snakes). How can these irrational fears be modified?
10. Discuss the applications of aversion therapy to correct problem behaviours and mention the practical and ethical difficulties of applying aversive techniques to sexual problems and alcoholism.

Annotated reading

Rachman, S. (1971) The Effects of Psychotherapy. Oxford: Pergamon.
> An account of the problems associated with psychotherapy and the way in which the behavioural approach deals with issues of treatment and training.

Kanfer, F.H. and Goldstein, A.P. (1975) Helping People Change: A textbook of methods. Oxford: Pergamon.
> An account of practical behavioural approaches to change.

Oakley, D. and Platkin, H. (1979) Brain, Behaviour and Evolution. Andover: Methuen.
> Undergraduate level synthesis of disciplines relevant to psychology. How evolutionary perspective can help our understanding of psychological questions.

Walker, S. (1976) Learning and Reinforcement. Essential Psychology Series. Andover: Methuen.
> Introductory text on key concepts to understanding behavioural approaches to change.

Boddy, A., Martin, F. and Jefferys, M. (eds) (1979) The Behavioural Sciences in General Practice. London: Tavistock.
> Primarily intended for general practitioners to enable the medical profession to acquire concepts relevant to their work so as to facilitate professional skill and expertise.

13

Counselling and Helping
Barrie Hopson

Opening remarks
DAVID GRIFFITHS

Counselling, as Barrie Hopson reminds us, has become an important part of the repertoire of the helping professions in the UK over the last 15 years or so. It follows that medical practitioners, many of whom will have the overall responsibility for clients' welfare within the Health Services, should have some understanding of the aims, nature and effectiveness of these psychological techniques. The following review provides the basis of such an understanding and attempts to provide answers to questions which should interest both the trainee and the more experienced clinician. For example, what is distinctive about counselling techniques? How does counselling differ from the everyday processes of help and support which untrained individuals provide for others? What are the characteristics of the effective counsellor? What are the goals of counselling? What are the most significant features of the process of counselling?

The review has a fair degree of success in securing Hopson's goal of 'de-mystifying' counselling. Many questions are, however, easier to pose than answer. Indeed, the chapter suggests and implies that there can be no simple or straightforward answers to important questions such as those which relate to the effectiveness of counselling and psychotherapy. Does it work? In other words, does it produce changes which clients would not enjoy if they had not received counselling? Such questions cannot be answered in a straightforward manner since outcomes and effects are likely to depend on the nature and extent of aims, the characteristics of both clients and therapists, the methods which are applied and other features such as the duration of the follow-up. No review of counselling could therefore be expected to include statements about effectiveness under these many combinations of conditions. Hopson does not claim to do this. Nevertheless, his chapter provides a comprehensive and useful introduction which makes a valuable contribution to an understanding of many features of counselling and psychotherapy.

Introduction
BARRIE HOPSON

From a situation in the mid-1960s when 'counselling' was seen by many in education as a transatlantic transplant

which they hoped would never 'take', we have today reached
the position of being on board a band-wagon; 'counsellors'
are everywhere: beauty counsellors, tax counsellors, investment counsellors, even carpet counsellors. There are
'counsellors' in schools, industry, hospitals, the social
services. There is marriage counselling, divorce counselling, parent counselling, bereavement counselling, abortion
counselling, retirement counselling, redundancy counselling,
career counselling, psychosexual counselling, pastoral counselling, student counselling and even disciplinary counselling! Whatever the original purpose for coining the word
'counselling', the coinage has by now certainly been de-
based. One of the unfortunate consequences of the debasing
has been that the word has become mysterious; we cannot
always be sure just what 'counselling' involves. One of the
results of the mystification of language is that we rely on
others to tell us what it is: that is, we assume that we,
the uninitiated, cannot know and understand what it is
really about. That can be a first step to denying ourselves
skills and knowledge we already possess or that we may have
the potential to acquire.

It is vital that we 'de-mystify' counselling, and to do
that we must look at the concept within the broader context
of ways in which people help other people, and we must
analyse it in relation to objectives. 'Counselling' is often
subscribed to as being 'a good thing', but we must ask the
question, 'good for what?'

Ways of helping

'Counselling' is only one form of helping. It is decidedly
not the answer to all human difficulties, though it can be
extremely productive and significant for some people, sometimes. Counselling is one way of working to help people
overcome problems, clarify or achieve personal goals. We can
distinguish between six types of helping strategies (Scally
and Hopson, 1979).

* Giving advice: offering somebody your opinion of what
  would be the best course of action based on your view
  of their situation.
* Giving information: giving a person the information he
  needs in a particular situation (e.g. about legal
  rights, the whereabouts of particular agencies, etc.).
  Lacking information can make one powerless; providing
  it can be enormously helpful.
* Direct action: doing something on behalf of somebody
  else or acting to provide for another's immediate needs;
  for example, providing a meal, lending money, stopping
  a fight, intervening in a crisis.
* Teaching: helping someone to acquire knowledge and
  skills; passing on facts and skills which improve
  somebody's situation.
* Systems change: working to influence and improve systems
  which are causing difficulty for people, that is,

working on organizational development rather than with individuals.

* Counselling: helping someone to explore a problem, clarify conflicting issues and discover alternative ways of dealing with it, so that they can decide what to do about it; that is, helping people to help themselves.

There is no ranking intended in this list. What we do say is that these strategies make up a helper's 'tool-bag'. Each one is a 'piece of equipment' which may be useful in particular helping contexts. What a helper is doing is to choose from his resources whichever approach best fits the situation at the time.

There are some interesting similarities and differences between the strategies. Giving advice, information, direct action, teaching and possibly systems change recognize that the best answers, outcomes, or solutions rely on the expertise of the helper. The 'expert' offers what he feels is most useful to the one seeking help. Counselling, on the other hand, emphasizes that the person with the difficulty is the one with the resources needed to deal with it. The counsellor provides the relationship which enables the clients to search for their own answers. The 'expert' does not hand out solutions. This does not deny the special skills of the helper, but does imply that having 'expertise' does not make a person an 'expert'. We all have expertise. In counselling, the counsellor is using his expertise to help to get the clients in touch with their own expertise. Counselling is the only helping strategy which makes no assumption that the person's needs are known.

Teaching, systems change, and counselling are only likely to be effective if the 'helper' has relationship-making skills. Giving advice, information and direct action are likely to be MORE effective if he has them. Systems change is different in that it emphasizes work with groups, structures, rules and organizations.

The counsellor possibly uses most of the other strategies at some time or other, when they seem more appropriate than counselling. The other strategies would have an element of counselling in them if the 'helper' had the necessary skills. For example, a new student having difficulties making friends at school could involve a counsellor, in addition to using his counselling skills, teaching some relationship-building skills to the student, getting the staff to look at induction provision, making some suggestions to the student, or even taking him to a lunchtime disco session in the school club.

Who are the helpers?

Strictly speaking we are all potential helpers and people to be helped, but in this context it may be useful to distinguish between three groups.

Professional helpers
These are people whose full-time occupation is geared

towards helping others in a variety of ways. They have usually, but not always, received specialist training. Social workers, doctors, teachers, school counsellors, nurses, careers officers and health visitors are a few examples. They define their own function in terms of one or more of the helping strategies.

Paraprofessional helpers

These people have a clearly defined helping role but it does not constitute the major part of their job specification or represent the dominant part of their lives, such as marriage guidance counsellors, priests, part-time youth workers, personnel officers and some managers. Probably they have received some short in-service training, often on-the-job.

Helpers in general

People who may not have any specially defined helping role but who, because of their occupational or social position or because of their own commitment, find themselves in situations where they can offer help to others, such as shop stewards, school caretakers, undertakers, social security clerks or solicitors. This group is unlikely to have received special training in helping skills. In addition to these groupings there are a variety of unstructured settings within which helping occurs: the family, friendships, and in the community (Brammer, 1973).

What makes people good helpers?

In some ways it is easier to begin with the qualities that quite clearly do not make for good helping. Loughary and Ripley (1979) people their helpers' rogue's gallery with four types of would-be helpers:

* the 'You think YOU'VE got a problem! Let me tell you about mine!' type;
* the 'Let me tell you what to do' type;
* the 'I understand because I once had the same problem myself' person;
* the 'I'll take charge and deal with it' type.

The first three approaches have been clearly identified as being counter-productive (Carkhuff and Berenson, 1976) while the fourth one certainly deals with a person's problems but prevents the person ever learning skills or concepts to enable him to work through the problem on his own the next time it occurs. The only possible appropriate place for this person is in a crisis intervention. However, even this intervention would need to be followed up with additional counselling help if the needy person were to avoid such crises.

Rogers (1958) came out with clearly testable hypotheses of what constitutes effective helping. He said that helpers must be open and that they should be able to demonstrate UNCONDITIONED POSITIVE REGARD: acceptance of clients as worth while regardless of who they are or what they say or do; CONGRUENCE: the helper should use his feelings, his verbal and non-verbal behaviour should be open to the client and be consistent; GENUINENESS: he should be honest, sincere and without façades; EMPATHIC: he should be able to let the client know that he understands his frame of reference and can see the world as he sees it, whilst remaining separate from it. These qualities must be not only possessed but conveyed: that is, the client must experience them.

Truax and Carkhuff (1967) put these hypotheses to the test and found considerable empirical support for what they identified as the 'core facilitative conditions' of effective helping relationships - empathy, respect and positive regard, genuineness, and concreteness - the ability to be specific and immediate to client statements. They differed from Rogers in that whereas he claimed that the facilitative conditions were necessary and sufficient, they only claimed that they were necessary. Carkhuff has gone on to try to demonstrate (Carkhuff and Berenson, 1976) that they are clearly not sufficient, and that the helper needs to be skilled in teaching a variety of life and coping skills to his clients. The other important finding from Truax and Carkhuff was that helpers who do not possess those qualities are not merely ineffective, for they can contribute to people becoming worse than they were prior to helping.

The evidence tends to suggest that the quality of the interpersonal relationship between helper and client is more important than any specific philosophy of helping adhered to by the helper. This has been demonstrated to be the case in counselling, psychotherapy and also teaching (Aspy and Roebuck, 1977). A recent review of the many research studies on this topic would suggest, as one might expect, that things are not quite that simple (Parloff, Waskow, and Wolfe, 1978), but after a reappraisal of the early work of Truax and Carkhuff and a large number of more recent studies, the authors conclude that a relationship between empathy, respect and genuineness with helper effectiveness has been established. They also shed light on a number of other factors which have been discussed periodically as being essential for effective therapists (their focus was therapy, not helping):

*   personal psychotherapy has not been demonstrated to be a prerequisite for an effective therapist;
*   sex and race are not related to effectiveness;
*   the value of therapist experience is highly questionable; that is, someone is not necessarily a better therapist because he is more experienced;
*   therapists with emotional problems of their own are likely to be less effective;
*   there is some support for the suggestion that helpers are more effective when working with clients who hold values similar to their own.

What they do point out is the importance of the match

between helper and client. No one is an effective helper with everyone, although we as yet know little as to how to match helpers with clients to gain the greatest benefits.

Helping and human relationships

Carl Rogers states very clearly that psychotherapy is not a 'special kind of relationship, different in kind from all others which occur in everyday life' (1957). A similar approach has been taken by those theorists looking at the broader concept of helping. Brammer (1973) states that 'helping relationships have much in common with friendships, family interactions, and pastoral contacts. They are all aimed at fulfilling basic human needs, and when reduced to their basic components, look much alike'. This is the approach of Egan in his training programmes for effective interpersonal relating (1975), of Carkhuff and Berenson (1976) who talk of counselling as 'a way of life', of Illich (1977) who is concerned with the de-skilling of the population by increasing armies of specialists, and of Scally and Hopson (1979) who emphasize that counselling 'is merely a set of beliefs, values and behaviours to be found in the community at large'. Considerable stress is placed later in this chapter on the trend towards demystifying helping and counselling.

Models of helping

Any person attempting to help another must have some model in his head, however ill-formed, of the process which he is about to undertake. He will have goals, however hazy, ranging from helping the person to feel better through to helping him to work through an issue for himself. It is essential for helpers to become more aware of the value-roots of their behaviours and the ideological underpinning of their proffered support.

> The helper builds his theory through three overlapping stages. First he reflects on his own experience. He becomes aware of his values, needs, communication style, and their impact on others. He reads widely on the experience of other practitioners who have tried to make sense out of their observations by writing down their ideas into a systematic theory ... Finally the helper forges the first two items together into a unique theory of his own (Brammer, 1973).

Fortunately, in recent years a number of theorists and researchers have begun to define models of helping. This can only assist all helpers to define their own internal models which will then enable them in turn to evaluate their personal, philosophical and empirical bases.

CARKHUFF AND ASSOCIATES: Carkhuff took Rogers' ideas on psychotherapy and expanded on them to helping in general. He has a three-stage model through which the client is helped to (i) explore, (ii) understand and (iii) act. He defines the skills needed by the helper at each stage of the process (Carkhuff, 1974), and has also developed a system for selecting and training prospective helpers to do this. Since the skills he outlines are basically the same skills which anyone needs to live effectively, he suggests that the best way of helping people is to teach them directly and systematically in life, work, learning and relationship-building skills. He states clearly that 'the essential task of helping is to bridge the gap between the helpee's skills level and the helper's skills level' (Carkhuff and Berenson, 1976). For Carkhuff, helping equals teaching, but teaching people the skills to ensure that they can take more control over their own lives.

BRAMMER (1973) has produced an integrated, eclectic developmental model similar to Carkhuff's. He has expanded Carkhuff's three stages into the eight stages of entry, classification, structure, relationship, exploration, con-solidation, planning and termination. He has also identified seven clusters of skills to promote 'understanding of self and others'. His list of 46 specific skills is somewhat daunting to a beginner but a rich source of stimulation for the more experienced helper.

IVEY AND ASSOCIATES (1971) have developed a highly systematic model for training helpers under the label 'microcounselling'. Each skill is broken up into its constituent parts and taught via closed-circuit television, modelling and practice.

HACKNEY AND NYE (1973) have described a helping model which they call a 'discrimination' model. It is goal-centred and action-centred and it stresses skills training.

KAGAN AND ASSOCIATES (1967) have also developed a microskills approach to counsellor training which is widely used in the USA. It is called Interpersonal Process Recall which involves an inquiry session in which helper and client explore the experience they have had together in the presence of a mediator.

EGAN (1975) has developed perhaps the next most influential model of helping in the USA after Carkhuff's and, indeed, has been highly influenced by Carkhuff's work. The model begins with a pre-helping phase involving attending skills, to be followed by Stage I: responding and self-exploration; Stage II: integrative understanding and dynamic self-understanding; Stage III: facilitating action and acting. The first goal labelled at each stage is the helper's goal and the second goal is that of the client.

LOUGHARY AND RIPLEY (1979) approach helping from a different viewpoint, which, unlike the previous theorists, is not simply on the continuum beginning with Rogers and Carkhuff. They have used a demystifying approach aimed at the general population with no training other than what can be gleaned from their book. Their model is shown in figure 1.

The helping tools include information, ideas, and skills (such as listening and reflecting dealings). The strategies

Figure 1

Model of helping
From Loughary and Ripley (1979)

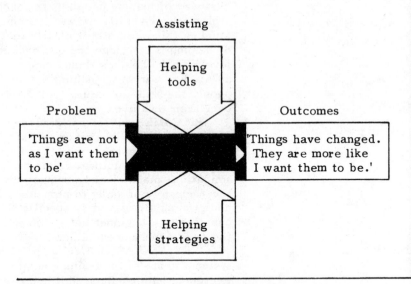

are the plans for using the tools and the first step is always translating the problem into desired outcomes. Their four positive outcomes of helping are: changes in feeling states, increased understanding, decisions, and implementing decisions. Their approach does move away from the counselling-dominated approach of the other models.

HOPSON AND SCALLY: we reproduce our own model in some detail here, partly because it is the model we know best and it has worked very effectively for us and for the 3,000 teachers and youth workers who have been through our counselling skills training courses (Scally and Hopson, 1979), but also because it attempts to look at all the aspects of helping defined at the beginning of this chapter.

Figure 2 outlines three goal areas for helpers, central to their own personal development. It also defines specific helping outcomes. Helpers can only help people to the levels of their own skills and awareness (Aspy and Roebuck, 1977). They need to clarify their own social, economic and cultural values and need to be able to recognize and separate their own needs and problems from those of their clients. Helpers see in others reflections of themselves. To know oneself is to ensure a clarity of distinction between images: to know where one stops and the other begins. We become less helpful as the images blur. To ensure that does not happen, we need constantly to monitor our own development. Self-awareness is not a stage to be reached and then it is over. It is a process which can never stop because we are always changing. By monitoring these changes we simultaneously retain some control of their direction.

>als of helping

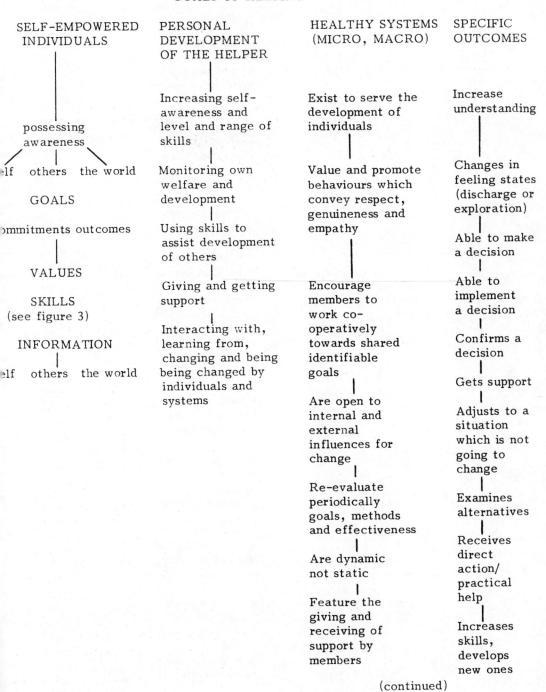

GOALS OF HELPING

SELF-EMPOWERED INDIVIDUALS	PERSONAL DEVELOPMENT OF THE HELPER	HEALTHY SYSTEMS (MICRO, MACRO)	SPECIFIC OUTCOMES
	Increasing self-awareness and level and range of skills	Exist to serve the development of individuals	Increase understanding
possessing awareness	Monitoring own welfare and development	Value and promote behaviours which convey respect, genuineness and empathy	Changes in feeling states (discharge or exploration)
ʒlf others the world	Using skills to assist development of others		Able to make a decision
GOALS	Giving and getting support	Encourage members to work co-operatively towards shared identifiable goals	Able to implement a decision
ɔmmitments outcomes	Interacting with, learning from, changing and being being changed by individuals and systems		Confirms a decision
VALUES		Are open to internal and external influences for change	Gets support
SKILLS (see figure 3)		Re-evaluate periodically goals, methods and effectiveness	Adjusts to a situation which is not going to change
INFORMATION		Are dynamic not static	Examines alternatives
ʒlf others the world		Feature the giving and receiving of support by members	Receives direct action/ practical help
			Increases skills, develops new ones

(continued)

Focus on
individual's
strengths
|
And builds on
them
|
Use problem
solving strate-
gies rather than
scapegoating,
blaming or focus-
sing on faults
|
Use methods which
are consistent
with goals
|
Encourage power-
sharing and enable
individuals to
pursue their own
direction as a
contribution to
shared goals
|
Monitor their own
performance in a
continuing cycle of
reflection/action
|
Allow people
access to those
whose decisions
have a bearing
on their lives
|
Have effective
and sensitive
lines of
communication
|
Explore differ-
ences openly and
use compromise,
negotiation and
contracting to
achieve a maxi-
mum of win/win
outcomes for all
|
Are always open
to alternatives

Receives
information
|
Reflects on
acts

From a greater awareness of who we are, our strengths, hindrances, values, needs and prejudices, we can be clearer about skills we wish to develop. The broader the range of skills we acquire, the larger the population group that we can help.

As helpers involved in the act of helping we learn through the process of praxis. We reflect and we act. As we interact with others, we in turn are affected by them and are in some way different from before the interaction. As we attempt to help individuals and influence systems we will learn, change, and develop from the process of interaction, just as those individuals and systems will be affected by us.

Having access to support should be a central concern for anyone regularly involved in helping. Helpers so often are not as skilled as they might be at saying 'no' and looking after themselves.

We would maintain that the ultimate goals of helping are to enable people to become self-empowered and to make systems healthier places in which to live, work and play.

Self-empowerment

There are five dimensions of self-empowerment (Hopson and Scally, 1980a).

*   Awareness: without an awareness of ourselves and others we are subject to the slings and arrows of our upbringing, daily events, social changes and crises. Without awareness we can only react, like the pinball in the machine that bounces from one thing to another without having ever provided the energy for its own passage.
*   Goals: given awareness we have the potential for taking charge of ourselves and our lives. We take charge by exploring our values, developing commitments, and by specifying goals with outcomes. We learn to live by the question: 'what do I want now?' We reflect and then act.
*   Values: we subscribe to the definition of values put forward by Raths, Harmin and Simon (1964): a value is a belief which has been chosen freely from alternatives after weighing the consequences of each alternative; it is prized and cherished, shared publicly and acted upon repeatedly and consistently. The self-empowered person, by our definition, has values which include recognizing the worth of self and others, of being proactive, working for health systems, at home, in employment, in the community and at leisure; helping other people to become more self-empowered.
*   Life skills: values are good as far as they go, but it is only by developing skills that we can translate them into action. We may believe that we are responsible for our own destiny, but we require the skills to achieve what we wish for ourselves. In a school setting, for example, we require the skills of goal setting and

action-planning, time management, reading, writing and numeracy, study skills, problem-solving skills and how to work in groups. Figure 3 reproduces the list of life skills that we have identified at the Counselling and Career Development Unit (Hopson and Scally, 1980b) as being crucial to personal survival and growth.

* Information: information is the raw material for awareness of self and the surrounding world. It is the fuel for shaping our goals. Information equals power. Without it we are helpless, which is of course why so many people and systems attempt to keep information to themselves. We must realize that information is essential (a concept), that we need to know how to get appropriate information, and from where (a skill).

Healthy systems

Too often counsellors and other helpers have pretended to be value free. Most people now recognize that fiction. Not only is it impossible but it can be dangerous. If we honestly believe that we are capable of being value free, we halt the search for the ways in which our value systems are influencing our behaviour with our clients. If we are encouraging our clients to develop goals, how can we pretend that we do not have them too? Expressing these goals can be the beginning of a contract to work with a client for, like it or not, we each have a concept, however shadowy, for the fully functioning healthy person to which our actions and helping are directed.

As with clients, so too with systems. If we are working towards helping people to become 'better', in whatever way we choose to define that, let us be clear about what changes we are working towards in the systems we try to influence. Figure 2 lists our characteristics of healthy systems. Each of us has his own criteria so let us discover them and bring them into the open. Owning our values is one way of demonstrating our genuineness.

What is counselling?

Having identified six common ways of helping people, counselling will now be focussed on more intensively, which immediately gets us into the quagmire of definition.

Anyone reviewing the literature to define counselling will quickly suffer from data-overload. Books, articles, even manifestoes, have been written on the question.

In training courses run from the Counselling and Career Development Unit we tend to opt for the parsimonious definition of 'helping people explore problems so that they can decide what to do about them'.

The demystification of counselling

There is nothing inherently mysterious about counselling. It is merely a set of beliefs, values and behaviours to be found in the community at large. The beliefs include one that says individuals benefit and grow from a particular

Figure 3

Lifeskills: taking charge of yourself and your life

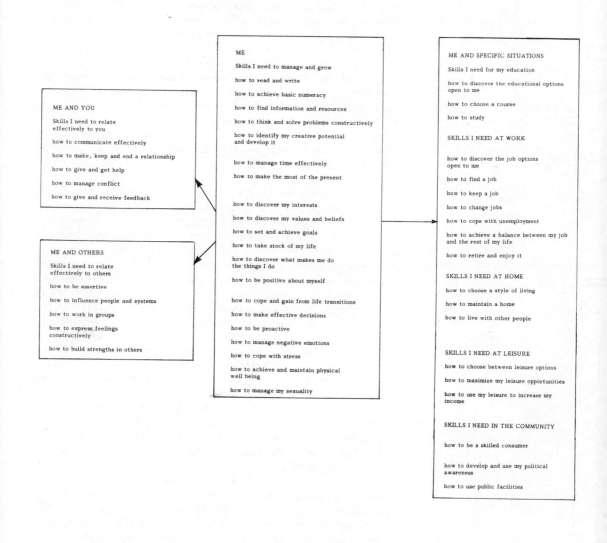

ME AND YOU

Skills I need to relate
effectively to you

how to communicate effectively

how to make, keep and end a relationship

how to give and get help

how to manage conflict

how to give and receive feedback

ME AND OTHERS

Skills I need to relate
effectively to others

how to be assertive

how to influence people and systems

how to work in groups

how to express feelings
constructively

how to build strengths in others

ME

Skills I need to manage and grow

how to read and write

how to achieve basic numeracy

how to find information and resources

how to think and solve problems constructively

how to identify my creative potential
and develop it

how to manage time effectively

how to make the most of the present

how to discover my interests

how to discover my values and beliefs

how to set and achieve goals

how to take stock of my life

how to discover what makes me do
the things I do

how to be positive about myself

how to cope and gain from life transitions

how to make effective decisions

how to be proactive

how to manage negative emotions

how to cope with stress

how to achieve and maintain physical
well being

how to manage my sexuality

ME AND SPECIFIC SITUATIONS

Skills I need for my education

how to discover the educational options
open to me

how to choose a course

how to study

SKILLS I NEED AT WORK

how to discover the job options
open to me

how to find a job

how to keep a job

how to change jobs

how to cope with unemployment

how to achieve a balance between my job
and the rest of my life

how to retire and enjoy it

SKILLS I NEED AT HOME

how to choose a style of living

how to maintain a home

how to live with other people

SKILLS I NEED AT LEISURE

how to choose between leisure options

how to maximize my leisure opportunities

how to use my leisure to increase my
income

SKILLS I NEED IN THE COMMUNITY

how to be a skilled consumer

how to develop and use my political
awareness

how to use public facilities

form of relationship and contact. The values recognize the worth and the significance of each individual and regard personal autonomy and self-direction as desirable. The behaviours cover a combination of listening, conveying warmth, asking open questions, encouraging specificity, concreteness and focussing, balancing support and confrontation, and offering strategies which help to clarify objectives and identify action plans. This terminology is more complex than the process needs to be. The words describe what is essentially a 'non-mystical' way in which some people are able to help other people to help themselves (see figure 4).

Training courses can sometimes encourage the mystification. They talk of 'counselling skills' and may, by implication, suggest that such skills are somehow separate from other human activities, are to be conferred upon those who attend courses, and are probably innovatory. In fact, what 'counselling' has done is to crystallize what we know about how warm, trusting relationships develop between people. It recognizes that:

* relationships develop if one has and conveys respect for another, if one is genuine oneself, if one attempts to see things from the other's point of view (empathizes), and if one endeavours not to pass judgement. Those who operate in this way we describe as having 'relationship-building skills';
* if the relationship is established, an individual will be prepared to talk through and explore his thoughts and feelings. What one can do and say which helps that to happen we classify as exploring and clarifying skills (see figure 4);
* through this process an individual becomes clear about difficulties or uncertainties, and can explore options and alternatives, in terms of what he might do to change what he is not happy about;
* given support, an individual is likely to be prepared to, and is capable of, dealing with difficulties or problems he may face more effectively. He can be helped by somebody who can offer objective setting and action planning skills.

Counselling skills are what people use to help people to help themselves. They are not skills that are exclusive to one group or one activity. It is clear that the behaviours, which we bundle together and identify as skills, are liberally scattered about us in the community. Counselling ideology identifies which behaviours are consistent with its values and its goals, and teaches these as one category of helping skills.

What may happen, unfortunately, is that the promotion of counselling as a separate training responsibility can increase the mystification. An outcome can be that instead of simply now being people who, compared to the majority,

Figure 4

The Counselling Process

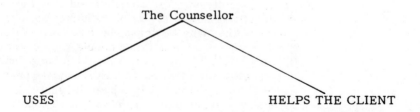

	USES	HELPS THE CLIENT
RELATIONSHIP BUILDING SKILLS	respect genuineness empathy	to feel valued, understood and prepared to trust the counsellor
EXPLORING AND CLARIFYING SKILLS	contracting open questions summarizing focussing reflecting immediacy clarifying concreteness confronting	to talk and explore to understand more about how he feels and why to consider options and examine alternatives to choose an alternative
	objective setting action planning problem-solving strategies	to develop clear objectives to form specific action plans to do, with support, what needs to be done

COUNSELLING IS HELPING PEOPLE TO HELP THEMSELVES

are extra-sensitive listeners, are particularly good at making relationships, and are more effective at helping others to solve problems, they have become 'counsellors' and licensed to help. A licence becomes a danger if:

* those who have it see themselves as qualitatively different from the rest of the population;
* it symbolizes to the non-licensed that they are incapable, or inferior, or calls into question valuable work they may be doing, but are 'unqualified' to do.

It is important to recognize that labelling people can have unfortunate side effects. Let us remember that whatever the nomenclature - counsellor, client or whatever - at a particular time or place, they are just people. All, at some time or other, will be able to give help, at other times will need to seek or receive help. Some are naturally better fitted to help others; some by training can improve their helping skills. All, through increased awareness and skill development, can become more effective helpers than they are now.

Counselling is not only practised by counsellors. It is a widespread activity in the community and appears in several guises. Its constituent skills are described variously as 'talking it over', 'having a friendly chat', 'being a good friend' or simply 'sharing' with somebody. These processes almost certainly include some or all of the skills summarized in figure 4. Often, of course, there are notable exceptions: for instance, we do not listen well; we cannot resist giving our advice, or trying to solve problems for our friends; we find it difficult to drop our façades and roles. Counselling skills training can help reduce our unhelpful behaviours and begin to develop these skills in ourselves, making us more effective counsellors, as well as simply being a good friend. In almost any work involving contact with other people, we would estimate there is a potential counselling component. There is a need for the particular interpersonal skills categorized here as counselling skills to be understood and used by people at large, but particularly by all people who have the welfare of others as part of their occupational roles. Specialist 'counsellors' have an important part to play, but it is not to replace the valuable work that is done by many who would not claim the title. Having said that, people sometimes think they are counselling, but in fact are doing things very far removed: disciplining, persuading people to conform to a system, etc.

Types of counselling

Developmental versus crisis counselling
Counselling can operate either as a RESPONSE to a situation or as a STIMULUS to help a client develop and grow. In the past, counselling has often been concerned with helping someone with a problem during or after the onset of a crisis

point: a widow unable to cope with her grief, the school leaver desperate because he has no idea what job to choose, the pregnant woman with no wish to be pregnant. This is a legitimate function of counselling, but if this is all that counselling is, it can only ever be concerned with making the best of the situation in which one finds oneself. How much more ambitious to help people anticipate future problems, to educate them to recognize the cues of oncoming crisis, and to provide them with skills to take charge of it at the outset instead of running behind in an attempt to catch up! This is counselling as a stimulus to growth: developmental as opposed to crisis counselling. All successful counselling entails growth, but the distinction between the two approaches is that the crisis approach generates growth under pressure, and since this is often limited only to the presenting problem, the client's behavioural and conceptual repertoire may remain little affected by the experience. There will always be a need for crisis counselling in a wide variety of settings, but the exciting prospect of developmental counselling for growth and change has only recently begun to be tackled.

Individual counselling

As counselling was rooted in psychotherapy it is hardly surprising that the primary focus has been on the one-to-one relationship. There are a number of essential elements in the process. The client is to be helped to reach his own decision by himself. This is achieved by establishing a relationship of trust whereby the client feels that the counsellor cares about him, is able to empathize with his problem, and is authentic and genuine in relating to him. The counsellor will enter the relationship as a person in his own right, disclosing relevant information about himself as appropriate, reacting honestly to the client's statements and questions, but at no time imposing his own opinions on the client. His task is to facilitate the client's own abilities and strengths in such a way that the client experiences the satisfaction of having defined and solved his problem for himself. If the client lacks information on special issues, is incapable of generating alternative strategies, or cannot make decisions in a programmatic way, then the counsellor has a function as an educator whose skills are offered to the client. In this way the client is never manipulated. The counsellor is negotiating a contract to use some skills which he, the counsellor, possesses, and which can be passed on to the client if the client wishes to make use of them.

Individual counselling has the advantages over group counselling of providing a safer setting for some people to lower their defences, of developing a strong and trusting relationship with the counsellor, and of allowing the client maximum personal contact with the counsellor.

Group counselling

Group counselling involves one or more counsellors operating

with a number of clients in a group session. The group size
varies from four to sixteen, with eight to ten being the
most usual number. The basic objectives of group and individual counselling are similar. Both seek to help the
clients achieve self-direction, integration, self-
responsibility, self-acceptance, and an understanding of
their motivations and patterns of behaviour. In both cases
the counsellor needs the skills and attitudes outlined
earlier, and both require a confidential relationship. There
are, however, some important differences (Hopson, 1977).

* The group counsellor needs an understanding of group
  dynamics: communication, decision making, role-playing,
  sources of power, and perceptual processes in groups.
* The group situation can provide immediate opportunities
  to try out ways of relating to individuals, and is an
  excellent way of providing the experience of intimacy
  with others. The physical proximity of the clients to
  one another can be emotionally satisfying and supportive. Clients give a first-hand opportunity to test
  others' perception of themselves.
* Clients not only receive help themselves; they also help
  other clients. In this way helping skills are generated
  by a larger group of people than is possible in
  individual counselling.
* Clients often discover that other people have similar
  problems, which can at the least be comforting.
* Clients learn to make effective use of other people, not
  just professionals, as helping agents. They can set up a
  mutual support group which is less demanding on the
  counsellor and likely to be a boost to their self-esteem
  when they discover they can manage to an increasing
  extent without him.

There are many different kinds of group counselling. Some
careers services in higher education offer counsellor-led
groups as groundwork preparation for career choices; these
small groups give older adolescents an opportunity to
discuss the interrelations between their conscious values
and preferred life styles and their crystallizing sense of
identity. Other groups are provided in schools where young
people can discuss with each other and an adult counsellor
those relationships with parents and friends which are so
important in adolescence. Training groups are held for
teaching decision-making skills and assertive skills. There
are also groups in which experiences are pooled and mutual
help given for the married, for parents, for those bringing
up families alone and for those who share a special problem
such as having a handicapped child. All these types of
groups are usually led by someone who has had training and
experience in facilitating them. The word 'facilitating' is
used advisedly, for the leader's job is not to conduct a
seminar or tutorial, but to establish an atmosphere in which
members of the group can explore the feelings around a

particular stage of development or condition or critical choice.

Another type of group is not so specifically focussed on an area of common concern but is set up as a sort of laboratory to learn about the underlying dynamics of how people in groups function, whatever the group's focus and purpose may be. These are often referred to as sensitivity training groups (e.g. Cooper and Mangham, 1971; Smith, 1975). Yet a third category of group has more therapeutic goals, being intended to be successive or complementary to, or sometimes in place of, individual psychotherapy. This type of group will not usually have a place in work settings, whereas the other two do have useful applications there. Obvious uses for this type of group occur in induction procedures, in preparation for retirement, in relation to job change arising from promotion, or in relation to redundancy. The second type of group is employed in training for supervisory or management posts, though one hears less about their use in trade unions.

Schools of counselling
Differences in theories of personality, learning and perception are reflected in counselling theory. It is useful to distinguish between five major schools.

1.   PSYCHOANALYTIC APPROACHES were historically the first. Psychoanalysis is a personality theory, a philosophical system, and a method of psychotherapy. Concentrating on the past history of a patient, understanding the internal dynamics of the psyche, and the relationship between the client and the therapist are all key concerns for psychoanalysis. Key figures include Freud, Jung, Adler, Sullivan, Horney, Fromm and Erikson.

2.   CLIENT-CENTRED APPROACHES are based upon the work of Rogers, originally as a non-directive therapy developed as a reaction against psychoanalysis. Founded on a subjective view of human experiencing, it places more faith in and gives more responsibility to the client in problem solving. The techniques of client-centred counselling have become the basis for most counselling skills training, following the empirical evaluations by Truax and Carkhuff (1967).

3.   BEHAVIOURAL APPROACHES arise from attempts to apply the principles of learning to the resolution of specific behavioural disorders. Results are subject to continual experimentation and refinement. Key figures include Wolpe, Eysenck, Lazarus and Krumboltz.

4.   COGNITIVE APPROACHES include 'rational-emotive therapy' (Ellis), 'Transactional analysis' (Berne) and 'reality therapy' (Glasser), along with Meichenbaum's work on cognitive rehearsal and inoculation. All have in common

the belief that people's problems are created by how they conceptualize their worlds: change the concepts and feelings will change too.

5. AFFECTIVE APPROACHES include 'Gestalt therapy' (Perls), 'primal therapy' (Janov), 're-evaluation counselling' (Jackins), and 'bioenergetics' (Lowen). These have in common the belief that pain and distress accumulate and have to be discharged in some way before the person can become whole or think clearly again.

There are many other approaches and orientations. The existential-humanistic school is exemplified by May, Maslow, Frankl and Jourard. Encounter approaches have been developed by Schutz, Bindrim and Ichazo, 'psychosynthesis' by Assagioli, 'morita therapy' by Morita, and 'eclectic psychotherapy' by Thorne. In the United Kingdom the biggest influence on counsellor training has been from the client-centred school. Behavioural approaches are becoming more common and, to a lesser extent, so are transactional analysis, Gestalt therapy and re-evaluation counselling.

Where does counselling take place?

Until recently counselling was assumed to take place in the confines of a counsellor's office. This is changing rapidly. It is now increasingly accepted that effective counselling, as defined in this chapter, can take place on the shop floor, in the school corridor, even on a bus. The process is not made any easier by difficult surroundings, but when people need help, the helpers are not always in a position to choose from where they would like to administer it. Initial contacts are often made in these kinds of environment, and more intensive counselling can always be scheduled for a later date in a more amenable setting.

What are the goals of counselling?

Counselling is a process through which a person attains a higher stage of personal competence. It is always about change. Katz (1969) has said that counselling is concerned not with helping people to make wise decisions but with helping them to make decisions wisely. It has as its goal self-empowerment: that is, the individual's ability to move through the following stages.

*   'I am not happy with things at the moment'
*   'What I would prefer is ...'
*   'What I need to do to achieve that is ...'
*   'I have changed what I can, and have come to terms, for the moment, with what I cannot achieve'.

Counselling has as an ultimate goal the eventual redundancy of the helper, and the activity should discourage dependency and subjection. It promotes situations in which the person's views and feelings are heard, respected and not judged. It builds personal strength, confidence and invites initiative and growth. It develops the individual and encourages control of self and situations. Counselling obviously works for the formation of more capable and effective individuals, through working with people singly or in groups.

In its goals it stands alongside other approaches concerned with personal and human development. All can see how desirable would be the stage when more competent, 'healthier' individuals would live more positively and more humanly. Counselling may share its goals in terms of what it wants for individuals; where it does differ from other approaches is in its method of achieving that. It concentrates on the individual - alone or in a group - and on one form of helping. Some other approaches would work for the same goals but would advocate different methods of achieving them. It is important to explore the inter-relatedness of counselling and other forms of helping as a way of asking, 'If we are clear about what we want for people, are we being as effective as we could be in achieving it?'

Counselling outcomes

This chapter has defined the ultimate outcome of counselling as 'helping people to help themselves'. A natural question to follow might be, 'to help themselves to do what?' There follows a list of counselling outcomes most frequently asked for by clients:

* increased understanding of oneself or a situation;
* achieving a change in the way one is feeling;
* being able to make a decision;
* confirming a decision;
* getting support for a decision;
* being able to change a situation;
* adjusting to a situation that is not going to change;
* the discharge of feelings;
* examining options and choosing one (Scally and Hopson, 1979).

Clients sometimes want other outcomes which are not those of counselling but stem from one or more of the other forms of helping: information, new skills, or practical help.

All of these outcomes have in common the concept of change. All counselling is about change. Given any issue or problem a person always has four possible strategies to deal with it:

* change the situation;
* change oneself to adapt to the situation;
* exit from it;
* develop ways of living with it.

Is counselling the best way of helping people?

In the quest for more autonomous, more self-competent, self-employed individuals the helper is faced with the question,

'If that is my goal, am I working in the most effective way towards achieving it?' As much as one believes in the potential of counselling, there are times when one must ask whether spending time with individuals is the best investment of one's helping time and effort.

Many counsellors say that time spent in this way is incredibly valuable; it emphasizes the importance of each individual, and hence they justify time given to one-to-one counselling. At the other end of the spectrum there are those who charge 'counsellors' with:

* being concerned solely with 'casualties', people in crisis and in difficulty, and not getting involved with organizational questions;
* allowing systems, organizations and structures to continue to operate 'unhealthily', by 'treating' these 'casualties' so effectively.

To reject these charges out-of-hand would be to fail to recognize the elements of truth they contain. One respects tremendously the importance that counselling places on the individual, and this is not an attempt to challenge that. What it may be relevant to establish is that counselling should not be seen as a substitute for 'healthy' systems, which operate in ways which respect individuality, where relationships are genuine and positive, where communication is open and problem-solving and participation are worked at (see figure 2). 'Healthy' systems can be as important to the welfare of the individual as can one-to-one counselling. It is unfortunate therefore that 'administrators' can see personal welfare as being the province of 'counselling types', and the latter are sometimes reluctant to 'contaminate' their work by getting involved in administrational or organizational matters. These attitudes can be very detrimental to all involved systems. The viewpoint presented here is that part of a helper's repertoire of skills in the 'tool-bag' alongside counselling skills should be willingness, and the ability, to work for systems change. Some counsellors obviously do this already in more spontaneous ways; for example, if one finds oneself counselling truants, it may become apparent that some absconding is invited by timetable anomalies (French for remedial groups on Friday afternoons?). The dilemma here is whether one spends time with a series of individual truants or persuades the designers of timetables to establish a more aware approach.

One realizes sometimes also that one may, in counselling, be using one's skills in such a way that individuals accept outcomes which possibly should not be accepted. For example, unemployment specialists in careers services sometimes see themselves as being used by 'the system' to help black youths come to terms with being disadvantaged. Such specialists ask whether this is their role or whether they should in fact be involved politically and actively in working for social and economic change.

Resistance to the idea of becoming more involved in 'systems' and 'power structures' may not simply be based upon a reluctance to take on extra, unattractive work. Some will genuinely feel that this approach is 'political' and therefore somehow tainted and dubious. It is interesting that in the USA during the last five years there has been a significant shift in opinion towards counsellors becoming more ready to accept the need to be involved in influencing systems:

> Their work brings them face to face with the victim of poverty; or racism, sexism, and stigmatization; of political, economic and social systems that allow individuals to feel powerless and helpless; of governing structures that cut off communication and deny the need for responsiveness; of social norms that stifle individuality; of communities that let their members live in isolation from one another. In the face of these realities human service workers have no choice but to blame those victims or to see ways to change the environment (Lewis and Lewis, 1977).

In this country, perhaps a deeper analysis is needed of the 'contexts' in which we work as helpers.

Can counselling be apolitical?

It is very interesting that in his recent book, Carl Rogers (Rogers, 1978) reviewing his own present position vis-à-vis counselling, indicates the revolutionary impact of much of his work as perceived by him in retrospect. Perhaps identifiable as the 'arch-individualist', Rogers signals now that he had not seen the full social impact of the values and the methodology he pioneered. He writes eloquently of his realization that much of his life and work has in fact been political, though previously he had not seen it in those terms. Counselling invites self-empowerment; it invites the individual to become aware and to take more control; it asks 'How would you like things to be?' and 'How will you make them like that?' That process is a very powerful one and has consequences that are likely to involve changing 'status quos'. Clearly processes that are about change, power, and control are 'political' (although not necessarily party political).

From this viewpoint counsellors are involved in politics already. As much as one may like there to be, there can really be no neutral ground. Opting out or not working for change is by definition maintaining the status quo. If the 'status quo' means an organization, systems or relationships which are insensitive, uncaring, manipulative, unjust, divisive, autocratic, or function in any way which damages the potential of the people who are part of them, then one cannot really turn one's back on the task of working for change. 'One is either part of the solution or part of the problem!' We have argued (Scally and Hopson, 1979) that counsellors have much to offer by balancing their one-to-one work with more direct and more skilled involvement in making systems more positive, growthful places in which to live and work.

To counsel or to teach?

Counselling is a process through which a person attains a higher level of personal competence. Recently, attacks have been made on the counselling approach by such widely differing adversaries as Illich (1973) and Carkhuff (Carkhuff and Berenson, 1976). They, and others, question what effect the existence of counsellors and therapists has had on human development as a whole. They maintain that, however benevolent the counselling relationship is felt to be by those involved, there are forces at work overall which are suspect. They suggest:

* that helpers largely answer their own needs, and consciously or unconsciously perpetuate dependency or inadequacy in clients;
* helping can be 'disabling' rather than 'enabling' because it often encourages dependency.

For counsellors to begin to answer such charges requires a self-analysis of their own objectives, methods and motives. They could begin by asking:

* how much of their counselling is done at the 'crisis' or 'problem' stage in their clients' lives?
* how much investment are they putting into 'prevention' rather than 'cure'?

To help somebody in crisis is an obvious task. It is, however, only one counselling option. If 'prevention' is better than 'cure' then maybe that is where the emphasis ought to be. Perhaps never before has there been more reason for individuals to feel 'in crisis'. Toffler (1970) has identified some likely personal and social consequences of living at a time of incredibly rapid change. Many, like Stonier (1979) are forecasting unparalleled technological developments over the next 30 years which will change our lives, especially our work patterns, dramatically. There are so many complex forces at work that it is not surprising that many people are feeling more anxious, unsure, pessimistic, unable to cope, depersonalized, and helpless. Helpers are at risk as much as any, but are likely to be faced with ever-increasing demands on their time and skills. Again, this requires a reassessment of approaches and priorities, which could suggest a greater concentration on the development of personal competence in our systems. We need to develop more 'skilled' (which is not the same as 'informed') individuals and thereby avert more personal difficulties and crisis. One view is that this, the developmental, educational, teaching approach, needs to involve more of those who now spend much time in one-to-one counselling; not to replace that work but to give balance to it.

Personal competence and self-empowerment, which are the 'goals' of counselling, can be understood in many ways. A recent movement has been to see competence as being achievable through skill development. 'Life skills' are becoming as large a band-wagon as counselling has become.

We are producing a series of Lifeskills Teaching Programmes (Hopson and Scally, 1980b) which cover a range of more generic personal skills: for example, 'How to be assertive rather than aggressive', 'How to make, maintain and end relationships', 'How to manage time effectively', 'How to be positive about oneself', 'How to make effective transitions', etc. (figure 3). The programmes attempt to break down the generalization of 'competence' into 'learn-able' units, with the overall invitation that, by acquiring these skills, one can 'take charge of oneself and one's life'. We have the advantage, working in a training unit, of being able to work directly with teachers and youth workers on the skills this way. Aspy and Roebuck (1977) have identi-fied that the most effective teachers are those who have, and demonstrate, a high respect for others, who are genuine, and display a high degree of empathy with their students. Many professional counsellors therefore should have the basic qualities required in teaching, and could make appre-ciable contributions by being involved in programmes in the community which encourage 'coping' and 'growth' skills. More personally skilled individuals could reduce the dependence, inadequacy and crises which are individually and collec-tively wasteful, and take up so much counselling time.

Towards a 'complete helper'

The argument here is for the development of more complete helpers, more 'all-rounders', with a range of skills and 'tool-bags' full of more varied helping equipment. It is possible to work to increase the level of skill in each particular helping technique and go for 'broader' rather than 'higher' skill development. This diagram (figure 5) could map out for individual helpers how they may want to plan their own development.

On a graph such as this an effective teacher may be placed typically along the line marked 'x'. A full-time counsellor working in a school or workplace may typically be indicated by the line marked 'o'. An organization-change consultant may typically be somewhere along the dotted line.

How much one wants to be involved in helping, at what-ever level and in whatever form, obviously depends upon many factors. How much one sees helping as part of the roles one fills; how much helping is part of the job one does; how much one wants to be involved as a part-time activity; how much helping is consistent with one's values, politics and personality; all will have a bearing on where an individual may wish to be placed on the graph. One person may decide to specialize in a particular approach and develop sophis-ticated skills in that field. Another may go for a broader approach by developing skills from across the range. Yet

Figure 5

Helpers' skills levels and possible approaches to increasing them

(What skills do I have and in which directions can I develop?)

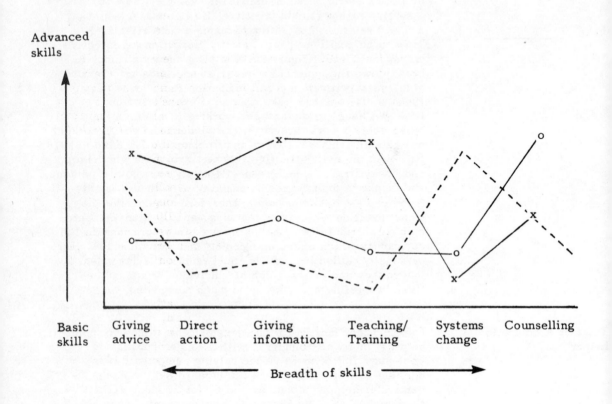

another may at particular times develop new specialisms as a response to particular situations or as part of his own personal career development.

What is advocated here is that basic helping skills can be regarded as essential life skills. These skills can be made available to, and developed very fully in, professional helpers and in those for whom helping is part of their job specification in the workshop, in hospitals, in the social service agencies or in education. They can also be taught to young people in schools and at work.

Counselling in the UK

It is interesting that 'counselling' was a term rarely used in Britain until the mid-1960s. According to Vaughan's analysis (1976),

> three factors gradually tended to focus more attention on this area. One was the emergence throughout this century of a wider band of 'helping' professions, such as the Youth Employment Service, the social work services, and psychotherapy, as well as other 'caring' organizations, such as marriage guidance, and more recently such bodies as the Samaritans and Help the Aged. A second was the development of empirical psychology and sociology, which began to offer specific techniques for the analysis of personal difficulties; and a third was the rapid spread from about the mid-1960s onwards of the concept of counselling as a specific profession derived almost wholly from North America, where it had undergone a long evolution throughout the century from about 1910. Thus today we have a situation comparable in some ways to that of the development of primary education in Britain before the 1870 Act. A new area of specialization seems to be emerging.

It is just because a new area of specialization is developing that people already engaged in, or about to involve themselves in, counselling need to think carefully of where and how they wish to invest their time and resources. Counselling clearly is an important way of helping people, but it is not the only way.

References

Aspy, D. and Roebuck, F. (1977)
Kids Don't Learn from People They Don't Like. Amherst, Mass.: Human Resource Development Press.

Blocher, D. (1966)
Developmental Counseling (2nd edn). New York: Ronald Press.

Bonnex, J.T. (1965)
Cells and Societies. Princeton University, NJ: Princeton University Press.

Boy, A.V. and Pine, G.J. (1968)
The Counselor in the Schools. New York: Houghton Mifflin.

Brammer, L.M. (1973)
The Helping Relationship. Englewood Cliffs, NJ: Prentice-Hall.

Burnet, F.M. (1971)
Self-recognition in colonial marine forms and flowering plants. Nature, 232, 230-235.

Carkhuff, R.R. (1969)
Helping and Human Relations. New York: Holt, Rinehart & Winston.

Carkhuff, R.R. (1974)
The Art of Helping. Amherst, Mass.: Human Resource Development Press.

Carkhuff, R.R. and Berenson, B.G. (1976)
Teaching As Treatment. Amherst, Mass.: Human Resource Development Press.

Coombs, A., Avila, D. and Purkey, W. (1971)
Helping Relationships: Basic concepts for the helping profession. Boston: Allyn & Bacon.

Cooper, C.L. and Mangham, I.L. (eds) (1971)
T-Groups: A survey of research. Chichester: Wiley.

Corey, G. (1977)
Theory and Practice of Counselling and Psychotherapy. Monterey, Ca: Brooks/Cole.

Corsini, R. (ed.) (1977)
Current Psychotherapies (2nd edn). Itasca, Ill.: Peacock Publications.

Egan, G. (1975)
The Skilled Helper. Monterey, Ca: Brooks/Cole.

Eibl-Eibesfeldt, I. (1971)
Love and Hate. London: Methuen.

Hackney, H.L. and Nye, S. (1973)
Counseling Strategies and Objectives. Englewood Cliffs, NJ: Prentice-Hall.

Hoffman, A.M. (1976)
Paraprofessional effectiveness. Personnel and Guidance Journal, 54, 494-497.

Hopson, B. (1977)
Techniques and methods of counselling. In A.G. Watts (ed.), Counselling at Work. London: Bedford Square Press.

Hopson, B. and Scally, M. (1980a)
Lifeskills Teaching: Education for self-empowerment. Maidenhead: McGraw-Hill.

Hopson, B. and Scally, M. (1980b)
Lifeskills Teaching Programmes No. 1. Leeds: Lifeskills Associates.

Illich, I. (1973)
Tools of Conviviality. London: Calder & Boyars.

Illich, I., Zola, I.K., McKnight, J., Kaplan, J. and Sharken, H. (1977)
The Disabling Professions. London: Marion Boyars.

Ivey, A.E. (1971)
Microcounseling: Innovations in interviewing training. Springfield, Ill.: Thomas.

Jackins, H. (1965)
The Human Side of Human Beings. Seattle: Rational Island Publications.

Kagan, N., Krathwohl, D.R. et al (1967)
Studies in Human Interaction: Interpersonal process recall stimulated by videotape. East Lansing, Mich.:

Educational Publication Services, College of Education, Michigan State University.

Katz, M.R. (1969)
Can computers make guidance decisions for students? College Board Review, New York, No. 72.

Kennedy, E. (1977)
On Becoming a Counsellor: A basic guide for non-professional counsellors. Dublin: Gill & Macmillan.

Lewis, J. and Lewis, M. (1977)
Community Counseling: A human services approach. New York: Wiley.

Loughary, J.W. and Ripley, T.M. (1979)
Helping Others Help Themselves. New York: McGraw-Hill.

Maslow, A. (1968)
Toward a Psychology of Being (2nd edn). New York: Van Nostrand.

Mowrer, O.H. (1950)
Learning Theory and Personality Dynamics. New York: Ronald Press.

Newell, P.C. (1977)
How cells communicate. Endeavour, 1, 63-68.

Parloff, M.B., Waskow, I.E. and Wolfe, B. (1978)
Research on therapist variables in relation to process and outcome. In S.L. Garfield and A.E. Bergin (eds), Handbook of Psychotherapy and Behavior Change: An empirical analysis (2nd edn). New York: Wiley.

Pietrofesa, J.L., Hoffman, A., Splete, H.H. and Pinto, D.V. (1978)
Counseling; Theory, research and practice. Chicago: Rand McNally.

Proctor, B. (1979)
The Counselling Shop. London: Deutsch.

Raths, L., Harmin, M. and Simon, S. (1964)
Values and Teaching. Columbus, Ohio: Charles E. Merrill.

Rogers, C.R. (1957)
The necessary and sufficient conditions of therapeutic personality change. Journal of Consulting Psychology, 21, 95-103.

Rogers, C.R. (1958)
The characteristics of a helping relationship. Personnel and Guidance Journal, 37, 6-16.

Rogers, C.R. (1978)
Carl Rogers on Personal Power. London: Constable.

Scally, M. and Hopson, B. (1979)
A Model of Helping and Counselling: Indications for training. Leeds: Counselling and Careers Development Unit, Leeds University.

Sinick, D. (1979)
Joys of Counseling. Mincie, Indiana: Accelerated Development Inc.

Smith, P.B. (1975)
Controlled studies of the outcome of sensitivity training. Psychological Bulletin, 82, 597-622.

Stonier, T. (1979)

On the Future of Employment. N.U.T. guide to careers work. London: National Union of Teachers.

Toffler, A. (1970)

Future Shock. London: Bodley Head.

Truax, C.B. and Carkhuff, R.R. (1967)

Toward Effective Counselling and Psychotherapy: Training and practice. Chicago: Aldine.

Tyler, L. (1961)

The Work of the Counselor. New York: Appleton-Century-Crofts.

Vaughan, T. (ed.) (1976)

Concepts of Counselling. London: Bedford Square Press.

Questions

1. What are the characteristics which distinguish counselling from other approaches to helping the individual? Illustrate your answer with as many clinical and practical examples as possible.

2. What are the characteristics of the good counsellor? In this context, consider the meaning of 'good' and how you would assess it. Do you think that the outcomes of counselling are determined by factors other than the characteristics of the counsellor? If so, give examples of these factors.

3. What are the main aims of counselling? How do the various 'schools' of counselling differ in their efforts to secure these aims for their clients?

4. Describe and discuss the conditions which appear to be necessary for effective counselling. To what extent are counsellors to be regarded as 'special' individuals who differ in important respects from the lay public?

5. If you were responsible for the selection and training of a group of lay counsellors (with no professional qualifications or previous training), what steps would you take? Consider the initial assessment, and also the steps needed to both train them and monitor their subsequent progress.

6. Compare and contrast any three 'schools' of counselling. If you have any preference between these approaches, indicate your preferred school and give your reasons.

7. Discuss the practical and ethical problems involved in the evaluation of counselling. Does counselling work?

8. Compare and contrast the approach of the counsellor with that of the behaviour therapist.

Annotated reading

Corey, G. (1977) Theory and Practice of Counseling and Psychotherapy. Monterey, Ca: Brooks/Cole.

This contains an excellent review of all the schools of counselling described in the chapter. There is an accompanying workbook designed for students and tutor which gives self-inventories to aid students in identifying their own attitudes and beliefs, overviews of each major theory of counselling, questions for discussion and evaluation, case studies, exercises designed to sharpen specific counselling skills, out-of-class projects, group exercises, examples of client problems, an overview comparision of all models, ethical issues and problems to consider, and issues basic to the therapist's personal development.

Corsini, R. (ed.) (1977) Current Psychotherapies (2nd edn). Itasca, Ill.: Peacock Publications.
An excellent introduction to the main schools of psychotherapy by leading practitioners who have been bullied to stick to the same format. Covers psychoanalysis, Adlerian, client-centred, analytical, rational-emotive therapy, transactional analysis, Gestalt, behavioural, reality, encounter, experiential and eclectic. Contributors include Carl Rogers, Albert Ellis, William Glasser, Alan Goldstein, Will Schutz and Rudolf Dreikurs.

Vaughan, T.D. (ed.) (1975) Concepts of Counselling. British Association for Counselling, London: Bedford Square Press.
A guide to the plethora of definitions of counselling. Uneven, illuminating, with some useful descriptions of developments in the UK.

14

Stress
David Griffiths

The experience and management of stress is of obvious importance to both psychologists and doctors. Stress is an inevitable part of life, and is involved in a wide range of experiences, such as birth or death; changes affecting education, work and home; legal proceedings and convictions; courtship, marriage and, for some, separation and divorce. Even experiences which are generally seen to be pleasant can also involve varying degrees of stress. For example, most of the people involved in weddings would agree that the enjoyment is generally diluted with varying degrees of stress associated with planning, organization, punctuality, speech making and many other factors. The honeymoon period, for many young couples, might be less rosy than they have expected since it involves the first steps in the adjustment to the more-or-less constant presence of their partner. On a day-to-day basis, life is rarely without the minor irritations of work, school and home worries, physical ailments and interpersonal discord.

It is also well established that anxiety or 'stress' is a common, and indeed normal, response to both physical illness and the medical or surgical procedures which are often necessary. Surveys reveal that fear of medical, surgical and dental procedures is widespread. For example, 75 per cent of patients experience pre-operative anxiety to some degree, and in many cases this amounts to a near panic state as the time of the operation approaches. In the period shortly before treatment begins, tooth extractions cause as much anxiety as major surgery. The experience of stress associated with dental treatment is, not surprisingly, associated with avoidance of treatment. In one survey, 49 per cent of a group of individuals who reported anxiety made routine visits to their dentist; this is considerably lower than the 65 per cent reported for a group who were not anxious.

In spite of the importance of stress, both as a common experience and clinical problem, it is only relatively recently that the concept has been subjected to a careful theoretical analysis, and also empirical investigation. An analysis of the use of the term indicates immediately that it is used in two different but closely related ways.

The stress situation
'Stress' is sometimes used to refer to those situations and

conditions which place individuals under some pressure, involve some adjustment in their behaviour and can cause changes which are unpleasant, sometimes maladaptive and even associated with physical damage. When the situation or stimulus is referred to, the term stressor is generally more appropriate, and definitions include such factors as 'personal life changes ... which alter the individual's social setting' (Rabkin and Struening, 1976), or 'any set of circumstances the advent of which signifies or requires change in the individual's ongoing life pattern' (Holmes and Rahe, 1967).

The stress response

Stress also commonly refers to the syndrome of responses and changes in behaviour which are associated with stress stimuli. Human and animal psychology provide many examples of stress responses. For example, experiments in Pavlov's laboratory demonstrated that disorganization of behaviour was commonly observed when dogs were presented with a difficult discrimination problem. If a semi-circle had been linked with an electric shock, and a three-quarter circle with a food reward, the presentation of an incomplete circle midway between the two originals might be associated with agitation and a refusal or inability to continue with the experiment. Masserman and his colleagues subjected cats to a stress situation which involved exposure to a sharp blast of air as they were opening a feeding box. Cats subjected to these situations manifested changes in their behaviour and appearance. For example, they lost their position in a dominance hierarchy and appeared dishevelled as a consequence of a reduction in their grooming behaviour. Under certain conditions, they also demonstrated a preference for alcohol rather than milk; the preference for milk returned, however, when the animal was removed from the stressor situation. In other studies, monkeys developed gastric ulcers when they were required to learn a complex discrimination task; exposure to weak electric shocks which were beyond their control was not, however, associated with similar changes and gastric damage.

As we see in due course, in human psychology stress responses are apparent both in normal individuals exposed to intense or frequent stressors and also in a variety of abnormal states where an extreme response such as anxiety and avoidance is produced by an unexceptional stimulus (as in anxiety or obsessional states).

Now that the distinction has been made between the stress stimulus or stressor, and the stress response, we might consider these two components of the stress experience in more detail. First of all, what are the situations which cause or elicit stress responses?

Life changes and life events

Most people assume that life events such as a birth or death in the family, a change of house or job, losing a valuable possession or being involved in a court case constitute a stress to the individual, and a considerable proportion of the 'small talk', which is such an important aspect of social interaction, is concerned with the significance, importance and effects of a wide number of life events. It is only relatively recently, however, that research investigations have clarified the perception, role and effects of life events using objective methods. The research has suggested a number of conclusions which are both interesting and clinically important; in addition, many of the results support the common-sense assumptions made about the importance of life events. The following are the most important conclusions.

1. PEOPLE PERCEIVE LIFE EVENTS WITH A FAIR DEGREE OF CONSISTENCY. In other words, individuals and groups tend to agree when they rate life events in terms of the degree of upset and distress which they produce. Paykel and his colleagues (1971) required their subjects to rate 61 events on a 0-20 point scale of distress. The ratings extended over the whole range indicating that there was considerable variation in the upset which the subjects judged to be involved. Judges also tended to agree in their ratings; other studies indicated a surprising degree of agreement across social and cultural groups, though small differences in ratings of the distress caused by life events have also emerged and have been related to social class, item order (in other words, the position of each life event in the overall list), and whether the rater has been exposed to the life event recently. Here are the values given to the five most distressing and the five least distressing items in Paykel's work; the means and standard deviations (s.d.) are provided and each rater was required to judge how upsetting an event would be to the average person. A high score indicates a greater degree of distress.

	mean		s.d.
Death of child	19.33	±	2.22
Death of spouse	18.76	±	3.21
Jail sentence	17.60	±	3.56
Death of a close family member	17.21	±	3.69
Spouse unfaithful	16.78	±	4.14

....

	mean		s.d.
Begin education	5.09	±	4.48
Child's engagement	4.53	±	4.57
Become engaged	3.70	±	4.64
Wanted pregnancy	3.56	±	5.39
Child married with respondent's approval	2.94	±	3.75

2. LIFE EVENTS ARE ANTECEDENTS AND AT LEAST PARTIAL DETERMINANTS OF A WIDE RANGE OF PROBLEMS, BOTH ORGANIC AND PSYCHOLOGICAL. In relation to

medical illness, life experiences have been associated with heart disease, tuberculosis, diabetes, accidents and many other disorders. In addition to demonstrations that life events are more common in the three to six months preceding the onset of organic disorders, a small number of studies (e.g. Holmes and Holmes, 1970) have shown relationships between life experiences and minor physical complaints (headaches, stomach discomforts, skin irritations, irritability, etc.) on a day-to-day basis. More complaints are reported on those days when life events and stressors are either present or more numerous. The research on psychological and behavioural disorders also indicates clearly that life events are part of the aetiology of breakdown and dysfunction.

Studies have demonstrated that life events either cause or precipitate depressive breakdown, suicide and also neurotic disorders (such as episodes of tension and anxiety). In the six months before the onset of a depressive breakdown, the patients involved reported almost three times the number of life events as a control group (Paykel et al, 1969). Events which were particularly important were those which involved an 'exit' from the individual's social scene (death, separation, departure of a family member) and events which were obviously undesirable (unemployment, demotion, serious illness, etc.).

Suicide attempts are also preceded by an excess of life events and stressors (Paykel et al, 1975) and the events tend to peak in the month prior to the attempt. Over the six months prior to the attempt, potential suicides have experienced four times as many life changes as a general population control group and one-and-a-half times more than a depressed group prior to the onset of a depressive breakdown. The differences between suicide attempters and the general population did not involve any specific type of experience. When suicide attempters were compared with depressives, however, they had clearly experienced an excess of certain types, such as events involving threat and those which were outside their control. In addition to the role of life events in precipitating depression and suicide, life changes have also been shown to be common antecedents of neurotic episodes identified in general practice (tension and anxiety, etc.) and also relapses in schizophrenic outpatients (cf. Birley and Brown, 1970).

3. THOUGH THE ROLE OF LIFE EVENTS AS A DETERMINANT OF VARIOUS DISORDERS AND PROBLEMS IS WELL DOCUMENTED, CARE IS ALSO NECESSARY IN THE INTERPRETATION AND EVALUATION OF SOME OF THE RESULTS. It is likely, for example, that some of the earlier studies failed to distinguish between life changes which produced psychological breakdown and other changes which might have been part of the same breakdown. A disturbed marital situation, for instance, might have produced a depressive response; it might also have been caused by a depressed state

associated with irritability in one of the partners. Failure
to make this distinction would tend to exaggerate the link
between life events and disorders such as depression.

More recent studies have been careful to identify only
those life events which are unlikely to be caused by the
condition being studied. Birley and Brown, for example,
have carefully identified those events which are clearly
'acts of God', fortuitous (e.g. a win on the football
pools), planned well in advance or beyond the individual's
control.

When this is done, the relationship between life events
and breakdown continues to be present; it is therefore clear
that the result cannot be explained entirely by confusion as
to whether life's events caused, or were caused by, the
disorder under examination.

One other conclusion which deserves to be stressed is
that, though life events have consistently been shown to be
related to various disorders, the correlations have usually
been low. In practice, this means that the occurrence of
life events increases the risk of physical or psychological
problems. Whether or not breakdown or illness occurs,
however, depends on other factors. What are these factors?

4. TWO MAJOR CATEGORIES OF FACTORS INFLUENCE
THE CONSEQUENCES OF LIFE EXPERIENCES. In other
words, they act as 'mediating variables' (Rabkin and
Struening, 1976) and influence the eventual outcome. These
are, first, the characteristics of the individual or group
who experience life events and, second, factors such as the
support available in the environment.

A wide range of individual characteristics are known
to affect the extent and type of response to a stressor.
Intelligence might be expected to be an asset since the
intelligent individual is more likely to be able to anticipate and to cope with various stresses more competently,
and Terman's research in America has shown that very intelligent individuals are also well above the average in
scholastic and work achievement. The advantages associated
with high intelligence can, however, be reduced or eliminated by factors such as high anxiety or neuroticism, and
it is known that intelligent but unstable individuals are
considerably less successful at school and work than their
stable counterparts. Neuroticism is also likely to determine
the individual's response to stressors since it is associated with a tendency to react quickly, excessively and
repeatedly to a wide range of stress experiences. Neurotic
individuals, for example, are more likely to become tense
and anxious when they experience a myocardial infarction
(Byrne, 1979).

One other example of a factor which can influence the
individual's response to stress is his experience of that or
other stressors in the past. On the one hand, repeated exposure to a stressor can allow the individual to habituate
to that stress and to cope with it more effectively and

without excessive emotional arousal. On the other hand, wartime research indicates that some cases of breakdown are produced by several unpleasant experiences rather than by one traumatic event (Eysenck and Rachman, 1965). These examples demonstrate very clearly that the factors which affect the individual's response to a stressor can be very complex, and the complex aetiology of abnormal behaviour is a theme which is given emphasis in David Shapiro's review of psychopathology (chapter 17).

In addition to the various factors within the individual, his environment is also clearly important. The degree of support which is provided by the environment is an obviously relevant consideration since social support can provide a very effective buffer for the afflicted individual (Rabkin and Struening, 1976).

Nucholls, Cassel and Kaplan (described in Rabkin and Struening, 1976) studied some of the factors which seemed to be associated with complications during late pregnancy and following delivery. Complications were not related to either life changes or social support when the two types of variable were studied independently. When they were studied together, however, some striking relationships emerged. Ninety per cent of the women with a low level of social support and a high level of life events had at least one complication; 33 per cent of those with a similar level of life change but more adequate social support experienced at least one complication. The results indicated very clearly that the effects of life experiences were influenced by the existence and degree of support provided by the woman's environment. Research on the community care of psychiatric patients discharged from institutions also indicates clearly that their adjustment in the community is related much more closely to the support which they receive there than to the treatments which they have previously received in hospital.

In summary, it is evident that life events can exert important effects on the individual. At worst, life events can contribute to psychological and physical breakdown. The individual's response to stressful experience is, however, clearly a function of many variables both in himself and his environment. Though the clinical research has concentrated on the adverse effects of life problems, it is also likely that the individual can benefit (e.g. in terms of skills which he acquires, lowered tension and increased confidence) from the adequate handling of a range of life events which are, for most people, inevitable.

Conflict and frustration

Stress stimuli can also be classified in terms of the type of response which they produce. The general characteristic of life events is that they involve change and adjustment from the individual; in other words, he is placed in a position where he must adjust his behaviour to suit a new set of circumstances. He is, therefore, obliged to act as a problem solver, and to change his behaviour so that he

continues to secure goals and aims which are important to
him. Two further categories of stressors which have attracted the attention of psychologists involve conflict and
frustration.

Conflict situations are those which are associated with
'the simultaneous presence of opposing or mutually exclusive
impulses, desires or tendencies' (Hilgard, Atkinson and
Atkinson, 1971). Conflict has been subjected to extensive
laboratory investigation, and researchers have distinguished
three basic categories of conflict. Each category involves
decision and choice between alternatives, and the basis for
differentiating between them involves the organism's direction of response. More specifically, whether the situation
elicits an approach or an avoidance response.

*   AVOIDANCE: AVOIDANCE conflicts involve choices be-
    tween two unattractive alternatives. For example, the
    student who finds it difficult to choose between study-
    ing and not studying; he is not keen on studying but
    anticipates that, if he does not, he will spend his time
    worrying instead. Similarly, the individual suffering
    from toothache is faced with the choice between two
    alternatives, both of which have unpleasant aspects.
*   APPROACH: APPROACH conflicts, on the other hand,
    involve the choice between two pleasant and attractive
    alternatives. For example, the choice between two
    equally attractive boyfriends, or between two or more
    motor cars. The difficulty of the choice, and the in-
    tensity of the resulting conflict, might be expected
    to vary with the degree of attractiveness of the
    alternatives.
*   The third category of conflict involves APPROACH:
    AVOIDANCE situations where the organism is attracted
    by some properties of an alternative but repulsed by
    others. The resulting conflict involves varying degrees
    of ambivalence. Approach-avoidance conflicts are com-
    mon human experiences. For example, the young man who
    anticipates that many of his needs will be satisfied by
    a female companion but that he will lose many of the
    assets of independence and freedom. A doctor might have
    to weigh the potential advantages of a therapeutic pro-
    cedure to his patient against the risks of failure or
    adverse side effects. Though it is dangerous to make
    general statements about the effects of the three categ-
    ories of conflict on human behaviour, there is some
    indication that approach-avoidance conflicts tend to
    have the most disruptive effects on behaviour and
    psychological functioning.

Hilgard, Atkinson and Atkinson (1971) have summarized
the main principles which have emerged from the investigations of approach-avoidance conflicts. Four are identified.
The first is stated as follows: 'The tendency to approach a
positive incentive is stronger the nearer the subject is to

it.' This is not necessarily to be interpreted in terms of physical proximity. It also implies, for example, that a car might be expected to appear more attractive near to the point at which the purchase is completed.

The second principle states that the strength of the avoidance response (in relation to an unpleasant alternative) is stronger as the organism nears the aversive object. For example, the greatest degree of discomfort, in relation to an examination, is likely to be experienced as the time of the examination approaches. A third principle is that the strength of the avoidance response (to an undesirable alternative) increases more rapidly than the strength of an approach response (to a desirable alternative). Discomfort in relation to an unpleasant choice increases more rapidly as the organism moves towards it, or towards the point of decision. Pleasure in relation to a positive or desired alternative does not increase as steeply as the objective is approached. Finally, the strength of both approach and avoidance is increased by the strength of various drive states. For example, intense sexual drive will naturally be associated with enthusiastic approaches to a receptive partner and with similarly enthusiastic attempts to evade the surveillance of third parties!

Frustration involves those situations which block or impede the organism's progress towards a desirable goal. For example, the best-known study of frustration involves observations of the behaviour of young children whose approach to a selection of attractive toys was blocked by a barrier (Barker, Dembo and Lewin, 1941). In this study, frustration involved a barrier in the physical environment. Another alternative might involve socially determined barriers: for example, the existence of rules or conventions which discourage young people from satisfying their sexual needs outside marriage and, in addition, the existence of social conventions which discourage a wide range of behaviours in the company of others. Frustration can also involve a discrepancy between the individual's goals and his capability. Low intelligence or the absence of appropriate training and skills can prevent the individual from securing many of the jobs which he might choose if he had the necessary attributes.

Some of the more obvious effects of conflict and frustration are considered in the next section, which is concerned with the nature of the stress response.

What are the main changes in behaviour under conditions of stress?

The following are some of the more prominent changes which can occur. It is important to remember, however, that whether these changes occur - and also to what extent they occur - will depend on a large number of variables such as the nature and intensity of the stress stimulus, the predisposition and previous experience of the individual, and the existence and degree of social support in the individual's environment. We have seen already that the adjustment of discharged psychiatric patients in the community is dependent on the support which they receive from their families and also other individuals and groups in their environment. Individual predispositions (e.g. their susceptibility to anxiety) are also important determinants of their response. The following list is therefore to be regarded as an inventory of possible changes rather than necessary components of the stress response.

Changes in tension, anxiety and general levels of arousal

The stress response often involves anxiety and tension as prominent components. Anxiety is recognized through changes in subjective feelings (varying degrees of discomfort and strain, etc.), overt behavioural changes (e.g. restlessness and fidgeting) and also physiological states (evident from pallor, perspiration, muscular tension, changes in breathing rate and skin conductance, etc.). A rather dramatic inventory of the changes associated with an intense stress (or fear) response is provided by Marks (1969); his list includes 'unpleasant subjective feelings of terror, a pounding heart, muscular tenseness, trembling, exaggerated startle, dryness of the throat and mouth, a sinking feeling in the stomach, nausea, perspiration, an urge to urinate and maybe to defecate, irritability ... a great urge to cry, run or hide, difficulty in breathing, paraesthesia of the extremities, feelings of unreality, paralysing weakness of the limbs and a sensation of faintness and falling'. These examples might be present, however, in extreme states; when the response is less severe, many of the changes listed might not occur at all, or might be weaker.

It might be useful to refer to the association between one aspect of the stress response (in this case, tension) and one example of a stressor (in this case, myocardial infarction). Byrne (1979) has provided a useful review of the association between myocardial infarction and anxiety. He refers, for example, to a study which showed that 65 per cent of a sample of 203 patients admitted to a coronary care unit manifested clinically significant degrees of anxiety and depression; in the majority, their stress response had apparently been present before hospitalization. Further evidence suggests that anxiety levels are at their highest after admission, and again near the point of discharge. Similar levels of anxiety are evident in medical emergencies, and previous research is claimed to demonstrate 'anxiety to be an integral component of illness behaviour, and to be associated with interpersonal difficulties during recovery'.

Aggression, irritability and hostility

The stress response can also be associated with marked changes in aggressiveness; this can become apparent, once again, in subjective feelings, overt behaviour and physiological states. Although there is general agreement that emotional states (such as fear, surprise and anger) cannot be distinguished in terms of the associated pattern of physiological change, there is at least one demonstration of distinctive and different patterns of change associated with fear and anger respectively. It is also evident, however, that there are wide individual differences in the pattern and intensity of physiological changes associated with stressors. In addition to the idiosyncratic pattern of responses in heart rate, breathing rate, palmar conductance and so on, it has also been demonstrated that the individual's pattern of response is consistent over time and occurs irrespective of the nature of the stress stimulus.

Aggression, and its various manifestations, has been specifically associated with frustration of goal-directed behaviour (Yates, 1965). An alternative to this model involves the study of the consequences of behaviour; aggression will persist if it is reinforced, and will disappear if its consequences are unpleasant (or non-existent). Aggression can also be directed towards the self (as in, for example, acts of self-mutilation and destruction) or towards other people. Scapegoating can be seen as an example of displaced aggression; in their discussion of aggression, Hilgard and his colleagues (1971) refer to the negative correlation between the price of cotton in America between 1880-1930 and the number of lynchings in southern states as a probable example of the mechanism of displaced aggression. As we see in due course, Janis (1969) has shown that patients who have not prepared themselves for the inevitable discomforts of surgery sometimes respond by blaming staff and directing their anger towards nursing and medical staff.

Social changes
The social behaviour of individuals under stress can change, though again this is not inevitable. Some investigations indicate that individuals who are subjected to experimentally induced stresses tend to seek the company of others who share the same stress, but are less likely to seek the company of individuals who are not being subjected to stress. Individuals who are exposed to chronic stress and deprivation - as in concentration camps during the Second World War - can develop a state of withdrawal and social indifference which can be difficult to modify when the stress is terminated. It is also important to remember, however, that the presence and behaviour of others can have a very significant effect on the individual's stress response. For example, discharged schizophrenic patients are more likely to experience a relapse and a recurrence of acute symptoms if they are exposed to close emotional involvement, and especially hostility, from their family.

Regression and disorganization of behaviour
The behaviour of individuals under stress can become very disorganized. Disorganization can manifest itself as inefficient problem-solving or the breakdown of skilled

behaviour. The behaviour of children who are prevented from reaching attractive toys can change dramatically, and the observations made by Barker, Dembo and Lewin (1941) indicated that the resulting changes involved behaviour which would be appropriate for children who were approximately 18 months younger than the study group. It was therefore possible to make a quantified estimate of the extent of deterioration in the maturity of the behaviour. At least two explanations have been offered to explain the changes. One suggests that the change involves a regression (in the face of stress) to a younger and presumably more secure level. The other suggests that the change in behaviour is a feature of disorganization associated with high emotional arousal. We shall often need to refer to the observation that extremes of arousal (such as panic or anger) are associated with a loss of efficiency in performance.

Rigidity

Animal studies (Yates, 1965) demonstrated as long as 30 years ago that organisms subjected to stress can develop rigid or stereotyped behaviour. For example, rats which were subjected to difficult discrimination tasks were observed to assume a rigid manner of response, and this was resistant to modification even when severe punishments were introduced. The animal might, for example, jump repeatedly to one side or the other if it had been previously required to jump to one of two possible reward boxes which were correct (food reward) or incorrect (animal falls into net) on a random basis.

Rigidity involves the reverse of flexibility, so the behaviour of the individual under chronic or intense stress might be expected to become less flexible and more rigid. Rigid behaviour can be observed, for instance, in certain categories of psychiatric disorder. For example, obsessional patients might involve themselves in repetitive and senseless rituals (counting, repeating words or phrases, cleaning themselves) though they are aware that their behaviour is unreasonable or irrational.

Coping or 'defence' mechanisms

Individuals also differ in the strategies which they adopt to reduce stress and discomfort. Clinicians are well acquainted with the strategies adopted by patients suffering from intense anxiety and phobic conditions. The two most obvious strategies are, of course, escape from the feared object and avoidance of the feared object (Eysenck and Rachman, 1965). Since both types of response are associated with reductions of anxiety and are therefore reinforcing to the individual, escape and avoidance behaviours become important and common responses in phobic conditions. In the short term, they avoid or reduce discomfort; in the long term, however, they tend to maintain the individual's disorder and his degree of handicap.

In addition to overt acts of escape and avoidance the individual can also reduce his stress by other responses.

The work of Janis (1969) is discussed shortly; he demon-strated that some individuals, faced with surgery, appear to deny their impending discomfort and direct their attention away from their inevitable stress. In the short term, their anxiety is reduced and they are placid and calm. When the inevitable discomfort of the surgery is experienced, how-ever, their response involves anxiety, distress and generally disturbed behaviour.

Attitudes and cognitions are also important factors which influence the individual's response to stress. The individual faced with the discomfort of dental treatment might convince himself that treatment is not really neces-sary, and manifest resistance to any cognition which is in-consistent with this belief. Smokers are also resistant to suggestions about the disadvantages of the habit (e.g. smell) and the dangers to their health. Both laboratory and clinical studies have demonstrated that the individual's overt behaviour and his physiological response to stress can be influenced very appreciably by his expectations. For example, subjects who believe that they are not responding physiologically to a phobic stimulus have been shown to manifest less fear under certain conditions when they are exposed to the phobic object. Laboratory studies have also demonstrated that physiological aspects of the individual's response to a stress stimulus (such as an electric shock) can be modified if he believes that he has some control over the stimulus. This effect is present even if the indivi-dual's belief is unjustified and he has no control at all over his fate.

Though this list of possible components of the stress response is not necessarily complete, it does include the more obvious and important components which are likely to be present. One further aspect of response needs to be dis-cussed, however, in view of its clinical significance and the assumptions which are often made about its importance as a response to stress. 'Tension' headaches are common experiences, and recent research has begun to clarify the variables and mechanisms which are involved.

Headaches
Headaches certainly deserve mention in a discussion of stress since they are commonly assumed to be implicated in a number of ways. 'Tension' headaches, and in excess of 75 per cent of all headaches are suggested to have a 'tension' component, are invariably assumed to be an important part of a psychophysiological response to stress. It is also in-ferred that 'tension' is an important part of the response; popular belief (apparently shared by experts and profes-sional 'helpers') suggests that local muscular tension in the head and neck is the basic problem and the 'cause' of the psychological experience of pain and other manifesta-tions of discomfort. The review and research reported by Clare Philips (1977) suggests very clearly, however, that many of the assumptions made about headaches are erroneous, and that a considerable amount of further research is

required to clarify the determinants and mechanisms involved in the experience of headaches.

In order to investigate three aspects of headaches, sufferers from 'tension' headaches were compared with migraine sufferers, control subjects and a small group of 'mixed' (tension and migraine) headache sufferers. The three areas of interest involved the role of muscular changes, the relationships between separate components of the headache phenomenon and, finally, the effect of biofeedback training.

The results on muscular tension provided some support for the importance of muscular changes. Tension headache sufferers were found to have higher levels of tension in frontalis muscles when compared with controls, though migraine sufferers were found to be the most tense group. Other muscle groups (e.g. temporalis and neck) were no more tense than for controls during non-headache or 'resting' periods. Muscular tension levels were significantly higher, however, during headaches, but the muscle group manifesting the highest level of tension coincided with the locus of the pain in only 40 per cent of the group. Furthermore, assessment of the muscular changes in response to a stressor revealed that the greatest changes often occurred in muscles which were not particularly tense during non-headache periods. The focus of the pain, the most reactive muscles and the highest level of 'resting' tension coincided in only one out of every four subjects.

These results suggest that headaches are not simply a matter of an abnormally sensitive and reactive muscle group, and the psychological experience of muscular change. This impression was further supported by other results concerned with the relationship between muscular tension, subjective experience (involving ratings of pain intensity and frequency) and overt behaviour (based on reports of analgesics taken over periods of a week). These measures were generally found to be unrelated. More specifically, muscular tension was not closely related to subjective pain experience or pill taking, and could not therefore be regarded as the organic basis for either the subjective experience of a headache or the behaviour undertaken to control the pain.

The final part of the investigation studied the effects of biofeedback training on muscular tension, pain reduction and pill taking. The biofeedback involved training subjects to reduce muscular tension in specific muscle groups by providing them with instructions and appropriate feedback on their success in reducing tension levels. In spite of the lack of a close relationship between physiological, subjective and behavioural measures, the reduction of muscular tension was associated with improvements in the pain experienced and pill taking. The improvements were not, however, synchronous. Pain experience reduced initially with muscular tension, but continued to improve when the reduction in muscular tension had ceased. Pill taking lessened, but again not in close association with pain experience or muscular tension. Philips suggests that improvements in experienced pain and pill taking are dependent on the reduction of muscular tension to a threshold level. If this suggestion is substantiated, then subjective and behavioural changes in 'pain' behaviour depend on the reduction of muscular tension to a specific level (which might differ between individuals) but, as long as the threshold level is reached, are not closely related to the extent of muscular change.

Although this research is based on a small number of subjects and Philips is careful to stress the limitations of her findings, a number of interesting conclusions are suggested. The first is that headaches are not simply a matter of the psychological experience of changes in muscular tension. In many individuals, muscular tension is not closely related to the experience of pain or behaviour such as the taking of pills or staying away from work. The second is that the phenomenon of headaches appears to be subject to wide differences between individuals. In practice, this means that muscular change, the experience of pain and overt behaviour are related in some individuals; in others, however, the changes which occur are unrelated. Tension headache sufferers are not, it would seem, a homogeneous group. A third conclusion is that techniques such as biofeedback training do offer some hope of relief to headache sufferers. A final conclusion about the efficacy of such techniques would be premature, however, since other investigations have reported that reductions in muscular tension cannot necessarily be generalized from one muscular group to another. Furthermore, the results of outcome studies specifically concerned with biofeedback techniques are not entirely positive and encouraging (Attfield and Peck, 1979).

Further research is obviously necessary and Philips' review mentions some of the difficulties. For example, the independence of separate aspects of headaches means that the selection of subjects for research projects cannot be simply a matter of either muscular tension or reported pain, or overall assessment by a clinician. Objective studies will need to involve a number of measures and the evaluation of the effects of treatment will need to allow for the possibility of quite specific changes. Headaches are, however, a universal experience: Philips experienced considerable difficulty in finding control subjects who had not experienced headaches for at least six months. It is also likely that headaches are of considerable social importance since they might be expected to be associated with decreased efficiency, and also loss of work and school. Further research might therefore be expected to bring some relief to the individual and to society, and also to increase our understanding of what is a common and interesting aspect of human experience.

The basis of individual differences

In our discussion of stress responses, we need to refer to individual differences frequently since it is a fact, apparent in laboratory studies and clinical investigations, that individuals vary in their behaviour. Some individuals respond quickly to stress, whilst others are slow to react or do not manifest any overt response. The intensity and pattern of responses also vary; some individuals continue to respond to a stressor whilst others habituate to it after a single experience. What factors underlie these differences, and influence or determine the individual's reaction? In addition, what are the factors which determine that the individual should vary in his response to stress and other experiences since it is apparent that human behaviour can be very inconsistent (Mischel, 1968)? Though the basis of individual differences is not considered in any detail, it would be useful to note at least some of the factors which determine the variations in stress responses.

It is more than 15 years since Eysenck and Rachman (1965) concluded that 'the genesis of anxiety states is by no means shrouded in mystery', and continued to review the factors which had been implicated as part of the aetiology of anxiety. Since anxiety is a prominent component of the stress response, the factors listed in this review might be repeated here as examples of the variables which influence the individual differences as in stress responses. The following seven sets of factors are discussed by Eysenck and Rachman.

Personality
The individual's response to a range of stressors appears to be affected by general predispositions to respond in certain ways. Neuroticism has been linked with the lability of the autonomic nervous system and it has been suggested that the neurotic is predisposed to respond quickly, in an intense manner and repeatedly to stresses. Measures of neuroticism have been shown to be associated with, for example, phobic behaviour and the anxiety generated by physical illness (Byrne, 1979). It also seems likely that the degree of neuroticism is influenced by genetic mechanisms (Shields, 1962). In spite of the importance of traits such as neuroticism, it has also been demonstrated that their effect is not sufficiently pervasive or intense to render behaviour consistent across different stimulus situations (Mischel, 1968). Other factors are also involved as determinants of behaviour.

Degree of confinement
Laboratory research involving animals demonstrates that physical confinement tends to increase the intensity of emotional response. Humans also appear to be more likely to experience similar changes if their emotional arousal is experienced in a situation where escape is difficult. Some constraints are physical (as in the case of the person who has a panic attack in a lift or train) whilst others are psychological and social (e.g. the lecturer who experiences intense anxiety during his lecture but feels unable to excuse himself until the lecture is completed).

Intensity of the unconditioned stimulus

The unconditioned stimulus refers to the stimulus which produces a spontaneous anxiety (or stress) response; for example, the intensity of an electric shock or of a scream in the dark. We have already noted that judges tend to agree in their ratings of the upset caused by common life events (Paykel et al, 1971). In addition to the intensity of the stressor, however, it has also been suggested that the type of stressor can be an important determinant of certain patterns of breakdown. We have seen that experiences of 'loss' are often antecedents of depression (Paykel et al, 1969).

Age

A number of reviews have demonstrated that the organism manifests a preparedness or sensitivity to different classes of stimuli at the various stages of its development (cf. chapter 6). Young infants are responsive to sudden noises and movements; older infants are more likely to manifest fear of strangers; pre-school children are more sensitive to animals; whilst fears of open spaces or social situations are more common at and after puberty (Marks, 1969).

Past experience and learning

The individual's response to stress can be influenced in quite different ways by his past experience. For example, a single traumatic experience can produce an anxiety response which is intense and proves difficult to modify; although ethical considerations prevent the experimental induction of such responses in human subjects, a small number of investigations do demonstrate that this is possible (Sanderson, Campbell and Laverty, 1963). A neurotic breakdown can also, however, be produced by a series of experiences which are mildly unpleasant, and anxiety states under combat conditions are reported to develop in this manner quite frequently. More recently, repeated exposure to noxious stimuli (in reality or imagination) has also been implicated as an important part of the development of some neurotic conditions (Eysenck, 1976). On the other hand, repeated exposure to low intensity noxious stimuli can also inoculate the individual against the development of an intense fear response. It seems likely that amongst the factors which determine the individual's reaction to repeated stressors is the presence and intensity, and also the degree of control over, his anxiety and general arousal. If the emotional response is weak or easily controlled, repeated exposure is more likely to have beneficial effects.

To complicate matters further, repeated exposure to stressors can sometimes alter the sequence or timing of the response rather than its intensity. For example, though it has been demonstrated that subjective fear decreases with increased experience of parachute jumping, some studies have discovered that trainee parachutists manifested increased physiological reactivity up to the point of jumping whilst experienced staff had an early (and sometimes equally intense) peak of arousal which was then followed by a sharp drop before the actual jump.

Type of conflict

We have already noted the different categories of conflict and also the suggestion that approach-avoidance conflicts are associated with greater emotional arousal and behavioural disorganization than other types.

The existence and strength of competing responses

Relaxation is antagonistic to anxiety and the induction of relaxed states is now generally agreed to be an important component of the treatment of anxiety and phobic conditions. One theory which attempts to explain the effects of relaxation suggests that it is effective because it lowers the organism's arousal to a point where it habituates more effectively to the stress stimuli (Lader and Matthews, 1968).

In addition to these seven factors discussed by Eysenck and Rachman, there are also a number of other factors which influence the individual's response to stress. Although there is considerable controversy about the role of cognitive factors as determinants of emotional state and disorder (cf. chapter 17), cognitive variables such as beliefs, attitudes and expectations have been found to be correlated with various aspects of the response to stress, and it is plausible to suggest that such factors do influence the individual's responses. For example, self-confidence has been found to predict the success of handicapped individuals, psychiatric patients and men who have suffered myocardial infarctions in returning to work, whilst measures of neuroticism have proved to be less successful predictors.

Fear and stress tolerance

It is clear that fear and stress are often undesirable to the extent that they can be associated with a number of adverse effects. We see this, for example, in the research on the effects of life events and changes. At the same time, we have to recognize that many stresses are unavoidable and are beyond the control of both the individual and the professional who is responsible for the patient's care. In addition, the management of stress need not necessarily have harmful consequences. On the contrary, it has been argued that successful management of stress can benefit the individual substantially to the extent that he acquires coping skills and self-confidence which allow him both to manage further stress more adequately and to act as an adviser and support to others who are experiencing difficulties. Irving Janis (1969) has argued that 'stress can bring about a positive change in the individual, make him more responsive to relevant warnings, cause him to make realistic plans for dealing with subsequent emergencies and sometimes even help him to develop greater emotional control'.

A striking demonstration of the importance of stress and the factors which influence stress tolerance is provided by the programme of research reported by Janis. His concern was with the response to surgery and the management of preoperative stress in a patient group. The research has attempted to answer three major questions. How do patients respond to surgical procedures? What factors determine their response? Can the adverse and potentially damaging aspects of patients' responses be modified? The work reported by Janis has involved a number of related stages.

* A pilot study, involving 23 patients, suggested that there were three broad categories of response to surgery, and also that the patient's psychological state before surgery was related to his condition and behaviour during the convalescent period. One group of patients was found to be apprehensive and generally upset (anxious, irritable, complaining, etc.) both before and after surgery. A second group was calm and placid before the surgery and appeared to be ideal patients in this respect; rather surprisingly, however, they were often found to be apprehensive, angry and resentful afterwards. Some of these patients blamed staff for the discomforts which were more realistically to be regarded as the inevitable consequences of the surgery. A final group of patients was moderately fearful before surgery, but adjusted well and did not have any difficulties afterwards.
* A second study involved a larger sample of surgical patients and confirmed the results from the pilot study. Placid and apparently unruffled individuals, who were least fearful about the impending ordeal of surgery, were more disturbed than others by the inevitable stress which followed. After surgery, they were more likely to be worried and irritable, and to manifest various aspects of a stress response. This again included a tendency to blame staff for their discomfort, and they were more difficult to manage within the hospital ward. Patients who worried about the surgery beforehand, however, were again found to be less disturbed afterwards. Individuals who experienced excessive apprehension beforehand, sometimes amounting to anxiety or panic states, often remained anxious and worried afterwards. The relationship between initial anxiety and subsequent stress tolerance seemed, in fact, to be curvilinear. The most adaptive response was made by those who were moderately anxious; the worst response was associated with the extremes of anxiety observed before surgery was undertaken.
* Janis attempted to explain his findings by investigating the mechanisms and processes which determined the patients' response, and especially their attempts to obtain or avoid information about the ordeal. He suggests that the moderately anxious are those who are motivated to obtain information, to anticipate the inevitable

discomforts and to prepare themselves. In the short term, they are more worried than some of their peers, but their worry is part of a coping process which is effective to the extent that their response after surgery tends to involve less stress and difficult behaviour. The patients who are placid before surgery, and often easier to manage on the ward, are in fact behaving in a defensive manner by avoiding information and almost denying the reality of the inevitable ordeal. Though they are more comfortable in the short term, they are subsequently less well prepared for the inevitable discomforts, and they cope less adequately during convalescence.

Those individuals who are very anxious and disturbed both before and after surgery are very probably neurotic individuals whose general anxiety level is high, and who respond to any stressor with the psychological and physiological aspects of high emotional arousal. Their arousal level is so high that their response to information about their ordeal is likely to be beyond their voluntary control and to involve a further exacerbation of their anxiety.

The form of the relationships between anxiety and the adaptiveness of the patient's response to surgery coincides with the curvilinear function between arousal level and effectiveness of performance associated with the Yerkes-Dodson hypothesis. The two extremes of arousal, both high and low, are associated with performance which is less effective. In this case, the coping of those individuals who were highly aroused, or overtly placid, was clearly less adequate than the group who experienced moderate but not excessive worry before surgery.

* Janis' hypothesis about the role and effects of information and the 'work of worrying' was given further support by a study of the differential responses of 'informed' and 'uninformed' patients to surgery. Informed patients were more fearful on the day of surgery, but appeared to tolerate the subsequent stress more adequately. Janis and his colleagues have also been careful to exclude the possible effects of a number of variables on their results. The 'fear' groups, for example, did not differ in terms of such factors as the type and extent of surgery, amount of pain, number of previous admissions or prognosis. Nor were the groups different in age, education and sex to an extent which might explain the differences in response.

* The acid test for this programme of research, and the underlying theory, was provided by studies which documented the effects of providing information to surgical patients. One study, described by Janis, was conducted by Lawrence Egbert at the Massachusetts General Hospital. Ninety-seven surgical patients were randomly allocated to an 'informed' experimental group or a 'no

information' control group. The information group was
briefed before surgery, and the medical and nursing
staff were not aware of whether or not the patient had
been prepared. The results were rather dramatic.

During the five days after surgery, the informed
group required half as much sedation as the controls;
they made fewer complaints and were considered to be
in better physical and emotional condition, and they
were discharged on average three days before the uninformed control group. Janis refers to similar results
which have apparently been derived from both a study of
paediatric surgery and dental treatment. In addition to
the support provided by these results for Janis' theory,
they also suggest that the role of information in facilitating the coping process is remarkably cost effective. The time required to provide information is
relatively small whilst the saving in staff time and
hospitalization would appear to be impressive.

* Janis concludes his discussion by considering the
practical problems of providing patients with, to use
his words, the 'proper dosage of fear'. His suggestion
is that 'moderately fear arousing messages about impending dangers and deprivations will function as a
kind of emotional inoculation, involving normal persons
to increase their tolerance for stress by developing
coping mechanisms and effective defences'. In practice,
however, it is often difficult to determine the correct
or optimal amount of information and fear for any individual. The aim is to provide information which will
motivate coping and adaptive responses, but will not
frighten the patient to the point where he avoids
consideration of and preparation for his ordeal.

Some of the studies reviewed by Janis suggest that
stressful information is more effective than neutral
information in encouraging coping responses; other
studies suggest the opposite. One solution seems to be
that the most effective level of fear involved in communications depends on the recipient. At low anxiety
levels, fear arousal will tend to increase the individual's receptiveness to the message and produce changes;
at high levels of anxiety, further arousal associated
with frightening communications is more likely to
stimulate escape and avoidance responses. Involvement
can be another factor. For example, moderate fear
arousal is more effective in changing the opinion of
smokers against smoking; strong fear arousal (e.g.
illustrations of the details of lung disorders) can
be more effective, however, in strengthening the
determination of non-smokers never to smoke.

In his concluding sections, Janis also refers to the potential importance of the manner in which frightening information is communicated to the individual in order to change
his behaviour. He refers to a study conducted by Mann on the

effectiveness of 'emotional role playing' in modifying the smoking habits of a group of female subjects. Smoking behaviour has, of course, proved to be notoriously difficult to change. Mann's technique required smokers to act the role of patients who were told that they had lung cancer. As compared with controls who listened to recordings of these scenes, attitudes towards the undesirability of smoking changed dramatically in the experimental subjects and, more significantly, so did smoking habits. The study also provided the opportunity to compare the effects of role-playing with government reports about the dangers of smoking, and suggested that the more active involvement of subjects produced substantially more change than the government's attempts at health education.

Janis' contribution to both the understanding of the determinants of stress, and also the clinical management of stress tolerance, are impressive. The work clearly needs to be replicated and extended and subsequent research in related fields tends to support both the importance of stress in the clinical situation and the difficulties (and also potential benefit) of controlling and reducing stress. It is important to note, however, that more recent research has not always been able to confirm findings such as the curvilinear relationship between anxiety and response to stressful treatments (Ley, 1977). On the other hand, the importance of anxiety and stress as clinical variables is indicated by a number of studies.

Byrne's (1979) review confirms the general conclusion that anxiety is the most likely response to physical illness; he suggests that anxiety and stress are also common responses to myocardial infarction. In addition to the individual's response to the physical pain and discomfort associated with an infarction, his own work leads him to suggest that further anxiety is caused by the information that the patient has suffered a 'heart attack'.

Byrne's results suggest that such factors as neuroticism or anxiety proneness, and also the sex of the patient, have significant effects on the intensity of the patient's stress response. Neuroticism and state anxiety (the latter involving a self-assessment by the patient of his current level of anxiety) were assessed in 120 individuals who had suffered a myocardial infarct and 40 controls who had suffered chest pains but, on further investigation, were found not to have suffered heart attacks. In both groups, those individuals who had higher scores on the questionnaire measure of neuroticism also had higher scores on self-ratings of their anxiety level. In addition, the group which had suffered confirmed myocardial infarctions was more anxious (but not more neurotic) than the controls. Women were not, in terms of the questionnaire scores, more neurotic than men, but they reported greater state anxiety.

Byrne suggests that it might be possible to identify those patients who are most likely to manifest stress responses, and to arrange for appropriate care as soon as possible. Such patients might need to be identified, however, by reference to their response to previous stressors and crises. Questionnaire measures of neuroticism might be of limited value in this respect since they would be difficult to administer to the patient, and the results might in any case be influenced by the patient's current level of anxiety.

What of the effects of general support and counselling on the outcome for patients who have suffered myocardial infarctions? The evaluation of counselling is certainly relevant to our discussion since it would inevitably involve a discussion of the nature and implications of the infarction, and also practical advice about methods of coping at home and work. The evaluation of the effectiveness of such counselling is not, however, entirely encouraging though the information available on outcome is limited. At this point, it is sufficient to consider two examples.

Kushnir et al (1976) studied the value of counselling before discharge on the subsequent adjustment of 35 men who had suffered their first myocardial infarction. The counselling was specifically, but not exclusively, concerned with work, sexual activity and driving. The outcomes were compared with those for 63 controls who had also suffered infarctions but were not provided with any counselling. Follow-up indicated that there were no differences between the groups in terms of the resumption of work, sexual behaviour or driving. The impression gained by the researchers was that factors such as the support provided by the general practitioner were more important as determinants of the resumption of a normal pattern of living. Further investigation has revealed, however, that individual differences between patients need to be considered when the outcomes of counselling are being evaluated.

Naismith et al (1979) randomly allocated 143 males who had suffered myocardial infarcts to either an experimental group who received counselling, or a control group who did not receive such attention. Outcomes were assessed after six months. Patients with higher scores on questionnaire measures of neuroticism and introversion had a poor outcome in the control group, but made a significantly better adjustment when counselling was provided. Outcome was assessed in terms of an overall assessment of success in returning to work, physical and emotional stability, and social independence (e.g. coping with family needs). The level of neuroticism and anxiousness was therefore found to be a predictor of the response to counselling, and to be of some practical value in selecting those individuals who would gain the most benefit from counselling. In addition, the patient's attitude to his illness and the future was also found to be important. Negative and unconstructive attitudes were associated with a poor outcome whilst individuals manifesting a positive and constructive outlook did substantially better at the follow-up stage.

Naismith and her colleagues suggest that counselling might be conducted by a suitably trained nurse and not necessarily (or even preferably) by a qualified doctor. They also suggest that a counsellor would constitute an important link between the hospital and community.

When the results of these investigations are considered together they suggest a number of conclusions. The manifestations of stress are a common and normal aspect of the individual's response to illness and also many aspects of medical and surgical treatment. The existence of a moderate stress response does not, however, necessarily imply that the patient's adjustment is maladaptive. Indeed, worrying can be an important part of the patient's preparation for inevitable discomfort. There are, however, wide individual differences both in the individual's response to diagnosis and treatment and also his ability to cope adaptively with discomfort and pain. We now have a basis for identifying at least some of those patients who are likely to respond adversely. Research on the role and importance of information suggests that a considerable amount can be done to control the patient's tolerance of stress. The outcome is dependent, however, on such factors as the type of help which is provided and, once again, there are wide individual differences in the response to counselling and other aspects of rehabilitation.

Summary

Stress is a universal and inevitable experience which can harm the individual and therefore deserves careful consideration from the professional whose aim is to understand and help his patient. The term 'stress' refers to two distinct but related aspects of the stress experience. The first involves the stress stimulus or 'stressor'; the second is the stress response. Life changes provide the organism with frequent and varying degrees of distress, and the link between life events and breakdown of psychological functioning is well documented. Most individuals respond, however, with behavioural and psychological changes which do not involve disorganization of an extreme kind. The components of a stress response include changes in anxiety and tension, irritability and aggression, alterations in social behaviour, the flexibility of behaviour and also various coping strategies which vary in their contribution to the resolution of discomfort in either the short or long term. Tension headaches are of importance to doctors and psychologists, and research has at last begun to contribute to the understanding of what now appears to be a complex combination of physiological and psychological changes which are not in perfect harmony.

There are wide individual differences in responses to stress. Most of the empirical research has been associated with the determinants of anxiety, but it seems likely that the general categories of variables implicated as determinants will also be found to have a similar role in relation to the syndrome of changes associated with stress. The basis for individual differences appears to reside in factors such as personality characteristics, the degree of freedom and control given to the individual, the severity and type of stressor, age, past experience, type and degree of conflict, cognitions and attitudes and the repertoire of coping responses available to the individual.

Although stress can have adverse effects, the great majority of individuals cope successfully and research in medical settings indicates that patients can benefit very appreciably from provisions such as counselling and information which prepares them for ordeals that are in any case inevitable. As usual, a great deal of research remains to be done in order to explore further the determinants and management of stress, but we can comfort ourselves with the thought that a healthy beginning has been made to the theoretical analysis of stress, its empirical investigation, and also to the clinical management of the individual under stress.

References

Attfield, M. and Peck, D.F. (1979)
Temperature self regulation and relaxation with migraine patients and normals. Behaviour Research and Therapy, 17, 591-595.

Barker, R.G., Dembo, T. and Lewin, K. (1941)
Frustration and regression: an experiment with young children. University of Iowa Studies in Child Welfare, 18, No. 386.

Birley, J.L.T. and Brown, G.W. (1970)
Crises and life changes preceding the onset or relapse of acute schizophrenia: clinical aspects. British Journal of Psychiatry, 116, 327-333.

Byrne, D.G. (1979)
Anxiety as state and trait following survived myocardial infarction. British Journal of Social and Clinical Psychology, 18, 417-425.

Eysenck, H.J. (1976)
The learning theory model of neurosis - a new approach. Behaviour Research and Therapy, 14, 251-267.

Eysenck, H.J. and Rachman, S. (1965)
The Causes and Cures of Neurosis. London: Routledge & Kegan Paul.

Hilgard, E.R., Atkinson, R.C. and Atkinson, R.L. (1971)
Introduction to Psychology (5th edn). New York: Harcourt Brace Jovanovich.

Holmes, T.S. and Holmes, J.H. (1970)
Short-term intrusions into the life style routine. Journal of Psychosomatic Research, 14, 121-132.

Holmes, T.H. and Rahe, R.H. (1967)
The social re-adjustment rating scale. Journal of Psychosomatic Research, 11, 213-218.

Janis, I.L. (1969)
Some implications of recent research on the dynamics of fear and stress tolerance. In Social Psychiatry, Proceedings of the Association. Baltimore: Williams & Wilkies.

Kushnir, B., Fox, K.M., Tomlinson, I.W. and Aber, C.B. (1976)

The effect of a pre–discharge consultation on the resumption of work, sexual activity and driving following acute myocardial infarction. Scandinavian Journal of Rehabilitation Medicine, 8, 155-159.

Lader, M. and Matthews, A. (1968)
A physiological model of phobic anxiety and desensitisation. Behaviour Research and Therapy, 6, 411 421.

Ley, P. (1977)
Psychological studies of doctor-patient communication. In S. Rachman (ed.), Contributions to Medical Psychology, Volume 1. Oxford: Pergamon Press.

Marks, I.M. (1969)
Fears and Phobias. London: Heinemann.

Mischel, W. (1968)
Personality and Assessment. New York: Wiley.

Naismith, L.D., Robinson, J.F., Shaw, G.B. and Macintyre M.M. (1979)
Psychological rehabilitation after myocardial infarction. British Medical Journal, 1, 439-446.

Paykel, E.S., Myers, J.K., Dienelt, M.N., Klerman, G.L. Lindenthal J.J. and Pepper, M. (1969)
Life events and depression. Archives of General Psychiatry, 21, 753-760.

Paykel, E.S., Prusoff, B.A., and Myers, J.K. (1975)
Suicide attempts and recent life events. Archives of General Psychiatry, 32, 327-333.

Paykel, E.S., Prusoff, B.A., and Uhlenhuth, E.H. (1971)
Scaling of life events. Archives of General Psychiatry, 25, 340-347.

Philips, C. (1977)
A psychological analysis of tension headache. In S. Rachman (ed.), Contributions to Medical Psychology, Volume 1. Oxford: Pergamon Press.

Rabkin, J.G. and Struening, E.L. (1976)
Life events, stress and illness. Science, 194, 1013-1020.

Sanderson, R.E., Campbell, D. and Laverty, S.G. (1963)
Traumatically conditioned responses acquired during respiratory paralysis. Nature, 196, 1235-1236.

Shields, J. (1962)
Monozygotic Twins Brought Up Apart and Brought Up Together. Oxford: Oxford University Press.

Yates, A.J. (1965)
Frustration and Conflict. Princeton, NJ: Van Nostrand.

Questions

1. 'Stress' is a term which is often used but rarely with any precision. What does the term mean to you?
2. Consider five stressful incidents which have involved you or members of your family. What aspects of these incidents made them stressful? What were the main changes in behaviour (in either you or your relatives) which were produced by these incidents?

3. Discuss the importance of life events in relation to both physical and mental health. What can a doctor do to help his patients to cope effectively with difficult life experiences?

4. Discuss the main changes which are caused by stress. How do individuals differ in their response to stress? What factors determine the individual's response to stress?

5. Discuss the clinical implications of our understanding of the psychological aspects of stress.

6. What has psychological research contributed to our understanding of headaches? Consider the practical value of this research.

7. Discuss the contribution of the psychologist to the management of stress associated with surgery. In addition, what can the doctor do to reduce the stress of the patient who is discovered to have curable cancer?

8. Discuss the relevance of our understanding of stress to: (a) the clinical management of reactive depression; (b) telling young parents that their baby is mentally deficient; (c) counselling patients who are soon to have surgery.

Annotated reading

Eysenck, H.J. (1976) The learning theory model of neurosis - a new approach. Behaviour Research and Therapy, 14, 251-267.

   This is more suitable at a postgraduate rather than an undergraduate level but is, nevertheless, a useful discussion of a contemporary psychological perspective of the nature of neurosis. It also illustrates the general strategy of applying basic empirical research to common human problems.

Janis, I.L. (1969) Some implications of recent research in the dynamics of fear and stress tolerance. In Social Psychiatry, Proceedings of the Association. Baltimore: Williams & Wilkies.

   This is hardly a recent reference but it is a very readable account of Janis' investigations of the determinants of pre-operative stress, and aspects of management. Enthusiastic students willl also need to be referred to Philip Ley's review (1977) referred to in chapter 18 of this volume which indicates that some aspects of Janis' results have not been supported by more recent research.

Marks, I.M. (1969) Fears and Phobias. London: Heinemann.

   A comprehensive and critical review of the aetiology and management of anxiety which will be attractive to medical students since it is written by an eminent psychiatrist and reflects a medical point of view. At the same time, the review is a competent and comprehensive summary of the research. It is still useful in spite of the fact that it is, once again, rather dated.

Strongman, K.T. (1978) The Psychology of Emotion (2nd edn) Chichester: Wiley.

This book provides a useful review of the determinants and nature of emotional response. It is not suitable for introductory courses with medical students but might be of some value to tutors and postgraduate students.

Rabkin, J.G. and Struening, E.L. (1976) Life events, stress and illness. Science, 194, 1013-1020.

A well-written and competent review of the research on life events which provides a realistic perspective of the research.

Depue, R.A. (ed.) (1979) The Psychobiology of Depressive Disorders: Implications for the effects of stress. New York: Academic Press.

This text has a broad interest in the phenomena associated with stress but depression is its major concern. Review chapters consider aspects of depression such as biological determinants and changes (e.g. genetics, biochemistry and physiology) and also social and psychological variables (e.g. life experiences, social pressures, self-esteem and learning). It is to be recommended because of its clinical relevance - depression is probably one of the most common disorders presenting in general practice and psychiatry - but it is also a comprehensive and competent review of theory and empirical findings. It is probably more suitable, however, for clinical trainees at the postgraduate level than as an introductory text.

Cooper, C.L. and Payne, R. (1978) Stress at Work. Chichester: Wiley.

As the title suggests, this book provides reviews of stress associated with work. Of particular interest are the chapters which are concerned with stressors in the physical environment (e.g. noise) but social and psychological determinants are also discussed. Stress management is also reviewed (Part 5) both in terms of individual coping and environmental design. The book is useful both as a source of specific references and a comprehensive review of stress associated with work.

Oborne, D.J., Gruneberg, M.M. and Eiser, J.R. (1979) Psychological aspects of stress. In Research in Psychology and Medicine. London: Academic Press.

This section contains eight papers delivered at an international conference on psychology and medicine. Papers are concerned with many aspects of stress but all are clinically relevant (for instance, the relationship between life stress and susceptibility to colds) and provide useful material for medical trainees at both the undergraduate and postgraduate levels.

15

Transition: Understanding and Managing Personal Change

Barrie Hopson

pening remarks
AVID GRIFFITHS

The review of stress, and more specifically the discussion of life events on pp. 297-300, has already indicated that the individual's experience can affect both his health and his psychological well-being. There can be little doubt, for instance, that life experiences (even pleasant events) do increase the risk of a broad range of physical and psychological disorders. In some cases, life events have a direct causal effect in producing a problem (e.g. experiences involving loss increase the risk of depression) whilst in others they maintain or exacerbate an existing condition (as in the effects of emotional involvement in the family on relapse in schizophrenia). Life events are, however, inevitable and affect most individuals. If this is accepted, what can be done to facilitate the task of coping with life's problems, and also deriving some benefit from the process?

Barrie Hopson's discussion of transitions attempts to facilitate the reader's understanding of what happens during life changes and also attempts to provide practical advice as to the most useful course of action. Since doctors are likely to be consulted by large numbers of patients who are coping with life's inevitable problems, a reading of Hopson's review promises to provide a considerable amount of relevant material whose theoretical interest is more than adequately complemented by its potential practical value. Patients will expect guidance from their doctors and this chapter provides principles and guidelines which the doctor will find extremely useful as an adjunct to his skill and common sense.

troduction
ARRIE HOPSON

In the ongoing flux of life, (the person) undergoes many changes. Arriving, departing, growing, declining, achieving, failing - every change involves a loss and a gain. The old environment must be given up, the new accepted. People come and go; one job is lost, another begun; territory and possessions are acquired or sold; new skills are learned, old abandoned; expectations are fulfilled or hopes dashed - in all these situations the individual is faced with the need to give up one mode of life and accept another (Parkes, 1972).

Today, more than at any other time in our history, people have to cope with an often bewildering variety of transitions: from home to school; from school to work; from being single to being married and - increasingly - divorced; from job to job; from job to loss of employment; retraining and re-education; from place to place and friend to friend; to parenthood and then to children leaving home; and finally to bereavements and death. Alongside these and other major life events people are having to learn to cope with the passage from one stage of personal development to another: adolescence, early adulthood, stabilization, mid-life transition and restabilization.

What is a transition?
We define a transition as a discontinuity in a person's life space (Adams, Hayes and Hopson, 1976). Sometimes the discontinuity is defined by social consensus as to what constitutes a discontinuity within the culture. Holmes and Rahe (1967) provide evidence to show the extent of cultural similarity in perceptions of what are important discontinuities, in the research they conducted to produce their social readjustment rating scale. The life changes represented here (see table 1), along with their weighted scores, were found to be remarkably consistent from culture to culture: Japan, Hawaii, Central America, Peru, Spain, France, Belgium, Switzerland and Scandinavia. For example, death of a spouse requires about twice as much change in adjustment worldwide as marriage, and ten times as much as a traffic violation. The correlation between the items ranged from 0.65 to 0.98 across all the cultures.

Another way of defining a discontinuity is not by general consensus but by the person's own perception. These two may not always coincide: for example, adolescence is considered to be an important time of transition in most western cultures, whereas in other cultures like Samoa it was not considered to be a time of stressful identity crisis. Also, in a common culture some children experience adolescence as a transition while others do not. Consequently it cannot be assumed that everyone experiences a transitional event (e.g. a change of job) in the same way.

Table 1

The Holmes and Rahe social readjustment rating scale

LIFE EVENT	Mean value
1. Death of a spouse	100
2. Divorce	73
3. Marital separation from mate	65
4. Detention in jail or other institution	63

5. Death of a close family member 63

6. Major personal injury or illness 53

7. Marriage 50

8. Being fired at work 47

9. Marital reconciliation with mate 45

10. Retirement from work 45

11. Major change in the health or
    behaviour of a family member 44

12. Pregnancy 40

13. Sexual difficulties 39

14. Gaining a new family member (e.g.
    through birth, adoption, oldster moving
    in, etc.) 39

15. Major business readjustment (e.g.
    merger, reorganization,
    bankruptcy, etc.) 39

16. Major change in financial state
    (e.g. a lot worse off or
    a lot better off than usual) 38

17. Death of a close friend 37

18. Changing to a different line of work 36

19. Major changes in the number of arguments
    with spouse (e.g. either a lot more
    or a lot less than usual regarding
    childbearing, personal habits, etc.) 35

20. Taking on a mortgage greater than
    $10,000 (e.g. purchasing a home,
    business, etc.) 31

21. Foreclosure on a mortgage or loan 30

22. Major change in responsibilities
    at work (e.g. promotion,
    demotion, lateral transfer) 29

23. Son or daughter leaving home (e.g.
    marriage, attending college, etc.) 29

24. In-law troubles 29

25. Outstanding personal achievement   28

26. Wife beginning or ceasing work
outside the home   26

27. Beginning or ceasing formal schooling   26

28. Major change in living conditions
(e.g. building a new home, remodelling,
deterioration of home or neighborhood)   25

29. Revision of personal habits (dress,
manners, associations, etc.)   24

30. Trouble with the boss   23

31. Major change in working hours or
conditions   20

32. Change in residence   20

33. Changing to a new school   20

34. Major change in usual type and/or
amount of recreation   19

35. Major change in church activities (e.g.
a lot more or a lot less than usual)   19

36. Major change in social activities (e.g.
clubs, dancing, movies, visiting, etc.)   18

37. Taking on a mortgage or loan less than
$10,000 (e.g. purchasing a car, TV,
freezer, etc.)   17

38. Major change in sleeping habits (a lot
more or a lot less sleep, or change
in part of day when asleep)   16

39. Major change in number of family
get-togethers (e.g. a lot more or a
lot less than usual)   15

40. Major change in eating habits (a lot
more or a lot less food intake, or
very different meal hours or surroundings)   15

41. Vacation   13

42. Christmas   12

43. Minor violations of the law (e.g.
traffic tickets, jaywalking,
disturbing the peace, etc.)   11

For an experience to be classed as transitional there should be:

* PERSONAL AWARENESS of a discontinuity in one's life space; and
* NEW BEHAVIOURAL RESPONSES required because the situation is new, or the required behaviours are novel, or both.

A person can sometimes undergo a transitional experience without being aware of the extent of the discontinuity or that new behavioural responses are required. This at some point will probably cause the person or others adaptation problems. For example, following the death of her husband, the widow may not be experiencing strain - she might even be pleased that he is dead - but suddenly she becomes aware that no house repairs have been done, and a new dimension or loss becomes evident along with the awareness of new behavioural responses required.

Why is an understanding of transitional experience important?

Life in post-industrial society is likely to bring more and more transitions for people in all arenas of living. Any transition will result in people being subjected to some degree of stress and strain. They will be more or less aware of this depending upon the novelty of the event and the demands it makes upon their behavioural repertoires. Thus, there is likely to be a rise in the number of people experiencing an increased amount of stress and strain in the course of their daily lives.

Many practitioners in the helping professions are dealing directly with clients who are in transition. It is vital for them to understand how people are likely to react during transition, and to recognize the symptoms of transitional stress. Professionals also need helping techniques to ensure that individuals cope more effectively with their transitions, and to make organizations and social groups more aware of what they can do to help people in transition.

Is there a general model of transitions?

As we began to discover other work on different transitions, a general picture increasingly began to emerge. It appeared that irrespective of the nature of the transition, an overall pattern seemed to exist. There were differences, of course, especially between those transitions that were usually experienced as being positive (e.g. marriage and desired promotion), and those usually experienced negatively (e.g. bereavement and divorce). But these differences appeared to reflect differences of emphasis rather than require a totally different model.

The major point to be made in understanding transitions is that whether a change in one's daily routine is an intentional change, a sudden surprise that gets thrust upon one, or a growing awareness that one is moving into a life stage characterized by increasing or decreasing stability, it will trigger a cycle of reactions and feelings that is predictable. The cycle has seven phases, and the identification of these seven phases has come about through content analysis of reports from over 100 people who have attended transition workshops for the purpose of understanding and learning to cope more effectively with transitions they were experiencing and through extending the findings reported above.

Immobilization
The first phase is a kind of immobilization or a sense of being overwhelmed; of being unable to make plans, unable to reason, and unable to understand. In other words, the initial phase of a transition is experienced by many people as a feeling of being frozen up. It appears that the intensity with which people experience this first phase is a function of the unfamiliarity of the transition state and of the negative expectations one holds. If the transition is not high in novelty and if the person holds positive expectations, the immobilization is felt less intensely or perhaps not at all. Marriage can be a good example of the latter.

Minimization
The way of getting out of this immobilization, essentially, is by movement to the second phase of the cycle, which is characterized by minimization of the change or disruption, even to trivialize it. Very often, the person will deny that the change even exists. Sometimes, too, the person projects a euphoric feeling. Those readers who recall seeing Alfred Hitchcock's film 'Psycho' will remember that Tony Perkins spent considerable time shrieking at his mother in the house on the hill. It is not until the end of the film that one learns the mother has been dead for some time, and it is her semi-mummified body with which he has been carrying on his 'dialogue'. That is an extreme example of denying or minimizing the reality of a major change in one's life. Denial can have a positive function. It is more often a necessary phase in the process of adjustment. 'Denial is a normal and necessary human reaction to a crisis which is too immediately overwhelming to face head-on. Denial provides time for a temporary retreat from reality while our internal forces regroup and regain the strength to comprehend the new life our loss has forced upon us' (Krantzler, 1973).

Depression
Eventually, for most people - though not for Tony Perkins in 'Psycho' - the realities of the change and of the resulting stresses begin to become apparent. As people become aware that they must make some changes in the way they are living, as they become aware of the realities involved, they sometimes begin to get depressed: the third phase of the transition cycle. Depression is usually the

consequence of feelings of powerlessness, of aspects of life out of one's control. This is often made worse by the fear of loss of control over one's own emotions. The depression stage has occasional high energy periods often characterized by anger, before sliding back into a feeling of hopelessness. They become depressed because they are just beginning to face up to the fact that there has been a change. Even if they have voluntarily created this change themselves, there is likely to be this dip in feelings. They become frustrated because it becomes difficult to know how best to cope with the new life requirements, the ways of being, the new relationships that have been established or whatever other changes may be necessary.

Letting go
As people move further into becoming aware of reality, they can move into the fourth phase, which is accepting reality for what it is. Through the first three phases, there has been a kind of attachment, whether it has been conscious or not, to the past (pre-transition) situation. To move from phase three to phase four involves a process of unhooking from the past and of saying 'Well, here I am now; here is what I have; I know I can survive; I may not be sure of what I want yet but I will be OK; there is life out there waiting for me.' As this is accepted as the new reality, the person's feelings begin to rise once more, and optimism becomes possible. A clear 'letting go' is necessary.

Testing
This provides a bridge to phase five, where the person becomes much more active and starts testing himself vis-à-vis the new situation, trying out new behaviours, new life styles, and new ways of coping with the transition. There is a tendency also at this point for people to stereotype, to have categories and classifications of the ways things and people should or should not be relative to the new situation. There is much personal energy available during this phase and, as they begin to deal with the new reality, it is not unlikely that those in transition will easily become angry and irritable.

Search for meaning
Following this burst of activity and self-testing, there is a more gradual shifting towards becoming concerned with understanding and for seeking meanings for how things are different and why they are different. This sixth phase is a cognitive process in which people try to understand what all of the activity, anger, stereotyping and so on have meant. It is not until people can get out of the activity and withdraw somewhat from it that they can begin to understand deeply the meaning of the change in their lives.

Internalization
This conceptualizing, in turn, allows people to move into

the final phase of internalizing these meanings and incorporating them into their behaviour. Overall, the seven transition phases represent a cycle of experiencing a disruption, gradually acknowledging its reality, testing oneself, understanding oneself, and incorporating changes in one's behaviour. The level of one's morale varies across these phases and appears to follow a predictable path. Identifying the seven phases along such a morale curve often gives one a better understanding of the nature of the transition cycle. This is shown in figure 1.

Interestingly, the Menninger Foundation's research on Peace Corps volunteers' reactions to entering and experiencing training (a transition for each person) produced a very similar curve. More recently, Elisabeth Kubler-Ross and those who joined her death and dying seminars have also charted a very similar curve of the reaction cycle people go through upon learning they are terminally ill, which is the ultimate transition.

Before proceeding, it is necessary to make it clear that seldom, if ever, does a person move neatly from phase to phase as has been described above. It can help someone in distress, however, to be made aware that what they are experiencing is not uncommon, that it will pass, and that they have a great deal they can do in determining how quickly it will pass.

It is also important to point out that each person's experience is unique and that any given individual's progressions and regressions are unique to their unique circumstances. For example, one person may never get beyond denial or minimization. Another may end it all during depression. Yet another might experience a major failure just as things begin to look up, and slip back to a less active, more withdrawn posture.

What is important is the potential for growth arising from any major disruption or calamity. One realizes this potential and moves toward it when one lets go and fully accepts the situation for what it is; one dies a 'little death' to become larger.

What effects do transitions have on people?

It is important to note here that all transitions involve some stress, including those considered by society to be positive changes, such as being left large sums of money, parenthood or marriage (Holmes and Rahe, 1967). Our own studies investigating this relationship show the following results:

* transitions are most stressful if they are unpredictable, involuntary, unfamiliar, of high magnitude (degree of change), and high intensity (rate of change);
* the incidence of illness is positively correlated with the amount of life change one undergoes;
* lack of feedback on the success of attempts to cope with

330

Figure 1

Self-esteem changes during transitions

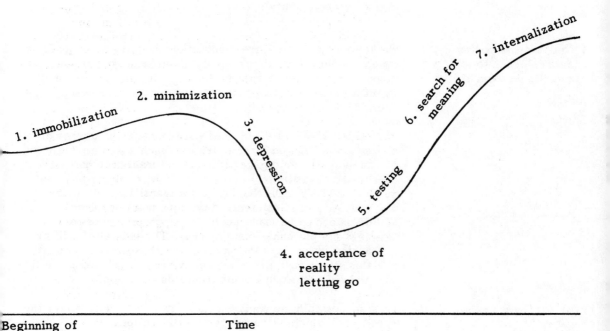

1. immobilization

2. minimization

3. depression

4. acceptance of
reality
letting go

5. testing

6. search for meaning

7. internalization

Beginning of
transition

Time

strain-inducing events causes more severe stress-
related diseases than when relevant feedback is present;

* interpersonal warmth and support during stressful
periods seems to reduce the impact of the stress;
* viruses alone do not cause illnesses. The incidence of
bad emotional experiences seems to upset the body and
allow the viruses to take over;
* hypertension occurs more often in environments characterized by high stressors and few ways of responding to
those stressors;
* the more major the life changes the higher the risk of
coronary heart disease.

**Every transition
contains 'opportunity
value' for the mover**

However undesirable a particular transition may be for the
mover, there is always opportunity for personal growth and
development contained within it. If one takes a severe

example such as death of a spouse, for the majority of those bereaved nothing will compensate for that loss. On the other hand, given that the loss is out of their control, what is under their control is what they decide to do with their lives from there on. There are opportunities for new relationships, travel, career change, new interests, etc. Obviously, during the grief process - which is essential - the opportunities are difficult and often obnoxious to contemplate but part of the 'letting go' stage involves doing exactly that. The Chinese have two symbols for the concept of 'crisis': one means 'danger' while the other signifies 'opportunity'.

What are the coping tasks relevant to all transitional events?

We believe that there are common elements in any transition, which enable us to talk generally about transitional behaviour. We also assert that in dealing with any transitional event a person has two tasks to perform as he moves through the phases of the model:

* MANAGEMENT OF STRAIN: to manage the degree of strain generated by the stress in such a way that the individual can engage with the external problems caused by the transition.
* COGNITIVE COPING TASKS: a transition will always necessitate adjustment. Any adjustment requires decisions to be made about the appropriateness of new and old behaviour patterns. The individual will be asking himself questions such as: (i) How can I accept this situation?; (ii) What behaviour is expected of me?; and (iii) What do I want from this situation?

How successfully he manages these two tasks determines the speed with which he completes the transition.

What are the coping skills relevant to transitions?

At the Counselling and Career Development Unit at Leeds University we have been working for a number of years on developing training programmes to help adults in transition and to teach transition coping skills to young people in schools and colleges.

We have developed a questionnaire to be used to help people identify the transition coping skills they already possess and which simultaneously highlights the deficits in their coping repertory. Table 2 reproduces the questionnaire designed for use with adults. People are asked to answer 'yes' or 'no' to all the questions. Each time they reply 'no', it suggests an area where they are lacking in some theoretical understanding of the nature of transitions, or deficient in cognitive or behavioural skills. Each of the items is dealt with briefly below, along with some teaching points we make to participants. In a workshop, this learning would take place experientially and participants would have an opportunity to develop and practise their skills. The

332

language used is written to convey the flavour of the workshop approach. The following text should be read in conjunction with the questionnaire.

Table 2

Coping skills questionnaire

1. KNOW YOURSELF
a. Would I have chosen for this to have happened?
b. Am I proactive in new situations: do I take initiatives, have a purpose as opposed to sitting back and waiting on events?
c. Do I know what I want from this new situation?
d. Do I know what I don't want from this new situation?
e. If I feel under stress do I know what I can do to help myself?
f. Do I know how to use my feelings as indicators of where I am?

2. KNOW YOUR NEW SITUATION
a. Can I describe the transition?
b. Do I know how I'm expected to behave?
c. Can I try out the new situation in advance?

3. KNOW OTHER PEOPLE WHO CAN HELP: do I have other people:
a. To depend on in a crisis?
b. To discuss concerns?
c. To feel close to - a friend?
d. Who can make me feel competent and valued?
e. Who can give me important information?
f. Who will challenge me to sit up and take a good look at myself?
g. With whom I can share good news and good feelings?
h. Who will give me constructive feedback?

4. LEARN FROM THE PAST
a. Is there anything similar that has happened to me?
b. Can I identify what I did which helped me get through that experience?
c. Can I identify what I would have done differently?

5. LOOK AFTER YOURSELF
a. Do I know how to use supportive self-talk?
b. Do I get regular exercise or have a personal fitness programme?
c. Am I eating regularly and wisely?
d. Do I know how to relax?
e. Am I keeping to a regular schedule?
f. Do I know my 'personal anchor points'?
g. Do I give myself 'treats' when under stress?
h. Do I have other people who will take care of me?

i. Can I survive?
j. Do I know when my low points are likely to be?

6. LET GO OF THE PAST
a. Do I easily let go of old situations?
b. Do I continually feel that this should not happen to me?
c. Do I know how to vent my anger constructively?

7. SET GOALS AND MAKE ACTION PLANS
a. Do I know how to set goals?
b. Do I know what my goals are for this transition and for my life generally?
c. Do I know how to make and implement action plans?
d. Do I know how to set priorities?
e. Do I know how to make effective decisions?
f. Do I know how to generate alternatives, because there is always an alternative?

8. LOOK FOR THE GAINS YOU HAVE MADE
a. Can I find one thing which is positive about this experience?
b. Can I list a variety of new opportunities that did not exist before or that I would not have thought of previously?
c. Have I learned something new about myself?

Know yourself

1. WOULD I HAVE CHOSEN FOR THIS TO HAVE HAPPENED? You may not have chosen this situation. This could make it more difficult for you to accept the transition. But it has happened. You now have three options:

(A) accept it and put up with it
(B) refuse to accept
(C) accept it and try to benefit from it

(A) will help you to survive. (B) will bring you nothing but bad feelings and worse; you will be less able to cope with the tasks facing you in the new situation. (C) will help you to grow in addition to merely surviving.

Given the inevitable, ask yourself the key question: 'What is the worst thing that could happen?' Having identified that, ask yourself if you can cope with that. Is it really so terrible?

It is essential to remember that problematic situations constitute a normal aspect of living. It is also useful to recall the variety of transitions that you have encountered and survived up until now. Through having survived you will probably have developed some skills. If, on looking back, you feel dissatisfied with how you managed a transition, it is important to ask yourself whether you had all the skills needed to deal effectively with that situation. More than likely you did not. Do not berate yourself for not having these skills. Instead be glad that you have identified the need for additional skills, for that in itself is the first stage of skill development.

2. AM I PROACTIVE IN NEW SITUATIONS: DO I TAKE INITIATIVES, HAVE A PURPOSE, AS OPPOSED TO SITTING BACK AND WAITING ON EVENTS? To be proactive involves a certain sequence of behaviour:

* knowing what you want;
* knowing alternative ways of achieving this;
* choosing one alternative;
* evaluating the results against your original objective.

The essence of proactive behaviour is that there is a REASON for it, even if the end result involves no action. The reason, however, must stem from what Maslow (1968) calls a 'growth' need as opposed to a 'deficiency' need. Deciding not to give a public talk (objective), and knowing various ways of avoiding this (knowing alternatives), choosing one, and thereby achieving the objective at first glance seems to fit the description of 'proactive behaviour'. However, if the reason is based on fear of making a fool of oneself, this would not be classed as proactive. If it were due to over-commitment, or the feeling that you are not the best equipped person to do it, that would be proactive.

3. DO I KNOW WHAT I WANT FROM THIS NEW SITUATION?

4. DO I KNOW WHAT I DO NOT WANT FROM THIS NEW SITUATION? If you are unclear as to what you want or do not want from a new situation this usually signifies a lack of knowledge about your own values or about what the new situation has to offer. There is an entire educational technology designed to help young people and adults to crystallize their needs and values. It has been developed in the USA and is known generically as 'values clarification' (Simon, Howe and Kirschenbaum, 1972; Simon, 1974; Howe and Howe, 1975; Kirschenbaum, 1977). Obtaining more information about the new situation is dealt with in the next section.

5. IF I FEEL UNDER STRESS DO I KNOW WHAT I CAN DO TO HELP MYSELF? Avoid situations where you might over-react. If you have recently separated from your spouse and it is still painful, do not accept an invitation to an event where you know you will encounter your spouse again. Make as few decisions as possible as you will not be thinking clearly enough. Do not make more than one transition at a time. It is amazing how often people choose one transition to be the stimulus for a host of others. If you have changed your job, do not change your spouse, residence and/or life style all at the same time. A new broom can sometimes sweep you over!

Look after yourself (see below).

Do not waste time blaming yourself (see below).

Remember that time itself will not eliminate the stress or heal you, it is what you do with that time. There are a variety of cognitive shielding techniques that you can use to minimize the strain. These all involve controlling the amount of stimulation in the environment. Some examples are:

* time management: making priorities;
* making lists;
* queuing: delaying decisions during a difficult period by queuing them up, dealing with them one at a time, and not thinking about future decisions until the time to make them arrives. Writing down a decision in a diary to be made at a future date is a good way of queuing.
* temporary drop-out: refusing to resolve decisions until after a recuperation period. This can appear initially as reactive; however, it is correctly termed proactive as the mover is deliberately opting out of the situation temporarily as part of a strategy to move in later and thereby more effectively.

There are now some excellent resources available for techniques of preventing and managing stress; for example, Sharpe and Lewis' 'Thrive on Stress' (1977), Lamott's 'Escape from Stress' (1975), and Forbes' 'Life Stress' (1979).

6. DO I KNOW HOW TO USE MY FEELINGS AS INDICATORS OF WHERE I AM? Many people, especially men, as a result of their upbringing are emotionally illiterate: that is, they have not developed the skills of 'reading' their own emotions. One's 'gut' feelings are the surest indicator of how one is coping at any particular time. The skill is in learning to recognize the changes in feelings when they occur and then having an emotional vocabulary to be able to label them correctly. Often when people are asked what they are feeling they will answer you in terms of only what they are thinking (see Hopson and Scally, 'Lifeskills Teaching Programmes no. 1 - How to manage negative emotions', 1980a; Johnson's 'Reaching Out', 1972).

Know your new situation

1. CAN I DESCRIBE THE TRANSITION? An essential prerequisite to successful transition coping is to know that you are in one. It is essential to be aware of when the transition began, where you are in relation to it and what are all the variables involved. For example, considering changing your job might involve geographical change, relationship changes, financial implications, holiday plans for this year, etc.

2. DO I KNOW HOW I AM EXPECTED TO BEHAVE? Transitions are naturally accompanied by stress even if they are

desired. Anxiety certainly increases the less information you have about your new situation. Collect as much data as you can about what others expect of you, what society expects and how you are to behave. You may decide not to live up to or down to those expectations, but again you need the initial data before you can make that decision. You also need to know the consequences of any decision before you make it.

You can ask people who have made a similar transition or indeed are presently going through the same transition. A variety of self-help and special interest groups have developed in recent years to provide mutual support and information to people undergoing similar transitions: antenatal classes, induction courses, orientation programmes, women's and men's 'rap' groups for people redefining their sex roles, widows' clubs, singles' clubs, one-parent family groups, etc.

It is important to remember that other people often forget, or in some cases are not even aware, that this is a new situation for you. They may need reminding. For example, one new day at the end of your first week at a new job constitutes 20 per cent of the time you have worked there. For someone who has been here for five years, one new day represents less than 0.4 per cent of the time he has been there. Consequently, his feelings about that day are likely to be quite different from your feelings about the same day.

3. CAN I TRY OUT THE NEW SITUATION IN ADVANCE?
Some transitions can be 'sampled' in advance, for example, starting a new job, moving to another country; even a divorce or death can sometimes be anticipated. Reading books about anticipated transitions can be valuable, as can talking to others who have experienced it, while remembering that no one will experience it just like you. Where appropriate you can visit places, meet people, watch films, etc., prior to your transition.

Knowing other people who can help
There is now considerable evidence to show the beneficial effects on stress reduction of talking problems through with people: friends, colleagues, even strangers.

We often make the mistake of expecting too few people, typically a spouse and children, to satisfy too great a proportion of our needs. Check the list in the questionnaire. How many categories of person do you have available to you in your life? Are there any gaps? How many different people make up your 'support' group? How dependent are you on one or two?

We are also better at developing some forms of support at the expense of others. For example, people are often better at developing friendships than relationships with people who challenge us. The challengers in most people's support systems are about as abrasive as a marshmallow. Yet sometimes challengers are exactly what we require to shift us out of stereotyped thinking. Who are the challengers in your support systems? Remember, you may not even like them.

Learn from the past

Our past is an important part of our present. Our past is the history of our successes and our failures and is thereby a record of our learning. As such, we can continue to learn from our past experiences. 'Mistakes' are another way of labelling 'opportunities for learning'. If we can identify times in the past when we have had similar feelings or experienced similar transitions, we have an opportunity to monitor those chapters of our history and evaluate our performances against the criteria of our own choosing. What did we do that really did not help the situation? What would we avoid if we were to have that experience again? Can we learn from that experience and generalize it to the new transition? A sense of one's own history is a prerequisite to a fully functioning present and a portent for one's range of possible futures.

Look after yourself

1. DO I KNOW HOW TO USE SUPPORTIVE SELF-TALK? Many of the problems we create for ourselves and much of the support that we give ourselves derives from the same source: our internal dialogue with ourselves. This dialogue continues throughout most of our waking hours. These 'cognitions' are vital to our survival and growth. They enable us to adapt to new situations, to learn, to feel and to enact cognitively a variety of scenarios without having to perform any of them. Ellis (1975), with his RATIONAL EMOTIVE THERAPY, for years has claimed that the way we think determines what we feel, with the corollary that if we can change how we think we can also change how we feel. His therapeutic method involves retraining people to talk internally to themselves to minimize the negative emotions which they otherwise would create. Ellis claims that most people carry a variety of 'irrational beliefs' in their heads unfounded in reality, but which result in their creating bad feelings for themselves as a result of 'shoulds' and 'oughts' which they believe are infallible. These beliefs usually belong to one of three categories, which Ellis calls the 'Irrational Trinity' on the road to 'mustabation':

* A belief that I should be a certain sort of person, or a success, or perfect, or loved by everyone, and if I'm not, I'm a failure and worthless;
* a belief that you, or other people, should do as I want them to do: love me, work for me, understand me, etc., and if they do not, it is terrible, and I deserve to be miserable or they should be made to suffer;
* a belief that things should be different; there should not be racial hatred, this organization should run better, our parents should not have to die, etc., and if things are not as I want them to be it is awful and

either I cannot cope and deserve to be miserable, or I
have every right to be furious.

Since it takes years to develop our patterns of self-talk,
changing them involves practice. There are a variety of
programmes now available for helping people to restructure
their self-talk into more supportive statements. Mahoney and
Mahoney (1976) call this process 'cognitive ecology':
cleaning up what you say to yourself.

2. DO I GET REGULAR EXERCISE OR HAVE A PERSONAL
FITNESS PROGRAMME? Physical fitness is related to one's
ability to cope with stress. It has also been shown to be
related to the ability to create effective interpersonal
relationships (Aspy and Roebuck, 1977) which in turn is related to stress reduction.
    You need to be fit to cope effectively with transitions.
Yet, of course it is often when we are most in need of
fitness that we are often least inclined to make time for
it. There are a number of well-researched fitness programmes
available (Health Education Council, 1976; Carruthers and
Murray, 1977; Cooper, 1977; Royal Canadian Air Force,
1978).

3. AM I EATING REGULARLY AND WISELY? Now is not
the time for a rash diet. Your body needs all the help it
can get. People in transition often have neither the time
nor inclination to eat wisely. There is sometimes a reliance
on quick junk foods, take-away meals or eating out. Remember
to eat something every day from the four major food groups:
meat, fish, poultry; dairy products; fruits and vegetables;
bread and cereals.
    Do not replace food with alcohol or smoking. Obviously
there are times when alcohol will help you get through a
lonely evening. You need a holiday from self-work as much
as from any other kind of work. The danger signs are when
alcohol or a cigarette is used as a substitute for meals.
    Be wary of developing a dependence on drugs at this
time. Sleeping tablets can sometimes be helpful during a
crisis, but get off them quickly. They can serve to prevent
you from developing healthier coping strategies.
    It is a good idea to acquire an easy to read book on
diet but one that is critical of food fads. The Health
Education Council's booklet, 'Look After Yourself' (1976),
contains a simple introduction to good nutrition, and
Breckon's 'You Are What You Eat' (1976) is a fascinating
survey of dietary facts and fiction, arguing strongly
against overdosing oneself with vitamins and dealing in a
balanced way with the hysteria over additives.

4. DO I KNOW HOW TO RELAX? There are two ways of
reducing stress. One is to organize your life to minimize
the number of stressors working on you. The other concerns
how to reduce the effect of stress WHEN it hits you. The

latter is typically the biggest problem when coping with a transition. Unfortunately, the very people who are most prone to stress illnesses often exacerbate the problem by packing their lives with transitions.

There are numerous relaxation methods, each of which have their advocates. A brief guide follows.

* Learn a relaxation technique. Progressive relaxation is simple and easy to learn. It is described in 'Exercises in Personal and Career Development' by Barrie Hopson and Patricia Hough (1973). It is described there as a classroom exercise. Transcendental meditation is now well researched and strong claims are made for it as a technique which directly affects the body's physiology. Most cities have a TM centre. You could also read 'The Transcendental Meditation Technique' by Peter Russel (1977). For those who do not enjoy the ritual cliquishness that accompanies TM, read Herbert Benson's 'The Relaxation Response' (1977).
* Direct body work to encourage relaxation: massage. The basics can be learned quickly on a course. If there is a Personal Growth centre near you, make contact as they might run courses. Read 'The Massage Book' by G. Downing (1972). You will need to keep an open mind regarding some of the sweeping generalizations made on behalf of some of these techniques.

5. AM I KEEPING TO A REGULAR SCHEDULE? If your internal world is in crisis, keep your external world in order. Keeping irregular hours, eating at strange times, going to lots of new places, meeting new people; all these can be disorientating.

6. DO I KNOW MY 'PERSONAL ANCHOR POINTS'? Toffler (1970) described this concept as one antidote to 'future shock'. When all around us things are changing we need an anchor point to hold on to. For some people it is their home, for others a relationship, children, a job, a daily routine, a favourite place or a hobby. Anchor points are plentiful, and it is vital to have at least one. In the midst of instability a stable base offers confirmation of identity, disengagement from the problem, and maybe even relaxation.

7. DO I GIVE MYSELF 'TREATS' WHEN UNDER STRESS? This list of tips has been packed with work. But play is vital too. If you are feeling low, or under stress, how about simply giving yourself a treat? It might even be a reward for accomplishing a difficult test or situation, but it does not have to be.

Draw up a list of treats. Try to become an expert on self-indulgence: a theatre trip, a massage, a book, see friends, make love, have a disgustingly 'bad for you' meal, take a holiday, or pamper yourself.

The only warning about treats is: do not spend so much time treating yourself that you use these as a diversion from coping directly with the transition.

8. DO I HAVE OTHER PEOPLE WHO WILL TAKE CARE OF ME? It is all right to be taken care of sometimes. Allow a friend, lover or colleague to look after you. If they do not offer, be proactive, ask them. Be brave enough to accept help from others. Recall what you feel when others close to you ask for help. There are pay-offs for helpers as well as those who receive help.

9. CAN I SURVIVE? Of course you can. You may doubt it at the moment. Perhaps it will help to remind yourself that what you are feeling now is normal for someone having experienced what you are experiencing. It is also necessary before you can move on to the next stage of finding out more about you and what this transition can do FOR you instead of TO you.

Do not worry about feelings of suicide. Sometimes survival does not seem like such a good idea. If these feelings really seem to be getting out of hand see a counsellor, ring a Samaritan, or consult a doctor; you will probably get more librium than counselling, but that can take off the pressure until you have regrouped your resources.

The feeling will pass. Talk to people, keep a regular routine, treat yourself; at the end of each day recall one good experience, then you can match it with a bad one, then another good experience followed by a bad one, etc., or contract with a friend to call you at certain times.

10. DO I KNOW WHEN MY LOW POINTS ARE LIKELY TO BE? These can usually be predicted quite easily; after a phone call to your children (in the case of a divorced parent), seeing your ex-spouse with a new partner, just seeing your ex-spouse, discovering a personal belonging of your dead spouse, seeing an old workmate (redundancy, retirement), etc.

Keep a diary or a journal. This will help you to clarify your thoughts and feelings as well as to identify times, places and people to avoid. If you are experiencing the loss of a love it is usually advisable to fill your Sundays, bank holidays and Saturday nights!

Let go of the past
1. DO I EASILY LET GO OF OLD SITUATIONS? Sometimes people cannot let go because they try too hard to hold on. It is permissible to grieve. Grief shows that you are alive. Think about what you are missing, feel it. Ask people if you can talk to them about it. They will often be too embar-rassed to mention it or worry that it will 'upset' you. Cry, rage, scream, recognize the loss, do not deny the pain. Wounds hurt when you dress them, but you know that is the

first stage of the wound getting better. It is permissible to feel anger too.

2. DO I CONTINUALLY FEEL THAT THIS SHOULD NOT HAPPEN TO ME? Then you are guilty of making yourself unhappy by hitting yourself over the head with 'shoulds' and 'oughts'. You need to look again at the section on supportive self-talk.

3. DO I KNOW HOW TO VENT MY ANGER CONSTRUCTIVELY? Allow yourself to feel the anger. If it is kept inside it will only hurt you. Feel angry at the person who left you, at the person who took something from you, at the world that let you down or at friends who cannot be trusted. Hit a pillow, scream aloud (in a closed car this is very effective; just like an echo chamber) or play a hectic sport. Do not hurt anyone, including yourself.

Anger is only a feeling. It cannot hurt anyone. Only behaviour hurts. Once the anger is cleared away, you are then freer to begin to evaluate, make plans and decide.

Set goals and make action plans

1. DO I KNOW HOW TO SET GOALS? Some people fail to manage their transitions effectively because they have not identified a desirable outcome. 'If you don't know where you're going, you'll probably end up somewhere else' (David Campbell, 1974).

It is essential to identify what you want to achieve in terms which are as behaviourally specific as possible, such as 'I want a new job worth £8,000 per annum where I have overall responsibility for financial operations of a medium-scale department.' 'In six months I want to be able to go out on my own, to visit friends by myself, and to have developed one new interest' (this was an objective of a recent widow in one of my workshops).

2. DO I KNOW WHAT MY GOALS ARE FOR THIS TRANSITION AND FOR MY LIFE GENERALLY? This requires the specific skill of knowing how to set, define, and refine objectives.

3. DO I KNOW HOW TO MAKE AND IMPLEMENT ACTION PLANS? Once the objectives are clear the action steps follow next. There are a variety of resources available with guidelines on making effective action plans. Carkhuff's two books, 'The Art of Problem Solving' (1974a) and 'How to Help Yourself' (1974b), are useful. An action plan needs to be behaviourally specific: 'I will make an appointment to see the solicitor tomorrow morning'. It needs to be in terms of 'what I will do now', not in terms of 'what I will do sometime', or 'what we will do eventually'. An action plan should read like a computer programme, with each step so clearly defined that someone else would know how to carry it out.

4. DO I KNOW HOW TO SET PRIORITIES? Having a variety of goals is one thing, having the time to achieve them all is another. Skills of time management are required along with a systematic way of measuring the desirability of one goal with another.

5. DO I KNOW HOW TO MAKE EFFECTIVE DECISIONS? Katz (1968) has talked about the importance, not so much of making wise decisions but of making decisions wisely. There are a variety of teaching programmes now available to help people become more proficient at making choices (Hopson and Hough, 1973; Watts and Elsom, 1975).

6. DO I KNOW HOW TO GENERATE ALTERNATIVES, BECAUSE THERE IS ALWAYS AN ALTERNATIVE? Often people do not make as good a decision as they might have simply because they have not generated enough alternatives. The techniques of 'brainstorming', 'morphological forced connections' and 'synectics' (all described in Adams, 1974) are all ways of doing this. The key quite often, however, is the belief that no matter now hopeless the situation, how constrained one feels, there is always an alternative, no matter how unpalatable it may initially appear, and that you can choose. This is the central concept in the model of the 'self empowered person' described by Hopson and Scally (1980b).

Look for the gains you have made
If gains are not immediately apparent, review the section again under 'Know yourself'. Have you had to cope with something with which you have not had to cope before? If so, this will have shed light on a new facet of your personality. What is it? Do you like it? Can you use it to any advantage in the future?

Quick check-list on client's transition coping skills

1. DOES HE KNOW WHAT HE WANTS FROM THE NEW SITUATION? If not, you must help him to define what he wants; getting him to be as specific as possible. He may not be used to thinking in terms of objectives. You will have to teach him. Write down options on a blackboard, flip chart, or a note book. Help him to evaluate the costs and benefits of different alternatives. Give him homework on this to be discussed at a future session.

2. DOES HE TEND TO BE PROACTIVE IN NEW SITUATIONS OR TO SIT BACK AND WAIT FOR THINGS TO HAPPEN? If he appears to be proactive, check out that it really is proactivity and not just acting to minimize anxiety, for instance jumping into something to alleviate ambiguity. If he is reactive you will need to point out that this will minimize his chances of getting what he wants and you will need to give him a task which is small enough for him to complete successfully (e.g. doing some homework) in order

to develop his confidence in the ability to make things happen. Give him a suitable book to read (see the section on self-help books) which is simultaneously instructive and a task to be completed.

3. DOES HE HAVE OTHER PEOPLE HE CAN RELY ON FOR HELP? Get him to specify who and what they can do for him. If he is deficient in help, steer him towards an appropriate self-help group.

4. HAS ANYTHING LIKE THIS HAPPENED TO HIM BEFORE? Look for links with previous experiences. Help him to discover what he did then which helped, and what in retrospect he would now choose to do differently.

5. HOW WELL CAN HE LOOK AFTER HIMSELF? Is he physically fit and eating sensibly? If not, advise him of the importance of this. Similarly, help him to discover the 'anchor points' in his life and persuade him to keep to a regular schedule. Encourage him to give himself a treat from time to time. Help him to identify when the low points are likely to be and to plan to minimize the impact of these: for example, always have something planned for Sunday when you are newly divorced.

6. CAN HE LET GO OF THE PAST? If not, encourage him to experience the grief and the anger as a way of discharging it and accepting that these feelings are normal and acceptable. They only become a problem if we can never let go of them.

7. CAN HE SET GOALS AND MAKE ACTION PLANS? Persuade him to begin thinking about specific goals as outlined under point 1. Help him define priorities, generate alternatives, and weigh them up.

8. CAN HE SEE POSSIBLE GAINS FROM HIS NEW SITUATION? Gently pressure him to begin to look for gains. The timing of this is vital. If he has not sufficiently let go of the past your intervention can appear heartless. Empathy is essential, but also you are trying to get him to see that however much he may not have chosen for an event to happen, that there will be something to gain.

Is it possible to train people to cope more effectively with transitions?

This has had to be empirically tested. Our general hypothesis is that people experiencing transitions will have similar tasks to cope with, namely, managing strain and dealing with cognitive tasks presented by the transition. We are assuming that to a considerable extent people's reactions to being in transition are learned as opposed to being inherited. To the extent that individuals' reactions are learned, we should be able to develop preventive, educative and re-educative strategies to help them manage their affairs and relationships more effectively at lower psychological costs, and derive greater benefits from the opportunity values embedded in every major transition.

This means that training programmes could be generated to help develop more effective coping styles for a number of people either (i) experiencing different transitional events, or who are anticipating transitional events, or (ii) as general training for any presently unknown future transitions.

We have already conducted a variety of transitions workshops in the UK, the USA and Scandinavia with populations including managers, trade unionists, counsellors, organization development specialists, social workers, case workers, teachers and youth workers. These have been primarily designed for participants who in turn will have to deal with individuals in transition. We believe that it is only possible to do such work when one has a clear understanding not just of a theoretical orientation, a collection of coping skills and teaching techniques, but also of one's own transitional experiences, skills and deficits, joys, confusion and sadness.

The final question is always 'why'? Why spend the energy, use the time, deplete the resources, all of which could be directed to something else?

We can only give our answer. A transition simultaneously carries the seeds of our yesterdays, the hopes and fears of our futures, and the pressing sensations of the present which is our confirmation of being alive. There is danger and opportunity, ecstasy and despair, development and stagnation, but above all there is movement. Nothing and no one stays the same. Nature abhors vacuums and stability. A stable state is merely a stopping point on a journey from one place to another. Stop too long and your journey is ended. Stay and enjoy but with the realization that more is to come. You may not be able to stop the journey, but you can fly the plane.

References

Adams, J.L. (1974)
Conceptual Blockbusting. San Francisco: Freeman.
Adams, J.D., Hayes, J. and Hopson, B. (1976)
Transition: Understanding and managing personal change. London: Martin Robertson.
Aspy, D.N. and Roebuck, F.N. (1977)
Kids Don't Learn From People They Don't Like. Amherst, Mass.: Human Resource Development Press.
Benson, H. (1977)
The Relaxation Response. London: Fountain Well Press.
Breckon, W. (1976)
You Are What You Eat. London: BBC Publications.
Campbell, D. (1974)
If You Don't Know Where You're Going You'll Probably End Up Somewhere Else. Hoddesdon, Herts: Argus Publications.

Carkhuff, R.R. (1974a)
   The Art of Problem Solving. Amherst, Mass.: Human
   Resource Development Press.
Carkhuff, R.R. (1974b)
   How To Help Yourself. Amherst, Mass.: Human Resource
   Development Press.
Carruthers, M. and Murray, A. (1977)
   F/40: Fitness on forty minutes a week. London: Futura.
Cooper, K. (1977)
   The New Aerobics. New York: Bantam.
Downing, G. (1972)
   The Massage Book. New York: Random House.
Ellis, A. and Harper, R. (1975)
   A New Guide to Rational Living. Hollywood, Ca:
   Wilshire Books.
Forbes, R. (1979)
   Life Stress. New York: Doubleday.
Health Education Council (1976)
   Look After Yourself. London: Health Education Council.
Holmes, T.H. and Rahe, R.H. (1967)
   The social readjustment rating scale. Journal of
   Psychosomatic Research, 11, 213-218.
Hopson, B. and Hough, P. (1973)
   Exercises in Personal and Career Development. Cambridge:
   Hobsons Press.
Hopson, B. and Scally, M. (1980a)
   How to cope with and gain from life transitions. In B.
   Hopson and M. Scally, Lifeskills Teaching Programmes
   No. 1. Leeds: Lifeskills Associates.
Hopson, B. and Scally, M. (1980b)
   Lifeskills Teaching: Education for self-empowerment.
   London: McGraw-Hill.
Howe, L.W. and Howe, M.M. (1975)
   Personalizing Education: Values clarification and
   beyond. New York: Hart.
Johnson. D.W. (1972)
   Reaching Out. Englewood Cliffs, NJ: Prentice-Hall.
Katz, M.R. (1968)
   Can computers make guidance decisions for students?
   College Board Review, No. 72.
Kirschenbaum, H. (1977)
   Advanced Value Clarification. La Jolla, Ca: University
   Associates.
Krantzler, M. (1973)
   Creative Divorce. New York: M. Evans.
Lamott, K. (1975)
   Escape from Stress. New York: Berkley.
Mahoney, M.J. and Mahoney, J. (1976)
   Permanent Weight Control. New York: W.W. Norton.
Maslow, A. (1968)
   Towards a Psychology of Being (2nd edn). New York: Van
   Nostrand.
Parkes, C. Murray (1972)

Bereavement: Studies of grief in adult life. London: Tavistock.

Royal Canadian Air Force (1978)
Physical Fitness. Harmondsworth: Penguin.

Russel, P. (1977)
The Transcendental Meditation Technique. London: Routledge & Kegan Paul.

Sharpe, R. and Lewis, D. (1977)
Thrive on Stress. London: Souvenir Press.

Simon, S. (1974)
Meeting Yourself Halfway. Hoddesdon, Herts: Argus Publications.

Simon, S., Howe, L.W. and Kirschenbaum, H. (1972)
Value Clarification. New York: Hart.

Toffler, A. (1970)
Future Shock. New York: Random House.

Watts, A.G. and Elsom, D. (1975)
Deciding. Cambridge: Hobsons Press.

Questions

1. What factors define a 'transition' or 'life event'? List the defining aspects of these experiences and relate these to six transitions which have occurred to you, or someone well known to you, over the last few months.

2. 'Stress damages, and often destroys people.' Is this inevitably true? Discuss.

3. Describe the changes in the individual which are likely to follow a serious event such as the loss of a spouse. Are these changes inevitable? What factors might be expected to influence the changes?

4. Consider the most stressful transition in your life so far. Use the questionnaire given in the chapter to evaluate how well you coped, and also to decide whether you could have dealt with it more efficiently.

5. Consider how a doctor can best help his patients to deal with important life stresses. List the most important steps to be taken.

6. To many doctors time is precious because of the volume of their clinical duties. In view of this, consider how the above discussion could be used to encourage patients to help other patients, or volunteers to help your patients.

7. What are the main steps which you could take to reduce patients' feelings of helplessness in the face of serious life changes such as redundancy, retirement or bereavement?

Annotated reading

Adams, J.D., Hayes, J. and Hopson, B. (1976) Transition: Understanding and managing personal change. London: Martin Robertson.

This is the first attempt to provide a conceptual framework to describe the psychological sequence of a transition. It is primarily a theoretical book, although some guidelines for the practitioner are available.

Hopson, B. and Scally, M. (1980) How to cope with and gain from life transitions. In B. Hopson and M. Scally, Lifeskills Teaching Programmes No. 1. Leeds: Lifeskills Associates.
This is for a classroom teacher of young people and consists of a series of carefully described group exercises to teach young people about transitions and how to cope more effectively with them.

Parkes, C. Murray (1975) Bereavement: Studies of grief in adult life. Harmondsworth: Penguin.
This book is about more than bereavement, although it is discussed at great length. Parkes generalizes from bereavement to other aspects of separation and loss in people's lives.

16

Pain
Colette Ray

Opening remarks
DAVID GRIFFITHS

The topic of pain, reviewed with impressive skill by Colette Ray, needs few words to justify its presence in a text intended for medical trainees. And yet, how many doctors are well acquainted with the extensive research on an aspect of experience which they have to cope with more frequently than any other professional group, with the possible exception of nurses?

The following review provides an overview of both theory and empirical findings. Pain is shown to be as much a psychological phenomenon as an organic entity. It can, for instance, be experienced in the absence of any physical pathology; it can also be absent when there is severe physical damage. When doctors refer to pain, they are referring to reports of its location, intensity, quality and fluctuation provided by their patients. Many of the findings discussed in this chapter suggest that such reports can be influenced by a wide range of psychological and social factors so that it is naïve to assume that they are determined exclusively by organic changes.

Another important part of the relevance of this chapter to doctors resides in Ray's conclusion that the doctor's behaviour can be an important determinant of the patient's experience of pain or 'pain behaviour'. To the extent that the doctor will often use reports of pain to determine diagnosis or evaluate progress, his own behaviour can actually influence the patient's report and contribute to errors in clinical judgements. Whilst an awareness of this possibility obviously does not provide any guarantee of its control, there are naturally many advantages in the doctor being well informed of the possible effects of his conduct.

The chapter also contains material which is as relevant to the researchers as it is to the clinician. 'Models' of pain, both psychological and organic, are considered at some length and the chapter provides a useful review of the many factors which can influence pain, and which can therefore be potentially useful in the control of pain. Pain control also receives Ray's attention and it is a tribute to her skill that she has produced a chapter which is as interesting and readable as it is clinically relevant.

What is pain?
COLETTE RAY

Pain may be defined as an unpleasant sensation which is focussed upon the body, and is often but not always associated with tissue damage. While it may be generally true that physical injury produces pain and that pain occurs as a result of injury, this is by no means always the case. There are many syndromes for which a somatic explanation is not easily available, and the source of the disorder can be attributed either to an abnormality in the way in which normal sensory inputs are processed or to psychological factors. Similarly, people may meet with injury but fail to experience pain as a consequence. This will sometimes happen if the damage occurs suddenly in a compelling situation, such as in battle or on the sportsfield, where attention and emotions are directed elsewhere. It is difficult, therefore, to determine in a priori terms when pain should and should not be experienced, and we must rely primarily upon the individual's own self-report to indicate whether it is present or absent and the intensity of his feelings. Given a similar degree of pain, however, any two people will react to this in different ways. They may vary in their evaluation of the symptom's significance; in their emotional reactions and expression of these; in the extent to which they complain verbally about the pain and the kinds of remedies they seek; and in the effect that the pain has upon their family, occupational and social activities. Such reactions to symptoms are distinct from the symptoms themselves and are generally referred to as 'illness behaviour' (Mechanic and Volkart, 1960). A number of factors will influence these behaviours, including the individual's personality and cultural background and the rewards and expectations associated with pain.

Personality and culture

It has been widely argued that pain will in some cases have a psychodynamic significance: that is, a psychological meaning and function. Freud regarded it as a common conversion syndrome, representing the transformation of a repressed drive into physical symptoms; the pain need not be created to achieve this end, but may be selected from a background of 'possible' pain as that which best fulfils a specific symbolic function. A state of emotional disturbance can also influence pain in a less specific way, if the person fails to recognize the true nature of the disturbance and seeks instead an explanation in terms of everyday physical symptoms which might otherwise be ignored. An individual who is generally over-preoccupied with physical concerns would be most likely to misattribute psychological distress to somatic symptoms in this manner. Engel (1959) has suggested that there is a 'pain prone personality', characterized by feelings of guilt which can be in part relieved by pain; other relevant characteristics he lists are a family history of violence and punishment, a personal history of suffering and defeat, a state of anger and hostility which is turned inwards rather than outwards and conflict over

sexual impulses. The immediate 'trigger' for pain in the
case of such a personality may be the loss of someone
valued, and several writers have seen physical pain as a
symbol of real or imagined loss.

People show consistency in their response to pain over
time, while there are distinct differences between people.
Generally speaking, women are more responsive than men, and
the young more than the old. The relationship between pain
responses and personality traits has been extensively
studied, particularly with respect to neuroticism and
extraversion. There is some tendency for the former to be
related to pain proneness, but many inconsistent findings
have been obtained both in the laboratory and in natural
settings. Extraverts under some conditions tolerate pain
better than introverts, but may in some situations report
more pain because of a greater readiness to brave the possibility of social disapproval. Many studies have looked
at pain in psychiatric patients, and at the personality
profiles of pain patients compared with those of control
samples. A relatively high incidence of pain is found in
psychiatric groups and pain patients have a more 'neurotic'
profile than control groups (see Sternbach, 1974). It is,
however, unclear to what extent personality disturbance
predisposes to pain and to what extent the experience of
pain causes emotional difficulties. The relative importance
of these two different effects will depend upon whether the
context is that of psychiatric patients who experience pain,
or pain patients without a psychiatric history; in the former case maladjustment is likely to give rise to physical
pain rather than the reverse, while in the latter emotional
difficulties will generally be a consequence, rather than a
cause, of pain.

Responses to pain differ not only between individuals
and groups within a society, but also between cultures. All
groups develop norms or expectations of how one should perceive and react to any particular situation, and individuals
will adopt these to the extent that they are part of or
identify with the group. Some norms are prescriptive: that
is, there is a certain pressure upon the individual to
conform with expectations in this respect, and deviation
will meet with disapproval. An example of such a norm relevant to pain behaviour would be the expectation that one
should not evade one's obligations by faking or 'malinger-
ing'. Descriptive norms, in contrast, do not imply an obligation to conform, but merely describe the behaviour
which is characteristic or typical of the group. Cultural
stereotypes suggest the existence of differences between
nationalities in their expression of pain, and there is
empirical evidence for such differences. Zborowski (1969)
studied a group of American male patients and compared
reactions for those of Jewish, Irish, Italian and Old
American descent. Both Old Americans and Irish Americans
were inhibited in the expression of pain, while the Italians
and Jewish patients were more reactive. These latter groups

both sought to draw attention to their pain by this expressive behaviour, but their underlying aims were different. The Italians were primarily concerned with obtaining relief from pain, while for the Jewish patients the primary concern was to discover the cause of the symptom. These cultural differences appear quite reliable, since Zborowski's findings were supported by those of a study in which the responses of similar groups were compared, but in a very different laboratory setting (Sternbach and Tursky, 1965).

Rewards and expectations

Learning theorists make a distinction between a respondent behaviour which is closely linked with the occurrence of a particular stimulus or situation and does not require any other support for its establishment or maintenance, and an operant behaviour which is not directly elicited by the stimulus but can become associated with it given appropriate conditions of reinforcement. Reinforcement is defined as any event which strengthens a behaviour; rewards will generally operate as reinforcers, as will the termination of an aversive stimulus, while punishment generally weakens behaviour. This kind of analysis may be applied to pain behaviour (Fordyce et al, 1968). We can assume that certain responses to pain will be directly elicited by the experience, withdrawal or crying for example, while others may be prompted by the experience but depend effectively upon the outcomes which they produce. An individual may thus adopt and maintain a number of pain behaviours because they bring rewards such as sympathy and nurturance, and enable him to avoid activities or obligations which he finds unpleasant.

Behaviour will not only be influenced by the rewards associated with different kinds of response, but also by an awareness of how other people react in a similar situation. The experience of pain may involve considerable uncertainty, and when faced with uncertainty people often look to others as guides to determine both how the experience should be interpreted and the norms governing behaviour in that situation. This process has been described as one of 'social comparison' (Festinger, 1954). We compare our own interpretations and reactions with those of others to decide whether or not they are valid or appropriate in the circumstances, and may seek a lead from another before making our own interpretation and response. Thus the presence of a calm individual to act as a model may reduce the response to a painful stimulus, and the presence of one who appears distressed may intensify the response. Such effects have been demonstrated in the laboratory, in studies where the experimenter recruits a confederate who supposedly undergoes electric shocks similar to those to which the subject is indeed exposed, and instructs him to react to these with or without expression of pain and distress. Both 'tolerant' and 'intolerant' models in such studies can change subjects' reports of the intensity of the pain they experience and their willingness to tolerate shocks of various intensities.

Similar effects can be observed in clinical settings; patients with problems or treatments in common will observe each other, develop expectations about pain intensity and the course of recovery, and learn the norms of pain expression within that group. Modelling processes will occur within the family but over a longer period of time. Children's reactions to pain will be influenced by their observations of their parents' behaviour, and the child whose parents focus upon his or their own pain symptoms and react strongly to these may come to react in the same way. This effect would initially operate with respect to specific situations but could then generalize to pain behaviour in general.

Theory and research

Early theories regarded pain as arising from the relatively direct transmission of signals from 'nociceptors' to pain centres in the brain, and the receptors, pathways and centres involved were thought to be specific to pain. The assumption of specificity does not, however, seem justified, and this simple model cannot account for many common pain phenomena, including the known effects of psychological factors such as experience, motivation, attention and emotionality. A recent theory which has attracted much interest is the gate-control theory (see Melzack, 1973). The gate referred to is a hypothetical mechanism at the level of the spinal cord, which is assumed to modulate signals from the periphery before they are centrally processed. It is suggested that this mechanism is situated in the substantia gelatinosa and has its effect by inhibiting or facilitating the transmission of signals from the dorsal horns to the adrenolateral pathways of the spinal cord. Activity in peripheral fibres will not only influence the transmission of pain signals directly but also affects the operation of the gate, as can central brain processes. Three distinct psychological dimensions of the pain experience have been related to these neurophysiological concepts. These are the sensory-discriminative, the motivational-affective and the cognitive-evaluative dimensions respectively. The first is associated with the rapidly conducting spinal systems projecting to the thalamus, the second with reticular and limbic structures, and the third with neocortical processes. The model is a complex and dynamic one, and can hence explain many diverse phenomena.

Some areas of research focus upon physiological aspects of pain, while others are more directly concerned with identifying those factors which can modify the experience. These investigations are carried out both in laboratory and in clinical settings. Experimental laboratory studies may be criticized on the grounds that the kinds of pain that can be induced and the conditions in which it is experienced are rather different from those that apply under natural conditions. They do, however, allow the researcher to control and monitor carefully the variables under study. Various methods

353

of inducing pain have been developed for this purpose. These
include application of heat or pressure; administration of
electric shocks; the cold pressor test for which the subject
has to immerse his hand in ice-cold water; and the sub-
maximal tourniquet technique which produces ischaemic pain.
Using such methods experimenters can study the effects of
various manipulations upon pain measures such as the
threshold, or the point at which the subject first reports
pain, and tolerance level or the point at which he requests
that the painful stimulus be terminated. Threshold and
tolerance levels are not appropriate for use in the context
of naturally occurring pain, and measures in clinical situations are primarily concerned with the assessment of
subjective intensity. Estimates of this may be obtained by
asking the patient to rate the symptom on a scale which is
gradated by numbers or by verbal descriptions representing
different levels of pain from mild to severe. The experience
of pain does, however, vary in quality as well as in degree.
Melzack and Torgerson (1971) have thus developed a questionnaire which enables patients to describe their symptoms
in terms of a wide range of adjectives such as sharp, tugging, aching, piercing, nagging and so on. These descriptions can be related to the three dimensions of pain
described earlier.

Somatic therapies

The chemical agents used in the treatment of pain are
numerous and varied in their nature. They include, first,
narcotic drugs such as opium, morphine and their deriva-
tives; these act centrally and produce both pain relief and
a state of tranquillity. There is, however, a risk of establishing a dependency and this obviously places constraints
on the way in which they may be employed. A second category
comprises the psychotropic drugs or minor tranquillizers and
anti-depressants; these are directed at the reduction of
emotional distress rather than the pain experience per se.
Third, there are agents which act peripherally and not
centrally; examples are the salicyclates and analine deriva-
tives, including aspirin and phenacetin. These have anti-
pyretic and anti-inflammatory properties which can reduce
pain, although not as effectively as the narcotic agents.
They can have physical side effects if taken in large
quantities or over long periods of time. Recent developments in the study of the brain's chemistry may provide new
directions in the psychopharmacological treatment of pain.
Opiate-binding sites have been discovered in the dorsal
horns and in the central nervous system, and there is much
interest currently in substances such as encephalin and the
endomorphins which are naturally occurring morphine-like
peptides. It seems that morphine and similar substances may
produce their effects by mimicking the action of these
endogenous peptides. However, we are still far from fully
understanding the properties of these compounds and the way
in which they interact with the complex anatomical
structures involved in the transmission of pain.

In many cases chemical therapies provide insufficient relief, or cannot be used in the quantities required for adequate relief because of their side effects, and other forms of physical treatment may then be demanded. Surgical procedures designed to interrupt the nervous system's transmission of pain signals have been carried out at many different sites from the periphery to the centre, but the general effectiveness of such procedures is disappointing. There have been some encouraging results, but in many cases where relief is obtained it may only be temporary. This outcome, in the context of the irreversibility of the procedures employed, has focussed attention on less drastic forms of treatment. One of these is to 'block' sensory input by injecting alcohol or a local anaesthetic agent such as procaine into the nerve root. Another is to increase this input by peripheral stimulation. This practice is conceptually similar to the 'counter-irritation techniques' that have been commonly used throughout history. These have included hot fomentations, vigorous massage, and the raising of blisters and dry cupping. For the latter a cupping glass, with the air partly withdrawn from it by means of an air pump or flame, was drawn across the skin, thus raising a painful red weal. Both nerve blocks and peripheral stimulation can be very effective in the treatment of appropriate syndromes. Not only may they have an immediate effect through restoring normal sensory inputs, but they can disrupt abnormal patterns of central nervous system activity and thus permanently affect the way in which pain is processed.

A method that may comprise important psychological as well as physical factors is acupuncture. This has only recently been applied to the control of pain and is most often used in the context of surgery. The procedure involves inserting needles into one or several skin areas, and these needles are then stimulated either manually or electrically. The successes claimed may be in part attributable to effects associated with peripheral stimulation, but Chaves and Barber (1974) have proposed a number of psychological bases for its apparent efficacy. These include the fact that a low level of anxiety is looked for in those selected for treatment by this method; the expectation among these patients that the experience will be pain free; a thorough preparation before surgery with a strong suggestion of pain relief, and exposure to models who have successfully undergone the experience; and the distractions associated with the general procedure which should draw attention away from the operation itself. These authors also suggest that the pain of surgery may be generally exaggerated, and point out that acupuncture is not generally used in isolation but in combination with sedatives and analgesics. The apparent success of acupuncture may then depend upon the existence of such physical and psychological supports, but as yet the relative contribution of these factors and of any direct somatic effects of the technique is unknown.

Psychological approaches to therapy

We cannot have direct access to another's experience and must make inferences about this on the basis of overt behaviours, such as motor activity, autonomic reactions, verbal descriptions, and so forth. Some psychologists argue from this that any distinction between experience and behaviour will be unproductive, and that the psychological analysis of pain and treatments for its relief should be directed at the behavioural level (Fordyce et al, 1973). With respect to therapy, typical goals would then be the reduction of help-seeking and dependent behaviour, a decrease in the medications taken, and an increase in physical and social activity. The therapist would first identify those behaviours thought to be undesirable within this framework, and would then seek the co-operation of the individual's family and friends in withdrawing the presumably rewarding conditions which serve to maintain these. For example, they might be advised to meet unreasonable requests for assistance with disapproval and reluctance, and to respond to legitimate demands or complaints helpfully but without the accompanying expressions of sympathy and concern which serve to reinforce these. At the same time, alternative desirable behaviours would be met with attention, approval and encouragement. This approach is most obviously appropriate where changes have occurred as a response to suffering, and have been maintained in spite of the removal of the pain source because they are found to fulfil other needs. It may also help in cases where the underlying condition cannot be alleviated, in this context by motivating the individual to lead as normal a life as possible in the circumstances, and to avoid the temptation of making a 'career of suffering'. A behavioural approach may not alter the intensity of the pain experienced, and pain may even intensify during therapy as physical activity increases. Nevertheless, a change at this level can have a positive impact on emotional adjustment and can improve the general quality of life for both the individual and his family.

Other psychological therapies attempt to modify the underlying experience of pain rather than the behaviours associated with this. One such approach is to provide training in the use of cognitive strategies which either direct attention away from pain or restructure the experience so that it is no longer distressing. The sufferer may be instructed to counter the pain when it occurs by attending to distractions in the environment rather than to his sensations, or by constructing fantasies and concentrating on thoughts which are incompatible with these. He may, alternatively, be advised to acknowledge the painful sensations but to reinterpret them in imagination as something less worrying or take a 'clinical' attitude which distances him emotionally. There have been many attempts to study the effectiveness of these strategies in laboratory experiments, but with suprisingly inconsistent results. One reason for the failure of some studies to demonstrate a positive effect may be the difficulty of ensuring that subjects follow the instructions faithfully. Those in the experimental group will sometimes reject the strategy suggested to them and substitute their own, while the control group may spontaneously employ strategies even though not instructed to do so (Scott, 1978). The very nature of the problem suggests that cognitive strategies in general play an important role in coping with pain, but it presents considerable methodological difficulties in establishing the effectiveness of a given strategy, either in absolute terms or in comparison with another strategy.

A third clearly psychological approach to pain therapy is that of hypnosis. Here the aim is to manipulate the experience directly by means of suggestion. There has been much discussion about the nature of hypnosis. Some have thought of it as a special state of consciousness or trance which is distinct from other experiences, but others have argued that it is an example of complete or almost complete absorption in a particular role and conformity with the expectations associated with this (Sarbin and Anderson, 1964). The subject has faith in the hypnotist's power to influence him, and is prepared to accept such influence to the extent that not only his outward behaviour but also his subjective experience will be modified. Hypnotic suggestion has been used for pain relief in surgery, dentistry, terminal care and obstetrics (Hilgard and Hilgard, 1975). Verbal reports of pain are affected by hypnosis, but involuntary physiological responses such as heart rate or galvanic skin responses are not generally affected. This indicates that there is still some sense in which the pain is present, and it has been suggested that the absence of the subjective experience of pain under hypnosis is a form of dissociation, with pain being processed at a preconscious, but not at a conscious, level. In one study subjects were trained to make two reports of pain simultaneously, one using a key press and another by verbal description, and the results supported the dissociation hypothesis. The key press response indicated more pain than the verbal report, although less pain than that reported verbally under comparable conditions but in a normal 'waking' state.

Hypnosis is not itself a means of preventing or alleviating pain, but a method for increasing the potency of the suggestion of analgesia made to the subject while in this state. Suggestion can have a powerful effect outside the context of hypnosis merely by creating the expectation of pain relief, and this is the basis of the well-known placebo effect. A placebo drug is a neutral substance which has a positive influence because of the expectations created by the context in which it is administered, and all treatments can be assumed to have some placebo element given that the subject is aware of their intended purpose. Substances which are known to be pharmacologically inert are thus used for comparison purposes in drug trials, rather than no treatment, in order to control for the anticipation of relief and provide a true baseline for evaluating the active and

specific influence of the drug on trial. It is estimated
that placebo treatments can alleviate surgical pain in about
one-third of patients; laboratory studies produce lower
estimates, but a significant proportion of subjects are
still found to benefit. The effectiveness of a placebo will
vary with the situation in which it is administered and with
the status and manner of the person who administers it,
since effectiveness will depend on expectations and the
latter will be influenced by these factors. It will vary
also with the individual to whom it is administered, and
people can be grouped as either 'reactors' or 'nonreactors';
the former are not only more responsive to placebos, but are
less differentially responsive to active drugs. While from a
methodological viewpoint placebo effects may often be regarded as 'mock' effects for which controls must be introduced,
from an applied perspective it is evident that the patient's
expectations can be construed as powerful and legitimate
agents of change. Their general influence will be added to
that produced by the specific nature of any physical or
psychological manipulation which is, with the patient's
awareness, diverted at the treatment of pain, and can
significantly enhance the therapeutic impact of these.

Psychological preparation for pain

The occurrence of pain may sometimes be anticipated before
the event: for example, if a patient is scheduled for an
unpleasant medical examination. Many of the treatments referred to earlier may be used as a form of preparation for
a painful experience as distinct from an agent for relief
once pain has occurred, but particular attention has recently been given to psychological preparation with an
emphasis on those forms which enhance 'cognitive control'.
These involve the provision of information which enables the
individual to predict accurately what will happen in the
situation and the nature of his experience, and instructions
in strategies which may be employed to maximize the chances
of successful coping. A number of laboratory studies have
investigated the effect of the former, 'informational control', and have found that the stressfulness of electric
shock and similarly noxious stimuli is reduced if subjects
are made aware in advance of the timing and intensity of
these and the fact that there is no danger of actual injury. The potential of the second kind of manipulation,
'strategic control', is demonstrated by the work of Turk
(1978) who has developed a procedure for enhancing subjects'
ability to control their response to painful stimuli, hence
increasing their resistance to stress and tolerance for
pain. The training procedure is quite complex. First, the
subjects are given general instruction in the nature of
pain; it is not considered essential that the explanation
should be theoretically valid, but merely that it should
provide a framework within which the experience may be
conceptualized and the recommendations for coping presented. In the second stage of the procedure the subjects are
trained to relax physically and mentally, and are provided

with a selection of varied cognitive strategies with which
to confront and control the pain. These strategies are
similar to those described earlier, comprising methods both
for redirecting attention and reinterpreting the experience.
In this context, however, they are presented as a 'package'
from which the subjects will select those suited to their
personal needs. At this stage they will also be asked to
generate feedback statements that can later be used to
foster a feeling of control while in the painful situation
and provide self reinforcement. The final stage is that of
rehearsal, where the subjects imagine the painful situation
and their reactions, and subsequently play the role of a
teacher instructing someone else in the procedure. This
training has been found to increase pain endurance considerably in a cold pressor task. Subjects were able to extend
the time during which they kept their hand in ice-cold water
by 75 per cent, from before to after training, and this compared with a 10 per cent improvement for a 'placebo' group
who had been given attention and encouragement but no instruction in specific cognitive techniques. The experimental
group also showed a significant decrease in pain ratings.

It might be argued that many of the laboratory studies
that have investigated informational control have involved
highly structured and artificial tasks, and that the results
might not be applicable to patients' experiences in clinical
settings. It might also be pointed out that the cognitive
training described above is highly complex; it has several
components and stages and is orientated towards the particular personality and needs of each individual. It thus
requires some investment of time and effort on the part of
both the trainer and trainee, and such elaborate procedures
might not be practicable in most naturally occurring situations. Similar, positive effects of preparation have,
however, been found both under hospital conditions and in
laboratory studies which have simulated these closely in
terms of the nature of the painful procedures employed and
the complexity of the preparation attempted.

Some of the most influential studies carried out in this
area have been those conducted by Johnson and her colleagues
(Johnson, 1975). In one of the first of these, male subjects
were exposed to ischaemic pain in the laboratory and were
either told what physical sensations they might expect as a
result of the procedure, or the procedure itself was described without elaborating the sensations associated with
it. It was found that the former preparation reduced distress, but the latter was ineffective in comparison with
a control group. The intensity of the sensations experienced
by the two information groups was the same, and the results
could not be accounted for by group differences in either
the degree of attention paid to these sensations or the
anticipation of possible harm. It seemed, then, that this
effect must have been due to the expectations held by subjects about what they were to experience, with more accurate
expectations being associated with lower levels of distress.
Further studies have used patients undergoing a variety of

stressful medical examinations or treatments, including gastroendoscopy, cast removal and gynaecological examination. These too point to the conclusion that providing information about what to expect reduces stress and unpleasantness, especially if this focusses upon what the subject will experience rather than the objective nature of the procedure.

The effects of psychological preparation have also been extensively studied within the context of surgery. This will be a stressful experience for most patients, and the anticipation and experience of pain will contribute to this distress. The kinds of preparation attempted in these studies have varied quite widely. Most have taken a broad approach, providing information about procedures and sensations, offering reassurance and emotional support and advising on how to cope with physical discomfort and difficulty. The effects of these interventions are consistently positive, with both reductions in subjective distress and improvement in post-operative measures of recovery. Two such studies which have focussed on pain are those of Egbert and colleagues (1964) and Hayward (1975). Wherever preparation comprises a number of different components it is difficult to determine which of these are responsible or necessary for the effectiveness of the whole. Some research has thus attempted to isolate and compare different kinds of preparation. It seems, for example, that providing instructions on how to cope with physical difficulties is not in itself very helpful, but is beneficial when presented against a background of accurate expectations (Johnson et al, 1978). Only one study has attempted any detailed training in cognitive strategies and looked systematically at the impact of this training. Langer and colleagues (1975) encouraged the development of coping devices, such as the reappraisal of threatening events, reassuring self-talk and selective attention, and showed a significant and independent effect of this instruction.

There is, then, evidence from a number of studies that the distress associated with an unpleasant procedure can be reduced by making the individual aware of what this involves from his point of view. It is, however, important to recognize that such information can only be expected to have a beneficial effect if it is presented in a reassuring way: creating an expectation of pain, whether accurate or not, can of course alarm the patient and counteract any positive effects of informational control. Instructions or training which help the individual to cope with physical or psychological stresses also have a role in the preparation for pain, and will enhance the effects of accurate expectations.

Final comments

The experience of pain depends upon a complex signalling system whose functions are determined by neurophysiological and biochemical influences which are not yet understood but are acted upon by physical and psychological factors of which we have some knowledge. These influences are many and varied, and provide a relatively broad scope for treatment. Some cases may call for one form of therapy rather than another, but for many a combination of physical and psychological approaches will present the most productive strategy.

A number of writers have called attention to the importance of the doctor-patient relationship in the treatment of pain. Szasz (1968) and Sternbach (1974) have pointed to motives which can cause the latter to resist abandoning his symptoms, and show how the physician may play a complementary role which facilitates these efforts: the patient who wishes to maintain his invalid status will have this claim effectively legitimized by the doctor who continues to treat him as though he were ill. Another common theme of doctor-patient interaction is an attempt by the patient to place responsibility for the outcome of treatment on the physician's shoulders, with the latter accepting this responsibility because of an eagerness to help and a reluctance to admit to the limitations of his professional skill. Such attitudes have been criticized as maladaptive. It has been argued that doctors should discourage passivity and helplessness, and cultivate a co-operative and problem-orientated relationship in which the patient takes an active role. This will involve confronting any undesirable attitudes he holds towards the pain, and emphasizing that the outcome of treatment will be determined as much by his own efforts as by what can be done for him. Sympathy and reassurance can reinforce pain behaviour and can foster a dependency which discourages self-help and the development of strategies for coping.

On the other hand, the total care of the pain patient should be concerned not only with the relief of pain but also with the psychological stress to which this suffering can give rise. The danger of emotionally isolating the patient is as real as that of over-protecting him. The attitude of family, friends and even professional helpers may be complex and emotionally charged, reflecting both an altruistic concern for the victim's welfare and personal fears and conflicts associated with suffering. The distress of the person in pain will in itself be distressing, particularly where it seems that there is little hope of providing immediate relief, and this can prompt either physical withdrawal or psychological distancing to prevent or defend against emotional upset. Moreover, pain is greatly feared, both for its own sake and because of its association with illness, injury and death, and contact with suffering can elicit anxiety about one's own vulnerability in this respect. This, too, can lead to avoidance or a reluctance to become practically and emotionally involved. Finally, while suffering is often unmerited, the recognition of this is disquieting, since it reminds us of the injustice of the world and our powerlessness in the face of events. Experimental studies have found that blameless victims are sometimes perceived as responsible for their fate, or are derogated so that this fate appears to be less unjust. We can predict from these studies that feelings towards the pain victim in real life might sometimes have a hostile element, and bear the implication that he is in some way to blame for his situation whether or not this is the case.

Few would dispute the importance of emotional support in alleviating immediate distress, and the availability of social support is a key factor in protecting an individual under stress from long-term maladjustment. It is therefore important to adopt a balanced approach in the care and management of the person in pain, helping him to help himself while at the same time providing the sympathy and reassurance to reduce anxiety and prevent despair.

References

Chaves, J.F. and Barber, T.X. (1974)
Acupuncture analgesia: a six factor theory. Psychoenergetic Systems, 1, 11-21.

Egbert, L.D., Battit, G.E., Welch, C.E. and Bartlett, M.K. (1964)
Reduction of post-operative pain by encouragement and instruction of patients. New England Journal of Medicine, 270, 825-827.

Engel, G.L. (1959)
'Psychogenic pain' and the pain prone patient. American Journal of Medicine, 26, 899-918.

Festinger, L.A. (1954)
Theory of social comparison processes. Human Relations, 7, 117-140.

Fordyce, W.E., Fowler, R.S. Jr, Lehmann, J.F. and de Lateur, B.J. (1968)
Some implications of learning in problems of chronic pain. Journal of Chronic Diseases, 21, 179-190.

Fordyce, W.E., Fowler, R.S. Jr, Lehmann, J.F., de Lateur, B.J., Sand, P.L. and Trieschmann, R.B. (1973)
Operant conditioning in the treatment of chronic pain. Archives of Physical Medicine and Rehabilitation, 54, 399-408.

Hayward, J.C. (1975)
Information: A prescription against pain. London: Royal College of Nursing.

Hilgard, E.L. and Hilgard, J.R. (1975)
Hypnosis in the Relief of Pain. Los Altos: Kaufmann.

Johnson, J.E. (1975)
Stress reduction through sensation information. In I. G. Sarason and C.D. Spielberger (eds), Stress and Anxiety: Volume II. Washington, DC: Hemisphere.

Johnson, J.E., Rice, V.H., Fuller, S.S. and Endress, M.P. (1978)
Sensory information, instruction in a coping strategy, and recovery from surgery. Research in Nursing and Health, 1, 4-17.

Langer, E.L., Janis, I.J. and Wolfer, J.A. (1975)
Reduction of psychological stress in surgical patients. Journal of Experimental Social Psychology, 11, 155-165.

Mechanic, D. and Volkart, E.H. (1960)
Illness behaviour and medical diagnosis. Journal of
Health and Human Behaviour, 1, 86-94.

Melzack, R. (1973)
The Puzzle of Pain. Harmondsworth: Penguin.

Melzack, R. and Torgerson, W.S. (1971)
On the language of pain. Anaesthesiology, 34, 50-59.

Sarbin, T.R. and Anderson, M.L. (1964)
Role-theoretical analysis of hypnotic behavior. In J.
Gordon (ed.), Handbook of Hypnosis. New York:
Macmillan.

Scott, D.S. (1978)
Experimenter-suggested cognitions and pain control:
problem of spontaneous strategies. Psychological
Reports, 43, 156-158.

Sternbach, R.A. (1974)
Pain Patients: Traits and treatment. New York: Academic
Press.

Sternbach, R.A. and Tursky, B. (1965)
Ethnic differences among housewives in psychophysical
and skin potential responses to electric shock.
Psychophysiology, 1, 241-246.

Szasz, T.S. (1968)
The psychology of persistent pain: a portrait of l'homme
douloureux. In A. Soulairac, J. Cahn and J. Charpentier
(eds), Pain. New York: Academic Press.

Turk, D.C. (1978)
Application of coping-skills training to the treatment
of pain. In I.G. Sarason and C.D. Spielberger (eds),
Stress and Anxiety: Volume V. Washington, DC:
Hemisphere.

Zborowski, M. (1969)
People in Pain. San Francisco: Jossey-Bass.

Questions

1. What cues might we use in determining whether a person
   is in pain and the degree of pain experienced?
2. Describe the range of chemical and physical therapies
   available for the treatment of pain.
3. Can pain be treated using psychological methods alone?
4. Write a short essay on the use of hypnosis and
   acupuncture in the treatment of pain.
5. What is a placebo effect? What role can it play in the
   treatment of pain?
6. How do factors such as personality and culture influence
   pain behaviour?
7. In what sense can it be said that pain is 'learned'?
8. What criteria might be employed in selecting one form
   of pain treatment rather than another?
9. What psychological preparation would you recommend for
   an adult who has to undergo an unpleasant medical
   examination or treatment?
10. What psychological preparation would you recommend for
    a child who has to undergo an unpleasant medical
    examination or treatment?

11. Discuss the possible disadvantages of being either too 'soft' or too 'hard' in one's attitude toward the pain patient.
12. Does pain have a biological function?
13. Describe and discuss examples of cases where pain can occur in the absence of physical injury.
14. Describe and discuss examples of situations in which injury may be sustained without a corresponding experience of pain.
15. Write an essay on 'The definition of pain'.
16. How important is an understanding of the neurophysiological and chemical mechanisms underlying pain for its effective treatment?
17. Write an essay on the experimental induction of pain. What methods have been used and to what extent are they justified?
18. Critically assess the relevance of experimental laboratory research on pain for the understanding and treatment of pain in real-life settings.
19. Compare and contrast two or more methods for measuring pain.

Annotated reading

Melzack, R. (1973) The Puzzle of Pain. Harmondsworth: Penguin.

Sternbach, R.A. (1974) Pain Patients: Traits and treatment. New York: Academic Press.
> Both of these books provide a broad introduction to physiological, psychological and social aspects of pain and its treatment.

Weisenberg, M. and Tursky, B. (eds) (1976) Pain: New perspectives in therapy and research. London: Plenum.

Sternbach, R.A. (ed.) (1976) The Psychology of Pain. New York: Raven.
> These are collections of papers, recommended for students who wish to consider issues and controversies within the area in greater detail than that provided by the introductory texts.

McCaffery, M. (1972) Nursing Management of the Patient with Pain. Philadelphia: Lippincott.

Fagerhaugh, S. and Strauss, A. (1977) Pain Management: Staff-patient interaction. Reading, Mass.: Addison-Wesley.

Hayward, J.C. (1975) Information: A prescription against pain. Royal College of Nursing.
> These three books focus applied aspects on pain, relating theoretical knowledge to problems of patient care. The text by J. C. Hayward describes a study concerned with the psychological preparation of surgical patients.

17

Psychopathology
D. A. Shapiro

Opening remarks
DAVID GRIFFITHS

Since as many as 20 per cent of hospital beds in the UK are occupied by patients suffering from psychological disorders, and surveys of general practice reveal that psychological problems constitute very large proportions of the GP's caseload, a discussion of psychopathology deserves a prominent position in any book on the relevance of psychology to medicine. To many doctors, however, psychopathology continues to be almost (if not completely) synonymous with psychoanalysis, in spite of the major developments in theory and practice which have occurred during the last two decades. One of the implications of David Shapiro's chapter is that Freudian theory has been overtaken and surpassed by a number of other theoretical models and, indeed, psychoanalysis takes up a very small part of the review.

Freudian theory has been supplanted by a number of both medical and psychological models, and Shapiro's overall aims are to describe and evaluate the contribution of these models to the explanation of psychological disorder. Though the treatment of disordered behaviour is not taken up in any detail, his review of theories has many implications for treatment, since each of the models reviewed has been the basis for a distinctive approach to therapy.

Doctors will naturally be most acquainted in the so-called 'medical' model, and this approach is evaluated at some length. Shapiro's conclusion is, however, that the medical model is not entirely satisfactory, and he continues to examine a number of psychological alternatives. These include the statistical model, which views disordered behaviour as the extreme of a continuum of behaviour with the normal defined by the most frequent; the learning theory model, concerned with the contribution of learning to the causation and maintenance of abnormal behaviours; the cognitive model, which focusses on the contribution of perceptions, attitudes and beliefs to psychopathology; and the socio-cultural model, which views psychological disorder as a function of the social environment rather than any pathology, either psychological or organic, within the individual.

Shapiro's conclusion is that no single model is sufficient to explain everything, partly because 'answers are inevitably complex, involving a large number of interacting factors'. This conclusion suggests that doctors who wish to specialize in the assessment and treatment of psychopathological conditions have a formidable task to master. To facilitate their progress, this chapter is a comprehensive and competent introduction to the topic of psychological disorder.

Introduction
D. A. SHAPIRO

'Psychopathology', literally defined, is the study of disease of the mind. The use of this term reflects our society's predominant approach to understanding and dealing with individuals manifesting problematic and distressing behaviour and experience. They are diagnosed and treated as patients by medical specialists (psychiatrists). Many psychologists are critical of this approach, and have attempted to provide alternatives. The main aim of this chapter is to present the contributions of a distinctly psychological approach to the problems of behaviour disorder. This offers considerable insights and has become an essential component of present day scientific and professional work in this field. On the other hand, it has by no means supplanted the medical approach. In particular, the descriptive classification of behaviour disorders developed by psychiatrists remains a useful way of introducing the enormous range and variety of disorders we need to consider.

The varieties of psychopathology

Although some variation exists in terminology and classification between different psychiatric texts and diagnostic practices, the broad outline of psychiatric classification can be summarized as in table 1. Of the four major categories, the NEUROSES are generally the least severe, in that the personality and perceptions of reality are fundamentally intact. The main characteristic uniting these disorders is the presence of anxiety or its presumed effects. Anxiety states are characterized by pervasive or free-floating anxiety, without any immediately obvious object or cause. Associated with this are such symptoms as palpitations, breathlessness, and tiredness. PHOBIAS are intense fears of objects or situations which do not objectively present any real danger of harm. The individual avoids the phobic situation and may suffer considerable hardship and inconvenience on account of this. In OBSESSIVE-COMPULSIVE DISORDERS, the individual is preoccupied with intrusive thoughts about some imaginary danger, and experiences overwhelming urges to act to overcome this; for example, a fear of spreading contamination may accompany a compulsion to wash the hands for an hour or more to ensure perfect cleanliness. A CONVERSION REACTION involves a paralysis, lack of sensation or sensory disturbance, without any physical disease process to explain it. In NEUROTIC DEPRESSION the individual experiences prolonged and very deep sadness, seemingly disproportionate to the circumstances, although it may be triggered by some external event such as the loss of a loved one.

Table 1

Major category	Neuroses (milder disturbances)				
Illustrative syndromes	Anxiety state	Obsessive-compulsive disorders	Phobias	Conversion reactions	Neurotic depression
Characteristic symptoms	Palpitation, tires easily, breathlessness, nervousness anxiety	Intrusive thoughts, urges to acts or rituals	Irrational fears of specific objects or situations	Physical symptoms, lacking organic cause	Hopelessness dejection

Major category	Psychoses (severe Non-organic disturbances		Personality disorders (antisocial disturbances)	Organic syndromes		
Illustrative syndromes	Affective disorders	Schizophrenia	Psychopathic personality	Alcoholism and drug dependence	Epilepsy	Severe mental handicap
Characteristic symptoms	Disturbances of mood, energy and activity patterns	Reality distortion, social withdrawal, disorganization of thought, perception and emotion	Lack of conscience	Physical or psychological dependence	Increased susceptibility to convulsions	Extremely low intelligence, social impairments

The second major group of disorders listed in table 1 is that of the PSYCHOSES. These are severe deficits in the individual's capacity to meet the ordinary demands of life, and are associated with such gross impairments in perception, memory and language that the individual's contact with reality is lost. However, these disorders are not associated with obvious disease of the brain, and so cannot be explained in straightforwardly biomedical terms. The two most important categories are SCHIZOPHRENIA and AFFECTIVE PSYCHOSIS. Schizophrenic symptoms are extremely varied, and most people receiving this diagnosis only show some of them. thought disorders include disturbances of its FORM (speech rendered incomprehensible through disorganization of ideas, such as fragmentation, non sequiturs and invented words or neologisms) and disturbances of its content, in unshakeable, false beliefs known as delusions. For example, many schizophrenics believe that others are plotting against them (delusions of persecution) or that they have special powers (delusions of grandeur). Perceptual and attentional symptoms of schizophrenia include environment, such as 'voices' heard speaking to the patient. The individual may also find it very difficult to attend to what is going on around him. motor disturbances in schizophrenia include strange grimaces or gestures, wild, flailing excitability, and (at the opposite extreme) prolonged immobility (catatonia). Affective or mood disturbances in schizophrenia range from lack of emotional responsiveness (flattened affect) to out of context responses (inappropriate affect). Schizophrenic patients are often very withdrawn and out of contact with the world around them, immersed in the private inner world of their disordered experiences.

Affective psychosis is a severely disabling disturbance of mood and feeling. There may be delusions, notably concerning the individual's bodily state, and rigidly held beliefs in the individual's unworthiness. There may be periods of extreme euphoria, in which the individual's mood is irrationally elevated. Levels of activity tend to vary with the person's mood, becoming slow and inert when depressed, and wildly energetic if euphoric. Difficulty in concentration and sleep disturbances are also common.

Personality disorders are deeply ingrained, motivational and social maladjustments. The most important is the PSYCHOPATHIC (sometimes termed sociopathic) personality, whose central feature is an apparent lack of self-controlling 'conscience'. Also included here are ALCOHOLISM and DRUG DEPENDENCE.

Table 1 also includes the category of ORGANIC SYNDROMES. These are behaviour disorders associated with identified brain disease. Some resemble the non-organic psychoses quite closely, but the more common ones, such as EPILEPSY and SEVERE MENTAL HANDICAP, have quite distinctive symptoms reflecting the known organic pathology underlying them.

Not included in table 1 are the PSYCHOPHYSIOLOGICAL DISORDERS, discussed later in the chapter. These are characterized by physical symptoms whose origins are in part psychological (emotional). These include asthma, essential hypertension, gastric and duodenal ulcers. More generally, the impact of psychological stress on a great variety of illnesses is becoming an increasingly important focus of medical and psychological research.

The medical model of psychopathology

Before describing psychological approaches to behaviour disorder, it is necessary to examine critically the predominant medical approach. This embodies three major assumptions, which are considered in turn.

The diagnostic system

The first assumption of the medical model is that the
various manifestations of abnormal behaviour can be classified, by diagnosis, into syndromes, or constellations
of symptoms regularly found to occur together. This system
has already been outlined in table 1, and the interested
reader should consult a psychiatric textbook for a fuller
treatment than can be presented here. Even our present brief
outline, however, reveals some conceptual difficulties with
the scheme. For example, the criteria for distinguishing
between one major category and another are complex, and
can be self-contradictory. Thus, the differentiation between
neurosis and psychosis on the basis of both the severity of
psychosis and the presumed importance of anxiety in neurosis
means that very severe, disabling anxiety, accompanied by
near-delusional irrational fears, can defy classification.

Scientific studies have attempted to ascertain the
utility of the diagnostic scheme, and results have been
rather disappointing. For example, studies of the extent of
agreement between two or more psychiatrists in diagnosing
patients have suggested that the diagnostic process is
somewhat unreliable. Beck et al (1962) found only 54 per
cent agreement between two experienced psychiatrists in
diagnosing patients. However, agreement was much higher
(81 per cent) concerning cases on which the psychiatrists
were most confident of their diagnosis, and other studies,
especially those in which psychiatrists use more precise
diagnostic criteria, tend to yield rather better results
than Beck's 54 per cent. Another problem is that individuals
placed within the same diagnostic category are found to vary
considerably in the symptoms they show, whilst some symptoms appear in several different diagnostic categories
(Zigler and Philips, 1961). Thus a diagnosis may not tell us
very much about the person's actual behaviour, despite the
somewhat misleading simplicity of table 1 and the textbook
accounts upon which it is based. This problem is especially
pronounced in relation to the considerable number of
patients who appear to fall into 'borderline categories'.

A third problem has been raised by social scientists,
who have pointed to the subjectivity and cultural influences involved in the act of diagnosis; one culture's schizophrenic might be another's shaman; similar acts of violence
might be deemed heroic in battle but psychopathic in peace
time. Hence, it is argued by Szasz (1961) and others, the
symptoms of so-called 'mental illness' are not as objective
as those of physical illness. A related point has been made
by Rosenhan (1973). He duped psychiatric hospital staff by
having 12 normal people complain of hearing voices. All were
duly admitted and given a psychiatric diagnosis, remaining
in hospital for an average of 19 days, despite behaving
normally. During that period, their essentially commonplace
behaviour was interpreted as significant by hospital staff
in the light of the initial diagnosis. Furthermore, the
psychiatrists were in error, in terms of psychiatric practice, in making that diagnosis on the basis of a single

symptom. Rosenhan argues that his study highlights the essential subjectivity of thinking within the medical model. However, this work has aroused considerable controversy, and Rosenhan's interpretation has been challenged. For example, given the fact that such symptoms are rarely, if ever, encountered in isolation in non-dissimulating patients, Rosenhan's study over-estimates the likelihood of errors of this kind by psychiatrists in everyday practice. Another example of the apparent subjectivity of psychiatric diagnosis has emerged from careful comparisons of American and British psychiatrists; the two groups use different diagnostic criteria and hence classify patients differently.

Despite these controversies, the psychiatric classificatory system survives. This is largely because no better descriptive classification has been developed, whilst improvements have been obtained in the performance of the psychiatric classification with its refinement in the light of earlier criticisms. Provided that its approximate and pragmatic nature are recognized, its retention can be justified.

Physiological basis of psychopathology
The second assumption of the medical model is that the symptoms of psychopathology reflect an underlying disease process, physiological in nature, which causes the symptoms. This assumption rests on three main lines of evidence. First, there is the evidence for genetic factors, obtained by examining the rates of disorder amongst the relatives of sufferers. To the extent that a disorder is heritable, its origins are considered biological in nature. Studies have examined the CONCORDANCE RATES (the percentage of relatives of sufferers who also suffer from the disorder in question) for parents, children and siblings of patients. Especial interest has been focussed on twins, comparing identical or monozygotic twins (who are genetically identical) with fraternal or dyzygotic twins (who are genetically no more alike than any pair of siblings). There is evidence from these studies for some hereditary involvement in schizophrenia, anxiety-related disorders, depression and antisocial disorders, with the evidence strongest in the case of schizophrenia. Although figures vary widely from one study to another, it appears that around half the identical twins of schizophrenics suffer from the disorder, whilst no more than one in ten of the fraternal twins of schizophrenics suffer from it (Heston, 1970; Gottesman and Shields, 1973).

It is, of course, very difficult to disentangle hereditary from environmental factors in the greater similarity of people who are more closely related. Identical twins may be treated more alike than fraternal twins by their families. Researchers have, therefore, taken especial interest in the relatives of patients who have been adopted in infancy, which effectively disentangles the environmental and genetic influences from one another. Sixteen pairs of

identical twins, adopted separately in infancy with one or
both diagnosed as schizophrenic, have been described in the
literature. Of these, ten pairs were concordant (both
schizophrenic) and six discordant (only one schizophrenic).
Larger-scale studies of children with schizophrenic mothers,
who have been compared with other adopted children, also
support the case for an hereditary influence in schizophrenia. Even without contact with the schizophrenic biological parent, the adopted child of such a mother is more
likely to develop schizophrenia or other psychopathology
than are other adopted children. On the other hand, it
is quite clear that hereditary factors alone cannot fully
account for the origins of schizophrenia or any other emotional or personality disorder. Even amongst the identical
twins of schizophrenics, many do not develop the disorder.
Both hereditary and environmental influences are important.

If we suppose that hereditary factors are important in
psychopathology, the next step is to identify the biological
mechanisms within the organism which might, under the influence of heredity, be responsible for the disorder. The
second major strand of evidence for the physiological basis
of psychopathology looks to the biochemistry of the brain to
provide such a mechanism. Biochemical research seeks to
explain the disturbances of psychopathology as due to mal-
functioning of brain tissues. The psychological effects
of drugs with known biochemical effects are of especial
interest here. Whilst a succession of biochemical factors
have been implicated in research over the years, none has
been conclusively demonstrated to cause a particular form of
psychopathology. There are three major difficulties faced by
this research. First, biochemical factors associated with
the presence of a disorder may prove to be a consequence
rather than a cause of the disorder. Hospital diets, different activity patterns, or characteristic emotional
responses may influence the biochemistry of disordered
individuals. Second, even if a biochemical abnormality is
not such a secondary consequence of the disorder, the fact
that it is associated with the disorder does not establish
it as the cause. Most psychologists assume that every mental
event or state has some physical correlate in the brain, but
this philosophical assumption does not mean that the physical event is in any sense the cause of the mental event.
Even if the cause of, for example, depressed mood were
purely psychological, we would still expect the brains of
depressed people to be physically different, in some way,
from those of non-depressed people. Third, the biochemical
processes in question are themselves poorly understood in
the 'normal' brain, so that the interpretation of comparisons between 'normal' and 'disordered' biochemistry is
very difficult. Biochemical research is obliged to employ
techniques and concepts which are generally acknowledged to
be necessarily crude, and can offer only global approxi-
mations to the workings of that vastly complex and little
understood system, the human brain. These three areas of

difficulty oblige us to be cautious in interpreting currently proposed biochemical origins of psychopathology.

Despite the above problems there are some promising lines of biochemical research. In the case of SCHIZOPHRENIA for example, it has been suggested that excess activity of dopamine, one of the neurotransmitters (substances employed by neurons to stimulate adjacent neurons), may bring about the disorder (Snyder, Banerjee, Yamamura and Greenberg, 1974). This theory gains support from an 'interlocking jigsaw' of evidence. The phenothiazine drugs which have been found to alleviate schizophrenia resemble dopamine closely in their molecular structure, and so could block the reception of dopamine by taking its place at receptors which normally receive it. These drugs also cause side effects resembling the symptoms of Parkinson's disease, which is known to be associated with dopamine deficiency. If the phenothiazines thus offset dopamine activity as well as alleviating schizophrenic symptoms, it seems reasonable to infer that untreated schizophrenics have excessive dopamine activity, or excessively sensitive dopamine receptors. Furthermore, amphetamine drugs produce a state resembling paranoid schizophrenia, and this 'amphetamine psychosis' is also alleviated by phenothiazines. Amphetamines also increase dopamine activity. However, the dopamine theory has yet to be universally accepted, as some research has failed to support it, and no specific brain pathways have yet been shown to exhibit dopamine malfunction in schizophrenia.

In the case of DEPRESSION, it has been proposed by different researchers that low levels of two neurotransmitters, noradrenaline and serotonin, may be involved. As with schizophrenia, evidence for this comes largely from the effects of drugs. Research on animals shows that drugs which relieve depression in humans increase the amounts of these neurotransmitters in the brain. Mood changes in depressed patients have also been shown to coincide with fluctuations in the levels of noradrenaline excreted in the patient's urine. There is also indirect evidence from studies of related chemical compounds in the cerebro-spinal fluid of depressed patients. These indicate the level of the neurotransmitter present in the brain and spinal cord, and suggest that serotonin is reduced in the brains of depressed patients.

In summary, the biochemical evidence is suggestive of, and consistent with, presumed physiological origins of psychopathology. However, it is not conclusive, nor can such evidence make a psychological explanation redundant. It is best seen as an important part of our attempt to understand the origins of psychopathology but one whose causal significance probably varies from disorder to disorder.

The third major strand of evidence for the physiological basis of psychopathology relates to those types of disorders which have been shown to have clear organic causes. Disease or damage to the brain can result in severe disturbance or impairment of behaviour. A classic example of this is 'general paresis of the insane', whose widespread physical and mental impairments were revealed by nineteenth-century advances in medicine to be due to the syphilis spirochete. This discovery encouraged medical scientists to seek clear-cut organic causes for other psychological abnormalities. Such organic causes have been identified only in the case of 'organic brain syndromes' with characteristically widespread cognitive and emotional deficits, epileptic seizures, and severe mental handicap.

ORGANIC BRAIN SYNDROMES are classified directly with respect to the brain disease or damage involved; although neuropsychologists and clinicians have found characteristic patterns of deficit typically associated with different brain syndromes, these are not sufficiently distinct from one another to serve as a basis for classification. The classes commonly found include infections, injuries, nutritional deficiencies, cerebro-vascular diseases, tumours, degenerative diseases, toxic conditions and endocrine dysfunctions. The variable symptoms associated with a given brain injury or disease suggest that the behaviour shown by a brain-damaged patient is not simply related to his neurological pathology. Other factors, including environmental influences and the functional organization of the individual's brain, are involved. Although little understood, these must interact in some way with brain injury to produce the observed symptoms.

EPILEPSY is a condition in which seizures or convulsions, to which every brain is susceptible to varying degrees under extreme circumstances, are more readily triggered by a wider variety of circumstances than in the general population. In a seizure, sudden changes in the usual rhythmical electrical activity of the brain accompany an altered state of consciousness. Individuals especially susceptible to such seizures typically show abormal patterns of brain activity in the electro-encephalogram (EEG), even between seizures. But their behaviour is quite normal between attacks, suggesting that the behavioural disturbances shown during attacks are simply the result of a brain abnormality. Attacks can be triggered by metabolic factors (such as low blood sugar levels), external stimuli (such as flashing lights or particular sounds or musical notes), brain infection or injury, and stress or emotional problems. Despite the apparently clear organic pathology, therefore, environmental factors play their part in triggering seizures, and sufferers can utilize this information in avoiding circumstances similar to those which have triggered previous attacks.

MENTAL HANDICAP (Clarke and Clarke, 1974) is defined in terms of an individual's extremely low score on a test of general intelligence, together with poor adaptation to social requirements and expectations, manifest before adulthood. Although definitions vary, most authorities consider that an intelligence test score in the lowest 2 or 3 per cent of the population is characteristic of mental

handicap. Within this group, the most severely handicapped
are most likely to suffer from clear-cut organic pathology.
Severe physical abnormalities often accompany such severe
mental handicap. Some of these illnesses can now be prevented or alleviated by attending to the individual's diet,
and by careful pre-natal care.

Most mentally handicapped people do not have clearly
identifiable physiological damage. This is especially true
of those whose degree of handicap is not too severe. These
individuals may have been reared in environments which
do not provide sufficient of the intellectual stimulation
necessary for normal cognitive development. On the other
hand, it remains possible that such individuals suffer from
organic disorders which are more prevalent amongst deprived
people, which have not yet been identified. Another view of
the relatively mildly handicapped is entirely statistical in
nature; every population must have its extreme members, and
no special explanation need be required for the presence of
the least gifted members of the population. But this argument is not well able to account for the fact that, given an
intelligence test score commensurate with mild handicap, the
individual may or may not in fact exhibit the adaptive
failures characteristic of handicap.

It is important to emphasize that the organic pathology
shown in organic brain syndromes and some mental handicap
does not preclude environmental influences upon the disorders. The behaviour of all such individuals can be enhanced or retarded by good or bad environments. Special
training, for example, attuned to the needs of a handicapped
person, can often impart skills and knowledge which are
acquired by others without such training, but which the
handicapped person lacks until such efforts are made. This
may require more repetitive practice, or a more gradual,
step-by-step build-up of a complex task, than is required by
non-handicapped people. The organic syndromes thus show us
that physiological factors cannot alone determine the course
of any psychological disorder. They may, of course, set
limits upon the behaviour attainable by an individual, but
within these limits a great deal depends upon the psychological impact of the environment. The precise nature of the
physiologically determined limits on an individual can only
be determined by appropriately shaped efforts to raise his
performance until those limits are reached.

The treatment of psychopathology
The third assumption of the medical model concerns the
proper action to take in dealing with psychopathology.
Persons exhibiting psychological problems are considered
best designated patients, offered predominantly physical
treatment in hospitals and clinics, and regarded as cured
or improved if their abnormalities are reduced. Critics of
the medical model, such as Laing (1964), Szasz (1961), and
others, regard this action by society and the doctors to
whom it assigns these responsibilities as unjustified

exploitation of an ill-founded metaphor likening psychological disturbance to physical disease. The psychiatrist's
best answer to this criticism rests upon the evidence that
physical treatments are indeed effective. Since the concern
of the present chapter is with origins rather than treatment
of psychopathology, we have space only to make some general
observations concerning this evidence, rather than
attempting to evaluate it in any detail.

For three reasons, psychologists are often inclined to
question the support given to the medical model by the
effects of physical treatments. First, although drugs and
electro-convulsive therapy (ECT) do appear capable of an
ameliorative or controlling effect on many of the symptoms
of psychopathology, this effect is by no means universal.
The best evidence for the effectiveness of treatments comes
from controlled trials, in which the average outcomes of
groups of individuals receiving different treatments are
compared. In any such trial, many individuals are not in
fact helped by the treatment, and very little is known about
why this is so. Second, the fact that abnormal behaviour can
be controlled by physical means does not demonstrate that
its origins are physical. The powerful tranquillizers used
in schizophrenia are often described as 'pharmacological
straitjackets'; in controlling the most disruptive and
violent symptoms of schizophrenia they may be merely
'restraining' the nervous system from activity much as the
physical restraints of the past restrained violent lunatics.
Proponents of this metaphor would deny that such restraint
constitutes effective treatment of the source of the
activities thereby restrained. Third, physical treatments
are disquietingly lacking in established scientific ration-
ales. We have relatively little theoretical basis for
knowing why these treatments work whatever the empirical
basis (in terms of controlled trials; Scovern and Kilmann,
1980) for believing them effective. ECT, in particular, has
no coherent rationale and a revealing history. On the basis
of a (subsequently discredited) belief that epileptics were
less prone to schizophrenia than the general population, the
induction of epileptiform seizures by chemical or electrical
means was introduced as a putative treatment for schizophrenia. Experience with the technique subsequently led
psychiatrists to consider it effective, not with schizophrenics, but with depressives. Until a coherent rationale
is developed, this serendipitous history will not endear the
method to psychiatry's critics.

In sum, the medical model gains some support from the
evidence, but is sufficiently defective and incomplete to
warrant the development of alternative and complementary
approaches. The remainder of this chapter is concerned with
five approaches which have been developed by psychologists
and social scientists. The contribution of each is assessed
with respect to some of the most important kinds of psychopathology. The evidence surveyed is, of necessity, very
selective, and a full appreciation of these approaches can

only follow more extensive study. Another limitation to be borne in mind is that the present emphasis upon ORIGINS of disorder entails a neglect of research on TREATMENT which is, in fact, complementary to the material presented here.

The statistical model

The statistical model identifies individuals whose behaviour or reported experience is sufficiently unusual to warrant attention on that basis alone. Using this approach, we say that a person is abnormal if he deviates from the average to a marked degree. In order to determine whether an individual is normal or abnormal in a given respect, we assess the relevant aspect (degree of anxiety experienced, or intelligence) and find how close or distant his score is from the average. For example, Eysenck (1970) defines basic dimensions of personality and uses laboratory tests and a personality questionnaire to assess a person's score on each. People scoring at the extremes on one or more dimensions are regarded as abnormal. For example, people who are very easily emotionally aroused (scoring high on Eysenck's 'neuroticism') and learn conditioned responses and associations easily (highly introverted, according to Eysenck) are likely to suffer from what psychiatrists term anxiety neurosis.

Although this approach appears commendably objective, it has serious drawbacks. Not all unusual behaviour is properly regarded as requiring study by abnormal psychologists. Exceptionally gifted individuals are an obvious case in point. The approach does not supply us with any basis for choosing which aspects of people to measure; some statistically abnormal behaviours are obviously more relevant than others, and we need more than a merely statistical theory to tell us which to consider, and why. The approach also gives us no basis for deciding where to draw the line between normal and abnormal behaviour; just how unusual does a behaviour have to be to count as 'abnormal'? On the other hand, this model is of value for its suggestion that 'norrmal' and 'abnormal' behaviour may only differ in degree, in contrast to the medical model's implication of a sharp division between normality and abnormality.

The psychodynamic model

The psychodynamic model is very difficult to summarize, as it is based upon theories developed early in the century by Freud, and revised and elaborated by him and subsequent workers within a broad tradition (Brown, 1961; Ellenberger, 1970). It shares with the medical model the assumption that disordered behaviour is a symptom of an underlying disturbance. But the underlying disturbance is psychological in nature, and concerns unconscious conflicts within the personality. The approach, developed in the study of psychopathology, also serves as a general psychological theory. Its central feature is the importance given to active forces within the personality not immediately available to introspection (i.e. unconscious); these forces are viewed in terms of a hydraulic metaphor, whereby they must be discharged once aroused. Freud viewed the personality as comprising the conscious ego, the unconscious id (source of primitive impulses) and partly conscious, partly unconscious, super-ego (conscience). Psychopathology is held to originate in unconscious conflicts arising from childhood experiences.

This can be seen most clearly in relation to the dynamic theory of anxiety and neurosis. This contrasts 'objective' anxiety, the ego's response to real danger, with 'neurotic' anxiety, the fear of disastrous consequences imagined to follow the expression of a previously punished id impulse. The child learns 'neurotic anxiety' when he is punished for being impulsive, whereupon the conflict between wanting something and fearing the consequences of that desire is driven from consciousness (repressed). According to this theory, pervasive anxiety is due to fear of the person's ever-present id impulses, and phobic objects, such as insects or animals, are seen as symbolic representations of the objects of the repressed id impulses. More generally, dynamic theory posits that the ego protects itself from threat by a variety of defence mechanisms, adjustments serving to keep from awareness anxiety-arousing thoughts. In addition to repression, these include denial of threatening facts about the outside world, rationalization (seeking a rational or socially desirable 'excuse' to conceal one's true reasons for an action), projection (attributing one's undesirable features to another person), reaction formation (concealing a motive from oneself by giving strong expression to its opposite), intellectualization (emotional detachment achieved by dealing with a threatening situation in abstract, intellectual terms), and displacement (gratifying an unconscious need in an alternative, more acceptable, manner).

Freud argued that these defence mechanisms are a commonplace feature of everyone's adjustment, but are used to an exaggerated extent in the case of neurotic patients, whose early emotional conflicts have not been satisfactorily resolved, resulting in particularly strong unconscious impulses. For example, the obsessive-compulsive person who is excessively neat and tidy is seen as exhibiting reaction formation against a desire to be messy, originating in a childhood rebellion against severe toilet training.

Dynamic theory views depression as a reaction to loss in individuals who are excessively dependent upon other people for the maintenance of self-esteem. The loss may be actual (as in bereavement) or symbolic (as in the misinterpretation of a rejection as a total loss of love); but in either case, the person who becomes depressed is considered to be particularly vulnerable to such loss experiences because his self-esteem depends upon the support and encouragement of others to an unusual degree. There are differences between dynamic theorists in their explanations for this vulnerability, but these need not concern us here. The depressed person is seen as expressing a child-like need for approval and affection to restore his damaged self-esteem.

In psychotic disorders, Freud held that the defence mechanisms were overstretched to the point of collapse, with the individual 'regressing' back to an early stage of development, before the ego was differentiated from the id, and hence before reality could be tested. The schizophrenic symptoms of passivity and withdrawal are said to reflect this regression; hallucinations and bizarre speech reflect the primitive inner world of 'primary process' thinking which predominates when contact with the real world is lost. Severe, psychotic depression is seen as a regression to the oral stage during which the infant derives pleasure from sucking and being comforted in totally helpless and dependent fashion.

Despite its considerable impact upon the ways in which we understand human motivation and psychopathology, psychodynamic theory has remained controversial. Most of the evidence in its favour comes from clinical case material, as recounted by practising psychoanalysts, whose work has been guided by the belief that unconscious conflicts must be brought to the surface for the patient to recover from the symptoms they have engendered. Whilst this method often yields compelling material which is difficult to understand without recourse to dynamic theory (Malan, 1979), it is open to criticism as insufficiently objective to count as scientific evidence. The distinction between observations and the investigator's interpretation of those observations, considered essential by most psychologists, is difficult to draw in this area. The statements made by patients are prey to the subtle influence of the ideas held by the person to whom they are made. Social psychologists who have studied the ways in which we influence each other in everyday conversation and psychotherapy are frankly sceptical about Freud's claim that the analyst functions as a purely passive 'blank screen' exerting no influence upon the patient's thoughts. Most of psychodynamic theory is difficult to prove or disprove by the clear-cut methods of investigation favoured by psychologists. This is partly because its central concepts are somewhat abstract, and partly because of a certain slipperiness of logic. For example, appeal to reaction formation to explain behaviour contrary to the predictions of the theory has been castigated as a 'heads I win, tails you lose' argument, unacceptable in science. It has also be pointed out that psychodynamic theory is based upon work with highly selected, probably unrepresentative, patients; these are typically middle class, whether in Freud's Vienna, or present day London or New York.

There is some scientific evidence which is at least broadly consistent with psychodynamic theory. For example, the evidence on cognitive deficits in schizophrenia is compatible with the idea of ego impairment, and many of the life events found by such workers as Brown and Harris (1978) to precede the onset of depression involve the kinds of loss implicated by psychodynamic theory. But such evidence can be interpreted in other, perhaps simpler, terms. Psychologists unsympathetic to dynamic theory maintain that it explains no scientific evidence which cannot be explained by competing theories of a more parsimonious nature.

On the other hand, proponents of dynamic theory can point to its value as a general framework within which to understand psychopathology, independent of the truth or falsity of specific propositions about specific disorders. For example, the impact of conflicts of which the individual is unaware, and the deployment of cognitive distortions (defence mechanisms) to cope with such conflicts have been amply confirmed by empirical research, as well as informing decades of clinical practice. The dynamic model is also important for giving us the first and most fully elaborated psychological approach to psychopathology.

The learning model

The learning model views psychopathology as stemming from faulty learning in the course of growing up, and conceptualizes this process in terms of well-established principles of learning, extensively studied in psychological laboratories. The earliest of these principles were based on Pavlovian or 'classical' conditioning, in which two stimuli are presented together until the response to one stimulus is also evoked by the other; and 'operant' conditioning, whereby behaviour with favourable consequences becomes more frequent. According to early proponents of the learning model, the symptoms of psychopathology were nothing more than faulty habits acquired through these two types of learning. The 'underlying pathology' posited by the medical and psychodynamic models was dismissed as unfounded myth.

For example, it is suggested that phobias are acquired by a two-stage learning process; first, fear is aroused in response to a previously neutral stimulus when this stimulus is presented in conjunction with a noxious stimulus; then the person learns to avoid the situation evoking the fear, because behaviour taking the person away from that situation is rewarded by the reduction in fear. This interpretation is consistent with the classic demonstration by Watson and Rayner (1920) in which the boy known as Little Albert was made fearful of a rat. However, the fact that a phobia can be induced in this way does not prove that naturally occurring phobias are brought about in a similar fashion. Furthermore, subsequent investigators have not been successful in replicating this result. Laboratory studies of human beings indicate that fears acquired by this process of CONDITIONING are not as long-lasting as the persistence of naturally occurring phobias would lead us to expect.

Another learning theory suggests that fears, phobias and other 'neurotic' symptoms are due to the social rewards or reinforcements they produce for the person. For example, a child may devise excuses to avoid going to school, including expressions of fear and anxiety. If the child's mother yields to these excuses, and rewards the child by keeping it at home with her and devoting her attention to it throughout the day, then the phobic behaviour is thereby strengthened. This may sometimes happen. But this theory is implausible in many cases because of the suffering and deprivation associated with fear, anxiety and avoidance behaviour.

Similarly, it has been suggested that schizophrenics fail to attend to relevant, social stimuli, and hence become socially isolated. Learning theory holds that hospitalized patients receive more attention and other rewards from hospital staff when they behave in 'crazy' ways, so that the frequency of this behaviour is increased by this reward. This idea of schizophrenia as a learned social role is apparently supported by research in which patients show themselves capable of manipulating the impression they make on others in order to achieve their desired ends (such as remaining in or leaving hospital). But the demonstration that schizophrenics, like other people, can do this does not prove that all their schizophrenic behaviour has arisen in response to the rewarding attention of other people.

An approach to DEPRESSION in terms of learning theory views this disorder as a reduction in activity following the withdrawal of accustomed 'reinforcement' (Lewinsohn, 1974). According to this view, the feeling of depression and the other symptoms associated with it are brought about when the person's behaviour receives few reinforcements. The rate of reinforcement available to a person is considered to be a function of personal characteristics (such as attractiveness to others), the nature of the environment, and the person's success in gaining reinforcements by the exercise of skills. According to this theory, a 'vicious circle' develops in depressed people. When they become depressed, their inactivity and withdrawal serve only to reduce yet further the rate of reinforcement available to them, as they fail to exercise the skills necessary to secure positive responses from others. Indeed, the only reward available may be accompanied by privately-held hostile and rejecting feelings towards the depressed person. But even though depressed people tend to be less well liked even than other groups of psychiatric patients, this does not prove that low reinforcement rate causes their depressed mood in the first place, although it may well serve to prolong and intensify the depression.

Some of the evidence for the reinforcement theory was thought to come from studies in which depressed people reported very few rewarding experiences (Nelson and Craighead, 1977). However, the validity of this evidence has been questioned, since subsequent studies have shown that depressed people have a distorted view of their world. For example, they may tend to remember more of the bad things that have happened, whilst forgetting the good things (Teasdale and Fogarty, 1979). They tend to set higher standards for themselves (Golin and Terrell, 1977), and so experience as failure a level of performance that happier people would consider moderately successful. This kind of evidence has been cited in support of an alternative psychological approach to depression, which sees the perceptual and cognitive distortions as bringing about the mood disturbance.

More recently, the symbolic and social aspects of learning have been widely studied, and incorporated into the learning model of psychopathology. For example, the fact that certain stimuli (such as spiders) are much more likely to become the objects of phobias than others has led to the idea of 'preparedness'. According to this theory, some associations are inherently more easily learned than others. This is attributed to biological 'programming' of the brain rather than Freudian symbolism. But the preparedness theory can claim to be a rival explanation for some of the facts about fear upon which dynamic theory is based.

Bandura (1969) has studied imitative learning, or modelling, in which the behaviour of observers is influenced by another's actions and their consequences. Experiments have shown how powerfully such observation can result in a vicarious acquisition of fear and courage, aggression and self-control. This has obvious implications for the transmission of psychopathology from one person (such as a parent) to another.

In general, the learning model provides a powerful set of principles governing the acquisition of problem behaviour. It has also inspired a vigorous approach to treatment, behaviour therapy, based on similar learning principles. But it is by no means sufficient to account for most psychopathology unaided by more complex formulations, and the evidence for its validity is not conclusive.

The cognitive model

Another laboratory-based psychological approach to psychopathology focusses upon thinking processes and their possible dysfunctions. Much of the impetus for this approach has come from psychologists keen to extend the learning approach to take account of more complex human behaviour. The cognitive model assumes that 'neurotic' problems reflect relatively mild errors in reasoning processes, whilst 'psychotic' disorders may reflect profound disturbances in cognitive function and organization.

Psychologists have been particularly interested in a cognitive approach to DEPRESSION. As described above, depressed people tend to have a distorted picture of the world, which accentuates unpleasant experiences, and set themselves high standards. According to Beck's (1967) cognitive theory of depression, the depressed person sees himself as worthless, the future as hopeless, and the world as meaningless. The feelings of depression are, in this theory, a consequence of the cognitive distortion. Although an episode of depression may be triggered by external events, the theory proposes that it is the person's perception of the event which makes it set off depressed feelings.

Of course, everyday observation and scientific research both testify to the fact that depressed people hold negative attitudes of the type emphasized by this cognitive theory. However, this in itself does not show that negative beliefs CAUSE depressive mood. The best evidence for this comes from experiments in which negative beliefs are fostered and mood changes observed as a consequence of the induced beliefs. For example, bogus psychological test results alleging that the individual is immature and uncreative lead to depressed mood in students. Similar results have been obtained in studies requiring normal subjects to attend to unpleasant thoughts (e.g. by reading depressing statements aloud). Whether similar mechanisms account for the longer lasting and more severe depressive feelings of clinical patients, however, is another matter. On the other hand, the promising results of 'cognitive therapy', in which the hypothesized cognitive distortions of depressed patients are modified directly, may be taken as indirect evidence for the theory.

Another theory of depression compares it to LEARNED HELPLESSNESS, a phenomenon first studied in the animal laboratory (Seligman, 1975; Abramson, Seligman and Teasdale, 1978). The basic idea is that depression ensues when a person perceives that his actions cannot affect what happens to him. This is based on experiments in which poor performance, inertia and apathetic mood are induced by prior exposure to insoluble problems. A great deal of research has been carried out on this theory, and it has become clear that the effects of uncontrollable outcomes depend upon how the subject interprets them. In particular, it is important to know how he believes his helplessness to have been caused. Psychologists have developed attribution theory to help examine beliefs about the causation of events. According to this theory, only if the subject attributes his helplessness experience to something common to a variety of situations (a global rather than a specific attribution), will that experience have effects beyond the situation in which the helplessness occurred. Again, only if the subject attributes his helplessness to something likely to endure over time (a stable rather than an unstable attribution) will the effects of the helplessness experience persist. Finally, attribution theory suggests that only if the subject attributes his helplessness to factors within himself (an internal rather than an external attribution) will he suffer the loss of self-esteem (or self-blame) characteristic of depression and emphasized by Beck's theory. For example, a woman experiencing rejection by a man would be much less severely affected by the experience if she believed that this was due to the man's happening to be in a rejecting mood (i.e. that other men, or this man on another occasion, could be expected to treat her differently, and she bore no responsibility for the event) than if she believed that she was unattractive to men (i.e. that all men would continue to reject her on account of her unattractiveness).

Studies of the attributional styles of depressed people have confirmed the importance of these concepts. Depressed people tend to attribute bad outcomes to internal, stable and global causes, whilst they attribute good outcomes to external, unstable causes. These attributional biasses sustain the depressive's pessimistic outlook. In general, depressed people tend to believe that they are personally incompetent (so that their negative beliefs are often specific to themselves rather than necessarily reflecting universal pessimism). In this context, it is very interesting to note sex differences in attributional style which may help explain the well-documented fact that more women than men become depressed. It appears that the attributional styles of women in general differ from those of men in general, rather as depressives do from non-depressives. In particular, women, like depressives, tend to attribute success to external and unstable factors, and failure to internal and stable factors.

A tantalizing paradox is presented by considering Beck's theory of depression, self-blame, alongside the learned helplessness view, emphasizing the experience of helplessness. It appears logically inconsistent to blame oneself, whilst also viewing events as outside one's control. Does this reflect a contradiction between psychological theories, or does it (more interestingly) point to illogical thinking on the part of depressed people? The evidence supports the latter interpretation, since depressives seem to experience both helplessness and guilt in relation to similar aspects of their lives. It is with respect to the same aspects of life that a depressed person tends to experience both helplessness and guilt. (This paradox is also found in non-depressed people, but to a lesser degree.) Blaney (1977) compares the theories of Beck, Lewinsohn and Seligman.

Psychologists have devoted considerable research efforts to precise descriptions of the cognitive deficits of SCHIZOPHRENIC patients through controlled laboratory experiments. For example, their impaired performance in tasks requiring selective attention to relevant information, whilst excluding from attention other, irrelevant information, has been well-documented. Schizophrenic patients are highly distractable. If we assume that this is a fundamental feature of the schizophrenic, it might help explain how irrelevant features of a situation acquire, for the schizophrenic, disproportionate importance, and become interpreted as part of his delusional system of beliefs, or how speech is disorganized by his shifting attention to distracting, irrelevant thoughts and mental images which a non-schizophrenic can readily ignore. On the other hand, this research has two severe limitations. First, most studies simply report that schizophrenics do poorly on the task under investigation. But this somewhat uniform pattern of results does little to identify the precise nature of

the schizophrenic deficit; it tells us little about schizophrenia beyond pointing to the general incompetence of
sufferers. Second, such findings do not give much insight
into the mechanisms underlying the deficits shown by schizophrenic patients. In particular, it is possible that much of
the difference between schizophrenic and other subjects is
due to what have been aptly termed 'nuisance variables':
factors arising from the socio-medical consequences of the
disorder, such as the effects of drugs, institutional diet
and routine, and patients' learning to play the 'sick
role'.

Recent research has tried to overcome these difficulties. For example, studies showing different kinds of impairment in different kinds of schizophrenic serve both to
identify specific deficits with specific disorders, and also
to overcome the 'nuisance variables' insofar as all patients
tend to receive broadly similar treatments in broadly similar institutional environments. For example, paranoid
schizophrenics have been found to lack the ability to acquire the knowledge required to solve a task, whilst non-
paranoids lack the ability to control their responses in
accordance with the knowledge (Gillis and Blevens, 1978).
Another approach involves the study of patients who are in
a state of recovery, and are therefore no longer subject to
the 'nuisance variables'. Such patients have been found to
show similar performance deficits on tasks requiring selective attention to those shown by patients who are still
showing symptoms and undergoing treatment (Asarnow and
MacCrimmon, 1978).

The cognitive approach is of great interest because it
combines the systematic and objective approach of experimental psychology with a thoroughgoing interest in an important aspect of human mentality. It is a very active
'growth area' of current research, and shows considerable
promise. It is perhaps too early, however, to evaluate many
of its specific theories, and it does carry the risk of
neglecting other aspects of human behaviour.

The socio-cultural model

The final model to be considered attributes psychopathology
to social and cultural factors. It focusses upon malfunc-
tioning of the social or cultural group rather than of an
individual within that group.

In terms of the socio-cultural model, schizophrenia has
been considered both in relation to the quality of family
life and to larger socio-economic forces. According to the
influential psychiatrist Laing (1964), behaviour labelled
schizophrenia is due to self-contradictory parental demands
('double binds'), to which no conventionally sane response
is possible. Although graphic accounts have been offered of
such patterns in the family life of schizophrenic patients,
there is no evidence that these problematic demands are
peculiar to such families. Furthermore, careful studies of
the conversations of families with both schizophrenic and

normal offspring strongly suggests that the disturbed communication patterns of the parents of schizophrenics are a response to the behaviour of the patient, rather than a cause of it. Indeed, the idea of 'double bind' now seems much more relevant to the origins of less severe disturbances than schizophrenia.

Looking beyond the family, social psychiatrists have noted the higher incidence of schizophrenia amongst the lowest socio-economic class, especially in inner city areas. The rate of schizophrenia in the lowest social class has been found to be as much as twice that in the next lowest class. The multiple deprivations of this way of life have been suggested as a major cause of schizophrenia. On the other hand, cause and effect could be the other way around, with persons developing schizophrenia 'drifting' into poverty-ridden areas of the city, either as a means of avoiding social relationships and occupational ties or as a result of impaired ability to hold a job and earn a living. Research attempting to resolve this issue has proved only that the answer is not simple; studies of the social mobility of schizophrenics have yielded varying results, although it appears that schizophrenic patients tend to achieve a lower socio-economic status than did their parents. Episodes of schizophrenia have been shown to be triggered by stressful life events, some of which may be more common or less offset by social and material supports amongst lower-class people. But it is less clear whether such events do more than affect the timing of an episode, rather than bring on the disorder in someone who would otherwise never experience it (Rabkin, 1980).

Socio-cultural approaches to depression have focussed upon the social circumstances and precipitating events associated with depressive episodes. Unlike schizophrenia, depression is not markedly more prevalent in lower social classes. Indeed, there is some evidence that at least some types of depression are more frequently found in the middle class. However, psychiatrists may very well be insensitive to depression amongst working-class patients, and this is consistent with the higher rates amongst working-class patients found in community surveys and with questionnaires completed by the patients. It has been suggested that striving personalities, successful in middle-class occupations, may be particularly vulnerable to depression, especially when confronted by failure.

The socio-cultural approach is of undoubted value as a critical challenge to orthodox views, and has generated much useful research into social and cultural factors in psychopathology. Its proponents have also contributed much to an increasing humanistic respect for the personal predicament of troubled individuals, and to the development of 'therapeutic communities' as an alternative to individually centred treatments. However, many of its propositions concerning simple cause-effect relationships have not stood the test of empirical research.

The psychology of illness

Laymen and scientists alike have long been intrigued by the possibility that physical illness may reflect psychological processes. In the period 1930-1960, research was concentrated on certain 'psychosomatic illnesses', such as ulcerative colitis, bronchial asthma and hypertension. More recently, however, interest has broadened to consider the extent to which psychological factors can contribute to ANY illness (Oborne, Gruneberg and Eiser, 1979).

The link between psychological states and illness is mediated by the physiological response to stress. The general characteristics of this response are well known, and readily understood in evolutionary terms as preparation for 'fight or flight' (short-term changes) or as protection against exhaustion or injury (longer-term changes) (Cox, 1978). However, repeated occurrence of these physiological changes can itself be damaging to health. For example, secretions of hydrochloric acid in the stomach can lead to ulceration of its lining. Release of the 'stress hormones', such as adrenalin and the corticosteroids, can suppress immune responses and lead to heightened susceptibility to many diseases ranging from virus infections, such as the common cold, to cancer (Rogers, Dubey and Reich, 1979).

Many environmental conditions and events have been implicated in ill-health, presumably because of their effects on such physiological mechanisms as those described above. These include noise and other physical hardships, highly demanding and/or repetitive jobs (whether physical or mental), catastrophic life events (such as accidents, illness or bereavement) and major emotional difficulties (such as marital discord). However, it would be misleading to conclude that these stresses are simple, unaided causes of ill-health, for at least three reasons.

First, the subjective distress and health effects experienced by different individuals subjected to apparently similar environments differ very widely. Some people seem to create their own stress, such as the so-called 'Type A' personalities (exhibiting competitiveness, aggressiveness, impatience, constant time pressure, striving for achievement and dedication to work) who have been found susceptible to coronary heart disease. Introverts are more susceptible to the common cold than are extraverts. These personality factors appear at least in part hereditary. Other factors influencing susceptibility reflect the impact of the environment. For example, rich and extensive social supports (furnished by good relationships with relatives, friends and neighbours) serve to protect individuals from the health consequences of adversity.

Second, cause-effect relationships are often two-way. For example, marital conflict, itself distressing, may reflect prior strains felt by the individuals involved. Few of the events implicated in psychological distress and ill-health are entirely independent of the state and behaviour of the person undergoing them. 'Vicious circles' develop in people's lives, as one stress leads to another. Illness is itself a powerful source of further strain.

Third, the effect of a given event or other stress on the individual is largely determined by the individual's appraisal or interpretation of the situation, rather than merely reflecting its 'objective' features as they might appear to an outsider. This is presumably one way in which personality affects susceptibility to strain and illness. The impact of noise, for example, is strongly influenced by how much the person feels able to control it. Even if the sound is uninterrupted, the mere knowledge that he can silence it if he wishes has been shown to diminish the individual's reaction to it.

In sum, the study of psychological factors and physical health demonstrates clearly the interaction between charac- teristics of the individual which may predispose him to susceptibility, and complex features of his environment which may serve to mobilize his stress response systems. For physical illness, as for psychopathology, we must posit multiple, interacting causes, rather than impute its origins to any one factor alone.

Conclusions

Each of the approaches surveyed has contributed to our understanding of psychopathology. The evidence presented for each is merely illustrative in view of the massive amounts of research which have been conducted. However, some general themes emerge from this material, with profound implications for how knowledge of psychopathology and its origins may be expected to develop in the future. These are considered pri- marily in relation to schizophrenia, although they arise equally for all the major disorders discussed here.

First, our classificatory system is inadequate, and this is reflected in the results of research. For example, the enormous diversity of disorders subsumed within the concept of schizophrenia has led psychologists into developing a dimensional approach to differences between schizophrenics. These include paranoid/non-paranoid (derived from the extent of the patient's delusions), acute/chronic (based on the length of hospitalization and the extent of clear-cut, in- tense symptomatology), and good/poor pre-morbid adjustment (based on the quality of social and sexual relationships before the onset of the disorder). Research has demonstrated important differences in the behaviour of patients differing in these respects, so that research into the origins of schizophrenia which assumes it to be a unitary condition may be doomed to failure.

Second, a need exists to integrate the diverse models and approaches. Steps in this direction are especially fruitful. For example, Zubin and Spring (1977) have proposed a 'vulnerability' model of schizophrenia. Within this model, attention is focussed upon the origins of an 'episode' of disorder. Each individual is held to exhibit a given degree of vulnerability, determined by both genetic and environ- mental factors. This is conceived as an enduring feature, or trait, of the individual. Unrelated to this vulnerability is the coping ability of the individual, which is a function

of how much effort he exerts and his skills and abilities.
When the individual meets a situation which is beyond his
coping ability, coping breakdown occurs. Whether or not
such coping breakdown results in an episode of schizophrenia
depends on how vulnerable the individual is. After the illness episode the patient returns to his pre-morbid adjustment. 'Chronic' schizophrenia, on this view, is a product
of institutional care and may reflect a series of episodes.
This formulation can account for the fact that neither
hereditary nor environmental predisposing factors can fully
predict the occurrence of schizophrenia, although their
influence is undoubtedly important. This account breaks new
ground by separating the individual's coping ability (which
serves to protect him from coping breakdown) from his vulnerability (which determines whether or not coping breakdown is followed by an episode of schizophrenia). Clearly,
individuals with good coping ability can be overcome by
particularly severe stress; if such an individual is vulnerable and hence suffers an episode of schizophrenia, his
coping skills will ensure good readjustment after the episode. In this he would differ from someone whose coping
abilities were less good, and who was therefore more liable
to recurrent coping breakdown.

The idea of vulnerability helps to explain some important research findings. For example, it has been found that
recovered schizophrenics, and non-sufferers identified on
the basis of family histories and circumstances as 'at risk'
for schizophrenia, resemble people currently suffering from
the disorder in a variety of ways. For example, in laboratory experiments they show similar difficulties with respect
to selective attention and the processing of information.
These presumably reflect their lifelong vulnerability,
although this can only be detected by very careful psychological testing and is not apparent in the person's everyday
life. This model combined factors emphasized by the medical,
statistical, learning, cognitive and socio-cultural approaches in a creative synthesis with powerful implications
for the understanding and management of schizophrenia.

Third, it is apparent that the diverse models and
approaches have more in common than is often acknowledged.
In relation to schizophrenia, for example, the breakdown of
ego functioning posited by psychodynamic theory corresponds
quite closely to the inability to process information and
sustain contact with reality identified by cognitive theory.
Advancing knowledge may diminish yet further the differences
in perspective amongst researchers, and herald the acceptance of a common language in which to describe behaviour
disorders.

Fourth, the manifest limitations of existing models has
stimulated the growth of alternative approaches, some of
which are particularly promising. For example, psychologists
studying stress and anxiety have developed a 'transactional'
approach (Cox, 1978) emphasizing the importance of the
individual's active interpretation, or even creation, of

apparently external stressful events and pressures. This approach views the individual as neither a passive victim of circumstances, nor as irrevocably programmed from birth to respond in a particular way however life treats him. Rather, it acknowledges that person and environment continuously interact with one another, such as to defy any simple one-way cause-effect analysis. For example, harassed executives and mothers of small children bring some of the stress they suffer upon themselves as they respond sharply to colleagues or children and thus contribute to a climate of irritation or conflict. The task of translating such apparently basic insights into scientific research has only recently begun, although the general idea can be traced through various theorists in social and clinical psychology, such as Lewin (1951) and Kelly (1955); but this kind of approach offers new hope for our future understanding of psychopathology.

Finally, what can the psychological study of psychopathology offer the professional? Those expecting certain answers to simple questions such as 'What causes schizophrenia?' or 'What makes Mrs Jones stay indoors all the time?' are bound to be disappointed. We have a long way to go before such questions can be answered with certainty. At present, it looks as if their answers are inevitably complex, involving a large number of interacting factors. On the other hand, the psychological approach teaches us a healthy respect for the complexity of the human predicament, and is a valuable corrective to any tendency to offer simplistic and often unsympathetic explanations of human distress. Furthermore, professionals will often find it illuminating to apply some of the approaches outlined here to understanding distressed individuals they encounter in their daily work.

References

Abramson, L.Y., Seligman, M.E.P. and Teasdale, J.D. (1978)
Learned helplessness in humans: critique and reformulation. Journal of Abnormal Psychology, 87, 49-74.

Asarnow, R.F. and MacCrimmon, D.J. (1978)
Residual deficit in clinically remitted schizophrenics: a marker of schizophrenia? Journal of Abnormal Psychology, 87, 597-608.

Bandura, A. (1969)
Principles of Behavior Modification. New York: Holt, Rinehart & Winston.

Beck, A.T. (1967)
Depression: Clinical, experimental and theoretical aspects. New York: Harper & Row.

Beck, A.T., Ward, C.H., Mendleson, M., Mock, J.E. and Erlbaugh, J.K. (1962)
Reliability of psychiatric diagnosis II: a study of consistency of clinical judgements and ratings. American Journal of Psychiatry, 119, 351-357.

Blaney, P.H. (1977)
Contemporary theories of depression: critique and

comparison. Journal of Abnormal Psychology, 86, 203-223.

Brown, J.A.C. (1961)
Freud and the Post-Freudians. Harmondsworth: Penguin.

Brown, G.W. and Harris, T. (1978)
Social Origins of Depression. London: Tavistock.

Cox, T. (1978)
Stress. London: Macmillan.

Clarke, A.M. and Clarke, A.D.B. (1974)
Mental Deficiency: The changing outlook (3rd edn).
London: Methuen.

Ellenberger, H.F. (1970)
The Discovery of the Unconscious. London: Allen Lane/
Penguin.

Eysenck, H.J. (1970)
The Structure of Human Personality. London: Methuen.

Gillis, J.S. and Blevens, K. (1978)
Sources of judgement impairment in paranoid and non-
paranoid schizophrenics. Journal of Abnormal Psychology,
87, 587-596.

Golin, S. and Terrell, F. (1977)
Motivational and associative aspects of mild depression
in skill and chance tasks. Journal of Abnormal
Psychology, 86, 389-401.

Gottesman, I.I. and Shields, J. (1973)
Genetic theorising and schizophrenia. British Journal of
Psychiatry, 122, 15-30.

Heston, L. (1970)
The genetics of schizophrenia and schizoid disease.
Science, 167, 249-256.

Kelly, G.A. (1955)
The Psychology of Personal Constructs, Volumes I and II.
New York: Norton.

Laing, R.D. (1964)
Is schizophrenia a disease? International Journal of
Social Psychiatry, 10, 184-193.

Lewin, K. (1951)
Field Theory in Social Science. New York: Harper & Row.

Lewinsohn, P.H. (1974)
A behavioral approach to depression. In R.J. Friedman
and M.M. Katz (eds), The Psychology of Depression:
Contemporary theory and research. Washington, DC:
Winston-Willey.

Malan, D.H. (1979)
Individual Psychotherapy and the Science of
Psychodynamics. London: Tavistock.

Nelson, R.E. and Craighead, W.E. (1977)
Selective recall of positive and negative feedback, self-
control behaviors, and depression. Journal of Abnormal
Psychology, 86, 379-388.

Oborne, D.J., Gruneberg, M.M. and Eiser, J.R. (eds) (1979)
Research in Psychology and Medicine, Volumes I and II.
London: Academic Press.

Rabkin, J.G. (1980)
Stressful life events and schizophrenia: a review.
Psychological Bulletin, 87, 408–425.

Rogers, M.P., Dubey, D. and Reich, P. (1979)
The influence of the psyche and the brain on immunity
and disease susceptibility: a critical review.
Psychosomatic Medicine, 41, 147–164.

Rosenhan, D.L. (1973)
On being sane in insane places. Science, 179, 25–258.

Scovern, A.W. and Kilmann, P.R. (1980)
Status of electroconvulsive therapy: review of the
outcome literature. Psychological Bulletin, 87, 260–303.

Seligman, M.E.P. (1975)
Helplessness: On depression, development and death. New
York: Freeman.

**Snyder, S.H., Banerjee, S.P., Yamamura, H.I. and Greenberg,
D.** (1974)
Drugs, neurotransmitters and schizophrenia. Science,
184, 1243–1253.

Szasz, T.S. (1961)
The Myth of Mental Illness. New York: Harper & Row.

Teasdale, J.D. and Fogarty, S.J. (1979)
Differential effects of induced mood on retrieval of
pleasant and unpleasant events from episodic memory.
Journal of Abnormal Psychology, 88, 248–257.

Watson, J.B. and Rayner, R. (1920)
Conditional emotional reactions. Journal of Experimental
Psychology, 3, 1–14.

Zigler, E. and Philips, L. (1961)
Psychiatric diagnosis and symptomalogy. Journal of
Abnormal and Social Psychology, 63, 69–75.

Zubin, J. and Spring, B. (1977)
Vulnerability - a new view of schizophrenia. Journal of
Abnormal Psychology, 86, 103–126.

uestions

1. Describe and discuss critically the 'medical' model of
psychopathology.
2. Describe and evaluate critically the statistical
approach to psychopathology. What are the ways in which
behaviour can be defined as abnormal?
3. How useful is the psychodynamic model of psychopathology? Discuss this question with special reference to
Freud's views.
4. Discuss critically the learning theory approach to
psychopathology. Do you consider this approach to be
useful? If so, justify your opinion.
5. Has the 'cognitive' model contributed to our understanding of abnormal behaviour? What are its main assumptions? Provide as many examples as possible to
illustrate your answer.
6. Provide examples of the contribution of social and
cultural factors to the determination and maintenance of

abnormal behaviour. Can psychopathological disorders be explained entirely by reference to social and cultural factors?

7. What has psychology contributed to our understanding of abnormal behaviour? What are its main assumptions? Provide as many examples as possible to illustrate your answer.

8. Compare and contrast the psychological and medical approaches to psychopathology. Are these approaches mutually exclusive or complementary?

9. Consider two psychiatric conditions (e.g. depression and schizophrenia). Now describe various theoretical explanations of these conditions, including both the medical and psychological. Indicate whether the various approaches have increased our understanding of these conditions.

10. 'Psychopathology is determined primarily by biological causes.' Discuss.

11. Consider the medical and psychological approaches to psychopathology in terms of their implications for treatment and management.

Annotated reading

Davison, G.C. and Neale, J.M. (1977) Abnormal Psychology: An experimental clinical approach (2nd edn). Chichester: Wiley.

> The chapter can provide no more than an introduction to psychopathology. This is the best of the textbooks available: it is readable, comprehensive and, in general, accurate. I have found it useful in teaching, and have drawn upon it extensively in drafting the chapter. If you want to follow up any aspect of the chapter in more detail, look up the topic in the Index of this book.

Hilgard, E.R., Atkinson, R.L. and Atkinson, R.C. (1979) Introduction to Psychology (7th edn) New York: Harcourt Brace Jovanovich (chapters 14, 15 and 16).

> Intermediate in length between the chapter and the Davison and Neale book, this group of chapters give a good general account. Chapter 14 reviews conflict and stress in terms of both experimental and psychoanalytic work; chapter 15 gives a good outline of much of the ground covered in this chapter; and chapter 16 discusses methods of treatment.

Spielberger, C. (1979) Understanding Stress and Anxiety. New York: Harper & Row.

> A very readable and well-illustrated introduction to experimental and clinical work on stress and anxiety, recommended for the student wishing to look further into these aspects.

Seligman, M.E.P. (1975) Helplessness: On depression, development and death. New York: Freeman.
Seligman presents his theory of learned helplessness in a very stimulating and engaging book. Although the theory was based on laboratory studies with animals, Seligman has injected a great deal of 'human interest' into this account. Students who are especially interested in the theory of depression should note, however, that Seligman's ideas have moved on since the book was written to incorporate attributional concepts.

Stafford-Clark D. and Smith, A.C. (1979) Psychiatry for Students (5th edn). London: Allen & Unwin.
The chapter does not attempt to do full justice to psychiatry. This is the most readable of the general textbooks on psychiatry, written for students rather than for practitioners. It is a good source for more details of psychiatric symptoms, disorders and treatments.

Sim, M. and Gordon, E.B. (1976) Basic Psychiatry (3rd edn). Edinburgh: Churchill Livingstone.
Concise and authoritative, with succinct descriptions of the phenomenology of psychiatric disorders.

Mayer-Gross W., Slater, E. and Roth, M. (1977) Clinical Psychiatry (3rd edn), revised by E. Slater and M. Roth. London: Ballière Tindall.
For many British psychiatrists and psychologists, this is the 'bible' of psychiatry. A very sound authority.

Clare, A. (1980) Psychiatry in Dissent (2nd edn). London: Tavistock.
Unlike the general psychiatric textbooks, this book investigates the history and problems of psychiatry in a critical fashion. It is by no means a 'radical' book, but it is well-written, scholarly and interesting.

Inechen, B. (1979) Mental Illness. London: Longman.
This reviews the field from a sociological viewpoint, and covers a good deal of research on social factors in psychopathology.

Rowe, D. (1978) The Experience of Depression. Chichester: Wiley.
A fascinating and well-observed study of the experiences of some depressed clients seen by this experienced clinical psychologist.

Bannister, D. and Fransella, F. (1980) Inquiring Man (2nd edn). Harmondsworth: Penguin.
A persuasive account of George Kelly's personal

construct approach to psychology and psychopathology, written by two of its leading exponents.

Freud, S. (1962 edn) Two Short Accounts of Psychoanalysis. Harmondsworth: Penguin.

These accounts, written in 1909 and 1926, give strikingly clear insights into Freud's thought at two important stages in the development of psychanalytic theory. First-hand acquaintance with Freud's writings is often more valuable than the distillations offered by commentators. On the other hand, students should remember that psychoanalytic thought has advanced since 1926.

The Journal of Abnormal Psychology, 1977, 84, 433-474.

Contains a series of papers critically discussing the Rosenhan study 'on being sane in insane places'. Well worth following up this interesting controversy.

18

What the Patient Should Know: Communication Between Doctors and Patients
David Griffiths

Communication between doctors and patients has not been subjected to a great deal of systematic and objective investigation by the medical profession and it has certainly not received the attention which it would seem to deserve in view of its importance. In the United Kingdom, the major contribution to the scientific investigation of this topic has come from Philip Ley and his colleagues. Ley has written extensively on doctor-patient communication (1972, 1977a, 1977b) and has conducted a number of interesting and important empirical studies. Indeed, any review of doctor-patient contact would necessarily rely a great deal on the work of Ley; this brief summary of major conclusions in relation to medical communication must acknowledge a considerable debt to him as it is extensively based on his work and reviews.

Ley argues cogently that doctors 'find it hard to take problems of communication seriously' and suggests two reasons for this. The first is that doctors believe that they can and do communicate effectively with their patients. The second is that doctors are busy people and communicating with patients might very often seem to be secondary to the pressing problems of diagnosis and treatment.

There are, however, many indications that communicating with patients deserves very serious attention. As we shall see, patients are often dissatisfied with the information which they receive. In addition, there are indications that patients often do not follow medical advice and that these failures of compliance are related to both the content of information (especially advice) given by doctors and the manner and behaviour of the doctor. It follows from the research that communication with patients is not managed as effectively as it might seem to be; patients often do not follow advice (in taking tablets, dieting and other aspects of treatment which the patient controls) so that both the treatment programme and the patient's welfare could be placed in some jeopardy.

The work which has been reported and reviewed by Ley and his colleagues suggests five overall conclusions which deserve very serious attention from staff involved in the provision of health care.

Patients are often dissatisfied with information and advice received from doctors

Surveys reported by Ley indicate that between 30 and 60 per cent of patients are dissatisfied with explanations, information and advice given to them by doctors. Studies also suggest that dissatisfaction with communication is not necessarily a feature of a general dissatisfaction with all aspects of care. In other words, we are not dealing with a sub-group of patients who complain about everything since the results demonstrate that patients who complain about consultations with doctors are often happy about other aspects of their care and treatment. Furthermore, dissatisfaction is not necessarily explained by a lack of interest or involvement on the part of the doctor; substantial numbers of patients continue to be unhappy even when doctors have made special efforts to communicate with them.

Finally, dissatisfaction is not reasonably explained as part of a general resistance to information which is often unpleasant and anxiety-provoking for the patient. Ley's review suggests that most patients are keen to secure information about their condition, even if such information relates to the presence of serious conditions such as cancer or the imminence of death. Although medical and other staff are reported to be ambivalent about the provision of such information, to a large extent because of the dangers of adverse effects on patients' morale and behaviour, there is also evidence to indicate that many patients benefit from such information and are, subsequently, able to make a very reasonable adjustment to an inevitably difficult situation. For example, studies of the effects of the preparation of patients for surgery indicate clearly that the patient who is forewarned and prepared for inevitable discomforts does make a significantly better adjustment and is likely to be discharged sooner. This is not to deny, however, that information can have adverse effects in some cases. For example, Byrne (1979) suggests that the more neurotic individual is likely to suffer an exacerbation of an already high level of anxiety when he is informed that he has suffered a heart attack.

Patients often do not follow medical advice

The percentage of patients who do not follow advice differs between studies. The range of non-compliant patients varies (Ley, 1977b) from 8 to 92 per cent and the average number from 38.6 to 54.6 per cent. It is also clear that non-compliance is found in quite different groups of patients and is certainly not limited to, for example, psychiatric patients who are already handicapped by a wide range of psychological problems which might be expected to affect their co-operation. Reviews and surveys indicate that rates of compliance (measured by interviews with patients, blood tests to detect the presence of drugs and tablets which are returned) can be low for psychiatric drugs, but also for the taking of antibiotics, anticonvulsants and iron compounds during pregnancy. In addition, medical advice on diet, exercise and child care is neglected or not followed by substantial groups.

Compliance has been found to be unrelated to social class, education and family size so that it is not simply a matter of misunderstanding because of low intelligence, or the existence of problems of management in large families. Non-compliance is, however, more likely in some circumstances; it is more likely if the treatment is painful or involves distressing side effects. Degree of staff control is also important. Amongst psychiatric patients, medication is not taken by considerably more out-patients than in-patients and the compliance of day-patients is intermediate (Wilcox, Gillan and Hare, 1965).

At this point, it is important to remind ourselves of the serious consequences of non-compliance by patients. Patients who do not follow advice will often be placing themselves at risk and will increase the probability that their treatment is going to be ineffective. The importance of anticonvulsants and antibiotics in this respect can be assumed, but recent research also establishes that the chance of relapses for psychiatric patients in the community is substantially higher if the patient is not taking his medication. Some patients do not suffer (Leff and Wing, 1971), but others will pay a heavy price for their behaviour.

Patient satisfaction and compliance are related and the relationship probably implies a causal link

The evidence which has been reported (and it must be admitted that there is not a great deal) appears to support the common-sense hypothesis that satisfied patients are more likely to follow the advice which is given to them. In fact, Ley's evaluation of the evidence suggests that patient compliance has a number of determinants and he bases his conclusion to a large extent on work in paediatrics.

Korsch and her colleagues (Ley, 1977a) studied several hundred child-care referrals in North America; mothers were interviewed seven to fourteen days after a paediatric consultation to establish whether they were following any advice which had been given. The results indicated that compliance was more likely:

*   if the doctor was friendly;
*   if the doctor engaged in some informal discussion;
*   if the doctor talked to the child;
*   if the doctor talked for a substantial proportion of the time;
*   if the doctor enquired about and tried to satisfy the mother's expectations and explained why some could not be met;
*   if the doctor took action to alleviate the mother's anxieties;
*   if he gave information in addition to asking questions.

This evidence is, of course, correlational and cannot be

regarded as conclusive proof that the doctor's interview behaviour causes satisfaction and compliance. We see in due course, however, that a small number of controlled studies do suggest that better communication leads to improvements in both satisfaction and compliance with medical advice. Before we reach that point, we need to take note of the research on comprehension and memory.

Patients sometimes fail to understand or they forget what they are told
Much of Ley's work has been concerned with a 'cognitive' hypothesis. Quite simply, this is the suggestion that communication between doctor and patient is unsuccessful because patients either do not understand what they are told or forget a great deal of what doctors say. As an example of problems of comprehension, Ley and his colleagues have estimated that between 25 and 60 per cent of the general population would find it difficult to understand X-ray informational leaflets. Verbal communication from both specialists and general practitioners might also be beyond the comprehension of many patients, though the content is often simple and straightforward to the doctor.

Ley suggests that at least three factors determine failures of comprehension. The first is that oral or written material is too difficult (in terms of vocabulary, complexity of terminology, etc.) for some patients. The second is that patients often lack very basic knowledge such as the location of vital organs, and misconceptions often seem to be the rule rather than the exception. Finally, many patients are diffident about making enquiries and do not, in practice, tell their doctors that they need more information. Each of these explanations is supported by a body of empirical research.

If information is understood, how well does the patient remember it afterwards? Once again, Ley and his colleagues have shown that substantial amounts of information are quickly forgotten. In fact, as much as 35 to 50 per cent of the information given is forgotten within 80 minutes of the end of a consultation. Forgetting is, however, selective; advice, which is often practically more important to the patient than other information such as diagnosis, is very vulnerable and tends to be forgotten more easily than diagnosis. To some extent, the forgetting of advice is explained by the tendency to give advice at the end of an interview. Patients tend to remember information given at the beginning of an interview more effectively and to forget the message given at the end. Forgetting is also likely to have a greater effect on information seen by the patient to be less important and patients apparently believe that diagnosis is more important than advice.

It is possible to improve both the comprehension and recall of medical information: these procedures, in turn, produce improvements in patient satisfaction and compliance
We have seen that some important determinants of patient

satisfaction and compliance have been identified; but is this knowledge of any practical value? Can it be used to improve comprehension and recall and, in turn, to reduce dissatisfaction and increase compliance? The answer is that this information has already been applied, with generally very positive results. Ley's own work demonstrates that substantial improvements in comprehension and memory can be produced without excessive increases in staff time or effort. For example, the following techniques have useful positive effects on the total recall of information by patients.

* Improving the comprehension of messages by using shorter sentences and simpler vocabulary. The improvement in the amount recalled, as reported by Ley, varies from 5 to 20 per cent.
* 'Explicit categorization': a term used by Ley to refer to attempts by a communicator to emphasize and label the main message given to the patient. The doctor might, for example, warn the patient that he is about to tell him about diagnosis, prognosis and practical advice. Improvements in recall vary from 6 per cent for diagnosis to 38 per cent for advice.
* Repetition of information: this is associated with improvements similar to those reported for the labelling of messages in 'explicit categorization'.
* Concrete and specific advice: if advice is given in a precise and concrete manner (for example, a weight reduction of one kilo a week or the avoidance of specific foods rather than general advice to 'cut down on food'), it can produce improvements in recall as high as 30 per cent.

What of the effects of better comprehension and recall on satisfaction and compliance? In addition to the correlational evidence which has already been mentioned, Ley and his colleagues have shown that satisfaction and compliance can be controlled through the manipulation of comprehension and recall. For example, Ley reports that an extra visit by the doctor to his hospital patients (lasting less than five minutes every 7-10 days) and which was intended to ensure that the patient understood important information about his case, resulted in satisfaction with communication in 80 per cent of a sample of patients. This was well above the 48 per cent who were satisfied with the normal control procedure (no extra visit) and the 41 per cent who received an extra visit during which the doctor discussed general aspects of the patients' stay in hospital. It need hardly be emphasized that the extra five minutes of the doctor's time was very cost effective in terms of the resultant level of satisfaction amongst patients.

What of the effects of better communication on the patient's response to advice? This is arguably more important since patients might be dissatisfied with communication and yet follow advice which, through the beneficial effects

of the treatment, will have a greater effect on their
health. Once again, however, the evidence is limited but
suggests clearly that the manipulation of communication does
produce more compliance with medical advice.

Two important experiments are reported by Ley and both
involve common medical problems. Both also support the
suggestion that compliance is greater if measures are taken
to improve comprehension and recall. In relation to psychiatric out-patients, specially prepared leaflets about the
effects of medication (and explaining factors such as the
delayed effects of some drugs and side effects associated
with others), had significant and beneficial effects on the
self-administration of both antidepressants and tranquillizers. These results are quite impressive, especially if
they are evaluated against the background of low compliance
in the taking of medication demonstrated by Wilcox, Gillan
and Hare (1965). Direct comparisons are not possible, however, since Wilcox and his colleagues studied phenothiazine
drug-taking so that the patients involved can be assumed to
be a different sample. Research involving obese individuals
on weight reduction programmes has also demonstrated that
carefully produced explanatory leaflets are associated with
substantially greater weight loss and another study has
shown that weight loss is likely to be greater if weight-
reducing groups are conducted in a manner which increases
their cohesiveness (cf. chapter 23).

On the basis of these studies, it seems fair to assume
that patient satisfaction and compliance are likely to be
improved if measures are taken to improve the comprehension
and recall of communications and also the social conditions
associated with the provision of information. More research
is required, but there is a strong suggestion that improvements in patient care (and potentially in outcome) are to be
expected at the cost of relatively small increases in effort
from medical and other staff. The exercise is, in other
words, likely to be cost effective in terms of the benefits
which might be produced by small increments in effort.

Ley's evaluation of the work of Janis (described in more
detail in chapter 14) and others on the management of pre-
operative stress also suggests quite clearly that adequate
preparation of the patient (through the provision of information, advice about self-management and encouragement for
emotional rehearsal as a preparation for inevitable discomfort) tends to lead to better adjustment post-operatively;
in addition to the reduction of the patient's distress and
frustration, there seems to be a reduction in the need for
analgesics and also in the length of the patient's stay in
hospital.

At the beginning of this section, mention was made of
the meagre attention which has been directed to the problems
and inadequacies of doctor-patient communication. At this
point, it is important to note the implications of those
surveys which indicate high rates of non-compliance in some
patient groups. If it is possible to assume that prescribed

treatments are likely to affect the course and outcome of illness, then patients' failure to follow advice and instruction is likely to have adverse effects on their progress and the value of the treatment. In view of the links between communication, satisfaction and compliance, it also follows that the outcome for the patient, and the effectiveness and efficiency of many medical and surgical treatments, will be determined - and to potentially large extents - by the careful provision of suitable communication.

Summary and conclusions   Empirical research and literature reviews suggest a number of important conclusions. The first is that many patients are dissatisfied with the information and advice given to them by medical staff. Patients often do not follow medical advice and their non-compliance is related to aspects of their satisfaction with information and advice provided by doctors. Improved communication with patients can be expected to lead to better compliance with medical instructions and potentially to better treatment and outcome.

The second is that many of the determinants of effective communication have been identified. More specifically, failure to communicate effectively with patients is associated with difficulties in comprehension and memory; in addition, aspects of the doctor's social behaviour, such as his friendliness, would also seem to be important. The third conclusion is that a number of techniques are available to improve both comprehension and recall. These include control of the content of messages (e.g. simple vocabulary and sentence structure), placing important messages near the beginning of an interview, emphasis and labelling of important messages, repetition, and the provision of specific as opposed to vague advice. The application of these techniques is cost effective to the extent that it involves fairly small additional work by staff.

A final conclusion is that improvements in communication are capable of having important causal effects on both patient satisfaction and compliance. It follows from this that effective communication could lead to more efficient use of resources and also better therapeutic outcomes for patients.

A great deal of empirical research remains to be done on the problems and determinants of effective and efficient communication with patients. For example, the area of individual differences amongst patients has not been adequately explored. This is an issue of considerable clinical significance since potentially threatening communications could have adverse effects on some patients to an extent which would impair, rather than facilitate, their subsequent management. Byrne (1979) has already suggested that neurotic patients are more likely to respond adversely to unpleasant communications (cf. chapter 14). Research will need to establish whether adverse responses occur sufficiently frequently even when the content of communications, and the manner of presentation, is adequate. If this is so, the next step would involve attempts to identify the factors which increase the probability of adverse responses. As a final step, the research would need to establish whether the identification of causes can lead to the identification of individual patients who are likely to respond adversely to threatening messages, for it is not necessarily true that the identification of predictor variables will allow the accurate prediction of an individual's response. For example, though neurotic individuals tend to respond excessively to stress, it does not follow that all neurotic individuals respond adversely to all stressors.

An additional area for research relates to the staff who communicate with patients. The research has concentrated on the role of the doctor and has neglected the involvement of other professionals such as nurses. Yet it is obvious, even to the casual observer at a visiting session, that nurses are often the major point of contact both for patients and their relatives. Nursing staff are unlikely to have the expertise of the doctor and do not have the advantages of his prestige. It cannot, therefore, be assumed that some of the results on doctor-patient communication will necessarily be replicated if communications between nurses and patients were studied.

One final area for investigation involves communication between staff; for example, communications between doctors and nurses, both in relation to individual patients and, more generally, on broader issues of treatment and care. For though it is easy enough to assume that staff communication is relatively free of the worst difficulties involved in communicating with a patient, some investigations suggest that staff understanding of the steps involved in basic treatment techniques can be very limited and that lack of understanding is not necessarily improved by well organized teaching workshops (Richards, Hill-Tout, Berry, Hassall and Griffiths, 1980).

References

Byrne, D.G. (1979)
Anxiety as state and trait following survived myocardial infarction. British Journal of Social and Clinical Psychology, 18, 417-425.

Leff, J.P. and Wing, J.K. (1971)
A trial of maintenance therapy in schizophrenia. British Medical Journal, 3, 599-604.

Ley, P. (1972)
Complaints made by hospital staff and patients: a review of the literature. Bulletin of the British Psychological Society, 25, 115-120.

Ley, P. (1977a)
Psychological studies of doctor-patient communication. In S. Rachman (ed.), Contributions to Medical Psychology, Volume 1. Oxford: Pergamon Press.

Ley, P. (1977b)
> Communicating with the patient. In J. C. Coleman
> (ed.), Introductory Psychology. London: Routledge &
> Kegan Paul.

Richards, E., Hill-Tout, J., Berry, N., Hassall, R. and Griffiths, D. (1980)
> An evaluation of a rehabilitation workshop. Medical
> Education, 14, 36-40.

Wilcox, D.R.C., Gillan, R. and Hare, E.H. (1965)
> Do psychiatric patients take their drugs? British
> Medical Journal, 2, 790.

Questions

1. Discuss the suggestion that patients who apparently disregard their doctors' advice are either stupid or awkward, or both.
2. What has psychological research contributed to the understanding and management of patients' compliance with their doctors' advice?
3. Why are patients apparently often unhappy with information and advice given by their doctors? Who should accept the responsibility for this?
4. What are the measures which can be taken to increase patients' compliance?
5. On the basis of the research on compliance, compile a list of practical advice which might be given to young doctors about the management of their patients.

Annotated reading

Ley, P. (1972) Complaints made by hospital staff and patients: a review of the literature. Bulletin of the British Psychological Society, 25, 115-120.

> As the title suggests, this paper provides a useful overview of the evidence on complaints made by both staff and patients. Though brief, it considers a number of essential issues and is also careful in the conclusions which it draws.

Ley, P. (1977) Communicating with the patient. In J.C. Coleman (ed.), Introductory Psychology. London: Routledge & Kegan Paul.

> This is probably the most readable summary of Philip Ley's work and yet provides a concise synopsis of its major conclusions and implications.

19

Psychological Aspects of the Response to Drugs
David Griffiths

Drugs and medication are clearly an important part of life in modern industrial societies, and are a major element in the therapeutic programmes associated with health care. In Great Britain, for example, tens of millions of prescriptions for medication are handed out by general practitioners each year. In addition, many millions of pounds are spent by the public in purchasing their own favourite medicines at chemists and other shops.

Many of these drugs are taken to alleviate psychological rather than physical problems, and our main interest is limited to these drugs. For example, tranquillizers such as Valium or Ativan are taken to reduce tension and anxiety. Anti-depressant drugs are taken to alleviate the various discomforts associated with a depressed mood. Though some of these psychological problems are caused, in turn, by physical conditions (e.g. agitation and depression as a response to a prolonged and painful physical illness) it is likely that a much greater number are caused by life stresses. Life events - such as birth, death, marriage or a change of house or job - are well-known antecedents of depression, tension and anxiety, and also suicide attempts. When these events occur, the general practitioner will often have to rely on tranquillizers or anti-depressants as the basis of his therapy, and the evidence suggests clearly that at least 75 per cent of his patients will come with psychological rather than physical problems. The psychology of drugs and medication - the general term for this area of study is psychopharmacology - involves a number of areas of interest.

Two major questions deserve our attention. First of all, what are the changes in behaviour and psychological functioning which are produced by drugs? In addition to the effects of drugs on emotional state and mood, we are also interested in the effects on learning, memory, attention and human behaviour more generally. Second, to what extent are the changes associated with taking drugs attributable to the effects of the drug on the brain and nervous system? As we shall see, the widespread observation that the psychological and behavioural changes apparently associated with a drug are also produced by a tablet which appears to be the drug but is, in fact, an inert substance suggests very clearly that drug response is influenced by other factors. The evidence and clinical experience point to the importance of attitudes and expectations, personality characteristics and also the social situation associated with the taking of medication.

The major concern of this section is those drugs which are known to have psychological and behavioural effects. The general term for these drugs is 'psychotropic', and there are a number of well-known categories.

* Tranquillizers: minor tranquillizers (Valium, Ativan) are used to alleviate tension and anxiety. Major tranquillizers (such as Largactil) are used to control more severe disturbances of behaviour associated with psychotic conditions.
* Sedatives or hypnotics: these have a more pervasive and retarding action on behaviour and functioning than tranquillizers and so are more likely to be associated with a loss of mental efficiency and feelings of drowsiness and even confusion. Alcohol and the barbiturates are examples of sedatives. Some of these drugs are also used to correct sleep disorders.
* Anti-depressants: as the name suggests, this category alleviates the range of problems and discomforts associated with depressed mood. Imipramine and Ludiomil are examples.
* Stimulants: drugs such as the amphetamines, and also caffeine, increase the level of psychological and physical functioning and are also sometimes taken because of their positive effects on mood and feelings generally.
* Hallucinogens: LSD is the best-known example of this category of drugs which have dramatic effects on a wide range of functioning such as perception, thought and feelings.

Though all drugs can be associated with a degree of dependence (so that the individual experiences discomfort when the drug is withdrawn), stimulants and hallucinogens have become more prominently associated with addictive problems and the tendency for some individuals to secure them in order to promote psychological changes in themselves. Addiction has become a major social and health problem and it is clear that drugs can cause as well as alleviate human misery.

Placebo effects

Many of the changes which follow the taking of drugs are now known not to be caused by the chemical action of the drug. In fact, the same changes occur if the individual takes an inert substance which has a superficial resemblance in appearance to the active drug. This is the phenomenon known as the placebo response and its manifestations are both well documented and dramatic.

The placebo response is demonstrated by an experiment conducted by Frankenhaeuser and her colleagues in Sweden (1963). Female volunteer subjects were assessed under three conditions and the order of these conditions was varied so that the observed changes were not determined by the order of presentation. On one occasion, subjects were assessed during a visit to the laboratory (ostensibly to acquaint them with the situation) when they were not given any tablets. On another occasion, they were given an inert preparation but told that it contained an agent which encouraged drowsiness and even sleep. On a third occasion, they were led to believe that they were being given a stimulant drug which would, for example, improve their alertness. No active substance was involved on any of these occasions. Assessments of the subjects involved physical variables (e.g. pulse rate, blood pressure), psychological response (reaction time) and self-assessments of speed, drowsiness, feelings and mood. The results showed that all of these measures were affected and the subjects responded to the inert substances in a manner consistent with their belief that they were taking 'stimulants' or 'depressants'. For example, the 'depression' condition was associated with feelings of being slow and drowsy; reaction times and physical measures manifested the changes which might again be expected if the subjects had taken depressant drugs, though the changes were not as intense as in the self-assessed measures.

A number of quite fascinating conclusions are suggested by investigations of the placebo response.

* The placebo response can involve widespread changes in physiological state, behavioural response and subjective experience. As we have just seen, changes in pulse rate and blood pressure can be identical, or very similar, to those observed when an active drug has been taken. Some investigations reveal that the subjective changes (e.g. tension reduction) are greater than those observed in controlled trials of tranquillizers!

* Some functions appear to be more sensitive to a placebo response than others. Simpler mental processes (such as reaction time or tapping speed) are more likely to be affected than complex processes (such as logical problem-solving). Speed of functioning is more likely to be affected than accuracy.

* Placebo responses can involve both improvement and deterioration in functioning. On the one hand, placebo responders have reported marked improvements in mood and feelings and their performance is more efficient; in other investigations, the placebo response has included drowsiness, nausea, dizziness, slowness, and a wide range of changes including a deterioration in efficiency.

* The placebo response can mimic changes associated with most drug groups. This can even include hallucinogenic drugs, since a number of investigators have documented hallucinations and other bizarre experiences in volunteer subjects who believed that they had taken an active drug but had, in fact, drunk distilled water!

What factors determine the placebo response? A number of investigators have attempted to identify the factors which determine the complex response to placebo preparations. Three broad sets of factors are clearly implicated.

First, a number of aspects of individual differences are important. More specifically, personality traits and expectations are clearly involved. For example, individuals who are suggestible, neurotic and acquiescent are more likely to manifest a placebo response. On the other hand, this is certainly not inevitable and many such individuals do not manifest such a response. The search for a 'placebo responder' - a personality type who is likely to respond to inert substances - has not been successful. In fact, the general conclusion is that there is no specific pattern of characteristics which distinguishes the individual who responds in this way.

Though the proportion of placebo responses is said to be constant across investigations (approximately one in three individuals), this proportion is made up of different individuals on separate occasions. This means, of course, that an individual might respond at some times but not at others, and that measures of personality (cf. chapter 11) are unlikely to be accurate predictors since they are relatively constant. Part of this variation with the individual's behaviour is determined by his expectations (as in the Frankenhaeuser experiment). It has also been demonstrated, however, that the placebo response can occur even if the subjects in an experiment are informed that they are to be given a placebo and not an active drug. One investigation showed that the placebo response did not correlate at all with the individual's belief that he was not taking an active drug!

The context or situation is also important as a determinant of the placebo response. The presence and behaviour of other people is known to be very important, and the general trend appears to be that group conditions facilitate and intensify the effects of medication. If the effects of alcohol are considered (and solitary drinking is generally agreed to be anything but pleasant) then the effects of a social group are already apparent. Other investigations have studied the effects of stimulants and depressants in a group situation, and have found that changes in the behaviour of the individual are influenced not only by the substance which he has taken but also by the drug taken by others who are present.

Finally, the characteristics of the drug are important. In addition to the obvious factors such as the type and dosage, factors such as the appearance of the capsule or tablet are well-known determinants of the response. For example, the colour of the preparation is one possible determinant; coloured capsules are generally held to be more likely to produce a response than a plain tablet. In summary, the body of research on the placebo response indicates very clearly that a large number of variables - in the person, situation and the drug - are potentially involved as determinants of the individual's response.

A number of important conclusions are suggested by this discussion of the placebo response. The overall conclusion must be that, to variable extents, the changes which follow the taking of drugs are not necesssarily produced by the chemical effects of those drugs on the nervous system. Variables such as expectation, personality, the admini- stration and social context and the appearance of the drug are also important potential determinants of the response. The determinants are so complex, however, that prediction can be rather difficult. Placebo responding is clearly not a fixed personality characteristic.

One final point involves the scientific evaluation of drug effects. It will be apparent that a placebo control is a necessary element of the design of an evaluative study. This involves a random allocation of subjects to a placebo and 'active' drug group so that a comparison of the changes in behaviour in the two groups allows the researcher to identify the kind or extent of behavioural change which is associated with the active component in the drug. Double blind trials involve situations where neither subject nor experimenter is aware of the nature of the pill which is taken; in other words, they do not know whether an active preparation or a placebo has been administered and are, therefore, less likely to be biassed in their assessments of the effects. The placebo effect can, however, be difficult to control since it is possible for a subject to identify a drug by such factors as its taste, and observers are some- times able to make similar identifications through such cues as the presence and nature of side effects. Guesses are often, however, incorrect and 'negative' placebo effects (the subject incorrectly believes that he has taken a placebo) can reduce or cancel the effects of an active drug. These factors must be taken into consideration in both group based and individual investigations (cf. chapter 1).

'True' drug effects

Although placebo effects can account for a considerable portion of the changes following drug administration, care- fully controlled studies also demonstrate that many drugs produce 'true' effects through their action on the brain and nervous system. Drugs can affect a wide range of behaviours and psychological functions and their effects are both in- teresting and often practically very important. In addition to the effects of medication on emotional and mood states, drugs can also have extensive effects on perception, think- ing, learning and memory, attention, sleep and dreaming and a broad range of other behaviours.

The widespread effects of drugs are of practical impor- tance as well as considerable theoretical interest. For example, some of the effects of drugs administered to alle- viate emotional and mood problems are such that they impair the individual's ability to function safely in his job or to

drive a car. A major tranquillizer might affect the individual's psychomotor and skilled performance, and also his
judgement, to an extent that he becomes a dangerous driver.
The situation is potentially serious and especially if
neither the patient nor his doctor is aware of the changes
in behaviour. Adverse drug effects are a very real danger,
since it is extremely difficult to predict the effects of a
drug with any degree of precision. The dangers of self-
prescribed drugs are, of course, already evident in relation
to alcohol: the relationship between alcohol and road accidents is well documented and it is likely that the link is
explained, at least to some extent, by the effects of
alcohol on risk-taking.

Functional and behavioural change

The effects of drugs on human behaviour can be both widespread and very specific. This discussion is limited to a
brief review of examples of the effects of drugs on functioning. If the reader wishes to extend his knowledge of
this fascinating topic, he might be advised to continue to
read Gordon Claridge's 'Drugs and Human Behaviour' for its
impressive combination of scholarship, practical relevance
and interest. What are the effects which drugs exert on
human behaviour? Here are some examples.

Emotion and mood

The most commonly used drug groups, tranquillizers and anti-
depressants, are used with the specific intention of alleviating anxiety, tension and depression. Once again, an
extensive review of the effectiveness of these drugs is not
undertaken here. Indeed, such a review would need to be very
lengthy in view of the large number of drugs which are now
marketed by pharmaceutical companies. The evidence for the
value of many of these drugs has accumulated, however, from
both clinical experience and, more importantly, controlled
clinical trials. Drugs such as Valium are prescribed very
frequently and the disappearance of this medication would
probably deprive doctors of an important therapeutic aid.

Whilst the beneficial effects of tranquillizers and
anti-depressants are generally demonstrated, their exact
role in the alleviation of the individual's problems might
be expected to vary. In some cases, and especially those
where the individual's emotional state can be viewed as a
response to a life stress or problem, the contribution of
the medication will often not be to solve that problem but
to reduce the distraction of the emotional state and to
reduce the anxiety or depression to a point where the
individual's problem solving efficiency is increased.

It is now generally accepted that the relationship
between efficiency (e.g. in problem-solving) and arousal
(associated, at least in part, with anxiety level) is curvilinear. This means that individuals at high and low arousal
levels are likely to be less efficient than those in the
middle part of the range. Anxious individuals are likely to

be at the upper extreme: that is, to be hyperaroused. The effect of a tranquillizer, therefore, will be to lower their arousal and their problem-solving efficiency might be expected to improve so that they should be more able to cope with life's problems. Figure 1 clarifies this relationship: the anxious individual might be at point B on the arousal continuum before he takes his medication but move to point A after administration, and be expected to be both more comfortable and more efficient.

Figure 1

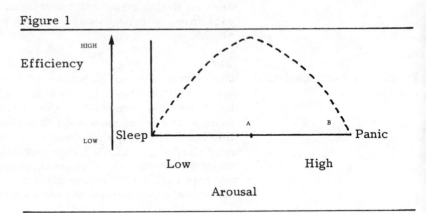

It also follows from the diagram that the effects of a tranquillizer on a person who is already at point A, and is not excessively anxious, will be to lower his arousal to a level where his efficiency will be correspondingly reduced.

Learning and memory

The process of learning is complex and involves at least three major stages. These are registration (when the material to be learnt is received by the organism), retention (storage) and retrieval (when the material is reproduced to influence behaviour). Within the retention stage, the mechanisms underlying short- and long-term storage are agreed to differ and there are strong indications that learning is particularly unstable in the period soon after registration. It is presumed, in fact, that various processes of consolidation are taking place at this time; if allowed to proceed, these result in a fairly permanent record being made.

What effects do drugs have on learning and memory? Though the use of categories such as 'stimulant' and 'depressant' suggests that drugs have a general facilitative or deteriorating effect on learning, the results of empirical research indicate clearly that the effects can be quite specific and depend on variables such as the point in the learning sequence when the drug is taken. One example suffices to demonstrate this point.

Steinberg and Summerfield (1952) were interested in the effects of depressant drugs on the acquisition and recall of verbal material. The general assumption, of course, is that learning is expected to be adversely affected by depressants such as alcohol, barbiturates and nitrous oxide. In one experiment, nitrous oxide inhalation was used because of the precision involved in its administration and the fact that it does not accumulate in the body. Steinberg and Summerfield required their subjects to learn and recall lists of nonsense words and their results were quite surprising. As expected, nitrous oxide administered before the learning began had an adverse effect on that learning. However, when the administration followed the acquisition phase, the retention and retrieval of the nonsense words was actually better! The effects, therefore, vary and depend on when the drug is taken in relation to learning. In this case, a depressant drug impairs acquisition but improves recent recall. One explanation for the positive effects on recent recall is that the drug prevents interference of the learning process during the stage when recently acquired material needs to be consolidated in memory storage if it is to be retained.

Attention

Stimulant and depressant drugs have, on the whole, predictable effects on tasks requiring prolonged attention. Such a task would involve, for example, protracted observation of a radar screen by an observer who is required to detect specific signals as they occur. Another possibility involves the observer who is required to listen to a list of digits and to detect specific numbers. Performance on such tasks is generally better after a stimulant and worse after a depressant. Talland and Quarton showed, for example, that the drugs methamphetamine and pentabarbitol have opposite effects on such tasks involving observer vigilance for periods of 60 minutes.

Investigators have also been interested in the psychological mechanisms through which drugs exert their effects on attention. One suggestion is that the observer involved in tasks requiring protracted attention will tend to have 'lapses' of attention or 'involuntary rest pauses'; these increase in frequency with time and, during a lapse, the electro-encephalogram can show signs of a sleep-like pattern. The effects of stimulant or depressant drugs, it is suggested, is to decrease or increase the rate of these pauses. One consequence is that those aspects of attention tasks which might be expected to be affected by drugs are those which are related to the involuntary pauses. It has been shown, for example, that amphetamines do not affect the rate of response on a reaction time test, but do reduce the error rate (i.e. missed signals). This is another example of the tendency of at least some drugs to have quite specific effects on behaviour. In practice, this means that a drug will be demonstrated to be exerting an effect only if important and relevant aspects of response are being monitored.

Drug profiles

Since drugs can have specific effects on behaviour and it can be both theoretically and practically important to identify these effects, researchers have been keen to develop techniques to identify the profile of effects produced by specific drugs. The general aim, of course, is to relate aspects of the stimulus (type of drug, dosage, etc.) to precisely measured aspects of the behavioural response. The technique involves the selection of a sample of subjects and also a battery of measures of their behaviour. Subjects can be animals (and often are in the initial trials) or humans, and they can be selected to represent specific sub-groups such as individuals who manifest abnormalities in their functioning. The measures are selected from a large number of possibilities; for example, assessments of learning, conditioning, memory, reaction time, attention, gross and fine motor co-ordination. Studies of the effects of medication on the unrestricted behaviour of children has involved such categories as locomotion, social responses, appropriate and inappropriate responses, and constructive and destructive behaviours. When baseline (i.e. non-drug) measures have been recorded, drugs are then administered and the measures are repeated so that the changes associated with the drug can be identified; comparisons will also need to involve observations of behaviour in response to inert placebos.

It is important to realize too that this technique can be applied to the behaviour of the individual as well as the behaviour of groups. This is especially important since individual differences in response are again a prominent feature of the results when drug responses have been objectively evaluated. We now turn our attention to the factors which influence and determine such differences in response.

Variation in the response to drugs

Two major aspects of individual variation in drug response have been studied. First, do individual differences in drug effects exist and how broad are they? Second, what factors determine differences in response?

The existence of individual differences, often dramatic in their extent, is a fact rather than a possibility. Individual differences are also an important factor since they mean that two individuals can respond in quite different ways to the same drug. In a clinical situation, such information can be of crucial importance because it suggests that some individuals might respond in an adverse manner to a drug which has beneficial results in the majority. An example of the importance of differences in response is provided by a study conducted by Klerman, Dimascio and their colleagues (1959). They monitored the response of two groups of subjects to two tranquillizers, phenyltoloxamine and reserpine. One group consisted of extraverts (A); the other group was more introverted and anxious (B). The A subjects were more hostile and negative in their attitudes to phenyltoloxamine whereas the Bs were more negative in their attitude to reserpine. Objective measures also indicated significant differences in both their behavioural responses and the physiological changes which occurred. On tasks such as serial addition, for example, the groups manifested contradictory and opposite changes to the same drug. Further experimentation demonstrated that the learning capacity of these separate groups was changed in quite different ways, and to the extent that one group would improve whilst the other would deteriorate.

These findings also illustrate rather dramatically the dangers of studies which involve groups and the assessment of the average response. For if the data from the A and B groups were combined, the drugs used would sometimes appear to have no effect since the average would now reflect two quite different modes of response which would cancel each other out in the calculation of statistical data.

What are the factors which determine individual differences in response? We have already referred to some of these factors in discussing the aetiology of the placebo response. The list is essentially the same and includes the following points.

Temporary and fluctuating states of the individual

Anxiety and tension levels are known to affect drug response. The point at which the sedative effect of a drug (measured by changes in the electrical activity of the brain and behavioural changes such as the slurring of speech) takes effect differs both within one individual over time and between different individuals. The individual's motivational level and his goals are also important. For example, the effects of a stimulant or depressant drug can be reduced by influencing the subject's motivation. Morphine addicts offered a shot of morphine immediately after a test of their reaction times responded more quickly, in one experiment, in response to the depressant drug pentabarbitol; if they were offered a shot after a delay, they responded more conventionally by slowing their responses.

Personality

An example of the importance of personality characteristics has already been discussed and the topic is reviewed by Paul Kline in chapter 11. The effects of personality can also be determined in a complex manner, which again makes prediction rather difficult in a clinical situation. For example, Rodnight and Gooch (1963) studied the effects of nitrous oxide on finger dexterity and mental arithmetic. The response was found to be related to combinations of neuroticism and extraversion, and not to extraversion or neuroticism independently. Among stable subjects, the introverts were more susceptible to the depressant effects of the nitrous oxide in terms of performance decrements. Amongst the extraverts, the more neurotic subjects were also more susceptible. The highest degree of susceptibility was found amongst those subjects who were both neurotic and extraverted. Once again, such findings underline the dangers of any research which determines the average response and neglects the potentially wide variation.

Context

The social situation can have a profound effect on drug response. Nowlis and Nowlis (1956) studied groups of four subjects who were allowed to interact with each other after taking various drugs. If subjects had taken the same drugs (Seconal, benzedrine, etc.) the reported effects were increased; for example, subjects on Seconal were more likely to use terms such as 'expansive', 'elated' and 'impulsive' to describe their state. If, however, a subject on Seconal was placed with others who had taken depressants or placebos, he was considerably more likely to describe himself as 'glum', 'dull', 'gloomy' and so on. The social context was clearly having an important effect and the practical implications of such findings in the clinical situation are not to be neglected.

Attitudes and expectations

Once again, some studies have shown that the effects of attitudes and expectations can equal the 'true' effects of the drugs. Alternatively, they can amplify or reduce the biochemically controlled consequences of a drug. The study of addiction provides many examples of the importance of cognitive factors such as expectations. Bozzetti and his colleagues (1967) have reported that dried banana peel, once commonly used as a 'psychedelic' drug, seems to contain no trace of any hallucinogenic agent. The conclusion would seem to be that the effects of the smoking of this substance could be explained entirely by expectation and suggestion. Expectation also appears to determine some of the effects of marijuana. Becker (1953), for example, has suggested that the experience of being 'high' is determined both by the presence of symptoms (which are physiologically determined) and the recognition of these changes, plus the making of a cognitive connection with the use of the drug. The direct effects are apparently not sufficient to produce the experience; the user must become aware of the effects and consciously connect them with the smoking of the marijuana.

Conclusions

Enough has been said to indicate that the psychology of drugs and medication deserves a considerable amount of attention from the clinician. Drugs obviously affect behaviour, but the mode of their effect can be complex. Some drugs have widespread and dramatic effects, whilst others have specific consequences and limited effects. Such findings are theoretically important and are also of clinical relevance since 'side effects' can constitute a serious hazard to the individual and others in his environment. The placebo phenomenon, however, demonstrates that many of the effects which are apparently produced by drugs are also present if the individual is given an inert substance which appears to be a drug.

The total response to a drug is clearly a mixture of biochemically and psychologically determined changes. In other words, the individual responds to the whole situation and not exclusively to the drug. In addition to the type and dosage of drug and other organic factors such as constitution and body build, the response to a drug is clearly affected by the individual's expectations and attitudes, his fluctuating feelings and motivation, and also more stable aspects of his personality. In practice, this means that precisely the same dosage of a given drug can have dramatically varying effects on different individuals, or even on the same individual at different times. Though the general classification of chemicals as 'stimulant', 'depressant', etc., has some value, it also has some limitations when the responses to drugs are studied in more detail.

References

Becker, H.S. (1953)
Becoming a marijuana user. American Journal of Sociology, 59, 235-242.

Bozzetti, I. Jr, Goldsmith, S. and Unger-Leider, J.T. (1967)
The Great Banana Hoax. American Journal of Psychiatry, 124, 678-679.

Claridge, G. (1970)
Drugs and Human Behaviour. Harmondsworth: Penguin.

Frankenhaeuser, M., Jaerpe, G., Svan, H. and Wrangsjae, B. (1963)
Psychophysiological reactions to two different placebo treatments. Scandanavian Journal of Psychology, 4, 245-250.

Klerman, G.L., Dimascio, A., Greenblatt, M. and Rinkell M. (1959)
The influence of specific personality patterns on the reactions to psychotropic agents. In J.H. Masserman (ed.), Biological Psychiatry. New York: Grune & Stratton.

Nowlis, V., and Nowlis, H. (1956)
The description and analysis of mood. Annals of the New York Academy of Science, 65, 345-355.

Rodnight, E. and Gooch, R.N. (1963)
A new method for the determination of individual differences in susceptibility to a depressant drug. In H.J. Eysenck (ed.), Experiments with Drugs. Oxford: Pergamon Press.

Steinberg, H. and Summerfield, A. (1952)
Influence of a depressant drug on acquisition in rote learning. Quarterly Journal of Experimental Psychology, 9, 138-145.

Questions

1. Discuss the ways in which an understanding of the

psychological aspects of the response to medication is important to the doctor. Wherever appropriate, provide examples of the practical implications of the research.

2. What is the placebo response? Discuss its clinical manifestations, its determinants and the clinical implications of the major findings on this phenomenon.

3. How do drugs affect behaviour and psychological functioning? Answer this question with reference to a wide range of behaviours and functions.

4. What are the psychological and social factors which influence the way in which the individual responds to a drug? What are the clinical implications of our understanding of these factors?

5. Assume that drug X is claimed to exert a mild tranquillizing effect. Design an experiment to test this claim, ensuring that your design also allows you (a) to monitor the effects of the drug on a range of behaviours and functions; (b) to detect individual differences in response; (c) to identify the factors which predict individual differences in response; (d) to detect changes in drug effects over time.

Annotated reading

Claridge, G. (1970) Drugs and Human Behaviour. Harmondsworth: Penguin.

Though this book might be out of print when students require it, libraries will presumably be able to obtain copies. For students, this book is an ideal introduction to psychopharmacology since it is well written, clear and interesting, and reviews aspects of psychopharmacology such as the classification of drugs, effects on psychological functioning, dependence and so on.

20

Mental Handicap
David Griffiths

Mental handicap refers to a group of conditions whose aetiology often involves organic causes but whose most obvious manifestations involve behavioural and psychological impairments such as low intelligence and a broad range of handicaps such as severely limited self-care and communication skills. The medical profession is obviously involved in the detection and diagnosis, assessment and care of the mentally handicapped. A major part of both assessment and management, however, involves psychological and behavioural techniques. For example, impairments in the ability to learn from experience are universal among the mentally handicapped; since psychologists have traditionally been very concerned with learning, it is not surprising that mental handicap has become one of the major areas of application for the large body of psychological research on learning and conditioning. It is also important that doctors should be aware of the developments and recent advances in the psychological aspects of mental handicap.

Mental handicap presents the Health Services with extensive problems. Approximately one in ten Health Service beds are occupied by the mentally handicapped in the UK. In addition, many more individuals are supported in the community and live with their families. A recent government report refers to a figure of 120,000 severely mentally handicapped individuals in England and Wales: of these, 50,000 are estimated to be children. Case registers suggest prevalence rates of 2.95 to 5.81 severely handicapped individuals per 1,000. Those mentally handicapped individuals who live in the community can, in addition, constitute a heavy burden to their families, so that an estimate of the number of mentally handicapped individuals is an underestimate of the total number in the community who are affected by mental handicap. An obvious, and quite recent, development has involved moving the focus of care from the institution to the community. While this has many advantages for the patient (who is able to live a more 'normal' existence close to those who love him) there can be little doubt that it sometimes involves considerable burden and distress for the family, since the requisite facilities (e.g. day-care centres) in the community are not always adequate for the needs of this group.

What are the major handicaps present among the mentally handicapped?

The two major categories of handicap involve low intelligence and social competence. In fact, mental handicap is usually detected and diagnosed by reference to low intelligence and limited social skills.

Intelligence, as we have seen, is most reliably assessed by the administration of standardized intelligence or developmental tests. These include a carefully selected set of problems (motor, perceptual, verbal, etc.) which allow the individual's performance to be compared either with his age group or (in the case of children and developmental tests) with different age levels. Test scores are then used to identify the individual's mental age: the age group which he most resembles in his test performance. For example, a mental age of 5½ years indicates that the individual is performing at the level of the average 5½ year old. Alternatively, and more commonly, the individual's intelligence quotient is determined. This indicates his standing relative to his own age group. An IQ of 100, for example, is arbitrarily defined as the average. Thus a 20-year-old individual with an IQ of 100 is at the average for 20 year olds. An IQ of 85 cuts off the bottom 16 per cent or so, while IQs above 115 are in the top 16 per cent for any particular age group.

As will be seen from the following diagram, the intellectual scores of the mentally handicapped are in the bottom part of the range. The severely mentally handicapped are those whose IQs are below 55: in other words, in approximately the bottom 0.1-0.2 per cent of the range. Those whose IQs are between 55 and 70 (about 2.1 per cent) manifest less severe degrees of mental handicap. Those individuals with IQs between 70 and 85 (approximately 12.6 per cent) are designated as borderline subnormal; while their handicaps are considerably less severe than those with IQs below 70, they are nevertheless known to have difficulty with a wide range of skills necessary for normal living.

Figure 1

Classification ranges based on standard deviations

From Gunzburg (1968) with the kind permission of the author and Ballière Tindall.

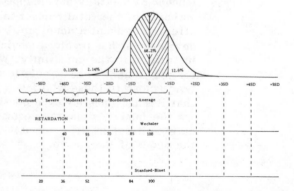

Impairments in social competence are probably more important practically than low intelligence. The mentally handicapped are unable to perform a wide range of skills and tasks which are necessary for normal living. These skills can be classified in different ways. One system of assessment, devised by Gunzburg, involves the following four groups of skills.

* SELF-HELP: for example, the individual's ability to feed and dress himself, move around the house and see to his own toilet needs.
* COMMUNICATION: the two main divisions involve the individual's ability to express himself (e.g. name objects, relate experience, make requests or indicate needs) and his ability to understand others (e.g. instructions, requests and explanations).
* SOCIALIZATION: those social skills which are necessary to harmonious interaction with others (e.g. play and social responses in children; co-operation and social graces in adults).
* OCCUPATION: various aspects of motor skill such as dexterity with the hands and fingers, and balance in standing and walking.

As a group, the mentally handicapped have gross limitations in their social competence. Without training, for example, the majority of the severely handicapped are unable to feed themselves or see to their own toilet needs; the level of vocabulary among the handicapped is generally less than that of the eight- to ten-year-old child, and many are able to communicate basic needs only with the aid of simple sign language. This means that the mentally handicapped are dependent on others: staff in institutions, their families at home. As we have seen, the burden involved can be quite considerable.

In addition to the limitations in social competence, the mentally handicapped can also manifest disordered behaviour which is an inconvenience or danger to themselves or others: for example, destructiveness or aggression. Various estimates suggest that approximately one-third of the severely handicapped manifest behaviour disorders, and these are sometimes sufficiently severe to require hospital care. Care may become difficult, or even impossible, outside an institution unless these problems are controlled.

Many manifestations of inability and handicap can be seen as the consequences of a basic and pervasive difficulty in learning which is generally characteristic of the mentally handicapped. Their learning is slow and inefficient, and learning often does not occur unless it is carefully planned and organized by staff. Whereas normal children learn and imitate spontaneously, this will often not occur amongst the mentally handicapped. As we shall see, their environment has to be carefully controlled to ensure that even the rudiments of a wide range of basic living skills are to develop. It is fortunate, however, that clinical experience and research have increased our understanding of the mentally handicapped's learning ability very considerably. Many of the principles which govern their learning are now understood, though the application of the principles in practice is often as much of an art as a science.

The nature of mental handicap

In the past, the care of the mentally handicapped seems to have been influenced by two general models. The first is an organic or medical model. The major assumption was that mental handicap was caused by a number of physical conditions (genetic disorders, post-infective damage to the brain and nervous system, the effects of traumatic injury etc.). The outcome was the range of impairments which we have considered. These were assumed, however, to be rigid and unchangeable since there was no cure for the underlying pathology. The second model was a more distinctly psychological model. Though it recognized that the underlying aetiology was physical, it tended to focus on low intelligence as the main reason for the social incompetence of the mentally handicapped. Psychologists were therefore primarily concerned with the assessment of intelligence, and it was assumed that intelligence determined the ceiling for the development of social skills; for example, a child with a mental age of five years would not be expected to develop a level of social competence above that age.

As a corollary to both models, the main aim of care was invariably seen to be 'tender loving care' usually within an institution. The alleviation of handicap through education and training was not attempted with any enthusiasm and consistency since it was assumed by both models that the impairments of the mentally handicapped were permanent and unchangeable.

Research and clinical practice have suggested clearly, however, that these models are inadequate and cannot be allowed to guide management and care. As we shall see, it is possible to modify the behaviour and competence of many mentally handicapped individuals, though the underlying organic pathology cannot be treated. The findings suggest very clearly that, though biological factors such as the type and severity of brain damage set certain limits on what can be done, training and education can nevertheless produce impressive improvements. Environment is the key to development; in practice, this involves a general background of varied experience, and well-organized programmes of training and education. In retrospect, those theories which assumed that the impairments of the mentally handicapped were unchangeable, prevented or discouraged attempts at training. Without training, the limitations in social competence did not change, and the theory seemed to be supported. This is an example, of course, of the self-fulfilling prophecy.

The inadequacy of these two models, both implying irreducible handicap, has been supported by three main sets of findings.

The intelligence of the mentally handicapped is not a rigid characteristic

It can and does change; given a stimulating and rich environment, the general trend is towards improvement. Clinicians have known for some considerable time that, if the mentally handicapped are re-tested over a period of years, test scores tend to increase in a manner which is not completely explained by practice effects on tests. When Clarke, Clarke and Reiman (1958) assessed the IQs of a group manifesting mild mental handicap and also 'dull normal' adolescents, over a period of approximately two years, they demonstrated many improvements. Though the correlation between earlier and later results was high at 0.897, closer inspection of absolute scores indicated average increases of ten points. In further experimentation, Clarke and Clarke have also demonstrated that intellectual growth is clearly related to the mentally handicapped individual's environment. When patients were re-assessed over a number of years after admission to hospital, it was discovered that those patients who had previously been in more adverse homes (judging by reports of neglect, cruelty, National Society for the Prevention of Cruelty to Children involvement, etc.) made larger improvements in test performance. The conclusion was that the development of intellectual skills in these individuals had been blocked or retarded by their environment. Admission to hospital meant a considerable improvement for them and this was reflected by increases in their intelligence test scores. The results, therefore, demonstrate both that environment affects competence and that development of intelligence can continue well into adulthood.

Social competence is not rigidly limited by intellectual level and mental age does not set a rigid ceiling to social competence

Gunzburg (1968) has shown this, quite simply, by assessing both mental age (a measure of intelligence) and social age (a measure of social competence). As figure 2 demonstrates, measures of social age are typically above mental age and they would seem to reflect the individual's experience and training rather than innate intellectual limitations. This is not to say that intelligence is unimportant since intellectual skills are a clear asset in, for example, social interaction. The results do show, however, that the level of competence in social skills is not limited by intellectual growth. As we shall see, the key to the development of social skills lies as much in the environment as in biologically determined functions.

The application of training and educational techniques changes social competence so as to narrow the otherwise substantial gap between the mentally handicapped and their normal colleagues

Methods of training, and their effects, are to be considered shortly and the general topic of behaviour therapy is also reviewed in chapter 12.

Figure 2

**Mental age and social age: based on assessments of 31
mentally handicapped persons aged 6–33 years**
From Gunzburg (1968) with the kind permission of the author
and Ballière Tindall.

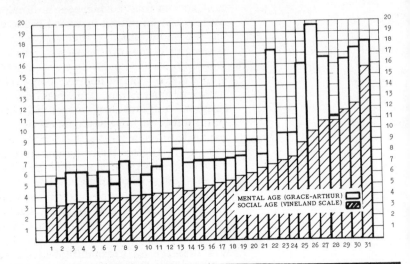

MENTAL AGE (GRACE-ARTHUR)
SOCIAL AGE (VINELAND SCALE)

The overall outcome of the research is that it is now
clearly recognized that the behaviour of the mentally handicapped can be modified. Social and intellectual competence
are not rigid and unchangeable, though a considerable amount
of effort and expertise is necessary to overcome the inefficient learning of the mentally handicapped and to help
them to exceed minimum standards of social competence.

**How do we modify the impairments of the mentally
handicapped?**
Training and habilitation, if therapeutic efforts are to be
successful, must involve a repeating cycle of four major
activities. These are:

* careful assessment;
* goal setting;
* active training programmes;
* monitoring of change.

The cycle will often take considerable time and effort to
complete since the learning of the mentally handicapped is
so slow. And when the cycle has been completed in relation
to one particular handicap (e.g. the inability to dress or
to speak) then it will inevitably need to be repeated in
relation to others. Let us now consider each of the
essential steps in more detail.

Assessment
Detailed and careful assessments are a necessary first step.

A number of assessment systems are available and we now consider one as an example. One commonly used battery of assessments was devised by Gunzburg and is called the Progress Assessment Chart. The overall aim is to provide a detailed and comprehensive picture of what the individual can do, on the one hand, and cannot do on the other. This is done by interviewing a parent or staff member who has had close contact with the mentally handicapped individual and can therefore be assumed to have a detailed knowledge of his behaviour. The major areas covered by the Progress Assessment Chart have already been noted to involve self-help skills (eating, mobility, dressing, toilet and washing activities), communication (both expression and understanding), socialization (play, home activities) and occupation (dexterity and agility). In excess of 100 items are included in the assessment, which is concerned with those attainments already present or which the handicapped individual could manage if the opportunity arose.

When the interview with the informant has been completed, each item achieved is then marked on the circular display illustrated in figure 3. The simplest items are on the inside while the more complex and advanced behaviours are sited on the periphery of the display. Three versions of the Progress Assessment Chart are available; these vary in the difficulty of the skills involved, and are used at the 0-2½ year level, 2½-8 years, and the adult level. The assessments in figure 3 involve a comparison of a normal child

Figure 3

Social attainment in a child and an adult of the same mental age (each numbered item refers to a specific behaviour or skill, and shaded items are those which are present in the individual's behaviour)
From Gunzburg (1968) with the kind permission of the author and Ballière Tindall.

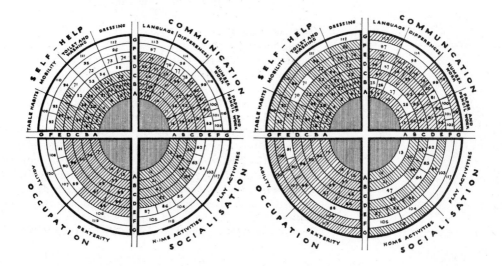

of 5 years 5 months with an 18-year-old mentally handicapped youth whose mental age is 5 years 5 months. Though the mental age of the two is the same, the mentally handicapped youth is more socially competent; this presumably reflects his wider range of experience. In addition, it is interesting to note that the pattern of attainments in the youth indicates the absence of a number of elementary skills; these have presumably not been encouraged by his training.

When Progress Assessment Charts, or other assessments, have been completed they can be useful in at least five ways.

* They provide a comprehensive summary of assets and deficits.
* They provide a rational basis for training; in other words, they indicate those areas which require modification, and also those which are already developed.
* They facilitate the monitoring of change and progress. Since change tends to be slow, records are essential to any unit concerned with the modification of the mentally handicapped's behaviour since staff are unlikely to be able to remember details for more than a small number of clients.
* They facilitate the selection of individuals for special training programmes. For example, a speech therapy or self-help training scheme might require that individuals whose deficits lie in these areas be differentiated from others who are either too severely handicapped to be suitable, and also those who do not require any help.
* They can be used to provide a guide to the attainments of groups of the mentally handicapped, and therefore a crude indication as to what can be expected in individual cases. As an example of the latter, figures 4 and 5 are again taken from Gunzburg, and compare the development of two specific PAC items for a normal group and a group of severely mentally handicapped children living at home with their families.

Goal setting

Assessment, as we have seen, is a step towards defining treatment goals for the individual. Goals can be any of a number of possibilities and will involve a statement of aims for training. For example, to train the client to dress, eat, and attend to his own toilet needs without help or, failing this, with a minimum of supervision; to use words to express needs ('toilet', 'food', 'dress', etc.); to attend to teaching efforts, or to play actively with other children; finally, to cope with a range of simple work activities such as manual assembly tasks or painting. Statements of goals will provide therapeutic efforts with direction and impetus, and allow training programmes to be planned and organized. The choice of goals will, however, be influenced by factors other than the patient's pattern of deficits. In

Figure 4

Ability to use table knife for 'spreading' butter, jam, etc.
From Gunzburg (1968) with the kind permission of the author and Ballière Tindall.

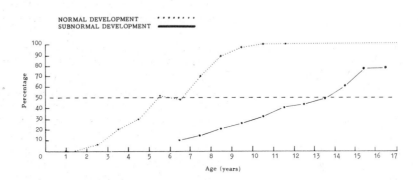

institutions, for example, much will depend on the staff who are available; an enthusiastic occupational therapist or nurse might have developed proficiency in training some specific skills rather than others, and staff interest may direct attention to some behaviours (e.g. dressing, toileting, shopping) rather than others. At home, those behaviours which cause the greatest disruption might become the initial targets for training (e.g. refusal or inability to eat, incontinence).

Treatment and training
There can be little doubt that effective training and education is the key to the development of social competence in the mentally handicapped and a number of training techniques have been developed. Two categories of training technique will now be considered: first, those techniques which are used to develop new behaviours and skills: and second, those techniques which are used to control and reduce maladaptive behaviours.

Habit and skill learning

The aim is to produce and maintain behaviours which are necessary for normal and independent living. In other words, to encourage the development of self-care skills, language and communication, social skills and work habits. The main method involves a range of training techniques based on operant conditioning and the hypothesis that behaviour is determined by its consequences. In practice, this involves the application of rewards or reinforcements which are made

Figure 5

Ability to relate experiences in coherent way
From Gunzburg (1968) with the kind permission of the author
and Ballière Tindall.

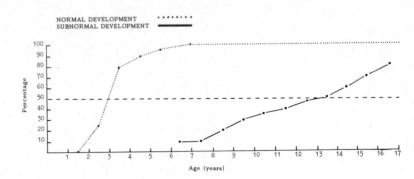

contingent upon the performance of well-defined behavioural
sequences. With the careful use of rewards, a wide range of
behaviour can be introduced into the repertoire of the
mentally handicapped individual.

Clarke (1965) and others have outlined a number of
principles which are important in the training of the sub-
normal. The following are some of the main principles which
have been discussed, and also some of the techniques known
to be useful.

Incentives and rewards
Lack of any apparent motivation often seems to be a barrier
to progress so that, in practice, a training programme will
need to identify those rewards which are effective as reinforcements in each individual case. Financial rewards will
often be of limited value, but other possibilities are not
difficult to suggest: for example, attention and praise,
food, tokens, and feedback using wall charts.

Breakdown of skills
Tasks such as dressing or independent eating are often too
complex to be learnt in their entirety, and will need to be
broken down into their constituent elements. These are then
learnt in an appropriate sequence.

Correct performance
When tasks are learnt by the mentally handicapped, care must be taken to ensure that the sequences learnt are correct and do not include inappropriate responses. There are at least two reasons for this. Correct movements are the easiest and inappropriate behaviours learnt by the mentally handicapped can be very difficult to change.

Spaced learning
Learning sessions will need to be brief to suit the often short attention span of the individual patient. In general, more effective learning is to be expected if training is provided through a number of relatively brief sessions.

Overlearning
Training should be continued well beyond the point where a task is performed successfully. Extended practice is necessary in view of the inefficient learning of the mentally handicapped.

Verbal reinforcement and instructions
Instructions and praise must be clear and simple so as to be appropriate to the patient's level of comprehension. It is unclear as to whether verbal accompaniments of learning (e.g. self-instructions) facilitate the acquisition of behaviours in the mentally handicapped as they do in normal children.

Accuracy
During the acquisition of a skill, accuracy (absence of errors) must be stressed rather than speed. In many cases speed will not be a realistic goal in view of the patient's handicaps.

Clarity and arrangement of materials
In order to avoid confusion, and also to reduce fumbling and clumsiness, the materials and steps of learning should be arranged as clearly and unambiguously as possible.

Generalization
Attempts must be made to ensure that skills learnt in one context are also used elsewhere by the client. For example, training should involve a number of staff rather than one; it is important to ensure that the rewards available during training are also likely to be available elsewhere. This might mean, for example, close liaison with the family so that parents are aware of a patient's capabilities, and allow him to do things for himself rather than do those things for him and deprive him of the opportunity to develop his independence.

Guidance, prompting and modelling
If a skill is not in the mentally handicapped individual's repertoire, it might be modelled for him, and his early

attempts might need to be physically guided by a trainer.
For example, in learning to eat the spoon might initially
need to be guided to the patient's mouth; in training a
patient to put on his trousers, this is initially done for
him and he is gradually encouraged to do things for
himself.

Successive approximation and 'shaping'

Since many behaviours will not be present in the individual's repertoire, it will often be necessary to begin with
behaviours which are relevant to the goals of training but
fall short of them. For example, an initial step in speech
training might involve the encouragement of any vocalization
or noise; a mentally handicapped child might be reinforced
for proximity to other children as an initial move towards
encouraging him to interact and play with them. If the initial steps are successful, the behaviour is then 'shaped' so
that it gradually approximates to the goal. This means that
rewards are gradually limited to those behaviours which we
wish to encourage. When, for example, the child is spending
more time near others, he will no longer receive reinforcements for this but will be rewarded when he responds to
others by touching or communicating.

Reverse order learning

Some complex skill sequences will be trained in reverse. For
example, teaching someone to put on trousers will begin by
requiring the client to pull up the trousers which have
already been slipped over his feet. When this is mastered,
he is then required to pull the trousers over his feet, and
so on. In this way, the patient learns initially those items
which are near the completion of the sequence, and therefore
gains the satisfaction of completing the task.

Control of maladaptive behaviour

In addition to deficits in their repertoire of behaviour,
the mentally handicapped also manifest behaviours which are
barriers to their normal development and integration into
society. Examples of such behaviours are self-injury, hyperactivity, destructiveness, socially withdrawn behaviour,
aggression and incontinence. Such behaviours cause inconvenience and even danger to others; they place a considerable burden on the families of the handicapped and can lead
to admission to hospital. There is, therefore, a clear need
to control and eliminate these behaviours, and the following
are some of the techniques used to do this.

Altering reinforcements

Some behaviours are clearly maintained by their consequences. Disruptive, aggressive, noisy behaviour might be reinforced by the attention it brings from parents or staff.
An important step in treatment will often be to encourage
others to disregard these behaviours and to withdraw their
attention. In practice, staff and parents might need to go
elsewhere so that their attention is completely withdrawn.

This might not be possible, of course, if the behaviour is dangerous to the patient or others: for example, physical attacks. In such an event, the mentally handicapped individual might need to be removed to an empty room, with a minimum of fuss, and kept there alone until the maladaptive behaviour has subsided. This is known as a 'time out' procedure.

Encouraging alternatives

Some maladaptive behaviours are controlled by reinforcing alternative and incompatible responses. Incontinence in an ambulant patient can be reduced by finding out (by repeated checking) when he is likely to wet or soil himself, and then encouraging him to use the toilet (by appropriate reinforcement) when he is likely to need to urinate or defecate. Aggressive behaviour can be reduced by rewarding socially acceptable behaviours, and classroom inattention by reinforcing attentive behaviour.

Extinction procedures

We have already referred indirectly to these procedures. The patient's environment is rearranged so that inappropriate behaviours no longer receive reinforcements, and therefore tend to disappear. A habit of head banging, for example, might decrease if the attention which it produces is withdrawn.

Restitution and over-correction

This involves a programme which encourages the individual to correct the adverse effects of any inappropriate behaviour. For example, the individual who can use the toilet and yet wets himself is encouraged to wash and change himself, and clean up any mess, whenever he is found to be wet. An aggressive act towards another might be followed by the encouragement of a range of comforting and social responses towards the other person.

Aversion therapy

This involves the linking of maladaptive behaviours with unpleasant consequences such as an electric shock. For example, a portable apparatus is used to give the patient a weak shock when he bangs his head against the wall. This technique obviously involves serious ethical problems and should certainly not be used until other less unpleasant methods have failed. In other words, it is a last resort. Provided that it is carefully and responsibly done, however, the technique can be of practical value in cases where all other techniques have failed, and the consequences of the continuation of behaviour (e.g. self-injury) are serious.

Is the training of the mentally handicapped effective?

The evaluation of training techniques involves a number of questions. Does training have useful effects on behaviour? What are the effective components of training? To attempt a review of the research would require a considerable effort, and more space than is available here. In general, however, it is clear that the results of well-conducted evaluative studies are very encouraging, and 'training programmes' produce adaptive changes in the behaviour of the mentally handicapped. The following is one example of an evaluative project reported by Gunzburg. The study was conducted in Slough, and evaluated the effects of a special training programme on a group of severely handicapped young adults. A group of 20 year olds was randomly allocated to two programmes of care. The experimental group (N=15) attended a training unit for approximately two years; their programme involved attempts to assess and improve their social competence. The control group (N=16) lived at home and attended day centres where the training was not as intensive. Progress was monitored by assessments before and after the two-year research period.

The groups had average ages of 19 years 3 months (experimentals) and 21 years 3 months (controls). Their respective mental ages at the beginning of the study were 5 years 11 months and 5 years 1 month, so that their IQs were below 30. At the follow-up assessment, after two years, their mental ages had increased (but not significantly) to 6 years 1 month (experimentals) and 5 years 2 months (controls). In other words, they had advanced two months over a period of two years. The programmes had therefore had little effect on their intellectual skills. When their social competence was considered, however, the results were rather more impressive.

At initial assessment, the average social ages were 7.62 years (experimentals) and 7.49 years (controls); in the follow-up study, the corresponding scores were 10.30 and 7.91 years. Both groups had improved, but the group subjected to special training had improved approximately six times more than their controls, and also more than would be expected in a period of two years. In conclusion, the groups were still handicapped at the end of the trial; but they were significantly less so, and the experimental group in particular had made substantial gains. The results also demonstrated that young handicapped adults continue to learn, and that learning capacity continues to be present well beyond the point of physical maturity.

In addition to group studies, the question of the value of training can be raised in relation to each individual client. The research literature does include, in fact, a large number of single case studies. In such studies, controlled assessments have been provided in a number of ingenious ways: these allow conclusions to be drawn about both the extent and the cause of improvements. Some studies involve controlled observation of the changes in behaviours subjected to training and others which are not subjected to any therapy. For example, some behaviours are 'treated' and these are expected to improve; others are untreated and these should not change. Some care is necessary, of course, to ensure that the 'treated' and 'untreated' behaviours are similar in terms of their complexity; this is partially controlled by using a sample of different behaviours in the 'treated' and 'untreated' categories.

Controlled observation can also be used to investigate the components of a treatment package which are effective. For example, how important is it to provide reinforcements contingent on the behavioural response which is being trained? This can be investigated by comparing the results of training under two conditions. One condition involves the provision of response contingent reinforcements; another involves the provision of the same number of reinforcements, but these are provided independently of whether the response is present or not. If contingent rewards are important, then progress in the first condition should be more marked.

Conclusions

Mental handicap presents the Health Services with a wide range of often severe problems. Social and medical advances have allowed the mentally handicapped to survive and to be recognized as a group which must be allowed the rights and privileges of the majority who are not handicapped. The application of psychological principles, research and techniques has made a major contribution towards the reduction of handicap and impairment, so that the mentally handicapped are more likely to be able to benefit from their right to a full and creative existence. The conscientious and enthusiastic application of educational techniques is making a major contribution to the development of independence and self-sufficiency, and this will increasingly benefit not only the mentally handicapped but also their families and those who are closely involved with their care.

Mental handicap has also been considered as an excellent example of the contribution which psychology can make to the understanding, assessment and modification of a range of serious impairments. Theory, research and practice have been closely integrated to demonstrate the potential contribution of applied research and clinical expertise to the alleviation of both suffering and impairment in the mentally handicapped and those who care for them in institutions and in the community.

References

Clarke, A.D.B. and Clarke, A.M. (1965)
Mental Deficiency: The changing outlook (2nd edn).
London: Methuen.

Clarke, A.D.B., Clarke, A.M. and Reiman, I.S. (1958)
Cognitive and social changes in the feeble-minded: three further studies. British Journal of Psychology, 49, 144-157.

Gunzburg, H.C. (1968)
Progress Assessment Chart of Social and Personal Development: Manual (3rd edn, revised and enlarged).
Birmingham: SEFA (publications) Ltd.

Questions

1. What are the most important psychological aspects of mental handicap which the doctor needs to know about?
2. Discuss the nature and aetiology of mental handicap. Compare the traditional medical and psychological viewpoints. How valid are these 'models' and how have they needed to change?
3. How are intelligence and social competence related to mental handicap?
4. Consider the advantages and disadvantages of caring for the mentally handicapped (a) in hospitals and (b) at home.
5. Discuss, with examples, the role of psychological assessment in the clinical evaluation of mental handicap in the family.
6. What methods are used to modify the behaviour of the mentally handicapped?
7. What practical and ethical problems are experienced by staff whose job involves the modification of the behaviour of the mentally handicapped?
8. How effective is the treatment of the mentally handicapped? In view of the severity of handicaps, and the limited gains which may be anticipated with many individuals, do you consider that treatment is worth while?
9. What would you tell the parents of a mentally handicapped infant about the prospects, in relation to their child, for the future?
10. Discuss the contributions of the members of a multidisciplinary team to the care of the mentally handicapped.

Annotated reading

Clarke, A.D.B. and Clarke, A.M. (1965) Mental Deficiency: The changing outlook (2nd edn). London: Methuen.
This provides reviews of the clinical manifestations of mental handicap, aetiology, training and management, and service organization and planning. It will be suitable for undergraduate and postgraduate students and allows for selective reading if particular aspects of mental handicap are of special interest. The various chapters discuss both biological and psychological aspects of mental handicap, and so facilitate an integrated perspective on the part of the students.

Gunzburg, H.C. (1968) Social Competence and Mental Handicap. London: Ballière, Tindall and Cassell.
This is a very readable and comprehensive discussion of the psychology of mental handicap which gives particular emphasis to assessment, training and management.

Yule, W. and Carr, J. (1980) Behaviour Modification for the Mentally Handicapped. London: Croom Helm.
This is to be recommended as a comprehensive review of the training and management techniques which have been found to be effective in both the acquisition of skills

and the control of undesirable behaviours. In addition
to the descriptions of specific methods, there are also
clear and practically useful discussions of the rationale for treatments, evaluation of effectiveness and
training of parents, teachers and nurses. Useful reading
as an introductory text and also with postgraduates, but
there are obvious advantages in ensuring that readers
have had some contact with mentally handicapped
individuals before they read this book.

21

Sexual Behaviour
David Griffiths

Though the traditional view that psychologists are preoccupied with sex is unjustified and is based on a confusion
between the psychologist and the psychoanalyst, psychologists are nevertheless concerned both with the investigation
of human sexual behaviour and with the treatment of sexual
difficulties. It has become increasingly obvious that sexual
behaviour is influenced by psychological factors such as
attitudes, emotional responses, personality, imagery and
learning, and that the clinician will need to be as aware of
the psychology of sex as he is of the underlying anatomy,
psychology and biochemistry. Psychologists and others have
contributed to our understanding of sex through a number of
survey investigations, and more recently laboratory studies;
in addition, clinicians have been keen to develop and evaluate treatment techniques to alleviate sexual inadequacies.
The importance of an understanding of sexual behaviour, for
doctors and other professionals, is underlined by a number
of factors.

Sex and human relationships
Sex is an inevitable and important part of a stable relationship between two individuals. Kinsey's research showed
that marital partners had intercourse, on average, 2.34
times per week. At the same time, any average figure is
misleading since it conceals the wide variations between
couples. Whatever the frequency, sex can strengthen or
weaken a human relationship, and there is a two-way effect
so that the broader relationship (warmth, support) can
influence sex, and the success of the partners in bed can
strengthen or strain the bond between them. In a clinical
situation, therapy for sexual problems appears to be less
successful if the couple also have a weak relationship.

Sexual problems
Though sex is traditionally viewed as pleasurable, it involves a considerable degree of distress and suffering for
many individuals. Surveys suggest, for example, that as many
as half of married couples experience persistent difficulties with the sexual side of their relationship. Premature
ejaculation, failure to have an orgasm and impotence are not
uncommon problems.

Sexual ignorance

There is widespread ignorance - both amongst professional groups and the general public - about sex. Myths and prejudice continue to influence sexual attitudes and behaviour, though there is an increasing body of reliable knowledge about sex. It is known, for example, that masturbation is quite common (especially in males) and does not cause any harm to the vast majority. The woman's satisfaction is not related to the size of her partner's penis. Though old age is associated with changes in sexual behaviour, it certainly need not be a cause of a loss of potency or interest. These are examples of facts, but myths continue to have more influence on sexual attitudes than does research.

Treatment needs

Surveys suggest that substantial numbers of patients have sexual problems, though they may not talk about these because of their own or the doctor's embarrassment. Though the estimates of sexual problems vary from 15 to 50 per cent, one reviewer concludes that 'Doctors are woefully ignorant about sex'.

Psychological and social determinants of sexual adjustment

Our understanding of sexual behaviour, and especially the factors associated with sexual adjustment, has developed on the basis of survey research, clinical practice and, more recently, direct observations of sexual activity. Though sexual activity does not lend itself easily to scientific scrutiny, and much of the research can be criticized for its inadequacies, a broad body of knowledge is developing which we can regard with a fair degree of confidence.

It is clear that sex cannot be considered in isolation from other aspects of the individual's behaviour. Sexual activity is intimately related to a whole range of social and psychological factors. The following are some of the social and psychological factors which need to be considered as part of the evaluation of sexual problems in the surgery or clinic.

Attitude and beliefs

As we have said, there is widespread ignorance about sex. Many are surprisingly unaware, for example, of the anatomy of the sexual organs. While this might not matter if there are no difficulties, it can be an important step to educate partners in the facts of their sexual anatomy. Expectations also differ for the sexes and there is a dual standard, so that sexual interest is expected of the male, and seen as a respectable sign of his virility; at the same time, there is a persisting belief that it is not 'natural' for the female to enjoy sex: she is assumed to accept sex as a duty to her husband, or in order to have children. Failure to experience an orgasm is generally seem as a problem in the male, but many females do not have orgasms and seem to accept this so that it is not presented to doctors as a problem. There is much guilt and embarrassment about masturbation, and also many beliefs about its harmful effects which are quite unfounded. Ignorance of the wide variation of normal sexual behaviour - its frequency, preferences for different positions during intercourse and so on - produces quite erroneous ideas of what is normal and abnormal, and what is healthy and 'perverse'.

Emotion

Embarrassment and fear over a perfectly normal and enjoyable biological function do seem to be the rule rather than the exception. This is important since anxiety can have a serious effect on sexual response: anticipation of 'failure' can, for example, generate anxiety which interferes with spontaneous sexuality and will cause the most respectable erection to wilt. Experts also suggest that the woman's sexual response, more than the male, is influenced by her emotional responses to her partner's personality. She is said to be influenced relatively less than the male by physical factors such as attractiveness and conventional aspects of beauty. There are also suggestions that, for the woman, sex is likely to be more pleasurable and satisfying if it occurs within a stable and enduring relationship. Research on young people in Britain indicates that boys seek sexual experience because of curiosity and such factors as the opportunity to prove their masculinity, whereas girls give 'love' as their reason.

Personality and individual differences

Individual differences in sexual needs, attitudes and behaviour are related to personality factors. For example, a German survey of 6,000 unmarried students found that extraverts masturbate less, pet to orgasm more, have intercourse more often and earlier, adopt a greater variety of positions, indulge in longer foreplay and are more likely to experience oral-genital sex than introverts. The differences between extraverts and introverts are greater for males than females, and this probably reflects the dominance of the male in determining patterns of sexual behaviour. Among males, neurotic individuals claim to have spontaneous erections more frequently, masturbate oftener and seem to have a greater desire for intercourse; amongst females, the more neurotic individuals seem to experience orgasms less frequently. These findings suggest that personality traits are important determinants of sexual differences: they could therefore play an important part in influencing sexual compatibility between couples.

Experience and learning

Sexual partners are involved in a process of adaptation to each other's preferences and behaviour, and processes of learning are clearly involved. The male, for example, may have to learn to delay his orgasm in order to allow his partner to climax. If he fails to do this, he loses his erection prematurely and his partner is unsatisfied. Over time, a process of habituation can reduce the attractiveness of a husband or wife as a sexual partner. On the other hand, familiarity can reduce anxiety and increase sexual pleasure. As we see in due course, the treatment of sexual problems invariably involves learning. For example, excessive self-awareness and anxiety about 'performance' can cause serious problems and need to be modified as part of treatment.

Imagery and fantasy

Imagery plays a very important role in sex. Masturbation, for example, is rarely a physical act of self-gratification. It is usually associated with fantasies: for example, the individual imagines that he is involved in a sexual act with others. The nature of the individual's fantasy is an important guide to sexual preferences and orientation. A homosexual orientation may be indicated by the choice of partners of the same sex in fantasy. Intercourse between partners frequently involves sexual fantasies which can be used to accelerate or retard sexual excitement.

Family and social background

Kinsey has shown that there are differences between social class groups in their patterns of sexual attitudes and behaviour. Middle-class individuals are more tolerant of masturbation as a normal activity and are more likely to provide their children with some form of sexual education. In general, however, parents play a limited role in sex education. In one survey, 67 per cent of boys and 29 per cent of girls were never given advice by their parents. Only 7 per cent of the boys were given advice by their fathers. Research also suggests that there are relationships between the sexual behaviour of teenagers and the attitudes of their parents. Sexually experienced boys are more likely to have parents who are less concerned with discipline and control. Sexually experienced girls are more likely to report poor relationships with their parents. Neil Frude's review of the family (chapter 9) provides more general discussion of sexuality within this context.

Differences between males and females

As we have seen when considering the importance of emotion, there are important psychological differences between males and females, so that it would be an error to regard the two sexes as having identical needs. Men appear to be sexually responsive most of the time whilst the responsiveness of the woman clearly varies quite considerably. As already mentioned, studies of the sexual behaviour of young people suggest that experienced females give 'love' as their motive whereas experienced males appear to be motivated by curiosity and 'adventure'; although experienced young females are sexually more active than males, they are more likely to be sexually active within one relationship, whereas the male is more likely to change his partner. Women's sexual responsiveness also appears to be affected more by the personality of their partners and relatively less (compared with men) by physical attributes. As we have seen, the differences in the sexual behaviour of introverts and extraverts are smaller in women than men. This has been explained by suggesting that men take the initiative and tend to be more dominant in sexual activity. Whilst this may be true, one study has demonstrated that whether sexual activity occurs is related more closely to the woman's characteristics (e.g. her religious affiliation and previous sexual experience) than to the male's various attitudes. These examples clearly support the existence of important differences between the sexes in the determinants of sexual responsiveness, patterns of sexual response and the role of sex within a relationship. Such differences are of considerable practical importance in the clinical setting, and to neglect them is likely to be to the disadvantage of the patient.

Scientific investigations

As we have already seen, our knowledge of sexual behaviour has developed from surveys, clinical experience and laboratory investigations. In order to consider a selection of this knowledge, we will now consider two large-scale surveys: Kinsey's pioneer work in America and a study done by Michael Schofield on the sexual behaviour of young people in Britain. Our brief consideration of basic research will then be concluded by looking at the laboratory-based investigations of William Masters and Virginia Johnson. The work of Masters and Johnson also provides a convenient introduction to treatment methods.

Kinsey's research

Kinsey was the first person to conduct a large-scale quantitative survey of sexual behaviour and it is difficult to avoid mention of this work in spite of its shortcomings. Kinsey's main technique was the interview, and his survey team interviewed approximately 12,000 Americans. The results were published in 'Sexual Behavior in the Human Male' (1948) and 'Sexual Behavior in the Human Female' (1953). The main results consist of extensive statistical data derived from the interview assessments. Selected aspects of sexual behaviour are, in turn, related to age, social class, education, marital status and geographical location. The following are a few examples of the findings.

1. MASTURBATION: this involves self-stimulation of the genitals, usually but not invariably to the point of orgasm. Kinsey showed masturbation to be a normal activity to the extent that 92 per cent of his males and 50 per cent of females had, at some time in their lives, masturbated. The reasons for not masturbating involved ignorance, religious taboos, lack of sex drive and (most commonly) alternative sexual outlets. Males and females of higher educational level tended to masturbate more frequently than those who

had received less education. Amongst the active male population, the average frequency of masturbation in early adolescence was nearly 2.5 times per week, but 17 per cent of boys masturbated four to seven times each week. The frequency for females was lower (once a fortnight being the median for adult females) and there was more variation between females than males. The frequency of masturbation changed, as might be expected, with age; it dropped more abruptly in the lower social levels (where there is more sexual intercourse) and less abruptly in the upper social levels (where there is less intercourse before marriage). Amongst females the frequencies were fairly uniform until the mid-fifties and thereafter they decreased.

There is no evidence (from this or other surveys) that masturbation is harmful. On the other hand, the conflict between the natural practice of masturbation and its social disapproval (one term for masturbation is 'self-abuse') can produce intense guilt and anxiety which could be harmful. Masturbation has, in addition, the useful function of tension reduction, and the masturbatory experience might also be regarded as providing learning which is a useful precursor to sexual activity with a partner.

2.   EXTRA-MARITAL INTERCOURSE: approximately 50 per cent of all married males had intercourse with women other than their wives; for women, the figure was about 25 per cent. The incidence of extra-marital sexual activity varied with such factors as age and social class; it was highest amongst young working-class males. It was also correlated with education; amongst women, for example, the incidence rose with higher education. In relation to men, Kinsey concludes that 'Extra-marital intercourse may occur irrespective of the availability or frequency of other sources of sexual outlet or the satisfactory or unsatisfactory nature of the sex relations at home. Most of the male's extra-marital activity is undoubtedly a product of his interest in a wide variety of experiences.'

3.   HOMOSEXUALITY: two important conclusions emerged. First, the incidence of homosexual behaviour is higher than most would assume. For example, 8-10 per cent of males (and 2-6 per cent of females) seemed to have been exclusively homosexual for at least three years between the ages of 16 and 55 years. Four per cent of males (and 1-3 per cent of females) appeared to be exclusively homosexual after the onset of adolescence. Second, there seems to be a continuum of sexual orientation with the exclusively homosexual individual at one extreme and the exclusive heterosexual at the other. In the middle is the ambivert (18 per cent of all males and 4-11 per cent of females) who is equally homosexual and heterosexual. This means, of course, that the assumption that an individual is either homosexual or heterosexual is incorrect. Heterosexuality is the commonest inclination (and has obvious biological importance) but a

substantial minority have homosexual interests to varying degrees.

How valuable is Kinsey's work? There can be little doubt that Kinsey made a tremendously important contribution to sexual research. He was able to change attitudes and set trends by conducting the research and publishing the results. He demonstrated that sexuality can be studied quantitatively. Furthermore, he was able to demonstrate the wide range of normality in sexual behaviour and to identify broad categories of variables (e.g. age and social class) which were related to sexuality. In spite of these substantial contributions and achievements, Kinsey's work does suffer a number of shortcomings.

The most obvious problem involves the difficulty of validating self-reports in interviews. It is very difficult to validate self-reports, especially self-reports of sexual activity. Kinsey was, however, able to demonstrate that similar results were derived from separate and independent samples, indicating that the results were reliable but again not proving their validity. Kinsey's work also suffered from a number of sampling and statistical problems. Some of the groups assessed were not statistically representative of their parent populations and, although statistical corrections were applied, there can be no safe alternative to hard data. A further problem involved the disadvantages of means and group data; a considerable amount of data was lost and the variations associated with, for example, personality differences were not studied. Finally, the validity of the results as a guide to current sexual behaviour must be questioned since Kinsey's data were gathered over 30 years ago.

Schofield: sexuality among young people

Michael Schofield's survey, described in his book entitled 'The Sexual Behaviour of Young People' (1972), tried to obtain facts about the sexual attitudes and behaviour of young people aged 15-19. More specifically his three aims were (i) to resolve the controversies about sexual activities in adolescence, (ii) to provide factual information about the sexual behaviour of young people in Britain, and (iii) to facilitate the comparison of his subjects with other groups, or future generations.

Schofield's main technique was a standardized and carefully developed interview; in addition, an attitude questionnaire was administered (partly to check the reliability of some of the interview data). A one in thirteen random sample of teenagers (1,873) was assessed in seven separate areas and the sample was carefully selected to be representative of the total population of 15-19 year olds in these areas. Though it is always difficult to make comparisons, Schofield's survey does appear to have been conducted more carefully than Kinsey's. The results provided valuable information about sexuality in the young, and examples are given below.

1. INCIDENCE OF SEXUAL EXPERIENCE: 20 per cent of
the young males were sexually experienced with at least one
partner, and 12 per cent of the young females. Promiscuity
did not, in general, seem to be a problem. Experience was
related to age; girls were initially ahead in kissing and
dating but were subsequently overtaken by the young males
when the more intimate aspects of sex were involved. Girls
were also more likely than boys to be introduced to sex by
older partners. The first experience of sexual intercourse
tended to be unplanned; half of the boys and two-thirds of
the girls did not enjoy their first experience and substantial minorities (18-39 per cent) continued to be unhappy
about their sexual experience.

2. KNOWLEDGE AND ATTITUDES: boys learned about the
'facts of life' at an average age of 12.5 years; the corresponding age for girls was 12.2. At 13, two-thirds of the
boys and three-quarters of the girls knew about the basic
facts of conception. Most boys (62 per cent) and many girls
(44 per cent) learnt about conception from friends and this
was often through playground anecdotes or obscene jokes. On
a more specific topic, more than half of the sample knew
nothing of the signs and symptoms of venereal disease. What
information was acquired was likely to come from friends,
television and books.
    What contribution did parents and schools make to sexual
education? Parents were found to play a negligible role,
especially the fathers. Sixty-seven per cent of the males
and 29 per cent of the young females were given little or no
advice by their parents. Only 7 per cent of the boys were
given any advice by their fathers. When advice was given,
it was often inadequate and limited to a discussion of the
biological, physiological and moral aspects of sex. Middle-
class children were more likely to receive adequate advice
than their working-class peers. Sex education provided at
school was also found to have its limitations. Twelve per
cent of boys and 18 per cent of females learnt about conception at school but this tended to be at 14 years or
later. Fifty-three per cent of the boys and 14 per cent of
the girls received no sex education at school. Once again,
the teaching tended to be concerned exclusively with the
biological aspects of sex.
    Approximately 80 per cent of the group claimed to know
about contraception but their knowledge was often limited.
Seventy per cent of the experienced girls and 51 per cent of
the boys were concerned about the dangers of pregnancy.
These dangers were very real since intercourse had on many
occasions been unplanned and contraception was not used; 25
per cent of the boys apparently never took precautions and
61 per cent of the girls never took precautions themselves
(though many of these would assume that their partners would
use contraceptives). Schofield suggests that approximately
one in three of sexually active young females become
pregnant.

There was also evidence of dual standards for young men and women. Sexual experience was more likely to be condoned in males and disapproved in females. For example, 51 per cent of the males wished to have premarital experience but 64 per cent were keen to marry a virgin. The greater acceptability of sex for males was also supported by the young women who were interviewed.

3. DIFFERENCE BETWEEN SEXUALLY EXPERIENCED AND THE OTHERS: the experienced and inexperienced groups were not distinguished by such factors as social class, position in the family, religious background, previous sex education or youth club affiliation. There was, however, a weak link between experience and education: the experienced were more likely to come from secondary modern and co-educational schools. Taken as a group, the sexually experienced were not more likely to come from broken homes or homes characterized by conflict between the parents. The results indicated, however, that it was important to separate the sexes when assessing the differences between the experienced and the inexperienced.

Experienced males were distinguished by four main types of characteristic. The first was opportunity and the lack of close surveillance and discipline from parents. The second was that they seemed to have reached puberty sooner. The third was a greater tendency to conform to their peers' standards and an antagonism to adult influence. The fourth was a tendency towards extraverted behaviour and a more tolerant and liberal attitude to moral questions. Experienced females, on the other hand, were differentiated by other variables. There was a greater tendency to find poor relationships with the parents and they were more likely to be unhappy with their work, have manual jobs, or to be unemployed. The extraversion noted in experienced males was not apparent in the experienced females. As with the boys, there was an antagonism to family influence and a preference for the advice of friends. Though these differences are interesting, it is not possible to conclude that they contributed in a causal sense to the sexual behaviour; some of the differences (e.g. the antagonism to parental influence) could possibly have been consequences of the young people's initiation of sexual experimentation.

The work of Masters and Johnson
Though the work of Kinsey, and probably Schofield to a greater extent, was conducted with persistence and care, there must remain some uncertainty about the truth of the self-reports provided by respondents. On the other hand, the direct observation of sexual behaviour in humans presents a wide range of obvious problems to the researcher. In spite of these, William Masters and Virginia Johnson have conducted a series of investigations which have made major contributions to our understanding of both normal sexuality and sexual dysfunction. The results of their laboratory

investigations are described fully in 'Human Sexual Response' (1980b) and an excellent and lucid summary of the major findings is given in 'Understanding Human Sexual Inadequacy' (1970) written by Fred Belliveau and Lin Richter.

The overall aim of the laboratory research was to document the physical and psychological changes associated with sexual activity. Individuals involved in sexual activity were observed and assessed directly under laboratory conditions; the investigations involved intercourse between partners, masturbation, and artificial and partner stimulation. Measurement of sexual activity was undertaken to an extent not previously achieved and the results have been both interesting and important.

1. THE SEXUAL RESPONSE CYCLE: the pattern of sexual response demonstrated by Masters and Johnson is consistent in men and women and also across different types of activity such as partner intercourse and masturbation. Four phases have been identified and each is associated with characteristic physiological and psychological changes. The EXCITEMENT phase is associated with initial erotic stimulation and can vary in length from minutes to considerably longer periods. In the woman it is associated with vaginal lubrication, changes in the vagina and position of the uterus, and widespread changes in muscles and blood vessels; penile erection is the most obvious change in the man but other changes involve the scrotum and nipples. If erotic stimulation is sufficiently long and intense, there is a build up of sexual tension to the PLATEAU phase. This is again associated with characteristic changes in both sexes; for example, the vaginal wall is distended so that the opening decreases substantially in size; involuntary muscular spasms are evident in both sexes, and the psychological experience of excitement and tension approaches its peak. The ORGASMIC phase involves dramatic elevations of breathing rate, blood pressure and muscular tension over normal levels. The male's ejaculation is heralded by the subjective experience of inevitability, and genital contractions in both sexes begin at 0.8-second intervals and decrease in duration subsequently. The RESOLUTION phase involves gradual decreases in sexual tension; the most obvious sign in the male is the loss of erection. In both sexes there is a decrease in the various manifestations of excitement and activity, both physical and psychological. Whereas the male experiences a refractory phase - a period during which he is incapable of further sexual response, and whose length increases with age - the woman is able to experience several orgasms, and the second or third (if they occur) tend to be the most pleasant. It must be emphasized, however, that there are wide individual differences within the general pattern of the four major phases. For example, some women do not experience the orgasmic phase and have a three-phase cycle. The intensity of the changes also varies with the type of experience.

Intercourse is associated, rather unexpectedly, with the least intense changes, and masturbation with the most intense.

2.   MYTH AND REALITY: Masters and Johnson's research also provides us with a reliable basis of factual knowledge which, in many instances, demonstrated the lack of validity of previously held beliefs. Sexual satisfaction was found to be unrelated to the size of the penis; in fact, the variation in the size of erect penises was very small. In the female, there is clearly one pattern of sexual response and it has not been possible to differentiate between two types of orgasm (based on the clitoris and vagina respectively) as had previously been believed. Simultaneous orgasms are not necessary goals for lovemaking and, indeed, such an aim can cause difficulties since it encourages a self-awareness in partners which disrupts the spontaneity of their lovemaking. Intercourse during menstruation does not usually harm the woman and seems largely to be a matter of personal preference. Old age is associated with changes in sexual response: for example, the excitement phase may proceed less quickly, orgasm does not always occur and the refractory phase can be considerably longer. Many of the changes associated with old age (e.g. cessation of sexual activity) are seen to be determined as much by expectation and anxiety as by the biological process of ageing. Masters and Johnson have also added further data to confirm the wide range of preference and sexual behaviour in individuals; the general criterion of normality which emerges is that sexual behaviour is to be considered normal as long as it is acceptable to both partners and does not involve a serious danger of damage to person or property!

Treating sexual dysfunction

The treatment of sexual problems involves a wide range of therapies and a review is not undertaken here. As an example of a consistent approach to sexual difficulties, however, the Masters and Johnson programme is considered briefly. Their treatment techniques have much to recommend them. They were derived from a firm basis of objective research; they are associated with an explicit model and philosophy of sexuality; they are now widely practised and are already being subjected to evaluative investigation.

What are the most common sexual problems? In the male, the most common problems seem to involve premature ejaculation and erectile problems. Premature ejaculation involves reaching a climax too soon for the partner who tends to have difficulty in reaching her orgasm because of, for example, her partner's rapid loss of erection. Erectile problems involve the inability to have an erection, or loss of the erection during (or even before) penetration. In the woman, loss of interest in sex (sometimes developing into an aversion to sex) and failure to reach a climax seem to be the commonest problems. Masters and Johnson have also been involved in the treatment of sexual problems in the aged.

The Masters and Johnson approach is governed by a number of explicit principles; for example, the assumption that most sexual problems are caused by attitudes, misconceptions and ignorance, and less often by psychiatric disturbance or physical problems. This is not to say that organic factors are unimportant: it is known, for example, that diabetes is associated with sexual difficulties and some drugs produce impotence as a side effect. Masters and Johnson conclude, however, that psychological factors tend to be more important in the majority of problems. When therapy begins, the focus is clearly on the relationship between the partners, and less on the partners as isolated individuals.

Therapy is provided by a male and female therapist because of the difficulty experienced by one sex in fully appreciating the experience of the other sex. Therapy procedures encourage the sexual partners to communicate with each other, both verbally and non-verbally. For example, the partners are encouraged to 'pleasure' each other during the early stage of treatment; this involves each partner in discovering the other's preferences for stimulation and then satisfying those preferences in lovemaking. Two important treatment aims are to abolish goal-linked behaviour (referred to as the pressure to 'produce, perform and achieve') and to discourage partners from observing their own behaviour. Fear of failure is seen as one of the more serious barriers to sexual satisfaction.

Treatment techniques are not described here in any detail since they are available in Masters and Johnson's 'Human Sexual Inadequacy' (1980a) and in the eminently readable book titled 'Understanding Human Sexual Inadequacy' by Belliveau and Richter. Two examples are considered briefly, however, to give a general idea of the approach. These are the programmes used to treat premature ejaculation, and failure to reach orgasm in the woman.

The initial stages of treatment are similar for all problems. Interviews with both partners are used to obtain case histories, derive relevant information, overcome anxieties and misgivings, and explain the treatment. Physical examination and laboratory tests are conducted and sexual education might be provided if required (e.g. by involving one partner in the physical examination of the other). When 'pleasuring' exercises have been described and initiated, partners return to discuss their progress. At this stage, attempts at sexual intercourse are banned as part of the treatment contract. After the initial sessions, treatment is tailored to suit the specific needs of each couple.

1. PREMATURE EJACULATION: as we have seen, this refers to the inability of the male to delay ejaculation for long enough to allow his partner to reach her climax. Without treatment, the problem tends to persist, can severely strain a relationship and can have severe effects on the male's confidence and his partner's frustration. Anxiety and self-preoccupation in lovemaking are commonly found in the male, though it seems that in some cases premature

ejaculation can be part of the male's lack of concern for his partner. In other words, some males consider sexual pleasure to be a male prerogative which is not enjoyed by women.

Treatment tries to instil confidence in the partners and to remove the pressure to perform by forbidding attempts at intercourse. After the 'pleasuring' exercises, the next stage involves training in ejaculatory control. When the male feels himself near to orgasm, his partner is instructed to cease erotic stimulation and to squeeze the penis in a predetermined manner in order to prevent the orgasm. Though this causes a loss of erection, sexual stimulation is again initiated and the 'squeeze' used as soon as the male again feels himself near to orgasm. The general aim is to increase the male's tolerance of sexual stimulation. When the male is able to enjoy stimulation by his partner for periods of 15-20 minutes, intercourse is attempted in a gradual manner, initially with the woman in the superior position and subsequently in a lateral position. Throughout the latter stages, the major principle is again to increase the male's tolerance of sexual stimulation whilst controlling his orgasm through the use of the squeeze technique.

2. FAILURE TO REACH ORGASM IN THE FEMALE: among the factors associated with female orgasmic dysfunction are religious prohibitions, parental overprotection, an unsatisfactory relationship with the male and sexual inadequacy (e.g. premature ejaculation) in the partner. Cognitive and emotional factors - such as ignorance and anxiety - can also play an important part. In some women, the failure to have an orgasm is specific to intercourse: they can reach orgasm without difficulty if they masturbate.

Treatment must involve a detailed analysis of the causes. Masters and Johnson stress the importance of exploring the marital relationship in some detail, and helping the partners to communicate at both a verbal and non-verbal level. Pleasuring exercises are used to encourage communication (e.g. to discover sources of sexual arousal). When genital and more intimate contact is initiated, the male is encouraged to cater for his partner's preferences rather than imposing his own, and both partners are advised about methods of stimulation during intercourse. Intercourse, as noted above, initially involves the woman in the superior position so that she has greater control over what occurs and the treatment programme involves both male and female as equal and active partners.

Is the treatment of sexual dysfunction effective?
This represents the acid test of our knowledge and expertise, since the understanding of sexual behaviour is of limited usefulness and the treatment techniques a waste of time unless the patient benefits in terms of a reduction of his problems. Masters and Johnson have, in fact, been keen to report on the outcomes of their own techniques. In

general, their success is high. For example, they report that treatment for premature ejaculation was unsuccessful in only four cases out of total of 186; the failure rate for the treatment of orgasmic problems in women was between 16 and 20 per cent in a sample exceeding 300 patients. It seems likely, however, that these reflect, possibly to a large extent, the composition of their patient groups. Their patients are clearly self-selected and well motivated; they are well above the average in education and income and include a substantial number of professional individuals.

At least one recent evaluative study has demonstrated that success rates are considerably lower than the overall 80 per cent suggested by Masters and Johnson (Mathews, Bancroft, Whitehead et al, 1976); there also seems support, however, for the greater effectiveness of this approach compared with other alternatives, though the outcomes are found to be subject to considerable variability. Further research is obviously necessary in order to assess accurately both the degree of success in alleviating sexual problems and to identify those factors which influence therapeutic outcomes. To date, however, the results are certainly encouraging enough to justify both a fair degree of confidence and the need for further investigation.

References

Belliveau, F. and Richter, L. (1970)
   Understanding Human Sexual Inadequacy. London: Coronet.
Kinsey, A.C., Pomeroy, W.B. and Martin, C.E. (1948)
   Sexual Behavior in the Human Male. Philadelphia and
   London: W.B. Saunders & Co.
**Kinsey, A.C., Pomeroy, W.B., Martin, C.E. and Gebhard,
P.H.** (1953)
   Sexual Behavior in the Human Female. Philadelphia and
   London: W.B. Saunders & Co.
Masters, W.H. and Johnson, V.E. (1980a)
   Human Sexual Inadequacy. New York: Bantam Books.
Masters, W.H. and Johnson, V.E. (1980b)
   Human Sexual Response. New York: Bantam Books.
Mathews, A., Bancroft, A., Whitehead, A. et al (1976)
   The behavioural treatment of sexual inadequacy: a
   comparative study. Behaviour Research and Therapy, 14,
   427-436.
Schofield, M. (1972)
   The Sexual Behaviour of Young People. Harmondsworth:
   Pelican.

Questions

1. Do you consider that doctors should have a thorough knowledge of the psychology of sexual behaviour: alternatively, is it sufficient to be acquainted with the medical (i.e. organic) aspects of sex?
2. What is meant by sexual adjustment? Discuss the social and psychological determinants of sexual adjustment.
3. What is 'normal' sexual behaviour? Consider the

relevance of sex research to this question, and also consider the relevance of the question to clinical practice.

4. Discuss critically examples of research into sexual behaviour. How useful has clinical research been in improving our understanding of human sexuality?
5. List the practical and ethical problems involved in scientific investigations of sexual behaviour. Have these problems been overcome by the sexual researchers?
6. Can sexual problems be treated? How? Are treatments successful?
7. List the implications of the psychological research on sexual behaviour for the general practitioner.
8. List the questions, or areas of enquiry, which you might wish to consider if you were assessing a young man or woman who was complaining of a sexual difficulty.
9. Is sex important to old people? What differences would you expect to find in the role played by sex in the relationships of younger and older couples?
10. Do you think that information about sex acquired from the 'mass media' could have any adverse effects? If so, how could these effects be avoided or reduced?

Annotated reading

Belliveau, F. and Richter, L. (1970) Understanding Human Sexual Inadequacy. London: Coronet.
 An interesting and readable summary of Masters and Johnson's research which considers both the laboratory investigations and the treatment techniques.

Jehu, D. (1979) Sexual Dysfunction. A behavioural approach to causation, assessment and treatment. Chichester: Wiley.
 This is a clear and broad discussion of sexual problems as viewed by a behavioural psychologist. It provides an up-to-date review of current knowledge and clinical practice. Specific sections discuss the characteristics of the behavioural viewpoint, the causation of sexual problems, categories of disorder and, finally, treatment and outcome. It is to be recommended as a useful and competent review which is also relevant to the clinical situation and could be expected to have many implications for decision and action in relation to patients.

Schofield, M. (1972) The Sexual Behaviour of Young People. Harmondsworth: Pelican.
 Also an interesting account of a very competent survey study which illustrates how careful methodology can be applied to sensitive aspects of human behaviour in order to increase our knowledge.

Schofield, M. (1973) The Sexual Behaviour of Young Adults. London: Allen Lane.
 This is a follow-up to Schofield's study of young people and reports on aspects of their sexual behaviour in

their mid-twenties. Among the topics discussed are sex education, contraception and venereal disease, and the results of this second extensive survey are discussed in terms of the implications for social policy and clinical practice.

Masters, W.H. and Johnson, V.E. (1980a) Human Sexual Inadequacy. New York: Bantam Books.

Masters, W.H. and Johnson, V.E. (1980b) Human Sexual Response. New York: Bantam Books.
The original texts are now available in paperback for those readers who are interested in details of both their theoretical approach, empirical findings and treatment methods. Both books are lengthy, illustrated and well referenced.

22

Insomnia
David Griffiths

We spend approximately one-third of our lives asleep. This is not, of course, constant throughout our life span since infants sleep for considerably more and the amount of time spent asleep then reduces with age. There are also wide individual differences at all age levels in the time spent sleeping. The range extends from the individual who is apparently quite happy if he has five to six hours sleep per day to the individual who appears to need at least twice this amount if he is to avoid tiredness and even some feeling of deterioration in performance and general efficiency.

It is hardly surprising that psychologists have been interested in sleep, and there is a large body of literature and research. Investigations indicate that sleep is neither a homogenous nor an inactive state. Electro-encephalographic studies show that there are four stages of sleep, each associated with characteristic EEG changes and also behavioural manifestations. The most widely researched stage is REM, or 'rapid eye movement' sleep, so named because its presence can be detected by eye movement. This takes up approximately one-quarter of the time spent sleeping and an individual who is aroused during this stage is very likely to report dreaming or dream-like experiences (Hilgard, Atkinson and Atkinson, 1971). REM sleep is suppressed by some drugs and often reappears in excess of the individual's normal pattern when the medication is withdrawn. Though there is little evidence to suggest that the individual is damaged by variation in sleep patterns and dreaming, it is generally agreed that sleep has a restorative function which makes it essential to the individual. Sleep deprivation can result in dramatic and often very disruptive changes in the individual's behaviour, and both cognitive problem-solving and motor skills can be seriously impaired if sleep deprivation is sufficiently severe.

Sleep is a normal and, it would also appear, a necessary function and it might be assumed to be an almost automatic response after prolonged activity and exercise. Sleep can, however, involve problems for substantial numbers of individuals and insomnia has become a topic of special interest to psychologists who are concerned about its description, aetiology and also its modification or treatment.

Research on the assessment, aetiology and modification of insomnia is extensive and this discussion attempts to answer a number of questions. What is insomnia? In other words, what are the sleep problems commonly reported by those unfortunate individuals who complain that they 'cannot sleep'? How is insomnia assessed, both clinically and in scientific studies? For example, are reports of their sleeping behaviour given by poor sleepers necessarily accurate and correct? What causes insomnia, and could the aetiology vary from one individual to the next? Finally, what can be done to treat and modify insomnia? How effective are sleeping tablets, and what other techniques have been used to modify the miseries which can be suffered by poor sleepers? It is possible to answer each of these questions and the following discussion attempts to review the present state of our knowledge.

What is insomnia?

The clinical presentation of insomnia commonly includes four areas of complaint by the individual. Though each specific complaint can appear in isolation, a number of studies suggest that sleep difficulties tend to appear as a syndrome. In other words, the problems tend to occur together.

The first type of problem involves reported difficulty in falling off to sleep. The individual may claim that it takes a long time to 'drop off', and objective studies of insomniacs have tended to select subjects who claim that it takes at least 30 minutes to fall asleep. Many insomniacs take considerably longer than this and the problem has often been present for some years. The second problem involves frequent disruptions of sleep. The individual wakes often and might again report considerable difficulty in getting back to sleep. The third problem is early awakening from sleep. In view of these difficulties, it is hardly surprising that poor sleepers also complain of excessive tiredness and fatigue, and are frequently concerned or anxious about their sleep pattern. Some degree of anxiety and depression is, therefore, quite common.

Poor sleepers or insomniacs are typically self-referred, so that their views of the existence and severity of their sleep problems often need to be verified by objective observation. Empirical studies have been undertaken to identify the exact behavioural differences between poor sleepers and others. For example, Monroe (1967) compared 16 poor sleepers with a group of matched control subjects. Poor sleepers, when observed under laboratory conditions, slept for less time, differed in their pattern of sleeping (e.g. they had markedly less REM sleep), took longer to fall asleep and woke up more frequently during the night. Monroe also records a strong impression that his subjects willingly rated themselves as good or poor sleepers and it seems likely that sleep behaviour is a stable aspect of the individual's self-image. Some of Monroe's poor sleepers also took periods in excess of an hour to fall asleep, and reported that this occurred quite regularly, so that the problem was persistent rather than transitory.

Monroe, and other investigators, also found that poor sleepers were distinguished by a number of signs of high physiological arousal. Insomniacs have been found to have higher temperatures and heart rate, higher muscular tension levels and also higher skin conductance; furthermore, such differences have been found to be present both during sleep and in the period preceding sleep. Poor sleepers and insomniacs have also been found to have more 'abnormal' scores and profiles on questionnaire measures of personality traits. For example, indices of neuroticism (anxiety, low self-confidence, tension) are often elevated in groups of poor sleepers.

As we shall see, it is impossible to ascertain whether both physiological and psychological signs of abnormality suggest a cause of the sleep problem or a consequence of the many stresses which can be associated with poor sleeping. Cause-effect relationships are notoriously difficult to establish in psychology and the problems of insomnia are no exception to this rule!

Another problem in relation to the investigation of insomnia involves the criteria for the identification of a group of sufferers. This is taken up in more detail in due course, but it is important to note at this point that Monroe's study involved students who responded to an advertisement and were subsequently selected since they satisfied criteria such as difficulty in falling asleep: other studies have involved individuals who presented with sleeping problems at clinics and were requesting help to modify their difficulties.

In general, however, studies of self-referred insomniacs seem to have produced results which are very similar to objective investigations of poor sleepers. For example, one study involved sleep polygraphs and behavioural ratings of 18 chronic insomniacs and 18 controls matched for age and sex. As might be expected, the insomnia sufferers took longer to get off to sleep, had less total sleep, slept for a smaller percentage of the time that they spent in bed and were awake for longer periods prior to getting up. There were also interesting, and clinically very important, differences in the reports of sleep difficulties given by the insomniacs and controls. Insomniacs tended to over-estimate the extent of their sleep problems (e.g. the time taken to fall asleep) whilst the control subjects tended to under-estimate such aspects of their sleep behaviour.

Possibly the most important development in sleep research has been the accumulation of objective data on sleeping behaviour which has been facilitated by laboratory sleep studies and apparatus such as the electro-encephalogram and the polygraph. American researchers have begun to collect data on the sleep behaviour of different age and sex groups; this work will eventually allow clinicians and researchers to compare the behaviour of specific individuals with normative data relevant to the appropriate age level and sex.

The importance of situational factors has also been recognized and at least one study has compared sleep behaviour in home and laboratory settings (Coates et al, 1979). The findings suggest consistency in sleep behaviour for groups but also the possibility of considerable variation between individuals so that, in some cases, the individual's sleep behaviour varies with the setting. This means that observations of sleep in one setting cannot be used as a guide to sleep in other settings.

And, as we see in a subsequent section, it cannot be assumed that self-report of sleeping behaviour is accurate. In many cases, there are gross discrepancies between self-report and objective measures of sleep.

How common is insomnia? It is not possible to give precise answers to this question since so much depends on how the term is defined and the manner in which information about poor sleeping is collected. Most surveys of sleep and sleep problems have relied on self-report by respondents and much of the information gathered has been taken from survey questionnaires. Self-report can be very unreliable and the use of questionnaire data does not normally allow any check on responses to ensure, for example, that respondents have understood questions adequately. In spite of these reservations, however, it is possible to state a number of tentative conclusions about the prevalence of sleep problems.

Sleep problems deserving the term 'insomnia' are common and affect quite large groups of individuals. Furthermore, sleep problems can be longstanding rather than necessarily transient phenomena. These conclusions are supported by a number of studies reported from quite different cultural settings. For example, a survey conducted in Melbourne indicated that about nine per cent of a large sample reported a troublesome degree of insomnia and a further 16 per cent complained of some difficulties with sleep. An American survey (Bixler et al, 1979) reported that 30 per cent of a Los Angeles sample reported current sleep problems and 52 per cent complained of either a current or past disorder affecting their sleep. This survey also indicated that those individuals who complained of insomnia were more likely to complain of other health, family and social problems. Self-reported sleeping difficulties could, therefore, be facets of general disturbance or even a general tendency to be dissatisfied with aspects of the individual's life experience.

General surveys usually fail to distinguish between transient and longstanding insomnia, and also between sleep problems which are secondary to other conditions (such as physical illness or depression) and insomnia which is present as a primary problem not produced by such conditions. Sleep problems do seem to be commoner in women, older age groups and lower class groups. Problems can also be very longstanding and one survey suggested that 18 per cent of those individuals who complained of insomnia reported that the problem had begun before the age of 20.

It will be obvious from this brief discussion that prevalence rates have not been established with any precision. Estimates tend to be high, however, and they also tend to vary: one survey estimates that between 13 and 26 per cent of those over 30 have some degree of sleeping difficulty. Whatever the precise rates, insomnia is a clinical problem of some significance. Another index of its clinical significance is that approximately 7-10 per cent of surveyed populations have been reported to be taking sleeping tablets.

How accurate are reports of the individual's sleep behaviour and especially the reports of problems provided by 'poor' sleepers?

This question is of considerable practical importance. As we have seen, surveys which attempt to estimate the prevalence of sleep disorders are dependent on the self-report of respondents. If self-reports are inaccurate, then the results of surveys are of limited value. In addition, most individuals treated for insomnia are selected on the basis of their complaints about their sleep difficulties. Some studies of the relationship between self-ratings of sleep and objective observations in the laboratory indicate that there is a close correspondence between the two categories of measures (Johns, 1977) and that self-report tends to be stable if it is repeated after a period of months. However, many other investigations indicate that self-assessments of sleep problems can be inaccurate and misleading when they are used as the sole measures of parameters of sleep such as the time taken by the individual to fall asleep after retiring, or the frequency of nocturnal wakenings.

Dement (1972) demonstrated that as many as 50 per cent of a group of 'insomniacs' seen at the Stanford Sleep Clinic showed little evidence of any problems according to objective EEG assessment. Carskardon and her colleagues (1976) were subsequently able to compare self-report and objective sleep records in 122 individuals who complained of longstanding insomnia and were not taking drugs. The discrepancies between subjective and objective measures were extensive. For example, 46 subjects complained that they took at least 60 minutes to get off to sleep. Of the total group, only six (13 per cent) actually took longer than 60 minutes in the sleep laboratory: 12 (26 per cent) slept after 30-60 minutes, eight (14.4 per cent) slept after 15-30 minutes and 20 (43.5 per cent) slept in less than 15 minutes. The investigators concluded that 'fewer than one patient in five with a complaint of very short sleep or very long sleep latency will have the complaint confirmed in a laboratory sleep recording'. This conclusion was further supported by the finding that at least 50 per cent of the self-reported poor sleepers could not be distinguished from a sample of normal controls in terms of total sleep time or time taken to fall off to sleep. In this particular study, the poor sleepers were distinguished from the controls most prominently by their tendency to wake more often during the night. Taken together, these studies indicate clearly that the reports of sleeping behaviour provided by 'poor' sleepers can be very misleading.

In conclusion, it is obvious that self-reports of sleeping problems are not sufficient in isolation, and need to be confirmed wherever possible by objective assessments. In practice, however, the facilities to provide objective assessments are usually not available. Descriptions and evaluations of medical and psychological treatments applied to alleviate insomnia have invariably used self-report both to select their patients and to evaluate outcomes. The inadequacy of this procedure, and its potential effect on outcome, is well demonstrated by a study reported recently by Borkovec and his colleagues (1979). When a criterion of 50 per cent over-estimation of sleep latency (in other words, the time between retiring to bed and falling asleep) was applied to a sample of complainants, 60 per cent were categorized as 'pseudoinsomniacs' (i.e. they over-estimated the problem by at least this amount) and the remaining 40 per cent were categorized as 'idiopathic insomniacs' (i.e. there was a fair degree of correspondence between the two types of measure). A controlled study subsequently attempted to evaluate the effects of tension release relaxation procedures, other relaxation procedures not involving tension release and a no-treatment control procedure. Tension release relaxation was more effective than the alternative in terms of subjective changes and the improvements were maintained at a 12-month follow-up. In terms of objectively measured changes, however, the tension release relaxation produced greater improvements in the 'idiopathic' group only. No significant changes were apparent in the 'pseudo-insomniacs'. If objective measures had not been available, the importance of confounding variables would not have been evident. The authors conclude that 'the presence or absence of an objectively defined sleep deficit would seem to be of obvious and fundamental importance in insomnia research'. The absence of objective measures needs to be considered again when evaluations of treatment techniques for insomnia are discussed.

What causes insomnia?

Sleep disturbances can be caused and maintained by any of a potentially large number of factors. Regestein (1976) has listed eight possibilities which we might consider. One involves work, social and recreational routines which do not allow the individual to develop and maintain regular sleeping habits. Another possibility is disturbance caused by environmental factors such as loud or unusual noises, though experience suggests that human beings can sleep under conditions involving a wide range of disturbances. A third possibility is insomnia caused by illness. Pain, fever, dyspnoea and many other conditions are, not surprisingly, associated with sleep problems. Personal and life crises, such as family deaths or examinations are a fourth example of a potential cause of sleep problems. Fifth, some individuals 'nap' during the day, so that their sleep over a 24-hour period is probably within normal limits but the problems experienced at night reflect a maladjustment in their pattern of sleep. Sixth, some drugs cause insomnia as a side effect. Caffeine, for example, can cause or aggravate insomnia. Insomniacs can also experience lighter sleep and wake more often if they take hypnotic medication. A seventh potential factor is old age and its associated biological and psychological changes. A number of surveys indicate that sleep problems are commoner in older age groups and there is a definite trend for the aged to have lighter sleep, more frequent awakenings and less total sleep. It has been estimated that nocturnal waking periods account for under 5 per cent of the time spent in bed by 20 year olds, but over 20 per cent at the age of 85.

One further factor listed by Regestein is personality disturbance. For example, a chronic maladaptive response such as anxiety in the individual's behaviour. Several American reviewers refer to the observation that insomnia sufferers often have abnormal scores on questionnaires which are claimed to detect various aspects of psychopathology. As many as 75 per cent of sufferers have been found to have abnormal scores on the Minnesota Multiphasic Personality Inventory. This is a widely used questionnaire which was designed to diagnose personality abnormalities. In relation to insomnia, what is being suggested is that it can be viewed as a facet of a general abnormality in behaviour. Indeed, we have already seen that many complaints of sleep disturbance occur in the absence of an objective abnormality in sleep behaviour.

Whilst sleep disturbance can certainly be viewed, in some individuals, as a symptom of a more general problem, it is unsafe to assume that this is always true. The validity of questionnaires such as the Minnesota Inventory is certainly not above question. More importantly, it seems likely that general disturbance in the individual's behaviour could often be caused by the insomnia. For example, chronic sleep problems might reasonably be expected to produce some degree of anxiety or depression. The basic problem, once again, is to establish the direction of causality. It is simply not possible to assume that any general disturbance which co-exists with insomnia is the cause of that insomnia. Indeed, many pervasive disturbances of behaviour are associated with sleep disturbance in some individuals but not in others. For example, insomnia is often used to diagnose depression; one study has demonstrated, however, that as many as a third of a group of depressed individuals did not have any problems in either falling or remaining asleep. Nevertheless, both personality and psychiatric disturbance remain to be considered as potential causes of sleep disturbance in some individuals. In such cases, the insomnia can be regarded as a secondary problem which is likely to improve when the underlying condition is successfully treated.

Many individuals suffer from sleep problems in the absence of personality and psychiatric disturbance and also in the absence of causation from any other of the factors which have been mentioned. Indeed, causational factors such as illness, life crises and environmental disruption might be expected to be self-limiting so that the insomnia would be transient rather than permanent. Yet many insomniacs have sleep difficulties which are longstanding and which can be confirmed by relatives and objective observations of their behaviour. Such individuals are sometimes assumed to be suffering from 'primary' insomnia. This condition can be a severe handicap both to the unfortunate sufferer and his family. What causes such a longstanding problem? Though there are again many possibilities, the psychological literature suggests three major problems. In addition to their theoretical importance, these factors need to be mentioned since they have been used to justify treatments for insomnia.

The first possibility is anxiety, or high physiological arousal. This theory suggests that the insomniac is too highly aroused and anxious to sleep; in other words, this state is incompatible with sleeping. Monroe (1967) suggests, for example, that insomnia is often a function of sleep-incompatible stress-induced physiological arousal. This theory does, in fact, have a considerable amount of objective support. Monroe has shown that insomniacs tend to be physiologically more aroused than controls both before and during sleep and Haynes and his colleagues have further supported the theory with indications that insomniacs score higher on questionnaire measures of anxiety. It also seems likely that high anxiety and sleep problems have reciprocal causal effects on each other, so that a 'negative feedback' loop or 'vicious circle' develops. High arousal prevents sleep: worry about sleep contributes, in turn, to further anxiety and arousal. If this occurs, a self-maintaining vicious circle is set up.

The second possibility can easily be seen as a part of the physiological arousal theory but it differs in that it concentrates on the cognitive aspect of insomnia. Insomniacs often complain that they are unable to sleep because of 'racing thoughts' or morbid preoccupations; these problems are seen as being beyond their control and prevent them from falling asleep. At least three themes seem to be common. These involve (i) preoccupations with attempts to fall as-asleep, (ii) general worries and (iii) specific worries about the adverse effects of sleep loss. It seems likely that these cognitions are integral parts of a state of physiological arousal. Nevertheless, the cognitive aspects of insomnia deserve separate mention since they have become the basis for a therapeutic approach which is considered in the next section.

A third theory suggests that insomnia is the consequence of 'bad habits'. The poor sleeper, it is suggested, behaves in a manner which is not compatible with sleeping. For example, insomniacs read in bed, watch television, study or listen to the radio. As a consequence the bedroom, normally associated with sleep, becomes a stimulus for activity and wakefulness through a process of associative learning. Bootzin (1972), suggests that 'the sleeping behaviour of insomniacs is considered to be under inadequate control of the relevant environmental stimuli'. Though the theory is attractive and plausible, the available evidence would not appear to support it. Haynes and his colleagues (1974) have demonstrated, for example, that though insomniacs are more anxious and physiologically aroused than controls, there are no significant differences in the frequencies of sleep in-compatible behaviours between insomniacs and a normal con-trol group. In spite of this finding, the theoretical model which stressed sleep incompatible behaviour has been the basis for a modification technique which again appears to have some success in modifying insomnia.

What conclusions are possible? Insomnia is clearly not a single entity since, in some individuals, it is secondary to other problems whilst, in others, it is present in isola-tion. Cause and effect relationships are difficult to estab-lish but it is likely that the pattern of aetiology needs to be considered in each specific case. The evidence certainly suggests the importance of physiological arousal and anxi-ety; in addition, however, the importance of cognitions and sleep incompatible behaviour need to be considered. As we see shortly, modification techniques have been developed to modify sleep problems indirectly through the control of anxiety, the sufferer's cognitions and also behaviours in the bedroom which might be expected to affect sleep.

Is it possible to treat insomnia?

The literature on the treatment of insomnia is very exten-sive and it is obvious that a large number of techniques have been used to try to alleviate the suffering of the poor sleeper. It is also encouraging to note, however, that des-criptions of treatment techniques and claims for their ef-fectiveness have been supplemented, in recent years, by an increasing number of objective and controlled investigations of the efficacy of treatment methods. The following are the major approaches to treatment; an attempt is also made to comment on the demonstrated effectiveness of each method, and the focus of attention is insomnia which cannot be regarded as a symptom of a disorder such as depression or physical illness. Where this occurs, treatment would involve the underlying disorder.

Medication

Drugs are, without doubt, the treatment used most commonly to control insomnia, and survey results suggest that 7-10 per cent of the population take sleeping tablets. In spite of the practical advantages of medication as a treatment, both clinical experience and research suggest that drugs do not solve the problems of insomnia and they involve a number of shortcomings and disadvantages.

Though hypnotics do appear to cure insomnia in some cases, in others the outcome is not necessarily positive and the sleep problem continues. In fact, drugs can lose their effect rapidly; one investigation indicated that four out of five hypnotics lost their effect within two weeks and another (Kales et al, 1974) demonstrated that insomniacs who were taking hypnotics had as much difficulty in falling and remaining asleep as a control group of insomniacs who were not taking any medication. The effectiveness of medication in controlling sleep problems clearly cannot be assumed without question.

The research also indicates that improvements in sleep behaviour associated with medication can disappear very rapidly when the drug is withdrawn. Drug withdrawal can also have other adverse effects whose consequence is to make the individual dependent on the drug. For example, many drugs suppress REM sleep; when the drug is withdrawn, REM sleep returns, sometimes in excess. Since this rebound effect involves dreams and sometimes nightmares, further sleep disturbance is the consequence. In effect, this means that medication actually causes sleep disturbance. Laboratory research indicates, in fact, that it can take as long as five weeks for the individual's sleep to return to normal after the withdrawal of a drug.

A final disadvantage of medication is that the individual develops a psychological dependence to the extent that he comes to believe that he cannot sleep adequately without drugs. He loses any feelings of control over his sleep and may believe that drugs are indispensable to him. It has been shown that any improvements in sleep behaviour (such as falling asleep sooner) are more likely to be maintained if the individual believes that the change was attributable to his own efforts and not produced by medication. The practical implication is that the individual's expectations need to be modified whenever drugs are used and feelings of self-control in the client need to be encouraged. It is also clear, however, that drugs are not entirely successful as treatments and other treatments need to be explored. At the same time, drugs and other medical treatments can have important effects on insomnia which is a symptom of, for example, depression or physical pain.

Psychotherapy

The rationale for psychotherapy as a treatment for sleep problems would be that insomnia is a consequence or symptom of a more pervasive conflict associated with unconscious and repressed strivings in the individual. Dream material is often analysed, in fact, as part of psychotherapy since dreams are considered to be potentially useful indicators of the individual's dynamics. It is not possible to make any conclusions about the effectiveness of psychotherapy in treating insomnia, however, since controlled studies have not been conducted which would allow any inferences to be made about the contribution of psychotherapy to any successful outcome.

Relaxation

Relaxation training (cf. chapter 12) is probably the most commonly used psychological treatment for sleep problems. The rationale for this technique resides in the theory that insomnia is caused by tension and high arousal; as we have seen, there is evidence to support this theory. What happens in practice is that poor sleepers are trained to relax themselves. This is done in a variety of ways. For example, some therapists utilize techniques which involve the tensing and subsequent relaxing of muscles; others do not use muscular tensing. Some therapists conduct therapy sessions in person whilst others use tape-recordings and group training sessions.

A number of objective and controlled evaluations are available and these suggest very clearly that relaxation produces clinically important improvements in sleeping which are maintained over follow-up periods. For example, Borkovec and his colleagues (1979) showed that the tension release relaxation technique was more effective in reducing sleep latency than relaxation which did not involve tension release. The superiority of this technique depended, however, on the characteristics of the insomniacs. When the outcome was measured in terms of subjective report of sufferers, tension release relaxation was more effective in both 'pseudoinsomniacs' and 'idiopathic insomnia'; when objective measures were used, however, the technique was superior only in the 'idiopathic' group. The extent of the improvement can be quite impressive. Borkovec refers to reductions in sleep latency from 42.3 to 12.5 minutes associated with relaxation compared with negligible changes observed in placebo treatment groups. The research also suggested that outcome is related to age: older insomniacs responded less well.

Relaxation is an efficient as well as an effective technique since it can involve as little as 30 minutes of a therapist's time; group treatment is also feasible and some therapists automate treatment by using tape-recordings. Improvements in sleep behaviour also occur when subjects have been instructed not to expect any. Furthermore, improvements tend to be stable over time and the client is encouraged as part of his training to assume control over his own behaviour.

Though there can now be little doubt about the potential value of relaxation, some caution continues to be necessary. For example, a number of the evaluative studies involve shortcomings. The majority of objective studies use students as subjects and there is evidence to suggest that their sleep problems are less severe than those suffered by older groups and the general population. In addition, the most common measure of outcome involves self-ratings; it has already been established that self-ratings can be very misleading. In spite of these limitations, relaxation is certainly a treatment of choice and especially in view of its economy.

In spite of the success of relaxation, other approaches need to be explored since relaxation is apparently not effective in 10-15 per cent of insomniacs; there are also indications that, though improvements are impressive, some insomniacs continue to take longer than normal to fall asleep. In one study, insomniacs treated with relaxation continued to take an average of 34 minutes to fall asleep, compared with 15 minutes for a normal control group.

Paradoxical intent

This technique involves the 'paradoxical' instruction to forget about sleeping and concentrate on other activities such as, for example, counting sheep! This example illustrates that the approach, despite its name, is hardly new. The rationale, however, is to relieve the insomniac's anxiety by modifying his goals and reducing the cognitions which are incompatible with sleep. In other words, his arousal is likely to be reduced if he is not trying to sleep. He might be instructed, as an alternative, to keep his eyes open and remain awake. Paradoxical intent has been used either alone or in combination with other techniques, such as relaxation. A small number of objective studies indicate that, as long as it is acceptable to the client, it can be effective in improving sleep behaviour even in individuals who have not responded to relaxation. The instructions involved are so brief that the technique is economical and can easily be added to other treatments to form a more effective therapeutic package.

Stimulus control

The theoretical assumption underlying stimulus control therapy is that, for the insomniac, the bedroom has been associated with sleep incompatible behaviour such as reading, listening to the radio or studying. The aim of this technique is therefore to control these behaviours so that bed and the bedroom can again be associated with sleep. Stimulus control treatment (Turner and Ascher, 1979) typically involves five steps. The sufferer is instructed (i) to go to bed only when sleepy, (ii) not to read, watch television, study or eat in the bedroom, (iii) to get up and do something if unable to sleep within ten minutes, (iv) not to nap during the day, and (v) to get up at a regular time. At least two carefully controlled evaluative studies have shown that this technique is associated with significant reductions in the time taken to fall asleep, fewer awakenings, more sleep and reduced feelings of fatigue. Improvements are also maintained over follow-up periods (nine months in one study) and stimulus control therapy has also been shown to reduce sufferers' dependence on medication. Once again, it is possible to conclude that this technique has much to offer the insomniac. Though its practical value has been demonstrated, however, the mechanisms which underlie its success remain to be clarified.

We have already noted that the evidence does not support the theory that insomnia is caused by sleep incompatible behaviours. Insomniacs are not likely to engage in such behaviours more than controls. In addition, recent research suggests that a therapeutic technique which violates the associative component of stimulus control therapy has the same degree of success.

Zwart and Lisman (1979) allocated students to five treatments which included stimulus control and 'counter-control'. The latter involved instructions which were contrary to the basic principle of stimulus control. Subjects were told to remain in bed if they could not sleep and to involve themselves in some activity; in addition, they were to engage in some activity in bed for at least 30 minutes each day. Both of these treatments produced improvements in the time taken to fall asleep; the improvements were greater than those associated with other techniques and occurred even though subjects were told not to expect changes. Zwart and Lisman suggest that the important factor underlying successful treatment may be the disruption of the 'difficult sleep onset period'. In other words, the syndrome of tension, worrying and arousal must be terminated and controlled and the stimulus situation (i.e. bed and bedroom) is not crucially important. Further research is needed to establish the validity of this suggestion but, once again, the research has produced techniques which are potentially very valuable in the alleviation of insomnia.

Other techniques

Though a number of other treatments have been investigated, outcomes are not as impressive as in the case of the treatments already discussed. Alternatively, evaluative research is simply not available. For example, a small number of researchers have tried to condition sleep behaviour by associating a stimulus (e.g. a metronome or counting) with a loss of consciousness produced by a hypnotic drug. There is some suggestion that the approach might be useful but there is also one demonstration that the conditioning of sleep responses was not successful.

Biofeedback techniques have also been applied to insomnia. The essential ingredient is self-relaxation focussed on specific muscle groups; polygraph techniques are used to monitor physiological changes and a signal (e.g. a tone) is used to provide immediate feedback to the individual of his success in self-control. One study (Haynes et al, 1977) compared biofeedback training with relaxation. In terms of improvements in the reported sleep behaviour of insomniacs, both techniques were more successful than control conditions but they did not differ from each other. There were, however, no significant differences in physiological measures (frontalis tension) in the three study groups either before or after training. In view of the economy of relaxation techniques, they would therefore appear to be the treatment of choice when compared with biofeedback. There is also at least one demonstration that relaxation is as effective as meditation techniques in the alleviation of sleep problems.

A word of caution

Though the conclusions mentioned in previous sections are supported by a body of evidence, a considerable degree of caution continues to be necessary in relation to the effectiveness of the various treatment techniques. Most of the evaluative studies are conducted on student samples and self-reports of sleeping behaviour are the most common outcome measure. Although self-report is an important measure, it has already been established that it can be a poor guide to objective changes. The studies of Borkovec and his colleagues also demonstrate the importance of including both objective and subjective measures.

Conclusions

Research on the assessment, determinants and treatments of insomnia will need to continue but clinical practice will obviously not be able to wait for the results since insomnia will continue to present as a problem in the meantime. What general principles should govern assessment and treatment? The studies which we have considered suggest implications for both.

The first principle is that careful and comprehensive assessment should be conducted on each individual case. Objective measurement, including sleep EEGs, is desirable but is likely to be beyond the capability of most treatment settings. As an alternative, it is clear that potential patients should be required to maintain records on their sleep behaviour for at least a week or two; wherever possible, these records should be corroborated by another observer such as a spouse so that there is some check on the reliability.

The research also has a number of clear implications for treatment. Caution is necessary about the use of medication to control insomnia. It is, of course, very easy to prescribe drugs, but the evidence indicates that their effectiveness can be limited and that they can actually cause quite severe problems, such as dependence and further sleep problems, so that the patient is in fact in an even worse condition. Psychological treatments do seem to offer more relief to the poor sleeper and the most realistic policy for the time being would seem to be to offer patients a combined package which includes elements of relaxation, stimulus control and paradoxical intent. Elements of these treatments are compatible and the whole package is economic to the extent that it involves a relatively small amount of therapist time, could easily be provided by an aide and could be provided on a group basis and with the use of automated devices such as audiotapes. A combined package would offer the best choice of success, and objective research might eventually identify the most effective components of the package so that treatment programmes can become both effective and efficient.

There can be little doubt that the prognosis for poor sleepers has improved quite considerably over the last decade and it should continue to do so if the impetus of the research is maintained.

References

Bixler, E.O., Kales, A., Soldatos, C., Kales, J.D. and Healey, S. (1979)
Prevalence of sleep disorders in the Los Angeles Metropolitan area. American Journal of Psychiatry, 136, 1257-1262.

Bootzin, R.R. (1972)
Stimulus Control Treatment for Insomnia. Proceedings of the 80th Annual Convention, American Psychological Association.

Borkovec, T.D., Grayson, J.B., O'Brien, G.T. and Weerts, T.C. (1979)
Relaxation treatment of pseudoinsomniac and idiopathic insomnia: an electroencephalographic evaluation. Journal of Applied Behavior Analysis, 12, 37-54.

Carskardon, M.A., Dement, W.C., Mitler, M.M., Guilbeminault, C., Zarcone, U.P. and Speigel, R. (1976)
Self-reports versus sleep laboratory findings in 122 drug free subjects with complaints of chronic insomnia. American Journal of Psychiatry, 133, 1382-1388.

Coates, T.J., Rosekind, M.R., Strossen, R.J., Thornsen, C.E. and Kirmil Gray, K. (1979)
Sleep recordings in the laboratory and home: a comparative analysis. Psychophysiology, 16, 339-346.

Dement, W.P. (1972)
Some must watch, while some must sleep. Stanford: Stanford Alumni Association.

Haynes, S.N., Follingstad, D.P., McGowan, W.T. (1974)
Insomnia: sleep patterns and anxiety level. Journal of Psychosomatic Research, 18, 69-74.

Haynes, S.N., Sides, H. and Lockwood, G. (1977)
Relaxation instructions and frontalis electromyographic feedback intervention with sleep onset insomnia. Behaviour Therapy, 8, 644-652.

Hilgard, E.R., Atkinson, R.C. and Atkinson, R.L. (1971)
Introduction to Psychology (5th edn). New York: Harcourt Brace Jovanovitch.

Johns, W.M. (1977)
Validity of subjective reports of sleep latency in normal subjects. Ergonomics, 20, 683-690.

Kales, A., Bixler, E.O., Tan, T., Scharf, M.B. and Kales, J.D. (1974)
Chronic hypnotic-drug use: ineffectiveness, drug-withdrawal insomnia and dependence. Journal of American Medical Association, 227, 513-517.

Monroe, L.J. (1967)
Psychological and physiological differences between good and poor sleepers. Journal of Abnormal Psychology, 72, 255-264.

Regestein, Q.R. (1976)
Treating insomnia: a practical guide for managing
chronic sleeplessness, circa 1975. Comprehensive
Psychiatry, 17, 517-526.

Turner, E.M. and Ascher, L.M. (1979)
A within subject analysis of stimulus control therapy
with severe sleep onset insomniacs. Behaviour Research
and Therapy, 17, 107-112.

Zwart, C.A. and Lisman, S.A. (1979)
Analysis of stimulus control treatment of sleep onset
insomnia. Journal of Consulting and Clinical Psychology,
47, 113-118.

Questions

1. What has psychological research contributed to the
   understanding of insomnia?
2. List those aspects of the psychological research into
   insomnia which the general practitioner should know
   about. Should this make any difference to the assessment
   and management of the patient who complains about a lack
   of sleep?
3. Discuss the problems which are experienced in the
   investigation of patients who complain of insomnia and
   also in the scientific investigation of insomnia as a
   general problem.
4. Comment on: (a) information which you would try to
   elicit from an insomniac patient, or members of his
   family, in interview; (b) the results of surveys of
   insomnia in the general population; (c) the causes of
   insomnia.
5. Discuss in detail the aetiology of sleep difficulties.
   Include in your discussion a critical consideration of
   the relationship between sleep problems and psychological disorder.
6. How is insomnia treated? Is medication the treatment of
   choice?
7. Compare and contrast the medical, psychotherapeutic and
   behavioural approaches to the treatment of insomnia.
8. Describe how you would design a study to evaluate the
   effectiveness of medical and psychological treatments of
   insomnia.

Annotated reading

Oswald, I. (1976) Sleep. Harmondsworth: Penguin.
This is a very useful and comprehensive introduction to
the study of sleep. It discusses methodology, the relationship between sleep and psychological functioning,
dreaming, hypnosis, drug effects and also some aspects
of sleep problems. At the undergraduate level, this is
probably the most readable text which is available.

Rachman, S.J. and Philips, C. (1978) Sleep disorders. In
S.J. Rachman and C. Philips (eds), Psychology and Medicine.
Harmondsworth: Penguin.
Covers much the same ground as this chapter, but

provides a readable and useful alternative viewpoint for students.

Lairy, C.G. and Salzarulo, P. (eds) (1978) The Experimental Study of Human Sleep: Methodological problems. Oxford: Elsevier Scientific.
The papers in this book were delivered at an international symposium held in 1974. This is not recommended as an introductory text, but is suitable for postgraduates and those with a special interest in the scientific study of sleep. Among the topics considered are the problems associated with objective investigation, theoretical models, the relationship between animal and human studies, relationships between experimental and clinical research, dreaming and problems of sleeping.

Williams, R.L. and Karacan, I. (1978) Sleep Disorders, Diagnosis and Treatment. New York: Wiley Medical.
This book is a collection of original reviews of sleep disorders. The chapters discuss the identification, assessment, aetiology and management of both primary and secondary (or symptomatic) sleep problems; in addition to general discussions and reviews, many practical issues are also considered so that the text has many attractions for a clinical readership.

Crisp, A.H. and Stonehill, E. (1976) Sleep, Nutrition and Mood. New York: Wiley.
The authors both describe and review a body of information on the relationships between sleep, activity level, nutrition and mood. The book will be most interesting to readers who have some clinical experience, and especially to advanced trainees and doctors with a special interest in psychological medicine. Many of the topics considered are, however, of general relevance; for instance, there are discussions of methodology and of the relationship between sleep and psychological disorders.

23

Obesity
David Griffiths

Obesity is a common problem and can involve quite serious complications. As one example of a study of the prevalence of obesity, Silverstone (1974) reports that a survey conducted in Richmond used an arbitrary criterion of an excess of 20 per cent over the median weight. The application of this standard indicated that 7.5 per cent of women under the age of 30 were overweight and 30 per cent or more of women over the age of 50. The percentage for all ages combined was 23.5 per cent for women (based on a sample of 715) and 15.4 per cent for men (where the sample size was 488). The incidence of obesity in Silverstone's sample also varied with both age and social class. The highest rates in women were for the older age group (31.6 per cent of the 50-65 year olds) and for social class groups 4 and 5 (35.5 per cent). A similar trend was obvious for the men but the absolute rates were considerably lower (18.2 per cent for the 50-65 years group and 18.4 per cent for social classes 4 and 5). Although the prevalence and incidence rates from other studies tend to vary (depending on such factors as the samples studied and the criteria used), it is apparent that obesity is a common problem.

Obesity has also been associated with a number of medical problems and, specifically, with high blood pressure, ischaemic heart disease and osteo-arthritis. It is, therefore, clearly a problem of some significance to Health Services and there are many indications that dietary problems can take up a considerable amount of the general practitioner's time. For example, one doctor (Chomet, 1974) reported at a conference that she saw, on average, six people per week who were seeking help with weight reduction and diet. She further estimated that this amounted to 288 consultations per working year, taking up a minimum of 100 hours of her time and sometimes being frustrating to the extent that patients would tend to regain weight losses unless they were provided with frequent support and surveillance.

In addition to the medical danger, the fact that so many individuals consult their doctors or attend weight reduction groups indicates that obesity is seen as being at the least an inconvenience, and often a problem. The general picture of the 'fatty' is that he is jolly, extraverted and happy. A more realistic view would seem to be that - partly because of the obvious physical inconvenience of being fat and partly because of factors such as social ridicule - obesity can be the cause of a considerable degree of distress and suffering. This involves both the obese individual and also close relatives and family. The following comments were made by a woman seeking help and illustrate common problems associated with overweight:

> I have always been fat and it has been the most important fact of my life. When I was young, it was difficult to play many physical games because I was slower than the others; the other children called me 'fatso' and many did not know my real name! Teachers often seemed to assume that, being fat, I was also likely to be lazy. Later on, young men were happy to treat me as a friend and were sometimes obviously more interested in me as a mother figure rather than a girlfriend. My self-confidence was pretty low, though I did not show this to other people, not even my close friends ... more recently I have got even fatter, in spite of the fact that I hate being fat and don't really want to eat so much. It is difficult to get around and to do things like jumping on a bus. In summer I sweat a lot, and have to change clothes often. The usual advice I am given is to eat less or to use my will power! People don't seem to realise that it is so much easier to preach than to practise!

The treatment of obesity has traditionally involved instructions about restrictions of food and calorie intake and also increased exercise and activity. Rapid treatment usually requires hospitalization and a starvation diet and is sometimes necessary if the obese individual needs surgery or other types of help for medical conditions.

Organizations are also available which offer help on a commercial basis. In addition to dietary advice in books, magazines and newspapers, weight-reducing groups are popular. These involve meetings at intervals of a week or so; group leaders provide information and advice on the techniques necessary to reduce weight, and meetings often involve commitments by individuals to lose specified amounts of weight and public weighings so that success or failure can be ascertained. Group pressures are, therefore, operating in a number of ways. Weight-reducing programmes, whether they involve grossly obese individuals or women who merely wish to be even thinner than they are, obviously involve a fair degree of time and effort, and also expense since many are organized on a commercial basis.

How successful are the various approaches to weight reduction? It is difficult to give an overall and general answer to this since, in addition to individual efforts to lose weight and commercial ventures, a large number of methods have been used. These include surgery and medication, and also hypnosis, psychotherapy and, more recently, behavioural therapies (Leon, 1976). In spite of the potential differences between treatments, however, reviewers have tended to be rather pessimistic in their evaluation of success.

The general trend would seem to be that some studies report initial success in reducing weight although follow-up studies indicate variable but often high relapse rates. Stunkard's (1958) conclusion is hardly recent but continues to be quoted so often that it still appears to be relevant. He commented that, 'Most obese persons will not stay in treatment for obesity. Of those who stay in treatment most will not lose weight and of those who lose weight, most will regain it'. As an example of evaluative studies, one prospective investigation (Lloyd, 1974) showed that, though most of a group of children lost weight during the first year of treatment, 80 per cent were again obese at follow up (up to 9 years).

Obesity is associated with many enigmas. For example, though it is associated with personal, social and physical problems - and many of these are quite serious - these problems are not sufficient to motivate the individual to lose weight and thereafter maintain a reduced weight status.

In view of the situation, we will presume that any help will be welcomed and continue to consider the contribution which psychology has made to the problems of obesity. There is, in fact, an extensive literature on psychological aspects of obesity and this might come as a considerable surprise to those who view obesity as a 'physical' problem. We therefore consider the following general question: how has psychological research contributed to the understanding and modification of obesity?

Two aspects of the psychological research are considered. First, what has psychological investigation contributed to the explanation of the behaviour of the obese individual? In psychological terms, what is the nature of obesity? Second, has the psychological research contributed anything to solving the apparently intractable problem of overweight? Has it produced successful methods of weight control?

What is obesity?

Psychological research has concerned itself with attempts to identify factors in obese individuals which predispose them to overweight. In other words, researchers have attempted to find psychological 'causes' in order to explain the occurrence of obesity and also in the hope that the discovery of psychological factors common to the obese will eventually lead to successful treatments. Two 'schools' of psychology have approached this problem in rather different ways, and these are outlined below.

The contribution of dynamic psychology
'Dynamic' psychology has tended to view obesity as a symptom of underlying psychological problems. Within this approach, however, a number of different causes have been suggested.

For example, the traditional (Freudian) view would be that obese individuals are either fixated at or have regressed to the oral stage of their development. At its most basic, the suggestion is that obese individuals have rather special needs for activities associated with the mouth; these needs are suggested to have been caused by experiences during the early years of life, and specifically when the infant is at its mother's breast. These are assumed to leave the individual with a need for oral stimulation. Eating is the most obvious oral activity and overweight is one prominent consequence.

Another dynamic explanation is that obesity is one symptom of a depressive state which, in turn, is caused by a feeling of helplessness and hopelessness associated with experiences of loss. It has also been suggested that overeating can be part of a defence mechanism; through eating to excess, for example, the individual is compensating for feelings of loss. In essence, food is being used to reduce discomfort and anxiety. Food is regarded, in other words, as having a very definite symbolic and psychological significance.

One final example of dynamic explanation of obesity is provided by Bruch's work. Bruch (1974) suggests that obese individuals have common factors in their early experience. More specifically, the mothers of obese individuals are believed to have pressed food on their children as a response to any stress and discomfort. Food is therefore used as a comforter and the obese individual develops a need to eat in order to maintain a psychological equilibrium. Bruch and her colleagues have also hypothesized that the mothers of obese individuals tend to press food on their children because of their own problems: they can, says Bruch, be experiencing a rejection of their children and attempt to compensate for this by being overprotective.

Though these explanations are interesting and invariably plausible, dynamic theory cannot really be said to have made vital contributions to the explanation of obesity. Many of the explanations are seductive in their simplicity, but much depends on whether the basic assumptions of dynamic and Freudian psychology are accepted. Freudian theory, in particular, has attracted a considerable amount of adverse review; the major criticisms are that it is unproven and, more than this, has not been formulated in such a way that it is capable of proof or disproof. It is, in fact, a creed rather than a scientific theory formulated so that it can be subjected to objective enquiry and verification.

Reviewers have also pointed to a number of other shortcomings which reduce the value of psychodynamic explanations of obesity (Leon and Roth, 1977). One is that the theories are based on an unrepresentative sample of the obese to the extent that they are derived from observations of those individuals who have sought psychiatric or other forms of specialized therapeutic help. Such individuals are likely to be a minority and it cannot be assumed that they are representative.

Theory has also been based on the information gathered by dynamically-orientated clinicians; this information might therefore be biassed by the clinician's selective attention to observations and inferences which are consistent with the theory he favours. For example, a significant number of obese individuals report that their mothers are overconcerned with food and eating (Silverstone, 1974) and this might be seen as support for Bruch's hypothesis about the role of the mother in the aetiology of obesity. Whilst it is consistent with such a theory, it does not prove the theory and other explanations are equally plausible. One is that obese individuals who suggest that their mothers were excessively concerned with food are, at least to some extent, responding to leading questions; another is that the mother's reported concern could, in some instances, be a response to the obesity rather than its cause. It also seems likely that maternal overprotection, focussing on food, is also present in individuals who do not subsequently become obese.

One further point requires to be stressed in relation to dynamic psychology and obesity. This is that there is a general lack of evidence about the effectiveness of treatments based on dynamic theory in reducing weight and treating obesity (Leon, 1976). Furthermore, there is at least one demonstration that a behavioural approach is more effective in producing and maintaining weight loss than both psychotherapy and group pressures (Wollersheim, 1970). Whilst it is unwise to rely on the results of one study, Leon's careful analysis of evaluative studies causes her to suggest that psychotherapy is not an effective treatment for obesity. As we see soon, other approaches which are not derived from dynamic theory seem to offer the best chance of success in the control of obesity.

In conclusion, neither psychodynamic theory nor psychotherapy can be claimed to have made any substantial contribution to the explanation and modification of obesity. Can other approaches claim to be more successful?

Cognitive and behavioural investigations

A large number of objective investigations have attempted to identify psychological factors which might either cause or sustain the problems of obesity. The best known example of such research is the work of Stanley Schachter. Schachter's (1967) work on the behaviour of the obese, and also his evaluation of results reported by others, lead him to suggest that obese individuals are more responsive to external cues than non-obese control subjects and are less sensitive to internal states such as the stomach contractions which are normally associated with hunger.

Stunkard and Koch had demonstrated that, whereas stomach contractions and reports of hunger were correlated in normal control subjects, such a relationship did not exist in the obese subjects who were studied. On the basis of this and subsequent investigations, Schachter concluded that 'the eating behaviour of the obese is relatively unrelated to any gut state but is, in large part, under external control: that is, eating behaviour is initiated and terminated by stimuli external to the organism'. Further studies demonstrated that obese individuals responded relatively more than their non-obese counterparts to such factors as taste, the prominence and appearance of food, and also time factors.

In practice, this means that the fat individual will eat relatively more of a tasty food, or a prominent and attractive meal; he is also likely to feel hungry and eat at certain times or in certain places which have become associated with eating and therefore act as stimuli to hunger. The obese are also more likely to eat even if they have eaten recently, so that satisfaction has less effect on their eating behaviour than it would have on a non-obese individual. The research on the receptivity to various stimuli amongst the obese is summarized and evaluated by Hodgson and Rankin (1978). They conclude that, though Schachter and his colleagues produced a body of evidence to substantiate the theory that the obese are affected relatively more by external cues, more recent work has failed to support the original theory and revisions are necessary.

A more recent study by Stunkard and Fox (referred to by Hodgson and Rankin) used careful and refined techniques to evaluate stomach contractions and self-reported hunger, and the results suggested that there is, after all, a relationship between stomach contractions and hunger amongst the obese. Furthermore, studies reviewed by Hodgson and Rankin now indicate that the obese are also responsive, in terms of their eating, to other 'internal' states such as moods. Hodgson and Rankin propose that Schachter's original hypothesis requires some modification and their conclusion is that 'compulsive eating is strongly influenced by food and mood cues rather than hunger pangs and eating pangs'.

Hodgson and Rankin also conclude that there might be individual differences within groups of obese individuals. This means, in practice, that the factors which produce and control eating are not necessarily the same; they vary considerably between individuals. The question of individual differences is also taken up at some length by other reviewers.

Are the obese a homogeneous group?

As we have seen, much of the work on obesity has assumed or implied that obese individuals share certain characteristics, whether these be dynamic traits or various kinds of response tendencies such as dependence on external cues. Careful and comprehensive reviews suggest, however, that it is fallacious to assume that the obese have a consistent 'personality'. Leon and Roth (1977) conclude that, in spite of the theory, objective research has failed to demonstrate that the obese are a homogeneous group to the extent that they share certain personality or behavioural 'traits'. Their conclusion is that 'there appear to be very few personality characteristics unique to the obese person'. A careful reading of their review suggests that there could be none.

It seems possible, therefore, that - in psychological terms - there does not seem to be an obese 'type', defined by specific characteristics. Even if further research were to demonstrate the existence of common characteristics, it would not necessarily follow that these characteristics had produced obesity. It is equally likely that characteristics (such as low self-esteem or anxiety) which might be common amongst the obese could be consequences of the obesity. It is also important to remember that a number of studies have failed to distinguish the obese from control groups. Silverstone (1974), for example, reports that in terms of questionnaire scores, the obese are no more neurotic than other groups. He also discovered, however, that those obese individuals who were neurotic made a significantly worse response to weight reduction programmes. They remained in such programmes for as long as their non-neurotic peers but failed to respond to the same extent in terms of a reduction in their weight. These results suggest that further progress in the explanation and modification of obesity might be expected if more attention is given to their response to treatment programmes, and much of the recent research does indeed suggest that the obese will benefit more from research concerned with therapeutic response.

To return to the issue of common traits amongst the obese, it is difficult to state any conclusion with complete confidence. This is partly because the failure to identify any common characteristics could be determined by limitations in the investigations and techniques which have been reported. For example, some projects have studied the behaviour of individuals who simply appear to be overweight, whilst others have defined obesity by an excess of 10-50 per cent above an ideal body weight calculated on the basis of height, sex and characteristics of the body frame. Many studies have utilized student samples only, whilst others have involved a wide range of age groups.

Though the effects of variations between studies is difficult to assess, it seems unlikely that inconsistencies of this kind are sufficient to explain the failure to identify common characteristics. In fact, most of the recent reviews conclude that the obese should be considered on an individual rather than a group basis. Leon and Roth (1977), for example, conclude that 'the search for a unitary explanation of obesity does not, at present, appear to be a fruitful avenue of exploration and the evidence strongly suggests that obesity is not a unitary syndrome'. This means that the individual who is 50 per cent above his ideal body weight might differ appreciably - in terms of psychological characteristics, and more specifically the psychological and social factors which influence and maintain his pattern of eating - from the individual whose degree of obesity is less extreme. Individuals who have been obese since childhood might be different from those where the development of the condition occurred during adult life.

It is already established, in fact, that even within a group of individuals who are classified as manifesting eating disorders, there are several patterns of overeating which are easily distinguished. Stunkard identified at least three patterns of excessive eating; these involved (i) individuals who consistently over-eat in the evening (especially when under stress), (ii) 'binge' eaters who have periods of high food intake, and (iii) individuals who, once they begin to eat, find it difficult to stop and do not become satiated in a normal manner.

An overall conclusion to this section is that, although we cannot be certain, the most reasonable assumption to make is that there are wide individual differences within groups of obese individuals. The practical implication is that the explanation of obesity, in clinical situations, requires a careful analysis of the behaviour of each individual. As we soon see, behavioural treatments applied to obesity have indeed adopted an inductive approach in many instances (but not always), and the overall success rates are probably better than those associated with the alternatives. At the same time, it also becomes clear that success rates (especially when careful follow-up is conducted) often fall far short of a complete cure for obesity.

The modification of obesity

How successful are the various techniques which have been applied to reduce weight and, in addition, to maintain a lower weight status? We have already referred to Stunkard's (1958) bleak observations about the lack of success in weight reduction programmes. More recently, Leon (1976) concludes that 'treatment results with traditional weight loss procedures are no more effective now than they were 15 years ago', and her comprehensive review suggests that most current approaches to weight reduction are not particularly successful. In relation to psychotherapy and hypnosis, Leon concludes 'that these procedures are effective only in isolated cases'; group support 'in and of itself was not associated with successful weight reduction and the lack of follow up statistics precludes judgments about weight maintenance'. Leon also reviews the usefulness of conventional medical and surgical procedures and concludes that medication has not produced a notable degree of success; surgery 'has produced substantial weight reduction but the physical side effects and complications are many'.

Does anything work? As we see below, it is possible to give a more positive answer to this question than might be expected on the basis of the lack of success of the treatments which have been mentioned. For the work on behavioural programmes of treatment does seem to offer a degree of hope to those who are keen to help the obese to control both their eating behaviour and their weight.

Behavioural treatment of obesity

The topic of behaviour therapy has already been discussed elsewhere, and notably by Beech in chapter 12. In relation to behaviour therapy applied to obesity, we might consider at least four questions. First, what are the assumptions which underlie the application of behavioural techniques? Second, what are these techniques? Third, are they successful? Fourth, which aspects of treatment programmes are most important in terms of their effects on weight reduction? Our answers to these questions are influenced very considerably by the comprehensive and competent reviews which have already been conducted by Hodgson and Rankin (1978) and Leon (1976). As will be obvious from the previous sections of this chapter, Leon's review is also concerned with a wide range of other treatments.

What are the assumptions which underlie the application of behaviour therapy?

Hodgson and Rankin draw our attention to two important principles of behaviour therapy. The first is that the basic model of behaviour involves the interaction between the individual, his behaviour and his environment.

In theory, the first step involved in a behavioural programme is an analysis of the stimuli and cues which elicit behaviour and also the consequences of that behaviour. In relation to eating, we have already seen how the eating behaviour of the obese can be linked with external cues such as the taste, smell or appearance of food; the obese are also more likely to eat when they experience certain states. For example, Conrad (1970) demonstrated that obese individuals subjected to social rejection ate more, whereas non-obese controls responded by eating less. One major aspect of a behavioural analysis therefore involves the detection of the cues (both external and 'state' variables) associated with excessive eating; in practice, the individual might be required to keep records so that associations between stimuli and eating become apparent.

In addition, the consequences of eating would also be investigated since, on the assumption that behaviour is influenced by its consequences, it would also be important to ascertain the changes contingent on eating for each individual. Self-report might indicate that eating was followed, for example, by a reduction in tension or anxiety. Such changes, contingent on eating, might then be assumed to act as reinforcements for the eating.

When a picture of the individual is derived, ideally from extensive observations, this should provide a detailed account of the relationships between his behaviour and both the antecedents and consequences. Under ideal conditions, the therapeutic programme should be derived from the idiosyncratic relationships evident between antecedents, behaviour and consequences for each individual. This does not necessarily occur in practice, since many weight reduction programmes are provided on a group basis and so do not necessarily cater for the idiosyncratic needs of the individual.

One further principle of behaviour therapy, again stressed by Hodgson and Rankin, is 'a strong respect for the client's right to share in decisions about treatment, strategies and goals'. In practice, this means that the therapist brings with him an expertise in the techniques of behaviour modification; these are made available to the client since the therapist acts as his adviser and the two collaborate in a joint venture to secure jointly agreed goals. Some treatment programmes involve an explicit contract between therapist and client; such contracts can contain statements of the goals of treatment and the functions and responsibilities which are to be assumed by both client and therapist.

What does a behavioural programme involve?
Hodgson and Rankin distinguish four categories of treatment in relation to obesity. The first involves reducing eating cues and coping with cues which cannot be avoided. In other words, this involves procedures to control the stimuli (or antecedents) associated with eating. In practice, the stimuli are identified; the next step involves their removal, or developing techniques to control their effects. For example, prominent foods are removed, or relaxation and activity are used to alleviate tension and boredom if these states are cues to eating.

The second approach involves changing the consequences of overeating. For example, the woman who overeats might be required to imagine adverse comments by her husband, or even to imagine him making love to another woman. An alternative approach involves the use of rewards for behaviours incompatible with excessive eating; avoiding a favourite food, or ceasing to eat before a meal is finished, might therefore be associated with images of the beneficial effects to the figure, or social approval from the therapist or a spouse.

A third approach, which has theoretical advantages but has not been extensively applied in practice, involves 'cue exposure'. This involves exposure to eating cues under conditions designed to prevent the usual response of eating. The client might, for example, ensure that his favourite food was prominently displayed in his home under conditions where his contract with the therapist specified that he was not to eat or touch the impressive display! The rationale underlying the approach is that the association between cues and eating is gradually broken.

Finally, a number of programmes involve a complex combination of techniques such as self-monitoring, self-reinforcement, cue avoidance, practice at slow eating or reduction of meal frequency. Here are a few examples of the steps involved in such a programme, though it must be stressed that there are numerous variations and that some of the steps taken have already been described in our brief mention of the other categories of treatment.

* A detailed analysis of the individual's eating pattern is undertaken. This can involve objective records of behaviour and extensive self-monitoring by patients. Such a behavioural analysis determines, for example, the cues which are likely to produce eating.
* Selection of specific and well-defined goals: although goals can involve specified amounts of weight loss, many programmes also concentrate on behavioural goals such as reductions in eating or meal frequency.
* Contractual agreement: for example, patients agree to restrict the times and places where they eat. In some cases, it might be agreed that eating is allowed only in specified places such as dining rooms.
* Graduated steps: in order to reduce the stresses likely to be associated with abrupt changes in behaviour, or rapid reductions in weight, some programmes involve a sequence of small changes. For example, eating behaviour is modified in carefully controlled steps; alternatively, the client is discouraged from losing more than two pounds per week.
* Stimulus control: for example, eating is restricted rigidly to certain specific conditions such as specified rooms in the house or times during the day.
* Self-monitoring and self-reinforcement: clients maintain diaries of their behaviour and weight status and reinforce themselves appropriately. For example, a specified weight loss might be reinforced by a treat such as a trip to the cinema. Or even a favourite food in small quantities! Alternatively, a lapse in behaviour might be associated with unpleasant images or self-induced feelings of nausea.
* Social support: families and spouses can support clients by agreeing to monitor their progress and providing a range of reinforcements which can include anything from encouragement to an enthusiastic caress!

Are behavioural programmes successful? If so, which of the many components of a programme are important?
Behavioural programmes do seem to offer a better chance of success than alternatives. In general, evaluative studies suggest that behaviour therapy is at least as successful as other treatments, and is often more successful in terms of the initial weight loss and also the maintenance of weight loss at follow up.

Levitz and Stunkard (1974) compared the outcomes for (i) behaviour therapy conducted by a professional therapist, (ii) behaviour therapy conducted by an experienced weight-reduction group leader, (iii) nutritional advice given by a group leader, and (iv) a group support programme involving periodic weighing, public announcements of progress, group discussions, etc. Behaviour therapy was associated with fewer drop-outs from treatment and was more effective in producing weight loss and maintaining it over a 12-month follow up. Hodgson and Rankin also refer to an investigation by Peruck and Stunkard which demonstrated that behaviour therapy conducted by relatively inexperienced therapists can be more effective than traditional calorie counting procedures administered by experienced personnel. Though behaviour therapy was placed at a disadvantage by using inexperienced therapists, approximately half of the subjects lost more than 20lb in weight compared with a quarter of the subjects in the more traditional programme. At a 12-month follow up, however, the traditional treatment group had caught up and approximately 60 per cent of both groups exceeded the 20lb criterion. At the five-year follow up, there had been some relapse and 20-50 per cent of both groups had maintained the 20lb loss. Throughout the follow up, the behaviour therapy group maintained a consistent improvement over the traditional treatment. As we have seen, however, the differences were small after the initial 12 months and both groups manifested a substantial relapse rate between one and five years after treatment.

Leon, and Hodgson and Rankin, all refer to a number of studies which have evaluated the effectiveness of behaviour therapy in the control of over-eating. As usual, it is impossible to compare many of these studies since they differ in such factors as the age and sex of subjects, criteria for selecting obese individuals, and the length of follow up. Some of the earlier studies did not include control groups, or they included control groups which did not receive the same amount of attention as the behaviour therapy group. Nevertheless, the general conclusion reached by these reviewers is that behavioural techniques tend to do at least as well as alternative treatments.

The differences between behavioural and other treatments are not, however, dramatic and follow ups tend to suggest that relapses, and the loss of initial improvements in weight status, are commonly observed. One possible explanation for this is that, although the theory underlying behaviour modification would tend to recommend that treatment should be tailored to meet the needs of the individual, most of the programmes involved in evaluative studies are provided on a standard group basis. Standard group treatment is practically more viable, but individualized programmes might be required if the weight losses are to be both more impressive and permanent.

Another factor which could contribute to the tendency of many clients to regain weight is that contact with individuals on weight-reducing programmes often ceases completely when the programme ends. This sometimes means that there is an abrupt loss of the support provided by the therapist and others. If this is a determinant of relapse, it might be rectified by the provision of 'booster' or support sessions which are provided after the termination of the intensive treatment programme. Though 'booster' sessions are justifiable on theoretical grounds, they might not provide a remedy to relapses in themselves since there is at least one demonstration (Ashby and Wilson, 1977) that the maintenance of weight loss over a 12-month follow up was not affected by either the frequency or content of booster sessions. As is so often the case in evaluation of psychological treatments, research will obviously need to continue for some time yet!

What are the factors which influence the effectiveness of behavioural programmes?

Once again, the available research does not allow us to identify all the important components of treatment. At the same time, a small number of well-conducted studies have identified some critical treatment variables. Mahoney (1974) has demonstrated that self-reinforcement for improvements in eating habits produces significantly greater weight loss than self-reinforcement of the weight loss itself; self-reinforcement of weight loss is, in turn, better than self-monitoring. Hodgson and Rankin also list a number of studies which suggest that self-management procedures using manuals can be as effective as treatment conducted by expert therapists; furthermore, simple methods such as monitoring mouthfuls of food, calorie counting and cue avoidance can be as effective as complex self-management procedures.

Whether the effectiveness of these simpler and more economical measures is maintained over longer periods remains, however, to be demonstrated in controlled studies using representative groups of clients. Though many questions remain to be answered, progress to date has been impressive and the amount and quality of research conducted on the behavioural approaches appears to be significantly better than that associated with many of the alternative approaches to weight reduction.

Conclusions

We have seen that obesity is a common problem which can cause varying degrees of both physical and psychological handicap to the sufferer. This, in turn, can involve a considerable burden to the Health Services. Unfortunately, the evidence on the effectiveness of a large number of treatments suggests that therapeutic outcomes are not impressive. Many patients fail to complete weight reduction programmes; others fail to lose weight while the general trend at follow up involves relapse and a return to the original weight status. Furthermore, the prognosis for obese individuals has not improved over the last 15 years or so. It is perhaps premature to be optimistic about the effectiveness of recently introduced treatments involving psychological and behavioural techniques. The results from a small number of evaluative studies suggest, however, that there is now reason for some optimism since behavioural therapy has consistently produced results which are at least as good as the alternatives. In addition, both theoretical considerations and empirical studies have begun to identify the variables in the individual patient, his environment, and also therapeutic programmes, which influence or determine outcomes.

Two aspects of obesity appear to be especially important if the management of overeating is to be successful. The first of these involves the need to increase our understanding of the factors which determine the individual differences within groups of obese individuals. If therapy is to be dramatically more successful, we need to identify (and control) those variables which, in each individual, control eating behaviour. As we have already seen, it is now assumed that the obese are not a homogeneous group. Behaviour therapy has provided us with techniques (e.g. behavioural analysis) which can facilitate our exploration of individual differences, and it remains to be demonstrated that these techniques can allow us to improve our understanding of individual clients.

The second problem which remains to be resolved is the maintenance of treatment gains. Relapses can be very common so that the original treatment programme ends up as being, at least to some extent, wasted effort. The problem of maintenance is, of course, a universal problem which affects the management of a wide range of problems. In relation to obesity, the long-term maintenance of improvements is now clearly recognized as an aim but not an achievement. Though a solution has not been evaluated, techniques such as self-control programmes and booster sessions do offer some considerable hope for the future.

References

Ashby, W.A. and Wilson, G.T. (1977)
Behaviour therapy for obesity: booster sessions and long-term maintenance of weight loss. Behaviour Research and Therapy, 15, 451-463.

Bruch, H. (1974)
Eating Disorders. London: Routledge & Kegan Paul.

Chomet, J. (1974)
Discussion following the paper on 'Psychological aspects of obesity' at a symposium on obesity, Royal College of Physicians. British Clinical Journal, 2, 274.

Conrad, E.H. (1970)
Psychogenic obesity. The effects of social rejection upon hunger, food cravings and food consumption. Dissertation Abstracts, 30, 4787-4788.

Hodgson, R. and Rankin, H. (1978)
Behavioural psychotherapy and obesity. Unpublished manuscript, Addiction Research Unit, Institute of Psychiatry, University of London.

Leon, G.R. (1976)
Current directions in the treatment of obesity. Psychological Bulletin, 83, 557-578.

Leon, G.R. and Roth, L. (1977)
Obesity: psychological causes, correlations and speculations. Psychological Bulletin, 84, 117-139.

Levitz, L.S. and Stunkard, A.J. (1974)
A therapeutic coalition for obesity: behavior modification and patient self help. American Journal of Psychiatry, 131, 423-427.

Lloyd, J. (1974)
   Childhood obesity. (Paper read at symposium on obesity, Royal College of Physicians.) British Clinical Journal, 2, 267-269.
Mahoney, M. (1974)
   Self-reward and self-monitoring techniques for weight control. Behaviour Therapy, 5, 48-57.
Schachter, S. (1967)
   Cognitive effects of bodily functioning. Studies of obesity and eating. In D.C. Gloss (ed.), Biology and Behavior: Neurophysiology and emotion. New York: The Rockefeller University Press and Russell Safe Foundation.
Silverstone, T. (1974)
   Psychological aspects of obesity. (Paper read at symposium on obesity, Royal College of Physicians.) British Clinical Journal, 2, 270-272.
Stunkard, A.J. (1958)
   The management of obesity. New York State Journal of Medicine, 58, 79-87.
Stunkard, A.J. and Koch, S. (1971)
   The relationship of gastric motility and hunger. Psychosomatic Medicine, 33, 123-134.
Wollersheim, J.P. (1970)
   Effectiveness of group therapy based upon learning principles in the treatment of over-weight women. Journal of Abnormal Psychology, 76, 462-474.

Questions

1. 'Obesity is a physical and medical problem. Psychology has little if anything to contribute.' Discuss.
2. What are the clinical implications of the psychological investigations of obesity? What aspects of the psychological research should be brought to the attention of clinicians?
3. Compare and contrast the medical, dynamic, cognitive and behavioural approaches to the understanding and management of obesity. Consider in detail the clinical implications of each approach.
4. Discuss the popular picture of the obese as 'jovial extraverts'.
5. What can be done to control and manage obesity?
6. What are the practical and ethical problems encountered in the treatment of obesity?
7. Describe and discuss critically the behavioural treatment of obesity.
8. Describe how you would design an investigation to evaluate the effectiveness of psychological treatments of obesity.
9. Research and clinical practice suggest that the maintenance of weight loss can be difficult to achieve. What methods could be used to help patients to maintain weight loss over long periods?
10. What factors would you consider if you were involved in the planning and subsequent organization of a weight

reduction clinic? Consider in detail both assessment, modification and maintenance of gains.

Annotated reading

Hodgson, R. and Rankin, H. (1978) Behavioural psychotherapy and obesity. Unpublished manuscript, Addiction Research Unit, Institute of Psychiatry, University of London.
> Though this review of the applications of behaviour therapy to obesity was used extensively in the preparation of the final chapter, unfortunately it has not been published and is not therefore generally available without direct contact with the authors.

Leon, G.R. (1976) Current directions in the treatment of obesity. Psychological Bulletin, 83, 557-578.

Leon, G.R. and Roth, L. (1977) Obesity: psychological causes, correlations and speculations. Psychological Bulletin, 84, 117-139.
> Both of these reviews will be available through libraries. Both are comprehensive in their scope and are also useful as sources of references. The style tends to be rather condensed, but the effort of reading is rewarded by the competence of the discussions and their wide scope.

Index

Index